W9-AMX-290

War, Politics and Superheroes

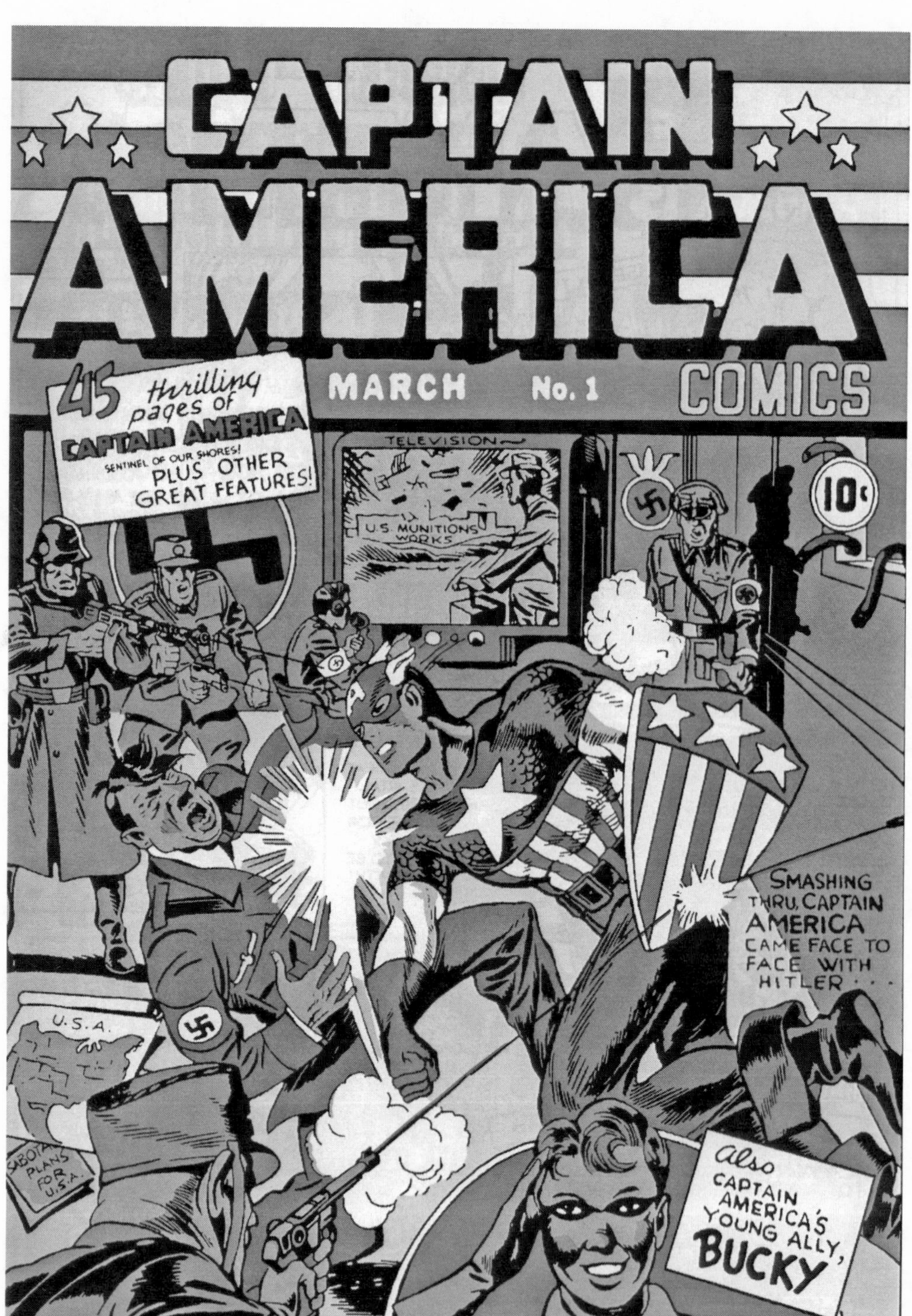
CAPTAIN AMERICA
45 thrilling pages of CAPTAIN AMERICA
SENTINEL OF OUR SHORES!
PLUS OTHER GREAT FEATURES!
MARCH
No. 1
COMICS
10¢
TELEVISION
U.S. MUNITIONS WORKS
SMASHING THRU, CAPTAIN AMERICA CAME FACE TO FACE WITH HITLER . . .
U.S.A.
PLANS FOR U.S.A.
also CAPTAIN AMERICA'S YOUNG ALLY, BUCKY

War, Politics and Superheroes

Ethics and Propaganda in Comics and Film

Marc DiPaolo

McFarland & Company, Inc., Publishers
Jefferson, North Carolina, and London

***Frontispiece:* The cover of the very first issue of *Captain America.* It was released by Timely Comics in December of 1940, a year before the U.S. officially entered World War II. The comic depicts Captain America — a creation of Jewish comic book creators Joe Simon and Jack Kirby — punching out Adolf Hitler.**

LIBRARY OF CONGRESS CATALOGUING-IN-PUBLICATION DATA

DiPaolo, Marc.
War, politics and superheroes : ethics and propaganda in comics and film / Marc DiPaolo.
p. cm.
Includes bibliographical references and index.

ISBN 978-0-7864-4718-3
softcover : 50# alkaline paper 

1. Superhero comic books, strips, etc. — History and criticism. 2. Comic books, strips, etc. — Political aspects. 3. Comic books, strips, etc. — Moral and ethical aspects. 4. Superhero films — History and criticism. 5. Propaganda in motion pictures. 6. Motion pictures — Moral and ethical aspects. 7. Superheroes — United States — History — 20th century. I. Title.
PN6714.D53 2011 741.5'352 — dc22 2011004691

BRITISH LIBRARY CATALOGUING DATA ARE AVAILABLE

Cover art by Mark Durr (based on the spoof of Shepard Fairey's HOPE poster in the 2010 film *Iron Man 2*)

Manufactured in the United States of America

McFarland & Company, Inc., Publishers
Box 611, Jefferson, North Carolina 28640
www.mcfarlandpub.com

For Brian

Table of Contents

Some people can read *War and Peace* and come away thinking it's a simple adventure story. Others can read the ingredients on a chewing gum wrapper and unlock the secrets of the universe.—Gene Hackman, as Lex Luthor, in *Superman: The Movie* (1978)

Acknowledgments

Comic Book Store Customer: Do you think that Superman is a Republican?

Comic Book Store Proprietor: No way! He's against the death penalty; he asked the U.N. to let him rid the world of all nuclear weapons in Superman IV; he's married to a feminist reporter; his archenemy is Lex Luthor, a billionaire arms dealer and Wall Street executive; and his father was a major environmentalist on Krypton.

Customer: But he wears the American flag as a costume! He's a patriot who believes in "Truth, Justice, and the American Way." Democrats hate patriotism, hate the American flag, and believe in the French Way.

Proprietor: Democrats don't all hate America. A lot of modern-day ones do, but other Democrats love America, and criticize it a lot because they love it. And JFK and FDR Democrats certainly didn't hate America. At the very least, Superman is an FDR Democrat, if not a Jimmy Carter Democrat. He sure as hell isn't a Reagan Republican.

Customer: Well, Captain America has to be Republican at least.

Proprietor: Are you kidding? He's a bigger pinko than Superman!

—*Conversation overheard in now defunct Staten Island comic book store Alternate Realm in the spring of 1998.*

After spending years of my life writing about serious literature, including the works of Jane Austen, Dante Aligheri, and British and American Romantic writers of the 18th and 19th centuries, it has been an enormous pleasure to turn the critical eye that I normally reserve for "high art" to the comic books and fantasy films that I have been a lifelong fan of. The result, I believe, is a work that combines the enthusiasm and occasional subjective tastes of a superhero devotee with the kind of objective, nuanced cultural criticism normally reserved for purely academic works. In a sense, this book is intended to be a more sophisticated version of the same kind of conversation that one might observe taking place between comic book fans, either in specialty stores, or in on-line chat rooms, or in articles written for websites like Ain't it Cool News, only those conversations tend to be a bit too acrimonious, evaluative, trash-talk-filled, bigoted, and trivia-centric for my taste. The slang term "meh" is often overused as a substitute for intelligent conversation, and there's also a lot of discussion about who would most likely win in a fight between Spider-Man and Wolverine or between Superman and the Hulk. The exchange between a comic book store owner and a customer quoted above is an unusually good example of such a conversation. Most are far less interesting. But that particular conversation raises an issue that is of central concern to me. The question of what kinds of political values superheroes represent, and what kind of values they instill in the adults who grew up reading superhero comic books and watching cartoons and films is the underlying concern of this book. What kind of heroism do superheroes represent, and is it a form of heroism worth emulating?

As I put the finishing touches on this book, I need to thank those who have granted me the opportunity to write it. First of all, the book is, in large part, an outgrowth of the research I did as a participant in two National Endowment for the Humanities Summer Seminar Grants for College Teachers. The first, "Adaptation and Revision: The Example of *Great Expectations*," was organized by Hilary Schor and Paul Saint-Amour and held at the University of California at Santa Cruz in July of 2007. The second, "The Decadent 1890s: English Literary Culture and the Fin de Siècle," was organized by Joseph Bristow at the William Andrews Clark Memorial Library, UCLA, from June 22 to July 24, 2009. These seminars, while seemingly far afield from superhero studies, helped me solidify my ideas about adaptation, pastiches, counterfactual narratives, social satire, British imperial history, the gothic genre, and the Victorian era roots of contemporary superhero narratives. Also, my interactions with fellow participants Diana Maltz and David King Dunaway, as well as with guest lecturers Margaret Stetz and Jay Clayton, further focused my thesis. I am also indebted to Ronald Herzman, Bill Cook, James Hala, Frank Battaglia, Wendy Kolmar, Nadine Ollman, and Blanford Parker for their intellectual guidance.

Also, I owe an enormous debt of gratitude to Marsha Keller and Fritz Kiersch, who both helped me, personally and professionally, when I needed help the most. Without them, I would have never managed to finish this book.

Several chapters in this work were featured in previously published anthologies, and have been collected, for the first time, together, in these pages. The Batman chapter was originally written for Lisa DeTora's book *Heroes of Film, Comics and American Culture* (2009), and the Wonder Woman essay first appeared in Terrence Wandtke's *The Amazing Transforming Superhero!* (2007). Both chapters have been updated and rewritten for this volume. The Punisher chapter is a heavily revised version of a paper with a very different title, and a very different focus, "The Dilemma of the Italian-American Male," which originally appeared in an anthology edited by Elwood Watson, *Pimps, Wimps, Studs, Thugs and Gentlemen: Essays on Media Images of Masculinity* (2009). The *Doctor Who* chapter originally appeared as an article in *The Journal of Popular Culture* Volume 43, Issue 5 (October 2010), which has graciously agreed to grant me permission to reprint my work here. The Spider-Man chapter began life as a paper I delivered at Peter Coogan's Comic Arts Conference during the San Diego Comic-Con on July 15, 2005.

I would also like to extend special thanks to David Sweeney, who offered helpful suggestions for focusing my argument better in the chapter on Wonder Woman; and Dr. David Silbey, author of *A War of Frontier and Empire*, who encouraged me to bolster my political and historical arguments in the chapter on Batman. I have also had the pleasure of twice teaching a cross-listed film and English course on "The Politics of Superheroes," once at Alvernia University and once at Oklahoma City University. The discussions I had with students about sex, violence, and political subtexts in superhero comic books, films, and television shows helped me formulate my work on this book, and I would like to single out the following former students for being particularly thoughtful and inspiring in their ideas: Joe Caputo, Mary Thacker, Alexander J. Hensley, John Hill, Sonia Topiarz, Rachel Penny, Orlando Santiago, Chris Stefanic, Alexandra Cardaropoli, Robert G. Ferguson, and Randall R. Beavers. Thanks also to Paul Sadaphal, John Nelka, and Matthew Rodriguez for sending excellent sources my way that I would otherwise have never found.

One of my goals in the production of this book was to provide art to better illustrate the concepts being discussed in the prose. This was particularly important in cases when the characters were obscure, or the storyline difficult to visualize. I owe thanks to many for their help in finding excellent examples of art for this book, including Christina Wolfe, of Oklahoma City University, and Miroslav Liwosz, of Alvernia University.

I would also like to thank Michael Shugrue and Ursula Melendi for giving me a lot of grief for "wasting my time and talents writing about comic books instead of continuing to write about more serious literature," and Peter DiMitri, the former comic-book-store owner quoted in the humorous dialogue about Superman's political party affiliation featured above. DiMitri absolutely loathes Spider-Man, Wonder Woman, and the Doctor, and his frequent, hours-long monologues against all of the above as suitable role models for children was still another source of inspiration for this volume. This book is, in part, my response to his regular attempts at the character assassination of my childhood heroes.

On a more personal note, I want to thank my wife, Stacey, my parents, Cathy and Ted, and my brother, Brian, for encouraging me in my career pursuits, supporting me emotionally and financially, stoking my imagination, challenging my intellect, and indulging me by listening to me talk at length about how great Wonder Woman is as a character, even if a lot of her comic books are mediocre. Finally, I need to thank my best friend from childhood, Mitchell Sherry. Mitchell got me excited about the world of comic books by showing me *The Thing* # 22, in which the Thing is forced to kill his own human alter ego, Ben Grimm, in an attempt to save the life of his true love, Tarianna. It was a work of gripping melodrama that captured my fifth-grade imagination and gave me a lifetime of reading pleasure. Mitchell also showed me, more than just about anyone, what it means to have integrity, be brave, tolerant of all peoples, and to challenge oppression and injustice when it rears its head. Mitchell was a true superhero in the best sense of the term, and continues to be an example that I am proud to follow.

Preface

> When we abstract images through cartooning we're not so much eliminating details as we are focusing on specific details. By stripping down an image to its essential "meaning," an artist can amplify that meaning in a way that realistic art can't. Film critics will sometimes describe a live-action film as a "cartoon" to acknowledge the stripped-down intensity of a simple story or visual style. Though the term is often used disparagingly, it can be equally well applied to many time-tested classics. Simplifying characters and images toward a purpose can be an effective tool for storytelling in any medium. Cartooning isn't a way of drawing. It's a way of seeing.— Scott McCloud, "The Language of Comics"

This book is about how superhero adventures comment upon — and sometimes shape — American public opinion and U.S. government policy. Barack Obama, Gloria Steinem, and Edward Said have all claimed to be inspired by the heroic examples of iconoclastic and anti-establishment superheroes such as Wonder Woman and Spider-Man. In contrast, Jack Bauer, the right-leaning, invincible counterterrorism agent from the television series *24*, reportedly inspired members of the Bush Administration to endorse torture as an acceptable means of fighting terrorism. Since superhero adventures have been in print and on film for more than seventy years, and have enjoyed a notable resurgence of popularity in the period following the terrorist attacks of September 11, 2001, an analysis of the influence of superhero narratives on generations of Americans is as timely as it is important.

As comic-book writer Mark Millar (*Wanted*, *Kick-Ass*) has observed, superhero stories are at their most popular and evocative when they respond to particularly turbulent political times, especially those marred by war and social unrest. The evidence bears him out, as all of the best-remembered, canonical "classic" superhero comic books, as well as the most successful film and television adaptations of comic books, were introduced during World War II, the swinging sixties, the Reagan/Thatcher era, and the Bush/Blair "war on terrorism." In other decades, superhero adventures were out of fashion or subject to censorship that artificially minimized their influence and popularity. The McCarthyist sentiments of the 1950s saw comic books blamed for juvenile delinquency and saddled with censorship that undercut comic book creators' artistic freedom and ability to produce worthwhile works. Notably, the Clinton years were good for the economy overall, but not for superheroes — the 1990s were the years in which Marvel Comics Group went bankrupt and the box-office mega bomb *Batman and Robin* made film studios swear off superheroes. Consequently, the present work will focus on four main periods of time in comic book history.

First and foremost, it is an exploration of how superheroes in print and on film responded to the war on terrorism, and the extent to which they either supported or vilified former United States President George W. Bush and former British Prime Minister Tony

Blair. Also examined will be the two periods in which most of the famous superheroes were first created: the Great Depression and World War II era, which gave birth to Superman, Batman, and Wonder Woman, and the sixties, in which Spider-Man, the Fantastic Four, the X-Men, Iron Man, the Hulk, and *Doctor Who* were first created. The 1980s was another critical period in comic book history, as the World War II–era characters were all radically revamped; their serialized stories began anew with a retelling of their "origin stories" set in the "present" of the 1980s, and their heroism was defined either in support of, or in opposition to, Ronald Reagan's America.

Superhero narratives, as they are traditionally understood, involve colorfully garbed heroic icons that demonstrate uncanny strength, intelligence, supernatural powers, and near-infallibility. Their amazing character traits may be a result of their divine or mythical origins, as in the case of Wonder Woman or Thor; alien heritage, as with Superman or "the Doctor" (from *Doctor Who*); or magic, as in the case of Zatanna Zatara, Doctor Strange, and Harry Potter. In contrast, there are other superheroes such as Iron Man and Green Lantern who are unremarkably "human," but are made supremely powerful by access to advanced technology, or, like Batman, Sherlock Holmes and James Bond, through spending years mastering fighting techniques and honing detective skills. Superheroes such as Aquaman, Spider-Man, and Tarzan are humans who mimic amazing abilities demonstrated in the animal kingdom. Finally, there are those superheroes such as Captain America and Asterix the Gaul whose amazing abilities are derived from performance enhancing drugs or magic potions.

Superheroes are commonly understood to be figures from the DC and Marvel Universe character roster, with Superman and Spider-Man respectively acting as the two multimedia corporations' respective mascots, intellectual properties, and cash cows; this book will not only discuss such figures in depth, but will also consider preternaturally heroic characters from related genres, such as science fiction, fantasy, horror, the crime thriller, and the espionage narrative because those characters represent similar political values and often influence, or are influenced by, traditional superhero stories. After all, to many genre critics, James Bond, Sherlock Holmes, the Doctor, and Harry Potter are as much superheroes as those that reside in Gotham City or the Baxter Building, and such a perception is far from inaccurate. For example, as super spies, Emma Peel and Jack Bauer do not appear to have "powers" such as flight, but they have an uncanny ability to survive any and all physical trauma, they triumph more than they fail, and they show the same grim determination that Batman does in his pursuit of the forces of evil. Indeed, all they need is a Batman mask and a cape and they are virtually indistinguishable from the Dark Knight. Batman himself has often been regarded by critics as part of the same Victorian Gothic lineage as Sherlock Holmes and Count Dracula — and may even be an amalgam of the two — so it is equally reasonable to consider Holmes to be, functionally, a superhero and Dracula a super villain, and any number of comic books, radio shows, or novels that pit Holmes against Dracula certainly feel like superhero stories.

Rather than follow a strictly chronological format, I have instead chosen to explore a selection of particularly evocative superheroes and consider how their portrayals have changed over time and how different writers have characterized them. These heroes primarily include Batman, Superman, Wonder Woman, Spider-Man, the X-Men, the Punisher, and the Fantastic Four, along with a variety of secondary characters, including James Bond, the Doctor, and Iron Man. These characters in particular have been chosen because they have the longest histories of numerous multimedia incarnations — ranging from animated cartoons, newspaper strips, tie-in merchandise, Broadway musicals, live-action TV shows, movies, and movie serials — and their memory has been revived in the public consciousness by a recent adaptation that has been, to one degree or another, widely seen and successful.

I have attempted to objectively examine the ethical codes these heroes represent, sometimes being quite critical of their actions and ideological beliefs. Consequently, while examining how these characters have changed over the years, I will be doing two things simultaneously — analyzing how they reflect and influence the hopes and fears of the average American during a given historical era, and evaluating whether the socio-political beliefs they promote during differing periods represent a healthy, moral, and ethical worldview, or if they have become the vehicle through which dangerous, divisive political propaganda is being spread through the mass media. This dual approach — part historical, part ethically evaluative — should differentiate this book from the secondary sources on superhero narratives that have come before.

The sly Asterix (front) and his invincible friend Obelix (back) defend their homeland, Gaul, from the invading armies of Julius Caesar. Asterix gains temporary super powers by drinking a "performance enhancing" magic potion made by the Druid Get*a*fix. René Goscinny and Albert Uderzo created *Asterix* in 1959, and recent film adaptations star Gérard Depardieu as Obelix. Fan art by Chryst Gaven A. Famorcan (courtesy Chryst Gaven A. Famorcan).

Leaving aside graphic novels themselves and coffee table books, including encyclopedias of superheroes and photo galleries of vintage memorabilia marketed to fans, there remains a rich variety of preexisting academic writing about superheroes published in book form. The works of literary and cultural critics who have already written about superhero adventures tend to form five groups. The first group includes books that are mainly concerned with the history of the creation of comic books, how they are written and produced, how they are marketed, the salacious, behind-the-scenes intrigues involving individual comic book creators and companies, as well as books about the culture of fandom, and the history of comic book censorship. Notable books in this vein include *Men of Tomorrow: Geeks, Gangsters, and the Birth of the Comic Book* (2004) by Gerard Jones, *Comic Book Culture* (1999) by Matthew J. Pustz, *Comic Wars: How Two Tycoons Battled Over the Marvel Comics Empire—And Both Lost* (2002) by Dan Raviv, *Seal of Approval: The History of the Comics Code* (1998) by Amy Kiste Nyberg, and *The Ten-Cent Plague: The Great Comic Book Scare and How It Changed America* (2008) by David Hajdu.

Umberto Eco is the most notable example of the second group of critics, which includes literary theorists, narratologists, and semioticians who use comic books as a means of understanding narrative technique, symbolism, and the structure of story. Such brilliant, erudite writers deserve the credit and the blame for making comic book scholarship a viable intellectual exercise.

The third group of serious secondary sources concerning superheroes includes books by writers such as Geoff Klock, who strive to elevate the respectability of the "graphic novel" among the literati by offering layered, insightful interpretations of landmark superhero comic books that are self-consciously "adult" or post-modern, including the perennially influential *Watchmen* (1986-1987), or graphic novels such as *Contract With God* (1978), *Maus* (1973–1991), *Palestine* (1996), or *Persepolis* (2003), which are not about superheroes but are, instead, autobiographical tales about the Jewish immigrant experience, the Holocaust, the Arab-Israeli conflict, and the Islamic radicalization of Iran following the 1979 revolution. These works are so well done that they challenge the notion that comic books are merely for kids, or a mass-marketed corporate product as healthy for the reading diet as potato chips are for the food diet. These are also the works most likely to find themselves on college syllabi, though even these are often looked down upon by literature purists, who agree with Harold Bloom that comic books have no place in the classroom, no matter how well-written or drawn they are, or how important and controversial their subject matter.

The fourth group of critics includes new historicists—such as Trina Robbins, Peter Coogans, Bradford W. Wright, and Will Brooker—who examine landmark superhero adventures as products of their time and as a means of determining that period's attitude towards issues such as gender, race-relations, and class.

The fifth group of superhero scholars includes cultural critics who, in a Leo Tolstoy–like fashion, worry about the moral repercussions of a populist narrative that reaches a wide audience of "Everymen" that appears to promote patriotism, violence, and anti-feminism, and that caricatures racial and ethnic minority "others" as evil or ignorant. Writers who express concern over the glorification of the male warrior image include Marina Warner and Leo Braudy, while Gerard Jones strove to respond to, and allay, these fears, with the book *Killing Monsters: Why Children Need Fantasy, Superheroes, and Make-Believe Violence* (2002).

The style and methodology of this book will blend the sensibilities of the fourth and fifth species of comic book critic. I will be examining the ways in which various superhero stories respond to issues of war, race, gender, politics, and religion in a manner born of a specific time and place. I will consider the extent to which these stories reflect the dominant values of the era, as well as the extent to which comic book writers and creators are rallying against the dominant spirit of the time and trying to influence public opinion. Whenever possible, I will use evidence from interviews with the storytellers themselves to reveal what social messages they intended to convey and how they hoped their audiences might respond.

The political messages embedded in these narratives by the creators, either deliberately or subconsciously, vary wildly from the radically liberal to the archconservative. I will be considering the possible effect these messages have on readers of all ages and the extent to which the messages point toward a more peaceful worldview or to a more martial one. Reading such stories with a moral eye is often a troubling prospect; I don't want to be dogmatic or paternalistic, nor do I endorse censorship. Conservative media pundits such as Bill O'Reilly and Michael Medved most often condemn art — both high and popular — from the vantage point of a self-appointed moral watchdog, and use "morals" as an excuse to promote censorship and to advocate for the cutting of funding for the arts. As a liberal moralist, I disapprove of O'Reilly and Medved's seeming attempt to silence secular humanist voices by publicly campaigning against bogeymen such as "Hollywood liberals" and "the liberal media." In contrast, I would like to demonstrate how it is possible to advocate for a medium that is often considered morally questionable — the super-violent, super-sexy superhero adventure — from an ethical perspective. In doing so, I want to demonstrate how tales of such dubious moral and literary merit could indeed, promote morals that would be good for people of any age any age, not just children, to adopt.

In fact, I believe that a somewhat moralist approach to the superhero genre is warranted, given the nature of the superhero narrative. Superhero stories bill themselves as tales of courage and friendship, representing American ideals at their best while attempting to pass on a strong moral code to the impressionable children who read comic books, play superhero video games, and watch superhero films. Since superhero stories make morals their business, it is useful to respond by analyzing the morals from a "moralist" perspective and judge these stories, at least to a degree, on their own terms before subjecting them to a deconstructionist analysis. Essentially, the moral framework for my analysis of these stories will not be the same one employed by contemporary conservative "moralists," but will be a continuation and modernization of the moralistic approach laid down by Leo Tolstoy in *What Is Art?* In this landmark work of art criticism, published for the first time in unexpurgated form in 1898, Tolstoy argues that bad art promotes social divisions, insular thinking, and conflict, while good art strives to convince the audience to set aside intellectual tunnel vision and embrace other cultures, perspectives, and individuals. At their most conservative, multimedia works of superhero art have advocated, to an unhealthy degree, that which Tolstoy argued is destructive, divisive propaganda. According to Tolstoy, such "bad" art conveys "the sentiment for the reverence of images, for [religious iconography], and for the king's person; of shame at betraying a comrade, devotion to a flag, the necessity of revenge for an insult, the need to sacrifice one's labor for the erection and adornment of churches, the duty of defending one's honor or the glory of one's native land" (Tolstoy 186). Certainly, Superman for one might well be seen as the physical embodiment of all of these "bad" ideals: a God-man dressed in the American flag that promises to fight for "truth, justice, and the American way."

However, comic books have, at their best, promoted values that Tolstoy would deem good, even within the basic framework of a melodramatic story that pits a superhero against a supervillain. In these instances, key moments of characterization, and sensitively written resolutions have altered the values that are promoted by the basically conservative character-type of the superhero, and changed the story structure enough to make a classically reactionary genre more progressive in tone. In stories such as these, the St. George figure sometimes decides not to kill the dragon after all. In fact, in some stories, St. George and the dragon decide they have a lot in common and become fast friends. These artfully written tales promote the more universal values that Tolstoy believed all good art should promote. As he wrote, "that same art [which could promote evil causes] can also evoke reverence for the dignity of every man and for the life of every animal; can make men ashamed of luxury, of violence, of revenge, or of using them for pleasure that of which others are in need; can compel people freely, gladly, and without noticing it, to sacrifice themselves in the service of man" (Tolstoy 186).

In addition, it is important to note that Tolstoy was an unrepentant advocate of "popular" fiction. Literary critics such as Harold Bloom and conservative thinkers such as Rush Limbaugh and Jeffrey Hart have decried the study of comic books and films in college classrooms and scholarship as frivolous and proof of the watering-down of education by radically leftist professors and administrators. (Limbaugh calls this process "filling young skulls with mush.") Other critics argue that comic books are too trivial to comment effectively on the most pressing political and social issues of our — or, for that matter, any — time. However, Tolstoy believed that the best way to change society was to transmit morally informed art to the masses, and I agree with him. Tolstoy felt that the most effective moral art would be accessible to the masses, and what stories are more accessible to the masses than superhero stories that are included in television shows, in films, on the internet, in video games, in newspaper strips, in graphic novels, and in monthly comic books? If any popular art has the potential to change public opinion for the better, especially now, it is the superhero story at the height of its popularity.

Chloe Moretz plays "Hit Girl," an 11-year-old assassin who slaughters a room full of Mafiosi in Matthew Vaughn's 2010 adaptation of the Mark Millar comic book *Kick-Ass* (Lions Gate). Critic Roger Ebert dubbed the film "morally reprehensible."

While my own personalized and modernized application of Tolstoy's thesis represents this book's philosophical foundation, I will more often quote directly from, and comment upon, scholarship by more contemporary thinkers who have made their careers analyzing art and society. In addition to the superhero narratives in comic books, television, and film that will serve as my primary sources, key texts cited will include gender criticism such as Leo Braudy's *From Chivalry to Terrorism: War and the Changing Nature of Masculinity* and Marina Warner's "Boys Will Be Boys" and "Fantasy's Power and Peril." Writings by film critics and scholars Roger Ebert, Molly Haskell, Pauline Kael, and Laura Mulvey will be referenced as a means of understanding the film adaptations of comic books, and my close-reading of landmark superhero narratives will build upon scholarship by Marshall McLuhan, Trina Robbins, Bradford W. Wright, and Will Brooker. Informing my discussion of the intersection of economics, religion, imperialism, and international conflict will be the works of George Orwell, Salman Rushdie, Noam Chomsky, Anthony Shadid, Lisa Finnegan, S.T. Joshi, and Wallace Shawn, among others.

While evaluating the political content of superhero stories, I will be using terms such as "liberal" and "conservative," which — as Orwell observed as far back as 1946 in his essay "Politics and the English Language" — have lost much of their meaning thanks to overuse, conflicting definitions, and misrepresentation. Indeed, I have already used such terms repeatedly in this preface. To clarify, when using such terms, I will be doing so both as a means of identifying the political bias of a given narrative, as well as identifying the extent to which the story fits Tolstoy's vision of "good" art. For example, when employing terms such as "liberal," "progressive," and "left-wing," I am suggesting that it promotes the universal, egalitarian, and populist ideals of Leo Tolstoy and would, therefore, be considered good art in his schema. Sometimes the authors of these stories have publicly identified themselves as left-of-center, or members of the Democratic, Green, Socialist, or Labor Parties of America or Great Britain, but often their exact party affiliation is a matter of conjecture. When identifying the story as "right-wing," "conservative," or "reactionary," I am arguing that it has the potential to promote the kind of sectarian and nationalistic worldview that would be repellant to Tolstoy, and would, therefore, potentially constitute bad art. Sometimes the authors of these stories proudly proclaim themselves as Tories, Republicans, Tea Party members, or Libertarians. Other times, they may be independents, conservative Democrats, or reluctant to disclose their party affiliations.

Ultimately, all of the above labels in this text are used in both a descriptive fashion and a highly evaluative manner. The positive connotation bestowed upon leftist labels and the negative connotation given right-wing labels will earmark me as left-of-center politically myself. Revealing my bias here saves me the trouble of disingenuously half-hiding it at the risk muddying the clarity of my voice. That having been said, my opinions of the quality of superhero narratives, and of the charisma of a given superhero, are not wholly dogmatic. For example, I begin the book with a highly positive portrayal of Batman, who represents conservative thinking at its best and its worst. Also, characters such as Green Arrow and Jean-Luc Picard do tend to fall flat as mouthpieces for liberalism, and do not have enough of a "soul" — that is, consistently nuanced, three-dimensional characterization — to engage my interest or respect, despite the fact that they represent well-meaning attempts by a collective of left-leaning writers to personify a worldview that I am in sympathy with. Significantly, I do not see my affection for the conservative Batman and my disdain for Green Arrow and Picard as inconsistency, but rather as proof that I am not an ideologue. I am capable of liking a character whose entire worldview makes me uncomfortable if that character is brought to life by storytellers with talent and an intelligent conservative vision.

In the Introduction, I will test cultural critic and feminist historian Marina Warner's thesis that superhero stories are fundamentally conservative and served to shore up support for the Bush-Cheney Administration following the attacks of September 11, 2001. The chapter will focus primarily on what kinds of heroism the superhero represented during the Bush administration, and will establish the methodology that will be employed to interpret superhero narratives throughout this book.

In the first chapter, I examine Batman, who strives to recreate a feudal world order in modern-day America by combining liberal sentiments such as anti-poverty measures and social programs with a tough-minded attitude towards crime fighting that gets him accused of being a fascist. Like Tony Blair, he is actually "Tough on crime and tough on the causes of crime." His adventures have always been political, but in recent years he has taken to defending Gotham City from terrorists like Osama bin Laden and corrupt corporate moguls modeled after the indicted Enron executives, making his stories more provocative than ever.

Chapter Two concerns Wonder Woman, who acted as a rallying symbol for the U.S. forces during their struggle against the Nazis in World War II, as well as an inspiration for the feminists of the 1960s and 1970s. In recent years, she has lost a large measure of her popularity thanks to a several-decades-long anti-feminist backlash led by conservatives, but her popularity is again on the rise, as she has become the subject of increased critical attention and comic book sales, a direct-to-video cartoon film released in early 2009, and a prominent role in episodes of the *Justice League* cartoon written by Dwayne McDuffie.

In Chapter Three, I consider how the character of Spider-Man has always been one of the most morally ambiguous superheroes, and how his status as a complicated, realistic figure can be particularly valuable for modern day Americans to contemplate during times as uncertain as those we live in today. His political ambivalence is rooted in the contrasting politics of his co-creators, Ayn Rand Objectivist Steve Ditko and hippie sympathizer Stan Lee, who infused Spider-Man with the conflicting impulses to both despise "the common man" as an ignorant bigot, and to do everything possible to help "the common man" rise above his lot in life. Both supremely selfish and supremely selfless, Spider-Man is a study in personal and political confusion, urbane humor, and Woody Allen–style neuroses. Part superhero, part–*Seinfeld* supporting character, Spider-Man's cultural confusion, financial difficulties, and problems relating to women make him easy for the insecure and inhibited to relate to.

The Punisher is spotlighted in Chapter Four as an example of an archconservative superhero who deals out death to virtually every criminal he faces. His hatred of street crime amounts to a pathological hatred of immigrants, including those from his own background, Italian Americans, and his massacring of such peoples amounts to an awful way of reversing an arguably too-liberal immigration policy. The Punisher is also interesting as a Vietnam Veteran, and his war scars are all the deeper than those suffered by World War II Veterans like Captain America because Vietnam was a far more politically divisive war. The Punisher is compared to characters such as Dirty Harry, who advanced conservative sentiments during the 1970s as part of a hippie backlash, as well as Judge Dredd, a British comic book character from the 1980s who satirized American machismo and gun-obsession.

Superman is the focus of Chapter Five. While previous critics have focused on his arguably unhealthy romantic relationship with Lois Lane, or his tendency to think with his fists, I will examine Superman as an FDR Democrat figure who defends the environment from destruction at the hands of Lex Luthor; who argued against nuclear proliferation during the 1980s; and who — bizarrely enough — took on the Ku Klux Klan *in real life*, and dealt a serious blow to their enrollment. This chapter will also consider the Jewish cultural origins of Superman, and his basis in the story of Moses and the legend of the Golem.

Chapter Six is about both the causes of the Iraq War and the nature of the alliance between the U.S. and Britain. In *Fantastic Four: Authoritative Action*, the Fantastic Four attempt to liberate the nation of Latveria from the tyrannical Doctor Doom, but find that the people they have come to save are just as afraid of the Fantastic Four as they were of Doom. The story is a commentary on both the "war on terror" and Operation Iraqi Freedom, as is *JLA: The Hypothetical Woman*, the James Cameron science fiction epic *Avatar*, and the revival of the television series *Battlestar Galactica*. However, the focus of the chapter is primarily on international views of the war on terror, and the portrayal of Americans, and their ally, Tony Blair, in British popular culture.

In order to provide a contrast with the mostly American characters being examined in the book, I focus on the British character "The Doctor" in Chapter Six. The alien from *Doctor Who* is an interesting amalgam of the characters Sherlock Holmes, Batman, and Superman; he has the powers of hypnosis, enhanced physical strength, the ability to put himself into a deep hibernation, and is even capable of full bodily regeneration when he is injured near to death. He is also, in many of his adventures on television and in comic books, an anti-imperialist who has spent much of his career fighting Nazi-like opponents and has, in his latest incarnation, taken to fighting American imperialism in a new series that is, arguably, staunchly anti-American. Controversial episodes of the new series include one that suggests that Bush staged 9/11 to justify his takeover of the Middle East and another that skewers Fox News and its owner, Rupert Murdoch, for killing real journalism. The chapter also examines the British characters James Bond and John Constantine, and considers how these characters have leveled serious criticisms against American imperialism.

Chapter Seven concerns the portrayal of the U.S. torture policy in popular culture, especially in the series *24* and in the "torture porn" film genre, which portrays torture as a necessary evil. In contrast, the Fantastic Four comic books and films took a strong stand against torture, as well as other Bush initiatives, including the Iraq War, the Patriot Act, and his anti-environmentalist programs. The most liberal member of the Fantastic Four, the Invisible Woman, was particularly aggressive in her defiance, showing that she had become more radical in the years since she was created to be a Cold War era love interest and homemaker.

Ron Pearlman has starred as the title character in both animated and live-action *Hellboy* movies produced and directed by Guillermo del Toro. In the comics, written and drawn by Mike Mignola, Hellboy protects our world from invasion by other-dimensional demons and H.P. Lovecraft–style tentacle monsters, but is feared by the very humans he protects.

In Chapter Eight, I examine the X-Men as representations of persecuted, sometimes closeted, homosexuality. Individual superheroes are often inconsistently portrayed as asexual, heterosexual, bisexual, or homosexual, and how they are portrayed by actors and authors, and how they are received by fans are indicators of how gays are perceived by society as a whole. But the multiethnic band of persecuted mutants featured in the X-Men have a broad appeal, and also speak to teenagers, Jews, and African Americans because of their status as disenfranchised, alienated Americans.

The ninth and final

chapter, "In Brightest Day, In Darkest Knight: President Obama vs. the Zombie Apocalypse" explores the American psyche during the Obama Presidency. Shortly after his 2009 inauguration, progressives around the world saw Obama as America's last hope to save itself before its whole culture collapsed into decadence and anarchy. His supporters had high expectations of a successful presidency characterized by sweeping (and necessary) reforms, but it soon became apparent even to his most ardent supporters that he alone could not save America from the horrific consequences of the worst economic depression in seventy years, two wars, a series of environmental catastrophes, systemic problems with immigration policy, rampant racism and homophobia, religious fanaticism, and fundamentally flawed health care, education, and financial systems nationwide.

With problems this calamitous, it is unsurprising that the allegorical "zombie apocalypse" that has been foretold by cult horror films, Heavy Metal concept albums, and video games since the 1968 release of *Night of the Living Dead* seemed to be imminent. Several comic books published since Obama's election have predicted that the apocalypse will, indeed, tragically happen on the watch of a president who *could have prevented it* had he faced less implacable opposition from the conservative, corporate establishment, or been elected a term sooner. Consequently, it is unsurprising that Antarctic Press released the comic book *President Evil* in 2009. The title depicted Obama and Hillary Clinton as pseudo-superheroes compelled to join forces with their political rivals, John McCain and Sarah Palin, to combat a zombie virus spread throughout America via the swine flu outbreak. As of the writing of this introduction, the comic book series has not yet completed the satirical narrative, and Obama has not yet completed his first term, leaving followers of both the comic book and current events in suspense regarding what forces will triumph in the end: the zombies or the president?

During the course of the book, I hope to demonstrate how the seemingly simple-minded medium of the superhero story raises questions that few products generated for mass consumption have dared ask. These stories are unsettling, and don't provide easy answers for the audience member. Instead, the comic books inspire us to meditate on the tense and controversial issues of our day and inspire us to think in unconventional terms. Years ago, Edward Said and Gloria Steinem found themselves inspired by the disreputable, anarchic images of comic books to become thinkers and activists who worked to change the world and make it a better place. As we read the comic books of today, and go to see a supposedly dispensable form of entertainment — the summer blockbuster movie based on such comic books — we need to consider whether we will use the action-packed story as a means of escape from the real world, and from responsibility in it, or allow the politics underlying the spectacle to make us directly wrestle with difficult issues, and inspire us to react with similar thoughtfulness and sensitivity to the pressing questions of our time.

Introduction

Are Superheroes Republicans? On The Avengers, Star Trek, *and* Watchmen

I'm a great believer that popular fiction, not just literary fiction, [can entertain an audience but, at the same time, take them into serious world issues, like John LeCarre does]. The great argument for politics as fiction is *1984*. If you imagine that George Orwell had written that book as a political tract about totalitarianism, it might well have been very good, but we would have forgotten it. But because he turned it into characters and a story and language and used his imagination, he created a work which changed the way that people thought about totalitarianism. I am not saying that my novel [*The Ghost*] is on that level, but in a humble way, that is also what I am trying to do.—Robert Harris[1]

I hated comic books growing up.... I didn't believe in the whole idea of a superhero.... Superheroes are bad role models for kids anyway. My favorite superhero growing up was the Hulk. I figured, he's green, I'm black—it's close enough. This guy is my hero. But did you ever see his TV show? Same dilemma *every week!* [Bruce Banner warns a bunch of punks] "Don't make me angry. You wouldn't like me if I was angry...." [Then t]hey would beat his ass like an animal. Then he'd get mad and turn into a monster and beat them up and keep on walking like nothing happened. I mean, what kind of role model is gonna fight that much? After five episodes, I was like, "Hey man ... maybe it's you!"—Dave Chappelle[2]

Do Superheroes Promote Violence?

While the comic books, films, video games, and television series featuring superheroes have been marketed primarily to children and adolescents, their content is often far more serious than their reputations would suggest, and people of all ages have been exposed to superhero narratives since the publishing debut of *Superman* in 1938. In fact, comic books have always been political, and have taken stands on controversial issues such as the death penalty, abortion, gay rights, and the environment. They have also reflected the mood of the public by being pro-war during wartime and pacifistic during peacetime almost as often as they have served as the voice of the minority opinion, crying for peace during wartime and advocating going to war when the public is reluctant to do so. Perhaps the most famous example of this occurred in 1941 when the Jewish writers of the *Captain America* comic book inspired widespread public debate by depicting Hitler as a comic book "supervillain" before the U.S. had entered World War II. However, several similarly controversial superhero stories have been produced since.

A 1963 comic book written by Stan Lee introduced high-tech weapons designer Tony

Stark, who built his first, crude Iron Man "battle-suit" as a means of escaping from a Communist prison camp in South Vietnam. As star and co-plotter of the story for *Superman IV* (1987), Christopher Reeve famously argued for nuclear disarmament during the Reagan administration. A 1992 comic book storyline reflected American dissatisfaction with how the first Gulf War concluded when it featured the Hulk single-handedly conquering a fictional country that symbolized Iraq (called Trans-Sabal), and his best friend, Rick Jones assassinated the dictator Farnoq Dahn, who was obviously a stand-in for Saddam Hussein.[3]

Generally speaking, politically themed superhero adventures tend to fall into three different categories: establishment, anti-establishment, and colonial. In the first category, the establishment narrative, the superhero acts to preserve the social status quo, and protects the government and the populace from invading foreign hordes, enemy saboteurs, and homegrown criminals and terrorists. In the second category, the anti-establishment narrative, the superhero stands in opposition to an evil governmental, corporate, or aristocratic villain (which is sometimes propped up by a misguided establishment hero). In the third category, the superhero travels overseas to an untouched, uncivilized country to civilize it and plunder its natural resources, often before a third power stakes claim to the land first.

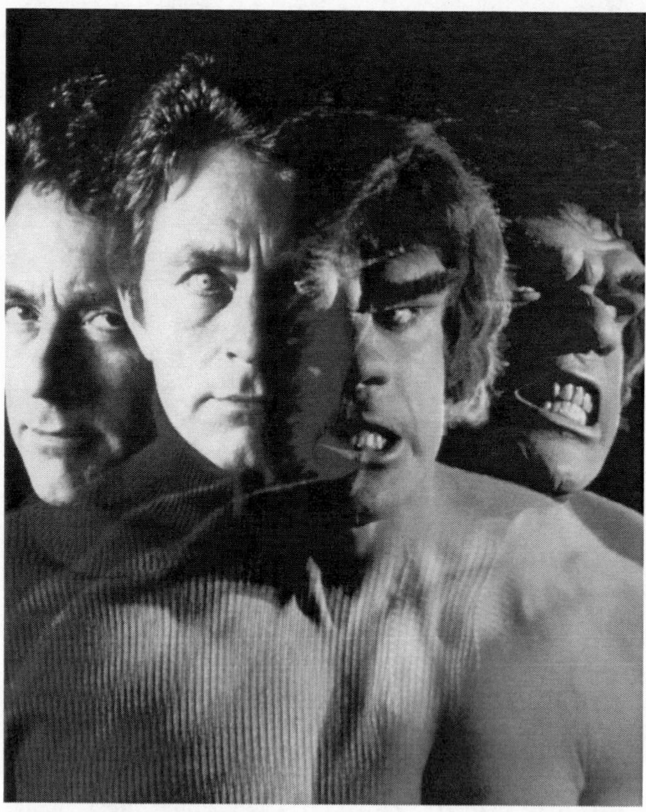

The Incredible Hulk **(1977–1982) television series starred Bill Bixby as Dr. David Banner, a gentle scientist cursed with a Jekyll-and-Hyde affliction that transforms him into the rampaging Hulk (Lou Ferrigno) anytime someone is foolish enough to make him angry. Dave Chappelle joked that he related to the Hulk as a child, but that the character is a bad role model.**

A striking example of an establishment narrative is the patriotic, World War II era *Batman* serial from 1943, directed by Lambert Hillyer. In the story, Batman and Robin protect America from the threat of evil Asian mastermind, Dr. Tito Daka (J. Carrol Naish). Daka has somehow escaped the Japanese American Internment program and based his terrorist activities in a now abandoned section of Gotham City called Little Tokyo. Driving home the serial's already apparent anti-immigrant and anti–Japanese message, a narrator intones ominously: "This was part of a foreign land, transplanted bodily to America and known as Little Tokyo. Since a wise government rounded up the shifty-eyed Japs, it has become virtually a ghost street...." One imagines that if Batman had been invented during the passage of the Alien and Sedition Acts in

1798, he would have been on hand to help John Adams apprehend "rude, smelly, big-nosed Frenchmen" too.

The 1966 Czech New Wave film *Who Wants to Kill Jessie?* is a brilliant, if largely unknown, example of the anti-establishment superhero narrative that features Playboy cover girl Olga Schoberová as Jessie, a leopard-skin-wearing heroine armed with a magnetic glove. The plot concerns a nebbish Czech scientist, Jindrich Beránek, who finds inspiration for his experiments by reading *Jessie* comic books filled with absurdly unscientific "scientific" devices (e.g., magnetic gloves). Jindrich is married to another scientist, Ruzenka Beránková, who has developed a device that can read people's minds when they dream—and delete those dreams if they are too revolutionary. Ruzenka tries the device on her husband and is appalled to find him dreaming about the voluptuous Jessie and her never-ending battle against the evil "Super Man" and the cowboy Pistol Nick. Ruzenka deletes Jindrich's adulterous dream, not knowing that an unanticipated side effect of this ultimate form of thought-control is that the censored material is magically transplanted into the real world. Consequently, the fictional characters Jessie, Super Man, and Pistol Nick materialize in Ruzenka's apartment, escape into the streets, and begin running amok around Prague, speaking in word balloons and ripping up lamp posts. While Ruzenka initially hopes to find a way to return Jessie, Pistol Nick, and Super Man to the realm of fantasy, she and Jindrich ultimately decide to trade up spouses. Ruzenka coerces the reluctant Super Man into cohabiting, and Jindrich wins Jessie. However, the moment a commitment is made, Jessie ceases being a mere "dream woman" and becomes a "real" woman, who has needs and demands outside of making Jindrich's sexual fantasies come true.

Who Wants to Kill Jessie? equates the constraints of marriage and domestic life with the limits of freedom placed upon individuals in Czechoslovakia's highly oppressive Communist regime, which seized control in 1948. In *Jessie*, wives, like Communist governments, curtail men's freedoms and insist on pure, loyal thoughts at all times. Arguably, the film is simultaneously anti-establishment, anti-marriage, and anti-feminist. Like other radical directors of the era, including Milos Forman, *Jessie* director Václav Vorlícek wanted "to make the Czech people collectively aware that they were participants in a system of oppression and incompetence which had brutalized them all" (Cook 705).

The third category of superhero narrative, the colonial tale, was a staple of the Victorian Gothic era, especially evident in the works of H. Rider Haggard, but the most memorable American Cold War–era example is the *Star Trek* episode "Friday's Child," written by Dorothy C. Fontana. United Federation of Planets representatives Kirk, Spock, and McCoy travel to the planet Capella IV, which has a primitive, tribal society blessed with rich natural resources. The Klingons pretend to be interested in negotiating for mining rights but are secretly interested in conquering the natives, whereas Kirk and the Federation forces want to offer the natives protection from the Klingons and the benefit of their civilizing, compassionate influence. The Klingons instigate a revolution, hoping to replace the current native leader, who is more sympathetic with the Federation, with a puppet leader who favors the Klingons. A small-scale guerrilla war ensues, the Klingons are defeated, and Kirk, Spock, and McCoy become the adoptive parents of the young native prince who assumes command of Capella IV. For a colonial narrative, the portrayal of the native people's is unusually sympathetic, especially as compared to the natives depicted in *She*, *King Kong*, and *Tarzan*, but there is an extent to which Kirk's smiling Colonial Ruler remains a Colonial Ruler nonetheless.

All three of these story types remain fixtures of the monthly comic books produced by the major companies, Marvel, DC, Image, and Dark Horse, and the film and television adaptations they generate. *Batman, The Punisher*, and *Iron Man* comics are consistently establishment narratives. *Wonder Woman, X-Men, Hellblazer*, and *Doctor Who* stories tend to be anti-establishment. *Indiana Jones, Doctor Strange, Birds of Prey*, and *Excalibur* tend to be colonial narratives.

While a variety of writers have crafted stories for these characters, those who are tapped to do so represent an elite minority, so the same handful of writers are famous for crafting stories for a variety of iconic characters. Writers such as Mark Waid, John Byrne, Gerry Conway, Dennis O'Neil, J.M. DeMatteis, Len Wein, and Jim Starlin have all written stories for the same group of heroes, including Superman, Batman and Wonder Woman, whose rights are held by DC Comics and Warner Brothers, and Spider-Man and the Fantastic Four, who are owned by Marvel Comics. Writers do not always announce their political biases in interviews, and they are not always in control of how their stories are interpreted by readers, so it is sometimes difficult to interpret the political messages in superhero stories. Since different writers handle the same character, sometimes a liberal writer will cast the heroic ideal as a liberal while a successor might portray that same hero as a conservative. As a case in point, liberal comic book writer Dennis O'Neil portrayed the Robin Hood–like Green Arrow as a Marxist revolutionary figure, while O'Neil's successors, Mike Grell and Brad Meltzer, portrayed Green Arrow as far more right-wing. Some fans only acknowledge the legitimacy of stories that present a superhero in a light that reflects their own politics, others demand consistency of characterization to aid their suspension of disbelief, and a minority are able to overlook the dramatic inconsistencies by arguing that the character is "going through a phase" or has understandably changed political allegiances during a turbulent time in American history.

Since these characters are not in the public domain, fans who attempt to write their own stories with established characters, or who try to reinterpret the classic visions of such characters in controversial ways, are often silenced by the rights holders in the name of copyright infringement. For example, the French awareness-raising organization AIDES attempted to use representations of Wonder Woman and Superman stricken with AIDS as a means of demonstrating that the disease could touch, and destroy, the lives of everyone, even those who believe themselves to be beyond AIDS's reach. Worried that the sight of a skeletal Wonder Woman lying in a hospital bed attached to an intravenous drip, or of an emaciated Superman breathing from an oxygen tank would somehow harm the image that the general public has of these characters, DC demanded that AIDES pull the ads from French subways and billboards. Consequently, AIDES was thwarted in its effort to get out the message that "AIDS touches us all" using those particular images, although those pictures can still be found online.[4]

In other instances, the publishers themselves have lent their characters to certain causes, as Marvel and DC have had occasion to publish comics to raise funds for UNICEF, and publisher Aspen MLT released an issue of *Fathom*— a comic about an aquatic, female superhero named Aspen — that raised funds for the National Wildlife Federation in the aftermath of the Deepwater Horizon oil spill.[5]

During election years, grass-roots campaigners like to co-opt copyrighted superhero imagery, largely because superheroes are so iconic and recognizable, as a means of making a political point. Buttons sporting a dramatic picture of Spider-Man boasting "Spider-Man for John Kerry" were illegally distributed in Manhattan during the 2004 presidential election between the Democratic Kerry and Republican incumbent, President George W. Bush. While liberals co-opted the image of Spider-Man in that instance, conservatives have done the same. A *Batman for President 2008* web site, created in January of that year, purported to support the fictional Batman as a real-life White House hopeful. The site campaign slogan read: "No welfare. No taxes. No mercy. Batman 2008."[6] During the 1988 Presidential Election, Republican Vice Presidential candidate and George H.W. Bush's running mate Dan Quayle famously declared, "I want to be Robin to Bush's Batman."

Gerald Scarfe, British editorial cartoonist for *The Sunday Times* and *The New Yorker*, is known for drawing President Obama as an appalled, miserable figure in an ill-fitting Superman costume, overwhelmed by being president in tumultuous times. In one cartoon, Scarfe depicts the "Kryptonian" Obama perched on a hill over the Gaza Strip, watching as it burns, uncertain what to do. In another, Scarfe identifies Obama as "the new broom," and shows the Superman figure sweeping up a floor covered in mountains of ticker tape labeled "deficit," "recession," "energy crisis," "Iran," "Iraq," "Afghanistan," "Russia," and more. Scarfe is one of several to depict Obama in this fashion. A survey of President Obama political cartoons displayed on the online art database DeviantArt.com in 2010 yields an array of positive portrayals of Obama as a superhero figure, sometimes dressed as Batman, Superman, or one of the Na'vi from James Cameron's *Avatar*, while anti–Obama art paints him as the Joker, *Mad Magazine* moron Alfred E. Neuman, or the Fascist Captain America villain the Red Skull, hiding under a smiling mask.[7] British journalist Ben Walters has condemned the representations of Obama as the Joker — perennially punctuated by the word "SOCIALISM" — as being particularly problematic. Not only is depicting a black man in "white face" racist, the connection between the Joker and Obama isn't funny because their personalities are nothing alike, suggesting that the image is meant only to demonize Obama, not comment substantively and incisively on his agenda, Walters observed.

Sometimes, stories and images not sanctioned by the copyright holders of individual superhero characters are successfully made available to the public, but they are generally satirical in tone, such as political cartoons in which famous figures are dressed as superheroes or supervillains, or *Mad Magazine* spoofs of superhero-themed films or television shows. Online communities publish fan-written "slash" fiction, which proposes, and dramatizes, straight and gay sexual relations between characters that seem to have chemistry together when in the same scene in a superhero adventure, but — for whatever reason — the official word from the copyright holders is that these characters are emphatically not romantically involved. For example, famous slash fiction stories posit a gay romance between Kirk and Spock, Batman and Robin, and Spider-Man and Harry Osborne, or enacted heterosexual encounters between Mulder and Scully, Superman and Lois Lane, and the Doctor and one of his various "Platonic" female friends before any of these characters eventually did have sex in the official, canonical versions of the superhero narratives endorsed by the copyright holders.

As a natural consequence of the multitude of storytellers who craft superhero adventures, and the changes in cultural values over the years in which the adventures are in production, superheroes become many different things to many different people. Children see superheroes as the adults they hope one day to grow up to be, people looking for religion in a secular age sometimes see superheroes as replacements for gods and angels, while others look to superheroes as moral and/or physical paradigms to live up to. Some enjoy the romanticism of superhero adventures and wish they themselves could perform feats of heroism, instead of living through their unremarkable day-to-day lives studying in an awful school or working long hours in a cubicle in a dead-end, middle-management job. The M. Night Shyamalan film *Unbreakable* (2000) also posited the notion that people with physical handicaps or debilitating illnesses such as asthma and allergies can live vicariously through superheroes, being physically active in the world of fiction when they do not feel capable of being physically active themselves on the football field. Indeed, the sheer number of superheroes with real or symbolic handicaps speaks to this phenomenon — Daredevil is blind, Tony Stark has an artificial heart, and both Oracle and *Avatar*'s Jake Sully are crippled.

Superheroes can mean all these things, and more.

When Andrew Garfield was cast as Peter Parker in the fourth *Spider-Man* film, he said he'd been preparing for the role since he was four years old, when he wore his first Spider-Man costume. He has always seen himself as Spider-Man. Garfield said that he feels like "every young boy who feels stronger on the inside than they look on the outside, any skinny boy basically who wishes their muscles matched their sense of injustice, God, it's just the stuff that dreams are made of, for sure."[8]

But how, one might ask, can the figure of the superhero — a muscle-bound, magically powered oaf dressed in wrestling tights that sport the colors of the American flag — be a figure of interest to both children and adults alike? Aren't superheroes too ridiculous to be taken seriously by adults, no matter how depressing the tone of their recent films, and no matter how much political commentary is shoehorned into the narrative between fight scenes with evil, effete opponents in equally colorful wrestling outfits? One answer is that adults shouldn't be interested in superheroes. They should be more concerned with the real world, real life, and more adult concerns. They should have moved on from comic books and should be reading real literature, watching serious dramatic films (directed by Lars von Trier, Nicole Holofcener, Peter Watkins, Jane Campion, and Noah Baumbach), they should be more actively engaged with greening the planet and spending time with their families. Judd Apatow comedies such as *The 40-Year-Old Virgin* functionally make this argument, simultaneously celebrating the male protagonists' encyclopedic knowledge of the popular culture of their youth while criticizing them for not moving on, maturing, leaving fantasy worlds behind, and learning how to have a serious, committed relationship with a woman.

In a similar manner, the documentary films such as *Trekkies* and movies like *Galaxy Quest* criticize devoted fans of shows like *Star Trek* for not understanding the difference between the real world and the world of fiction, and for becoming experts in speaking Klingon or learning the schematics of the Starship *Enterprise* instead of learning a real foreign language or taking up the study of actual engineering as it exists today. The point is well taken, but pointing to fanatical devotion of a hobby and laughing at it does not explain the devotion, nor does it offer any kind of insightful commentary as what kind of appeal fantasy franchises might have to casual, or saner, audience members. The fact remains that, as ridiculous as some individuals look dressed up in Halloween costumes when going to see the release of a new franchise film, or when attending the annual San Diego Comic-Con, superhero movies and video games are currently a national phenomenon, and their success cannot be accounted for by fanatical fans alone.

Indeed, much of their success comes from their obvious relevance, and their uncanny ability to speak to contemporary concerns — especially of the young. Consider how effectively superhero stories have been able to comment on our own love-hate relationship with our bodies in the last several decades — directly confronting issues such as plastic surgery, performance-enhancing drugs, and the amount of time we spend sitting in chairs and surfing the internet instead of moving about physically. Several superhero stories written since the creation of the internet have acted as commentaries on the divide between the "real" world — offline — and the world of fiction — "online" — and tied those parallels into waking and dreaming, and our public personas and our deepest, innermost desires. Depictions of the Internet as a therapeutic domain in which we all seek refuge, self-actualization, and liberation from an oppressive, hive-minded "real" world include *Voyager: Unimatrix Zero* (2000) and the anime *Paprika* (2006). Unsurprisingly, those stories are also about the threat that one day, the Internet will stop being a place of refuge and become, like the real world, a domain of rules, regulations, and corporate and religious oppression. And our secret anxieties that our online personas — or "avatars" — are more "real" than we are have inspired the films *Avatar* and *Gamer* (both 2009). These fears also underpin the comic book *Birds of Prey*, in which real superheroes act like video game characters "controlled" to a degree by Oracle (a.k.a. Barbara Gordon, who fought crime as Batgirl before she was crippled by the Joker). In the comic, Oracle works from a home base, seated in front of a computer screen, and commands her field agents, Black Canary, Huntress, Hawk, Dove, and Zinda Blake, to perform the physical, heroic tasks that she is no longer capable of.

In addition to sometimes serving as metaphors for the Internet generation and the gamer generation, superhero stories can also be about other contemporary issues, such as steroids, plastic surgery, genetic engineering, and cybernetic implants. As humans continue to use science to improve the human body, growing new tissues, manipulating the human genome, and inserting plastic, metal, silicone, and microelectronic parts into our bodies, we wonder when we cease being human and have become either an inhuman, programmable cybernetic organism (like the Cybermen or the Borg), or a real-world Captain America or Johnny Mnemonic created by science. And who gets to decide which humans are granted the gift of artificial "superpowers" and who gets to design and distribute these superpowers?

In 1998's "Pumped, Pierced, Painted, and Pagan," conservative thinker Joe Woodard expressed concerns about the ever-inflating statistics of teenage girls who have ask for breast implants for birthday presents since *Baywatch*'s Pamela Anderson attained fame and notoriety for her silicone-padded bosoms as *Playboy*'s Playmate of the Month in February 1990. Unfortunately, comic books, with their improbably proportioned heroines — sometimes sporting a 15-inch waist and a 38 KKK bust-size — merely exacerbate the problem. They, too, were likely influenced by Pamela Anderson, as Brian Pulido's bosomy Lady Death debuted in 1991 and Jim Balent's depiction of Catwoman as a purple-clad vixen with massive mammaries burst onto the scene in 1993. Thankfully, in 2001, Darwyn Cooke and Ed Brubaker dialed down Catwoman's physique and gave her a marginally more modest beauty by basing her on Diana Rigg's Emma Peel from the British spy series *The Avengers*. The physical proportions of Vampirella were also made marginally less absurd in 2010, and she now wears more clothes as well.

Steroids are as much of a concern to comics readers as breast implants, as Superman noticeably became steroid-enhanced in his look in the 1990s, completing a decades-long metamorphosis from a man with the body of a 1930s era professional wrestler to Christopher Reeve's fit, swimmer's physique to the muscles upon muscles body of a Sylvester Stallone or an Arnold Schwarzenegger. Chris Bell's documentary *Bigger, Stronger, Faster* (2008), chronicles America's love/hate relationship with steroids, observing that our culture promotes winning at all costs, to the point of encouraging cheating, while maintaining a Puritanical abhorrence of steroids. The documentary asks the viewer to consider why the American people love Arnold Schwarzenegger and hate Roger Clemens when the two men reportedly both committed the same offence. The documentary also simultaneously praises and criticizes Vice President Joe Biden's idealistic desire to strip the professional sports world of performance enhancing drugs as a noble effort doomed to failure and as a narrow-minded condemnation of steroids when other forms of "performance enhancement" that are not illegal in the sports world are just as problematic.

Captain America is a superhero created by government-manufactured performance enhancing drugs as a weapon of war against the Axis Powers in World War II. His opposition to Hitler absolves him of much, if not all, of the negative associations of anabolic steroids. In contrast, the French comic book and film character Asterix the Gaul presents a more satirical view of steroids. Set in Ancient Gaul circa 50 B.C., the Asterix stories involve an idyllic forest village filled with freedom fighters that succeed in beating back the unjust rule of Julius Caesar and the Roman Empire by fueling themselves with a magic potion that acts as the ultimate performance enhancing drug. The druid who creates the potion is often called Getafix ("Get a fix"), but some British parents groups objected, so the character has been renamed Vitamix, and his magic potion is now referred to as a "vitamin potion" to skirt the drug connotations. (The drug themes and Ancient Roman setting also account for why the cartoon is famous worldwide, but has never been released on home video in the United States.)

While the drug themes in *Asterix* have often been an embarrassment to fans of the character, in at least two instances the drug humor is funny and intelligent, and acts as an effective satire of the issue of steroids in sports. In *The Twelve Tasks of Asterix* (1976), Asterix reveals that sports in his village are dull because egalitarian concerns dictate that all the participants in sports be granted free magic potion, which means that "it's not very exciting ... because we all get [to the finish line] at once and we have to draw lots for the winner. Heh-heh-heh." In *Asterix at the Olympic Games* (2008), Asterix uses the potion to cheat at discus throwing and his fat friend Obelix uses it to cheat at shot-put. Brutus protests, and Asterix and Obelix are forced to take "beetlyzer tests"—they breathe into giant beetles that inflate in the presence of drugs. They're disqualified, but Brutus is also disqualified for doping in a wrestling match. In the final chariot race, Brutus cheats again by taking Getafix's potion, but Getafix colors the potion blue and it dyes Brutus's tongue, revealing to everyone that he cheated.

These themes are, of course, political, but they speak to issues that many people across the political spectrum can relate to. Where superhero stories get even more politically thorny is when they address issues of war and empire—especially military conflicts based in the Middle East. And yet, several critics have argued that the September 11, 2001, attacks on the World Trade Center and the Pentagon account for the boom of popularity of superheroes in recent years. If that is the case—and it appears to be so—then one must ask the obvious question: why?

In the past ten years, some of the highest-grossing summer blockbusters of all time have featured classic superhero icons, such as Spider-Man and Batman, or belong to the genres of heroic fantasy, such as *Lord of the Rings* and *Harry Potter*, or the spy thriller, starring James Bond and Jason Bourne. All three genres are part of the same category of "Hero Myth" tale that has been a staple of Western literature since long before St. George slew his first dragon. In an interview published on the website *Superhero Hype* on September 12, 2008, Jon Favreau, the director of *Iron Man* (2008), speculated that 9/11 set the stage for the current superhero craze. He observed that, in the years immediately following the 9/11 attacks, American audiences craved escapism, and movie storylines that featured easily identifiable heroes and villains, which was why *Lord of the Rings* and *Spider-Man* held such appeal at that time. He indicated that, as deceptively simple and provocative as those films were in their iconography, they still featured tortured heroes wrestling with issues of power and responsibility that helped audiences work out their own feelings about the current state of the world without speaking directly to those fears.

According to Favreau, the passing of seven years since 9/11 has enabled superhero films to hold onto their initial popularity while gradually pushing the envelope and dealing more overtly with politics and the war on terror. Hence, as he observes, a Batman film like *The Dark Knight* (2008) featuring the Joker as the ultimate terrorist, and his own film, *Iron Man* (2008), in which American scientist and arms dealer Tony Stark is wounded in a roadside bombing in Afghanistan and becomes Iron Man initially to keep a piece of shrapnel from moving too close to his heart and killing him. Such a film, with its prominent use of Afghanistan as a setting, and its employment of Semitic villains, would not have been possible had the film been made closer to 9/11, he argued.

While Faveau's analysis of the popularity of the superhero genre during the Bush Administration is presented in a largely positive light, many cultural critics and academics have traditionally expressed a much more negative assessment of superheroes and what they represent. In *The Mechanical Bride* (1951), cultural critic Marshall McLuhan expressed concerns that superheroes constitute an appealing form of pro-war propaganda that, across the board, encourages a militarist worldview and represent a form of American Fascism:

> The attitudes of Superman to current social problems ... reflect the strong arm totalitarian methods of the immature and barbaric mind.... Superman is ruthlessly efficient in carrying on a one-man crusade against crooks and anti-social forces ... [with no] appeal to process of law. Justice is represented as an affair of personal strength alone. Any appraisal of the political tendencies of "Superman" (and also its many relatives in the comic-book world of violent adventure...) would have to include an admission that today the dreams of youths and adults alike seem to embody a mounting impatience with the laborious processes of civilized life and a restless eagerness to embrace violent solutions... [349–350].

Recent critics writing in a similar vein have seen a potential inspiration for the rampant use of steroids in sports and lament an American culture so enamored of muscle-men that the California electorate actually voted in weight-lifter-turned-actor Arnold ("The Terminator") Schwarzenegger to the governorship of California. They also see an uncomfortable similarity between the Superman from the planet Krypton and the "Superman" of Hitler's Aryan race.

In "Fantasy's Power and Peril," an editorial published in *The New York Times* on December 16, 2001, feminist historian and folklorist Marina Warner expressed concern that the success of the Harry Potter series and *Lord of the Rings* suggested that the Western world was embracing a dangerous, black-and-white, Christian versus Muslim view of the world. As Warner wrote at the time, "Myths in which heroic figures are pitted in mortal combat against diabolical enemies have gained fresh energy in popular culture since Sept. 11." Such stories have been a part of Western tradition since the times of ancient Greece, and count among them landmark texts such as *Beowulf*, but Warner worries over their continual influence. "[T]his tradition assumes there is only one way to view the world: as a titanic battle between good and evil, with the triumphant goals of destruction, extermination, and annihilation. Mythology and history suggest alternatives: fantasies of reconciliation and redemption, for example."

Warner noted that it is difficult to tell whether popular culture artifacts merely reflect the society that produces them or if they, in turn, affect that society. In either case, the militarist tone of films made during the Bush years was a great cause for concern. Warner observed that such films encouraged angry and wounded Americans to look upon all of their enemies, especially Osama bin Laden, as fantasy villains akin to Sauron, Voldemort, or "the lethal, foreign antagonists of James Bond." Because the superhero film phenomenon had not yet hit its stride, Warner did not include comic book supervillains such as Doctor Doom or the Joker among this roster, but such figures fit the picture Warner paints, as well as prove that her predictions were arguably prescient. Bin Laden also has echoes in the religious-fanatic Cylon robots of *Battlestar Galactica*, who are bent on murdering every neo-pagan human from existence, and Count Dooku, the cave-lurking terrorist leader of the *Star Wars* prequel trilogy.

Conversely, Warner's discussion of mythic heroes could also extend from Harry Potter and Aragorn to superspies James Bond and Jack Bauer, the Harry Truman–like female President Laura Roslin from *Battlestar Galactica*, the slightly more liberal and pacifistic hero "the Doctor" from *Doctor Who*, as well as traditional superheroes Superman, Batman, and Spider-Man. All the heroes mentioned above were featured in popular movies, television series, comic books and video games in the years following September 11; some of these narratives embraced the classic vision of the mythic hero wholeheartedly, and without irony or criticism (*Lord of the Rings*), while others painted a more ambivalent (*Battlestar Galactica*), or sometimes satirical (*Doctor Who*) portrait of heroism. It is also significant to point out that heroic, iconic imagery surrounded first the heroic police and firemen who strove to rescue people still inside the Twin Towers immediately following the attack, then President George W. Bush and British Prime Minister Tony Blair, who forged an Anglo-American alliance against terrorism, and protected Western democracies from the evils of Islamo-fascism. Each of these figures were seen, especially in the first years following the attacks, as modern-day Beowulfs fighting foreign Grendels, and the romanticism of such representations arguably laid the groundwork for widespread public acceptance of the wars in Afghanistan and Iraq, the use of torture as a means of fighting terrorism, and the institution of the Patriot Act, which granted the U.S. government greater latitude in investigating the lives of its own citizens.

The connection between superheroes and the heroes of 9/11 was drawn virtually immediately, and was cemented by the comic book publishing companies DC and Marvel themselves. Indeed, two special graphic novels called *9/11* and the magazine *Heroes* were published shortly after 9/11, and featured police officers and firemen working alone, and alongside superheroes such as the X-Men and Fantastic Four to clear the rubble from Ground Zero, rescue survivors, and take the wounded to nearby hospitals. While some readers found this direct mixing of "real" and "fictional" heroes in questionable taste, some of the discomfort they felt was mitigated by the fact that the proceeds from the sales of these items were intended for the families of the victims of the attack. Some of the most emotionally charged moments from the collections of portraits and short stories included art that proclaimed the police and firemen who raced into the falling towers the real heroes, and suggested that the campy and fictional "superheroes" of both the Marvel and DC universes could never live up to the example of such heroism. Another pivotal entry included a short story in which Superman apologized to the reader for failing to leap from the pages of his comic book into the real world and prevent the September 11 attacks.

Other reactions to September 11 were more ambivalent. Comic book writer J. Michael Straczynski was initially reluctant to write a 9/11 story in the pages of *The Amazing Spider-Man* when he was asked to do so by editors at Marvel, but he eventually crafted a tale in which Spider-Man arrives at Ground Zero when it is too late to prevent the destruction of the World Trade Center. Horrified witnesses demand to know where Spider-Man was and how he let it happen. Notably, the story condemned not only the 9/11 terrorists, but also arch conservative Americans, such as Jerry Falwell, who expressed the belief that New Yorkers brought the devastation upon themselves by angering God with their abortions, promiscuous sex, and gay lifestyles.[9] Even at the height of America's anger and grief, Straczynski demonstrated with this story that he was thinking clearly, and holding firm to his center-left political beliefs during one of America's darkest hours.

Because the rights to characters such as Spider-Man are owned by corporations, and not held by their creators, a variety of writers, artists, and filmmakers have told stories with iconic DC and Marvel characters. The different writers have a degree of leeway in the stories they tell with these characters, provided they respect the work done by previous writers in the name of preserving a storytelling "continuity" for the sake of the fans, and that they do not tell a story that is so unpleasant that it risks angering fans, lowering a given character's "stock," and threatening the company's ability to sell merchandise with the characters. Some writers who have spent periods of their lives writing adventures for a given character have been politically liberal, some conservative, and some have strove to be more "apolitical" (although that term often implies a degree of unacknowledged conservatism). Consequently, it is possible for a superhero to represent radically different ideologies during the course of his or her career, depending on who has written the stories and whether they were published during a relatively conservative decade, such as the 1950s, or a more liberal one, such as the 1990s.

In fact, a great many of the people who write and draw comic books describe themselves as politically liberal in interviews. Many of them were either immigrants themselves, or descended from Jewish, Italian, or Hispanic immigrants who expressed sympathies with the poor and disenfranchised peoples of America, and throughout the world. Indeed, Jewish writers and the artists such as Jack Kirby, Will Eisner, Bob Kane, and Jerry Siegel and Joe Schuster essentially created the comic book industry in the late 1930s and early 1940s, imbuing their colorful protagonists with a very particular set of American values — New Deal–era progressive political sympathies and the working-class values of the urban Jewish immigrant.[10] Even though these values arguably fell out of favor in the conservative 1950s and during the Reagan Revolution of the '80s, they endure as the ideological backbone of the comics industry, making superhero comics

Alanna Wolff and Jeff Byrd, the stars of Batton Lash's *Supernatural Law* series, are heroic attorneys who represent monsters — including the Frankenstein monster. In addition to paying humorous tribute to classic horror films, these unsavory clients symbolize society's most vulnerable, and most persecuted citizens (courtesy Batton Lash).

consistently more left-leaning tonally than much of the rest of American popular culture. Working in the same left-leaning, blue-collar tradition, several notable British writers with Labour Party sympathies have taken over iconic American characters in recent years and written adventures with progressive moral messages attached.

Academic scholarship often perpetuates the view that comic books are essentially power-fantasies for right-wing adolescent males. And yet, as independent comic book writer and artist Batton Lash observes, liberal ideologies underpin most modern comic books. In an e-mail interview on September 20, 2010, Lash explained that he rarely reads mainstream superhero comic books known for providing social commentaries, "mainly because most of the writers in comics seem to get their understanding of the national scene from either Jon Stewart or Keith Olbermann! If super-heroes must be burdened with making political statements, I'd like to see a wider range of viewpoints."

Lash sees himself as primarily an entertainer, but his 30-year-old series *Supernatural Law* is as intelligent and political as it is funny. The series is about two attorneys, Alanna Wolff and Jeff Byrd, who represent "monsters" that look like classic Universal Studios monsters, such as Dracula and the Wolf Man, but really symbolize some of the most abused and persecuted members of our society. Something like a cross between *Ally McBeal* and *The Addams Family*, Lash's series began life as a comic strip, became the comic book *Wolff & Byrd: Counselors of the Macabre*, and evolved into a webcomic at www.supernaturallaw.com. What makes it notable is how daring it is in its handling of political issues ranging from protecting the First Amendment (it satirizes the EC Comics trials of the 1950s, in which Dr. Frederick Wertham played a large role), to advocating a woman's right to choose, to skewering political extremists.

As Lash explains, "What interests me and fuels the satire is the hypocrisy and disingenuousness of politicians, public figures and institutions (See *W&B* #17, 'A Case for Ygor'). Also, zealots of both sides of a heated issue fascinate me. The extremists don't realize that they practically agree with each other! (*W&B* #16: 'Sodd, We Hardly Knew Ye' and W&B #10: 'I'm Carrying Satan's Baby'). I consider myself an independent, and if pressed, I would say my stories have a libertarian point of view. I believe the individual is responsible for his/her own actions (*W&B* #17: 'The Death and Times of "Dr. Life"') and the state — especially in their zeal to do well 'for the children' — will ultimately oppress people and hinder free speech (see *W&B* #4, 'A Host of Horrors'). Recently, I have dealt with the issue of gay marriage ('The Life-Partner of Frankenstein,' published online) and returned to a free-speech issue (*SLaw* #41: 'The Works Speak For Themselves')."

Despite the controversial nature of these subjects, Lash has been thankfully free of a large-scale reader backlash. "[I've had] no guff from parent's groups or conservatives — I don't think I'm big enough to be on their radar! Some liberals told me I shouldn't do the 'Satan's Baby' story [in which Rosemary from *Rosemary's Baby* asks Wolff for help procuring an abortion when she discovers she is pregnant with the antichrist] because they were convinced 'right-wingers' would burn my house down, but there was no problem at all."

Lash has the freedom to present his views, as they are, in a comic property he has control over. Other comic book writers and artists who are hired to craft stories for heroes that have been in existence for decades, and serve as a major cash cow for publishers, video game makers, and film and television shows, have to be more careful and more subtle about the way they use the characters to make a political point — especially if they weren't the ones to create the characters in the first place.

Furthermore, the subversive storytelling approach—in which liberal writers co-opt conservative adventure narratives to promote moderate-to-progressive politics—is not always effective. Readers who approach heroic fiction hoping to see St. George slay the dragon at the end often feel cheated when the dragon is spared. These more politically conservative readers often feel misled by the macho trappings of the genre—conned into immersing themselves in a tale saturated by hippie values and the preaching of a left-wing propagandist writer, and they are angered at being tricked into reading a story they would have avoided had they known its political bent. On the other hand, some who come to an adventure story hoping for a bloody climax are given pause when the hero spares his opponent, and are asked to question what it was they were expected to "get" from their superhero narrative—escapism? Bread and circuses? A treatise on "just war?" Or a complex look at contemporary social mores?

Matthew J. Costello labeled the incongruous comic book phenomenon of the muscle-powered superheroes promoting a leftist agenda as "Liberalism with a Fascist Aesthetic" (215). Sometimes liberal comic writers have been adept at imbedding progressive ideas within the seemingly reactionary medium, convincingly portraying a physically perfect specimen as a spokesperson for progressive social ideals. For example, during the 1980s, the left-leaning *Babylon 5* creator J. Michael Straczynski scripted episodes of the cartoon *Masters of the Universe*, featuring the renowned He-Man and Skeletor. It was, by and large, a cheesy, "sword and sandal" cartoon that combined imagery from *Clash of the Titans* and the *Star Wars* films in an effort to sell action figures to impressionable boys. However, thanks to the efforts of writers such as Straczynski, who tried to give the series a serious mythological foundation, and who attempted to flesh out the characters, certain episodes were actually pretty good. Some were intelligent and progressive, and one of Straczynski's, which filled out the back-story of the Sorceress of Castle Grayskull (a previously underutilized female character), is fondly remembered as one of the best episodes of the series.

But not everyone who spent the 1980s watching the adventures of He-Man agreed that writers such as Straczynski were successful in elevating a money-making endeavor like *Masters of the Universe* into worthwhile art. Humor columnist Dave Barry had a lot of fun at the expense of cartoons like *Masters of the Universe,* which professed to endorse liberal values such as pacifism and multiculturalism while featuring as a protagonist a muscle-bound thug who ended each adventure by beating the stuffing out of his opponent. To Barry, superhero narratives that attempt to offer positive instruction to little boys essentially do so as a pretense. As he wrote in *Dave Barry's Complete Guide to Guys* (1995), little boys have a genetic tendency towards being bullies that cartoons marketed to them take advantage of, and encourage:

> The TV cartoon shows aimed at little boys [are] ... infested with characters who have biceps the size of prize-winning hogs and names like Commander Brock Gonad and his Hard Punchers of Justice. In an effort to please government regulatory agencies and child-psychology experts, these shows pretend to involve uplifting themes such as racial tolerance, ecological awareness, and non-violence, but in fact they almost always involve macho behavior:
>
> COMMANDER GONAD: Uh-oh, Sarge, looks like we have company!
>
> SERGEANT STEROID: It's Anthrax, the evil villain from the planet Polluto! With no concern whatsoever for the environment! And it looks like he has...
>
> ANTHRAX (in evil voice): That's right, you fools! I have the Giant Atomic Fluorocarbon-Emitting Hairspray Container of Doom, and I am going to spray the entire Earth and destroy every living thing on it!

SERGEANT STEROID: Uh-oh! That would mean...

ANTHRAX: Yes! That would mean the extinction of the Spotted Owl. HAHAHAHA!

COMMANDER GONAD: We've got to stop him! By nonviolent means if at all possible! Listen. Anthrax! Be reasonable!

ANTHRAX: No!

COMMANDER GONAD: Okay, then! (He beats the shit out of Anthrax.)

SERGEANT STEROID: Whew! That was a close one!

COMMANDER GONAD: Yes! Every species is important, which is why we need to protect our planet and recycle whenever possible and eat hearty nutritious meals including the breakfast cereals advertised relentlessly on this program!

SERGEANT STEROID: Part of this complete breakfast! By the way, action figures based on our characters are available in toy stores everywhere! Sold separately!

COMMANDER GONAD: Collect them all! Speaking of licensed characters, look who's here! It's Corporal Token!

CORPORAL TOKEN: That's right! Please note that I am an African American!

COMMANDER GONAD: Right on, "homes!" "What it is!" And here's Lieutenant Woman!

LIEUTENANT WOMAN: Speaking of owls, please note that I have an anatomically impossible set of hooters!

(General laughter)

Barry is indeed correct in pointing out that even politically "progressive" comic books often suffer from unconvincing and racist portrayals of minority figures, the sexual objectification of women who are supposed to be "feminist" because they are effective fighters despite their ample bosoms, and the highlighting of a pacifist hero who uses violence to solve all problems. Essentially, Barry views the concept of "liberalism with a Fascist aesthetic" as the product of political idiocy and marketing crassness, but he is not always correct. Sometimes liberal writers of superhero narratives are amazingly successful in crafting counterculture narratives or stories that protest the current social order. And it isn't always a con "to please government regulatory agencies and child-psychology experts" either.

For example, during the 1940s, psychologist William Moulton Marston created a pacifistic, socialist, feminist superhero with the express purpose of convincing a generation of children to embrace peaceful dialogue instead of turning to violence as an easy solution to every problem. Sure enough, real-life feminist Gloria Steinem has declared that comic book feminist Wonder Woman was one of her early inspirations for leading a life of activism. As she wrote in an essay paying tribute to the character, "haven't comic books always been a little disreputable? Something that would never have been assigned in school? The answer to these questions is yes, which is exactly why they are important. Comic books have the power—including over the child who still lives within each of us—because they are not part of the 'serious' grown-up world" (355). Certainly, for Steinem, Wonder Woman's message of female strength and solidarity was powerful indeed, partly because it came from a storytelling medium that the establishment frowned upon.

Another famous cultural and literary critic who was inspired by an early exposure to comic books is Edward Said, author of *Orientalism* (1978). In his introduction to Joe Sacco's graphic novel *Palestine* (1996), Said praises the very traits of comic books that Barry mocks—the oversexed women, the recourse to violence, the absurd pseudo-science, and the lack of subtlety. For Said, the anarchic images contained in comic books helped free him of the oppressive, doctrinaire environment of the British high school that, not coincidentally, had a strict ban on comic books.

Said believed that, ostensibly, the comic book ban was aimed at the "slang and violence which ruffled the pretend calm of the learning process." Also dangerously significant:

> ... and perhaps more important though never stated, there was the release provided to my sexually repressed young life by outrageous characters (some of them like Sheena of the Jungle, dressed far too skimpily and sexily) who did and said things that could not be admitted either for reasons of probability and logic or, perhaps more crucially, because they violated conventional norms — norms of behavior, thought, accepted social forms. Comics played havoc with the logic of a+b+c+d and they certainly encouraged one not to think in terms of what the teacher expected or what a subject like history demanded.... Besides, comics provided one with a directness of approach (the attractively and literally overstated combination of pictures and words) that seemed unassailably true on the one hand, and marvelously close, impinging, familiar on the other. In ways that I still find fascinating to decode, comics in their relentless foregrounding ... seemed to say what couldn't otherwise be said, perhaps what wasn't permitted to be said or imagined, defying the ordinary processes of thought, which are policed, shaped and re-shaped by all sorts of pedagogical as well as ideological pressures. I knew nothing of this then, but I felt that comics freed me to think and imagine and see differently [ii].

Indeed, there are a great many forces in society that discourage free thinking, using one's imagination, and asking difficult questions. And as difficult as it is to think and to question authority during peacetime, it is even more difficult to do so during times of war. As Lisa Finnegan observed in *No Questions Asked: News Coverage Since 9/11* (2007) reporters were amazingly reticent to question President Bush's policies in the wake of the attacks on September 11, 2001. According to Finnegan, reporters were so afraid of appearing unpatriotic in light of the attack that they did not widely report on the administration's policy decisions which curtailed American civil liberties, they did not do much to question the wisdom of Bush's decision to conquer Iraq, and they did little to criticize him for alienating the United States from its European allies. Interestingly enough, as serious news journalists tossed softball questions at the president, supposedly escapist, juvenile forms of entertainment placed his actions under great scrutiny. While Bush's policies faced little opposition from the Democrats and few questions from the press, television comedians and comic book writers were often bold in their criticisms of the Bush administration, with *Saturday Night Live* script writer Tina Fey seeming particularly brazen in her condemnation of conservatives at a time when such sentiments were often labeled treasonous. It was also intriguing how readily script writers of superhero comic books and movies risked retaliation from conservative fans by pressing their criticism of the administration. After all, were they not afraid that their comic book sales would drop, as did the sales of albums cut by country music's Dixie Chicks, after they publicly proclaimed themselves ashamed of being from the same home state as the president? And how did a big-budget film like *V for Vendetta* even get made, let alone released into theaters, given that its anti–Bush sentiments are extreme enough to make it seem essentially pro-terrorist? Rush Limbaugh would argue that these things happen because the media is fundamentally liberal, but select programming on NPR, MSNBC, Comedy Central, and PBS, plus a handful of Oscar-nominated box office flops with liberal narratives released each year do not a liberal media make.

Some of these politically themed superhero stories were careful not to be too overt in their criticism in an effort to dodge possible boycotting. Like the great fables of the past, which disguised the fact that they were political satires by casting members of the animal kingdom in the roles of public figures, contemporary liberal superhero stories comment on real-life figures such as President Bush and Osama bin Laden by reinventing classic heroes and villains as commentaries on parallel figures in real life. In casting characters such as

Batman and Thor in the role of Bush, villains such as Ra's al Ghul in the role of Osama bin Laden, and Doctor Doom as a stand-in for Saddam Hussein, comic book writers were able to make their criticisms appear marginally less strident, giving themselves the freedom to write speculative stories about real people.

The first superhero stories to appear openly critical of Bush were the various Superman monthly periodicals. On the eve of George W. Bush's real world installation into the White House, writer Jeph Loeb crafted a story in which Superman villain and amoral robber baron Lex Luthor is elected President of the United States in the fictional world of the DC Universe. When asked by a fan why anyone in their right mind would vote for Lex Luthor — the lunatic who dropped a nuclear bomb on California in the first *Superman* film as part of an elaborate plan to make a billion dollars on a real estate swindle — Loeb replied, "This is almost too easy ... who's president now?" For Loeb, there was little difference between Bush and Luthor, so there was little reason to assume that Luthor would lose a presidential election, no matter how infamous his crimes. Despite the fact that the subsequent storylines featuring President Luthor could not deliver on the promise of the provocative concept, the power of the visual of a comic book "supervillain" as President was remarkable, and the storyline was popular enough to be introduced into two television series featuring Superman and Luthor as lead characters, the live-action *Smallville* and the cartoon *Justice League Unlimited*, and was adapted into the straight-to-video cartoon film *Superman/Batman: Public Enemies* (2009).

The Mighty Thor comic books of 2003 and 2004 also accused Bush of being too publicly pious and warned readers that he might be tempted to impose his form of Christianity on both the American people and the world at large. These criticisms were veiled, to an extent, by the fact that the comic books were technically about the Norse god Thor and not the President of the United States. However, the stories were so clearly an allegory for contemporary world events that they were as much about Bush as they were about Thor. In a series of books written by Dan Jurgens (including "Gods on Earth," "Spiral," and "Gods and Men"),Thor reveals his godhood to humanity and demands that all the peoples of the world acknowledge his existence and pay him worship. He hopes that, in making this revelation, all other religions will cease to exist, effectively putting an end to religious sectarian violence. Also, in transporting Asgard to the skies above Manhattan, Thor hopes to inspire humans to fear his proximity enough that no more international conflicts, or even street crime, will mar human existence on earth. His enterprise, in effect, imposes peace on earth by removing human free will.

In response, there is a general outcry against Thor's attempt to assert his will over all of humanity. Atheists, Roman Catholics, and members of other religions unite in protest against the establishment of Norse mythology as the official world religion and several nations launch military attacks against Asgard. Thor responds angrily to these attacks and crushes all opposition. The harshness of his response causes his friends to desert him, and more opposition to rise up. Spider-Man, Iron Man, and Captain America lead a superhero rebellion against his rule, and they are defeated. A street-level, hit-and-run insurgency begins, and Thor even manages to capture and kill many of those insurgents, but that doesn't stop a new rebellion from beginning, or treachery from simmering within his own administration. By the time he is done, Thor's misguided quest to bring peace to the world has effectively cost him his soul and his ideals, and has destroyed everything that he hoped to save. In the end, Thor is forced to go back in time and warn his younger self not to assert his will so mightily over those who treasure their free will above being saved from themselves, thereby preventing himself from making such a colossal mistake. The time-travel move was intended to restore Thor as a figure of heroism so that readers might accept him as a role model once again, even after his fall from grace. However, the move did not entirely work because, at a loss for how to continue the comic book after such a powerful storyline, Marvel temporarily canceled the *Thor* comic book and gave the character a rest until the summer of 2007, when the comic began again from #1. Of course, while Thor was granted a second chance, and an opportunity to undo his grievous error, in the real world, America cannot take back its actions on the world theater. What America has done, it has done; there is no symbolic reset to issue #1.

There have been several decades worth of comic books featuring characters such as the Thor of Marvel Comics, and I am, in effect, cherry-picking by choosing a storyline such as *The Mighty Thor: Lord of Asgard* to prove that superhero stories are liberal. Certainly, there are countless other Thor stories that have far more conservative sensibilities than Jurgen's swan song storyline. Indeed, Thor was initially designed by comic creators Stan Lee and Jack Kirby to be a Cold War–era hero, defending America from Soviet spies, neo-Nazis, and supervillains such as Mr. Hyde and Cobra, in an age of American paranoia fostered by the Soviet Sputnik program.

The launching of *Sputnik 1* in 1957 has long been recognized as a major historical and cultural event in the history of the Cold War, inspiring massive government investment in the space program, grants for scientific research and funding for affordable college education (especially in the sciences), and a shift in the representation of the iconic American hero from cowboy to cosmonaut (or, as allegorically retold in *Toy Story*, from Woody to Buzz Lightyear). The 1960s television series *Star Trek* also embodies the shift from America's pastoral concern with the Western frontier of the past to its futurist interest in "space ... the final frontier." *Star Trek*, like the Marvel Comics produced during the same period, was influenced by a variety of incompatible 1960s ideologies and storytelling tropes. These values included the liberal hopes and fears of the civil rights and feminist movements and Great Society progressivism underscored by "trippy" psychedelic imagery, Theremin and sitar music, and a rainbow color palette. *Star Trek* and 1960s Marvel superhero comics also dramatized, in their characters and situations, the clash between Victorian and Love Generation sexuality, as well as the disconnect between America's Cold War militarism (and World War II nostalgia) and its fervent desire for world peace and nuclear disarmament.

That is why, while many cultural critics look to early Marvel comics as examples of Cold War propaganda, those readings are often not quite complex enough. Certainly the space race helped fuel the birth of modern science fiction, and gave American heroes ready-made foes to face in order to demonstrate their patriotism and heroism, but *Star Trek* and Stan Lee Marvel Comics narratives were half-hearted in their demonizing of the Red Menace, even including prophecies of a future time in which East and West could live together in peace and mutual understanding. While Stan Lee did set the early Iron Man adventures in Vietnam, he did so with reservations, admitting that he understood little to nothing about the war and why it was being fought. However, he knew that the war was unpopular with the Marvel readership, and deliberately designed Iron Man to be everything the readership hated as a creative challenge to see if he could convince a liberal reader to find a "military industrial complex" billionaire protagonist likeable despite his conservative politics. Lee said he was not trying to change his readership's politics, but to see if Tony Stark, a Howard Hughes style inventor and munitions maker, could be successfully presented as a redeemed anti-hero, and reformed womanizer, despite the fact that "nobody likes someone who just makes munitions."[11]

Thor and the Hulk in particular spent their first few years fighting an array of Communist menaces, before moving on to fighting more apolitical foes culled from mythology and monster movie matinees. Even when the villains were Communists, such as Emil Blonsky (a.k.a. the Abomination), the evil they represented seemed like pro forma propaganda. One could almost imagine Stan Lee's thought processes on this score: there were publishing deadlines to be met and a new villain-of-the-month was needed, so the new villains were Commies because ... well ... Commies were not supposed to be nice, and who really cares why they're bad? What is important is that they have "cool" powers with which to menace the Hulk. Consequently, most of the "red menaces" faced by the Marvel superheroes in the early days rapidly faded into oblivion — the evil astronauts the Red Ghost and the Super Apes had surprisingly little staying power as *Fantastic Four* foes — or quickly turned into heroes (Natasha Romanova, a Russian Spy known as the Black Widow, is now a trusted member of the U.N. peacekeeping force S.H.I.E.L.D. and the American superhero team the Avengers). The most obvious exception to this trend is Iron Man, who is perennially facing Russian and Asian menaces, whether they are the Mandarin, a mystical riff on Genghis Khan; Ivan Vanko, the Russian foe known as the Crimson Dynamo (or Whiplash in *Iron Man 2*), and the Japanese Fujikawa Corporation, which humiliates Stark by buying out his family business, Stark Enterprises. However, in contrast, Spider-Man had virtually no Communist menaces in the first place. There was the Chameleon, a Russian spy, and Kraven the Hunter, who was only Russian because he was based on General Zaroff, the memorable Cossack villain from Richard Connell's *The Most Dangerous Game*. Other Spider-Man villains are middle-aged Caucasian males with superpowers inspired by those found in the animal kingdom.

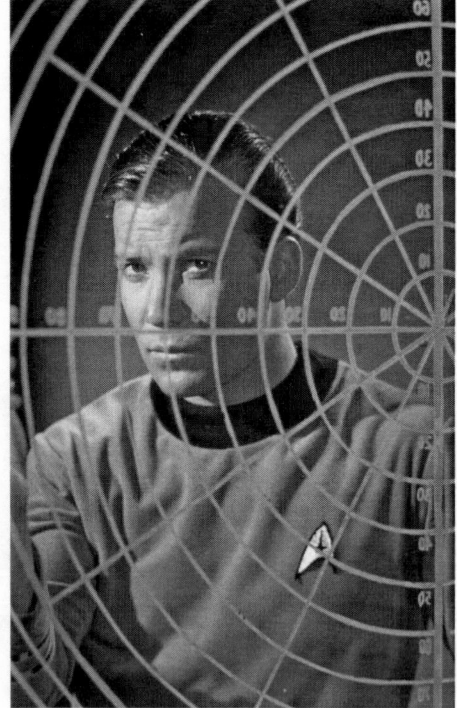

William Shatner plays James T. Kirk, captain of the U.S.S. *Enterprise*, during the Cold War–era science fiction series *Star Trek* (1966–1969). The 1957 launching of *Sputnik 1* is often cited as the inspiration for the science fiction renaissance that saw the creation of *Star Trek* and the Marvel superheroes.

Also, heroes designed by Stan Lee and his artist collaborators to be politically right-of-center have moderated their views over the years. The most obvious example of this is Doctor Stephen Strange, the elitist surgeon who became an unlikely magician after a car accident disfigured his hands and ended his lucrative medical career. While Strange originally espoused some of artist Steve Ditko's Ayn Rand–influenced libertarian and Objectivist philosophies, Strange has not often expressed similar views since. Indeed, in *Doctor Strange: The Oath* (2006-2007) writer Brian K. Vaughan pitted the once aristocratic surgeon against the American pharmaceuticals industry, demanding that they stop suppressing the cures to diseases in order to get rich off of the regular sales of medicines that merely treat symptoms. The story could be read as a symbolic call for greater government regulation of, and reform of, the crumbling health care industry, exploitative insurance companies, and greedy pharmaceutical businesses, not unlike similar calls for reforms led by Paul Krugman, Nicholas Kristof, and Barack Obama, and none of these egalitarian figures tend to endear themselves to the libertarians and Ayn Rand disciples of today.

Furthermore, even the original Lee-Ditko stories can be read as subversive works. Dr. Strange frequently left the confines of his unhealthy physical body to explore our world, and other dimensions, in the freedom of his astral form — invariably needing to hide his now soulless body in a safe place before embarking on a quest. While this can be read as a metaphor for an Objectivist's quest for personal fulfillment and evolution, it need not be interpreted in this fashion. As critic Douglas Wolk observed in 2007, Dr. Strange would often liberate himself from the laws of physics and the recognizable world:

> ... floating freely in other-dimensional space filled with curving, scribbly design elements. There are almost no right angles in Ditko's Doctor Strange stories other than panel borders. Over and over, though, there are visions of weird shaped portals through which even weirder planes of existence can be seen, and the implication is that the rectangles on the printed page act as the same sort of portal for the reader.... Every few panels, there's a new psychedelic explosion.... Doctor Strange was, whether or not Lee and Ditko admitted it (they didn't) or even intended it, a vehicle for talking about drug culture [159–160].

In a similar fashion, many of the young people who read Stan Lee's Cold War comics in the sixties related to all that was subversive in the content, and chose to deliberately overlook anything that was a product of half-baked, reactionary politics. As critic Robert Genter has observed, it is striking that, in a 1965 poll, student radicals in California named Bob Dylan, Fidel Castro, Spider-Man and the Hulk as their favorite anti-establishment icons:

> Of course, the super heroes at Marvel remained committed to the Cold War long after many of their readers had taken to the streets to protest the war in Vietnam. But to youth fighting a cultural and political war against "the one-dimensional man" of the Cold War order, the alienated but confident heroes of Marvel comics served as an emblem of an authentic subjectivity deemed lost, expressing the existential anguish of a generation growing up under the threat of nuclear catastrophe. As an undergraduate at Stanford University explained in 1966, "Spider-Man, my favorite, exemplifies the poor college student, beset by woes, money problems, and the question of existence. In short, he is one of us" [974].

Like the Marvel Comics of the 1960s, the classic incarnation of *Star Trek* presented a commentary on the Cold War that mixed conservative and liberal messages to a nigh incoherent degree, partly because of the differing politics of the various script writers and producers. On the one hand, individual episodes of *Star Trek* seemed to embrace a cartoonish, propagandist vision of the United States (in the guise of the United Federation of Planets) as purely "good" and the Soviet Union (in the guise of the Klingon Empire) as purely "bad." On the other, an imperfect-but-still-progressive form of multiculturalism was imbued into the series by the presence of a multiethnic cast of secondary and tertiary hero characters, the insertion of Jewish cultural rituals and values into the series mythology by Leonard Nimoy and several franchise writers, and by persistent efforts by stories to show the "good" side of the villains. Finally, the Federation makes peace with the Klingons in *Star Trek VI: The Undiscovered Country* (1991), a film clearly designed to end the saga of the 1960s–era *Star Trek* on a hopeful, progressive note.

The ideological inconsistencies and incoherence that characterized *Star Trek* adventures throughout the franchise's history had the odd effect of empowering viewers to make for themselves what they would of *Star Trek*'s message. *Star Trek* fans of a more conservative bent, or those who have an enthusiasm for military history and battle tactics, have a tendency to favor *Trek* adventures that are centered on space-ship battles or macho revenge narratives, such as "Balance of Terror" and *Star Trek II: The Wrath of Khan*, while more liberal-minded Trekkers embrace the environmentalist message of *Star Trek IV: The Voyage Home* or the condemnation of racism evident in "Let That Be Your Last Battlefield." (And, of course, in a less overtly political manner, fans of comedy embrace "The Trouble with Tribbles," and lovers of romance enjoy "This Side of Paradise.") It is possible for the same audience member to aesthetically appreciate all of the above *Star Trek* adventures, irrespective of their political messages, simply because they are entertaining. However, one frequently finds conservative *Star Trek* fans that detest the "preachy liberal episodes" and liberal fans of the broader *Star Trek* universe who prefer the pacifism and science represented by *Star Trek: The Next Generation,* and see it as a superior show, in part, because it appears more liberal and less masculine in its sensibilities, and because Captain Picard is perceived to be a gentler soul than Captain Kirk.

Dr. Strange is a sorcerer character that explores other dimensions in his astral form. He must hide his physical body whenever his spirit "leaves" it so that none of his enemies will kill him while he's "out." From *Strange Tales* #143 (April 1966) illustrated by Steve Ditko and written by Stan Lee.

In understanding how political symbolism and subtext work in superhero stories, it is important to be aware that the politics of a given storyteller and the politics of the individual fan often determine how that story is received. It is also important to be aware of industry trends, and the life cycles of long-lasting fictional characters that have changed over time, not only because of historical trends, shifting fan bases, and the idiosyncrasies of individual storytellers, but also for marketing reasons. A study of the general arc of most officially sanctioned superhero stories, such as *Superman* comic books published by DC Comics group, reveals that superhero narratives that remain in constant production for decades tend to follow four stages of narrative development. In the first phase, a passionate creator designs a superhero character for a publisher on a work-for-hire basis. The creator is not a rich person, and is happy with the work-for-hire contract, not dreaming that the character will one day become a cultural icon worth billions. He puts a lot of work and creative energy into the character, infusing it with his personal political, religious, and cultural beliefs. For example, Jerry Siegel and Joe Shuster, created Superman to be a populist hero, champion of the everyman, and representation of Jewish heroism in the tradition of the golem, Moses, and the Hebrew Judges. In contrast, Steve Ditko designed Spider-Man and Doctor Strange to be the living embodiments of Ayn Rand's Objectivist philosophy. Finally, William Moulton Marston crafted Wonder Woman to personify feminism, socialist values, and a completely uninhibited sexuality, devoid of unhealthy American Puritanism, and open to bisexuality and bondage.

The second phase begins when the creators stop writing or drawing their characters. This can occur for a variety of reasons. They either grew weary of writing for their heroes on an underpaid basis, become disenchanted with their own characters, retire, die, or are fired. What little control they once had over the destinies of their creations shifts to the publisher, who assigns other writers and artists to craft stories for the character. While the first replacement creative team strives to mimic the storytelling style of the original team, so as not to alienate fans, the ultimate result is a watering-down of the character. During this phase, the character becomes a pure corporate cash cow, and its likeness is marketed to action figure makers, video game companies, Saturday morning cartoon producers, and even featured on an array of merchandise that has little, or nothing, to do with the character, such as soda cans, garbage cans, school supplies, toothpaste, and so on. The recently departed creators of the character become bitter that they were left out of the lucrative merchandising deals struck by the publisher, and are upset to see the tamer, more apolitical versions of their characters marketed to the general public as inoffensive kids' fare. Hence, the appearance of Spider-Man in *Spider-Man and His Amazing Friends*, a sweet cartoon that bears little or no resemblance to the comic books Ditko created, and the insertion of Wonder Woman and Superman in the bland and safe cartoon *Superfriends*, which presents a tame version of the Justice League in which all the heroes have essentially the same cardboard, "heroic" personality and are the "buddies" of the kids watching TV. *Superfriends*, unsurprisingly, was free of Marxist political messages and sexualized bondage imagery.

In stage three of the development of the superhero narrative, the company notices that the public has grown weary of a character, and allows a new writer to come on board the comic book to provide a radical, deconstructionist take on the character, emphasizing its fallibility, tendency towards Fascism, and satirizing the more ludicrous conventions of the superhero genre. The 1980s was replete with this kind of storytelling, including Frank Miller's portrayal of Superman as a crony of Ronald Reagan in *The Dark Knight Returns*, Peter David's portrayal of Spider-Man as a bitter and vengeful figure, and Alan Moore's deconstructionist vision of the superhero genre as a whole in *Watchmen*.

Stage four sees the comic book companies at a loss to know how to proceed with telling monthly stories with characters who were so completely dismantled during the deconstructionist era. In consequence, they turn to fan writers, who grew up reading the characters and know by heart all of the adventures produced during stages one through three, and have a complete vision of the character as it was originally intended to be, as it was mass-marketed to parents and children, and as it was psychoanalyzed, killed, and dissected during the 1980s. The fan writers — in the mold of Mark Waid, Kurt Busiek, and Geoff Johns —

then produce a new, "greatest hits" version of the character, that is an amalgam of the figure seen in stages one through three, and inform their narratives with a fourth-wall-breaking, "knowing wink" tone to other fans. There is a general, "gee whiz" tone of "Look! This is how the character was always meant to be! And isn't it cool that an actual fan is writing the character now! Yay!" imbued in these stories. Stage four tales tend to be very divisive. They are either adored or loathed. Probably the most successful Stage four tales of a particular superhero concern Batman. *Batman: The Animated Series* reveled in the more supernatural elements of the character, while grounding him in an art deco reality and stories replete with film noir genre conventions. In contrast, another Stage four production, the film *The Dark Knight,* refrains from a fourth-wall-breaking narrative tone, strips the Batman character of all of its romanticized and unrealistic elements, and presents a vision of what Batman would be like if he lived in the real world. Both stage four visions of Batman are wildly popular. In contrast, stage four visions of Spider-Man, including the comic books *Ultimate Spider-Man* and the Sam Raimi trilogy of *Spider-Man* films, were embraced by the public at large, but were too post-modern and sly in their tone to appeal to a small, hardcore base of fans, who, ultimately, enjoy only the adventures of their favorite superhero produced in stage one by Steve Ditko and Stan Lee.

James Bond also works well here as one final example of the four phases of a superhero's career from outside the world of comic books. The original Ian Fleming novels, which constituted his personal vision of the character, represent stage one. The early Sean Connery films, which are fairly faithful adaptations of the novels, are also widely considered stage one adventures in their own right. However, the mass-marketed stage two of 007's fictional lifetime was certainly well underway by the time of the production of the Roger Moore film *Moonraker* (1979), which strayed far from Fleming's original vision of the Bond character, but successfully cashed in on the public enthusiasm for *Star Wars* by staging an atypical, space-based Bond adventure with mass audience appeal. The stage three, deconstructionist era of Bond adventures came in the form of Pierce Brosnan's *GoldenEye* (1995), in which Bond found himself at a loss for villains to fight following the end of the Cold War, and when his new, female boss "M" declared him a "sexist, misogynist dinosaur." A perfect example of a stage four Bond film is 2006's *Casino Royale,* starring Daniel Craig, which returns to the Ian Fleming source material, maintains *GoldenEye*'s deconstructionist tone, but retains the overblown action scenes popularized by the Roger Moore Bond films.

Even when taking into consideration all of the above factors — authorial intent, fan reaction, and the editorial and marketing intentions of the copyright holders — it is sometimes difficult to determine whether or not something is to be read naively, as a straightforward narrative, or whether a fascinating subtext is there to be unearthed with a little digging. The process of unpacking symbolism and reading for subtext is perennially unpopular with college students, who believe their English professor is out to play a trick on them when arguing that *A Modest Proposal* is meant to be read ironically, or that *Moby-Dick* is a metaphor for the power of an angry and unjust God. Certainly, in his preface to *Lord of the Rings,* J.R.R. Tolkien took to task anyone who would dare see his epic tale as an allegorical retelling of World War II. But, in "The Death of the Author" (1967), Roland Barthes gives license to every reader to find in a given work what meaning they will, and completely disregard issues of authorial intent, which are ultimately irrelevant. Meaning is made by the reader, not the author, Barthes argues, and there is an extent to which Barthes argument liberates scholars to make what they will of a given text without having to phone living authors to check to make sure the interpretation is "correct." However, one must strive, at the very least, to make an interpretation of a given text justifiable on the basis of textual evidence, or no one else will take such a reading seriously. In that case, the reading has failed, and the critic needs to reread the text in question to determine what went wrong.

Ideology and Subtext in Superhero Stories

How does one know when one has arrived at a justifiable, if not a spot-on, reading of a politically charged superhero comic book?

Here, I must confess to an example of my own limitations in this area. While I pride myself on my ability to recognize irony and properly interpret satire—a skill lacking in many Americans, who are unaccustomed to irony, but that is well-honed in the British, who make an art of it—I must confess to have been wholly wrong about comic writer Mark Millar for several years. My earliest exposure to his writing was the incredible body of work he produced for the *Superman Adventures* (1996–2002) comic book, easily the best Superman ongoing series in decades, in large part because of his contribution to it. I found it difficult to pigeonhole his politics, but I marveled at his ability to tell concise, traditional-style Superman narratives that were exciting and imaginative. Other *Superman* comics of recent years have demonstrated the questionable tendency to serialize storylines that last for more than a year before providing an unconvincing and bland resolution.

When I read his miniseries *The Ultimates* (2002), however, I began to suspect that Millar was conservative to a troubling degree. The idealized physical figures of the classic Avengers—Thor, Captain America, Iron Man—drawn by Millar's collaborator, Bryan Hitch, were a sight to behold. Recruited by a then-popular President George W. Bush and a Nick Fury drawn to resemble Hollywood superstar Samuel L. Jackson, this modern iteration of the Avengers talked breezily about pop culture, employed ruthless, Jack Bauer–style tactics in fighting their enemies, and trash-talked France. The rampaging Hulk boasted an enormous erection and was on a quest to rape his true love Betty before Captain America stopped him, and Ant-Man brutalized the Wasp in a domestic violence scene that was shockingly cruel.

Throughout, Millar's intended tone was difficult to ascertain. These superheroes were not acting like heroes, but the art made them appear to be gods. Aside from gratuitous references to Hollywood C-list actors Freddie Prinze, Jr., and Shannon Elizabeth, very little seemed to indicate a humorous tone, but the disconnect between the heroic art and the unheroic actions of the main cast should have been my clue. The comic, which I had read as a paean to the Bush Administration, was, in actual fact, a savage satire of it. I was not alone in missing this completely. Part of the problem was that Millar's subversive storytelling was obscured by Marvel Comics' probable motivations in publishing *The Ultimates*. Essentially, the comic book seemed like a clever marketing strategy designed to re-launch a moribund *Avengers* comic book franchise and begin pre-production on an *Avengers* film franchise. Consequently, *The Ultimates* read as a rough draft script, storyboard art, and costume design for a future *Avengers* film that would be non-satirical in tone and likely star Samuel L. Jackson as Nick Fury. And the eventual development of an *Avengers* film starring Samuel L. Jackson bore out the truth of these assumptions. Some of Millar's jokes were likely lost under the weight of those concerns.

Furthermore, my initial view of Millar as frustratingly conservative seemed confirmed by trailers for *Wanted* (2008), a film based on a Millar comic book that seemed to cast as its heroes an underground community of assassins. The film, indeed, plays like a recruitment video for Eric Harris' and Dylan Klebold's Trenchcoat Mafia, and Roger Ebert noted that it lacked "two organs" he needs to see in a film in order to fully enjoy it—a brain and a heart. Not so Millar's original miniseries, which is replete with angry satire and ironic humor, condemning American society for its lack of genuine heroes and its elevation to the highest stratum of society the worst kinds of criminals, rapists, and killers. That comic book, depressing and gothic in tone as it is, is clearly the work of a writer with a brain and a heart. In essence, the film with Angelina Jolie and Morgan Freeman was a loose adaptation that completely failed to translate to the screen the true spirit of Millar's story, while getting some of the major plot points and trappings correct. If the perceptive Roger Ebert could make the same mistake about Millar that I did, then I was at least in good company.

Adding to the confusion, during the 2008 presidential election, Millar wrote a comic book called *War Heroes* for Image Comics that took place in a near future in which John McCain was president of the United States, not either Democratic contender Barack Obama or Hillary Clinton. In Millar's story, McCain bribed American citizens into signing up to fight in Iraq and Afghanistan—and, provocatively, for a future invasion of Iran—by promising them superpowers. Millar got the idea when he heard McCain promise to stay the course in Iraq even if it takes 100 years to bring the war to a close. This prospect deeply disturbed Millar, who was also concerned that the decimated American economy would offer future young Americans no other career paths but the military. Hence, *War Heroes* was an even darker take on the concept of the "militarization of superheroes" that he introduced in *The Ultimates*.[12] But Millar was chagrined to learn that, as with *The Ultimates*, many readers, such as myself, missed the satire of *War Heroes*:

> It's amazing how many people seem to think this is a neo-con comic. Same thing happened on *Ultimates*, when it was clearly anti-war through and through.... In my story, America is clearly engineering terror attacks as a means to garner control back home, enslave the population, and send kids with nothing to lose into the Gulf. It's fake terror to justify an aggressive foreign policy.... There's nothing duller than some worthy anti-war [commentary]. We know it's wrong, illegal, and ill-considered. You don't need me to tell you that....[13]

Since celebrities like to make themselves look good in interviews, it is always wise to view defensive assertions skeptically, but Millar's bibliography bears out his claims. Any time his satire is unclear, the fault generally lies with his collaborators, who are not working in the same subversive spirit, or in the reader, who completely misses the tone.

In contrast, Sylvester Stallone's objection to having his films characterized as conservative is far less credible. As he stated in a 2008 interactive fan interview hosted by AintIt CoolNews.com:

> I do get offended at the [Rambo] character being politicized. Rambo questions the leadership of [this] country to the point where he doesn't even live in it.... Rambo is completely apolitical, but once Ronald Reagan declared Rambo a Republican, the media decided to make me into a right wing dartboard.[14]

It is difficult to see how Rambo, a character who fought alongside the Mujahideen against the Soviets during the Soviet-Afghan War in *Rambo III* (1988) could be considered apolitical. *Rambo: First Blood Part II* (1985) expressed laudable concern over the fate of American POWs left behind in Vietnam, but was possibly more potent as a fantasy scenario in which an invincible American Green Beret goes back to Vietnam and uses modern-day weaponry to exact a brutal revenge upon Vietnamese forces on behalf of an America still reeling from its defeat in the war. And *Rambo* (2008) shows the protagonist single-handedly decimating the forces of Burma's military junta with an enormous .50-caliber machine gun, purportedly to bring to the attention of the American audience the plight of the Burmese people. The film also symbolically expresses solidarity with pacifist human rights activist Aung San Suu Kyi, the rightfully elected leader of Burma who was, at the time of the film's release, languishing in a Burmese prison operated by her political enemies. Ironically, the brutal tactics Rambo employs in her name would likely appall Suu Kyi, who advocates passive resistance in opposition to the junta. Another admirer of Suu Kyi, John McCain, advocated U.S. intervention in Burma during the 2008 presidential election, which may well have influenced Stallone's decision to support McCain over Obama.

Rocky IV (1985) depicts America as a land of plenty in which every self-made millionaire has the right to buy himself a robot butler, and the Soviet Union is presented as a frozen wasteland policed by KGB agents. The film casts Rocky Balboa as an honorable Everyman who faces certain death with bravery and integrity, and does not sink low enough to use steroids when he trains for a boxing match (heh, heh, heh). Rocky's opposite number, the steroid enhanced Ivan Drago, is the merciless, emotionless murderer of the charismatic Apollo Creed, and his trainers are hateful con artists and collectivists. At the end of the film, Rocky defeats Drago and makes an impassioned plea for greater understanding and a future peace between America and the Soviet Union, but few viewers, by this time, would be eager to make peace with the evil empire that claimed Apollo Creed's life.

Stallone's most liberal film, *Judge Dredd* (1995), is a satire of American machismo and unwavering faith in its laws and criminal justice system. The title character is an extreme right-wing law enforcement officer who faces off against in-bred religious fanatic hicks in a post-apocalyptic rural America. *Demolition Man* (1994) is a conservative satire of the politically correct, pacifist world of *Star Trek: The Next Generation*, with a little liberal criticism of the fast-food industry thrown in for good measure.

Finally, it would be difficult to argue that Stallone's *The Expendables* (2010) is a hymn to feminism, pacifism, and world peace, although it is theoretically possible.

Despite Stallone's claims to the contrary, most of his films do, indeed, play like Republican propaganda, whether they were intended to or not. Consequently, it is reasonable for any critic to claim that Stallone and his movies are right-of-center politically.

Using the examples of Stallone and Millar as a springboard, here it will help to consider how several politically themed superhero narratives may (or may not) have been misinterpreted by their readership — or, to put it another way, read in a spirit not intended by the author. Perhaps the best example of this comes from a story in *The Amazing Spider-Man* #574 in which Peter Parker's high school nemesis, the bully Flash Thompson, loses his leg serving heroically with the American forces stationed in Iraq during Operation Iraqi Freedom. The issue is "dedicated to the men and women who serve, have served, and will serve in Iraq and Afghanistan with bravery and honor. (With special thanks to Sergeant Jeffrey Guerin, U.S. Army 25th Infantry Division.)" The letters pages of *The Amazing Spider-Man* issues #579 and #580 were filled with letters praising the story, as relatives of servicemen and patriotic Americans noted that they cried over the real and fictional stories of American soldiers related in #574. One letter published in #579, was by Robbie Doughty, a serviceman who lost his left leg below the knee to an Improvised Explosive Device in Iraq in 2004. He said he was moved by the realism of the story, though he was at first reluctant to read it, and expressed hopes that Flash would learn to walk again on an artificial leg as he did, a mere 30 days after the explosion. Doughty finished by including a picture of himself and writing, "I hope you can tell the rest of Flash's story at some point. Thank you for honoring those that have served in the War on Terror, especially those that lost their lives and those of us that left part of us there. That was one of the best comics I've ever read in my entire life."

A far less admiring letter, written by Uros Smiljani, appeared in *The Amazing Spider-Man* #592. Smiljani wrote:

> I know it is difficult to make any kind of profound geopolitical analysis and definitive statement in barely two dozen pages but that comic is simply shameful. Sure, I have seen your American readers getting themselves worked up with patriotic inspiration over it and I guess it's a job well done, but seriously does no one realize how ugly and offensive this issue was? How (dare I say it) racist it was? Hey, I know you've probably never been called racist before (much less by a Serb, eh?) but believe me, I have lived through four dirty wars in the last 18 years and I know racist discourse when I see it (much because Milosevic's regime I lived under used it. A lot.): blonde, handsome Aryan Americans who are just trying to make the neighborhoods of Middle Eastern cities free of those evil-looking, brown-skinned, pain-loving, narcotics-popping insurgents. Who just happen to be DEFENDING THEIR HOME CITIES against an invasion from another continent. Does not anyone see the bitter, bitter irony here?

Editor Stephen Wacker corresponded with the letter writer, asking Smiljani if he was sure he wanted to stick to the term racist. Smiljani replied that he believed that Guggenheim's story was more of a product of "cultural insensitivity" that tends not to go noticed until "someone from the other side points it out." He added, "I know most readers will feel unjustly assaulted which of course was not my intention as I am sure most of them are nice people, but that's the risk of talking about such topics."

Writer Marc Guggenheim responded by stating, "it might surprise you to learn that I lean very far to the left of the American political spectrum. I opposed the invasion of Iraq and believe that the offensive in Afghanistan was poorly handled. I don't feel that either engagement was undertaken with the goal of establishing democracy in either region." He added that the story of Flash's injury was told from Flash's perspective, which did not provide Guggenheim the opportunity to represent the Iraqi perspective on the war. "Nor was there an opportunity to voice my personal view that while I support American troops 100%, I don't believe their lives are being lost in a just or well-planned war. As a writer, sometimes all you get to do is tell the story being told."

This extended socio-political conversation, which played out over a series of Letters to the Editor, is one of the most fascinating public readings of a comic book ever. It puts to shame the absurd, unintelligent mudslinging political exchanges featured in online "talk-backs" and chat rooms, because every letter published, irrespective of its political perspective, was intelligent and compassionate. All of the people quoted above seem like good people with legitimate perspectives on the Iraq War, and their letters play off one another in a fascinating and, frankly, refreshing way. If only all political discourse was as intelligent when unmediated by the "Letter to the Editor" page format.

As potentially offensive as Smiljani's perspective on the Iraq war would be to an American reader, his musings seem tame when compared to the portrayal of the war on terror in the political cartoons of controversial Brazilian artist Carlos Latuff. Latuff has appropriated the image of the American superhero as a means of condemning American, British, and Israeli militarism, which he sees as this generation's Nazism. Much of his art is focused on the Arab-Israeli conflict, the wars in Afghanistan and Iraq, and the belief that the West has committed an endless series of war crimes against the civilians of the Middle East in order to corner the market on oil. In his cartoons, Latuff spins the normal dramatic conventions of superhero comics on their heads. Instead of showing Superman triumphantly defeating terrorists, he has terrorists defeat Superman in a dramatic moment meant to elicit cheers of approval from the onlooker. Latuff has drawn several cartoons in which Superman is shown machine gunned to death by an Iraqi insurgent armed with Kryptonite bullets. He has depicted a blindfolded Captain America held hostage by rebels, and forced to testify on tape that, "America is FUCKED in Iraq." He created an Iraqi superhero, Captain Iraq, and drew American-style comic book covers in which Captain Iraq breaches White House security and kidnaps George W. Bush from the oval office.

The images of a dead Superman, a captured Captain America, and an invaded White House are very disturbing to the American sensibility, but Latuff says his audience is not the suburban American middle class, but "freedom fighters around the world." As he writes, "I expect to see my art being appropriated by common people worldwide, see these examples of my cartoons being converted into posters for Gaza massacre demonstrations."

Latuff feels that the depictions of Superman and Captain America as evil are only natural given contemporary American international policies:

> During World War II it was very common seeing comics where Superman or Captain America fought the Nazis and the Japanese. Such superheroes were the representation of the US/Western values of democracy, freedom, and all that bullshit. Washington is always blabbing about freedom for justifying wars and invasions. Now US "heroes" are no longer battling Nazis, but killing scores of people resisting the occupations of Iraq and Afghanistan, and funding the immoral and illegal repression of the Palestinians by Israel. And when US soldiers are blown up in pieces by a roadside bomb in Iraq, it's as if Captain America and all his power wasn't enough to subdue people's will.[15]

While he maintains that he is not anti–Semitic but anti-imperial, Latuff has awakened the ire of many Jews by characterizing their treatment of the Palestinians as a Holocaust perpetrated by Jews. He has stated that he is not biased against all Jews, but critical of the actions of the Israeli government. Certainly, he has been an equal opportunity critic of imperial regimes, and has portrayed former British Prime Minister Tony Blair as a hippie wearing a shoulder bag of Iraqi skulls, and drawn President Barack Obama as a war criminal who has disgustingly been awarded the Nobel Peace Prize. He has also drawn President George W. Bush using Fox News as bait on a hook to catch American public opinion in support of the Iraq War, and depicted American soldiers stationed in Iraq as "slasher movie" villains Freddie Krueger, Chucky, and Jason Voorhees. Latuff is unsurprised that such cartoons make him very unpopular with the targets of his savage satire, and isn't bothered by criticism: "There are many people from US who are supportive of my views, but most of them prefer to call me names. The same thing with Israelis. But I really don't care. My focus is on those who are suffering from state terrorism, mainly in the Third World."[16]

Since Latuff's topics are inherently controversial and his art highly inflammatory, it is unsurprising that his work has provoked strongly divergent reactions depending on who is looking at it. One could well understand why Israelis would view Latuff's cartoons as prejudiced against Jews, and grasp why the individuals he has targeted with his satire, including lawyer Alan Dershowitz, would find his cartoons disgusting and offensive. On the other hand, the distinction Latuff draws between the Jewish people as a large group of individuals and the Israeli government's oppressive policies is as valid and graspable as the distinction between the the Bush Administration and the American people (who were divided over Bush's policies), and the Blair Administration and the British people (who turned on Blair over Iraq).

One could also imagine someone with Smiljani's view of the Iraq War agreeing with all of Latuff's cartoons. Finally, it would be easy to see why someone with political views similar to Guggenheim's would be sympathetic to Latuff's characterization of the war, and of Bush and Blair, but would reject the uniform portrayal of American troops as war criminals and horror movie villains.

It is usually at this point in discussing the portrayal of whole groups of people as "good" or "evil" that the specter of statistics rears its head. There are those who might say, if above x percentage of American troops are war criminals, then Latuff's cartoons are justified, and if below x percentage of American troops are war criminals, then they are not. Similar arguments could be made about the percentages of Italian Americans in the Mafia justifying or not justifying the prevalence of the Mafia stereotype in the mass media, or about the *realism* of the characterization of most Muslim characters featured on the television series *24* as terrorists.

Delving deep into these controversial waters, British born art historian and visual culture scholar David Wall wrote in "It is and it isn't: Stereotype, Advertising, and Narrative" (2008):

> Just as with [political campaign advertising, the action series] *24* can offer its consumers a multiplicity of intentions, consequences, and meanings at one and the same time, dependent on culture, context, and audience. And to criticize it on the grounds that it misrepresents Muslims does not get us very far. While *24* is undeniably the product of a set of wider cultural politics, which routinely represents Muslims and Islam negatively, we should remember that the media also generates some positive images of Islam. But to engage in the sort of analysis whereby we trawl the media and simply count off each negative image against a positive one and see what total we end up with is missing the broader point. If this kind of misrepresentation were the main problem then the only corrective necessary would simply be to make lots of television shows featuring Muslims as special needs teachers or acrobats. A show such as *24* needs to be assessed not in terms of the supposed accuracy or inaccuracy of its representations but in terms of what Ella Shohat and Robert Stam (1994) call "a specific orchestration of ideological discourses." In other words, how are those representations arranged and how do they reimagine, rearticulate, and reinstate wider cultural politics? [52].

For Wall, negative stereotyping of people of color in the media has one core motivation: the justification of Western imperialism. It is a potent point, in line with Marina Warner's and Marshall McLuhan's, and represents a legitimate condemnation of the portrayal of Asian and Middle Eastern cultures in particular as villainous and irredeemable in superhero narratives. Obviously, dramatic narratives require conflicts, and conflicts require antagonists and protagonists, but such conflicts need neither be populated by disgustingly Satanic villains, nor go to the opposite extreme, and present a universe of bland, unthreatening opponents who are merely misunderstood and easy to talk down, like those in *Star Trek: The Next Generation*. A balance can, and should, be achieved.

However, the point remains that, as Millar and Guggenheim demonstrate, people who go looking for conservative propaganda in superhero stories will find it there, thanks in part to the tunnel-vision perspective created by the assumption in the first place. It takes savvier readers to find the real perspectives at the core of the narrative, and separate the problematic racial, sexual, and violent elements of the narrative from the subversive spirit of these often divisive and exploitative elements. After all, a political message is not truly subversive if it is obvious, and readers should keep in mind how often someone like Millar's work is misread before leaping to conclusions about the author. Having already made the mistake once with Millar, it is my goal to provide better, closer readings of source texts in this book. Acknowledging that there will be times I will present a reading not initially intended by the author, my hope is that it will still be a valid reading and an interesting one, and justifiable on the grounds of Barthes' "Death of the Author."

The following represents the methodological approach I will use when determining the extent to which a superhero narrative is progressive or reactionary, and the extent to which it is meant to be satirical or taken seriously.

First, one can judge how central political commentary is to the narrative when analyzing how deeply integrated into the plot and characterization the political commentary is. If the political commentary is confined to a few throwaway lines of dialogue, it is difficult to build a case that the narrative represents a thoughtful or fully developed political commentary. If the entire conflict is political in nature, and the resolution directly confronts the political issues raised in the plot's exposition and development instead of dodging them, then the tale is likely one worth dissecting. *Mission Impossible 3* is a perfect example of this first kind of story, and *Watchmen*—both the comic and the film adaptation—is the ideal example of the second.

Roberto Orci and Alex Kurtzman are Hollywood screenwriters adept at crafting incomprehensible films populated by characters who lack credible motivations for the extreme actions they take in the stories. They sometimes try to make their films topical, but the political dialogue is window-dressing to serve as the justification for a series of action set pieces. For example, Billy Crudup's villain in *Mission Impossible 3* (2006) makes some sort of evil speech related to the Bush Administration and the war on terror, but he races through his monologue at such high speeds that, if you blink, you will miss what he has said about Iraq and Afghanistan. This rapid-fire speech was probably not Crudup's fault, but the script's, and the studio's expectation that a modern-day film audience lacks the capacity to pay attention to extended dialogue-heavy segments sandwiched in between action segments.

The Orci and Kurtzman scripts for *Transformers* (2007) and *Star Trek* (2009) also fail to properly explain the motivations of the villains or say anything interesting about modern politics. Indeed, the *Transformers* franchise in general has little literary or dramatic worth, and was created to help sell toys to young boys in an era when President Reagan relaxed restrictions against marketing to children (Suellentrop, *Wired*). The multimedia franchise is bolstered by the imaginations of the *Transformers* fans that imbue the flimsy material with their own potent fantasies of family cars and household devices turning into robots (Frus). *Transformers* also benefits from the emotional associations built into its iconography, and hero Autobot leader Optimus Prime is easy to love because he is a red-white-and-blue-painted cab over truck that transforms into a fatherly, compassionate John Wayne figure. He is a heroic stereotype, but he is hard to dislike, and many children cried over his death in *Transformers: The Movie* (1986). None of this makes the Transformers franchise any more intelligent and socially aware, however. Simon Furman's 1993 comic series *Transformers: Generation 2* remains the only Transformers story worth seeking out, and it is good largely because of Furman's imaginative myth-making surrounding the origins of the robot species.

There are only two possible political readings of the series. The original cartoon depicts Autobots and Decepticons fighting over earth's oil resources, making it clear to children how much of the industrial world needs oil to survive. The Michael Bay film series shows the American military stationed in the Middle East suddenly unable to control its own superior technology, as U.S. Army tanks and helicopters come frighteningly to life and seem to defect to the Taliban and the Iraq insurgency, killing American troops instead of the enemy. But that, essentially, is all there is to say about overt politically commentary in *Transformers*.

Other superhero stories with paper-thin plots and virtually absent political subtext include *G.I. Joe: The Rise of Cobra* (2009), which downgrades the war on terror to a family squabble and a lovers' spat, the incomprehensible theatrical cuts of *Supergirl* (1984) and *Daredevil* (2003), and *Spider-Man: Maximum Carnage* (1993), a plotless, overlong marketing initiative and transparent attempt to imitate and compete with the far superior *Batman: Knightfall* (1993).

In contrast, the comic book *Watchmen* (1986–1987), written by Alan Moore and illustrated by Dave Gibbons, is brilliant, unparalleled political commentary based in the superhero genre. A radically liberal story made palatable to a conservative comic book reading audience via the inclusion of a right-wing protagonist named Rorschach, *Watchmen* is an indictment of Reagan-era militarism and a funeral dirge for American progressivism. By the 1980s, the heroes of the counterculture, feminist, and civil rights movements had all either been assassinated, turned unexpectedly Republican, or grown into fat, aging shadows of their former selves, like the superheroes that comprise the cast of *Watchmen*. While many of them had contented themselves with combating street-crime in cities slipping into anarchy (thanks to Reaganomics), the brilliant Ozymandias realizes that there is no greater supervillain to combat than the power-mad President of the United States, Richard Nixon (the symbolic stand-in for Ronald Reagan). As his fellow superheroes fruitlessly investigate a nonexistent serial killer, Ozymandias plots to save the world from being obliterated in an inevitable nuclear war between the U.S. and the Soviet Union. His ruthless plan involves giving the Republicans and the Communists a small taste of what nuclear war would really be like, in the hopes that the

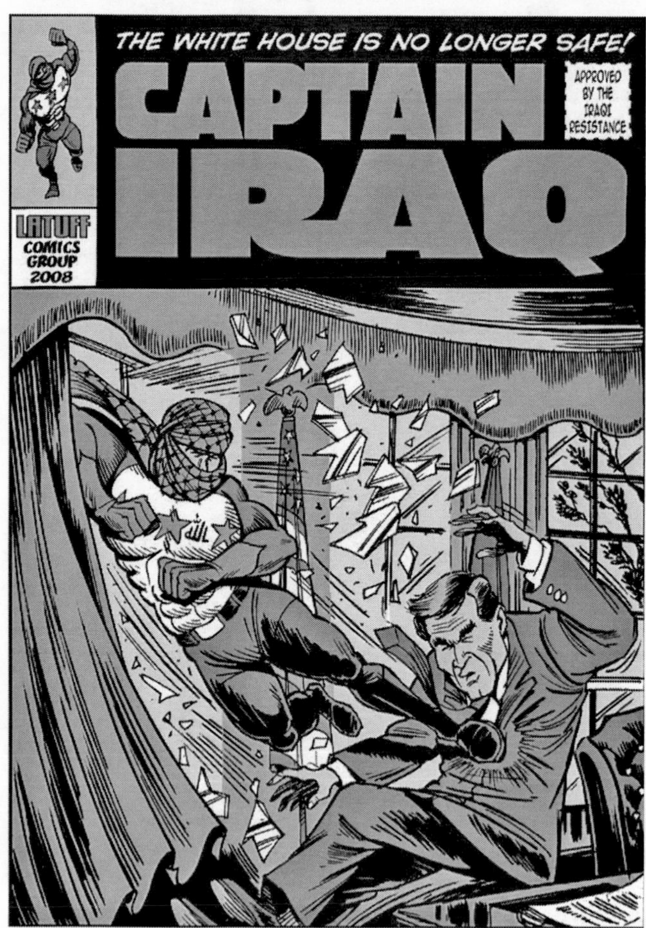

Brazilian artist Carlos Latuff has garnered controversy for condemning American imperialism and offering sympathy for the U.S.'s opponents in the wars in Iraq and Afghanistan. In this mock-up comic cover, Captain Iraq kidnaps sitting president George W. Bush from the White House to arrest him for war crimes (courtesy Carlos Latuff).

widespread devastation and loss of millions of innocent lives would make them rethink their eagerness to push the button.

As comics scholar Douglas Wolk aptly observed:

> *Watchmen* systematically undermines the entire premise of adventure stories: not only that evil can be vanquished and that doing good can save the world but that "good" and "evil" are easy to apply. It upends the principles of heroic victory and heroic self-sacrifice, and at the end it looks like saving the world may not have been a good idea anyway. And its big love scene is scaldingly bitter: "Was it good for you?" one of the lovers asks helplessly. "Did the costumes make it good?"
>
> But *Watchmen* is still a pleasure to read, because it is also a first-rate adventure story of exactly the kind it has a grudge against.... There's an aerial rescue, a prison break scene, a showdown at a secret hideout, and exquisitely fleshed-out characters [240–241].

The political commentary never stops, and is noticeable even in the action segments, making the graphic novel one of the most literary and mature superhero narratives ever published, and the film adaptation far too cerebral for movie audiences looking for cheap thrills and cool explosions. But that, of course, is what made the film a masterpiece as well, and why Roger Ebert rightly declared it one of the best superhero films ever made.

Of course, what is true for one Alan Moore comic is true for many. Readers interested in other intelligent political commentaries from Moore may look no further than his tenure writing *Swamp Thing* stories. The character appeared in a cheesy Wes Craven B-movie in 1982, but the Moore comic book, surprisingly, is outstanding. Especially compelling is Moore's satire of 1980s America in the "American Gothic" storyline, which introduced another iconic comic hero, John Constantine. In the story arc, Swamp Thing travels across America, encountering a series of traditional Universal Studios Monsters who were "explicitly connected with one of the monsters of the American national psyche: the werewolf story was also about repressed feminism (think lunar cycles), the zombie story concerned America's gun fetish, and so on" (Wolk 231–232).

Examples of superhero narratives by other writers that offer incisive political commentaries include *Mr. Freedom, Asterix the Gaul, The Fantastic Four: Authoritative Action, Marvel's Civil War, Wonder Woman: Gods and Mortals*, and *Barack the Barbarian*.

The most problematic category of superhero narrative is the one that has smart political commentary in the first half of the film, but degenerates into an escapist action tale in the second half and fails to resolve, or even address, the points it made in the final act. The most obvious examples of these superhero stories include *X-Men: The Last Stand* (2006), which offers an excellent commentary on gay rights for the first half of the film and then shelves the politics in time for an extended siege segment, and *Avatar* (2009), which left major plot threads unresolved, presumably in the service of a sequel.

The remaining question at hand is, once a story seems to treat political issues seriously, what is the best way to determine whether a film is liberal or conservative in its sentiments? Superhero story or not, clues can be found in how the narrative in question depicts violence, sexuality, nature, women, and issues of race and class.

If a given narrative condemns violence in general, and shows death as ugly and bloody, then it likely represents a pro-pacifist form of liberalism (*Doctor Who: Survival, Duck Soup*, and *Sophie Scholl*). If it celebrates violence against an oppressor, it represents an angry, revolutionary species of leftist politics (*Machete, Jennifer's Body, The Baader-Meinhoff Complex*). If the violence celebrates the glory of war, and if it concerns the squashing of revolutionary or invading hordes to protect the current ruling class, then the story is more conservative (*The Lord of the Rings, Conan the Barbarian, Die Hard*).

If the narrative depicts sexuality as natural, sex as fun and beautiful, and challenges Puritanical prudery and homophobia, then the story is liberal, whether the sex is explicit or not (the *Watchmen* film and non-superhero stories *Harold and Maude, Gods and Monsters,* and *Smiles of a Summer Night*). If the woman is portrayed as a sex toy for the man, or if the lovers are killed shortly after copulating — symbolically receiving a death sentence for being sexually active — then the story is conservative, whether or not nudity is depicted (*Transformers, Piranha 3-D, Hollow Man*).

If the story depicts the natural world, and the animal kingdom, as friendly and beautiful, and worth conserving (*Aquaman, Beastmaster, Bambi*), then the story is liberal. If the natural world is filled with dangerous monsters that need to be destroyed or subdued to make the world safe for humanity, then it is conservative (*Jaws, The Birds, Outbreak*). Unless, of course, the film warns about the dangers of global warming, deforestation, pollution, and the extinction of animal life; then it is liberal (*The Day After Tomorrow, Silent Running, We3*).

By and large, superhero stories offer dreadful portrayals of women and are clearly reactionary conservative in this matter at least. There appear to be two major choices of female lead character: the damsel in distress and the emotionless, voluptuous vixen in painted-on clothing who never has sex but is great at karate. These dreadful portrayals of women essentially provide masturbatory fantasies for the predominantly male readership, and indulge in the male gaze Laura Mulvey described in "Visual Pleasure and Narrative Cinema" (1973).

The damsel in distress is generally chained up or knocked unconscious, left sprawled across the floor or a bed, legs open, mouth ajar. This female character template serves the function of inspiring lust and action on the part of the hero, but does little herself to advance the story. To this extent, the hero's love interest is "the perfect woman" as described by Victorian satirist Max Beerbohm in his "Defense of Cosmetics" (1894):

> [I]t is, from the intellectual point of view, quite necessary that a woman should repose. Hers is the resupinate sex. On her couch she is a goddess, but so soon as ever she put her foot to the ground — lo, she is the veriest little sillypop, and quite done for. She cannot rival us in action, but she is our mistress in the things of the mind. Let her not by second-rate athletics, nor indeed by any exercise soever of the limbs, spoil the pretty procedure of her reason. Let her be content to remain the guide, the subtle suggester of what we must do, the strategist whose soldiers we are...

The ultimate example of the woman in "repose" in recent superhero stories is Megan Fox in *Transformers*. A highly sexualized, erotically idealized female figure draped over a car or motorcycle invariably evokes lust in the heterosexual male onlooker, which accounts for the instant fame Fox achieved merely by leaning low over the hood of a yellow Camaro wearing a flimsy pink belly shirt and an impossibly short denim skirt — a "money shot" featuring a pose that the male audience read as an unequivocal sex invite.

Interestingly, Megan Fox made a film that condemned men for sexually objectifying and raping women —*Jennifer's Body* (2009). She also slammed the Walt Disney Company for raising young girls such as Miley Cyrus and Vanessa Hudgens to be Lolita-style sex symbols: "Fuck Disney. They take these little girls, and they put them through entertainment school and teach them to sing and dance, and make them wear belly shirts, but they won't allow them to be their own people. It makes me sick."[17] This feminist streak stood in stark contrast to Fox's status as a sex symbol, and her defiance of director Michael Bay and frequent outspoken comments helped cut her career short. The fact that *Jennifer's Body* was marketed to the wrong audience and was a financial failure didn't help her either. Still, it was largely Fox's outspokenness that made it difficult for her former fans to continue imagining her in a state of repose, so her character was dropped from *Transformers 3*.

***Watchmen*, both the 2009 film and the 1987 graphic novel by Alan Moore and Dave Gibbons, is one of the greatest superhero narratives ever written, as well as a powerful, left-wing satire of Reagan-era America. The Comedian (Jeffrey Dean Morgan) has spent a lifetime using his superpowers to help President Nixon win Vietnam, pacify hippie protestors, and crush the civil rights movement, but he has done all this at the cost of his soul.**

The super ninja woman is active, but scenes of her leaping about in a cat suit, beating men into submission, as in the segment in which Scarlett Johansson (as the Marvel character Black Widow) pummels an entire corridor of men into unconsciousness in *Iron Man 2* (2010), are specifically designed to make viewers wonder: "What would it be like to have sex with *her*?" That the Black Widow character has little to do in the film otherwise, and lacks cohesive characterization, merely compounds the problem.

Female superheroes have their defenders. As Famke Janssen, the actress who played Jean Grey in *X-Men* and dominatrix Xenia Onatopp in *GoldenEye*, observed, "We've always been ready for female superheroes. Because women want to *be* them and men want to *do* them."[18]

Another defender of female superheroes is Gerard Jones, who wrote in *Killing Monsters* (2003):

> The current generation of adolescent boys love active, powerful, threatening female figures—often as protagonists and often ... as a heroic surrogate for the boy himself.... Girls have long been known to identify with male fantasy figures. Now it looks as though young boys are finally learning the same art.... By combining the "frailties" normally allowed to women in commercial entertainment with the power and anger allowed men, they become much more complete characters [160–161].

This is often true. Some of the best of these female protagonists include Ellen Ripley from the *Alien* franchise, Kitty Pryde of the *X-Men* and *Excalibur*, Judge Cassandra Anderson from *2000 AD Comics*, Emma Peel from the British spy series *The Avengers*, Laurie Juspeczyk from *Watchmen*, Maureen O'Sullivan's Jane Parker from *Tarzan and His Mate* (1934), Buffy Summers from *Buffy the Vampire Slayer*, Xena from *Xena: Warrior Princess*, Lisbeth Salander from the *Millennium* trilogy, Pam Grier from *Jackie Brown* (1997), and Leela and Barbara Wright and Sarah Jane Smith from *Doctor Who*. Furthermore, the Invisible Woman, Lois Lane, Catwoman, and Mary Jane Watson can be excellent or dreadful characters depending on how they are written and how they are drawn.

However, as nice as it is for men to have female characters to relate to, there is a troubling tendency in hero narratives of the past two decades to make the heroine functionally the male reader, but dressed in a too-perfectly proportioned "wet dream" female body. The woman then becomes the male reader himself and the male reader's sex fantasy all at once, and little concern appears to be paid to the female reader and whether or not these concessions to male tastes have cut her out of the equation altogether. Luc Besson's films in particular consistently feature idealized female warriors who are at once guardian angels of the protagonist (modeled after Besson himself), the sex fantasy of the protagonist, and the protagonist's "female side." The classic Besson man/woman/angel/fetish is an uncannily slender and athletic figure, with long, shapely legs and intense eyes, and is fundamentally innocent *despite* the evils of the world that she has directly experienced and the sins that she herself has committed. She inspires the men around her to embrace life and reform their character by overwhelming them with her awe-inspiring innocence and sexual presence. This character template was featured in *La Femme Nikita* (1990), *Leon* (1994), *The Fifth Element* (1997), *The Messenger* (1999), *Angel-A* (2005), and *Banditas* (2006).

A refreshing departure from this mold of female comic book character is Batton Lash's Alanna Wolfe, the defense attorney from *Supernatural Law*. Wolff is professionally dressed, slender, not buxom. She is a real woman and a real feminist — not a ninja — and that makes her, easily, one of the best and most important women in comics. She gets the message out without the over-the-top sex appeal of a Wonder Woman type, while still being a pretty, older woman.

Lash was consciously moving away from the stereotypical comic book woman when he created her. "In real life, I always liked the Alanna Wolff–type. But it seemed (in 1979), that the only type of female lead in comics was either built like Wonder Woman or Angelfood McSpade! I like a woman in a business suit and tie and most of my female friends wore glasses, so that seemed like a natural to me," he said in an e-mail interview on September 20, 2010.

In *Watchmen* (Warner Bros., 2009), Nite Owl (Patrick Wilson) and Silk Spectre (Malin Åkerman) pause in the midst of their efforts to break fellow superhero Rorschach out of prison to appreciate how sexy they both look in costume — and how much of an adrenaline rush it is beating up corrections officers and rioting prisoners.

Sexy or not, invincible or not, if the female character is presented as having a fully developed personality, graspable motivation, subjectivity, and a soul, then the story is arguably presenting a more enlightened, liberal view of women. If the woman is a mere symbol of male desire or saintly victimhood, then the story is conservative.

Depictions of race are even more appalling in comics than depictions of woman. As Dave Chappelle joked, many superhero stories are prejudiced. He offered, as case in point, "...you'd never see Batman in a housing project wasting his time."[19] Nor, for that matter, are you likely to often encounter a black superhero. There are some notable exceptions, such as the Green Lantern John Stewart, Marvel's Black Panther, Afro Samurai, and Static Shock, but they are the exception rather than the rule. One is far more likely to see a black character as a villain, a crack addict, or a confidant for the main hero. In these roles, the black character is supposed to act as multicultural window-dressing to a fundamentally conservative story, or add a layer of gritty urban realism, but he is not important in and of himself. The same can be said of Asian and Native American characters. They can appear as sidekicks and servants (Kato in *Green Hornet,* Tonto in the *Lone Ranger,* Wong in *Doctor Strange*), or villains (The Mandarin in *Iron Man,* Ming the Merciless in *Flash Gordon,* and the "Injun" hordes of countless Westerns). If the non-white character is presented as a "real" person, with graspable thoughts, feelings, and motivations, is important to the plot, and does not seem to be behaving in a purely stereotypical fashion, then the story is liberal (the *Justice League* cartoon, *Black Panther*). If the non-white character is mere cannon fodder for action sequences, a smiling servant, a Satanic villain, or mere comic relief, then the story is conservative (see virtually every cop show on television).

Similarly, if gay, lesbian, bisexual, and transgendered characters are presented as human beings and not judged for their sexual orientation then the story is liberal (*X-Men, Doctor Who,* and Jeremy Brett's *Sherlock Holmes*). If non-heterosexual characters are presented as immoral, evil, or are figures of pure comedy and caricature, then the story is conservative (*Conan the Barbarian, Diamonds Are Forever*). Notably, *Batman Forever* (1995) muddies these waters by presenting the bisexual Batman and Robin positively, and presenting the gay Riddler as a grotesque, evil figure.

In terms of class representation, most American popular culture narratives depict middle-class protagonists because most writers in Hollywood and the publishing industry are middle class and write about themselves. Consequently, mainstream stories tend to depict middle-class fears of both the very poor (potential rioters and muggers) and the very rich (who can fire you and steal your retirement). This seeming equal opportunity bashing is self-serving and uncritical of the middle-class worldview, and tends to range from the apolitical (a synonym for mildly conservative) to the reactionary, depending on the story. If the poor characters are depicted sympathetically and the wealthier characters are shown to be parasitical, the story represents liberal, anti-corporate perspectives (*The Girl with the Dragon Tattoo, Columbo*). If the rich are respectable and the great unwashed are dangerous menaces, then the story is conservative (*Batman, Uncle Scrooge*).

Finally, and most importantly, tone is vitally important in determining how to read a story. On the surface a story may celebrate the values of one political philosophy to an extreme degree, but still subtly caricature and condemn that same movement to the point that the tale's *real* message emerges as the exact opposite of its *apparent* message (see Mark Millar's superhero satires, *Watchmen, Mr. Freedom,* and *A Modest Proposal*). The question of tone is particularly vexed when the story is very, very violent. Extreme violence is often funny, and there is a moral question as to whether the natural inclination to laugh is cathartic, releasing pent up aggression in a heavily policed and repressive society, or a sign of moral corruption. In their contrasting reviews of the Mark Millar film *Kick-Ass* (2010), Harry Knowles argued that laughing at a little girl while she commits mass murder is funny and liberating, while Roger Ebert described it as "morally reprehensible."

Applying this schematic to superhero, science fiction, and horror films yields some fascinating results. For example, the *Planet of the Apes* series emerges as the most politically liberal commercial franchise in history. The series promoted a strong anti-war message throughout, except in *Conquest of Planet of the Apes* (1972), which expressed solidarity with the radical wing of the civil rights movement and advocated a race rebellion. The series boasts a strong female lead in Zira (Kim Hunter), makes a plea for animal rights, champions Darwinism over Creationism, chafes at class differences, and condemns racism and extremist nationalism in all its forms. In the realm of the superhero narrative, *Watchmen* emerges as one of the most left-wing superhero stories of all time, using a satirical tone to present a thoughtful, staunchly liberal worldview through a conservative surface narrative. *John Constantine: Hellblazer* and *Doctor Who* are also consistently leftist in a similar vein.

The schematic also reveals that the *Transformers* franchise is one of the most conservative superhero narratives in history. The original cartoon had no female characters at all and the Michael Bay films paint women as fools, damsels in distress, and sex objects. *Transformers: Revenge of the Fallen* (2009) is replete with racist stereotypes and prominently features urban ghetto Transformers. Violence is depicted as glorious and operatic, and the Peter Parker–style hero Sam Witwicky grows into manhood on the field of battle. Coherent political commentary is consistently absent and the screenplays are juvenile across the board. Working-class characters are depicted as morally suspect (Megan Fox and her absent, criminal father), while members of the American military industrial complex are largely heroic, if sometimes comical and bureaucratic, figures. It is hard to get more right wing than *Transformers*. And that, of course, might be forgivable if the *Transformers* films and TV shows had any artistic merit whatsoever. However, as a group, *Transformers* stories are among the most absurd, poorly made narratives in the history of popular culture, and inspire many viewers to positively reassess Ed Wood's body of film work in comparison, and appreciate it for its originality, "no-budget" bravado, and narrative coherence.

What is interesting about the methodology presented above is that it not only reveals obvious far-right and far-left narratives, but also indicates how difficult it is for many narratives to be purely liberal or conservative. A superhero story might have an excellent black protagonist, but depict women as sex objects, as *Black Dynamite* (2009) does. The *Alien* films boast a wonderful female protagonist in Ripley, demonstrate socialistic solidarity with the working classes against the evil Weyland-Yutani Corporation, but depict the alien villains as wholly irredeemable (and dangerously female) and seem to promote genocide as the only logical course of action. The *Asterix the Gaul* comic books are gleefully anti–Imperialist, celebrating a socialistic band of French peasants who rise up in opposition against the imperialism of the Roman Empire. The comic, produced in the aftermath of World War II, can be read as an anti–Fascist allegory, and condemns 20th century commercial culture, unrestrained capitalism, and the crimes against the environment committed in the name of industrialization. And yet, this liberal comic strip has no strong female leads and revels in racial and ethnic stereotypes for comic purposes, sometimes to a troubling degree. (But sometimes it is just funny, and mostly harmless.)

That is why, as useful as this methodological schematic is, most narratives need to be judged on a case-by-case basis. Sometimes their relative progressivism or conservatism is difficult to gauge when some elements seem progressive and others do not. Nevertheless, close-readings of given texts often yield conclusive evidence on one side or the other. When they do not, the muddled political tone will be reported honestly.

When writers working in a mass-marketed genre engage in political dialogue with their audience, they are likely doing so in part because they feel passionately enough about a given political issue that they need to express their views. They are also expressing these views, at times, in the service of a dramatic story. Finally, they may entertain some hopes that, should they express their political views intelligently and clearly enough, they will meet with approval from readers who already agree with the political point, and perhaps even get readers on the other side of the debate to reconsider their position.

While few superhero stories have had a noticeable effect on the real world, some have, against all likelihood, changed the real world in large ways and small, as the television series *24* and the *Superman* radio show did. Other stories were intended to change the world, but failed to make much difference. Ultimately, as Wolk argues, comic book writers like Grant Morrison (*All-Star Superman, Seven Soldiers of Victory, X-Men*) hope to perform a certain kind of magic when they write comic books.

> The premise, though, is that when two-dimensional characters and their stories take on enough complexity and depth, they effectively become real, bursting through the fourth wall or the surface of the page, slipping into their reader's world and changing it with the energy of the fantastic. Morrison desperately wants to inscribe that idea into reality, and [his] astonishingly ambitious [body of work] glimmers with the faint, startling light of magic [Wolk 288].

This book will consider several key superhero adventure stories that were excellent works of art, and passionate political pleas that fell upon deaf ears, as well as the select few, surprising tales that successfully changed the world — in ways large and small — with their powerful political statements.

One

Batman as Terrorist, Technocrat, and Feudal Lord

Guns are for cowards. People carry them because they are afraid.—Batman[1]

You must begin a reading program immediately so that you may understand the crises of our age.... For the contemporary period, you should study some selected comic books.... I recommend Batman especially, for he tends to transcend the abysmal society in which he's found himself. His morality is rather rigid, also. I rather respect Batman.—Ignatius J. Reilly, from John Kennedy Toole's *A Confederacy of Dunces*[2]

I want to be Robin to Bush's Batman.—Dan Quayle

Batman versus Osama bin Laden

When Frank Miller announced that he would be crafting a graphic novel in which Batman would confront real-world terrorist Osama bin Laden, journalists across the country picked up the story and reported on it with a combination of amusement and amazement. As NPR's *Morning Edition* noted on Feb. 16, 2006:

> The Joker and the Riddler can rest easy—"The Caped Crusader" will be taking on Osama bin Laden. The cartoonist says it's silly for Batman to chase old villains out of Gotham City when there are real threats out there. Miller admits it's a piece of propaganda. But hey, it worked for Superman and Captain America, who both punched out Hitler.

Here NPR perpetuates the widely held public perception that comic books are predominantly escapist, apolitical, kids' adventures and the least likely place to find meditations on contemporary political and military conflicts. Yet, it simultaneously establishes that comic books have been political and socially relevant all along. Miller's *Holy Terror,* in fact, is only the latest in a long line of political and (sometimes) socially insightful Batman stories, including a 1943 movie serial, *Batman Begins* (2005), *Batman Returns* (1992), *The Cult* (1988), *A Death in the Family* (1989), *Venom* (1991), *No Man's Land* (1999), and *Dark Detective* (2005). Since announcing the project, and proudly declaring that it will "offend just about everyone," Miller has struggled to complete it, and has, at various times, removed Batman from the story, placed him back in, and removed him again. Should Batman ultimately appear in the finished product, *Holy Terror* would be the second story to feature a confrontation between Batman and Osama bin Laden, the first being depicted allegorically in *Batman Begins.*

Batman Begins reintroduced American audiences to Bruce Wayne, an orphaned billionaire philanthropist who secretly fights crime by night as Batman. The film was released after a string of Batman narratives that condemned American corporate, political, and military leadership. The *Batman* films from the 1990s tackled issues of sexism and corporate corruption, and Frank Miller's comic book narratives from the 1980s, *Batman: Year One* and *The Dark Knight Returns,* raised the question of whether or not Batman was himself a terrorist or quasi-fascist dictator. In examining these adventures and building on previous scholarship by Will Brooker, Geoff Klock, and Aeon J. Skoble, this chapter will demonstrate how each Batman story operates as social commentary. Each of these Batman stories can stand alone as an individual work of art or product of its time, yet each functions as a piece of the much larger narrative of Batman that exists in the collective consciousness of fans who work to reconcile inconsistencies and to decide who the definitive Batman truly is and what form of heroism he represents.

As Brooker (1999) has observed, Batman has changed much since he was created by Bob Kane in 1939, engaging in adventures that reflect the times in which they were crafted. In his first decade of adventures, Batman was equally likely to fight gangsters, vampires, and Nazis, as well as classic villains such as the Joker and Catwoman. In the 1950s, a smiling Batman faced aliens and nuclear-age menaces akin to those found on the silver screen in *Them!* (1954) and *Forbidden Planet* (1956). In the 1960s, his comic book exploits took a psychedelic turn, and the Adam West television series he inspired became an instant camp classic. The depressed 1970s were characterized by darkly Gothic, often supernatural stories drawn by Neal Adams and Marshall Rogers, who emphasized Batman's toned musculature and newly brooding countenance.

Batman's adventures during the 1980s were gritty, violent, and "For Mature Readers Only," featuring critically acclaimed stories by Jim Starlin, Alan Moore, and Frank Miller that pitted him against Communists, Muslim terrorists, the Radical Christian Right, and President Reagan himself. From 1989 to the turn of the century, *Batman* enjoyed renewed mainstream popularity with four major feature films and a new television show, *Batman: The Animated Series,* which followed the 1990s movie thriller trend of glorifying their colorful villains at the expense of the hero, who was sometimes reduced to the role of boring supporting player. Significantly, as the first major live-action Batman adventure since the 9/11 attacks, *Batman Begins* reflects the hopes and anxieties of modern urban American culture just as closely as previous incarnations of Batman reflected their times. Perhaps unsurprisingly, it is hard for some fans to embrace all of these portrayals of Batman, and readers tend to prefer the version of Batman they grew up with. However, recent comic book stories by Neil Gaiman (*Whatever Happened to the Caped Crusader?*) and Grant Morrison (*The Return of Bruce Wayne*) have presented all iterations of Batman as equally valid and part of the character's rich past.

Given varied Batman portrayals over time, it seems natural that each actor who has played Batman on film and television has interpreted the character in his own way. Adam West was astonishingly straight-laced, innocent, and earnest as Batman, and his wealthy alter ego Bruce Wayne, in the 1960s television series. Michael Keaton made a strong impression as Wayne in two Tim Burton–helmed films —1989's *Batman* and 1992's *Batman Returns*— presenting him as a likeable, socially inept eccentric prone to brooding before his oversized fireplace like a classic Orson Welles movie character. In *Batman and Robin* (1997) George Clooney was a charming, Cary Grant–style Bruce Wayne, but he wasn't a very good Batman; he seemed uncomfortable acting in the rubber superhero suit and tried too hard to be "funny." Christian Bale, famed for playing insane, murderous yuppies, as in *American Psycho* and *Shaft* (both released in 2000) portrayed Wayne as a benevolent American prince who grows from a self-involved, vengeful young man into a mature "Feudal lord" dedicated to helping the people of Gotham instead of wallowing in his own anger and personal demons.

Just as longtime Batman aficionados draw upon decades' worth of print and cinematic adventures to create a composite, *ur*–Batman in their minds, the film *Batman Begins* drew upon dozens of classic adventures to create an archetypal image of Batman and an original, yet recognizable story. The Bruce Wayne of *Batman Begins* is the sane, intelligent, moral man of the classic comic book adventures written by Steve Englehart, Mike W. Barr, Gerry Conway, and Denny O'Neil. The urban "realism" of the film derives from the Frank Miller Batman stories *The Dark Knight Returns* and *Batman: Year One*. The dramatic tone, ensemble cast, complex narrative, and the inclusion of mafia don Carmine Falcone are all inspired by Jeph Loeb's miniseries *The Long Halloween* (1996–1997). The Joe Chill story and the doomed romance with Rachel Dawes have echoes in Barr's *Batman: Year Two* (1987). The film also owes a debt to *Batman: The Animated Series*, previously regarded by many fans as the most "faithful" adaptation. The fidelity of the film to the source material owes much to the fact that the plot and the script were shaped by comic book writer David S. Goyer, and to the fact that studio executives finally began to capitulate to the fans (who were tired of seeing unfaithful and, in their view, poorly made superhero films) after the commercial and critical failure of *Batman and Robin*.

Faithful as the film is to Batman stories of the past, *Batman Begins* is obviously rooted firmly in the present and clearly reflects contemporary anxieties about the destruction of the World Trade Center, the "war on terror," and the invasion of Iraq. The film's signature adversary, Ra's al Ghul, wants to destroy Gotham because its decadence personally offends him. Director and cowriter Christopher Nolan acknowledged during a 2005 interview with Scott Holleran of *Box Office Mojo* that the film does, indeed, reflect the troubled times we live in, but that he made these connections unconsciously, seeing them only after he had completed the film. As he explained, "[W]e wanted to allow the influences to just naturally find themselves in the story. We didn't want to be conscious about it, because then it would be insincere. But, definitely, the broad strokes, the villain that threatens you — the things you find frightening — those are going to be influenced by what's going on in the world. I see the parallels now, but it certainly wasn't conscious."

Although the Gotham City of *Batman Begins* derives certain significant architectural features, like its elevated train, from Chicago, its overall feel is certainly inspired, in part, by the archetypal "corrupt" New York of the 1970s, which looms large in the public consciousness thanks to films such as *The French Connection* (1971) and *Taxi Driver* (1976). But *Batman Begins* blends the visual feel of the dirty, overtly "immoral" New York with the more subtle corruption that infests the cleaner, tourist friendly New York of today. Even after Mayor Rudolph Giuliani helped "clean up" the city with his tough-on-crime measures, Manhattan remains a place in which the citizens fear falling victim to criminal activity, a fear that now includes the machinations of Wall Street executives and Muslim terrorists. Ever since the September 11 attacks and the Enron scandals, New Yorkers have felt a specific combination of fear, fury, and moral outrage that has been kept alive by similarly troubling events that took place over the following decade, including the global financial meltdown, the Bush-Obama bank bailouts, and the failed Times Square bomb plot of 2010.[3] These feelings are best exemplified by a segment in the Spike Lee film *The 25th Hour* (2002) in which Edward Norton's character suffers a meltdown in a New York bar and curses President Bush, Osama bin Laden, Wall Street executives, the police, minorities, and himself for destroying New York and "the American Dream."

In *Batman Begins*, the title character is pitted against an amazing array of enemies, including an evil university professor, a corporate mogul, drug-dealers, a mafia don, corrupt police officers, rioting escapees from a lunatic asylum, an army of ninjas, and international terrorist Ra's al Ghul ("Demon's Head" in Arabic). By the end of the film, Batman foils Ra's al Ghul's plan to destroy Gotham City and manages to root out much of the corruption that has tainted the police department and his family business, Wayne Enterprises, but the war against crime has only just begun.

Of all the villains populating *Batman Begins*, Ra's al Ghul is presented as Batman's arch nemesis, who seeks to gas Gotham with a toxin that will cause the city to "tear itself apart through fear." Ra's al Ghul, the ultimate terrorist, forces Batman to fight a literal "war on terror." The film's villain is an amalgam of three comic book characters: Dennis O'Neil's original "Ra's al Ghul," Sam Hamm's "Ducard," and Mike W. Barr's "Reaper." The comic book character's Arab ethnicity is changed for *Batman Begins*. The character is played by Irish actor Liam Neeson (*Michael Collins, Schindler's List*). Thus, the extent to which viewers will agree that Ra's al Ghul is a commentary on Osama bin Laden will depend on how they view bin Laden.

Batman — here played by Christian Bale in *Batman Begins* (Warner Bros., 2005) — is best known for rescuing damsels in distress such as Rachel Dawes (Katie Holmes) from the likes of Scarecrow. He is not, however, well-regarded for his ability to stay in a committed, romantic relationship with women.

In *Legacy of the Prophet*, journalist Anthony Shadid (2002) explained how bin Laden's message of "defending Palestinians, ending sanctions on Iraq, and curtailing near-total U.S. sway over the region" was seen as heroic and appealing to many Muslims who viewed the 9/11 attacks as a self-defense response to unjust American foreign policy (693). Leo Braudy's *From Chivalry to Terrorism: War and the Changing Nature of Masculinity* (2003) notes that the 9/11 attacks were motivated by a warrior culture's disgust with American capitalism because it fosters three philosophies a warrior despises: secularism, pacifism, and feminism (202–203).

The implication here is that America inspired wrath because it is "godless." President Bush has commonly referred to the September 11 attacks as an attack on "freedom." On the other hand, bin Laden himself gave these reasons for orchestrating the attacks in a "Letter to the American People" released on November 24, 2002:

> You attacked us in Palestine. ... in Somalia; you supported the Russian atrocities against us in Chechnya, the Indian oppression against us in Kashmir, and the Jewish aggression against us in Lebanon. Under your supervision, consent, and orders, the governments of our countries, which act as your agents, attack us on a daily basis. These governments prevent our people from establishing the Islamic Shariah, using violence and lies to do so. These governments give us a taste of humiliation and place us in a large prison of fear and subdual.[4]

Compare these words to those Ra's al Ghul expresses as his motivation in attacking Gotham City with fear gas. As he says to Batman, "The League of Shadows has been a check against human corruption for thousands of years. We sacked Rome. Loaded trade ships with rats. Burned London to the ground. Every time a civilization reaches the peak of its decadence, we return to restore the balance.... No one can save Gotham. When a forest grows too wild a purging fire is inevitable and natural. Tomorrow the world will watch in horror as its greatest city destroys itself."

The use of words like "corruption," "decadence," and "injustice" reflect those used by jihadist fanatics appalled by American excesses. Ra's al Ghul is a lunatic who is too driven by "righteous" fury and ideology to be reasoned with. This is far from the view of bin Laden as a militant revolutionary figure staunchly opposed to American imperialism, as asserted by many of the Muslims interviewed in Shadid's book, or by bin Laden himself in his "Letter to the American People." But it is also possible that one of the reasons Nolan muddied Ra's al Ghul's ethnic background was to underscore the similarity between Muslim and Christian fundamentalists who believe that sinners should be purged from the world to make society more righteous and acceptable to God.

For example, novelist Salman Rushdie has argued that the "'clash of civilizations' theory is an oversimplification: that most Muslims have no interest in taking part in religious wars, that the divisions in the Muslim world run as deep as the things it has in common" and that the "real wars of religion" are "the wars religions unleash against ordinary citizens within their 'sphere of influence.' They are the wars of the godly against the largely defenseless: American fundamentalists against pro-choice doctors, Iranian mullahs against their country's Jewish minority, the Taliban against the people of Afghanistan, Hindu fundamentalists in Bombay against that city's increasingly fearful Muslims." He concludes, "the real wars of religion are also the wars religions unleash against unbelievers, whose unbearable unbelief is re-characterized as an offense, as sufficient reason for their eradication" (382). Rushdie has had personal experience with such persecution since, after publishing *The Satanic Verses* (1988), he was condemned for blasphemy by the Ayatollah Khomeini, the Islamic fundamentalist leader of Iran, and condemned to death. Living in fear from the price placed on his head, the Bombay-born author lived life out of the public eye, and under guard, in England for many years.

One of several cultural critics who cited Muslim and Christian fundamentalists as equally dangerous, Rushdie has called upon like-minded progressives worldwide to stand up to their pernicious influence. Rushdie's argument was validated to a considerable degree when, on the eve of 9/11, the Rev. Jerry Falwell, founder of the Thomas Road Baptist Church and Republican Party stalwart, argued that the secularization of American culture caused God to "lift the veil of protection which has allowed no one to attack America on our soil since 1812" and allowed the 9/11 attacks to occur. "I really believe that the pagans, and the abortionists, and the feminists, and the gays and the lesbians who are actively trying to make that an alternative lifestyle, the ACLU, People For the American Way, all of them who have tried to secularize America. I point the finger in their face and say 'you helped this happen,'" he said, citing Proverbs 14:23 as the basis for his accusation.[5] While Falwell eventually apologized for the assertion, National Gay and Lesbian Task Force Executive Director Lorri L. Jean said, "The terrible tragedy that has befallen our nation, and indeed the entire global community, is the sad byproduct of fanaticism. It has its roots in the same fanaticism that enables people like Jerry Falwell to preach hate against those who do not think, live, or love in the exact same way he does."[6]

It is this kind of fanaticism, found at home and abroad, in almost every ideological tradition, that Ra's al Ghul embodies, potentially making him as much a Timothy McVeigh figure as an Osama bin Laden figure. Of course, if Ra's al Ghul is *Batman Begins*' ultimate fundamentalist terrorist figure, that suggests Batman, the one who stands between al Ghul and Gotham City, is a commentary on the United States government. Like President George W. Bush, who made his principle concern national security, Batman is open to great praise for using a firm military hand in protecting his home from foreign threats, but he is also open to great criticism for curbing civil liberties. A critical question is, therefore, to what extent do *Batman Begins* and other classic Batman stories present Batman as violating civil rights? Also, to what extent do these adventures, by extension, suggest that Batman harms the very same American people he is trying to protect?

In *How to Read Super Hero Comics and Why* (2002), Geoff Klock observes many problematic elements built into the classic super hero narrative, not the least of which is an inherent strain of fascism. As Klock observes, Batman is depicted as a violent fascist in Miller's *The Dark Knight Returns*. The landmark story criticizes both Batman and then President Ronald Reagan for highly martial tactics and a too–Puritanical worldview. According to Klock, "Batman's use of conspicuous force parallels the Reagan-era cold war politics ... 'fighting crime' in a conspicuous display of power ... to impress the population they want to control.... Batman becomes the worst sort of reactionary fascist terrorizing people into his control with cheap theatrics" (45–46). At the climax of the story, Reagan orders the American military — and Superman — into the fictional islands of Corto Maltese as a means of ending a 1980s–era Cuban Missile Crisis. Instead of backing down, the Russians respond in kind by detonating a warhead that plunges America into a nuclear winter. For his part, Batman's own uncompromising tactics provoke a confrontation between him and Superman in which Batman is beaten near to death and is forced to go into hiding (see Chapter Five for more). As *Batman Begins* demonstrates, the parallel between Reagan and Batman drawn by Miller in *The Dark Knight Returns* is easily updated by substituting Bush for Reagan. Notably, in the film, Bruce Wayne's butler Alfred acts as his conscience and questions whether the allure of Batman and all of his army-issue toys is enough to cause Bruce to become lost in a crazed, martial persona and lose all connection to reality. Meanwhile, in the "real" world, presidential advisors tend to be high-ranking party members and members of the military industrial complex, often advocating doctrinaire thinking and extreme, single-minded courses of action, insulating the Oval Office from alternative perspectives represented by members of the opposing political party, international allies, journalists, and social activists. They are hardly the moderating influence that Alfred is on Batman.

Still, critic Aeon J. Skoble offers a more balanced view of Batman: "[d]espite Batman's willingness to break rules, he has always been cautious and measured in his use of violence, he has refused to cross certain lines, and he has consistently interfered with and apprehended only criminals" (33). According to Skoble, Batman's methods are appropriate given how crime-infested Gotham city is portrayed as being, and how operatically evil his opponents are. Therefore, when pacifist or liberal characters criticize Batman on the news or at a peace rally, the criticism rings hollow and hypocritical, as he is being attacked by the very people who would not otherwise be able to survive in Gotham City without his protection (2005, 33). The vision of Batman that Skoble presents here is ultimately the one that *Batman Begins* embraces. Even as the film draws parallels between Batman and President Bush, making both look heroic in the process, it distances Batman from Bush by emphasizing his greater restraint, intelligence, social liberality, wiser choice of battles, and superior tactics.

But what exactly makes Batman heroic? What would motivate a man to dress up as a bat, shirk the company of women, and take up residence in a cave surrounded by an arsenal of weapons? And can a man who chooses to do so be considered anything but a maniac? These are the key questions asked by *Batman Begins.* Who is Batman? What motivates him to do what he does? And is he a hero or a lunatic?

The Batman of *Batman Begins*

Batman Begins won the support of comic book aficionados across cyberspace as a "traditional" and pitch-perfect portrayal of Batman, while simultaneously providing a reflection of the contemporary American social and political environment. The self-appointed protector of the crime-infested Gotham City, Batman vows to battle corruption at every level of society, making Gotham safe once again for all. He uses "theatricality and deception" as a weapon "to turn fear against those who would prey upon the fearful."[7] Dressed in a mask, a cape, and bullet-proof body armor, Batman relies on his keen instincts as a detective, formidable martial arts expertise, and an assortment of high-tech gadgets and weapons to *capture* his opponents—not *kill* them.

In this film, Bruce Wayne was traumatized as a child when he saw his parents gunned down in an alley by a drug-addled mugger. After spending years brooding over their deaths, and nursing a burning desire for revenge, he decides to channel his rage and frustration into a more positive and selfless direction. He becomes the Batman to protect the people of Gotham City from harm so that they never have to experience the pain that he did in losing his parents. Wayne chooses the bat as his avatar because he was afraid of bats himself and wanted criminals to share his dread. In both the film and comic books, Wayne developed a primal fear of the animal after falling down a well on the family estate and landing in the future Batcave. His fall into the cave frightened the bats into flight, and their storm of flapping wings terrified him in nightmares for years to come.

The *Batman Begins* origin story is slightly different from the one presented in the comic book *Batman: Year One* (1988) in which Bruce's parents are killed after seeing a revival of the Tyrone Power film *The Mark of Zorro.* The Waynes are accosted in an alley outside the movie theater by a mugger, who shots them dead. In this version, Bruce's child-mind determined that, since super heroes like Zorro do not exist in real life, he would become one.[8] Given the innocent, wish-fulfillment nature of his quest to become a real-world Zorro, Bruce behaves with the purity of a child even as an adult; and his greatest flaw is that he is prone to see the world in the stark black-and-white morality of a child. Consequently, it is no surprise that, in *Batman Begins,* the college-age Bruce Wayne is portrayed as a frightened and angry child on the inside, who eventually grows into his role as feudal lord of Gotham City. As an anonymous crimefighter, he becomes a mature man who has conquered his demons. However, there are key moments in the story, such as when Batman leads the police of Gotham City on a high-speed car chase inside his tank-like Batmobile, when Alfred accuses Bruce of *still* behaving like a child.[9]

As an orphan who cannot escape the pain of his father's death, Bruce seeks father substitutes in Alfred Pennyworth (Michael Caine in *Batman Begins*), his policeman friend Jim Gordon (Gary Oldman), and scientist and Wayne Enterprises director Lucius Fox (Morgan Freeman). The young Bruce Wayne even develops affection for the seemingly wise Ra's al Ghul. Although Wayne may be faulted for investing too much in Ra's al Ghul, his taste in father figures is otherwise exceptional, as the other men are invaluable aids in his mission to clean up Gotham City and all are good at helping him maintain a sense of fairness. All of them understand his human need to decompress and, occasionally, take the Batman mask off.

At the same time, in the original comic books that inspired *Batman Begins*, Wayne feels a kinship to other orphans and will adopt an orphaned child in a heartbeat and invite him (or her) to join his extended Bat-family as a fellow soldier and playmate in his war games. He invariably asks them to assume a colorful identity as he has — but only his favorites get to wear the "Robin" costume. And, whenever these partners show signs of not wanting to play any more, either because they have begun to mature or have expressed a desire to strike out on their own, Batman petulantly disassociates himself from them before they have a chance to say goodbye. He is usually too wounded to part with them on good terms. These adolescent-level friendships and intimacy issues are among the most damning signs of Batman's immaturity.

Another hallmark of Batman's innocence is his refusal to use firearms because the memory of the gun that killed his parents is too painful. Instead, he uses potentially lethal weapons such as throwing stars, gas bombs, and armored cars in a non-lethal way to capture his opponents. *The Dark Knight Returns, Batman* (1989) and *Batman Returns* (1992) are the exceptions that prove the rule, although the former takes place in the future and is, technically, "non-canonical," and the latter are "looser" adaptations of the comic. In fact, Batman stamps all of his weapons with his "Bat insignia," calls them by rather endearing names like "the Batmobile," and "the Batarang," and treats them almost like toys in an elaborate game of one-upmanship against his criminal opponents. In this light, Batman's adversarial relationship to the Riddler is particularly "chummy," especially since the Riddler exercises similar restraint himself, tending not to kill civilians and to place Batman into easily escapable deathtraps, just for a lark.

The campy 1960s *Batman* television series had a lot of fun with Batman's utility belt, giving him a weapon for every occasion. *Batman: The Movie*— a 1966 theatrical release with the same cast and crew as the television show — even went as far as showing Batman fending off a shark attack with an aerosol can of "Bat-Shark Repellent" that he had handy for *just such an occasion*, so he would never have to kill a shark. In contrast, *Batman Begins* goes to great lengths to provide the title hero with a far more verisimilitudinous high-tech arsenal reminiscent of the James Bond films. His new weapons include an armored car that becomes the first Batmobile and a memory cloth cape that allows him to soar like a base-jumper across the rooftops of Gotham City. Perhaps most notable of all is his body armor, a near-bullet-proof Nomex suit designed for advanced infantry, but never issued on the battlefield because a "soldier's life is not worth three hundred grand."[10]

The restraint with which Batman uses his weapons of war is striking, suggesting that one day the American military might be able to do the same, defeating its international enemies in combat with a minimum of bloodshed. Indeed, another multi-billionaire super hero, Tony Stark, made just that assertion when—in the Marvel Universe—he became President Bush's Secretary of Defense in *Iron Man: The Best Defense* (2004) and promised that his technology could ensure that "no one need ever die in war again"—on either side. All opponents could be captured rather than killed, and all U.S. soldiers would be too well-armored to fall to enemy fire.[11] In a similar vein, 2008's *Iron Man* film features a scene in which, thanks to the sophistication of his targeting systems, the title character is able to pacify an insurgent uprising in Afghanistan without injuring any civilians in the crossfire. The scene is powerful, partly because many audience members wished that U.S. forces would be able to avoid collateral damage in the real world as well, and not just in the make-believe world of a summer blockbuster superhero movie. The scene is also arguably offensive because—to date—civilian casualties remain a reality in all armed conflicts, including the wars in the Middle East. As Scott Peterson observed in "'Smarter' Bombs Still Hit Civilians" (2002), civilian casualty rates continue to climb even as America deploys more and more "smart bombs," largely because the U.S. relies on air-based attacks to keep American casualties low, and enemy combatants deliberately locate weapon stores and training camps near civilians to turn the tide of international opinion against the U.S. when they are killed (180).

Nevertheless, the dream of a war with no civilian casualties—and even no enemy combatant casualties—persists. Batman has employed a similar martial strategy in the fictional world of Gotham City. Batman wants to liberate his home city from the rule of criminals, terrorists, and robber barons. He wants to orchestrate a regime change. To all of his enemies, he is a Dark Knight, a masked avenger, but to the innocent, he is the Caped Crusader, fighting to protect them from harm. And yet, both Batman and Tony Stark may be suffering from delusion. They may think that their motives are purer, and that they are kinder, than they really are.

A scene from Bruce Wayne's favorite movie, *The Mark of Zorro* (20th Century–Fox, 1940), which inspired him to become Batman. Zorro (Tyrone Power) crosses swords with his enemy, Captain Esteban Pasquale (Basil Rathbone).

Commenting on the *Iron Man* story, comic book scholar David Sweeney observed that, despite Stark's good intentions, "fascism is still fascism, conquest is still conquest." Sweeney also notes that "suicide bombings or hunger strikes or self-immolation ... work as a protest against the West because it relativises our

Liberal Humanist value system."[12] A similar objection can just as easily be leveled against Batman's war on crime. Therefore, Batman's quest for justice easily begs the question: what right does Bruce Wayne have to take it upon himself to confront the evils of society? Aren't his violent means and angry rationale little different from the methods and motivations employed by the very criminals and madmen he has sworn to defeat? Isn't Batman himself, arguably, a terrorist, if not a fascist dictator in making? The question is a fair one.

The simplest answer is that the storytelling conceit of the Batman universe is that Batman has an unerring inner moral compass that prevents him from doing wrong, so he deserves the trust and respect of the reader. In his world, villains, following long-standing melodramatic tropes, announce their intentions in advance and perform obviously evil acts. There is little need for speculation about their possible innocence and no need for "absurd" notions such as due process. Even in more morally ambiguous Batman stories, in which Batman's actions are questioned by a narrator, most readers are willing to give Batman a lot of moral latitude in his crime-fighting methods. Luckily, Batman has the script on his side, so if he were to ever, say, imprison a terrorist suspect, there would be no question either of the suspect's guilt or of his right to a fair trial. And, as a lone crusader, Batman does not have to worry about leading an army into a foreign country on the basis of faulty—possibly doctored—evidence. But real-world defenders of "truth" and "justice" are rarely as infallible as fictional characters in hero narratives. Batman, as just such an infallible hero, provides a site for a reassuringly consistent view of good and evil in the universe of Gotham.

There is another, even more interesting reason that Wayne feels he must assert his will over Gotham City: heredity. Dubbed "the prince of Gotham" by the tabloids, Wayne feels a feudal obligation to protect the citizens of a city that he frequently refers to as "his." His wealthy family presided over Gotham for generations, and its rule has always been just, providing a general moral compass for society. The Waynes were abolitionists, and they used the system of caverns that would later become the Batcave to shelter escaped slaves as part of the Underground Railroad.[13] Bruce's father, Thomas, a beloved and gifted physician, never cheated on his wife, despite much temptation, and created the Wayne Foundation to fund orphanages, environmental initiatives, journalist grants, hospices, and national defense. There is little to condemn in their record as the unelected rulers of Gotham City.

Bruce Wayne, thus, is a feudal prince who happens to live in a democratic society. He embraces the values of an older social order by offering the citizens of Gotham his charity and his protection. By doing so, he effectively condemns wealthy capitalists who shirk their civic responsibilities and view the common people as commodities to be exploited. Wayne is noble and humanitarian, a true "compassionate conservative" who is more like Jane Austen's Mr. Darcy or Mr. Knightley than the Enron or Halliburton executives we are more used to seeing in the news today. As the Prince of Gotham, Wayne feels a responsibility to imprison the irredeemable, to heal the mentally ill, and to protect the innocent from harm. And so, simultaneously underlining the hero's duality and his feudal worldview, the comic book portrays Bruce Wayne as the Feudal Lord and Batman as the "Dark Knight" who carries out Wayne's will, acting as his sword of justice.[14]

This desire to protect his city is at the heart of the restraint Batman employs when using his high-tech weapons. He feels a feudal lord's desire to protect his subjects from each other and from themselves. In effect, Batman is fighting an urban war against his own serfs, so he cannot afford the luxury of hating even the worst of his adversaries. On some level, he cares for all of them—his former best friend Harvey Dent (Two-Face), the pathetic Ventriloquist, and the mischievous Riddler. He feels a measure of responsibility for "creating" the Joker—the evil clown who is his most deadly and persistent foe. And Catwoman, the Phantasm, and Ra's al Ghul's daughter Talia are as much love interests as they are opponents.

Aside from the fact that they are all, effectively, his "subjects," Batman's villains are connected to him in an even more visceral, symbolic way. The vast majority of them are dark reflections of Batman himself and they frequently parody or pervert his intentions and method of operation. Indeed, their very existence is an indictment of his entire enterprise. For example, in both *Batman: The Animated Series* and *The Dark Knight* (2008), the vigilante Two-Face is portrayed as a more obsessed version of Batman who goes too far to stamp out crime, either by killing criminals, or not worrying enough about causing collateral damage as he attacks them and their businesses. His rage is fueled by the fact that criminals scarred his once handsome face and condemned him to a life without love. As a figure who suffers from multiple personality disorder, Two-Face represents Bruce Wayne's fears that Bruce and Batman are two distinct people and that Bruce himself suffers from the same disorder.[15]

Like Two-Face, Ra's al Ghul is a zealot who represents the kind of warped, vigilante thinking that Batman himself could have embraced, had his life taken a darker turn. In *Batman Begins*, Ra's is a zealot who has a zero-tolerance policy towards criminals and wishes to see them executed even for comparably minor infractions. He believes that criminals thrive when society's leaders are too lenient with them and that Thomas Wayne was too softhearted in trying to rehabilitate criminals and drug addicts, as evidenced by his death at the hands of one of the people he was trying to protect. For Ra's al Ghul the message of Thomas Wayne's murder is clear. Gotham City is too far gone to be saved. It should be destroyed. These insane conclusions represent the ultimate end of the vigilante philosophy embodied by darker "superheroes" such as the Punisher or Charles Bronson's character from the *Death Wish* films. As Nolan explained in his *BoxOfficeMojo* interview, his goal was to distinguish Batman from such characters and argue that Bruce Wayne is a hero because he is not motivated by revenge but by justice and altruism.

The Joker, meanwhile, represents a different kind of commentary on Batman. He counters Batman's desire for order with a need to create chaos. His seemingly motiveless crimes are essentially the angry cries of a deranged child who is frustrated by the hypocrisies and compromises of the adult world. Also, while Batman uses "safe" weapons, the Joker enjoys killing people with lethal toys—party balloons filled with poison gas instead of helium, joy buzzers that electrocute people, teddy bears filled with explosives, and a novelty lapel flower that squirts acid instead of water. And whenever Batman is able to disable the Joker's twisted toys with his own, more high-tech gadgets (which are, themselves, like toys because they are non-lethal, "play" weapons with Bat-logos stamped on them), the Joker expresses jealousy that Batman has access to better toys. As Jack Nicholson's Joker wondered in *Batman* (1989) "Where does he get those wonderful toys?"[16]

The Joker debuted in *Batman* #1 (1940) and he bore some resemblance to two iconic silent-film characters—with a personality similar to the mysterious, titular crime lord *Dr. Mabuse* (1922) and a physical appearance reminiscent of Paul Henreid's rictus grin from *The Man Who Laughs* (1928). A Moriarty figure, the Joker could announce his high-profile crimes in advance and still succeed despite the police's and Batman's best efforts. The Joker's early comic book crimes were violent and grotesque, but the character softened into a Mad Hatteresque figure in the 1950s and 1960s as the comic book lightened in tone (see Caesar

Romero's Joker from the *Batman* series). The Joker was re-imagined in the 1970s and 1980s in response to the emergence of celebrity serial killers such as Charles Manson and the Zodiac Killer, and to the sickening pointlessness of the Cleveland Elementary School murders, in which a teenager, Brenda Ann Spencer, shot eight children and three adults with a rifle in order to "liven up" her Monday.[17] The Joker's logic is often similarly appalling. A figure of arrested development who enjoys goading Batman into "coming out and playing" with him by killing as many innocent people as possible, the Joker represents the greatest challenge to Batman's anti-killing stance. In fact, in the miniseries *The Joker's Last Laugh* (written by conservative comic book writer Chuck Dixon), Batman's ally Barbara Gordon asserts that the Joker is an irredeemably evil, utterly insane mass murderer who should be put down like a mad dog.

The Dark Knight's representation of the Joker (an Oscar-winning performance by the late Heath Ledger) is a more "realistic" one than Nicholson's, evoking Malcolm McDowell's role in *A Clockwork Orange* (1971). This Joker is also more of a force of nature than a mere man — an agent of chaos that forces Batman to use more ruthless means. The Joker's identity is shrouded in mystery, and he lies about his past, but he repeatedly alludes to a loveless, miserable childhood. Unlike Batman, who had a fine home and loving parents, the Joker refers to a horrific father-figure, a home life marred by domestic violence, and a failure to find romantic love. Consequently, the Joker's hatred of his father and of women causes him to lash out at authority figures and disfigure anything he perceives to be beautiful.

In *The Dark Knight*, Ledger's Joker acts like a homicidal answer to the Marx Brothers; he disrupts black-tie affairs, mocks judges and policemen and American aristocrats, and points out how everything in society is really just a sick joke. Like the comic book version of the character — who has done everything from exploiting legal loopholes in U.S. patent law (*The Laughing Fish*) to attempting to solve famine in Ethiopia with genocide (*A Death in the Family*) — this Joker's mockery of the wars in the Middle East and government corruption again resemble the manifesto of a terrorist. Consequently, Ledger's Joker works well as a follow-up villain to Ra's al Ghul, since both villains are striking out at a modern American society that they find morally repellent.

Heath Ledger's Oscar-winning turn as the Joker in *The Dark Knight* (Warner Bros., 2008) captivated audiences and presented Batman with yet another classic, anarchic villain redefined and reinterpreted as a commentary on America's most persistent terrorist adversaries.

Perhaps the most interesting character trait of the Joker is his secret death wish. At least three times in the film, the Joker tries to goad Batman into killing him, both to free himself of his own inner turmoil and to prove, conclusively, that Batman is a hypocrite and his vow not to kill will be broken during its first real test. But the Joker is surprised to learn that Batman is "incorruptible" and won't rise to take the bait, even after the Joker kills Batman's childhood sweetheart, Rachel Dawes. The other test of Batman's character comes in the form of the high-tech device he creates to monitor the private phone calls of every person in Gotham City. The device proves essential in finally tracking down and apprehending the Joker, but the scientist who inadvertently inspired Batman to create it, Lucius Fox (Morgan Freeman), believes that it is fundamentally "unethical" and "dangerous," as it provides the user the ability to spy on thirty million people, affording "too much power for one person." Even though capturing the Joker is essential to preserving public safety, Fox feels that the device represents Batman's choosing to sacrifice freedom for security. Vowing not to work for a fascist, Fox threatens his resignation, but his faith in Batman is restored when Batman destroys the device the moment the Joker is captured. The implication of this decision is that, ultimately, the Joker fails to push Batman into becoming a full-fledged, permanent fascist or a technocrat. He just pushes Batman into *briefly* becoming a tyrant.

Despite Batman's occasional questionable acts during the course of the film, he impresses the audience with his selflessness when he goes to great lengths to save the life of a man bent on revealing his true identity to the world. Furthermore, he ultimately assumes responsibility for crimes he did not commit in an effort to preserve the good name of his friend Harvey Dent, and to prevent the morale of the people of Gotham from being destroyed should they learn of Harvey's transformation into Two-Face.

However, Two-Face and the Joker are not the only Batman villains who act as shadowy reflections of Batman, and who cause the people of Gotham City to second-guess their champion, both in his roles as Batman and Bruce Wayne. Oswald Cobblepot, or "The Penguin," serves a similar function in the Batman comic books, cartoons, and films. Penguin is a rich, cultured enemy with ambitions to be the one true feudal lord of Gotham City.

Unlike Bruce Wayne, however, Penguin wishes to use his wealth and privilege for his own personal gain, not for the good of the people. He persistently attacks Wayne's reputation and attempts to orchestrate hostile takeovers of Wayne Enterprises. Perhaps most interestingly, he is the villain who most often tries to sabotage Batman's weapons by removing their safety features. In doing so, he hopes that Batman might one day accidentally kill an innocent person with the sabotaged weapons, and end his career as Batman out of a sense of guilt. If that ever came to pass, Batman would be removed as an obstacle to Penguin's plans, and Penguin's ascent to domination over Gotham would be assured. "The Penguin" works well as an avatar for Cobblepot because it is an animal that seems to be wearing a tuxedo. Therefore, cartoonists often render it as a ridiculous figure with delusions of grandeur (e.g., the stumbling maître d' penguins from *Mary Poppins* who try and fail to behave in a formal manner). Hence the reason why the Penguin featured in *Batman Returns* (1992) is

Burgess Meredith as the Penguin in the classic 1966 series *Batman*. The Penguin strives to make his fortune, illegally, in order to have enough money to buy his way into "the old boys' network."

dressed in a tuxedo, but is sometimes distracted by his quest for gentility when he sees a tasty-looking raw fish. It is also why he alternates between declaring "A penguin is a bird that cannot fly. I am a man." and "I am not a man! I am an animal!" He wants to be larger than he is, but is frustrated and feels worthless every time Batman foils his plans to regain his lost aristocratic title and wealth.

Significantly, artist Joe Staton drew the Penguin as the spitting image of Richard Nixon in *Penguin Triumphant* (1992). The script by John Ostrander involves Penguin striving to escape his humble beginnings through Gordon Gekko–style insider trading, so it appears to have more in common with Oliver Stone's *Wall Street* (1987) than with the details of the Watergate scandal. However, Penguin's sleazy criminal activities, delusions of grandeur, and hatred and jealousy of the privileged, Ivy League smart set, has echoes in the rise and fall of the 37th president of the United States. Like the simultaneously released *Batman Returns*, which saw Penguin manipulating the American political system, *Penguin Triumphant* transformed Penguin from the gentleman gangster created by Bob Kane into a figure who satirizes class division in American society, and the fundamentally corrupt "Old Boys Network" found in Wall Street and Washington, D.C.

A thug and a thief with a veneer of respectability, Penguin eternally fails to ingratiate himself with the members of the American oligarchy, who are arguably far more evil, and far more successful in their criminal endeavors than Penguin will ever be. After all, Richard Nixon was successfully removed from office, but the corporate machine that had backed his candidacy, and that has been consistently undermining democracy in America for generations, remained all-but untouched. Indeed, commentators as diverse as Paul Krugman, Michael Moore, Noam Chomsky, Howard Zinn, and Ralph Nader have assailed the forces of the American oligarchy for decades, to little effect, and it remains to be seen what substantive challenges to the oligarchy's supreme authority will be made by the legislative initiatives of President Barack Obama.

With villains such as the Joker and Penguin constantly menacing its citizens, Gotham City is undeniably an appalling place to live. It is corrupt on all levels, its architecture is a Gothic nightmare, and it seems as if the sun stopped shining over its rooftops twenty years ago. But it is Bruce Wayne's home — and he feels that it can still be saved.

Deadlier Than the Male: Batman's Problematic Relationships with Women

One of the main problems Batman has had from the outset of his career as Feudal Lord crime fighter is that he cannot find a Lady of the Manor to stand at his side. Most of the women he encounters — Vicki Vale, Silver St. Cloud, Rachel Dawes, and even the heiress Julie Madison — find his desire to reshape the modern, democratic world into a neo–Medieval society highly questionable at best, if not outright delusional. Catwoman understands his motivation, and is sympathetic to it, but believes that marrying him and becoming, functionally, a Disney Princess in a castle in "New York" is a betrayal of her feminist sensibilities. Several *Justice League* and *Trinity* adventures indicate that Wonder Woman, a socialist princess with superhuman powers, is attracted to Batman, but believes that men are fundamentally sexist and incapable of a romantic partnership of equals. Also, as a pacifist, she finds Batman's methods too violent. The only woman who has a truly Medieval world view, and who wants to marry Batman and work to reshape the world in a new, better image, is

Talia, the amoral daughter of Ra's al Ghul, who hopes to become feudal lord of the entire world. In *Batman: Tales of the Demon* (1971, 1991) and *Son of the Demon* (1987), Batman does indeed marry Talia, and she becomes pregnant with his child, but when Talia realizes that Batman will make an overprotective, controlling husband, she fakes a miscarriage and ends their relationship.

Talia notwithstanding, Batman has been, thus far, incapable of finding a woman to marry and be the mother of his child. Consequently, he has resorted to "adopting" young men and women as wards so they can be the heirs to his feudal empire and keep his dreams alive once he becomes too old to continue being Batman. His first ward, Dick Grayson, was a circus acrobat whose parents were killed by the Mafia. Since Grayson was touched by the same violence Bruce was, Bruce felt a kinship with Grayson and functionally adopted the boy. To the world at large, Grayson was Bruce Wayne's ward, while Dick's alter ego, Robin, was Batman's crime-fighting partner. This legendary "Dynamic Duo" is the most well known of the Batman and Robin partnerships, but not the only one. Grayson was the first of several of Batman's children to serve as a partner and successor-in-training, including substitute Robins Jason Todd, Tim Drake, and Damien Wayne (Bruce's recently revealed, now-ten-year-old son with Talia al Ghul), and Terry McGinnis, who becomes Batman in a cyberpunk future (*Batman Beyond*).

Most contemporary fans of the Batman saga are uneasy about the character of Robin, because he interferes with their "willing suspension of disbelief" when reading a Batman story. They do not believe it is realistic that Batman would drag a young child into battle with him, as Robin can be anywhere between eight and eighteen years old, depending on the story. (Amusingly, Christian Bale has threatened to handcuff himself to a radiator and not go to work if producers propose to insert Robin into one of his Batman films.) Fans also associate the Boy Wonder with campy exclamations of surprise at the levels of nefariousness the Batman rogue's gallery is capable of, often to the effect of "Holy Giant Killer Robots, Batman!" And then, of course, there is another controversy at the core of the Batman/Robin relationship: are they lovers?

As Brooker has written, many fans who are invested in Batman being a heterosexual, tough-as-nails woman-hater have no patience for a funny, possibly homosexual Batman. The homosexual subtext of the Batman comic books, and superhero comics in general (see Chapter Eight), was pointed out as early as 1954 by psychiatrist Dr. Fredric Wertham in *Seduction of the Innocent,* in which he argued that children could be harmed by the homoerotic aspects of the Batman/Robin relationship. DC Comics discourages portrayals of Batman and Robin as a gay couple, as in August of 2005, when it pressured the Kathleen Cullen Fine Arts gallery in New York to remove artwork by Mark Chamberlain depicting Batman and Robin kissing in varying states of undress.[18] Despite the suppression of this particular exhibit, Robert Smigel's "Ambiguously Gay Duo" cartoons featured on *Saturday Night Live* remain a well-known comedic riff on the taboo romance.

It isn't clear if the root of the objection to the Batman and Robin relationship is generally inspired by homophobia, pure and simple, or if the discomfort stems more from the sizable age gap between mentor and protégé, which suggests incest or pedophilia. Significantly, the straight-to-DVD film *Mystery of the Batwoman* (2003) hints strongly that a similarly taboo romance blossomed between a mature Batman and a possibly sixteen-year-old Batgirl. In the "real world" State of New York (where Gotham City is located), even "consensual" sex is considered third-degree rape when someone over 21 has intercourse with someone under 17, and carries penalties of up to four years in prison.[19] In theory, those who are not perturbed by *their* age difference, or Batman's Lolita complex, should not be bothered by the May/December nature of a Batman/Robin romance. Addressing this contentious issue, longtime comics editor Denny O'Neil has stated that, officially, Batman is attracted to women but doesn't act on that attraction (Brooker 1999). This position implies that, in O'Neil's eyes, a celibate Batman has had sex with neither Robin nor Batgirl. But O'Neil is not the final word on the subject, and certainly Vivid Video's *Batman XXX: A Porn Parody* (2010), suggests that Batman has had plenty of sex, and once participated in a threesome with Robin and Catwoman.

On the other hand, the women in the Joel Schumacher films are mainly background characters. In *Batman Forever*, Dr. Chase Meridian (Nicole Kidman) shamelessly throws herself at a distant Batman, and seems to win him over, but Roger Ebert observes that the most romantic scenes are between Bruce and Dick Grayson. Meridian does not return for the next film, a theme taken up by online slash fiction in which Batman breaks up with Meridian so he can focus on his sexual relationship with Robin. Julie Madison (Elle Macpherson), Bruce Wayne's fiancée in *Batman and Robin,* is featured in only two or three scenes, and Batgirl (Alicia Silverstone) pales in comparison to the more psychologically complex Barbara Gordon of the comic books (see *Batgirl: Year One, Showcase Presents: Batgirl,* and the *Birds of Prey* trade paperback library). Also, the seductress Poison Ivy (Uma Thurman) is most threatening when her pheromones are strong enough to briefly turn Robin's attentions away from Batman.

While many fans disliked the Schumacher *Batman* films specifically because of their homosexual subtext, the films also happen to be garish, poorly written, poorly acted, and poorly directed. They seem more like spoofs of *Batman* than adaptations. As Virginia Postrel observed in "Superhero Worship" (2006) in *The Atlantic*, the best superhero movies have "engaged their subjects without emotional reservation." She specifically notes that "campy mockery exemplified by the *Batman* television show or Joel Shumacher's disastrous *Batman & Robin*, featuring a smirking George Clooney in the lead" (140–141), failed in this respect. In contrast, the Tim Burton films, *Batman* and *Batman Returns* take some important liberties with the comic books, especially by allowing Batman to kill and by presenting entirely new interpretations of classic villains (especially Catwoman), which resulted in initially negative fan reactions that didn't prevent the films from being financial blockbusters and pop culture phenomena. In fact,

From left to right: Robin (Burt Ward), Batgirl (Yvonne Craig), and Batman (Adam West) from the television series *Batman* (1966). Batman is rumored to have had relationships with both Robin and Batgirl, although DC Comics' official position is that he has been romantically involved with neither.

the Burton films also romanticize the Joker, Catwoman, and the Penguin in a manner that is sometimes subversive and progressive in a positive sense, and sometimes morally questionable. The films are inspired, if flawed, and offer intriguing commentaries on the Batman universe. What makes Burton's films both interesting and uncomfortable to watch is that they invite audience sympathy with Batman while dwelling on his flaws—especially his alienation from women and his investment in preserving a flawed social order. As such, they deconstruct the Batman myth in an intelligent manner, rather than content themselves with mocking the surface silliness of the Batman stories, as the Schumacher films do.

In *Batman* (1989), Keaton's Dark Knight and Nicholson's Joker battle to the death for control of Gotham City. Both men are presented as funny, theatrical, anti-social, and disturbed, hearkening back to the overstated comic book catchphrase that they are "two sides of the same coin." However, the film is most concerned with exploring their mutual fear of women and their different reactions to this fear. The Joker's main targets in the film are women. Nicholson's Joker blames his girlfriend for his disfigurement in an accident at a chemical plant, so he disfigures and murders her in retaliation. When he plots to poison the inhabitants of Gotham with deadly laughing gas, his first step is to taint cosmetics products, claiming two supermodels and a female newscaster as his first victims. When the Joker sees a possible soulmate in photojournalist and fellow artist Vicki Vale (Kim Basinger), he demonstrates his love for her by alternatively flirting with her, kidnapping her, and trying to burn her with acid.

Dina Meyer as Barbara Gordon in the television series *Birds of Prey* (2002). Barbara's career as Batgirl was cut short when she was raped and crippled by the Joker in *The Killing Joke* (1988). She then became Oracle, internet researcher and combat tactician to Batman, the Justice League, and the Birds of Prey.

Bruce Wayne is also attracted to Vale, and the only way he knows how to act on this impulse is to have sex with her on their first date and then never call her again. He has learned to keep women at a distance because he sees them as a distraction from his mission to bring law and order to Gotham. However, his aging butler, Alfred, coaxes him to pursue the relationship with Vale, warning him that without a woman to love Bruce was functionally as dead as his parents. As a matchmaker, Alfred is intrusive in the extreme, betraying his fears that his master is too far gone to woo a woman without being coerced into it. Alfred even takes it upon himself to reveal Bruce's double-life to Vale by allowing her access to the Batcave. By the end of the film, the Joker is killed and Wayne finds himself open to romantic love for the first time since becoming Batman. He appears ready to work on the relationship himself, without any further prompting from Alfred. However, as *Batman Returns* reveals, Vale leaves Bruce because she is too disturbed by his need to continue being Batman to remain in the relationship.

This depiction of the romance with Vale reflects the comic book source material. As a child-man, Wayne has never fully learned to understand women or communicate with them. For example, Batman is clearly attracted to Catwoman, but her unpredictable actions and morally grey worldview deeply disturb him, no matter how good she is at heart. In fact, Batman appears to equate female sexuality with danger and death, possibly because he blames his parent's violent ends on his mother's alluring pearl necklace, which attracted the murderous mugger's attention. These secret Oedipal fears manifest themselves most dramatically in the elfin form of Poison Ivy, an insane environmentalist who can hypnotize or kill men with one kiss, and who lives in greenhouses populated by giant, wet, toothy Venus Flytraps. A previously underutilized villainess who gained prominence during the age of AIDS, Poison Ivy foregrounds all of Batman's worst fears about all women.

In *Batman Returns*, Bruce Wayne is confronted with grotesque doubles of himself as a corporate mogul and as an American aristocrat. He suffers a crisis of faith that causes him to wonder if his naïve aspirations to heroism have any place in the dark, *film noir* world he inhabits, in which everyone is corrupt to some degree.[20] The main villain, Max Shreck (Christopher Walken), is a real-estate tycoon, department store owner, and investor named after the star of F.W. Murnau's *Nosferatu*. Shreck publicizes a bogus energy crisis to gain support for an unnecessary power plant, but Bruce Wayne and Gotham City's mayor squash his schemes. Shreck retaliates by funding a recall campaign to replace the mayor in the wake of a sudden outbreak of urban chaos, which Shreck is secretly orchestrating through his underworld connections. Shreck's candidate for mayor is the Penguin. In a cynical commentary on the American political process, Shreck's campaign savvy makes the grotesque Penguin — who was born disfigured thanks to aristocratic inbreeding — attractive to the voting public, who see him as an aristocrat returned from exile who has heroically forgiven the wealthy parents that forsook him. The film's plot, which seemed ludicrous in 1992, in retrospect appears to have predicted many of the events leading up to California's 2003 recall of Governor Gray Davis, especially the state's electricity crisis (2000–2001) and Enron's behind-the-scenes role in the affair.[21]

By the end of the film, Wayne succeeds in exposing the Penguin as a fraud using hi-tech recording and broadcasting devices to disrupt one of Penguin's press conferences. Wayne also temporarily thwarts Shreck's plans to build a power plant. However, he does not find a way to decisively defeat Shreck, or strip Shreck of his wealth and power. Therefore, the film suggests that Shreck is above the law and beyond the reach of both Bruce Wayne and Batman. Shreck even claims to be as permanent and unassailable as Gotham City itself. "I am the light of the city and I am its mean and twisted soul," he says. Like Bruce Wayne, who is part Donald Trump, part vampire, Shreck *is* contemporary patriarchal capitalism. The angry tone of the film suggests that, in the real world, businessmen are more like Shreck, and "trust fund goodie goodies" like Bruce Wayne exist only in the realm of fiction. But Bruce Wayne is too invested in the system as it is — his feudal variant of benign capitalism — that he does not see that he is, arguably, as much a problem as Shreck is. Wayne cannot see that the roots of society's evils can be traced to inequalities built into the unacknowledged American class system and in its imbalanced capitalist economy. So the moral of *Batman Returns* is that "problems cannot be solved within the mindset that created them."

The born-to-the-purple Bruce Wayne is very good at fighting street crime or foreign enemies with his impressive arsenal and cool Batmobile, but he is clueless when it comes to combating the real evils of capitalist society. Therefore, Wayne has no real understanding of poverty, racism, or the inequalities suffered by women in a male-dominated system. Ironically, while Shreck *is* decisively dealt with at the end of the film, it is not by Batman, but by Shreck's personal secretary, the lower-middle-class Selina Kyle, who is in a better position than Wayne to know just how evil men like Shreck are.

Kyle, played by a frumpily costumed but still quite gorgeous Michelle Pfeiffer, lives in a run-down Gotham City apartment, alone except for the stray cats who visit her for food and shelter. Romantically frustrated, financially strapped, and nagged by the mother she doesn't call enough, Kyle is eager to impress her boss and graduate from secretary to personal advisor and confidant to Shreck. Researching Shreck's business ventures to better advise him, she stumbles across evidence that his power-plant plans are an attempt to *drain* power from Gotham, rather than *provide* power to the people. When Shreck realizes that Kyle has found him out, he kills her by pushing her through the window of his high-rise office building. What Shreck doesn't anticipate is that the many stray cats that Selina has been caring for discover her broken body in the alley below and mystically breathe life back into her, granting her nine new lives.

Back from the dead and furious, Kyle returns to her apartment and destroys her doll house, stuffed animals, and pink clothes, effectively cleansing herself of girlhood. The scene is powerful as Kyle destroys these symbols of passivity and domesticity that brainwashed her into investing in a man like Shreck. Selina then uses her domestic arts to sew herself a black leather costume. Then she arms herself with a low-tech bullwhip, which she adopts instead of the too-phallic alternative, a gun. Reborn as Catwoman, Kyle launches an extended campaign against Shreck by attacking him where it will hurt the most — his wallet. She breaks into his department store after closing time, chases the useless guards away, and blows up the store using an aerosol can, a microwave, and a gas line. (A nice, no-frills approach. No C-4 for Catwoman.) These weapons are low-tech in comparison to Batman's, but are just as non-lethal. The explosion is an act of revolution, carried out mercifully, when no guards, customers, or Shreck employees are still in the store; but it brings down the wrath of Batman, who tries to bring her to justice for property damage and domestic terrorism.

In *Batman Begins* (Warner Bros., 1992), Michelle Pfeiffer plays Catwoman as an anti-hero who understands far better than Bruce Wayne does that white-collar, corporate criminals are the most dangerous after all, and the most in need of being brought to justice by any means necessary.

She evades capture long enough for Batman to get to know her — both in her Catwoman and Kyle identities — and to fall in love with her. When he discovers that her ultimate goal is to assassinate Shreck, he tries to dissuade her to save her from her own darkness. Catwoman isn't interested in being dissuaded, however. She says, "Don't give me a killing-Max-won't-solve-anything speech, because it will. Aren't you tired of this sanctimonious robber baron coming out on top when he should be six feet under?" Batman responds by declaring that she doesn't have the right to kill him, asking, "Who do you think you are?"

At the end of the film, Catwoman captures Shreck and is about to kill him when Batman intervenes, promising Catwoman that he finally has enough evidence to turn Shreck in.

> CATWOMAN: Don't be naïve. The law doesn't apply to him or us.
>
> BATMAN: Wrong on both counts. Why are you doing this? Let's just take him to the police. Then we can go home ... together.

Batman continues to speak softly to Catwoman, pleading with her, and unmasking to show her Bruce Wayne's face. After a long moment of indecision, Catwoman replies: "Bruce, I would love to live with you in your castle forever, just like in a fairy tale. [Pause.] I just couldn't live with myself." Then she kills Shreck and disappears into the night. Batman does not pursue her. The film ends shortly afterwards.

This resolution represents an interesting reversal from the comic book, where Catwoman is always begging Batman for a relationship, and he always spurns her for being too corrupt for him. Here Batman *wants* the relationship, but Catwoman doesn't want to betray her principles, or compromise her independence, by marrying a rich prince after all. It is a great tragic ending. As satisfying as it would have been to see a Batman-Catwoman relationship, it is good that Selina Kyle doesn't "sell out," and a pleasant surprise that she doesn't wind up safely jailed or killed at the end. Unsurprisingly, *Batman Returns* had been widely criticized for being a bleak and angry film. It certainly is, but it is also an excellent, thought-provoking film, especially since Catwoman is a marvelous character who has a very legitimate point about the evils of "sanctimonious robber barons"—both in the world of Batman and in "the real world." Clearly, Batman thinks she does, or he would have tried harder to capture her after she killed Shreck.

Having It Both Ways

When asked if the Batman story is "pro-vigilante" or "anti-vigilante," *Batman Begins* auteur Christopher Nolan observed that "it's kind of both at the same time. It's enjoying something and questioning it."[22] Certainly that is the case when one considers, side-by-side, *Batman Begins*, which presents a largely positive portrayal of Batman, and *Batman Returns*, which is more concerned with the limits of Batman's power and heroism, despite his likeability and his good intentions. The two films represent two polar opposite perspectives on the character that are equally valid.

Admittedly, there are many problematic elements to the Batman story featured in films, comic books, and cartoons. The story is consistently sexist in its thinking and its almost uniformly male cast of characters. It is in love with technology and weaponry—a narrative about boys with toys. It is, therefore, obviously the product of adolescent male power fantasies and wish-fulfillment. It is also, in this day-and-age, a potentially dangerous narrative that can be easily exploited as propaganda that supports the excesses of American imperialism and global capitalism.

However, at its best, the Batman story is about justice, restraint, and the desire to take a stand against evil—to make society as a whole the better for the effort. It is about a man who has the power, the money, and the influence to behave self-indulgently, but who, instead, uses moderation and behaves selflessly. It is possible for a fan to embrace Batman's more problematic character traits—his flirtation with fascism, his sexism, his single-mindedness—and that is, of course, not desirable. But it is also possible for someone to enjoy the heroism that Batman represents, and to strive to find a real-world way to emulate it, while being critical of the Batman universe and aware of the limitations of Batman's philosophy. It is in Batman's nobility—his desire to protect and improve his home city—that he has a renewed appeal for modern audiences. He is especially appealing to the modern day New Yorker, who fears that the city might be too far gone to save, or that it might be attacked by a real-life Ra's al Ghul. He is an exhortation not to give up, but to remain hopeful, and to keep striving for a better future.

Two

Wonder Woman as World War II Veteran, Feminist Icon, and Sex Symbol

Don't kill if you can wound, don't wound if you can subdue, don't subdue if you can pacify, and don't raise your hand at all until you've first extended it.—Wonder Woman, quoting an old Amazon saying[1]

[People tell me that] having Wonder Woman as a role model helped them get out of an abusive relationship, or that it got them to keep going to the gym and take care of themselves ... I've had young girls tell me that she helped them stand up to bullies at school. I've even had people go as far as to say it stopped them from committing suicide because that's not something that she would do. People relate to her in a really emotionally deep way that I had no idea about before I started writing comics about her.—*Wonder Woman* comic book writer Gail Simone, author of *Wonder Woman: The Circle*[2]

Who Is Wonder Woman?

A warrior pacifist, a feminist sex symbol, a foreign royal–turned–American immigrant, and a devout pagan living in a secular age, Wonder Woman is a heroic figure who embodies a set of seemingly contradictory character traits. These traits, all of which have been a part of her persona since she made her debut in *All Star Comics* #8 in December of 1941, conspire to make her a highly complex and controversial figure. Torn between being an escapist action hero and an activist role model for young women around the world, Wonder Woman satisfies both roles when she is presented as having a charismatic, three-dimensional personality that comfortably contains these contradictions.

Unsurprisingly, different creative teams on the comic book from different decades have pulled the character towards the political right (see comics written and drawn by Frank Miller and John Byrne during the 1990s) and towards the left (George Perez's stories from the 1980s). But the character has been at her most interesting, both dramatically and socially, during periods of great social unrest and military conflict—when she was a New Deal patriot during World War II, a symbol of ascendant feminism during the 1970s, a voice of the opposition during the Reagan years, and a meditation on power and responsibility during the current War on Terror. It is during these eras of global conflict that she speaks as a priestess praying for a time when soldiers will finally lay down their weapons and men and women from all cultures will finally live in peace.

The stories which come closest to convincingly depicting Wonder Woman as a soldier of peace are the original, World War II era comic books and the episodes of the television series *Wonder Woman* (1975–1979) featuring actress Lynda Carter's pitch-perfect portrayal of the heroine. Both the early comic books and the 1970s television adaptation cast the Amazon princess as more of a negotiator than a warrior, more of a women's advocate than a pin-up girl, but they also present her as a rich, complicated figure who has the potential to be all of the above. Nevertheless, cultural critics such as Gloria Steinem and Matthew J. Smith have correctly asserted that Wonder Woman should ideally promote peace over war, feminism over conservatism, and multiculturalism over American Imperialism because she acts as one of the few progressive alternatives to the male-centric sensibilities still dominating popular culture. Also, it is vitally important to preserve Wonder Woman's legacy as an inspiring and empowering role model for young women, especially in light of the startling testimony to the power of the character offered by Gail Simone.

Unfortunately, Wonder Woman's status as an icon of feminism and an advocate of peace during wartime has often been undermined by those who are invested in domesticating the character and making her less threatening to sensitive male egos. In some instances, more politically reactionary writers of the comic books have directly challenged her feminism by charging her with hypocrisy and "exposing" her divided loyalties. In other cases, artists and merchandisers have sold Wonder Woman posters, action figures, and comics that represent her as a wet dream in a star-spangled thong and not as a "real" woman with a soul and a life beyond the one conferred on her by a lecherous male gaze. And so, even though the character has made a career of fighting Nazis and nuclear-armed terrorists, her greatest enemies have consistently been those in the real world who would censor her comic books and marginalize her significance in the history of both the feminist movement and "heroic fiction." After all, as one of the earliest popular icons of twentieth-century feminism, Wonder Woman deserves to be treated with respect by those who currently write adventures with the character, and should not be sanitized by clever marketing, turned into a one-dimensional fetish object, or appropriated by a writer who opposes everything she stands for.

Creating an Icon: The World War II Era Comic Books

Wonder Woman, a princess of the Amazons also known as Diana of Themiscyra, was created in 1941 by psychologist William Moulton Marston, a student of the psychological effects of mass media on the individual spectator, an advocate of the reformation of criminals, and an early developer of the lie-detector test. According to biographer Les Daniels, Marston believed that the antisocial, violent tendencies in humanity were undesirable masculine traits that were best subdued by the socializing and loving influence of a powerful maternal figure. He felt that society in general would be a more peaceful place if "women's values" were cherished and if men willingly submitted themselves to female dominance. For Marston, the inducement for men to relinquish their power and reform the excesses of the patriarchy would be the sexual appeal of the dominant female.

Marston created the comic book character Wonder Woman to be both strong and sexy, as a means of encouraging women to emulate her unapologetic assertiveness. He also hoped to convince men that strong women were more beautiful than passive ones and were worthy of love and respect instead of fear. Therefore, Marston designed Diana's adventures to advance his political agenda and psychological views, while hoping that her serialized exploits would offer an alternative to the grotesque comic books that flooded the market, such as *Dick Tracy*, a strip saturated with violence that gave him great personal reservations.

As Marston explained in *The American Scholar* (1943):

> It seemed to me, from a psychological angle, that the comics' worst offense was their blood-curdling masculinity.... It's smart to be strong. It's big to be generous, but it is sissified, according to exclusively male rules, to be tender, loving, affectionate, and alluring. "Aw, that's girl stuff!" snorts our young comic reader, "Who wants to be a girl?" And that's the point: not even girls want to be girls so long as our feminine archetype lacks force, strength.... Women's strong qualities have become despised because of their weak ones.[3]

As a devotee of Classical mythology, Marston found a precedent for his empowered female hero in the story of the Amazons — a race of proud women warriors from ancient Turkey who were subdued by Hercules and whose queen, Hippolyta, was ruined by her love of men. Marston crafted Wonder Woman to be the greatest member of this warrior race.[4]

According to Daniels, Marston was encouraged to use the Amazons as models for his super heroine by his creative collaborators and muses, lawyer Elizabeth Holloway Marston and psychologist Olive Byrne (or Richard), the mothers of his children with whom he had a polyandrous relationship. Whether Wonder Woman's Amazon heritage was Marston's idea, or Holloway's or Byrne's, the Greco-Roman underpinnings of the comic book represented a significant departure from the precedent set by the *Superman* adventures, which, as a secularized retelling of the Moses story, was based in Judeo-Christian lore and tailored to more contemporary sensibilities.

To help make the Amazons more successful role models for women, Marston rewrote the end of the established narrative, explaining that they eventually escaped their Greek captors. The first *Wonder Woman* comic book, which Marston wrote under the pen name Charles Moulton and which was drawn by artist Harry (H.G.) Peter, reveals that Hippolyta prayed to the Goddess Aphrodite for deliverance from Hercules and his men. Aphrodite granted the Amazons freedom from bondage provided they left the "civilized" world and founded a colony of exclusively women on "Paradise Island." Freed of their chains, the women would also have to permanently wear the manacles Hercules had placed upon their wrists as a grim reminder of what happened when they once allowed themselves to be dominated by men. Having fulfilled their end of the bargain, the Amazons earned the gift of eternal life, as well as superior strength and access to highly advanced technology, including invisible planes and telepathic communicators. The goddess also rewarded Hippolyta with a fatherless daughter — Diana,

To many, Lynda Carter "is the living, physical embodiment" of Wonder Woman — a gorgeous actress who brings "a sense of grace and style and dignity" to the character. From a promotional photograph for the second season of *Wonder Woman* (Warner Bros, 1977).

the only offspring ever produced on Paradise Island.[5] And so, the Amazons lived in peace and isolation for thousands of years ... until the outbreak of World War II.

Naturally, World War II was *the* significant historical influence on the Golden Age of comic books, and *Wonder Woman* was no exception. In 1942's *Wonder Woman* #1, Marston reveals that "The planet earth ... is ruled by rival Gods—Ares, God of War, and Aphrodite, Goddess of Love and Beauty." One of Peter's panel illustrations dramatically depicts the male Ares and the female Aphrodite facing off against one another in the stars with the Earth positioned as a contested prize between them. Ares proclaims, "My men shall rule with the sword!" and Aphrodite challenges, "My women shall conquer men with love!" The image strikingly crystallizes Marston's view of the world as defined principally by gender conflict, as opposed to by class, religious, or cultural strife, all of which would be equally valid ways of understanding the history of civilization and of warfare.[6]

Later in that same comic book, the narrator reveals that Ares has orchestrated World War II to set the world aflame. To wrest control of Earth from Ares, Aphrodite commands that the Amazons end their long period of isolation. They would send the wisest and strongest Amazon to aid the Allies. This "Wonder Woman" would protect the American home front from Axis spies and terrorists, promote the importance of women's rights, and preach the promise of peace. Again, global conflict is defined as a clash of male and female ideals as opposed to a clash of empires or of cultures. The result, while simplifying the root causes of World War II from a historical perspective, offers some intriguing food for thought, especially given the Nazi regime's anti-feminist policies.[7]

Even as Aphrodite orders the Amazons to join the Allied side, the tranquility of Paradise Island is disrupted by the unexpected arrival of the first man in history to set foot on its shores. U.S. Army Intelligence Captain Steve Trevor crashes his plane on the beach after losing an aerial engagement with the Germans. As Diana tends to his wounds, both patient and nurse find themselves falling in love with each other. Eager to separate her daughter from Trevor's corrupting influence, Hippolyta holds an Olympics-style contest to determine which Amazon would become Wonder Woman, Aphrodite's champion and Trevor's escort home. She forbids her daughter from participating in the contest, but Diana enters in secret, as a masked contestant, and proves herself to be legitimately the best athlete on an island of superpowered women. Winning the right to the title Wonder Woman, Diana forsakes her immortality for love and for duty by leaving her home and her people.[8]

Heartbroken at losing her daughter, Hippolyta nevertheless gives Diana her blessing and sews her daughter an ambassadorial uniform made of the colors of American flag, a symbol of Diana's pledge to protect Democracy and to adopt America as her new homeland. Hippolyta also gives her a golden lasso that has the magical ability of forcing those caught in it to tell the complete truth. Upon arrival in Washington, D.C., Diana assumes the identity of war office secretary Diana Prince and disguises herself in dowdy clothes and oversized glasses. From that vantage point, Diana monitors enemy activity. She also remains close to Trevor, the man she loves but is wary of becoming romantic with, partly because he is so enamored with his dream-visions of Wonder Woman that he cannot see the beauty lurking behind his secretary's plain façade.

This "origin" is perhaps one of the richest in comic book history, and the story of how the daughter of a queen became a superhero remains one of the best *Wonder Woman* stories, which is why it is so often retold—as it was in the Carter television series, 1987's *Wonder Woman Vol. 2* #1, the premiere episode of 2001's *Justice League* cartoon, and 2009's straight-to-DVD *Wonder Woman* cartoon where the heroine was voiced by Keri Russell. In each retelling, certain elements of the story are changed, or given a different amount of dramatic weight, either through dialogue, visuals, or the structure of the plot and, consequently, the central themes of the story change to match the times and a given creator's voice. Sadly, as compelling as the origin story is, it has not penetrated the public consciousness the way that Superman's origin story has—*everyone* knows about Krypton and the Kents—so there was no guarantee that anyone reading this would have known Wonder Woman's story in advance. This is ironic since her origin was complete and complex from the beginning, while the back stories given to Superman and Batman evolved incrementally over the course of many years and through contributions from a variety of writers.

Americans basically know what Wonder Woman looks like, thanks largely to merchandizing and a fond (if often vague) memory of the old television show, and they have a general idea that she is a feminist. But they are unlikely to know the full political and thematic significance of her exploits, nor are they likely to know that she was created during World War II as a patriotic feminist symbol akin to Rosie the Riveter. Indeed, Rosie the Riveter is an ideal parallel figure for Wonder Woman since, as merciful as the Amazon was to her enemies, there was no question which side she was on during World War II: America's. And she states repeatedly that she fights for America because America fights for women's rights around the world.[9]

Marston and Peter pitted their Amazon champion against Nazis who were bloodthirsty pawns of Ares. They were insane, had no moral center, and sported stereotyped names and features. They were also frequently portrayed as sexually repressed or would-be rapists, greeting the sight of Wonder Woman's exposed flesh with either too much moral outrage or too much lust, and failing the test of reacting to Diana's appearance in a well-adjusted manner.[10] Hitler himself appears in *Wonder Woman* #2 (Fall 1942), as a drooling maniac eager to shoot his own best men for insubordination even as he absorbs subconscious psychic commands from Ares to escalate his military campaign against the Allies.[11] This scene is emblematic of *Wonder Woman*'s consistent portrayal of the Nazis as "evil" pagans and Diana as a "good" pagan. Diana's paganism, a worship of Aphrodite, is shown to be maternal, environmentalist, and "natural," while Hitler and the Nazis worship Ares in a manner that is industrial, marshal, and anything but "natural." Perhaps the most imaginative story that illustrates this is the adventure from February 1943's *Sensation Comics* #14, in which a fir tree in the snow-covered border between the United States and Canada literally talks to Wonder Woman, betraying the nearby location of a secret Nazi base. As the story's narrator and central character, the fir tree is effusive in its praise of Diana's virtue and helps her rescue the mother of two small children from being raped and killed by Nazi soldiers.[12]

Not *exactly* figures of fun, Wonder Woman's enemies were still not granted depth of characterization or any kind of respect as worthy opponents, nor were they given the forum to express a cohesive political philosophy. The inevitable consequence is that she is pitted against straw man opponents who are no match for her super powers, even if they attack her in tanks, submarines, planes, or with an entire army of storm troopers. Nor are they any match for her ideologically because their philosophy is empty and inarticulate. Indeed, they are only interesting as threats when they discover how to nullify her super powers. In a weakness that resembles Superman's vulnerability to Kryptonite, the earliest *Wonder Woman* adventures feature a heroine who loses her powers when she allows herself to be manacled by a man.[13] Diana is in danger only when she is tied up, and the real suspense derives from the audience wondering whether she will trick her way out, or whether the local Holliday College for Women sorority sisters she has befriended will come to her rescue.

Despite the uninteresting villains (which have plagued *Wonder Woman* adventures from the beginning) the early Marston-penned comics are compelling reads primarily in their political commentary and in their depiction of female friendship. The aforementioned Holliday College women appear frequently during Marston's tenure on the comic book, which lasted until his death in 1947. Their leader, the comically overweight Etta Candy, is a loyal friend to Diana, rather than a rival who is envious of the Amazon's perfect figure. Depictions of female friendship are rare in popular culture, as they are in literature; so, the camaraderie between Wonder Woman and the women she encounters in her 1940s adventures, be they sorority sisters, nurses, teachers, or even misguided villainesses, may be found in precious few places, before or since, with the notable exceptions of Alan Davis' *Excalibur* and Gail Simone's *Birds of Prey* comic books.

Although the sensibilities of an action-oriented comic strip are not conducive to showing Diana merely "hanging out" with other women characters and enjoying their company, the women in these early adventures are always there to help one another, rally together under a united political front, and even go to prison to protect one another. Their feelings of sisterhood are presented as strong enough to encourage women on the side of the Axis to reconsider their allegiances and join their sisters on the side of "right" and democracy. In these comic books, Wonder Woman advocates a new standard of sisterhood that challenges the jealous female competition fostered by the dominant patriarchal cultural climate. She also expresses concern with the plight of the poor, working woman during wartime. In these ways, Diana questions the American culture that she champions, showing that it is possible to be a patriot and still be a progressive. In typical New Deal fashion, her somewhat Marxist-feminist leanings are not traitorous, but help inspire improvements in the American standard of living, making the United States stronger as it continues its conflict with Nazi Germany.

For example, in *Sensation Comics* #7, Diana encounters a grieving mother whose son, Danny, died of undernourishment after she could no longer afford to buy milk for him.[14] Wonder Woman promises to send milk to Danny's equally undernourished sister every day, and to investigate the causes of the price-gouging. She confronts the head of the International Milk Co., Mr. DeGyppo, who resents her claims that the company is behaving immorally since, "Everything we do is absolutely legal!" (105) In retaliation, Diana attacks the milk company's public image by organizing a massive protest featuring banners that read: "The International Milk Company is starving America's children!" (110) Thanks to the publicity provided by print journalists and newsreel grinders, her protest is a success and milk is made affordable once again.

In a story with similarly populist and feminist overtones, the following issue sees Diana confronting department store owner Gloria Bullfinch for underpaying her overworked female employees. While Bullfinch wines and dines in high society, her staff is suffering from exhaustion and cannot afford to pay for the medicine they need to keep grinding away at their grueling jobs. When one employee collapses and another steals medicine on her behalf, Bullfinch's lackeys see to it that the sick one is fired and the thief is imprisoned. Infuriated by this injustice, Wonder Woman hypnotizes Bullfinch into thinking that she is a working-class woman and orders Bullfinch to take a job in her own department store. Once she is sure that Bullfinch has learned her lesson, Wonder Woman lifts her spell and allows Bullfinch to reassume control of the store. Fortunately, Bullfinch's latent feelings of sisterhood are awakened and she learns to value the women in her employ, offering them more equitable pay and more reasonable work shifts.[15]

Like DeGyppo, Bullfinch was seduced into working against the best interests of her country by a foreign spy of the opposite sex. Consequently, the presence of that "alien" enemy elides the possible criticism that the comic book is anti–American and anti-capitalist. Still, Wonder Woman's insistence on combating homegrown economic evils — war profiteering, low wages, etc. — as well as enemy soldiers and saboteurs suggests that her patriotism and her allegiance to democracy and capitalism, depend entirely on America delivering on its promises of *true* freedom and *true* equality for all. The implication is that, should America ever stray from the path of righteousness, Wonder Woman will cease wearing the colors of the American flag.

(In fact, in the 1978 comic book "Superman vs. Wonder Woman: An Untold Epic of World War II," written by Gerry Conway and drawn by Jose Luis Garcia-Lopez, Superman fights to make sure that America develops nuclear technology before the Axis does, while Diana fights both Superman and the Axis to make sure that *no one* develops nuclear technology, because she doesn't trust America, or any other nation, with such destructive power.)

The two Marston stories described above are emblematic of the early Wonder Woman adventures, which provide a vision of female friendship and solidarity that has inspired generations of women — including luminaries such as the previously mentioned Gloria Steinem, Judy Collins, and a host of others — to fight for the betterment of women's positions in society. Steinem, who honored her childhood hero by printing a "Wonder Woman for President" headline on the cover of the first issue of her *Ms.* magazine (December 1971), has written extensively about the appeal of the character, but has also acknowledged that the Amazon's relationship to men is as problematic as her relationship to women is admirable. As she explained in a 1995 essay on the heroine,

> Of course, it is also true that Marston's message wasn't as feminist as it might have been. Instead of portraying the goal of full humanity for women and men, which is what feminism has in mind, he often got stuck in the subject/object, winner/loser paradigm of "masculine" versus "feminine," and came up with female superiority instead.... No wonder I was inspired but confused by the isolationism of Paradise Island: Did women have to live separately in order to be happy and courageous? No wonder even boys who could accept equality might have felt less than good about themselves in some of these stories: were there *any* men who could escape the cultural instruction to be violent?
>
> Wonder Woman herself sometimes got trapped in this either/or choice, as she muses to herself: "Some girls love to have a man stronger than they are to make them do things. Do I like it? I don't know, it's sort of thrilling. But isn't it more fun to make a man obey?" [276–277].

Steinem is correct in identifying Wonder Woman's conflicted heart, especially concerning her relationship to Steve Trevor. It is interesting that Diana is so uneasy around Trevor, the man she loved enough to sacrifice immortality for. After all, Trevor is hardly presented as a male chauvinist. He is a capable soldier, spy, and tactician who expresses unwavering admiration for Diana's unearthly power when a lesser man might feel threatened by her. (During one adventure, when he fails to jump out of the way of an explosion, as she does, she asks, "Are you hurt, Steve? Why didn't you jump like I did?" To which he replies, "Jump like you? What am I, a kangaroo?") He gives credit where it is due, invariably telling his superiors that they have Wonder Woman to thank, not him, whenever she saves the day. In fact, Trevor appears to only have two flaws: he is probably a little too militaristic for Diana, and he consistently fails to react correctly to her clothing.

Diana's fashion sense is symbolically linked to her politics. Her half-nakedness is part

In *Superman vs. Wonder Woman* (DC Comics, 1978, page 31), Superman takes Franklin Delano Roosevelt's word that the United States will never use the atom bomb while he is president. However, Wonder Woman indicates to her mother that she believes a future president will.

and parcel of her political agenda, so those who are uneasy about her clothes are often uneasy about her broader message of female empowerment. When Diana confronts the world with her exposed flesh, she expects a well-adjusted reaction. The first time she encounters American clothing in *All Star Comics* #8, she is puzzled by how conservative the women's fashions are. "There's so much material in these dresses ... but they *are* cute!" she says, talking as if she had the sensibilities of Eve before the Fall. Leaving the store after choosing to stay dressed in her Wonder Woman costume, Diana encounters throngs of people on the streets who "are amazed to see the scantily clad girl walking about so unconcerned." When old women react with jealousy ("The hussy! She has no clothes on!" "The brazen thing!") and young men with lechery ("Ha! Sour grapes, sister! Don't you wish you looked like that!"), Diana is mildly put out that her body causes such a stir in either direction. While she does blend in with mainstream American society by dressing conservatively as Diana Prince, she finds the clothes as confining as if she were wearing a corset or a nun's habit, so, when she transforms from Diana Prince to Wonder Woman for the first time, she shouts with triumph, "It feels grand to be myself again!" as she discards her civilian attire.[16]

Even though Trevor does not react with lust or fear to her half-nakedness, as those on the streets do, he does deify "Wonder Woman," and Diana does not feel that his reaction to her is healthy. When she rescues him from the Nazis, he exclaims, "Wonder Woman! My beautiful angel!" And she replies, "What's an angel? I'd rather be a woman."[17] Deifying "Wonder Woman" seems to be an understandable sin for the oft-rescued Trevor to commit, but it is also too much for Diana to deal with. She wants him to see her as a flesh-and-blood woman, and not as a romanticized ideal. Trevor also compounds this mistake by writing off his secretary—the more plain Jane, dressed down Diana Prince—as a possible romantic interest. He does not see the potential of an ordinary woman to be extraordinary, nor does he see that there are many kinds of female beauty, not just the flashy Amazonian kind.

Because Wonder Woman herself has such anxiety about male/female romance, her relationship with Steve Trevor has always been a non-starter. In fact, like the Lois Lane/Superman relationship, which treaded water for decades, the Diana/Trevor relationship was always a challenge for writers to keep interesting. More often than not, the solution was to write Trevor out of the comic book, or to kill him, only to resurrect him from the dead later on. However, when the saga of Diana of Paradise Island briefly came to an end in 1986 with the publication of issue #329, that "Final Issue" featured the marriage of Diana and Trevor and their bodily assumption into Mt. Olympus. Obviously, the "match made on Olympus" ending seems too "pat" and too "domestic" an end for the Wonder Woman saga. On the other hand, each time Trevor, or any of Diana's other love interests, disappears from *Wonder Woman* adventures, many fans lose hope that Diana will ever be able to find love, or demonstrate to her readers how a true (heterosexual/homosexual/polygamous) romantic relationship of equals can be achieved.

It is significant that the Wonder Woman who appears in comic books today, the same one that was revamped and modernized during the 1980s in a story crafted by George Perez, left Paradise Island purely out of a selfless sense of duty, charged with preventing Ares from escalating the Cold War tensions between Russia and the United States into a nuclear conflict. She had no real romantic interest in Steve Trevor. As with the early Marston issues, Perez's adventures showed that Wonder Woman's most rewarding relationships were with female friends, especially mother-figure and Harvard University Professor Julia Kapatelis, and Julia's daughter, Vanessa, who looked up to Diana as an older sister. Her asexuality assured, the new Wonder Woman has sometimes been criticized by readers for being frigid, and writers have addressed the issue by suggesting that she has unrequited romantic feelings for Superman, that she had brief flirtations with Aquaman, and feels unresolved sexual tension whenever she is with Batman, who is equally attracted to her but also equally afraid of the opposite sex, dooming the relationship even before it begins.[18] When writer/artist Phil Jiminez challenged this frustrating cycle by proposing a storyline in which Wonder Woman would finally lose her virginity to African American character Trevor Barnes, the resultant racist fan outcry over the sexy, inter-racial relationship prevented the story from reaching its intended climax.[19] Diana's dalliance with Hindu god Rama was also cut abruptly short when protests from the religious community deemed the romance sacrilegious.[20]

Both a sex symbol and an icon of 1960s feminism, Emma Peel (Diana Rigg) partnered with John Steed (Patrick Macnee) to expose Soviet spies who had infiltrated every level of British society. The chess motif, a symbol of the Cold War clash of East and West, recurs in the television series *The Avengers*.

The sexual content of the comic book has always been controversial, to the extent that the Holliday girls were written out of the series following the publication of *Seduction of the Innocent* (1954). The book was a study of juvenile delinquency in which social critic and psychologist Dr. Frederic Wertham pointed to the lesbian overtones of Wonder Woman's relationship to the sorority sisters. Following the publication of Wertham's book, *Wonder Woman* became far more conservative in its sensibilities. Since the dominant cultural mood of the McCarthy-era 1950s suggested that it was not possible to be both a progressive and a patriot, Diana chose patriotism over feminism and socialism. She fell silent on political issues and became more of a fickle flirt. Before long, the Amazons disappeared from the narrative and Wonder Woman took to studying karate under Chinese mentor I Ching after losing her super powers. This era of the comic book modeled its Wonder Woman after Emma Peel from *The Avengers*.

Both a sex symbol and an icon of 1960s feminism, Emma Peel (Diana Rigg) partnered with John Steed (Patrick Macnee) to expose Soviet spies who had infiltrated every level of British society—from department stores, to nanny training agencies, to the secret recesses of MI-5. Sexy and tough, Emma Peel appealed to both men and women because of Rigg's ability to be dignified and assertive, even when wearing an S&M outfit as part of her "cover" while on assignment infiltrating the Hellfire Club. A fan of the series, comic writer-artist Batton Lash observed that, "Mrs. Peel wasn't a 'girly-girl' and she and Steed were not lovers, but associates with mutual respect. They liked each other!" Their platonic relationship helped inspire Lash's characterization of the professional relationship between Alanna Wolff and Jeff Byrd in *Supernatural Law*.

Similarly, the Avengers inspired Wonder Woman's romance-free relationships with the hard-bitten male detectives, police officers, and spies she worked alongside to fight crime and terrorism in the 1960s. These comic stories, in turn, inspired the 1974 Cathy Lee Crosby *Wonder Woman* television movie, in which the title heroine faced off against an international spy ring led by Ricardo Montalban.[21] Thanks largely to an intervention by Steinem, who hated the new direction the comic book had taken, the Amazons and the "original" version of Wonder Woman returned to the comic book in 1973. Two years later, a television pilot inspired by the early Marston comic books appeared, *The New Original Wonder Woman* featuring Lynda Carter, and it soon evolved into a television series.[22]

Lynda Carter: *The New Original Wonder Woman*

Given the timing of *Wonder Woman*, which ran from 1975 to 1979, the series served as a celebration of the then-recent strides made by the women's movement. It also acted as a tribute to the super heroine who, as a creation of the 1940s, helped lay the groundwork for feminism's contemporary successes. As the series' executive producer Douglas S. Cramer observed, "*Wonder Woman* came along at a time in the 1970s that was absolutely right ... [when] the women's movement was hitting its stride, where feminism and all that it conveyed ... was ... exploding across the country."[23] It was also the era when other strong and sexy superheroines could be found on television shows such as *Charlie's Angels* (1976–1981), *The Bionic Woman* (1976–1978), and *The New Avengers* (1976–1977).

In the 2005 DVD release of the entire *Wonder Woman* series, the legacy of the show was examined, as was its portrayal of the character, both as a feminist icon and a sex symbol. Naturally, much attention was paid to the revealing costume that Carter wore in the title role. After all, as sexy as Wonder Woman was in the comic book, it was even sexier seeing a flesh-and-blood woman on television wearing such a revealing outfit — especially a woman as beautiful as Carter. In an admittedly self-promoting DVD special feature, "Beauty, Brawn, and Bulletproof Bracelets," the subjects interviewed agreed that, as sexy as Carter was, and as revealing as the costume was, the television Wonder Woman was remarkably "sexy" and "not sexy" at the same time. Carter herself remarked that the costume, "felt like a second skin. I really didn't feel too self-conscious oddly. Maybe I should have but, you know, don't forget, this was the 'ban the bra' time, this was sexual freedom, this was bikinis and midriffs and that was the timing and I really wasn't thinking of being sexy either." Carter added that she was always determined to play Wonder Woman as an inspiration to women, and that is why few women saw her as a threat to their self-esteem.

Painter Alex Ross, whose depictions of Wonder Woman rank with Garcia-Lopez's and Perez's as among the most recognizable artistic renderings of the character, also felt that Carter's look in the costume was striking but not threatening to women. He said: "Here's this woman — a very gorgeous woman — running around half-naked, essentially wearing ... a swimming outfit and somehow she comes across as not being ultra sexual and, in fact, she is this symbol to young women — or women of any age — as not being defiled by that exposure. Essentially, the character was taken as what [she] ... was meant to be, as an object of energy in motion, not as of corrupted sexuality or something that was just ... for the boys."

But it is also important to point out here that Steinem felt that Carter's Wonder Woman was "a little blue of eye and large of breast" for her taste, so it is conceivable that Carter's stunning looks were off-putting to other women viewers. On the other hand, it is also possible that Carter's good looks had exactly the effect on the male viewers that Marston wanted his Wonder Woman to have — they were initially attracted by her beauty, and later learned to respect her intelligence, spirit, personality, and good deeds.

The early installments of the series were remarkably faithful to the spirit of the comic book, including all the major elements of the mythos and episodes directly adapted from Marston tales. The Nazis remained Wonder Woman's main foes, but they were presented in an even more broadly comic fashion on television (closer to Nazis found on *Hogan's Heroes* and *'Allo 'Allo* than to those in *Schindler's List*). Their philosophy was just as empty as before, only now the series could operate with the knowledge that the Nazis were ultimately vanquished. In fact, the show had an air of nostalgia about it, hearkening to the "simpler times" of World War II, when it was easier to be a liberal patriot than it was in the years following Vietnam and Watergate.

In general, Diana was as reluctant to use force in the series as she was in the comic, and virtually always contented herself with rendering her enemies unconscious or tying them up until they were arrested. Also, as with the comic book, she would reason with opponents before fighting them and, in the case of Fausta, the Nazi Wonder Woman, convinced her enemy to defect to America, a land that treated its women better.[24]

One minor difference from the comic book was the placing of Diana in the position of yeoman, rather than secretary, in her civilian guise. Also, the Holliday girls were notably absent, but Etta Candy was included as another of Trevor's female staff members. Most significantly, most of the trappings of Greek mythology were removed from the series, and the secret of the Amazon's power was revealed to be superior technology fueled by the discovery of Feminum, a rare element unearthed in the mines of Paradise Island. The move made the show less mystical than the comic, but the fact that Wonder Woman now only had her mother to answer to, and not the gods as well, helped make the character more assertive and more of a free agent.[25] Indeed, Carter's Wonder Woman goes to America to fight the Nazis and to be with Steve, but she is not spurred on by a command from Aphrodite. Therefore, Diana's dramatic choice is not to obey Aphrodite over her mother, but to defy her mother despite her own misgivings about breaking her mother's heart.

As Nina Jaffe, author of several children's books featuring the heroine, including *Wonder Woman: The Journey Begins* (2004) explains, "To be like her mother, she has to defy her mother. Queen Hippolyta led her own people in a battle for freedom. At a certain point, Wonder Woman realizes that she wants to take on the challenges that someone like her mother would and, in order to do that, she has to rebel. She has to disobey her mother."[26] The television pilot movie emphasizes this domestic, generational element of the conflict above the feelings of love Diana has for Steve, and the shift in emphasis makes for a rewarding and fascinating mother-daughter conflict on screen.

While Hippolyta loves Diana, she grows concerned that her daughter has become too involved with Trevor, too warlike, and too prejudiced against the Nazis. These concerns are dispelled during the two-part adventure "The Feminum Mystique," in which the Nazis discover Paradise Island and conquer it. The Nazi ringleader (John Saxon) forces the Amazons to mine Feminum for Hitler, and plans to send the women back to Berlin "for study and possible breeding." While the Amazons are genuinely horrified that war has come to their home and haven, some viewers may suspect that Hippolyta allowed the Nazis to conquer the island just to see if they were are as bad as Wonder Woman reported they were. When Hippolyta is convinced that the Nazis are genuinely evil and beyond reasoning with, she decides that they have failed her test and orders Diana to lead a rebellion to liberate the Amazons.[27] One of the Amazons who helps Diana overthrow the Nazi rule is Drusilla, a younger-sister figure played by Debra Winger, who is clearly inspired by the DC comics character Donna Troy (a.k.a. Wonder Girl).

Of course, while Hippolyta reveals in this story that she suspects her daughter and Major Trevor have a sexual relationship, it is not clear that she is correct in this assumption. The first season episodes feature several sly remarks that, like the double entendres peppering John Steed and Emma Peel's dialogue in *The Avengers* (1961–1969) series, makes viewers wonder whether the lead characters are lovers or just friends joking with one another, since no romantic encounters occur during the actual episodes. Whether or not their relationship is a sexual one, both Diana and Trevor are presented as equally respectable, heroic figures, and they work well together as a team when taking on villains like the Nazi counterfeiter codenamed "Wotan" in "The Last of the Two Dollar Bills." Episodes such as this present a model friendship/romance that serves as the 1970s "television action series" equivalent of a Spencer Tracey and Katharine Hepburn romance of equals.[28]

The sometimes arch, sexy dialogue between the leads is also part of the somewhat campy quality to the series. The show is never as campy as, say, the Adam West *Batman* television series, mostly because Carter plays Wonder Woman with great seriousness and integrity, and does not mock her own character. To that extent, the show fits perfectly Susan Sontag's definition of successful camp. According to Sontag, camp is "high spirited and unpretentious" (278), is anti-elitist in its sentiments, and features garish costuming, a fascination with the androgyne, and a "relish for the exaggeration of sexual characteristics and mannerisms" (279). Carter's Wonder Woman is certainly "flamboyantly female" thanks to her grand beauty and buxom figure. Also, as far as Sontag is concerned, the best "camp" is played as serious, while "camping," done deliberately, is less successful. At times, the series features guest actors in the role of villains, such as the Nazis in the premiere television movie, who are "camping" in a manner that is wince-inducing, while Carter's performance is more successful because it is serious without being humorless.

The series as a whole also grew less light-hearted during its second season as its setting was brought into (what was then) the present. It was revealed that, following the defeat of the Nazis, Wonder Woman returned to Paradise Island for several decades to live in peace with the Amazons. When word eventually reaches her of the existence of an underground, international terrorist ring armed with nuclear weapons, her fear of nuclear war prompts her to return to America to lead the fight against terrorism. Since the series moves from taking place during a "nostalgic" conflict of the past to a "realistic" conflict of the present, the tone becomes notably more somber. When Diana returns to the U.S., she is a veteran at overcoming culture shock and acclimates more easily the second time assuming an American identity. However, she is understandably shocked by the inflation that has raised rents markedly since the 1940s and is disappointed that women haven't come further in achieving equality with men since the end of the war.[29]

Wonder Woman as Feminist, Feminazi, Neo-Conservative, and Sex Symbol

It is somehow appropriate, perhaps symbolic, that the Carter series was cancelled in 1979. Its final episodes marked the end of the liberal 1970s and the beginning of twelve years of the Ronald Reagan and George H. W. Bush administrations, as well as the feminist backlash that accompanied them. During this time period, Wonder Woman's perception among the general public suffered. Even during the presidency of Bill Clinton, and the all-too-brief resurgence of feminist sentiments during the 1990s, the character was oddly absent from the public scene. This was especially strange, given the cult fandom generated by derivative characters such as *Xena: Warrior Princess* and *Buffy the Vampire Slayer* on television. In fact, Wonder Woman was a source of embarrassment to Lucy Lawless, the actress who played Xena. For years, Lawless refused to consider playing Wonder Woman, even though she was already playing an anti-hero variation of the character, because she saw the character as silly and one-dimensional. She even-

Xena (Lucy Lawless) looks remarkably like a Wonder Woman dressed in somber colors. More militant than Diana, Xena's circular weapon is a chakram instead of a coiled lasso, and she is more apt to brandish a sword and slay her enemies. Unlike Diana, who is innocent and unfailingly noble, Xena is haunted by a past as a war criminal that she strives to atone for.

tually relented and voiced Diana in a 2008 straight-to-DVD cartoon film *Justice League: New Frontier,* in part because she regarded Darwyn Cooke's interpretation of the character as more flawed and complex.

The sales of the *Wonder Woman* comic book, which have often not been good, were particularly low during the 1990s. As in the I Ching period, several of the writers and artists attached to the series tried to make the character more accessible to the largely male, conservative comic-book-buying audience by emphasizing her sexuality and/or downplaying her feminism. These alterations made Wonder Woman more like Jim Balent's ultrasexy 1990s era Catwoman, and Brian Pulido's ultimate "bad girl" Lady Death—hot, but in a very non-political, non-threatening way. During this period, readers of the comic paid far more attention than usual to Diana's breasts, and much less attention to what she was saying.

It was around this time that independent writer-artist Joseph Michael Linsner created "Dawn," the embodiment of the Earth Goddess, Gaea, who looked like a red-headed Wonder Woman—or Bettie Page. Unlike Wonder Woman, Dawn wears a wide variety of outlandishly erotic outfits, including a Gothic electric blue variant of a Disney Princess gown, low-riding jeans and a tight white T-shirt, and whips and chains and thorny roses over either a crimson suit of armor or a green teddy. An advocate of religious freedom who spent one storyline protecting teenage Wiccans from murderous, right wing Christians (1999's *Dawn: Return of the Goddess*), Dawn's political messages are punctuated by her sexiness in a very Marston-like manner. What is surprising is just how sexy she is. Wonder Woman, sultry as she can be, is a much tamer visual image than Dawn, who has been known to wear little more than knee-high boots, a bustier, and a pair of panties with a zipper running along the bottom for easy vagina access. Interestingly, annual conventions such as DragonCon often include Dawn lookalike contests judged by Linsner, with a sizable number of women dressing in these various outfits, suggesting that the character speaks to more than just men looking for a little soft-core comic book fun.

During a period when Dawn and Lady Death ruled the comic book shelves, it was beginning to look as if Wonder Woman was hopelessly out-of-date and, interestingly, nowhere near sexy enough for modern tastes. Fortunately, despite her lapse in popularity, some of Diana's appeal was rediscovered thanks to her inclusion in the *Justice League* cartoon (2001–2006), and many episodes of that series, especially those written by Dwayne McDuffie and Stan Berkowitz, depict her as a compelling, three-dimensional character. However, this new version of Diana is quite marshal and humorless—far more so than Carter's and Marston's visions of the character ever were—making her more like the imperious Batman or the belligerent Hawkgirl than she really should be.

In many ways, the Wonder Woman of the modern era featured in the *Justice League* cartoon is a top-to-bottom reinvention of Diana crafted by Alex Ross and Mark Waid for *Kingdom Come* (1996). That miniseries featured a bitter Wonder Woman of the future who has failed in her mission to bring peace to "man's world" and been exiled from Paradise Island. Stripped of her idealism and air of wise, "experienced innocence," this Wonder Woman is a tragic, Xena-like figure who attempts to bring peace to planet Earth by effectively trying to coax Superman into conquering the planet for her. When he appears not up to the task, she takes the lead, showing a growing militancy and mental instability as she dramatically kills one of her opponents, a Yugoslavian supervillain called Von Bach. Eventually, the paternalistic Batman and Superman try to get Diana to stand down and see reason, hoping to help her rediscover her inner idealist and become the "real" Wonder Woman once again. In these scenes, Superman and Batman appear to be morally and mentally centered, even as they themselves have made deeply flawed decisions and demonstrated Fascistic tendencies of their own throughout the story, while Wonder Woman seems consistently hysterical.

Ultimately, the tragic events of the story grant Wonder Woman a moment of clarity, and she rejects her new, warlike persona in favor of her classic role as ambassador of peace. Newly reformed, she is now a suitable mate for Superman, and becomes pregnant with his child. In an epilogue, Batman is named the baby's godfather. There is a happy ending here, especially for those who always saw DC Comics' three most iconic heroes as members of the same family anyway. It was also good to see Wonder Woman portrayed as a central figure in the DC Universe when she had been largely absent from major storylines for years. But there was an extent to which she was not recognizably the Wonder Woman of old.

Still, despite her antihero portrayal, Wonder Woman was saved from being a wholly unlikable character in *Kingdom Come* by Alex Ross' stunning artwork — which grants Wonder Woman sophistication, intelligence, and charisma as well as beauty — and by her awe-inspiring depiction as one of the most formidable combatants in the history of comic books. At times painted to resemble a Wagnerian Valkyrie or a Joan of Arc leading fighting men into battle, Wonder Woman is a sight to behold on the battlefield, dressed in golden armor, brandishing lances and axes, and fearlessly confronting an army of super-powered opponents. For many comic readers, those images of Wonder Woman clashing dramatically with Batman in a fierce aerial duel in *Kingdom Come* are *the* most memorable and iconic representations of Wonder Woman, and have effectively replaced the gentler, more conciliatory depiction of the character from the Marston comic books and the Lynda Carter series.

Since *Kingdom Come* and the *Justice League* cartoon reminded comic book fans that the character had great potential, Wonder Woman has had a renewed presence in the DC Comics line of comic books, playing especially prominent roles in *Justice League of America* comics and in epic graphic novels and miniseries such as *The OMAC Project* and *New Frontier*. However, the Wonder Woman who has appeared in these stories represents a significantly different brand of feminism than the one from the television series. Unlike earlier incarnations of the character, who would never consider killing, the new Wonder Woman is presented as too pragmatic and too ruthless to spare the life of an opponent she sees as both deadly dangerous and irredeemable. On the one hand, her position is presented as far more reasonable than Superman's and Batman's, who argue the position *that used to be taken by Diana herself* that it is always wrong to kill an enemy, even if that enemy is Adolf Hitler or the Joker. On the other hand, in both storylines, Diana is presented as being *too* violent and *too* ruthless to be truly heroic, and her honor and purity are somewhat stained by the blood on her hands.

In *New Frontier* (2004), during a segment set in Indo-China shortly before the Vietnam War, Wonder Woman liberates a group of women who have been raped and imprisoned by guards and enables the former victims to avenge themselves by machine-gunning their oppressors to death. A shocked Superman protests her role in the execution of the rapists instead of joining her and the vindicated women in a drink from a celebratory goblet of mead, so she demands that he leave. In *The OMAC Project* (2005), telepathic villain Maxwell Lord robs Superman of his free will and orders the Man of Steel to kill Batman and Lois Lane. When Wonder Woman determines that the only way to free Superman from Lord's influence is to kill Lord, she does so without compunction or guilt. Footage of her snapping Lord's neck with her bare hands is soon made public, causing Wonder Woman to be publicly disgraced, accused of betraying her pacifist convictions, and put on trial for murder. Although she is eventually cleared of all charges, she still surrenders her costume and title to skulk off into exile for a year. In both *New Frontier* and *The OMAC Project*, Diana has to suffer great public disgrace, penance, and physical beatings before either Superman or Batman deign to forgive her.

These storylines are not the only recent ones in which Diana has been criticized by her fellow heroes for being too much of an ideologue, too militaristic, and too underdressed. In *Wonder Woman: Spirit of Truth* (2001), Superman tells Diana that she is too much of an aristocrat and too arrogant for people to relate to, let alone listen to. He advises her to humble herself, live like a common woman, and dress more conservatively when visiting Muslim countries so as not to frighten the natives. In *JLA: Golden Perfect* (2003), even Wonder Woman's Lasso of Truth rebukes her for being too much of an ideologue. When Wonder Woman grows too overzealous in her potentially misguided protection of a young, Messianic boy, the lasso disintegrates, and the very concept of "truth" as a reality binding, Platonic form vanishes. Consequently, math and science no longer "work," fact and fiction blend, and the world is almost destroyed in a mystical tidal wave of moral relativism that sweeps creation. Only when Wonder Woman supplicates herself before the Fates is the lasso repaired, "truth" restored, and the created order stabilized. In addition to the humiliations Diana has suffered in these stories, she has been effectively fired and replaced on no less than three occasions since her life story was begun anew in 1987. First she was replaced by the Amazon Artemis, then by Hippolyta herself, and, most recently, by her former sidekick, the "Wonder Girl" Donna Troy. Diana has been killed and resurrected, made a goddess and then kicked out of Olympus, and her fellow Amazons have seen their Paradise Island invaded, destroyed, and shunted off into another dimension an absurd number of times.

Admittedly, many of these stories, on their own, have their share of high drama. Some, especially *New Frontier*, are wonderfully written and include some classic moments with the character. However, *collectively* these stories seem to rebuke Wonder Woman harshly even as they work to restore her to a position of prominence in the comic book world. The modern-day Diana is strong and admirable, but she is also frightening and reckless in a way that she arguably would not be if more women writers and artists were assigned to craft her adventures. While this latest version of Wonder Woman gets to play an interesting role as an agent of chaos in the DC universe, she is arguably the epitome of the "Feminazi" that Rush Limbaugh made famous in the 1990s when he compared abortion rights activists to perpetrators of the Holocaust. These days, Wonder Woman is a ruthless, sexless woman with blood on her hands who has more in common with her archenemies the Nazis than she would ever be willing to admit. The male writers who have penned her stories of late love to imply that Diana would be a lot nicer, and a lot happier, if she'd just have sex with Batman or Superman, put some more clothes on when she goes out in public, and shut up with the annoying politics already.

Even as the darker Wonder Woman has gained prominence in the comic book world, writers such as Phil Jiminez have worked hard to write and draw stories with the character that are truer to the legacy of a more liberal, kind-hearted Wonder Woman from both the early Marston comics and the Carter TV show. According to Jiminez, he draws Wonder Woman to look as much like Carter as possible because she "is the living, physical embodiment of this character." She brings to Wonder Woman "a sense of grace and style and dignity [and regality] which you don't often see in most female characters ... in comics today," who are usually presented "as sex vixens or ... kittenish or just as men in women's clothes."[30]

As an openly gay creator, Jiminez's more politically liberal sentiments have informed the way he writes the character. Sadly, but not unexpectedly, Jiminez's highly political tales garnered their share of negative fan reaction. For example, in *Wonder Woman*, Vol. 2, #170 (July 2001), Jiminez wrote a story in which Lois Lane interviewed Diana on a talk show modeled after "The View," and Diana openly discussed her political and religious philosophies. This is one of the monologues Jiminez, and co-scripter Joe Kelly, wrote for her:

> Women and their children must no longer fear abuse. *Anywhere* in the world. They must be given information that will help them remain economically self-sufficient, and in control of their bodies and reproductive lives. [My] Foundation's mission statement promotes the liberation of men, women, and children from the terrible problems that stem from antiquated religious philosophies and patriarchal fear — by educating them about alternatives. All human beings deserve to live on this planet without threat of violation, physical or spiritual, simply because of the body they were born in, the gender they were born to, or the region in which they live.

This dialogue provoked an angry letter from a pro-life Christian reader, Chris Jackson of Greenville, NC, which was published a few months later, in issue #173. Jackson felt that Wonder Woman's dialogue was an attack on "freedom of religion" and amounted to Marxist, anti–Christian, and pro-choice propaganda. As he wrote, "you've lost a longtime reader. Let me fill you in on a little secret: Most of us don't buy comic books to have our personal beliefs ridiculed or stoked by some funnybook writer." Editor Eddie Berganza replied to the letter by saying, "Wow. Sorry that Diana's message of tolerance exposed your intolerance. ... [i]f you feel that 'valuing each other simply because we exist' is a wrong message, then Diana would ask you to look more closely at the teachings of your beliefs."

In a September 14, 2010 e-mail interview with the author of this book, Jiminez revealed that, despite Jackson's anger:

> most of the responses to that issue were positive, and many still hold it up as a high point in her recent publishing career...
>
> As most know, I think that Diana is an inherently political character — she's about feminist politics, humanist politics, sex politics, the politics of war, etc. — and that fact is probably her downfall. What makes her so fascinating and endearing to me is also what makes her so controversial and so unlikeable to some; it's also one of the things that make her such a difficult property commercially. Wonder Woman's womanness is such a vital component of her character; I really think it's quite off putting for most men and many women who prefer to see her as just "one of the guys" so they aren't confronted with the very deep issues she was created to contend with.

It is, indeed, notable that often when great writers such as Jiminez, Trina Robbins, or Greg Rucka tackle Wonder Woman's liberal political beliefs — say, by having her fight domestic violence in *The Once and Future Story* (1998) or write a controversial non-fiction book analyzing contemporary culture in *Down to Earth* (2003–2004) — conservatives complain and respond by not buying the comic. DC Comics responds in kind by minimizing the political content or placing a greater emphasis on fight scenes with mythological opponents such as Circe or Medusa. Oftentimes fans claim they are reacting to bad writing more than bad politics, or they argue that controversial politics have no place in comic books marketed to children. Whatever the reason, the consequence is that the traditional-yet-still-progressive Wonder Woman has been replaced by a militant Wonder Woman — who, despite being a murderess, is more palatable to an audience that prefers to see an aggressive feminism unleashed on America's enemies in place of the more pacifistic feminism that is critical of American conservatism. Consequently, Wonder Woman has been, to a great extent, transformed from a nice person with accessible flaws into a Marvel Comics–style anti-hero, like the murderous Wolverine or the self-loathing Punisher. While some fans like a Marvel-style Wonder Woman better, Jiminez doesn't like how the heroism has been stripped away from so many DC characters like Wonder Woman in the name of making them "realistic":

Wonder Woman (voiced by Shannon Farnon) starred in the TV series *Super Friends* (Warner Bros., 1980–1984), alongside Batman and Robin, Superman, the Wonder Twins, the space monkey Gleek, and Aquaman and his trusty seahorse steed. In the series, Wonder Woman's relationships with these characters were always friendly and professional, even as they found themselves in stressful, face-to-face confrontations with the likes of a giant praying mantis. In comics such as *The OMAC Project, JLA: A League of One, New Frontier*, and *Kingdom Come*, Wonder Woman often finds herself in bitter conflict with her Super Friends (a.k.a. the members of the Justice League).

> For what it's worth, and I'm in a tiny minority I'm sure, I'm rather sick of "flawed" characters — because "flaw," it seems to me, is like a codeword for something else. Often, it allows characters not just to have problems, but to have PROBLEMS — drug addiction; gambling problems; dark, bloody pasts full of violence, etc. "Flaws" allow hero characters to be "morally ambiguous" and, quite frankly, I'm not sure what good that does any of us, if these characters are in anyway supposed to act like role models. It's one thing for a character to have a character flaw like self-doubt; or a hefty ego; or to be an irritating chatterbox, or a bit of an impulsive hothead. It's quite another for a character to behave so badly they could be considered villainous.
>
> My favorite comic character when I was a teenager was Donna Troy, the Wonder Girl of the *New Teen Titans*.... What I loved about her was that she wasn't overly flawed; she was a good, just, moral character, who did the right thing because that's what you were supposed to do. She got angry, she made mistakes, she tried to hard to be perfect, but it seems to me, these "flaws" are just as valid as a drug addiction or murderous streak. When I was younger, I was always attracted to characters who helped me think about my own sense of moral purpose in the world; if I had to choose between a straight character like Donna Troy whose biggest in-story character flaw was trying to be too much, too perfect, to too many people, and a gay character whose "flaw" made him/her almost impossible to discern from the villains s/he fights, I'll take Donna Troy any day. My role models, gay or straight, are people who remind me to do good, to be good, to make the world a better place. My boyfriend is an extraordinary human being in this way. I seek inspiration in my heroes, not validation; I have no need to have my own darker impulses justified by the characters I read about. But I do

have a need to see more people doing good than people doing bad (of course, my versions of "good" and "bad" may differ from everyone else's). I want to be reminded by my fictional, costume-wearing super-powered heroes that goodness and decency are possible and desirable traits worth celebrating.

Fortunately, the comic book portrayal of Wonder Woman as "ultimate badass" has evolved since her more single-minded portrayal in *Kingdom Come*, and the stories it influenced, and she became a more nuanced, sympathetic character in the hands of her first regular women writers: Jodi Picoult and Gail Simone. Picoult's Wonder Woman (from 2009's *Love and Murder*) was a good-humored and approachable portrayal of the character, harkening back to the innocent-but-wise Wonder Woman of the Perez era. But Picoult's tenure was sadly brief and artistically compromised by having to dovetail with the ultra-dark 2007 miniseries *Amazon's Attack*, written by Will Pfeiffer, in which the Amazons grow weary of American militarism and invade Washington, D.C. The tone of Picoult's writing was nigh irreconcilable with a miniseries that features a bewitched Hippolyta slicing the head off of the Lincoln Memorial, and it was not long before Picoult departed as writer. *Birds of Prey* veteran Gail Simone succeeded Picoult in 2007 and was the regular writer until July 2010.

Simone has revealed in interviews that she was initially reluctant to write Wonder Woman stories both because she was daunted by the responsibility of writing for a feminist icon, and because she feared she would be artistically pigeonholed as a woman writer of women's comics. However, after a grassroots fan campaign inspired DC Comics executives to approach Simone to take over the comic book, she found herself growing to love writing for the character. Perhaps most significantly, like George Perez, Phil Jiminez, and Dwayne McDuffie, Simone succeeded at presenting a version of Wonder Woman that synthesized the best elements of the ultimate warrior figure found in *Kingdom Come* with the peacemaker Gloria Steinem saw as the definitive vision of the heroine.

Simone frequently dramatized Wonder Woman's nearly supernatural ability to successfully call a truce in the middle of a fight-to-the death, and to transform an archenemy into a close friend simply by showing sisterly or maternal concern for her opponent, or candidly admitting her own imperfections. The effects of these scenes were often simultaneously inspiring and humorous, as when a grudge match between Wonder Woman and Giganta ends with the two of them sitting together on a beach, commiserating about how difficult men are to date.[31]

Equally dramatic, often in a thrilling and shocking manner, are moments when Diana encounters a wholly irredeemable, Satanic villain, and realizes her only option is to kill it, as she does in both *Ends of the Earth* (2008) and *Rise of the Olympian* (2009). Indeed, after seventy years of unending combat with Ares, the God of War, Wonder Woman finally loses patience with his interference in human affairs and decides to bury an axe in his head, killing him instantly.[32] It is the kind of brutal, decisive act that one might more expect from Conan the Barbarian than the superhero most likely to quote Mohandas Gandhi, but Simone grants Wonder Woman the power and the moral authority to slay the God of War with relative impunity, especially after the devastation and untold suffering he has caused in his lifetime.

And yet, Simone's version of Diana is not just a warrior. Her Wonder Woman also retains some of the humor and sensitivity found in Picoult's characterization, and she is not too proud to bake mouth-watering desserts for members of the Justice League or engage in *Sex and the City*–style banter with "sister" superhero Black Canary. Simone gradually developed a fun, believable friendship between the two characters, and has revealed that Canary deeply respects Diana, who she regards as superior to both Superman and Batman because Diana encompasses both of their one-dimensionally "light" and "dark" personalities and value systems.[33] Canary's respect for Diana does not prevent her from teasing Wonder Woman for being a closeted lesbian and having breasts that are considered "a national treasure" on nerd lust websites, but it is through this teasing that Simone explores their genuine affection and easy rapport.[34]

Black Canary's jokes about Amazonian sexual proclivities notwithstanding, Simone's Wonder Woman notably initiated a romance with U.S. government national security agent Thomas Andrew Tresser and considered having his child. However, in Simone's stories, Diana's deeper motivations are never instantly apparent or uncomplicated. For example, Diana's interest in motherhood may have had more to do with her concern over the future of a depleted Amazon race than it does her affection for Tresser.[35] Maternal anxieties are a recurring theme in Simone's stories, as Wonder Woman is frequently faced with wounded child figures, including her space-gladiator cousin Theana, the vengeful Children of Ares, and Achilles, the reluctant son of Zeus. In *Wonder Woman: The Circle* (2008), Simone also revealed that Wonder Woman's birth was nearly prevented by Alkyone, a member of Hippolyta's imperial guard, who feared that other Amazons would be jealous if the queen, and the queen alone, were allowed to become a mother.

For Simone, Wonder Woman is a morally complex figure living in a media age in which motivations are oversimplified or deliberately misrepresented by political opponents. In the comic book world, as in real life, pundits on conservative talk radio or liberal MSNBC often try to paint the motives of public figures as purely selfish or purely selfless, liberal or conservative, hawkish or dovish, "good" or "evil." That is why two of Simone's most evocative stories with the character involve Wonder Woman's public image. The first, *A Star in the Heavens*, involves Diana's fears that an upcoming Hollywood movie about her life would amount to a Michael Bay–style special-effects spectacular featuring crude sex jokes and intimations that feminists are frigid and complain too much about men leaving the toilet seat up. Diana's fears wind up being well founded, as the film clearly depicts Hercules as a hero who tamed cold Amazon hearts, while Diana and her mother are portrayed as sex-starved wenches fighting one another for the right to visit his bedchamber.[36]

The second, *A Murder of Crows*, features five demonic private school boys who undermine Wonder Woman's reputation among the general public by gossiping about her and intimating that she is an intellectual elitist, socialist, and glory-seeker. The villains are clearly Simone's swipe at conservative pundits such as Glenn Beck, Rush Limbaugh, and Sean Hannity, who make millions of dollars a year destroying the reputations of liberal activists and casting aspersions on the motivations of President Barack Obama, whom Wonder Woman clearly represents in this unusually effective political allegory.[37]

Wonder Woman in the 21st Century

One of the problems many superheroes face is that, over the years, they become rarefied and sanitized caricatures of themselves, burdened by decades worth of previous adventures' continuity. Hence the occasional "rebooting" of their narratives, in which their origin story is retold in a modern context, their appearance and personalities are given refits, and an attempt is made to simultaneously bring the character back to its roots and transform it from a figure of fan nostalgia to one of contemporary relevance. In some cases, these attempts at making an old character "trendy" were disastrous (the American *Godzilla*). In other cases, the general public felt their interest revived in the franchise while some fans of the original version were disappointed (J.J. Abrams' *Star Trek*). In a very few instances, the re-imagination was an enormous success with fans and lay viewers alike (the Daniel Craig *Casino Royale*).

Beginning with issue 600 in June 2010, J. Michael Straczynski — screenwriter of *The Changeling* (2008) and creator of *Babylon 5*— was brought on board to give Wonder Woman just such a radical refit with a storyline called *Odyssey*. As a plot device to change Wonder Woman's entire life story, Straczynski has a time-traveling villain destroy Paradise Island when Wonder Woman is still a baby. The surviving Amazons flee to New York and form an underground society of their own within the city, where they raise Diana to adulthood as both a full-fledged Amazon and a modern American woman. This version of Diana has supernatural visions of her old life and a desire to change history back to its original path, to restore both her traditional timeline and the Amazon society.[38]

There were many reasons for this sudden, radical revision of the character's look and history. According to Straczynski, over the years, Wonder Woman has "ossified" to the point where readers see the character as matronly, if not grandmotherly, and are disturbed by the prospect of her "telling a joke, or being flirty, or dancing." "When people start to see your character as a grandmother, or a prude, or inflexible ... something's profoundly wrong," he said.[39]

Dissatisfied with her new costume, Wonder Woman lassos artist Jim Lee and confronts him about the "look" he designed for her in 2010 ("Wonder Woman Vs. Jim Lee" illustrated by Dean Kotz).

His goal in the character redesign is to make Wonder Woman more like the leather pants–wearing Trinity from the *Matrix* films — "strong, sexy, dynamic, powerful." Indeed, her new costume, designed by renowned comic book artist Jim Lee, blends a Trinity-inspired street-fighter look with the classic Wonder Woman costume; it replaces the oft-criticized star-spangled shorts with dark blue tights, and deepens the color scheme from sky blue to midnight blue and bright red to maroon. She retains her lasso and a more stylized rendering of her belt, bracelets, "WW" chest logo, and tiara, and adds a necklace and short blue jacket as accessories.

The wardrobe change garnered a characteristically shrill response from Fox News, as an article by Jo Plazza ("New Wonder Woman Loses Patriotic Costume in Favor of 'Globalized' Duds") decried the deemphasizing of the American flag elements in the new outfit. The story did, however, quote Lynda Carter's reaction to the new costume: "[Wonder Woman's] got an attitude, and if this is the new thing she wants to wear, well by God she's going to wear it," Carter said. "And I like that. And I hope somewhere in the story someone mentions, where's the old one? And she says, 'Get over it.'"

While the new look had its detractors, Straczynski observed that "virtually every woman I know tends to look at her current costume and say, 'How does she fight in that thing without all her parts and pieces flying out?' She needs to look as strong, capable and resourceful as she is. As another female friend put it, 'What woman wears the same outfit for sixty years without accessorizing?'" His intention in updating the character is to be true to her spirit, and not make her unrecognizable, as she was when she sported "a regrettable mod look of the 60s."[40]

Ultimately, the *Odyssey* story was almost universally condemned by fans. However, the Straczynski reboot did herald a broader, universe-wide reboot of the DC universe (dubbed the post–*Flashpoint* "DCnU") in 2011, complete with 52 new superhero comics beginning at #1. A retooled version of Superman was fashioned by Grant Morrison and George Perez, the Justice League was reinvented by Geoff Johns, and a *reboot of Straczynski's reboot* of Wonder Woman was launched with Brian Azzarello's *Wonder Woman* #1).[41]

But the various "Dianas" featured in comic books and on screens are not the only possible iterations of the character. There is also the iconic figure that is bigger than any one writer, artist, or flawed superhero narrative. More than anything, that figure is an ideal. As Lillian Robinson, author of "Wonder Women: Feminism and Super Heroes," observed, Wonder Woman *is* still relevant. She can still be a hero, and a role model, even to the young women of today:

> Anyone who realizes that she has the power within her to make changes, not just for herself, but for women, can be Wonder Woman. You have to take what she does and extend it into the terms of your real world. If you want to fly through the glass ceiling, if you want to bring about an end to domestic violence, if you want to bring pay equity for working women, she's there to be that kind of icon.[42]

Whether Wonder Woman will succeed in inspiring young women today will partly depend on who gets to tell stories with the character, and on how her image is "marketed" to the young. If her comic books continue to be drawn by artists who are masters at rendering Diana as luscious eye-candy for horny men of all ages, women will likely be too disgusted by the display to embrace the character as anything more than a degrading, *Sin City*–style pretense at feminism.[43] If she is used only as an image to merchandise, perhaps as one of many "outfits" to slip on a Barbie doll, then her feminist message truly will be smothered by corporate suits. And if she continues to be an Amazon in the traditional sense, a relentless, bloodthirsty foe of Third World dictators, then her appeal will not outlive the marshal sensibilities of the Bush-Cheney White House years. However, it is equally possible that Robinson is right, and the world is waiting for Wonder Woman to return as a positive role model for women across the world. With luck, Wonder Woman stories of the future, whether written by women or men, will do the character justice. If so, perhaps these creators will have better luck presenting a progressive Wonder Woman to the public whose appeal will hearken back to the heyday of the original 1940s comic books and the Lynda Carter television series, which inspired men and women alike to work towards the creation of a more just and peaceful world where men and women could finally face one another as equals, and not as rivals.

THREE

Spider-Man as Benedict Arnold, Objectivist, and Class Warrior

Did it ever occur to you that maybe ... just maybe ... if you're nice to people, they might *let* you rule the world?—Spider-Man, speaking to Ra's al Ghul[1]

I was always into the Spider-Man/Batman model [of superhero]. The guys who have too many powers, like Superman, that always made me think they weren't really earning their superhero status. It's a little too easy. Whereas Spider-Man and Batman, they have some inner turmoil. They get knocked around a little bit.—Barack Obama[2]

Spider-Man Stories in the Age of Enron

Between 2002 and 2007, within the cultural context of both the Enron scandals and the Bush-era "war on terror," the Sam Raimi–directed trilogy of *Spider-Man* movies were made and released. Class conflict issues have formed the subtext of Spider-Man stories since the beginning, but stories of recent years have dealt more directly with corporate malfeasance and economic injustice in America thanks to the Enron scandals, the middle class squeeze, the Bush-Obama Wall Street bailouts, and anxieties over the conservative policies of the past several presidents. If there is a consistent theme to Spider-Man narratives, it is that the superhero's alter ego, Peter Parker, wants to be rich, famous, and recognized, and he will take virtually every opportunity that arises to jump social classes. His desire to be rich isn't completely selfish since he often needs money to pay for his ailing Aunt May's frequent, skyrocketing medical bills, but he also feels entitled to wealth because he is a genius with unrealized potential, and a large grant—or, at the very least, a living wage—could help him finally realize that potential.[3]

One of the central themes of Spider-Man stories produced during the Bush era is that corporations have so stacked the deck against financial upward mobility, and so decimated the American middle class, that Peter will never rise to a position of wealth and power unless he sacrifices all his ideals in the process, and becomes a de facto member of the Bush Administration. As a young man tempted to abandon traditional family values of selflessness and decency on the road to making his fortune in the big city, Peter resembles the callow, corruptible protagonists from *Great Expectations*, *The Great Gatsby*, and *Wall Street*. The key moral question surrounding this conflict is: will Spider-Man be able to retain his status as a hero if he sells out and becomes an official member of the right-wing American establishment?

While ostensibly a satire of Spider-Man by libertarian comic book writer Peter Bagge,

The Megalomaniacal Spider-Man (2002) posits the somewhat plausible idea that, if Peter had grown up without his Uncle Ben's strong moral example, he would have become the greedy CEO of Spider-Man, Inc. In the story, Peter becomes enraptured by the writings of Ayn Rand, takes advantage of his fans, and refuses to do a fundraiser for UNICEF because he despises the United Nations.[4] While Peter has not grown quite so selfish and mercenary in his regular monthly comic book, he has come close on more than one occasion.

For example, in a 2008 storyline written by Dan Slott, "Peter Parker: Paparazzi" (*Amazing Spider-Man* #558–560), Peter checks his morals at the door of *The Daily Bugle* and decides to earn more money than he ever dreamed of by obtaining compromising photographs of a Hollywood movie star and his secret new love. When Peter accepts the job, he loses the respect of his highly principled mentor, Joe "Robbie" Robertson, and his best friend, Harry Osborne, who has himself been dogged by paparazzi for most of his life. Later, Peter gets to know the Hollywood actor he is stalking and feels intense guilt when the actor turns out to be a nice person. When Peter tells his boss, newspaper magnate Dexter Bennett, that he has the pictures, but won't sell them to the paper at any price, Bennet ruthlessly blacklists Peter out of a career in journalism. In this story, as in many previous misadventures in which Peter is tempted to the dark side, he invariably chooses to do the right thing in the end but only after he has committed himself so much to the wrong cause that he cannot extract himself from the dark path he has chosen without great personal cost.

To best understand Peter's recurring dilemma, one needs to take a closer look at the "real world" corporate culture that Spider-Man has alternated between opposing and joining forces with, especially the corporate culture as symbolized by Enron. When the Enron Corporation went bankrupt in 2001, its employees' retirement plans, based heavily on the value of the energy company's stock, were devastated. Naturally, several executives with foreknowledge of the company's precarious position granted themselves "golden parachute" retirements before the company imploded, so they did not suffer the same fate. Nevertheless, in 2004 and 2006, two central figures in the Enron scandal — Ken Lay, Enron's CEO and Chairman, and Jeff Skilling, Enron's president — were convicted of multiple federal felony charges, including doctoring accounting records and defrauding shareholders.[5] Liberal activist and social commentator Barbara Ehrenreich was surprised by the trial verdicts, noting that, historically, very few corporate criminals are ever punished for their crimes. She observed that, "what was at stake in the Enron trial was not just criminal justice, but democracy itself. Call it the first outbreak of the next American revolution — against our overfed, unappointed, corporate royalty."[6] She added:

> American corporations ... live in a bubble of privilege, generally exempted from scrutiny until, as at Enron, they go wilding and suck their companies dry. Their pay is set by their true class peers, the CEOs who populate boards of directors, and these fellows know that rising pay for one CEO lifts all yachts, for the simple reason that CEO pay is often based on a survey of other CEOs' pay. There is no limit, in other words, to their plunderings.[7]

Notably, the charges against Lay were vacated in the wake of his death, and the U.S. Supreme Court vacated several of the charges against Skilling on June 24, 2010.[8] However, in the wake of the Enron scandal, and reports of corporate abuses that have been aired since the start of the Great Recession, populist anger against white-collar crime has been at a boiling point.

Spider-Man has largely been recognized as the ultimate "Everyman" superhero, as much a "regular guy" as a demigod. Given the contemporary "regular guy" anger, one would assume that Peter would be equally angry with evil corporations. However, in a sense Peter is somewhat naïve about corporate corruption. A part of him embraces Ayn Rand's view of corporate success as the greatest sign of freedom in a democracy. Most of the time he also believes that the best way to go from being penniless to being well paid is to become multibillionaire Tony Stark's toady, not to pit himself against Stark, corporate America, and the military industrial complex. That is, in his mind, a battle he cannot win.

The Temptation of Peter Parker

Superman was born great. Batman became great through years of training. Spider-Man had greatness thrust upon him. As unlikely an agent of "divine will" as David, a shepherd chosen to become king of the Israelites, Peter Parker was an orphaned science geek who received his super powers during a freak accident at a science exhibition. In the first Spider-Man story, *Amazing Fantasy* #15 (1962), an irradiated spider bit Peter's hand, preternaturally endowing him with "the proportionate strength of a spider," the ability to stick to any surface, a sixth sense warning him of imminent danger that he playfully calls a "spider sense," and uncanny speed and agility.

Unlike the exceptionally selfless Superman, Spider-Man's first instinct is not to use his amazing new powers to help other people, or to fight crime, but to seek fame and fortune. Keeping his new powers a secret from his guardians, Aunt May and Uncle Ben, Peter sews himself a red-and-blue spider costume and uses his expertise as chemist and engineer to design a super-glue "webbing" and a wrist-gun to fire it.[9] Thus garbed, he begins a career as a professional wrestler and featured guest on television variety shows such as *The Tonight Show* and *The Ed Sullivan Show*. Unconcerned with anyone but himself, Peter fails to intervene when he has the opportunity to apprehend a fleeing mugger, because crime fighting doesn't concern him. Tragically, Peter later returns home to discover that the same thief he failed to capture broke into the Parker family home and shot and killed Uncle Ben. In the aftermath of the killing, Peter adopts Uncle Ben's moral code that "With great power comes great responsibility," and he dedicates the use of his powers to stopping criminals so that no one else will have to lose a loved one to violent crime the way that he did.

From *Spider-Man* (Sony Pictures, 2002): Tobey Maguire plays the nerdy-but-handsome Peter Parker, the high school science whiz and freelance newspaper photographer who moonlights as Spider-Man.

Peter's ambition to look out for himself and only himself is one of the reasons he remains haunted by the memory of his Uncle Ben, even sometimes seeing visions of his disapproving uncle when he strays from the path of righteousness. Spider-Man is both guilty and not guilty of his uncle's death, but he blames himself entirely for it because his real sin was not in his failure to catch the thief before the murder was committed, but in the shame he felt about his failure to follow the example of his uncle's simple blue-collar decency. The first *Spider-Man* film (2002), directed by Raimi, makes this theme even more overt than the original comic book does when it includes a scene in which Peter angrily tells his uncle to "stop pretending to be" his father when Ben expressed concern that Peter was becoming aggressive, self-centered, and secretive. It was to be their last conversation before Ben was killed.[10]

Raimi's *Spider-Man* film is both a faithful adaptation of two of the character's most famous comic stories—the origin story from *Amazing Fantasy* #15 and *The Death of Gwen Stacy*—and a pseudo-remake of the Douglas Sirk film *Written on the Wind* (1956). Multi-billionaire scientist Norman Osborne (Willem Dafoe) is disappointed in his complacent son Harry (James Franco), who has no natural scientific aptitude. Norman secretly wishes that his son's lower-middle-class best friend Peter (Tobey Maguire) were his real heir, because Peter is an undiscovered child prodigy languishing in public school, and he lavishes attention on Peter, making Harry secretly jealous. Meanwhile, Peter's childhood sweetheart, Mary Jane (Kirsten Dunst), initially chooses to date Harry over Peter, mainly because Harry is wealthy, but she later repents the decision and chooses the financially struggling Peter as a more appropriate love interest. (Amusingly, these relationship dynamics are exactly the same as in *Written on the Wind*, in which Rock Hudson plays the role of "Peter," Robert Stack is "Harry," and Lauren Bacall is "MJ.") Corporate America is portrayed poorly in the film. Peter's guardian, Uncle Ben, is laid off from his job as an electrician after a lifetime of faithful service at the same job, while Norman Osborn is removed as CEO from the corporation he himself founded by board members who hope to boost market share values with a change of leadership. Uncle Ben is resigned to his fate and his own inability to find a new job at his age, but Osborne fights back. He becomes the Green Goblin, an evil Objectivist in a Kabuki mask who, unlike Ayn Rand, is known for flying on a bat-shaped glider and throwing grenades and giant razor blades at his enemies—especially the members of Oscorp's board of trustees. The Goblin attempts to recruit Spider-Man as an ally, because he sees in Spider-Man a kindred spirit—another extraordinary individual oppressed by the unintelligent and jealous masses—but Spider-Man refuses to join the Goblin in his crime spree. In the conflict that follows, the Green Goblin is killed.

Interestingly enough, the soap opera–style narrative does not end when the film does. In the fashion of the comic books, and the *Lord of the Rings* trilogy, Spider-Man's story stretches into the next two films, making the *Spider-Man* trilogy as much one film as it is three distinct films. In *Spider-Man 2*, a 2004 film co-written by Pulitzer Prize–winning author Michael Chabon, Peter has spent so much time as Spider-Man that he is squandering his college education by sleeping through class and neglecting his assignments, thereby alienating himself from mentors such as Dr. Connors, who could potentially open up doors for him in the scientific research community after graduation. Meanwhile, Peter struggles to pay the exorbitant rent for his squalid Manhattan apartment, making money by delivering pizzas and getting paid paltry sums from newspaperman J. Jonah Jameson for his Spider-Man photographs. Fortunately, by the end of the film, he finds a way to be both Peter Parker and Spider-Man comfortably. He also redeems himself in the eyes of Dr. Connors and wins the ever-opportunistic Mary Jane away from Jonah's celebrity astronaut son, John.

At the beginning of *Spider-Man 3* (2007), Peter is blissfully happy because he is in love with Mary Jane and has become famous and respected as Spider-Man, even if the world doesn't yet recognize the scientific genius of Peter Parker, college undergraduate. As he says to Mary Jane, half-thoughtfully, half-boastingly, "I'm just a nerdy kid from Queens. Do I deserve this?" However, Mary Jane's acting career crumbles even as Peter's reputation as a superhero soars, so she is forced to watch, jealously, as her boyfriend is becoming a success while her dreams start to slip away. One of the film's central themes is life's uncertainty and the unscrupulous things people are willing to do to ensure their own success and financial security. The film features a sympathetic, working-class villain in the form of Flint Marko (a.k.a. the Sandman), who turns to crime to raise money to pay the hospital bills for his dying daughter, and an unredeemable cretin of a freelance news photographer, Eddie Brock, who is willing to fake news photographs to make a name for himself.[11]

Since Sandman is suffering from some of the same financial troubles Peter has been, and needs to secure affordable treatment for his daughter, he is presented as someone who needs to be sympathized with, not imprisoned or killed. Once Spider-Man learns this, he and Sandman come to an understanding of one another, and forgive each other. The mutual understanding that follows results in an ending that confounds all audience expectations: Peter and Mary Jane end their romance, but remain friends, and the hero does not dispatch the villain like Saint George slaying a dragon.[12]

Coincidentally or not, the comic books published during the same period that these films were released were equally focused on the socio-economic status of the entire cast of characters. Class injustice and the evils of multinational corporations were central to the *Ultimate Spider-Man* stories written by Brian Michael Bendis, which feature a high school age Peter Parker at the start of his career, and *Amazing Spider-Man* stories written by J.M. Straczynski, which feature a "thirtysomething" version of the character. In one of Bendis' most overtly political narratives, *Ultimate Spider-Man and His Amazing Friends*, Spider-Man has an unexpected heart to heart with one of his rogue's gallery, the Shocker, who turns out to be no mere thug, but a former inventor with a grudge against his old employer, the corporation Roxxon, which stole the patents for his inventions. Shocker says:

> Let me be the one that tells you how it is! In the big boy world [...] rich people screw *everyone*! And not in a cliché way ... in a truly mean, nasty, uncaring, inhuman way.
>
> They ... take those who are creative or ... imaginative, ... and they *steal* from them and then they destroy them. Why? Because they *hate* those of us who are creative. They *need* us and they *hate* us. They hate us because we are what they know they will *never* be ... they will never have that feeling, that *rush*, to have invented something from nothing.
>
> So yeah, a big company like Roxxon hires a guy like me to create for them and then when they get my best work ... do they reward me? No.... They ruin me.

Spider-Man can relate to the Shocker's anger because, despite his ability to invent an array of gadgets, he has never successfully sold a patent, joined a think tank, or translated any of his genius into regular income, and he still has trouble paying rent each month [see pp. 266–267 for *Big Time* discussion].[13] However, Straczynski introduced the idea that Peter would eventually want the salary and medical benefits of a full-time job, and wrote a storyline in which Peter became a chemistry teacher at the same high school he had attended years before. Straczynski's veteran, thirtysomething Peter is more gregarious than the emotionally stunted teenage Spider-Man, especially since he has both a happy and a dramatically interesting marriage to MJ, but his success does not make him selfish or forgetful of his responsibilities to others. Straczynski's Spider-Man embraces egalitarian politics, often heroically defending the poor, the homeless, and the orphaned. He famously depicted Spider-Man at Ground Zero on the morning of September 11, 2001, helping police, fire fighters, and EMT workers clear the rubble, treat the wounded, and remove the bodies of the dead.[14]

Straczynski's Spider-Man was not the same loner and misanthrope he had occasion to be in the past; he was now a team player eager to enlist and serve his country as a soldier against the war on terror. Responding to Captain America's call to become part of a superhero team called the New Avengers, Spider-Man quickly showed signs of becoming a central and indispensable member of the group, and his deduction skills led them far in their first major confrontation with the neo–Nazi terrorist group Hydra.[15] In fact, in a surprising and near-unprecedented moment, Captain America himself praised Spider-Man for his heroism, and the compliment was granted the dramatic weight of a king bestowing a knighthood on a serf.

However, Spider-Man's sudden success and respectability as a superhero did not satisfy him, since he remained a relative underachiever in his civilian life. Peter finds himself in a philosophical mood one day, and asks his high school students a question that is not directly applicable to science class:

> PETER: The question is ... is the system fair to the least of us?
>
> FIRST STUDENT: I ... uhm ... I didn't study this part of—
>
> PETER: It's not a study question. It's a *you* question. What do *you* think? We know the system works for guys with lots of money, for corporations, but is it fair to everybody else?
>
> SECOND STUDENT: I get it, but, like, what's the point? You go to a big important college, you got big important family ... you got it made. ... You think anybody from here ever made it big? Ever went anywhere?
>
> PETER: I came out of here. I graduated from this very high school.
>
> SECOND STUDENT: [Is silent for a moment and looks down, then says] Yo, no disrespect, but ... I think you just kinda made my point. Y'know?[16]

Significantly, this conversation sets the stage for the Marvel Universe's *Civil War*, in which Spider-Man is finally given the opportunity to achieve complete respectability, but the cost is betraying many of his friends in the superhero community. True to form, it is a cost he is initially willing to pay. In 2006 and 2007, Straczynski worked with a team of writers—including Mark Millar, Paul Jenkins, and Brian Michael Bendis—to craft a storyline called *Civil War*. In *Civil War*, the superheroes of the Marvel Universe are so divided over the debate that raged in this country during George W. Bush's presidency, between those who

Spider-Man arrives at Ground Zero on September 11, 2001, too late to prevent the al-Qaeda–hijacked airplanes from crashing into the World Trade Center. He encounters survivors of the attack, who demand to know where he was. From *The Amazing Spider-Man* volume 2 #36 (Marvel Comics, December 2001, written by J. Michael Straczynski and illustrated by John Romita, Jr.).

favor protecting civil liberties over strengthening national security and those who believe the reverse — that suspending civil liberties during wartime is necessary for the preservation of public safety — that they literally went to war with one another over it.

For example, in 2003, in our reality, U.S. Attorney General John Ashcroft advocated the U.S.A. Patriot Act as a means of closing "gaping holes in law enforcement's ability to collect vital intelligence information on terrorist enterprises," of "meeting the challenges posed by new technologies and new threats," and increasing cooperation between law enforcement agencies (99). Constitutional law Professor Susan Herman, in contrast, wrote in 2001 that the Patriot Act was a frightening expansion of the powers of the Executive Branch of government and another step towards the totalitarian, Big Brother society predicted by George Orwell in *1984* (109). By and large, the *Civil War* storyline portrayed the faction represented by Tony Stark (a.k.a. Iron Man), which favored national security over civil liberties in the style of John Ashcroft, as the villains. The group led by Captain America, which opposed the government's initiatives to limit the rights of the individual, in the spirit of Susan Herman, was portrayed as the story's heroic underdogs.

The initiating incident of the *Civil War* storyline is the nuclear destruction of Stamford, Connecticut, which was obliterated by the incompetence of inexperienced superheroes who, unsupervised by the U.S. military, accidentally caused a nuclear-powered supervillain to detonate. The event mirrored the trauma caused by 9/11 in our world and the resulting wave of public anger and panic. Anticipating a public outcry demanding that all rogue superheroes reveal their secret identities to the world and only fight crime under the auspices of the police and the American military, Stark advocates that the superhero community support, and comply with, the U.S. Superhero Registration Act. The Act, an expansion of the principles that had previously been included in the Mutant Registration Act, demands that all rogue superheroes, Spider-Man included, publicly reveal their secret identities and sign up with a recognized branch of law enforcement, homeland security, or the military. All heroes who fail to register are considered criminals and traitors, and find themselves as hunted and reviled as the supervillains they had once pursued.

Faced with a choice of either becoming as much of a wanted man as Doctor Octopus or finally finding respectability by standing tall beside Stark, Peter joins Stark (see *The Road to Civil War* and *Civil War*). He does so partly in response to years of reading J. Jonah Jameson's editorials, which perpetually ask what right Spider-Man has to fight crime if he is not a licensed or deputized member of a legitimate law enforcement organization. In signing up with Stark, Spider-Man thinks that he will finally be free of Jonah's defamatory newspaper editorials. At Stark's request, and with the blessing of Aunt May and Mary Jane, Spider-Man calls a press conference and unmasks on live television, thereby encouraging other superheroes to follow suit in the name of full disclosure and a safer America.

Thanks largely to Spider-Man's example and the public anger over Stamford, Stark soon wins popular support for the Registration Act. However, the American people do not realize that Stark is growing rapidly more zealous in his efforts to imprison insurgents and crush political opposition to his agenda. In fact, Spider-Man is shocked when he learns that Stark has secretly begun imprisoning anyone who opposes his initiative — even superheroes labeled "traitors" because of their conscientious objections to his leadership — in an "other"-dimensional prison in the Negative Zone that serves as metaphor for America's extraordinary rendition policy and the detainment of enemy combatants in Guantanamo Bay.[17] Angered that these captives for life have been imprisoned without trial or possibility of reprieve, Spider-Man has the unpleasant realization that he has dedicated himself to the wrong side. Once Peter tells Aunt May and Mary Jane what Stark has done, they agree that it is time for them to leave Stark's protection and go on the run. Peter defects to Captain America's army of insurgents, officially announcing the reasons for his change of allegiance on Channel 9 News:

> We all want to be safe. We all want to know we can go to bed at night and have a good chance of waking up without somebody in a costume blowing up the building. But there's a point where the end doesn't justify the means, if the means require us to give up not just our identities, but who and what we are as a country....
>
> ... I was brought up to believe that some things are worth dying for. If the cost of silence is the soul of the country ... then the price is too high.
>
> I cannot, in good conscience, continue to support the Registration Act as it has been created and enforced. I was wrong. And from this day on, I will do everything in my power to oppose the act and anyone attempting to intimidate and arrest those who also oppose the act, in the cause of freedom.[18]

No sooner is the speech broadcast than Stark orders Peter's arrest on the grounds of high treason. For his part, Captain America was delighted by Peter's change of heart. However, as poetic as this speech is, many of those who had been with Captain America from the beginning of the Civil War were reluctant to accept Peter on their team because of the damage he had done to their cause. Two other major consequences came of Peter's disassociating himself from Stark and the protection of the U.S. Government. First, shocked by the revelation that Spider-Man has been secretly working for him all these years, Jonah publicly fires Peter and threatens the journalistic fraud with a multimillion-dollar lawsuit for undermining the reputation of *The Daily Bugle.* Secondly, finally aware who his longtime nemesis really is, the Kingpin of Crime orders an assassin to murder the three Parkers. Aunt May is shot and fatally wounded, leaving Peter feeling responsible for her death.[19] Unusually for comic books, the *Civil War* story has a tragic ending. When Stark ultimately defeats Captain America's forces, the Captain is assassinated and Spider-Man is forced to become a fugitive. Stark, meanwhile, has won, but he has to face the reality that his former friends have all come to hate him for the tyranny of his rule, and his few allies are comprised largely of new recruits to his cause and a handful of comrades from the original Avengers.

By the end of the *Civil War* storyline, Spider-Man is a man with few friends who is seen as a Benedict Arnold by most everyone except the New Avengers, his immediate family, and his eternally loyal first girlfriend, Jonah's secretary Betty Brandt. He is fully aware that, should he be captured, he will likely be imprisoned in the Negative Zone, the very same facility that outraged him and inspired him to betray Stark. Had such a story been written, it would have demonstrated the extent to which Stark, and the U.S. government of the Marvel Universe, had become unjust, jailing heroes such as Spider-Man for opposing America's abandonment of human rights. Such a story would also have evoked Henry David Thoreau's 1849 tract, *Civil Disobedience,* in which he expressed the notion that "Under a government which imprisons any unjustly, the true place for a just man is also prison" (9).

Despite the presence of some occasionally well-expressed conservative sentiments by Stark and his compatriots, the *Civil War* story as a whole, and the Spider-Man installments in particular, are essentially an indictment of President George W. Bush's policies. By presenting a world in which Spider-Man, the Everyman hero, is a fugitive from the U.S. government, *Civil War* asks us the extent to which average citizens of the *real* world—who are guilty of no crime but being liberal, criticizing Bush, or striving to redeem the United States' status in the court of world opinion—can be spied upon, publicly condemned, branded traitors, and even imprisoned. They ask us to remember that dissenters are often the bravest, and most patriotic, among us, despite the fact that they are derided and vilified by the establishment and by television pundits.

As S.T. Joshi observed in *The Angry Right: Why Conservatives Keep Getting It Wrong* (2006):

> We are..., at this moment, having to deal with the historical accident that a conservative Republican was (however illegitimately) in the White House during the terrorist attacks of 9/11. This provided a splendid opportunity for conservatives to jump on the patriotism bandwagon and hamstring their opponents. The slightest criticism of George W. Bush and his military policies (or even his social and economic policies), no matter how blundering, hypocritical, self-serving, or politically motivated those policies were, caused conservatives to circle the wagons and defend their dubiously elected president at all costs — even at the cost of winking at their party's derelictions. It is perhaps no accident that accusations that every liberal, or every member of the Democratic Party, is a traitor surfaced after 9/11, and involved ... a radical rewriting of history not only that Democrats were soft on Communism (conservatives' wild exaggerations of Communist infiltration of American government and society conveniently forgotten) but also soft on terrorism [256].

In the cultural context of an American society in which self-styled patriots Michael Savage, Anne Coulter, and Sean Hannity acted as treason police, condemning liberal college professors, reporters, and social activists for undermining national security, stories such as *Civil War* ask readers to revaluate what heroism truly is and what patriotism really means. Certainly, Stark is a patriot in his desire to protect American lives and public safety, but is not Spider-Man at least as patriotic, if not more so, for questioning and defying Stark? Finally, is Spider-Man not truly the most idealistic and self-sacrificing of heroes? After all, he gave up his dreams of being wealthy, established, respected, and the personal assistant to one of the most brilliant scientists in the country, Tony Stark, to become a fugitive from the law and an exile, merely because he objected to the way the United States treats its suspected lawbreakers.

Spider-Man's close friend and mentor Tony Stark (Iron Man) becomes his worst enemy in *The Road to Civil War*, *Civil War*, and *The Amazing Spider-Man: Civil War* (2006–2007) (art by Clayton Crain from 2007's *The Amazing Spider-Man: Civil War* collection).

However, it is equally possible to have a very different, very unfavorable view of the character, his actions, and the dangerous example he sets to others.

Certainly newspaperman J. Jonah Jameson has little good to say about the man. And he may have a point.

Spider-Man: Hero or Menace?

Classic comic-book villain J. Jonah Jameson has run this front-page headline time and again over the years in his newspaper, *The Daily Bugle*, as part of his smear campaign against Spider-Man. Jonah's motivations for hounding Spider-Man often emerge as suspect in the comic books, since many stories suggest that Jonah is attacking Spider-Man primarily because anti–Spiderman propaganda sells a lot of newspapers. There is also the possibility that Jonah attacks Spider-Man for some secret, psychological reason. In a private moment depicted in 1964's *Amazing Spider-Man* #10, Jonah confesses to himself that:

> All my life I've been interested in one thing—making money! And yet, Spider-Man risks his life day after day with no thought of reward! If a man like him is good—is a hero—than what am I? ... Spider-Man represents everything I'm not! He's brave, powerful, and unselfish! ... I'd give everything I own to be the man he is! But I can never climb to his level! So all that remains for me is—to try to tear him down—because, heaven help me, I'm jealous of him.[20]

This interpretation of Jonah, crafted by Spider-Man's creators Steve Ditko and Stan Lee, has guided future writers, who tend to depict Jonah as a perpetually angry, miserly figure who is at once comical and villainous. Some writers have departed slightly from this model, suggesting instead that Jonah is secretly racist—despite his (sometimes) amicable friendship with African American colleague Joe "Robbie" Robertson—and refuses to cheer Spider-Man's heroics because he believes that a black man is hiding underneath the Spider-Man mask. This idea is not as odd as it might seem when one considers that Jack-in-the-Box, the Spider-Man tribute character featured in Kurt Busiek's *Astro City,* is an African American disguised by clown makeup. Furthermore, in interviews, Stan Lee has speculated that the Spider-Man costume makes the hero popular with nonwhite readers because they can more easily imagine themselves in his costume than in one without a mask.

Just as J. J. Hunsecker was a commentary on Walter Winchell in *The Sweet Smell of Success* (1957) and Charles Foster Kane was essentially William Randolph Hearst in *Citizen Kane* (1941), Jonah has been refitted to become a symbolic commentary on Glenn Beck, the Fox News commentator who frequently portrays President Obama as a dangerous socialist with "a deep-seated hatred for white people or the white culture."[21] The title character of Fred Van Lente's "The Extremist" (2010) adores Spider-Man with the same fervor that many of Obama's supporters have demonstrated, and is determined to kill anyone in the media who unfairly criticizes Spider-Man. The Extremist's two main targets are Jonah and Mark Branden, a Glenn Beck lookalike who draws frantic chalkboard charts to demonstrate that Spider-Man and Captain America are two "Super-Marxists" intent on taking over America. In one broadcast, Branden claims that Spider-Man is "the most mysterious costumed Commie of all" who flip-flops unsettlingly between two costumes: a friendly American flag–colored one and a scary black one. Following the broadcast, Branden finds himself ambushed by the Extremist. Branden begs for his life, yelling, "It's show business! A TV show! I don't mean any of that stuff!" but the merciless Extremist murders him. Despite having his own issues with the press constantly attacking him, Spider-Man is horrified by this show of "support" and denounces the Extremist. He then successfully prevents the Extremist from killing Jonah.

While many interpretations of Jonah undermine his credibility and present him as a comic villain, there are several Spider-Man writers that have portrayed Jonah positively, giving credence to his claims that Spider-Man *is* actually a supremely powerful loose cannon running amok around Manhattan *à la* Will Smith's Hancock. These writers depict Jonah as being akin to his Biblical namesake, proving his worth by defying a Godlike figure with the power to crush him in retaliation. In fact, Spider-Man *is* often incompetent, selfish, and dangerous to be around, as he has caused billions of dollars in property damage in his very public fights with supervillains. Additionally, many of his friends and relatives have been kidnapped, maimed, and killed precisely because they are close to him. Therefore, Jonah raises a legitimate question. It *is* equally possible to see Spider-Man as both a hero and a menace, and this fundamental paradox is one of many that lie at the heart of the character.[22]

However, ever since making the vow to use his powers to help people in need and to bring criminals to justice, Spider-Man has been very successful at both. He has saved countless lives, and imprisoned an array of thieves and murderers. Comic book adventures written by Roger Stern, Marv Wolfman, and Tom DeFalco make Spider-Man appear particularly heroic, in both the stature of the villains he defeats and in the good deeds he performs on behalf of friends and strangers.[23] Arguably, the comic book writer who is most overtly concerned with Peter Parker's moral compass, and who writes the most intentionally morally ambiguous Spider-Man stories is Peter David. David wrote a series of memorable Spider-Man adventures during the 1980s that ranged in tone from screwball comedies to dark social commentaries, and the villains he created represented a cross-section of the social anxieties of the Reagan-era, including Mohawk-sporting street punks, glassy-eyed religious cultists, and slick corporate moguls. David enjoyed playing with the personalities of long-established characters, particularly focusing on the darker side of Peter Parker while working overtime to soften the portrayal of Jonah. In fact, David's version of Jonah is the one who finally repents his crusade against Spider-Man and makes peace with the crime fighter in a pivotal tale called "Point of View."

Newspaper publisher J. Jonah Jameson gloats as his longtime nemesis, Spider-Man, is publicly disgraced. Illustrated by Steve Ditko, prose by Stan Lee. From "The End of Spider-Man!" in *The Amazing Spider-Man* #18 (Marvel Comics, November 1964).

The story, from *Web of Spider-Man* #13 (1986), begins

when Jonah publishes an article that falsely accuses Spider-Man of chasing a defenseless pedestrian into the path of an oncoming truck and almost killing him. This latest smear is too much for Spider-Man and he snaps, deciding to physically attack Jonah in retaliation for his endless series of blistering editorials. Spider-Man crashes through the window of Jonah's office, corners him, and slams him up against the wall. He demands to know why Jonah has been crucifying him in the press all these years. Hasn't he done a lot of good? Hasn't he saved Jonah and his son from danger, time and again? Jonah looks bravely at Spider-Man and yells: "You can't lay it all on me! I never made anything up! I interpret facts, like any journalist. All my paper does is reflect the public's perception of you!"

Spider-Man yells back, "Don't give me that! You're the one who made them believe I was a menace!"

"Oh, really, Spider-Man?" asks Jonah. "Look at yourself, you're so blasted smug. Either you were always the menace I said you were, or I've managed to convince you that you're a menace, because you're sure acting like one! And frankly, masked man, I didn't think I was that good a writer."

The rejoinder has too much truth in it for Spider-Man to ignore. After a long silence, he says, "You stink, Jonah, you really do," and then leaves, with nothing else to say. But Jonah is left shaken, considering for the first time that he might have gone too far.[24]

The dramatic issue featured a confrontation that was a long time coming, and it is noteworthy because there was a sense that both of these characters were deeply flawed people, sympathetically presented, and representing a legitimate "point of view." Instead of providing a pat resolution and a fortune-cookie moral at the end of the tale, David presents a delicious moral ambiguity, leaving the reader to ponder the questions he raises well after the story ends.

The Roots of Spider-Man's Moral Ambiguity and Psychological Complexity

Tobey Maguire, the actor who has played Peter Parker in the *Spider-Man* film series, believes that Peter Parker appeals to young people because he experiences what they often experience — the same "existential doubts and conflicting desires about who they are and where they stand in the world." According to Maguire, *Spider-Man* stories are "about identity and self-discovery and figuring out a little more about who you want to be and who you think you should be. That's what's so intriguing about the *Spider-Man* concept — the fact that Peter Parker openly raises his doubts so that the readers of the comic strip could share his worries and fears. He's not an all-powerful, all-knowing cardboard cutout superhero. He's not a superhero at all, by that standard. He's very mortal, someone who agonizes a lot about his role in life."[25]

Indeed, as Maguire indicates, Spider-Man is a surprisingly complex character. Seymour Chatman, a scholar who has studied movie adaptations of literature, wrote that people often have strong personal connections to fictional characters who possess conflicting personality traits, and whose behavior is not predictable. "We remember the[se characters] as real people.... Like real-life friends and enemies, it is hard to describe what they are exactly like.... The great round characters seem virtually inexhaustible objects for contemplation" who offer us insight into ourselves and our fellow beings" (132–133).

Chatman's description of the classic "round" character applies here. Spider-Man always seems to be changing, aging, and evolving. He inspires strong feelings of intimacy, both from his fans and from the storytellers who've crafted many of his adventures. Longtime fans often say that they like Spider-Man because he is both a loser they empathize with and a hero they emulate. It sounds like a fundamental contradiction, and it is, but the fans are not wrong. Spider-Man is the quintessential loser-hero. While Superman is clearly a physical and moral paradigm and his secret identity of Clark Kent is a naïve, rural Midwesterner overwhelmed by the big city, the concept of Spider-Man is enough of a departure from (and spoof of) the Superman template to necessitate being understood in a different light. One cannot comfortably designate Spider-Man as the hero and his civilian identity of Peter Parker as the loser, since the distinction between Parker and Spider-Man is generally not as sharp as the distinction between Kent and Superman or Wonder Woman and Diana Prince. Somehow, Spider-Man has managed to embody a number of fundamentally contradictory traits over the years. He has been loser and winner, hero and menace, geek and stud, and — as inconsistent as his characterization might appear — he has been believably the same person since his creation.

The roots of Spider-Man's complexity go back all the way to the early days of the comic book, and the first several years of issues produced by script writer Stan Lee and plotter and artist Steve Ditko. The two creators had diametrically opposed political perspectives and vastly different personalities. Ditko was a conservative Objectivist and devotee of Ayn Rand while Lee had more egalitarian views and greater sympathy with the hippie movement. Ditko has been characterized as being more introverted, while Lee is an extrovert and consummate showman. Since they are so different, their collaborative efforts in the comic book medium are rich and multilayered. In fact, their clash of perspectives can actually be seen playing out in their Spider-Man stories; their opposing narrative voices offer two different takes on the events of each issue, creating a constant dramatic tension and moral ambiguity in both the plotting and the characterization of Peter Parker.

Lee's accounts of the creation of Spider-Man, from *Origins of Marvel Comics* and his interview with Kevin Smith (*Stan Lee's Mutants, Monsters, and Marvels*), are consistent. Lee says he wanted to create an inexperienced superhero with insect powers that was the same age as the youngsters who read comic books. He wanted it to be like having the teenage Robin as the main character of the comic book or granting Archie or Jimmy Olsen superpowers instead of making the title character an adult between twenty and thirty-five years old, as usual. Lee wanted the stories to be rich in humor and to focus on everyday problems that were easy to relate to. According to Lee, Marvel's publisher, Martin Goodman, thought that an incompetent insect boy would be a wholly unlikable central character and a comic book featuring him would not sell well, since people hated insects and didn't like reading about ineffective protagonists. Still, Lee managed to sneak Spider-Man into the last issue of a canceled science fiction anthology comic book, *Amazing Fantasy* #15 (1962), and the character was a surprise hit.[26]

When the monthly Spider-Man comic book, *The Amazing Spider-Man*, launched shortly thereafter, Ditko continued on as Lee's co-plotter and artist — drawing a series of adventures that included the first appearances of most of the comic's classic villains and supporting characters.[27] As with many collaborative endeavors, especially films and comic books, there has been debate over which of the two men conceived the basic stories and characters, especially since Ditko did not draw the issues based on written scripts, but after informal, undocumented brainstorming sessions with Lee. Since Ditko rarely gives interviews, and Lee claims that his memory of the 1960s is terrible, it is necessary to look to other sources for information about Lee and Ditko's creative differences. Ditko's replacement on the book, John Romita, related his own account of the controversy:

"What I gather happened is that Ditko's plots were very personalized," Romita remembers. "In other words, they were sort of conservative and hard on beatniks and things like that and Stan would modify them. Ditko kept complaining, 'Don't change my plots.' Ditko would come in with one perspective and one attitude, and Stan would change it. By the time he got to ink it, Ditko saw that it was a different story, and I think he just finally got fed up and told Stan he was leaving" (Arehart 82–83).

Ditko's hero, Rand, was twelve years old when the Bolshevik Revolution swept through Russia and turned her bourgeoisie Jewish family into refugees that fled to the United States. The suffering she endured at the hands of Communism inspired her to be an ardent supporter of capitalism, and she made her career writing melodramatic novels that were as much political manifestos as narratives. Her works, especially *Atlas Shrugged* and *The Fountainhead*, remain widely read, and are frequently cited in polls as second only to the Bible as books that changed the lives of their readers. While she remains disparaged by most literary scholars and criticized by the left, her publicly influential defenders include Alan Greenspan, Ron Paul, and Chris Matthews (Heller).

According to Rand biographer Anne C. Heller, the author is one of the chief architects of modern American culture:

> Her controversial themes and racy romantic themes made her famous in the 1940s and 1950s. She attracted a youthful right-wing following in the 1940s and 1950s and became the guiding spirit of libertarianism and White House economic policy in the 1970s and 1980s....
>
> As a deconstructionist of liberal American economic and political assumptions, considered against a background of twentieth century Russian history, she displayed breathtaking insight and remarkable courage. Whatever one thinks of her program of rational selfishness, egoism, and unregulated capitalism, her ability to spot and skewer cowardice, injustice, and hypocrisy is at least as keen and passionate as that of her ideological opposite, Charles Dickens [xii–xiii].

For his part, Ditko shared Ayn Rand's impatience with hypocrisy, and incorporated a satire of the 1960s college protest movement in the final issue of *Amazing Spider-Man* that he drew and co-plotted in 1966 before his resignation—#38.[28] The scene involves Peter arriving on Empire State University's campus and being accosted by protestors who wish him to join in on "protesting tonight's protest meeting!" They give him a serious of reasons why he should participate, most of which sound morally and intellectually bankrupt. Various hippies say things like, "Aren't you interested in saving the world?? Anyway, it's an excuse to cut classes!" Another adds, "And maybe you'll get your picture in *Newsweek*." As further incentive, one beatnik says, "If you join our protest meeting, we'll join one of yours some time," while an additional voice in the chorus proclaims, "If you've nothing to protest, don't worry about it! That won't stop us!" Peter looks at them with disgust and says, "I haven't got time! Besides, I've nothing to protest about!" This gets the students fired up, and they lambast him. "Nothing to protest about?? What are you some kinda religious fanatic or somethin'?" one student cries, while others join in with, "Gowan back to Squaresville, you rosy-cheeked reactionary!" Peter is ready to start punching out the lot of them, but he grits his teeth and stalks away. Here, again, is an indication not only of Ditko's right-leaning politics, but Peter Parker's. Whatever sympathy the Lee-Ditko Spider-Man may or may not have with liberal causes, he certainly finds undergraduate activists tiresome, bubble-headed hypocrites.[29] And yet, there are indications that Lee took steps to soften the dialogue featured in this scene, and that he allowed the protestors to get in the last word because he himself sided with them over Peter Parker. And, based on Romita's accounts, it seems fair to assume that Ditko didn't like the idea of seeing his avatar, Peter Parker, chided for being a reactionary and a religious fanatic in his own comic book.

According to Romita, another source of creative contention between Lee and Ditko involved how they would best resolve the mystery of the Green Goblin's secret identity. Lee liked the drama of revealing that the Goblin was Norman Osborne, the father of Parker's best friend, while Ditko felt that it be too much of a coincidence for there to be such a connection between the two superpowered adversaries in their civilian identities. Instead, Ditko wanted Spider-Man to unmask the Goblin eagerly, only to be surprised when the villain wound up being someone unremarkable and anonymous — just a guy named "Joe."[30]

Comic book and television writer Mark Evanier, who has spoken to Ditko about the early days of Spider-Man, has largely substantiated this version of events. Ditko did not approve of Lee's dialogue or narration and felt that Lee was making Spider-Man too emotionally troubled and not heroic enough. However, Evanier believes that Ditko could have lived with the changes made to Spider-Man's character and to individual plots — including the Goblin mystery resolution — if he had received more credit for creating the characters and crafting the plots. Ditko also felt cheated out of his fair share of the merchandising royalties that Spider-Man earned for Marvel through toys, clothes, cartoons, movies, and memorabilia, by the stipulations of his work-for-hire contract.[31]

"Although he was subject to the same chiseling work-for-hire contracts as Kirby," Ditko lobbied for, and achieved, a plotting credit that artists such as Kirby failed to achieve, Ditko biographer Andrew Hultkrans observed.[32] Hultkrans believes that the early campaigns for more credit were inspired by Ditko's Objectivism, "with its hatred of creative dilution and unearned rewards" (217). Certainly Ayn Rand's iconic architect hero of *The Fountainhead*, Howard Roark, didn't stand for any of his buildings being modified, even though compromising his aesthetics would have meant providing cheap housing for the urban poor. Like Ditko, Roark wouldn't have liked anyone meddling with his artistic vision, or underpaying or under-crediting him for his work.

Both Evanier's and Romita's accounts of Ditko's grievances are substantiated by the Spider-Man stories from the time, which parallel the actual Lee-Ditko creative differences with the fictional conflict between photographer Peter and Jonah. Peter would take pictures of Spider-Man in action that would make Spider-Man look heroic, and sell those photos to Jonah without making it known that he was Spider-Man. Then Jonah would write a newspaper article around the art that would be critical of Spider-Man. Peter would also perpetually feel underpaid for his pictures, making paltry freelance wages even as his art helped Jonah's newspaper outsell all opposition and make Jonah wealthy. In a further parallel, Ditko clearly draws Peter to look like himself, and he drew Jonah to resemble Lee.

Interestingly enough, Lee himself revealed in an interview with Kevin Smith that Jonah is, indeed, a caricature of him, and an accumulation of all of his most loathsome traits.[33] Instead of being angered by the way Ditko drew him into the comic book as a villain, he publicly appears delighted that he is, essentially, Spider-Man's chief antagonist. In fact, he has often expressed a desire to play Jonah in a film or television adaptation of the comic book, but admits that he would probably not be as good at the part as J. K. Simmons has been in the *Spider-Man* motion pictures.

Putting Ditko's royalty woes aside for the moment, if he felt that his creative vision had been interfered with, and never made it to the printed page, then what kinds of stories did Ditko want to tell with Spider-Man? It stands to reason that Lee's vision of the character as a hapless wisecracker is not necessarily the same one that Ditko embraces. In fact, Ditko's plots seem to present Peter *as anything but* a trivial gadabout. For Ditko, Peter is a misunderstood genius suffering from the cruelty of fate and the stupidity of his peers. Although Peter got his spider powers by accident, he developed his webbing and web shooters on his own. He put his webbing to highly creative use—creating gliders, parachutes, projectiles, and even fake bat monsters to distract his enemies. He designed and sewed his own costume, developed the spider-tracer, and managed to create a potion to cure Dr. Connors of being the Lizard. Also, Ditko's Spider-Man was not powerful enough to defeat his enemies in straight combat, so he often used his scientific knowledge to thwart his opponents. The standard formula of the Ditko story was that he would encounter a new menace, such as the Vulture or Electro, be soundly defeated in a straight fight, and he would return home to develop a scientific method of defeating his more powerful opponent in a rematch. For example, to better prepare for his next encounter with the dangerous supervillains, Peter would develop an insulated costume to protect himself from Electro's hand-thrown thunderbolts or create a jamming device to cancel out the antigravity engines that give the Vulture the gift of flight.

While the Ditko stories did feature moments that trivialized Peter, Ditko's Peter was not a fool. In fact, the real tragedy of Ditko's Spider-Man is not that Peter is flawed; it is that the world he lives in is unjust and anti-intellectual, and Peter had the disadvantage of being born working class—or lower-middle class—instead of into an upper-class household. If he had come from a rich family, he would have been able to go to the best science schools, work in the finest labs, and become an innovator of the first order, like Reed Richards or Tony Stark. Instead, Peter languishes in a public school, tormented on a daily basis by handsome-but-clownish jocks like Flash Thompson, and ignored by suburbanite girls. Time and again, Spider-Man goes to established scientists like Richards and Connors for help and support, and he is invariably rebuffed. Therefore, when Ditko's Spider-Man feels anger at being unappreciated and behaves selfishly and arrogantly, declaring that he can do so because he is better than everyone else, he has a point.

Ditko also seems to be sympathetic with several members of Spider-Man's rogues' gallery, who are also misunderstood scientists. Doctor Octopus in particular is remarkably like Peter, a socially awkward man in glasses teased by his coworkers. Of course, "Doc Ock" crosses the line into becoming overtly evil in a way that Spider-Man never does, by murdering, kidnapping, stealing, and blackmailing to get revenge against the society that mocks him. He also cares more for his science projects than for the general public, and is willing to risk multitudes of human lives in the name of seeing one of his experiments come to fruition. In other circumstances, Ock and Spider-Man would be friends, and the fact that they are bitter enemies is one of the interesting twists of fate that governs the sensibility of the book. In fact, had things turned out differently, it could just as easily have been Doctor Octopus the superhero and Spider-Man the supervillain.

Lee's dialogue muddies the water further. Unlike the Objectivist Ditko, Lee loves to deflate characters with big egos and delusions of grandeur. That's why Lee writes Flash Thompson as being far more eloquent than any schoolyard bully should be, and why Lee seems to tacitly agree with Flash that the morose, withdrawn Peter brings the teasing and public ostracizing on himself. It is also no accident that Flash idolizes Spider-Man and hates Peter. Nor is it a coincidence that the dialogue Lee writes for Spider-Man is a lot like Flash's dialogue. Just as Flash skewers Peter for being an elitist, Spider-Man teases his often-nerdy opponents in the same manner to throw their concentration off during a fight. On rare occasions, the insults are politically oriented, as in 1964's Lee/Ditko romp, *Amazing Spider-Man Annual* #1, in which Spider-Man accuses incompetent villain Kraven the Hunter of being unable to grasp when he's beaten in a straight fight, just like most Republicans after their candidate loses a presidential election: "You never give up, do you?!?! I bet you're still wearin' a Vote-For-Dewey button!" (20).[34] Often, his quips are less political references than pop culture ones, as in a late–1980s David Michelinie story, when he would easily defeat a room full of hired thugs and then proclaim that he gets better workouts watching Paula Abdul dance on an MTV music video.

However, most often, Spider-Man's gibes resemble the kinds of schoolyard bully insults that one would normally associate with Flash. In fact, it is likely that he sometimes quotes the things bullies would say to him, or to similarly unpopular students; since he saw the hurt feelings they caused in the school yard, he could be assured they would work at least as well in life-and-death combat. Hence Spider-Man's propensity to tease Doctor Octopus for looking like Elton John and insinuate that Bonesaw McGraw is gay. This Bugs Bunny–like character trait of Spider-Man's has survived for decades, and still resurfaces today. In *Ultimate Spider-Man Vol. 2: Learning Curve* (2001), writer Brian Michael Bendis has Spider-Man read a list of fat jokes off of a sheet, successfully whipping the portly Kingpin of Crime into a blind rage. Spider-man says, "You are so fat that when you cut yourself shaving, marshmallow fluff comes out.... You are so fat that your high school yearbook photo was taken from a helicopter.... If you were a truck, you'd have a 'wide load' sign. When you back up we can hear a beeping sound."

In general, many of Spider-Man's jokes are "groaners"—the kind of cheesy attempts at levity one might expect from an uncle who tries too hard to be entertaining at a family reunion—but the character is often very funny, and his sense of humor can be one of his most endearing traits. He certainly teases friends and allies as often as he needles his enemies. During his brief partnership with Batman, Spider-Man never let up teasing Batman about all of his various "Bat-weapons," wondering how they seemed to appear from thin air when they were most needed, and expressing envy over the amount of money clearly required to purchase them all.[35] Similarly, when Spider-Man meets Wonder Woman for the first time, she uncharacteristically tries to arrest him without speaking to him first because she had heard he was a wanted man. Spider-Man manages to evade her attempt to lasso him, yelling, "I don't believe in 'magic lassos' but I'm still not going to let you tie me up—not on our first date!" Eventually, Spider-Man convinces her that he is innocent of the charges against him and she offers a heartfelt apology. Once this misunderstanding is resolved, Spider-Man says, "By the way, do you think it's too early in our relationship to consider marriage?"[36]

As funny as this constant teasing and wisecracking may be, Peter's remarks could sometimes be regarded as mean-spirited, and it is likely that Ditko himself was not a fan of Spider-Man's razor-sharp wit. Consequently, while Ditko constructed the stories to be sympathetic to the gifted Peter and the misunderstood geniuses he is reluctantly forced to fight, Lee's mouthpieces are the wisecracking Spider-Man and Flash, who get their kicks skewering elitists. But, as striking as Lee's text-based changes are, Ditko's visual framework remains, and the two narratives play off one another, creating a dramatic tension and layers of irony that are interesting to consider.

In fact, the complex Spider-Man character template forged by these two incompatible visions was so successful that it spawned a series of imitators over the decades, including younger, hipper versions of the Flash (Wally West), Green Lantern (Kyle Rayner), and Robin

(Tim Drake), as well as Spider-Man–like supervillains Deadpool, Wesley Gibson (*Wanted*), and Kevin the Serial Killer (*Sin City*). But the most successful Spider-Man variant of all was his female counterpart, Buffy the Vampire Slayer. Though in the same female superhero lineage as Wonder Woman, Buffy, like Peter, is a wisecracking, acrobatic high-school student who initially hides her superheroic extracurricular activities from her mother (her Aunt May). At school, Buffy is hounded by female bully Cordelia Chase (a Flash Thompson equivalent) and Principal Snyder (Jonah), but her greatest foes are not her mentors, as Spider-Man's are, but her string of abusive, deceitful boyfriends.

Despite the difficulties Lee and Ditko had in working together, they somehow managed to create a character that is so memorable that he remains beloved to this day. Indeed, even as Spider-Man remains a lucrative source of inspiration for films, video games, action figures, and a vast array of memorabilia, he continues to spawn a variety of imitators—similar superhero characters that strive to duplicate the popular appeal of Spider-Man, with varying degrees of success. While some succeed (Buffy) and some falter (Kyle Rayner), Spider-Man remains.

Moral Ambiguities Surrounding Spider-Man's Friends and Enemies

John Romita, Ditko's replacement on *The Amazing Spider-Man*, had political views that were more in line with Lee's. According to Romita, he plotted the stories and Lee was a gifted collaborator who specialized in dialogue and characterization. Their working relationship appears to have been amicable, and the supporting characters that Romita created with Lee seemed more amicable, too. While Ditko's stories featured policemen, reporters, and young people who were all fundamentally corrupt, Romita introduced noble members of each group who were instantly likeable precisely because they offered a breath of fresh air from the loathsome characters who had come before. Captain Stacy was a wise policeman who deduced that Peter was Spider-Man and admired the young man for his courage. Joe "Robbie" Robertson was the African American city editor of the *Daily Bugle* who exuded the same kind of integrity that actor Sidney Poitier had been bringing to the movie screen during the time the stories were published. Robertson acted as Jonah's conscience and worked, often in vain, to keep the *Bugle*'s inflammatory anti–Spider-Man articles in check. Like Captain Stacy, Robertson acted as the sort of surrogate father figure Peter had lacked since the death of his uncle, and there were regular hints that he, too, knew who Peter really was.

Romita's villains were noticeably more evil than those created by Ditko, and more macho and muscular. The Kingpin and the Rhino were hallmarks of the Romita era, formidable fighters with the builds of sumo wrestlers who had no regard for innocent life and property. With Ditko gone, there was no more need for Flash Thompson. Inspired by the selfless heroism exemplified by his hero, Spider-Man, Flash enlisted in the military and was shipped off to Vietnam. He was written out of the book and did not appear again for several years, when he returned from combat duty with Vietnamese lover, Sha Shan. Meanwhile, Jonah remained a thorn in Spider-Man's side. He was one of the reasons that Peter was demoralized enough to briefly give up being Spider-Man in the famous fiftieth issue, "Spider-Man No More," which served as the inspiration for *Spider-Man 2*.

Despite Jonah's pernicious influence, Romita's Spider-Man existed in a much brighter world overall than Ditko's. Romita's Peter was handsomer and more sociable than Ditko's, and his good-luck streak was improving. In fact, removed from the fundamentally unjust, gothic universe that Ditko created, Romita's Peter starts to seem less of a victim and more of a whiner. After all, how could anyone who now seemed to have the pick of either "wild child" Mary Jane Watson (whom Romita designed to look like Ann-Margret) or the luminous, virginal Gwen Stacy allow himself the luxury of depression?

Lee left the title after writing slightly more than a hundred issues. Gerry Conway, one of the most influential and long-running writers to shape the character, replaced him. Conway felt that Romita's escapist adventure stories had represented too much of a honeymoon for the character, and he made a point of stepping up the dramatic intensity of the comic. He promptly had the Green Goblin murder Peter's first love, Gwen, by throwing her off the Brooklyn Bridge. In the following issue, Peter's desire for revenge is satisfied, if indirectly, when a trap intended to snare Spider-Man accidentally kills the Goblin.[37]

Conway had returned Peter to a dark and unjust world, and his Peter was understandably a misanthrope. However, Conway recreated some of the intriguing moral ambiguity of the original stories by having Peter direct some of his anger at his friends, who do not deserve ill treatment from him. Conway allowed Peter to be particularly rude to seemingly inoffensive characters such as Mary Jane, Betty Brant, and the Human Torch, most likely out of latent resentment that MJ and Betty were both former romantic interests, and out of jealousy for the Human Torch's high living and glamorous lifestyle. (The Human Torch was rarely without a sexy girlfriend or wicked cool sports car.) Although Conway occasionally went far enough that he began to cast Spider-Man in the light of an anti-hero, he usually made Peter's displays of temper justifiable enough to be understandable considering the stress he was under. The most uncomfortable scene that Conway wrote in this vein occurred during the "Death of Gwen Stacy" storyline. As Peter is about to leave his apartment to track down and kill Norman Osborne, his roommate Harry Osborne, suffering from the effects of drug withdrawal, begs him to stay and help see him through the ravages of going cold turkey. The chief irony of the situation is that Harry is the Goblin's son, but Harry doesn't know about his father's alter ego. Given a choice between killing Harry's mentally ill father and staying at the apartment to help Harry heal, Peter chooses to leave Harry shivering on the floor. In that moment, Peter chooses revenge over compassion; punishing the son for the sins of his father. Suddenly, readers find themselves wondering if Jonah has been right about Spider-Man all along.

From *Spider-Man 3* (2007): Spider-Man (Tobey Maguire) punches Flint Marko (Thomas Haden Church), only to discover why he is called "The Sandman."

In fact, like Conway, future writers and artists who would be assigned to a Spider-Man comic book consciously recreated the moral ambiguity of the early Lee-Ditko tales in their own adventures. The creative teams who would handle the character in later years would often lean more towards one creator's view of Spider-Man than another's, including either more of Ditko's political worldview, or more of Lee's humor and romantic sensibilities, if not find their own unique way of blending the two styles. Still, the dramatic ironies, the contradictions, and the unanswered questions that were an indirect consequence of the creative conflict between Lee and Ditko formed an enduring air of moral ambiguity around Spider-Man and the universe he inhabits.

Indeed, one of the strengths of the Spider-Man saga is that it continually pulls the rug out from under readers, revealing secret sides to personalities of longstanding characters that readers had thought they knew. Evil characters like Sandman would suddenly reveal a hidden noble streak, while moral paradigm characters such as Gwen Stacy and Joe "Robbie" Robertson would unexpectedly reveal a darker, hidden past. In *Sins Past*, Straczynski depicted the saintly Gwen Stacy as secretly a "fallen woman"—someone who cheated on Peter with Norman Osborne, became pregnant out of wedlock, and then fled to France to give birth to the Goblin's twin children. It was this story that revealed why the Goblin *really* killed Gwen: Osborne wasn't out to break Spider-Man's spirit; he was avenging himself on Gwen, who bravely defied the evil billionaire and would not allow him custody of their children. The classic melodrama is wonderfully written and beautifully illustrated but, unfortunately, Spider-Man fans largely rejected the storyline as borderline offensive and too incredible to be believed. (Gwen was just *too good a girl to do such a thing* as have sex with Norman, they argued.)

Conway crafted an elaborate storyline which revealed that Robbie survived an upbringing in a crime-infested neighborhood only because he did not call the police when he witnessed the neighborhood tough, Lonnie "Tombstone" Lincoln, commit murder. Had Robbie done "the right thing" at the time, Tombstone would surely have killed him as well. After years of feeling guilty for letting a murderer walk, Robbie finally turns state's evidence against Tombstone. The decision goes far towards undoing the damage that Robbie did, but the revelation that he withheld evidence in a criminal case causes Robbie to briefly lose the respect of his friends and sees him spend time in prison for obstruction of justice.[38]

In addition, after decades of seeing Jonah as little more than a comic foil for Spider-Man, readers were surprised to learn in a story written by Roger Stern that he was a crusading, anti-crime journalist throughout his career, and even had the guts to confront the Kingpin of Crime. The Ditko-influenced J.M. DeMatteis brought a freshness and realism to Aunt May's character that was rarely seen before, as she had previously been portrayed as frail, annoying, and uniformly wrong about everything. DeMatteis recast Aunt May as a witty, wise, three-dimensional character. At the same time he reinvented Aunt May, DeMatteis also reinvented Spider-Man's villains, making them far more frightening, and far more sympathetic, than they had been since Ditko created them. He was especially renowned for giving cardboard characters such as Kraven the Hunter and Electro complicated backgrounds and personalities, and offering them chances at redemption (see *Kraven's Last Hunt, Soul of the Hunter*, and 1993's "Light the Night" from *Spider-Man* #38–40). Of course, some fans have chafed at the Spider-Man tradition of using flashbacks to change characters' motivations and to offer different perspectives on long-established events. They call this narrative tactic "retconning" (a colloquial collapsing of the phrase "retroactive continuity") and the term has a largely negative connotation. However, retconning is justifiable so long as it produces a good story and adds to the richness of the comic's history. The storytelling technique also has the benefit of building upon the time-honored tradition of Spider-Man comic books offering multiple and conflicting perspectives of major events and lacing stories with moral ambiguities. Also, the Spider-Man universe exists as part of the tradition of Gothic storytelling, and one of the principal tenets of Gothic storytelling is that no one is ever just what he or she appears to be. The good thing about this storytelling tradition is it guarantees that characters in *Spider-Man* will continue to be round enough, and complicated enough, to keep readers interested in their fates.

Perhaps the most significant retooling of a character in the history of the Spider-Man story is the revamping of Mary Jane. She was originally crafted to be the "bad girl" and a dead-end romantic interest for Peter, while Gwen Stacy was presented as the "good girl" and the right person for him to marry. In some ways, their love triangle was a mirror of, and commentary on, the love triangle between Archie, Betty, and Veronica, with MJ as an edgier version of Veronica. This dynamic, and these portrayals of MJ and Gwen, lasted until Gwen Stacy was killed and MJ was briefly written out of the comic book. Then, during the mid–1980s, writer Tom DeFalco nearly single-handedly recreated the character of Mary Jane, changing her from a carefree, "bad girl" character into the sensitive woman who becomes Peter's first confidant and first real friend.

In fact, DeFalco presented Mary Jane as a parallel character to Peter.

While Peter's guardian, Uncle Ben, represented the working class at its best, and Peter felt guilty wanting to rise to a higher social stratum in life, Mary Jane's father represented the worst traits stereotypically associated with blue-collar life: alcoholism and domestic violence. The women in MJ's family, meanwhile, smoked, cursed, were saddled with too many children, and had no hope of a better future. This bleak domestic scene left MJ with a strong desire to cut all ties to her roots and do her best to class jump, even if it meant pretending to be wealthier than she really was and recklessly throwing herself in the arms of every rich bachelor in town until one of them snapped her up. Hence, the reason MJ was long portrayed as a carefree party girl with a bad reputation. Her desire to leave her poor background behind is often undermined by self-doubt. Secretly, she fears that a "white trash" girl like her isn't deserving of success, no matter how brightly she smiles or how much makeup and stylish clothing she puts on. In fact, she says as much in *Spider-Man 3* when she notes that a bad newspaper review of her singing and acting on Broadway reminds her of how her father used to insult her, validating the deep fears her troubled childhood had ingrained in her. But MJ is not a purely selfish character, by any means. In a memorable storyline written by Conway, MJ finds out that her cousin Kristy has developed bulimia and anorexia. Because Kristy was long jealous of MJ's model figure, MJ feels responsible for the eating disorder. Instead of once again running from a family member in need, MJ stays by Kristy's side, nursing her back to health and mentoring her until Kristy is ready to begin a new, healthier chapter in her life.

By giving Mary Jane a previously unrevealed harrowing childhood, DeFalco made Mary Jane one of the most interesting nonsuperpowered women in comic books. While Mary Jane had once been a flirt and a gold-digger that many comic book fans disliked intensely, suddenly she was far more three-dimensional and sympathetic. In the process of reinventing MJ, DeFalco helped move the comic book away from some of the sexist characterizations of women it had seen in the past while laying the groundwork for the marriage between Peter and MJ that would follow a few years later. But even the marvelous relationship between Peter and MJ that DeFalco helped establish is not without its own ambiguous qualities. In a wonderful dramatic contradiction, Peter and MJ are meant to be together, and have one of the best romances in comics, but there will always be a part of Peter who wishes that Gwen were still alive so he could have married her instead.[39]

From *Spider-Man 3* (Sony Pictures, 2007): Peter Parker's best friend Harry Osborne (James Franco), and his girlfriend, Mary Jane Watson (Kirsten Dunst) look on, amazed, as the Sandman disrupts a pro–Spider-Man rally.

These kinds of moral ambiguities are disturbing to some readers, who like good guys to be good, bad guys to be bad, and marriages to be blissfully happy and uncomplicated. However, other readers see such morally ambiguous characters and situations as part of the realism of the *Amazing Spider-Man* comic books, as well as part of their appeal. Whatever Peter Parker is — hero or menace — he is a complicated man. And his moral code is equally complex. Perhaps unsurprisingly, in the wake of the 2006 film *Spider-Man 3*, which focused on Spider-Man's less savory personality traits, some parents complained that Spider-Man's complex morality makes him a bad role model for children. Quite the reverse is true. The Spider-Man comic books are profoundly moral, precisely because Spider-Man is deeply flawed and deeply thoughtful about his limitations, his responsibilities, and the goodness that lurks within many of his adversaries. He is never certain what "the right thing to do" is, and he does not take for granted that he has all the answers. He questions the world, and himself, constantly, and he tempers his righteousness with self-awareness. In this way, at least, Spider-Man is a refreshing change from American fictional characters that are stalwart, unemotional, unquestioning, and anti-intellectual. His self-doubts invite readers to consider the morality of his actions, and of the actions of the characters around him. Better still, morally ambiguous Spider-Man stories invite readers to reflect upon their own propensity to be self-righteous and certain of the correctness of their opinions.

And there's humor along the way.

When Spider-Man changed sides during the superhero Civil War, he was, unsurprisingly, unpopular with both factions. A notable exception on Captain America's side was the Falcon, who tells Spider-Man that he respects him for being brave.

> FALCON: I mean, it takes a lot of courage to change your mind about something after going so far down the road. Saying "I was wrong" has to be the hardest sentence in the English language.
>
> SPIDER-MAN: Actually, the hardest sentence in the English language is "What are you doing with my wife?" There's never a really good answer to that one.

Spider-Man deflects the seriousness of Falcon's compliment with a joke, in part because he does not want to be thanked for doing the right thing too late. But the legitimacy of Falcon's point remains. It is, indeed, incredibly difficult to admit a mistake, especially if the person admitting the mistake is a powerful figure, or a world leader. Contrast Spider-Man's humility and self-doubts with George W. Bush's constant, unwavering insistence that he was unquestionably correct in all of his decisions, and his irritation with the press or anyone else who would question the wisdom of his actions.

While Superman and Wonder Woman may be good role models for children because of their selflessness and egalitarian politics, Spider-Man is a good role model because he is imperfect, and because he questions his own actions and motivations. Sometimes he teaches his readers to be better by behaving worse than they do. And his constant striving to be a better person inspires, even as he fails time and again to achieve his personal and professional goals. He has also shown, quite dramatically, that sometimes the most patriotic person is the one who defies his own government, protests its evil actions, and breaks its unjust laws. In the end, Spider-Man is an essentially tragic character that serves others and behaves selflessly, sacrificing his own dreams of self-fulfillment in the process, even though his only rewards are public condemnation, relentless persecution, poverty, and loneliness.

Four

The Punisher as Murderous Immigration Officer and Vietnam War Veteran

In certain extreme situations, the law is inadequate. In order to shame its inadequacy, it is necessary to act outside the law. To pursue ... natural justice. This is not vengeance. Revenge is not a valid motive. It's an emotional response. No. Not vengeance. Punishment.—Frank Castiglione (a.k.a. The Punisher)[1]

Political language ... is designed to make lies sound truthful and murder respectable.—George Orwell[2]

The Emotional Scars of War

The animated prologue to *The Punisher: Extended Cut* (2006) acts as a disturbing commentary on both Desert Storm and Operation Iraqi Freedom. The segment—which takes place before Frank Castle has become the invincible, mass-murdering vigilante known as the Punisher—updates the title character's wartime experience to Desert Storm, rather than Vietnam, as it was in the *Punisher* comic books. According to the film, in 1991, Castle's platoon enters Kuwait City in search of "escaped Republican Guard suspects" who "tortured and killed two U.N. Peacekeepers." Ambushed in a town square by the very Republican Guard suspects they are pursuing, they suffer heavy losses. It is only thanks to Castle—who runs out into the open and, with preternaturally good aim, wounds and captures the enemy combatants—that the rest of the unit survives the unexpected assault. Castle then delivers the two prisoners to the major in charge of his unit.

CASTLE: Secure the prisoners.

MAJOR: Secure them? We're gonna terminate these murderers right here, right now.

CASTLE: You're not authorized to execute these prisoners, sir. There's no justice in that.

MAJOR: They're not soldiers, they're terrorists.

CASTLE: They say the same thing about us.

MAJOR: Where's the justice in what they did?

CASTLE: You pull that trigger, you're guilty of murder, sir.

After convincing the major not to kill the prisoners, Castle walks off, disgusted with how bloodthirsty his comrades are. Unfortunately, one of the captives proves suicidal, lunges for a grenade on the major's belt, and blows himself and the rest of Castle's unit to smithereens. Castle looks on in horror from outside the blast radius at his former comrades, who are dead because he showed a defeated enemy mercy. In this moment, the Punisher is born, and Frank Castle loses all willingness to give a murderer a second chance.

The scene is effective, and helps explain how Castle developed his harsh sense of "morality," but what conclusions are viewers supposed to draw from this scene? Is the Geneva Convention a bad idea? Is it impossible to reform or deprogram criminals and terrorists? Are all enemy combatants, especially Muslim enemy combatants, suicide bombers who should be shot on sight rather than captured? While the "war on terror" certainly involves fanatical opponents who cannot be reasoned with, who would love to see America and Israel wiped off the map, there are too many Muslims in the world to paint with the same broad brush that this segment would like to hand viewers. Thinking in those terms leads dangerously close to advocating a policy of endless warfare in the Middle East, and endorsing a genocidal campaign against members of the Islamic faith, rather than supporting a policy that involves the possibility of diplomacy, redemption, and peace. Abdulaziz Sachedina, chair of Religious Studies at the University of Virginia, is one of many scholars who have warned against this kind of fatalistic thinking. In "From Defensive to Offensive Warfare: The Use and Abuse of Jihad in the Muslim World" (2002), he argues that Muslims are not uniformly fanatical in their thinking about religion, international relations, and *jihad*, as they are often portrayed in the media, and that Westerners need to be aware of this to aid in more nuanced, peaceful negotiations in the future.

The segment in the *Punisher* film is meant to be taken seriously by audience members, who are supposed to condemn Castle for being naïve in granting the enemy mercy, and who are meant to celebrate his hardening into the Punisher. On the other hand, a similar wartime back-story provided for the Punisher in the comic books is far more satirically written, criticizing the Punisher for losing his humanity. In stark contrast to the film, rather than validate American aggression abroad, this comic book also blames American imperialism above all else for creating the monster that is the Punisher. Writer Garth Ennis suggests that lunatics like Frank Castle are a natural consequence of the insane culture of the United States, with its brutal capitalism, gun-crazy culture, terrible racial injustices, and imperialist wars overseas. Ennis, a native of Northern Ireland, expressed these views eloquently in the ultra-violent comic book *The Punisher: Born* (2003), which retains the Vietnam War setting the character was originally designed to inhabit rather than updating the military engagement to Desert Storm. Nevertheless, the story takes a revisionist look at the character's fictional origins.

Traditionally, Frank Castle has been portrayed as a normal, law-abiding citizen who returned from an honorable tour of duty in Vietnam to become a police officer and live a normal life with his wife and children. When his family witnesses a mob hit during a picnic in the park, they are at the wrong place at the wrong time, and are machine-gunned to death by the Mafia. Even though Castle physically survives his own wounds, he has been transformed mentally into the Punisher, a merciless, one-man army who declares war on the Mafia and all other hardcore criminals around the world. While this origin has been widely referenced by comic books for years, and embraced by fans of the character, both the Desert Storm back story of the *Punisher* film and the Vietnam-set *Born* miniseries represent a departure from the established origin, arguing that the Punisher was in fact born on a battlefield overseas and not thanks to a domestic tragedy that occurred stateside after his military service ended.

In *Born*, Ennis tells the story of Castle's service in the Vietnam War, making it evident that he grew to enjoy killing for its own sake during his repeated tours of duty as a marine, sniper, and member of black ops between 1968 and 1971. As the war was becoming more unpopular back home and it looked like Castle's unit would be withdrawn from their position near the Cambodian border, he took extreme steps to prolong his unit's stay so he could continue fighting to the last possible second.

Throughout the story, Castle demonstrates a twisted sense of mercy and morality in the field, prefiguring the odd moral code he adopts as the Punisher. When his unit captures a female Viet Cong sniper, one of his men rips her uniform off and begins raping her. Castle shoots and seriously wounds the sniper to save her from the rape, telling his men, "No rape. We're here to kill the enemy. That's all." Later, Castle finds the would-be rapist alone, washing his face off in a lake. Castle places his boot on the back of the rapist's head, pushing him underwater and drowning him.

The Punisher's ruthlessness in wartime is contrasted with the comparable innocence of one of his platoon, the sweet, blonde-haired Stevie Goodwin, who wonders aloud, "Why can't we stay out of the rest of the world?" and hopes that Vietnam is a bad chapter in an otherwise glorious history of the United States. Another member of the platoon, Angel, is a black soldier who chastises Goodwin for his naïveté. During one of the key scenes in the story, he says, "I keep hearin' you talk about this idea you got—this *real America*? It's a fuckin' dream, man. It belongs in ... the Wild muthafuckin' West. That's the real America, right there: back when you was shootin' each other, rapin' red Indians an' callin' me nigga.... An' don't be given me none o' that shit 'bout how there's good along wit' the bad. How all everybody gotta do is work hard an' they gonna make it. There's good for you and there's bad for me, Stevie. Ain't no more to it than that." Angel adds, "All I got waitin' for me's a ghetto fulla death." Angel's speech not only reveals a lot about his character, his life, and his relationship to Stevie, it also serves as the moral backbone of the story, simultaneously indicting both the insane Frank Castle and the insane United States of America that created him.

The Punisher: Born grows more satirical, violent, and supernatural as it progresses, building to a surreal climactic battle scene. The story ends with a massive Viet Cong attack on Firebase Valley Forge in which both Angel and Stevie die. Castle is the only survivor. As he stands alone, killing hundreds of enemy combatants single-handedly, Castle hears the voice of the devil offering a gift:

> *Castle loves war.*
> *Vietnam may be ending, but Castle can have another war—an endless one.*
> *But there will be an unnamed price.*
> *All he has to do is say "Yes."*

Castle madly cries "Yes!" to the unseen, demonic speaker, and survives the battle. The demon has granted Castle some form of invulnerability, and promised Castle a never-ending-war-on-crime. In the epilogue of *Born,* Castle returns home from duty and is greeted at the airport by his wife and children. It is only then that Castle learns that his deal with the devil will cost his family their lives. As he looks upon his wife and children, the vision of a skull appears over them, and the voice of the demon asks, *Remember I said there would be a price?*

In addition to satirizing the destruction caused by American military action abroad, *Born* is about the terrible psychological scars that Vietnam veterans brought back with them from their wartime service. Even though most veterans did not return to witness their families killed by the Mafia, many did effectively lose their families to the war. They found themselves unable to reconcile the evils they had witnessed—and in some cases had committed—with a placid domestic life. Their families could not understand the depths of their guilt, or their pain, and many of their marriages ended in divorce. According to William P. Mahedy, author of *Out of the Night: The Spiritual Journey of Vietnam Vets*:

> Religious America, Christian America, was complicit in two assaults on the faith of its young veterans. The first was perpetuating the war itself while tolerating the endorsements and mythology that surround war in our culture. The second was scapegoating the veterans, laying full responsibility for what happened on their shoulders. Scapegoating amounted to an implicit recognition that war was evil. Like Pontius Pilate ... the American people washed their hands of the war, assuaging their own consciences by treating the veterans as moral outcasts....
>
> Vets were considered moral outcasts, baby killers, perpetrators of atrocities. One did not associate with such people and retain one's own sense of self-worth. The message from these guardians of America's conscience was clear: Vietnam veterans were pariahs. They were immoral and evil people. To their own peer group, those with whom they had grown up, with whom they shared the same Little League games, rock music, sexual adventures, they had become nonpersons [41, 46–47].

The 1982 film *First Blood* dramatizes the suffering, unemployment, and social castigation that fictional Italian American vet John Rambo (played by Sylvester Stallone) endured upon his return home from his tour of duty. When he goes to a small town to visit a former comrade-in-arms, the local sheriff persecutes him and arrests him for vagrancy. When Rambo is tormented in the police station, he suffers a flashback to his time as a prisoner of war and breaks out, starting his own, personal Vietnam War on the American home front, killing the police and members of the National Guard to win back his freedom and self-respect. When he is finally captured by his former commanding officer from the Green Berets, he explains why he suffered such a violent breakdown:

> Nothing is over! Nothing. You just don't turn it off. It wasn't my war. You asked me, I didn't ask you. And I did what I had to do to win. But somebody didn't let us win. Then I came back to the world and I see all the maggots at the airport protesting me, spitting, calling me baby killer, and all kinds of vile crap. Who are they to protest me, huh? Who are they, unless they been me and been there and know what the hell they're yelling about?
>
> ... for me civilian life is nothing. In the field, we had a code of honor. You watch my back and I watch yours. Back here, there's nothing...
>
> Back there I could fly a gunship, I could drive a tank, I was in charge of million-dollar equipment. Back here I can't even hold a job parking cars!

Sylvester Stallone from *Rambo: First Blood Part II* (Lions Gate, 1985). The Rambo character is indicative of how Americans regarded the Vietnam War in the 1980s.

Since the war never ended in Rambo's mind, he brought the war home with him and fought it anew on the streets of America. The Punisher did much the same thing. And the *Punisher* comic books, much like the crime exploitation films and the horror movies of the late 1970s and early 1980s that inspired them, brought images of the Vietnam War home to an "underground" audience to contemplate. Horror movie make-up man Tom Savini was a Vietnam War vet who explained that he worked out his experiences on the battlefield by recreating war wounds and corpses he saw first-hand in the zombie make-up he did for films such as *Dawn of the Dead* (1978). As David J. Skal writes in *The Monster Show*, "Horror films of the seventies and eighties began exhibiting symptoms remarkably similar to some of those suffered by victims of posttraumatic stress syndrome: startle reactions, paranoid, endless-scenes of guerilla-like stalking, and, like traumatic flashbacks, repeated images of nightmare assaults on the human body, especially its sudden and explosive destruction" (311). Other violent films, whether they were "slasher" films like those in the *Friday the 13th* series, rape revenge films such as *I Spit on Your Grave* (1978) and *Last House on the Left* (1972), or "you killed my family, prepare to die" films such as *Death Wish* (1974), all brought the war overseas back home.

The War on Crime

In some cases, the protagonists of 1970s and 1980s exploitation films started out not as battle-scarred veterans, but as liberal intellectuals who are shocked out of their too-rosy worldview by having their cozy world interrupted by rape and murder. Charles Bronson's character in *Death Wish* was both a Korean War veteran and a "bleeding-heart liberal," but his years of service in the medical corps did not spare him the horror of returning home one night to find his wife savagely beaten and his daughter raped and catatonic. A more cerebral take on this exploitation film formula was attempted in *The Brave One* (2007), in which Jodi Foster plays Erica Bain, a sweet-natured NPR radio-show host modeled after Terry Gross who turns into a murderous Punisher figure after she is raped and her fiancé is murdered during an ill-fated nighttime outing to Central Park. Following her transformation, Bain simultaneously sees liberal characters as naïve, yet wishes she was still like them. The film also symbolically links her personal trauma to the trauma suffered by New Yorkers, and the United States, following 9/11. It is a meditation on the war on terror as being perpetrated by a mentally unbalanced, "raped" America, and mourns the nation's move to the political right even as the film seems to support a conservative philosophical perspective.

Erica Bain is one of many crimefighting women found in books, comic books, and films over the last several decades that have at least one brutal rape written into their history, often as their raison d'être. A surprising number of women in superhero stories have also been raped, either as the incident that inspired them to become crimefighters or as the most traumatic moment in their career, which nearly resulted in their loss of powers and will to live. Barbara Gordon (*Batgirl/Birds of Prey*), Julie Winters (*The Maxx*), Echo (*Dollhouse*), Beatrix Kiddo (*Kill Bill*), Black Canary (*Green Arrow/Birds of Prey*), Starfire (*Teen Titans*), and Lt. Tasha Yar (*Star Trek: The Next Generation*) have all been raped, while Judge Anderson (*2000 AD*) and Lisbeth Salander (Stieg Larsson's *Millennium Trilogy*) have been subjected to both rape and brutal paternal abuse. At least two superheroines, Mirage (*Team Titans*) and Ms. Marvel (Marvel's *Avengers*), have been impregnated by rape. Characters who have been victims of extreme domestic violence and psychologically damaged by their lovers include Janet van Dyne (Marvel's *Avengers/The Ultimates*) and Buffy Summers (*Buffy the Vampire Slayer*). Several of these characters were killed off in storylines following their rape, including van Dyne and Yar. As Gail Simone's website *Women in Refrigerators* has suggested, these rapes and murders are sometimes indicative of the misogyny of the storyteller, sometimes form a condemnation of the sexism of society, and are sometimes a plot device used to justify the "entertaining" carnage and bloodshed which follows when the rape victim seeks revenge.

What makes Stieg Larsson's heroine, Lisbeth Salander, 2000 AD's Judge Anderson, and Joss Whedon's heroines Buffy Summers and Echo, stand out from the others is that their attackers are not muggers or gang-bangers encountered in an overnight corner deli, a nocturnal jog through central park, or in a cabin in the woods. "Respectable" members of the community—including corporate executive, mayors, lawyers, social workers, honors students, professional athletes, judges, and even fathers—brutalize these women. Their attackers also tend to get away with their crimes because they are unassailable public figures and are not immigrants or urban ghetto residents. They are protected by their suit-and-tie, a bought-and-paid for mass media, and a legion of high-paid lawyers and lawmakers. In Larsson's first Salander story, aptly called *Men Who Hate Women* overseas (but not in America, of course), one of the few remaining champions of investigative journalism, Mikael Blomkvist, writes an exposé in Stockholm's liberal activist periodical *Millennium* accusing one of Sweden's untouchable industrialists, Hans-Erik Wennerström, of heading a criminal cartel. Blomkvist's story, despite being essentially true, is discredited. Blomkvist is found guilty of libel, publicly disgraced, and sentenced to three months in prison. Such is the fate of the idealistic liberal who tries to expose evil in the upper echelons of society by working, in a civilized fashion, within a system designed to preserve the power of the establishment.

Noomi Rapace as Lisbeth Salander in Daniel Alfredson's film adaptation of Stieg Larsson's *The Girl Who Played with Fire* (Music Box Films Home Entertainment, 2010). Lisbeth is the avenging angel that destroys "men who hate women" by burning them alive.

Blomkvist's misfortunes underscore how impossible it is for anyone to take on an amoral, all-powerful corporate executive. Hence the importance of Salander, who has no illusions about what it takes to defeat monsters in positions of authority: anonymity, social isolation, computer-hacking savvy, and a willingness to be as ruthless as they are. She is, arguably, a Punisher character, more than willing to execute wealthy despots to bring their reign of terror to an end. However, she is a Punisher character who seems far more intent on dealing out justice to the people really responsible for society's ills — those at the top of the food chain — than the Punisher, who is more concerned with street crime. Also, Lisbeth does not kill legions of criminals, but cherry-picks the worst of the lot. Those she targets are men who feel that they are above the law, and have chosen to indulge their basest impulses, and embrace their inner Fascist, at the expense of the Swedish people in general, and women in particular. These men rape the legal system, rape the economy of their home country, and physically rape every woman they can get their hands on. They rape.

Buffy the Vampire Slayer, *Dollhouse*, and *Judge Anderson: Psi-Division*, all explore similar themes, although Buffy focuses on domestic level crimes, such as college frat boys date raping high school girls and Mayors representing the interests of demonic backers over the interests of their constituents. These angry liberal Furies have the superpowers needed to effectively combat the men in authority, demonstrating that no lone mortal — no mere Mikael Blomkvist — can bring them to justice. A female superhero is needed to get the job done. Only someone like Lisbeth Salander, or perhaps Selina Kyle, can identify the *real* enemy and intuit what needs to be done to take him down.

As compelling as these stories of righteous anti-corporate women are, most vigilante narratives are not angry liberal screeds, but angry conservative screeds. Unconcerned with corporate excess, or crimes committed by good, white, Christian men, most "Punisher" tales are instead interested in seeing the dangerous hippies and brown people of the world brought to the sword for leading a fundamentally corrupt life. Of course, these brown people demonstrate their corruption in such tales by raping white women — just as they have done throughout the history of American film, ever since D.W. Griffith's *Birth of a Nation* (1915). That racist epic portrayed the KKK as a group of vigilantes formed to protect white women from being molested by the freed slaves, and to prevent black men from being voted into elected office. The film's lionizing aesthetic paints the Klan as positively as most Justice League stories paint Superman, Batman, and Wonder Woman, and it is a deeply shocking viewing experience. However, when one thinks about it, one does not have to go far from *Birth of a Nation* to reach *Dirty Harry* or *The Brave One*. The vigilantes in these films kill ruthlessly, in violation of the victim's constitutional rights, and of their human rights. The viewers are supposed to excuse all this because the villains are depicted as mad dogs that need to be put down, and undeserving of human rights.

Whether the vigilante killer is male, like Bronson, or female, like Erica Bain, when they are the main character of a crime exploitation film, their motivations and actions are rarely called into question. In fact, as victims themselves of violent crimes, they are above reproach. After all, since Dirty Harry's wife was killed by a drunk driver, his rage at a lazy, permissive, drug-addled hippie society is understandable, and the revenge he seeks upon the criminals and the liberals who let them roam free to harm decent Americans is intended to be applauded by the audience. The films in the vigilante genre made throughout the 1970s and 1980s, especially those in the *Dirty Harry* film cycle, feature as villainous figures the hippies who stayed behind while the vets fought Vietnam. Other fools and evildoers include feminists, social workers, liberal activists, lenient judges, slimy lawyers, and pin-headed politicians who are "too soft on crime." The anti-liberal sentiments expressed in these films added fuel to the resurgence of the right wing, that grew steadily throughout the 1970s and resulted in the Reagan revolution of the 1980s. As historian Bruce J. Schulman observes:

> The New Right charged the liberal establishment with immorality. Liberal elites in the universities, the press, and the government, conservatives declared, had undercut traditional notions of decency and undermined established sources of authority. In the New Right's terms, the nation's ruling class displayed contempt for "family values." Thus, efforts to protect and restore family values formed [a] major component of the emerging New Right agenda [201].

And what is the antidote to a permissive society in which cops, judges, and Democrat elected officials are too soft on crime? Who can restore law, order, morality, and family values to a crime-infested nation?

The Punisher, of course. Or the Boondock Saints. Or Dirty Harry.

Of all of these characters, Dirty Harry is the most famous and the most effective. The first, and most obvious, reason for Dirty Harry's fame is that he is brilliantly played by screen icon Clint Eastwood, and he boasts uttering the classic movie line, "Go ahead! Make my day." The other thing that makes Dirty Harry such an effective character is that he is based, in part, on a real police officer. Retired San Francisco Police Inspector Dave Toschi, who famously investigated the Zodiac Killer case, has the distinction of being the partial inspiration for two of cinema's most memorable screen police officers: Steve McQueen's Bullitt, who wore his gun over his chest the way Toschi did, and Clint Eastwood's vigilante cop "Dirty" Harry Callahan, who was able to do in the movie world what Toschi was unable to do in the real world — bring the Zodiac Killer to justice.[3]

In 1968 and 1969, the Zodiac Killer terrorized the American populace, threatening to kill randomly in a wide variety of East Coast locales — targeting taxi cab drivers, lovers in public parks, and schoolchildren. As Toschi found it increasingly difficult to coordinate his investigative efforts with police forces based in other jurisdictions, and was frustrated by failing to gather enough evidence to arrest the chief suspect in the case, Arthur Leigh Allen, the mood of the public began to darken. Many increasingly conservative Americans felt that liberal lawyers and bureaucrats were more concerned with the Constitutional rights of criminals than keeping innocent people safe. It seemed as if the liberal elite were conspiring to keep the Zodiac Killer free to murder again. When members of the Charles Manson "Family" murdered pregnant actress Sharon Tate and several of her friends during a home invasion in the dead of night on August 8, 1969 these fears grew even deeper.[4] For many cultural critics, the Manson Family murders and the Zodiac killings, along with the widely publicized acts of violence involving the Hells Angels that occurred on December 6, 1969 at the Altamont Free Concert, helped finish off what little 1960s counterculture idealism remained following the 1968 assassinations of Martin Luther King, Jr., and Bobby Kennedy, and the election of Richard Nixon to the presidency.[5]

The film *Dirty Harry* (1971) was a reflection of the grim mood gripping the nation at the time. The title character's chief opponent, Scorpio, randomly snipes innocent civilians and culminates his reign of terror over the city by hijacking a school bus filled with children. Enraged with an incompetent mayor and cadre of officials who seem unable to do anything but concede to Scorpio's demands, Dirty Harry goes rogue, tracks down Scorpio on his own, frees the school children, and summarily executes Scorpio with his impressive .44 Magnum.

Robert Graysmith, a historian of classic unsolved crimes, ultimately chronicled the exploits of the Zodiac Killer in the non-fiction book *Zodiac*, and that book, in turn, inspired the 2007 film *Zodiac*. The film depicts an incident that was likely invented by screenwriters for dramatic purposes but which, nevertheless, is one of the most evocative segments in the movie. The film depicts an evening in which Graysmith (played by Jake Gyllenhaal) goes to see the film *Dirty Harry* the same night that Dave Toschi (Mark Ruffalo) does. Toschi is appalled by the similarities between the Scorpio killer and the Zodiac Killer and walks out on the film before it ends. Graysmith later finds Toschi in the lobby and informs him that Scorpio was reassuringly dispatched at the end of the film. He leaves unsaid the fact that Scorpio's real-life counterpart remains at liberty, but another theatergoer is not as considerate of Toschi's feelings.

As the crowd lets out of the theater, one patron recognizes Toschi and calls out, "Dave! That Harry Callahan did a hell of a job on your case!"

"Yeah," Toschi replies. "No need for due process, right?"

Although it seems unlikely that this event transpired in real life, the scene was still pivotal because it underlined, quite effectively, one of the key themes of the movie, which is that it is very easy for one madman, like the Zodiac Killer, to frighten the public into accepting a loss of liberty, even essential liberties such as due process. During times such as these, it is easy to forget that Founding Father Benjamin Franklin believed "those who would give up essential liberties to purchase a little temporary safety deserve neither liberty nor safety" (Isaacson 169).

Like the screen incarnation of the real-life Toschi, the late film critic Pauline Kael condemned the film *Dirty Harry* for promoting extremist, essentially Fascist values. She wrote in a review that "[t]his right-wing fantasy about the San Francisco police force as a helpless group (emasculated by unrealistic liberals) propagandizes for para-legal police power and vigilante justice.... [The film is] a remarkably single-minded attack on liberal values, with each prejudicial detail in place—a kind of hardhat *The Fountainhead*. Harry's hippie adversary is pure evil: sniper, rapist, kidnapper, torturer, defiler of all human values. This monster—who wears a peace symbol—stands for everything the audience fears and loathes. The action genre has always had a fascist potential, and it surfaces in this movie."[6]

One of the reasons Kael loathed the film is because it was dramatically effective conservative propaganda that made Dirty Harry's position seem to be the only logical, moral, and just position, whereas well-intentioned liberals were clearly evil in their desire to place the importance of civil liberties over public safety. Indeed, those who watch the first *Dirty Harry* film, or many of its sequels, might be inclined to find the conservative logic underpinning the franchise beyond reproach. However, all one needs to do is look at Dirty Harry's position from another angle, and the flaw in his argument becomes clear.

Dirty Harry's logic that the problem of crime can be solved by killing all criminals is akin to Victorian-era serial killer Jack the Ripper's reasoning that killing prostitutes can rid the world of venereal disease. Historians theorize that the Ripper was probably stricken by a venereal disease, such as syphilis, which he caught by visiting prostitutes. In revenge, he began a campaign of slaughtering and desecrating the bodies of prostitutes who worked the Whitechapel district of London. In an anonymous letter to the police, the Ripper boasted, "I am down on whores" and "shant quit ripping them till I do get buckled [arrested]" (Underwood 76). There are indications that his murdering of prostitutes constitutes a cleansing of immoral elements in the city, and measures against the further spread of sexually transmitted disease. This twisted logic—that murder is a good way to prevent the spread of disease—is not far removed from the argument that executing more criminals can abate crime. This logic is also similar to the logic employed by environmental terrorists, both in the real world and in the world of comic books (such as Ra's al Ghul and Poison Ivy), who murder polluters as a means of ending pollution, or pro-life murderers who shoot abortion doctors to prevent the killing of unborn children. The motivations of these murderous figures are graspable, and they sometimes elicit support from the general public, who see them as folk heroes and are glad that someone is doing the dirty work for the government and taking measures to purge society of its most loathsome elements. Nevertheless, there is a lack of human feeling at the core of their revolutionary movements that makes them little different from the forces they see themselves as opposing. Oftentimes, they are far, far worse.

The Marvel Comics "superhero" the Punisher is cut from the same cloth as perennially popular antiheroes such as Dirty Harry, only he operates within a world dominated by superheroes such as Spider-Man, Daredevil, and Ghost Rider. However, when the Punisher leaves the world of comic books behind and graduates to films of his own, his universe is stripped of super-powered elements and he even more resembles the characters that originally inspired him — the film vigilantes played by Clint Eastwood and Charles Bronson. The Punisher has appeared in three eponymous films, a direct-to-video release in 1989 featuring Dolph Lundgren as the Punisher and two theatrical releases featuring Thomas Jane (2004's *The Punisher*) and Ray Stevenson (2008's *The Punisher: War Zone*) respectively playing the title role. In addition to the films, the Punisher has appeared in cartoons and video games, and has inspired a number of novelty T-shirt designs and action figures. Originally created as an adversary for Spider-Man in "The Punisher Strikes Twice!" (*The Amazing Spider-Man* #129, 1974), Frank Castiglione gradually evolved from a sympathetic villain to a deeply troubling hero as his popularity grew and he graduated from Spider-Man supporting character to the star of his own comic books. Despite his popularity among comic books fans, the Punisher's films were box office disappointments and his iconography remains more famous than the character himself— the skull emblem that he wears on his shirt has become so ubiquitous that many people who buy and wear Punisher T-shirts in the real world aren't aware they are wearing Punisher merchandise *per se*, but just think it is a "cool skull T-shirt."

Thomas Jane stars in *The Punisher* (Lions Gate, 2004) as the fan-favorite title character.

Many comic book writers take a sympathetic view of the Punisher and see him as an average citizen who has been pushed too far. Inside all of us lurks a potential Punisher, once someone harms our family. In this view, the Punisher is not insane, but exercising a natural instinct to protect and avenge loved ones. This interpretation of the character is easy to accept and relate to when one considers the character's origin story, or the visceral appeal of films such as *Taken* (2008), in which a special forces character played by Liam Neeson goes to any and all lengths to rescue his daughter, who has been kidnapped and sold into white slavery. After all, who would not go to extreme lengths to protect one's family? Who would not cheer as Neeson, finally, successfully rescues his daughter when the weak and corrupt French police force lacked the will to do what needed to be done?

Characters such as the Punisher or the hero of *Taken* become more problematic, however, after the family member in question is rescued or avenged, and the angry white male protagonist continues to wage an indiscriminate war on crime with the same savage intensity he had employed while out to avenge a wronged family member. It is also important to point out that exploitation films, and action films in general, tend to win over enthusiastic audience support for a murderous rampage by making it in retaliation for the death or kidnapping of a child or the brutal rape of a beautiful young woman. For example, David Mamet made the Untouchables' war on crime in the name of a little girl who was accidentally killed by a bomb planted by a gangster at the start of *The Untouchables* (1987) film. He did this, presumably, because he anticipated that audience members who regularly partake of alcohol in a post–Prohibition era would not sympathize with Eliot Ness if he traveled Chicago machine-gunning Italians to death in retaliation for the illegal distribution of alcohol. Consequently, even when revenge is not originally a motivation for a character as he is originally envisioned, it is often later written into his background to act as a justification for any killings he perpetrates in the name of justice. While Robert E. Howard's Conan the Barbarian is a wandering adventurer who is not generally motivated by revenge, writer-director John Milius seemed to feel that a modern-day audience would respond better to Conan if he murdered dozens of cultists in retaliation for the burning of his village and the murdering of his parents in *Conan the Barbarian* (1982). Killings perpetrated on the battlefield, or in the name of revenge, or perpetrated by *24*'s Jack Bauer in the name of national security on the eve of nuclear war are graspable to many Americans. Otherwise, mass murder is not something most people feel comfortable cheering on; hence the use of the dead child, parent, or wife as, effectively, a plot device and a sop to the troubled conscience of the audience member.

The Punisher's creator, Gerry Conway, came up with the basic premise and look of the Punisher, and artist John Romita finalized the design for penciller Ross Andru to draw in the final comic book. As Conway explains, "My idea of the Punisher was that he was a guy who was driven by his need for vengeance but was not so driven that he couldn't see what was going on around him." Conway did not intend to present the Punisher as insane, but he acknowledges that writers who have written the character since have done so.

Interestingly, Conway never referred to the character as anything but the Punisher, but writer Steven Grant made the swarthy figure an Italian in 1986's *The Punisher* #1. Grant's script revealed that the Punisher was born Frank Castiglione to Mario and Louise Castiglione, Sicilian immigrants living in New York. The parents Americanized the family name to "Castle" in 1956, when Frank was six. Since Frank had an Italian surname for the first few years of his life, and then saw his surname changed at an impressionable age, the change probably contributed to his conflicted feelings about his own ethnicity.[7]

Future writers, such as Mike Baron, expanded upon the Punisher's Italian background by revealing that Frank Castle was a Roman Catholic who had briefly studied to become a priest but left the seminary when he discovered that he had difficulty forgiving those who confessed to committing grievous sins during the Sacrament of Confession (see the 1989 graphic novel *The Punisher: Intruder*). It was later revealed that Castle met his future wife,

Maria Falconio, after leaving the seminary, and that he enlisted in the Marines and fought in Vietnam after his marriage. By making the Punisher a former seminarian, the comic book achieved three things: it added a layer of characterization to a fairly one-dimensional figure; it tapped into the evocative hypocrisy best exemplified by Michael Corleone in *The Godfather* films of the churchgoing murderer; and it gave the Punisher a history of religious zealotry.[8] This zealotry transferred from traditional Catholicism — which has come to embrace a "consistent life ethic" over the past several decades, opposing the death penalty, abortion, and euthanasia — to a harsh, fanatical mission to kill virtually every career criminal he encounters.

Mike Baron is one of the writers who has written the Punisher in a highly sympathetic light, and he is not the only creative figure at Marvel Entertainment who seems to regard the character with a measure of understanding, perhaps even a little admiration. According to Ari Arad, an executive at Marvel Studios who worked on the 2004 film adaptation, the Punisher is not insane, but a man whose morality is so different that it makes him a pariah. "His system of ethics, his moral code, is very different from most people's, but it is specific and it exists. He doesn't kill innocent people. He has a benchmark for people that deserve to die and he's going to kill them, but it is not an arbitrary benchmark and it is not one that he violates."

Somehow surviving all of his run-ins with criminals, and never successfully being contained by the police, the Punisher's war on crime has lasted (in the fictional timeline of his comic book adventures) for thirty years. Law enforcement characters within his comic book adventures have charged him with the deaths of *thousands* of criminals. While the character exists in a universe of superheroes, he himself is not supposed to have any superpowers, but his longevity and invincibility cannot be accounted for by normal means (not even his nifty Kevlar body armor), so certain writers have suggested that he has been granted supernatural abilities, either by God or the devil, to wage his war for so long, as Garth Ennis did in *Born*.

Offering a more positive portrayal of the character than Ennis does in *Born*, the 2004 *Punisher* film goes to great lengths to justify Castle's murderous campaign against Howard Saint by having Saint responsible for the deaths of Castle's entire extended family. In the film, Saint sends his hired killers to the Castle family reunion and they machine gun everyone in attendance. The film also strives to justify Castle's decision to quit the police force and take the law into his own hands: Castle is unwilling to go to the police or the judiciary system because (in the extended cut of the film), his African American partner, Weeks, helped Saint find and eliminate Castle's family members. Saint is also, presumably, the richest man in Tampa, and has the police in his pocket.[9]

The police are not always evil in the Punisher universe, but they are usually ineffective. The Lundgren film, for example, portrays the police as weak and inefficient, but not corrupt.[10] In that version of the story, Louis Gossett, Jr., plays Castle's former partner, Jake Berkowitz, who is a decent man that hopes to capture Castle and get his friend treatment for mental illness. When Berkowitz is finally reunited with his former partner, he cries when he sees just how much of the humanity has been burned out of Castle's eyes. Louis Gossett, Jr.'s character also provides a heart, humanity, and decency to a film that is otherwise cynical and coldhearted. He is the moral center of the story, and his perspective represents a genuine alternative to the worldview offered by the mentally ill Punisher. Since Berkowitz exists as a goodhearted cop in the Lundgren film, the movie raises the possibility that the Punisher could have, if he wanted, fought crime more mercifully and within the system, alongside his old friend. The excuse the Punisher uses that he alone can fight crime has even less resonance in the comic book universe, in which characters like Spider-Man and Daredevil are arguably just as effective at fighting crime while still being merciful. However, it is important to note that, while Spider-Man and Daredevil are presented as effective crimefighters while appearing in their own comic books, when they guest star in the Punisher comic books, they are shown to be as misguided and ineffective as any liberal cop or official in a *Dirty Harry* or *Death Wish* film. So, even Spider-Man and Daredevil are not impressive enough figures to be immune from liberal-bashing in exploitative entertainment.

Still, of all of the superheroes, Spider-Man is the most sympathetic to the Punisher, because he has lost so many loved ones to criminals—including Uncle Ben, Gwen Stacy, Capt. George Stacy, Jean DeWolffe, and Nathan Lubensky—and his first instinct each time one of his loved ones is killed is to seek murderous revenge. So far only chance, acts of God, and a last-minute change-of-heart have prevented him from walking the same path as the Punisher, but the real thing keeping Spider-Man from ever killing a criminal is Marvel Comics Group, which would probably never allow Spider-Man to become a murderer on the off chance that it will hurt the sale of Spider-Man merchandise to children. A hero for kids shouldn't kill, after all.

A different kind of Roman Catholic than the Punisher, Daredevil ruthlessly fights street crime, but his Catholic upbringing has long prevented him from taking the lives of his opponents, even those such as Bullseye, who murdered Daredevil's girlfriends Elektra and Karen Page. (*Shadowland* changed this.) However, the Daredevil character played by Ben Affleck in the 2003 movie, did indeed, kill at the start of the film, but repented his murderous ways and made a point of not killing the Kingpin of Crime at the end of the film.

The Punisher has always been supernaturally good at determining who is "bad" and who is "good," and neither the Punisher nor readers of his magazine have been challenged by a highly publicized story in which Castle has accidentally killed a child or a falsely convicted criminal. The closest the Punisher ever came to killing an innocent man was Spider-Man himself. In the first-ever Punisher story, Castle is tricked into believing that Spider-Man murdered "innocent" businessman Norman Osborne. When he finds out that Osborne was the Green Goblin, and that Osborn had been killed in a freak accident while fighting Spider-Man, he breaks off his attack on Spider-Man and goes off in search of the truly guilty men. But the Punisher's near-disastrous mistake in attacking Spider-Man does not cause him to rethink his never-ending mission to fight crime, or his constant use of lethal force. Nor does the Punisher believe that criminals can ever be rehabilitated, no matter the circumstances.

Some Punisher stories try to evoke audience sympathy with the character and attempt to justify his mad quest, while others assume a more ironic, satirical, or critical distance. The Punisher's role in the Civil War over the Superhero Registration Act emphasized his bizarre code of ethics while making him seem both noble and mentally unhinged, especially when compared to Spider-Man and Captain America. In one of the story's major ironies, Iron Man offers amnesty to former supervillains who chose to embrace Registration, while condemning superheroes who opposed it to life sentences in prison without trial or hope of parole. Consequently, evil characters such as Venom, the Green Goblin, and Bullseye were pardoned even as Captain America and Spider-Man (after his defection from Iron Man's side to Captain America's) were declared public enemies and hunted by Iron Man.

In stories written by Mark Millar (*Civil War*) and Matt Fraction (*Punisher War Journal: Civil War*), the Punisher chose to side with Captain America once Iron Man began recruiting former villains. Castle dramatically saves Spider-Man's life when he is ambushed by Iron Man's mercenaries and brings the wounded hero back to the rebel superhero base of operations. Captain America reluctantly considers inviting the Punisher to join their side permanently, despite the Human Torch's objections that such an alliance amounted to getting into bed with Hannibal Lecter. The situation changed dramatically, however, when supervillains who opposed registration made overtures of friendship to Captain America within earshot of the Punisher.

1ST SUPERVILLAIN: You guys ain't the only ones scared we're headed for a police state, Captain. The super criminal community's more concerned about [Tony] Stark's plans than anyone.

2ND SUPERVILLAIN: We just came by to let you know we're here if you need us. Only fair if Iron Man's got supervillains on his side, right? Whaddaya say?

THE PUNISHER: [Instantly machine guns the two to death, then looks confused when the gathering of superheroes is watching him, aghast.] What?

CAPTAIN AMERICA: [Punches the Punisher to the ground] You murderous piece of trash!

Captain America continues beating the Punisher, who refuses to fight back. He merely protests that he had only killed bad guys, but accepts the punishment meted out to him by his commanding officer. When the scuffle is over, and the Punisher is led out of the room as a prisoner, witnesses speculate why the Punisher merely took the beating. Spider-Man suggests that Captain America must be the Punisher's hero. "Cap's probably the reason he went to Vietnam," he said. "Same guy, different war."

Captain America flinches and gives Spider-Man an icy stare. "Wrong. Frank Castle is insane." In the Marvel Universe, Captain America has the same moral authority as Superman, so his pronouncement on the Punisher bears enormous moral weight. It is one of the most dramatic and intriguing scenes featuring the Punisher since his creation, probably because it was not a Punisher story, but one that he was a guest character in. When the Punisher is featured in his own comic book or film, he is portrayed far more positively.

As a general rule, the Punisher seems at his most insane whenever he meets another superhero and argues that they are weak for being against the death penalty. Although cut from the same cloth as the Punisher, Ghost Rider, the "Spirit of Vengeance," is actually far more fair-minded than Frank Castle, and he does not kill. Johnny Blaze, a stunt motorcycle driver inspired by Evel Knievel, turns into a leather-clad skeleton with a flaming head when he is in the presence of evil. Rather than kill the sinner, Ghost Rider uses his "penance stare" to make the offender feel the full ramifications of the pain that he has wrought upon his victims. This punishment represents true balance — a literal "eye for an eye" — that is not possible outside of supernatural means, and a "fairness" the Punisher never even tries to achieve. Although Ghost Rider (played in the 2007 film adaptation by Nicolas Cage) is an angry character, he is more about balance and justice than the Punisher, giving exactly what was got and not escalating violence by making all crimes death-penalty offences. In contrast with Ghost Rider, the Punisher may be read as a morality tale warning against the spiritual emptiness, never-ending horrors, and perpetually escalating cycle of violence that ensues when the thirst for vengeance overtakes the need for justice.

But Ghost Rider may still be too bleak a figure to truly provide an alternative to the Punisher's worldview. Batman and Wonder Woman provide starker contrasts. In a particularly satisfying moment from *JLA/Avengers,* Batman prevents the Punisher from gunning down a group of drug dealers and takes measures to end Castle's career as a glorified serial killer by beating Castle to a pulp and leaving him for the police. In a more improbable, somewhat satirical adventure with a double entendre for a title—"Bullets and Bracelets: The Final Thrust" (1996)—Wonder Woman takes pity on the Punisher, attempts to mentally rehabilitate him, and falls in love with him. The two marry and have a child together, Ryan Castiglione, but the formerly pacifistic and socialistic Wonder Woman finds her worldview darkened by her husband's insanity, while she does little to lift him from depressed memories of his first family. They divorce and Wonder Woman assumes custody of the baby as the Punisher returns to his insane war on crime. Since the story was a spoof, it is not considered a "real" or "canonical" adventure for either Wonder Woman or the Punisher. Nevertheless, it was clever of the writer, John Ostrander, to pair polar opposite "superheroes" the Punisher, who is bloody Fascism incarnate, with Wonder Woman, who believes in redemption and often successfully negotiates peace with her enemies rather than use force against them.

The title character of the film *Ghost Rider* (Sony Pictures, 2007), starring Nicolas Cage as Johnny Blaze, a stunt motorcycle rider who is possessed by the skeletal "Spirit of Vengeance."

Other comic book characters appear to have been created as a commentary on the Punisher, or a corrective to his pernicious influence in comic books, since many parents and older fans were disturbed by how popular the Punisher became with angry adolescent readership during the 1980s and 1990s. For example, DC comics created Helena Bertinelli, an Italian American character who became the avenging Huntress when rival gangsters killed her Mafia Don father. She killed many of those responsible for her father's death, but she was ultimately rehabilitated, renounced murder, and became a crime fighter in the vein of the anti–death-penalty Batman. The story of her retreat from psychological darkness into the light was related in the *Justice League* animated series and *Birds of Prey* comic books written by Gail Simone.

Another response to the Punisher came from overseas. During the 1980s, British comic-book writer John Wagner created Judge Dredd to spoof characters such as the Punisher, and to critique the extreme, militaristic American conservatism of the Reagan administration. Dredd imprisons people for jaywalking, destroys illegally parked cars, beats senseless those who speak disrespectfully to the police, maims thieves, and kills or gives life sentences to anyone who commits any crime more serious than those already mentioned. In fact, in the universe of Judge Dredd, sugar is a dangerous narcotic, and Dredd, who acts as a state-sanctioned Judge, Jury, and Executioner, kills anyone he finds with the illegal white powder. The satirical tone of *Judge Dredd*, which carried over into the 1995 film starring Sylvester Stallone, mocks conservatives by taking their repressive philosophy to its ultimate conclusion. In fact, Judge Dredd's archenemy, Judge Death, is a zombie who has determined that, since all sins are committed by the living, life itself must, therefore, be a sin. Consequently, Judge Death kills *everyone* he meets. In the world of Judge Dredd, Dredd can only act in a heroic fashion when he is pitted against a character as operatically evil as Judge Death. Under other circumstances, Dredd is the villain of his own comic book.

One of the only nice, intelligent characters in the Judge Dredd universe is Judge Cassandra Anderson, a psychic colleague of Dredd's with a mordant sense of humor. She has the uncanny ability to capture and contain Judge Death's disembodied spirit in her mind like a genie in a bottle. Artist Brian Bolland designed Judge Anderson to look like Blondie lead singer Deborah Harry, and Olivia Thirlby was cast to play her in her rookie days opposite Karl Urban's more seasoned Judge Dredd in the second Dredd film. However, when it comes to common sense, Dredd is the true rookie and Anderson the wise, practical one. In *The Batman/Judge Dredd Files* (2004), the seemingly unstoppable Judge Death arrives in Gotham City and begins slaughtering everyone in sight. Investigating where the invincible zombie came from in the hopes of finding its Achilles' heel, Batman is accidentally teleported through dimensions to Dredd's universe, where Dredd promptly arrests the new arrival for carrying unlicensed weapons. Batman pleads with Dredd to return with him to Gotham and stop Death, but Gotham is outside Dredd's jurisdiction, and Dredd says simply that he doesn't make deals with convicted criminals. Disappointed with Dredd's tunnel-vision, Anderson frees Batman from captivity and travels with him to Gotham to stop Judge Death. Meanwhile, a vengeful and humiliated Judge Dredd heads off in hot pursuit — eager to stop *them*, not Judge Death.

The telepathic superhero Judge Cassandra Anderson (left) is the only one capable of defeating the near-invincible zombie, Judge Death (right). Illustrated by Matt Haley. Judge Anderson and Judge Death © Fleetway Pub.

After serving as a supporting character in 2000 AD's *Judge Dredd* for several adventures, Anderson graduated to her own spinoff title, *Anderson: Psi-Division.* Her most famous adventure, *The Possessed,* is a powerful, Sacrifice of Abraham narrative in which she is compelled to murder an innocent child to prevent the gates of hell from opening upon the world. Anderson resigned from the Fascistic Psi-Division after the events of the story *Engram,* when she discovered that her superiors wiped her memories of being molested by her father as a child — not for her own personal benefit, but to make her a "better" officer.

If only most *Punisher* comic books were written with a measure of self-awareness and irony, as the Judge Dredd and Judge Anderson tales are. Instead, there is an extent to which the Punisher comics, lurid as they are, strive for a realism that appears to endorse the Punisher's actions, and a radical form of conservatism, that is quite disturbing. On the one hand, the comic books like to present the Punisher as an equal-opportunity killer, since he has slain street gang members, corporate criminals inspired by the Enron offenders, Muslim terrorists, and members of the Italian, Irish, Japanese, and Russian mobs. However, there still seems to be a racist overtone to the comic as a whole and, no matter how many Waspish U.S. Senators he assassinates for political corruption, the Punisher still seems to be most at his most ecstatic when he breaks into a warehouse and begins machine gunning legions of Italians, Japanese ninjas, and non-white foes with gold teeth.

The Punisher has the most personal anger for the Italians, because it was they who killed his family. Consequently, the adventures in which he squares off against the Mafia are the ones that have the most dramatic resonance. For example, in "Red X-Mas," writers Jimmy Palmiotti and Justin Gray introduced a close circle of Mafia widows who decide to avenge their husbands' murders by putting a contract out on the man who killed their mates — Frank Castle. Ringleader Regina Napolitano, who lost three husbands to Castle's crusade, talks the other widows into contributing $5,000 apiece to hire Suspiria (an in-joke reference to Dario Argento's ultra-violent Italian horror film), a female assassin from Sicily. The leather-clad S&M sexpot Suspiria fails to kill Castle and, in an ironic twist, the two later become lovers because of their mutual love of carnage. In the meantime, Castle tracks down and kills Regina, and warns the other widows to donate several thousands of dollars to charity and leave the country or he will hunt them down one by one. As he puts it, "Just because you married a bunch of greaseballs, doesn't make you gangsters. I'm giving you a stay of execution."

Here, Frank Castle seems to hold Italian Americans in the same high regard that James Bond does. In Ian Fleming's novel *Diamonds are Forever* (1956), Bond says, "There's nothing extraordinary about American gangsters.... They're not Americans. Mostly a lot of Italian bums with monogrammed shirts who spend the day eating spaghetti and meat-balls and squirting scent over themselves. ... greaseballs who filled themselves up with pizza pie and beer all week and on Saturdays knocked off a garage or drug store so as to pay their way at the races." Such sentiments are unsurprising coming from James Bond, who never has anything good to say about any Americans, whatever their ethnicity, occupation, or place of residence, save his CIA-agent friend Felix Leiter. When an Italian American starts talking about his own kind in similar language, it is more noteworthy.[11]

In the Boaz Yakin script of the film adaptation starring Dolph Lundgren, Castle's vendetta against the various Italian crime families has weakened their hold on the city to the extent that the Japanese Yakuza is able to move in on their territory. While the Punisher is initially delighted to see a gang war brewing and jokes that he can finally go on vacation and let the Yakuza finish off the Italians for him, he feels compelled to help his enemies when Yakuza boss Lady Tanaka kidnaps the children of all of the Mafia dons and threatens to sell them into slavery. The Punisher reluctantly teams up with the same gangster who ordered his family killed, Gianni Franco (played by Jeroen Krabbe), in order to rescue the children, who he sees as innocent of any wrongdoing and undeserving of being punished for their fathers' crimes. At the end of the film, the Punisher rescues the children, but kills Franco in front of his own son, Tommy. The Punisher warns Tommy not to grow up to be like his father. "You're a good boy, Tommy. Grow up to be a good man ... because if not,

I'll be waiting." This horrifying and evocative finale inspired a variety of similar scenes in later comic books in which the Punisher, dressed in the garb of Santa Claus, would kill criminals in front of children and then pause to explain to the shocked little ones, "They were naughty." The unsubtle message is, "Be good little children, or the Punisher will come to get you." Like Santa Claus, the Punisher *knows* if you've been bad or good, so be good *for goodness sake*.

But *how* does he know? Is it that pact he made with Satan in Vietnam? Is he a good guesser? Does he *really* know? What if the Punisher accidentally killed someone who was innocent? The answer to this final question was a long time coming, but it was addressed, somewhat ineffectively, in the 2008 film *Punisher: War Zone*. The movie features the requisite cartoon Italian villains, each one more loathsome and inhuman than the next, ranging from aging, invalid mob boss Gaitano Cesare to his vain and primping nephew Billy Russoti (whose good looks would be destined to be destroyed by the Punisher), and Billy's insane brother, Loony Bin Jim. The film begins when the Punisher decides to wipe out the entire Cesare crime family while they celebrate foiling the Justice Department's attempt to break up their crime ring. As the Punisher shoots and stabs his way through every Guido in sight, he accidentally kills an undercover, Italian American FBI agent, Nicky Donnatelli, a character in the same mold as real-life law-enforcement legend Joe Pistone.[12] Realizing he has finally killed an innocent person by mistake and committed the kind of evil act he has sworn to punish, Castle considers ending his career as the Punisher. Actor Ray Stevenson's performance is compelling here, as Castle considers the possibility that he may be a villain after all, but the film ultimately cannot resolve this moral dilemma satisfactorily because of Marvel Studios' desire for there to be more *Punisher* films. The logic of the story — and the character of the Punisher — demands that the anti-hero *punish* himself, by either turning himself in or killing himself, or that he be relieved of the burden of his guilt by discovering that Nicky Donatelli was corrupt after all. None of these things happen. Instead, the almost-retired Punisher is forced back into action when he learns that Russoti has targeted the widow Donnatelli and her young daughter for death. In another interesting dramatic wrinkle, the Donnatellis remind Castle of his murdered wife and daughter, and he sees himself as symbolically being given a second chance to protect his family from being killed by the Mafia.

Meanwhile, Russoti builds a coalition army of criminals with which to face off against the Punisher, appealing to black, Latino, and Asian gang members to join forces against the prejudiced Punisher, who kills people who look "different." He further asserts that the police don't try hard to end the Punisher's reign of terror because they, too, are secretly racist. Russotti's provocative — and valid — line of argument aside, the film elicits audience sympathy with the Punisher and the Donnatelli family, and archconservative viewers are likely to celebrate as the Punisher succeeds in protecting the Donnatellis by slaughtering an army of gangsters and street criminals, leaving no one left alive to threaten them. When the dust settles, Frank Castle does not retire from being the Punisher, nor does he attempt to embrace a normal life by connecting more emotionally, and permanently, with the Donnatellis.

One of the recurring themes of revenge-based Punisher stories is that the Mafia makes a habit of murdering entire families, whether they be innocent bystanders who witnessed something unfortunate, or the family members of cops, rival Dons, or "rats." This is a storytelling tactic designed to make them seem particularly evil and win audience support for the Punisher's quest to exterminate Mafiosi. However, it is important to note that, in the real world, Italian gangsters are not this evil. According to Barry Harvey, a twenty-four year veteran of the Pennsylvania State Police's Organized Crime Division, "One of the unique things about the Mafia is that they are a criminal organization with tradition and rules, a code of conduct if you will, ways of doing things. Unlike some portrayals, they are not random killers. They do not kill people's wives and families even to get even. They accept the fact that they can be killed at any time as part of their 'occupation' but wives and families are usually off limits. They are very specific killers. So the depiction of them killing a family and then this Punisher taking revenge on them is very far from the truth."[13]

Because the Punisher is such a one-note character, he tends to be at his most interesting when he is sparing lives rather than taking them, but he is still more iconic in his "boogeyman of the underworld" persona than he is a three-dimensional character. That is why, when screenwriter Michael France was assigned to write a first draft of a screenplay for the 2004 adaptation of *The Punisher*, he felt the challenge was to make the character fresh when the "'you killed my family—prepare to die' story and character had been done a thousand times."[14] France felt that the key to the character was the fact that, on the one hand, Castle enjoyed killing criminals, and on the other, he hated his existence as the Punisher and would "trade anything at all to have his family back." To tackle this duality in the Punisher, France rewrote the origin story a little, placing Castle in the same situation as Joe Pistone was in the film *Donnie Brasco*. In France's version, Castle was an undercover FBI agent and family man who had infiltrated the Mafia and was enjoying both his existence as a mobster and as a husband and father. Unsure who "the real Frank" was, father or gangster, Castle decided to quit the FBI and leave the evil influence of the Mafia behind. Unfortunately, his extraction from the field doesn't go well, his cover is blown, and his old associates seek revenge by killing Castle's family. As France explains, "Frank Castle the family man dies with his family and he reverts to the man he's been pretending to be for years while undercover: a completely ruthless psycho who goes after the mobsters who killed his family."[15]

France's idea played up the Punisher's Italian identity and blurred the distinction between Castle and the gangsters he fought by making Castle the son of a mobster. "I had another character angle which was so dark I understand why [it didn't make it into the final film]. In the movie, Frank's father is a lawman played by Roy Scheider. But in my drafts, I established that Frank's father was actually a hitman in New York City named 'Il Punisco'—'The Punisher'—and Frank was always ashamed of that. He joined the FBI to prove that he wasn't at all like his father—but the fact is, he was such a good killer that every day he was on the job as an undercover cop, he was proving that he was exactly like his father."[16]

The film that was eventually made seemed reluctant to engage in Italian stereotyping, avoiding revealing that, according to the comic books, Castle's birth name was Castiglione. It also dropped France's idea for the Punisher's father as Il Punisco, and changed the guilty party responsible for the Castle family killings from the Costa family to Howard Saint, a figure who is presumably not Italian even though Italian American actor John Travolta plays him. While Italian villains are not present, other villains in the film are far more stereotypical, including a steroid enhanced Russian assassin similar to *Rocky IV*'s Ivan Drago, and the Toro Brothers, Hispanic gangsters inspired by the Spider-Man villains the Lobo Brothers. Still worse, the film features a psychotic gay assassin named Quentin Glass and Saint's bloodthirsty wife, Vivian, who coaxed her husband into having Castle's entire family killed instead of just putting a hit on Castle himself. Despite the fact that the audience is meant to feel somewhat sorry for Vivian and Quentin in the end, when they fall victim to Castle's elaborate (and cruel) revenge scheme, their respective sexual orientation and gender cast the film's already politically incorrect sensibilities in an even darker light. Interestingly, in making the villains a multi-ethnic cast of stereotyped villains instead of a group of Italians, the film goes from being potentially offensive to Italians, and prejudiced against Italians, to potentially offensive to women, gays, Hispanics, Russians, and other groups who might see themselves in the Punisher's squalid rogue's gallery. And, as much as the Punisher hates his own people, this is not the first time he has slaughtered unflatteringly portrayed members of other minority groups. Therefore, the recent Punisher film is not the first film to seem racist against just about everyone.

Unlike the Punisher, who kills plenty of non–Italians, but who reserves a special hatred for his own people, the Irish-American vigilantes Connor and Murphy MacManus featured in *The Boondock Saints* (1999) are functionally protectors of the Irish American community in Boston. After hearing a sermon during Sunday mass about the importance of fighting evil in society, the MacManus twins defend the local Irish bar from being shaken down by Russian Mafia extortionists. They kill the gangsters in self-defense and become neighborhood heroes. Afterwards, the MacManus brothers go on a killing spree, focusing their attention on purging Boston of the Russian and Italian mobs, but claiming to be against all criminals who prey upon the innocent. Like the Punisher, the Boondock Saints are religious fanatics who think God is on their side when they kill criminals. While a gay FBI agent played by Willem Dafoe briefly pursues these "Boondock Saints," his character ultimately comes to see the wisdom of their actions, and does not arrest them. There is some indication that he even joins them at the end of the film.

The Boondock Saints was written and directed by Troy Duffy, who reportedly felt compelled to write the screenplay as a form of therapy after he saw a murdered woman being removed from an apartment across the hall from him. As Duffy explained in an interview:

> I decided right there that out of sheer frustration and not being able to afford a psychologist, I was going to write this, think about it. People watching the news sometimes get so disgusted by what they see. Susan Smith drowning her kids ... guys going into McDonald's, lighting up the whole place. You hear things that disgust you so much that even if you're Mother Teresa, there comes a breaking point. One day you're gonna watch the news and you're gonna say, "Whoever did that despicable things should pay with their life."[17]

Duffy's rage at the sight of the murdered woman is understandable. Nevertheless, there is a disturbingly racist overtone to the film *The Boondock Saints*. In fact, one of the Italians, who ultimately joins forces with the MacManus brothers against his own people, tells a racist joke in which a genie solves all of white America's "problems" by teleporting all Hispanics to Mexico and all blacks back to Africa. The joke is not only mean-spirited, but makes one wonder if the Boondock Saints are not performing the same function as the genie, only by killing minorities instead of deporting them. The symbolism of the MacManus brothers as guardians of American "whiteness" is particularly ironic if one considers the fact that, when the Irish first came to America, they were greeted with terrible racism from the whites who already lived here, and were the targets of NINA ("No Irish Need Apply") laws. So the anger and hatred that the Boondock Saints level against immigrants who came to America after them seems hypocritical in the extreme.

Of course, people who embrace racist sentiments always like to have a justification for their feelings, and many racists blame the conditions of the inner cities on the minorities who live there, and not on the businessmen who own the buildings in that part of the city. Irish-Americans tend to be particularly unforgiving of those blacks and Hispanics who moved into neighborhoods they had previously occupied, shortly before those same neighborhoods appeared to go steeply downhill. The same is often true of Italian Americans.[18]

Ironically, such justifications have been most effectively countered by a voice for tolerance that comes from the unlikeliest of quarters, the Irish American, right-leaning Fox News personality who bills himself as a moderate: Bill O'Reilly. Using personal memories and anecdotal evidence rather than statistics, O'Reilly nevertheless gives a reasonable response to Italian Americans who blame the wrong people for the deterioration of the neighborhoods they used to live in. As O'Reilly writes in *The O'Reilly Factor: The Good, the Bad, and the Completely Ridiculous in American Life* (2000):

> The attitude of my [prejudiced] friend's parents came, I think, from the history of our lily-white town. Levittown was populated in the 1950s, mostly by whites who fled Brooklyn after World War II. This sudden exodus was caused by evil real estate agents. They began buying up small apartment houses and moving black families in. This was not an enlightened plan to promote integration and harmony among the races. They knew that many Irish, Italian, and Jewish families would succumb to prejudice—and to well-placed rumors—by selling their row houses in a panic....
>
> Real estate prices dropped drastically in many working-class sections of Brooklyn. The real estate people, the blockbusters themselves, snapped up the houses cheap. Then they subdivided them, squeezing two black families into a one-family structure. One thing led to another, and the quality of some neighborhoods spiraled downward fast. The agents, now acting as landlords, made a killing on rent but provided little maintenance....
>
> Naturally, many of the blocks owned by blockbusters began to deteriorate. Some whites blamed the black renters for this decline, but they were looking only at the surface. The slums had been created by blockbusters, and they were never really held accountable. Setting one race against another, they used fear and prejudice to make money, not caring that well-kept, peaceful neighborhoods were destroyed [156–157].

While there is evidence to support O'Reilly's claims, such a reflection on the creation of "bad neighborhoods" rarely filters into popular crime narratives, be they *Punisher* comic books or episodes of *NYPD Blue*, which are more concerned with depicting the punishment of an individual criminal for a particular crime rather than with looking at the root causes of poverty, crime, and race and class divisions. Only the comic book *Green Lantern/Green Arrow*, written during the activist 1970s by Dennis O'Neil, dares to show a superhero (the Robin Hood–like Green Arrow) join a gang of minorities in attacking a fat, white businessman for being a slum lord rather than depict a superhero defending a "respectable businessman from an unreasonable mob." It is a striking, progressive image, watching the Caucasian Green Arrow condemn the greedy white businessmen, but it is, again, the exception that proves the rule. Far more common in the world of comic books is the sight of the Punisher acting as racial purist, killing a black or Hispanic mugger/rapist in an alley after the grotesque criminal accosted a pretty white woman at the point of a switchblade. Iconic, and disturbing, scenes such as those demonstrate why, arguably, the Punisher reflects and amplifies the tendencies of conservative readers to, in a racist fashion, scapegoat entire groups for the problems of society without thinking of meaningful ways of dealing with poverty and crime. Obviously, the white-supremacist, wish-fulfillment fantasy of the Punisher is not a meaningful way of thinking about how to fix the problems of the decaying inner cities in America, but many reactionary readers seem to think it is.

Perhaps the most provocative and revolutionary exploitation film to come out of the new wave of post–*Grindhouse*, post–*Saw* revival of the exploitation film is *Machete* (2010). In it, the title character (Danny Trejo) is hired to assassinate Senator McLaughlin (Robert DeNiro) to prevent him from bringing to fruition a plan to deport hundreds of illegal immigrants. Machete is double-crossed by his rich employer, Michael Benz, who is secretly a

McLaughlin supporter that never wanted the assassination to succeed. Instead, Benz hoped that Machete's foiled assassination attempt would inflame anti–Mexican sentiment among white Americans, thereby ensuring that McLaughlin's racist initiatives would move forward. However, according to the deep-voiced narrator of the coming attraction to the film, Benz and McLaughlin have "fucked with the wrong Mexican," and have to face the wrath of Machete, a former Mexican Federale.

In an attempt to simultaneously advertise the then-upcoming film and protest stringent new Arizona immigration legislation, writer-director Rodriguez crafted a Cinco de Mayo "message" from Machete that dedicated the film "to Arizona." The coming attraction garnered criticism from the *New York Post* and Fox News for baiting a race war between whites and Latinos. In response, Rodriguez argued that his carefully edited trailer made the film look more like an exploitative race war film than it actually is to make his timely protesting of the Arizona legislation more potent. Whether the racial conflict is overt or marginally more subdued, the film and its two "fake" trailers express a potent and deeply affecting outrage over the racism that Hispanics and immigrants, both legal and illegal, face in their daily lives. At the very least, the Machete character, film, and IDW comic book series stand as an alternative, an antidote, and a rebuke to films such as *The Boondock Saints*, although some critics might justifiably argue that the *Machete* film exhibits the same kind of racism only reversed.

Unfortunately, a lot of those who write stories for characters such as the Punisher do not appear to be aware of the racist dimensions of the character. Some are, and present him as a villainous figure in stories such as *Born* and *Civil War*. Other stories are crafted by creative teams with ambivalent feelings for the character, and the result is a work that is hard to decode as either racist or satirical, but that seems to lean towards racism, like the uncomfortable viewing experience that is Martin Scorsese's *Taxi Driver*. Certainly, an argument can be made that a fun action story is a fun action story, and that an academic who overanalyzes fun pop culture artifacts is being a killjoy and accusing the average person of racism unfairly merely because that person enjoys watching a fun flick with Steven Seagal or Chuck Norris. And the troubling nature of Punisher stories shouldn't be overstated. However, there is something troubling about a person who adores exploitation stories and rape revenge stories to the exclusion of other kinds of narratives, and who does not take an ironic or detached look at the reactionary values imbedded in these tales.

A racist Senator (Robert DeNiro) and his evil aide (Jeff Fahey) "fuck with the wrong Mexican" in *Machete* (Sony Pictures, 2010). The Mexican in question, Machete (Danny Trejo, pictured above), exacts his revenge in the film's climax.

In the book *Killing Monsters*, Gerard Jones considers the arguments that violent video games and films in which children are asked to play (or relate to) a main character who violently, and realistically, kills high numbers of human opponents are harmful to their young psyches. On the one hand, Jones cites the work of U.S. Army psychologist Dave Grossman, who "described operant conditioning methods used during the Vietnam War that resembled some of today's video games and revealed that some military units are now using those same video games to train soldiers" (166). On the other hand, he agrees with forensic psychologist Helen Smith, who cites that, statistically, children have become less violent in the years since violent video games debuted. Jones feels that, rather than jerking violent video games and comic books out of the hands of young people, we should be asking them what they like about such images. "And I believe something good will come of the asking alone," he concludes (182).

However, such cynical entertainment, be it a *Punisher* comic book or a video game such as *Grand Theft Auto*, may well contribute to the "mean world syndrome" that media scholar George Gerbner argues is fostered in those who spend too much time immersed in violent media. Prolonged exposure to any violent media, including the news, makes viewers more insecure and vulnerable than those who spend less time immersed in violent media. As Gerbner writes, "if you are growing up in a home where there is more than, say, three hours of television per day, for all practical purposes you live in a meaner world—and act accordingly—than your next-door neighbor, who lives in the same world but watches less television. The programming reinforces the worst fears and apprehensions and paranoia of people" (40).

Interestingly enough, Ray Stevenson, the actor who played the role of the Punisher in the film *The Punisher: War Zone* (2008), was concerned that the character not be seen as a role model, or even as a superhero, by impressionable audience members. In fact, before accepting the role, he asked the creative team behind the film to avoid glorifying the Punisher. As the tall, swarthy British actor explained, "I made it very clear that people shouldn't walk out of the cinema wanting to be Frank Castle. I think America has suffered more than enough with anti-social kids shooting their schoolmates. I didn't want to encourage any of that attitude. There is no way to justify vigilantism in modern society."[19]

The Punisher comic books belong to the same disturbing pop culture family as 1970s and 1980s slasher movies, exploitation crime films, and rape revenge narratives. All were inspired by the Vietnam War and endorsed a conservative worldview. Unsurprisingly, in the political environment created by Operation Iraqi Freedom, the Punisher returned to star in two feature films and Quentin Tarantino and Robert Rodriguez gleefully helped resurrect the 1970s exploitation film with their 2007 *Grindhouse* double feature, "*Death-Proof*" and *Planet Terror*.

And everything old is new again.

FIVE

Superman vs. Ronald Reagan and the Ku Klux Klan

Every time I throw a punch in the name of peace, I feel as if I've failed.— Superman[1]

I actually think it's a sign of a malformed personality, people who don't like Superman. In fact, nearly all of my friends say "Oh, I hate Superman," and I ask why, and they say "Oh, cause he's such a goody-goody." So it's like "Don't you like nice people?" Y'know, "What is wrong with you?" And they say "Oh, I prefer Batman, he's more sort of evil and bad-ass." But who would you rather hang about with? Who's a better role model with a more kind of positive outlook on the world? I think it's the same kids that carve a swastika into the vestibule at school — that's the kind of person who doesn't like Superman.— Mark Millar, *Superman* comics writer[2]

The Death of Superman and the Destruction of Krypton

In the 21st century, a whistleblower intent on exposing evils committed by governments, corporations, or underground organizations need go no further than the website WikiLeaks to anonymously post exposés that newspapers and television stations are too frightened to make public. In the 1940s, no such avenue existed, so when Florida-born human rights activist Stetson Kennedy went undercover to become a member of the Ku Klux Klan and discovered their secret codes, rituals, and meeting places, he had nowhere to take the information. And, after all, several Klan members were high-ranking members of the local criminal justice system.[3]

Left with little alternative, Kennedy approached the producers of *The Adventures of Superman* radio show, starring Bud Collyer, and offered the writers accurate background information on the Klan to help them portray the KKK as realistic opponents of Superman. The producers were delighted with this development, especially as the end of World War II had robbed them of ripped-from-the-headlines opponents for Superman to combat, other than less-than-frightening Neo-Nazis and gangsters. When the serial "Clan of the Fiery Cross" broadcast its first episodes, members of the Klan group that Kennedy infiltrated were astounded that their most prized secrets had been broadcast for the whole world to hear. One member was chagrined to find that, when he had returned home from work, his son was playing Superman and his neighbor's child the evil Klansmen that his son was gleefully defeating. In an effort to save face, the Klan members rapidly wrote up new secret codes and new rituals, and hoped that they could move on from the embarrassment afforded them by the radio show. Naturally, Kennedy provided all of these new rituals to the Superman writers immediately, and they were all included in the next episode. When Kennedy attended the following meeting, he discovered that the entire chapter had disbanded in defeat.[4]

This was a significant, and memorable, victory for human rights in America, but Kennedy's battle against racist underground organizations was far from over. He would spend the rest of his life battling the Klan, and similar organizations, and publishing exposes about their activities online at StetsonKennedy.com, and in books such as *The Klan Unmasked* (1954) and *The Jim Crow Guide* (1956). However, before he had these other venues through which he could expose to the world the evils of the Klan, he had the fictional character Superman to use as his avatar and mouthpiece. In the Superman vs. the KKK affair, Stetson Kennedy became the fictional Superman and Superman became the real-life Stetson Kennedy. While *The Adventures of Superman* radio serial has significance for fans of the character for introducing both boy photographer Jimmy Olsen and the radioactive rock Kryptonite — the only thing that can harm the invincible Superman — the "Clan of the Fiery Cross" is definitely that radio show's finest hour.[5]

And Superman's.

A popular misconception about Superman is that he is obsolete because he represents quaint, establishment ideas; apparently, he's as hip and relevant to the modern world as Ward Cleaver.[6] Another common complaint heard about Superman is that he is, as a God-like figure, too powerful for anyone to relate to. However, there are legions of far more reactionary superheroes — and far more all-powerful ones — who remain astonishingly popular with a right-leaning superhero fan base. After all, what superhero is more invulnerable, more politically retrograde, and more beloved than the Punisher? Superman at least has Kryptonite as a weakness. The Punisher is a one-man army and cannot be killed. So the truth must lie elsewhere.

In actuality, Superman represents a form of patriotic, transcendentalist liberalism that has fallen out of favor since the Reagan Revolution's repudiation of the politics of the New Deal and the eroding of Lyndon Johnson's Great Society. Liberals since the 1970s have lost their faith that their movement will ever gain momentum again, and that lack of faith undermines their patriotism and their interest in the Utopian hopes for a better future that Superman represents. Conservatives, for their part, pay lip service to liking Superman because his costume is made from the colors of the American flag, but they secretly suspect that he represents liberal ideas, so they steer clear of reading his stories.

Superman writer and historian Mark Waid also sometimes falls into the trap of describing Superman as an establishment figure and protector of the status quo, but he comes closer to the truth when he writes in "The Real Truth About Superman: And the Rest of Us, Too" (2005) that Superman's ideals seem out of place in a world in which "unrestrained capitalism always wins, where politicians always lie, where sports idols take drugs and beat their wives, and where white picket fences are suspect because they hide dark things" (5). Waid correctly argues that young people have no incentive to imitate the selfless Superman because they learned in history classes what rewards "moral visionaries and inspirational figures ... from Bobby Kennedy to Martin Luther King to Mohandas Gandhi" get "for their efforts: a bullet and a burial" (5–6).

Significantly, President Obama, the first president since Lyndon Johnson to make some headway in restarting the legacy of progressivism, and reigniting the fires of FDR's New Deal for the present day, was frequently dressed as Superman in political advertisements and cartoons when he launched his campaign for the presidency of the United States in 2007. This was no accident. Obama was the first liberal leader in decades to embody Superman's values: hope, patriotism, liberalism, transcendentalism, and a Utopian future. He ultimately became not only the first African American President, but the most widely recognized African American Superman in history (see Chapter Nine).

While Superman himself doesn't exist, and was certainly not around to prevent or mitigate the effects of the 9/11 attacks, the Deepwater Horizon oil spill, or the earthquakes in Haiti, he has served as a potent symbol for progressive political causes. Superman has fought for liberal ideals through the actions he has performed and the scripted dialogue he has delivered, and through artwork and social awareness campaigns that have included representations of Superman, including Superman-themed AIDS awareness campaigns and UNICEF world hunger relief initiatives. As a science fiction character, Superman also works well, directly and indirectly, as an advocate for the funding of scientific research and space programs, and on scientific initiatives to protect the environment and lessen the destructive effects of global climate change. Superman's interest in scientific research and environmentalism is a natural outgrowth of his own life story, which began with an ecological disaster and a voyage across the stars.

The Superman story has changed somewhat in its telling over the years, but what follows is a blending of the most iconic elements of the origin story related in *Superman: Secret Origin* (2009–2010), *Last Son* (2008), *Man of Steel* (1986), *Superman* #1 (1940), and *Superman: The Movie* (1978). On the planet Krypton, chief scientist Jor-El has unearthed evidence that the planet is about to be destroyed and that the Elders of Krypton must move swiftly to either find a way to avert the disaster or evacuate the planet. (The exact nature of the threat changes, but usually involves Krypton being drawn into its solar system's red sun, or that sun going supernova.) The bureaucrats choose neither course of action, and threaten to imprison Jor-El if he spreads panic. Jor-El's more ruthless friends, General Zod, Ursa, and Non, attempt to save Krypton by conquering it and forcing the implementation of Jor-El's recommended emergency measures. Their rebellion fails when Jor-El himself exposes their treason, and they are exiled to the Phantom Zone, an other-dimensional prison that he designed. Unimpressed by Jor-El's act of good will, the council continues to refuse taking action to prevent the impending destruction of the planet.

Jor-El and his wife Lara place their infant son, Kal-El, in a small rocket ship programmed to land on Earth. Jor-El predicts that Kal-El, who looks like an Earthling, will be able to blend in, but will likely develop superhuman abilities not possessed by those on Krypton because of the radiation he will absorb in proximity to Earth's yellow sun. After traveling several years across space, little Kal-El lands in a field in rural Kansas, where the kindly, childless Methodists, Jonathan and Martha Kent, discover him and raise him as their own child. Fearful that the U.S. government would try to take the boy from them, they hide Kal-El's rocket and the alien technology on their farm in Smallville, Kansas, and encourage the boy, who they have named Clark Kent, to hide his powers from the world.

Even as a boy, Clark has superhuman strength, can leap far, and has hair that is impossible to cut with scissors. As a teenager, Clark develops an array of fantastic powers, including heat vision, flight, and super speed. Knowing that he'll need a disguise for when he uses his powers, Martha sews him a superhero costume from the red, yellow, and blue clothes he was swaddled in as an infant. The S insignia on his chest, in actuality the emblem of the house of El, inspires the name Superboy. After he is active as Superboy, saving lives and property from Kansas tornadoes, Clark confides his alien identity to his first girlfriend, Lana Lang, who loves Clark but hates his powers and his Superboy identity. He also encounters time-traveling teen heroes known as the Legion of the Superheroes, who help him understand his powers better than his "normal" parents can.

When Clark reaches college age, he uses the alien technology he finds in the Kryptonian rocket to build a Fortress of Solitude — a miniature planet Krypton — in the Arctic, and immerses himself in his heritage. Afterwards, Clark travels to Metropolis — a city much like Manhattan — and takes a job as a reporter at the newspaper *The Daily Planet* under editor-in-chief Perry White. As a reporter, Clark uncovers crimes, natural disasters, and social evils that he can fight when he transforms into Superman, the adult version of his Superboy persona. While he is able to do some good surreptitiously at first, Superman is revealed to the world, and becomes a household name, after he dramatically rescues *Planet* reporter Lois Lane from falling to her death. The moment Superman is exposed, he inspires a lifetime of undying love from Lois Lane, and a lifetime of burning hatred from Lex Luthor, a megalomaniac intent on world domination, who intuits that Superman is the only man in the world who can stand in his way.

The actor who played the definitive screen version of Superman in four films, Christopher Reeve, explained that he strove to emphasize Superman's accessibility in his performance. "Superman is a big fish in a small pond," Reeve said. "He's Superman on Earth only because he's in a different solar system. If he'd grown up on Krypton, if Krypton had not been destroyed, he might have been average — nothing special about him. That allowed me to underplay the character and make him quite casual" (Fussman).

And yet, Superman's casualness belies his underlying heroism. In a 1987 interview with *Starlog Magazine*, Reeve revealed that he defined a hero as "somebody who will make sacrifices for others without expecting a reward," and noted that, when he plays Superman, he tries to make that idea integral to the character. When interviewer Clifford Meth asked, "How about Christopher Reeve? Is he a hero?" Reeve replied, "I don't know. I don't start leaping to those conclusions."

Christopher Reeve as the definitive screen Superman in *Superman II* (Warner Bros., 1980).

Whether or not Reeve considered himself a hero, he worked to make the world a better place in his eyes. One of the most obvious examples of Reeve's social and political activism is the antiwar story he conceived of for *Superman IV: The Quest for Peace* (1987), in which Superman called for an end to the nuclear arms race during a U.N. address:

> For years I've lived among you as ... a visitor. I've felt great joy at your magnificent accomplishments, but I've also seen the folly of your wars. As of today, I'm not a visitor anymore, because the earth is my home, too. I can't stand idly by and watch us stumble into the

> madness of possible nuclear destruction. And so I've come to a decision. I'm going to do what our governments have been unwilling or unable to do. Effective immediately, I'm going to rid the planet of all nuclear weapons.

In 2003, film critic Barry Freiman observed that, "Superman's proactive involvement in world affairs seemed somewhat irrelevant to movie reviewers in 1987 who saw that we had already won the Cold War. But much of Superman's dialogue is apropos to current ... world events, giving the film an entirely new perspective." *Superman IV* suffers from poor editing and appalling special effects, but it also speaks to issues of the devaluing of farmland and the problem of urban sprawl (Superman won't sell the Kent farm to an investor who wants to build a strip mall) as well as the problem posed by the corporatization of journalism (a Rupert Murdoch–style businessman named Warfield buys *The Daily Planet* and turns it into a *New York Post*–style tabloid with lurid headlines such as "World on the Brink!"). Furthermore, the fact that Luthor grinds Superman's peace movement to a halt by consolidating the world's businessmen and munitions makers in opposition gives the film a sharp satirical edge and social relevance that elevates otherwise B-movie material into a narrative worth thinking about.

Reeve's other Superman films were notable in their environmentalist themes, and representations of the villainous Lex Luthor as the ultimate corporate criminal who rapes the environment and undermines democracy in the name of making a profit. The first film, like the fourth, warns of nuclear war and crimes against the environment, just as *Superman III* (1983) is a not-very-successful meditation on out-of-control computer technology and the industrial world's addiction to crude oil. Finally, in *Superman II* (1980), the Fascist Kryptonian trio General Zod, Ursa, and Non escape from the Phantom Zone and conquer Earth while Superman is busy romancing Lois in the Fortress of Solitude and considers stripping himself of his powers to live a domestic life as her husband. That film could easily be read as an indictment of the former leaders of the 1960s counter culture movement who contented themselves with settling into suburban domesticity in the 1980s as reactionary elements took over American social and political life.

The Reeve Superman films are also superb at emphasizing how incredible Superman's powers are. Since they take place in the "real" world, the few supernatural elements in the stories are all related to Krypton, and Metropolis itself is a gritty, grimy construction instead of a "city of the future." Consequently, Superman's uniqueness is emphasized in a way that the comic books never can, in a world in which he operates as a member of the Justice League alongside other superheroes with equally amazing abilities. The films also startle viewers by occasionally unveiling a super power not normally associated with Superman, like the ability to time travel, bestow amnesia with a kiss, or remove the S-emblem from his chest and throw it as a weapon at his enemies. These somewhat bizarre abilities elevate Superman to a godlike status and make viewers wonder what other powers he is hiding, and what secret ability he might unveil next. In contrast, the Superman in the comic book tends to stick — boringly and exclusively — to flight, super-speed, strength, heat-vision, and really cold breath.

As dramatic and heroic as Reeve's actions were in his four *Superman* films, nothing could prepare his fans for the events that would define his life in the real world. Everything changed in May 1995, when Reeve was thrown from his horse. He suffered a spinal injury, which left him a quadriplegic. Devastated, Reeve was contemplating suicide when his friend Robin Williams and his wife Dana helped him recover from the shock of the tragedy and dedicate himself to finding a way of getting out of the wheelchair and walking once again.

Reeve became a passionate advocate for stem cell research, which he believed might hold the key to restoring his mobility. He explained in 2001 that the spinal cord injury he suffered produced a condition called demyelination:

> ... in one very small segment of my spinal cord, about the width of your pinky, the coating, myelin, which is like the rubber coating around a wire, has come off. And that keeps signals from the brain from getting down into the body. So the human embryonic stem cells could be cultured and then sent right to the site, and they would know that their job is to remyelinate. And then the signals from the brain would go down properly, and I would get recovery of function [qtd. in Foreman, 32].

Although he campaigned as Christopher Reeve, for many of those who listened, it was a wheelchair-bound Superman who was making the appeal for research funding. Indeed, Anne Coulter was one of many critics in the Republican Party who believed that Reeve's potency as a symbol muddied the waters of the ethical debate over stem cell research too much, making the harvesting of embryos for research—which she considered the height of immorality—seem like a good idea because Reeve's status as an unassailable victim made his reasoning hard to question.

"A few months before Cardinal Ratzinger became Pope Benedict XVI, he called the power of cloning 'more dangerous than weapons of mass destruction.' Inflammatory statements, but he wanted to make a point about humans tampering with the sacred.... Such interventions, including in vitro fertilization, cannot be condoned in the Vatican's eyes. 'Man is capable of producing another man in the laboratory who, therefore, is no longer a gift of God or of nature,' Ratzinger said. 'He can be fabricated and, just as he can be fabricated, he can be destroyed'" (Furcht 238). These objections extended naturally to abortion and to embryonic stem cell research, and the Catholic Church has stood firm in opposition to these practices.

Scientist Spencer S. Stober and theologian Donna Yarri outlined the scientific benefits to stem-cell research, and the moral and theological objections to it, in their collaborative work of scholarship, *God, Science, and Designer Genes* (2009):

> The issue of stem-cell research, or therapeutic cloning, is a very complicated one. Oftentimes people ask others: Do you believe in or support stem-cell research? But as we have seen, the possible answers must be much more nuanced than simply "yes" or "no." Many individuals do not even have basic knowledge of how embryos are formed, let alone stem-cell lines. With regard to this research, we must ask: Are we talking about adult stem cells or embryonic stem cells? Are we talking about techniques involving harm to embryos, or would those techniques that do not harm embryos belong in a different category? It is likely that these ethical concerns regarding stem-cell research would largely go away if we are eventually able to either create embryonic-like versatility in adult stem cells or if we could perfect techniques that would never harm embryos [124].

However, Stober and Yarri acknowledge that as long as stem-cell research is done in part using techniques that destroy embryos, the ethical concerns about when life begins, where the embryos come from, and whether the rights of the embryo somehow trump the rights of people like Reeve will remain (124). Stober and Yarri also indicate, provocatively, that stem-cell research has the potential to lead to cures for all known diseases and injuries, and to the human body's ability to continually regenerate itself to the point at which death itself is cured and human immortality is assured. But the elimination of death opens up a host of other social, ethical, and theological concerns, and the technology is a ways away from achieving that panacea, Stober and Yarri explain (124).

Despite the objections of American conservatives and the Roman Catholic Church, Reeve pushed on with his campaign, frustrated by the knowledge that most Americans supported him, but that the authorities did not:

> We have a government that, generally speaking, does not respond to the people. Seventy percent of the American public supports embryonic-stem-cell research. And yet it has already been banned by the House and is stalled in the Senate. And we have no federal policy. All the excitement generated in 1998, when embryonic cells were first identified, has pretty much died down because scientists don't know what's going to happen in the future. Probably the saddest thing is that most young doctors who would like to go into stem-cell research say, "I can't go into that because this may not be going anywhere for a while, and I've got to pay off my student loans" [qtd. in Fussman].

Reeve observed that the politicians who tend to support stem cell research are those who have been touched by disease and disability, such as Senator Tom Harkin, whose nephew has a spinal cord injury, and Nancy Reagan, who began lobbying for the restrictions that President George W. Bush placed upon stem cell research in 2001 to be relaxed to help find a cure for the Alzheimer's Disease her husband, Ronald Reagan, developed. And yet, Nancy Reagan's turnabout on health research also frustrated Reeve:

> ... you think back to the early '80s, when she and her husband were in office and opposed federal funding for AIDS research. Thousands of people died. It's helpful that she's asking senators to back therapeutic cloning to create more stem-cell lines. But the way I see it, she's doing it now only because Ronnie doesn't recognize her. Why do people wait until it hurts? [qtd. in Fussman].

Frustrated with science's snail's pace, Reeve formed the Christopher Reeve Paralysis Foundation in 1999 (Furcht 24). He also publicly condemned the inconsistency of the developed world's handling of the controversy, noting that there was government support for all forms of stem cell research in Britain, Sweden, Belgium, Switzerland, Israel, Singapore, and Japan but not in the United States, France, Germany, and Italy (Furcht 166). Reeve and a group of scientists even filed a lawsuit against the federal government in May 2001, *Thompson vs. Thompson*, with the plaintiffs claiming that the Bush administration illegally withheld federal funding for stem cell research that could save lives. They withdrew the lawsuit a week later, after Bush underlined his administration's policy on national television (Furcht 172).

In 2004, nine years after the horse-riding accident, Reeve died from an infection caused by a bedsore. DC Comics was one of many publications that called Reeve's death the Death of Superman, and several artists painted memorial portraits of the actor and activist, one poignantly depicting the shadow of Superman falling over an empty wheelchair. In his lifetime, Reeve failed to see the changes he wanted in federal stem cell funding, but his legacy lived on after his death. In April 2005, Dana and 200 wheelchair bound advocates of the Christopher Reeve Paralysis Act gathered in Washington, D.C., to support the legislation, which would fund a clinical trial network for people with spinal injuries. Dana explained that one of Reeve's lessons to the world was that a wheelchair was something to aspire to get out of, not get used to. "Although Chris has died, I know the work he did has not died," Dana said in a speech to the crowd (235–236 Furcht).

In 2009, five years after Reeve's death, the newly elected President Obama lifted the restrictions imposed upon stem cell research by President Bush, and began to rejuvenate a field of medical research that had lain dormant throughout the Bush Administration.

Just as Reeve advocated for scientific funding and the education of the general public about issues in healthcare and cutting-edge research, the *Superman* universe has continually inspired comic book readers and movie viewers to learn more about science fact as well as science fiction. Like the *Star Trek* television series, which inspired researchers to finds a means of developing Captain Kirk's communicator in real life (cell phones), the Superman universe posits a world in which humans can travel to other planets with ease, cure spinal injuries, replace an oil dependent lifestyle with a fission-powered world, and repair damage done to the environment and animal life on earth through cloning technology and water and air purifiers. Anyone reading a *Superman* comic book that involves Luthor extending his own life by growing a new body for himself, to replace the one ravaged by cancer, must take a moment to wonder if such a miracle might ever be achieved through science in real life. In another dramatic DC universe story, Barbara Gordon, who was confined to a wheelchair after being shot in the spine by the Joker, recovered some small ability to move her legs and feet after being exposed to Superman villain Brainiac's nanite technology, which wrote therapeutic repairs into her DNA. As much as they wanted to see her recover completely, and resume the career as Batgirl that the Joker cut short, DC writers and editors decided not to cure Barbara yet. Instead, they let her remain the wheelchair-bound Oracle, personal researcher and advisor to Superman, the Birds of Prey, and the Justice League. The decision was made because there were not enough handicapped superheroes in the DC universe to justify "curing" one, and because it would have been odd to see Barbara Gordon escape from her wheelchair in the world of fiction when Reeve had never had that opportunity.

A poster from a health awareness campaign launched by AIDES (a French organization dedicated to combating HIV/AIDS and viral hepatitis). It is designed to illustrate that AIDS touches everyone, even those who think they are impervious to the disease, such as Superman.

In addition to the Superman universe's concerns with medical technology and space program funding, the comic books, movies, and TV shows are also notable in their championing of environmentalist causes and their warnings concerning the reality of global climate change. The first Reeve Superman film was released in the 1970s, a period when ecological concerns were high, and the public was concerned over deforestation, the effects of DDT, and the "greenhouse effect." Indeed, Superman's father, Jor-El, played in the film by Marlon Brando, became a patron saint of the environmentalist movement. Jor-El's opposition to the council of Krypton has been seen as heroism by environmentalists, and not as akin to Chicken Little's warning that the sky is falling. Environmentalists also view the Kryptonian elders' refusal to act in the face of evidence of imminent environmental catastrophe as illustrative of the general response of authority figures in our world.

While some of the moral objections to stem-cell research are understandable, what is far less understandable is the public skepticism surrounding global climate change. Given the overwhelming scientific evidence that supports the reality of climate change, it is alarming how many climate change skeptics and deniers are scattered throughout the world. Much of this skepticism may stem from the simple fact that American science education is shoddy at best.

The media, acting in its own profit-driven self-interest, also shares some of the blame. A number of books by reputable academics have been published over the last several years that cover the apparent intent of the news media to obscure the truth about climate change and sew seeds of doubt in the public mind about its scientific basis. These exposes include *Climate Cover-Up: The Crusade to Deny Global Warming* (2009) by James Hoggan and Richard Littlemore, *Censoring Science: Dr. James Hansen and the Truth of Global Warming* (2008) by Mark Bowen, *Requiem for a Species: Why We Resist the Truth About Climate Change* (2010) by Clive Hamilton, and *Merchants of Doubt: How a Handful of Scientists Obscured the Truth on Issues from Tobacco Smoke to Global Warming* (2010) by Naomi Oreskes and Erik M. Conway.

As in the case of stem cell research, much of the objection to global climate change data is based in religious views, and public skepticism of the motivations of scientists remain rooted in fears of their atheism and adherence to Darwin's theory of evolution. Emblematic of this line of argument is Rush Limbaugh's *The Way Things Ought to Be* (1992). As an unofficial official spokesman of the Republican Party, Limbaugh writes:

> My views on the environment are rooted in my belief in Creation. I don't believe that life on earth began spontaneously or as a result of some haphazard, random selection process; nor do I believe that nature is oh-so-precariously balanced. I don't believe that the earth and her ecosystem are fragile as many radical environmentalists do. They think man can come along all by himself, and change everything for the worse; that after hundreds of millions of years, the last two generations of human existence are going to destroy the planet. Who do they think we are?
>
> I resent that presumptuous view of man and his works. I refuse to believe that people, who are themselves the result of Creation, can destroy the most magnificent creation of the entire universe [152].

Responding directly to Limbaugh, Leonie Haimson, Dr. Michael Oppenheimer, and Dr. David Wilcove wrote *The Way Things Really Are: Debunking Rush Limbaugh on the Environment* (1995), noting:

> Rush Limbaugh's best-selling books *The Way Things Ought to Be* and *See, I Told You So* are full of statements on the environment that are misleading, distorted, and factually incorrect. Indeed, Limbaugh's claims often fly in the face of carefully considered scientific evidence, and put him in opposition to the views of the most eminent scientific experts, as reflected in the conclusions of such esteemed bodies as the National Academy of Sciences and the World Meteorological Organization.
>
> Though Limbaugh likes to frame the debate as a contest between him and the "environmental wackos," it is really Limbaugh's word against the overwhelming tide of scientific knowledge.

The environmentalist movement, which floundered for much of the 1980s and 1990s, was rejuvenated by the release of Al Gore's documentary *An Inconvenient Truth* (2006), in which the man who was almost the 43rd president of the United States argues that climate change "is really not a political issue, so much as a moral one," and that the environmental consequences of human-generated greenhouse gases will be catastrophic if they are not curbed immediately.

In 2008, Canadian science journalist Marq De Villiers wrote *The End: Natural Disasters, Manmade Catastrophes, and the Future of Human Survival* (2008). In the book, he argues that humans need to do more to adapt to a world in which weather patterns have grown noticeably more severe and the environment as a whole has become hostile to humanity. He is particularly frustrated by the amount of time wasted by climate change deniers, and even by those who refuse to believe in Darwin's theories of evolution, which are universally accepted as fact, not wide-eyed notions, by the scientific establishment:

> [The debate over the truth of evolution is] of all of the quarrels of our time perhaps the most deeply irrelevant, joined in its fatuity only by religious quarrels over, well, nothing—Protestant against Catholic, Old Believers versus New, Sunni versus Shia. Perhaps five angels, or fifty can dance upon the point of a needle, but none of their dancing will affect the course of the tsunami that will be rolling someone's way quite soon. Or the hurricane that will be coiling its deadly way across the Caribbean this summer. Or the earthquake that will tumble down cities. Or the volcano fire that will spread its pall of ash and destruction across towns and villages not yet known. Or the rising sea levels that will swamp coastal communities. This is surely where our attention must be focused [324].

As De Villiers argues, the time wasted in these squabbles is precious, and it is running out:

> Earth has time. But we don't. There would be life, but it wouldn't be *our* life, or even life as we more or less know it. The planet won't die, but the version of the planet that makes our existence agreeable or even possible could do so with ease. Either human-caused or natural calamities or both in concert could make it happen
>
> This is the vulnerability we need to confront and then devise policies that would maximize our chances of keeping ourselves alive and well. It remains possible. We are an inventive species as well as a destructive one. We now need to invent not just new science but a new politics. We are doing plenty of the first. And we are beginning to do the second, with climate change the engine that's driving us [322–323].

Unfortunately, Glenn Beck, *The Wall Street Journal*, and the rest of the mass media machine operated by Rupert Murdoch continue to undermine public confidence in the idea that there is anything whatsoever to worry about. And the good work that Gore achieved in his Inconvenient Truth campaign is being eroded by naysayers and by the public belief that, in a time of economic hardship, environmental legislation and green technology is a luxury issue that cannot afford to be funded. What these skeptics don't know is that the green movement could revitalize the economy and save the planet. They also don't seem to realize that delaying action is also a luxury that cannot be afforded.

In a brilliant satire of climate change skeptics, the "fake" newspaper *The Onion* published an article on July 30, 2008, that aptly cast Al Gore as the Planet Earth's equivalent of Jor-El of Krypton. The Onion headline read: "Al Gore Places Infant Son in Rocket to Escape Dying Planet." According to the report:

> Former vice president Al Gore—who for the past three decades has unsuccessfully attempted to warn humanity of the coming destruction of our planet, only to be mocked and derided by the very people he has tried to save—launched his infant son into space Monday in the faint hope that his only child would reach the safety of another world.
>
> "I tried to warn them, but the Elders of this planet would not listen," said Gore, who in 2000 was nearly banished to a featureless realm of nonexistence [the Phantom Zone] for promoting his unpopular message. "They called me foolish and laughed at my predictions. Yet

even now, the Midwest is flooded, the ice caps are melting, and the cities are rocked with tremors, just as I foretold. Fools! Why didn't they heed me before it was too late?"

Left with no other choice but to send his son away from our dying Earth, Gore declared his hope that, one day soon, his son will arrive in a new home, "where the sky is clear, the water is clean, and there are no Republicans" (see *The Onion*).

Superman as Moses, Christ, and Jimmy Stewart

Superman has lived many lives throughout his career, and has been portrayed in a variety of ways. Each television series that has featured the character has its own narrative arc, or continuity, and presents different interpretations of the subject matter. Consequently, the Superman featured in the Kirk Alyn movie serials of 1948 and 1950 is not the same Superman featured on the radio serials, nor is he the same character as he is in the 1950s George Reeves television series *Adventures of Superman*, or in the romantic comedy series *Lois and Clark: The New Adventures of Superman* (1993–1997), or in the 21st century teenage angst soap opera *Smallville*. Superman has also been reinvented time and again, and has had a series of alternative fictional lives in his home medium of the comic books. The first version of Superman lived primarily during the eras of the Great Depression and World War II and grew to be an old man by the time of *Crisis on Infinite Earths* (1984). The reinvention of the character that followed *Crisis*'s remaking of the entire DC Universe, John Byrne's *The Man of Steel* (1986), suggested that the then-current version of Superman began his heroic career during the Reagan years. Future retellings of Superman's origin, including Mark Waid's *Superman: Birthright* (2003–2004) and Geoff Johns' *Superman: Secret Origin* (2009–2010), drew Superman's arrival date on Earth even closer to our present day.

The *Superman* films with Reeve seem to portray the title character as a Christ figure, with Jor-El of Krypton playing the role of God the Father, who loved humanity enough to give the people of Earth his only son. This metaphor is carried further in *Superman Returns* (2006), when Superman nearly dies saving Earth from a kryptonite-powered engine of destruction, and seems to fall to his death, his arms outstretched like the crucified Christ. In *The Death of Superman* (1992), Superman falls in battle against a genetically engineered Kryptonian super soldier known as Doomsday. Provocatively, artist Dan Jurgens depicts Lois weeping over Superman's dead body, cradling him much like the Virgin Mary cradles her dead son in Michelangelo's Pieta. Kal-El's resurrection not long after further cements the Christ/Superman parallel. Finally, the epic narrative *Kingdom Come* (1996) is a secularized version of Nikos Kazantzakis' novel *The Last Temptation of Christ* (1960), with Superman inserted into the role played by Christ in the novel and Wonder Woman in the place of Judas Iscariot.

But Superman is not always meant to symbolize Christ. Indeed, new media critic Marshall McLuhan interpreted the character as a Guardian Angel figure, and was troubled by America's decision to embrace such a problematic role model:

> Like Superman, [the Angels of the Judeo-Christian tradition] require neither education nor experience, but they possess, without effort, flawless intelligence about all things. Men have dreamed about becoming like these beings for quite a while. However, fallen angels are known as devils. And imperfect men, possessing superhuman material power, are not a reassuring prospect [350].

The depiction of Superman that was most prevalent from the late 1990s through roughly 2004 was driven primarily by writer Jeph Loeb, who wrote both the character's comic book adventures as well as shaped his portrayal on the television series *Smallville*. By and large, Loeb's Superman is purely good primarily because he is purely innocent. What that pure innocence signifies is open to interpretation, but he lacks any real understanding of evil, and is often incompetent at fighting it, despite his amazing strength, largely because he does not understand it. In a sense, Loeb's Superman is reminiscent of the angel Uriel from John Milton's *Paradise Lost*. In Milton's epic poem, Uriel is charged with guarding the sun (and, by extension, Earth) from Satan, but Satan is able to trick his way past Uriel by disguising himself as an angel that Uriel has never seen before. Since the story takes place at the dawn of Creation, and "sin" is a new concept, Uriel is unfamiliar with the very concept of a "disguise," so Satan discovers that Uriel is strikingly easy to trick. Nevertheless, a feeling of unease overtakes Uriel because he does not understand how there could be an angel that he has never met, and he raises the alarm. However, he raises the alarm too late. Satan has already tempted Adam and Eve into original sin and humanity has Fallen.

In Superman stories such as *Superman for All Seasons* (1998), written by Loeb and drawn by Tim Sale, a rookie Superman confronts the multi-billionaire businessman and criminal mastermind Lex Luthor and is horrified by the extent of Luthor's evil. Luthor sees the city of Metropolis as his, and he demonstrates this by putting his name, Donald Trump–style, on virtually every business in the city—LexCorp, LexTowers, LexBank, and every conceivable other permutation. When Superman first arrives in town, indirectly challenging Luthor's position as the King of Metropolis, Luthor threatens to release a deadly toxin that will wipe out the entire populace if Superman doesn't go back where he came from. Unlike Luthor, this version of Superman never saw himself as making some sort of power play for control of Metropolis. This Superman merely saw himself as someone with the power to "help" and all he intends to do is "help" by saving lives, preventing property damage, and keeping the peace. Superman cannot conceive of how anyone can be vindictive, jealous, and imperialistic enough to make such a threat, or to see himself as "master" of a city.

On the other hand, it may be overstating things to argue that Loeb's Superman is merely meant to be "angelic." Loeb's Superman is a throwback to the values of the New Deal era, and a reincarnation of the classic Frank Capra hero, played by Jimmy Stewart and Gary Cooper, who act as the embodiment of Franklin Delano Roosevelt's progressive values and political platform. So Loeb's Superman is much like Jimmy Stewart's character, Jefferson Smith, from *Mr. Smith Goes to Washington* (1939). Loeb portrays Superman as pure and idealistic as Jefferson Smith, while he casts Lois in the Jean Arthur role, Clarissa Saunders—the cynic with the heart of an idealist who protects Smith as best as she can from the vultures circling Washington, D.C. This Frank Capra film dynamic amounts to a fascinating reversal of gender stereotypes that was ahead of its time, casting the man as charming and naïve and the woman as the hard-bitten, scrappy fighter. Capra had presented much the same dynamic in 1936's *Mr. Deeds Goes to Town*, in which Jean Arthur's jaded reporter Babe Bennett sets out to expose "humanitarian" millionaire Mr. Deeds (Gary Cooper) as a loathsome fraud only to discover that he is a genuine social reformer with a heart of gold. Instead of exposing his goodness as a veneer, her cold facade is stripped away, and Babe finds herself becoming more idealistic in Mr. Deed's presence. Here again, Jean Arthur's character inspires Loeb's characterization of the modern-day Lois, who is married to Clark. And Gary Cooper, like Jimmy Stewart, is the charismatic socialist that the Loeb Superman is based on. Consequently, the marriage between Superman and Lois depicted in the 1990s and 2000s comic books is also defined by an intriguing gender-role switch, in which Superman behaves like a stereotypical wife—deferential to the mate, affectionate, eager to make dinner by collecting

Chinese food from China — while Lois is the overworked, distracted, and aggressive "husband."

Again, the Loeb conception of Superman as part–Frank Capra–hero, part–Uriel is merely one of many depictions of the "last son of Krypton." Perhaps most interestingly, special graphic novels and miniseries dubbed Elseworlds also posit a number of unique, and often radical, reinventions of the character. Two of the most striking Elseworlds included *Superman: Red Son* (2003), written by Mark Millar, which posited a Superman whose rocket landed in Russia during the Cold War and a Superman who grew up fighting for Communism that eventually conquers the world. Another unusual tale, *Superman: War of the Worlds* (1999), written by Roy Thomas, shows Superman fighting the Martian villains from the classic H.G. Wells novel, but the humans he protects from occupation are just as frightened of Superman as they are the aliens, even as he proves himself a friend, time and again. This second tale features a heartbreaking scene where Lois refuses to allow Superman to embrace her because she believes he is an alien. Unable to meet Superman's gaze, she says, "I know I shouldn't feel that way — after all, you just saved our lives — but I can't help it! After seeing what those things have done to humanity, I just can't bear the thought of an alien creature touching me — not even you. Maybe — in time — when all this is forgotten — I'll feel differently — but right now — please understand, Clark. Please say you understand." The next drawing depicts Superman looking down, his eyes closed, and his features pulled taught. "Oh, yes, Lois. I ... understand" (53).

Since the story is set in an Elseworlds universe, and is outside what fans refer to as "continuity" or "canon," it posits an ending to the Superman saga in which he dies saving the world from the Martian threat. Lois and Luthor discover the dying Superman and are there to hear his final words. Struggling to speak, he says between breaths, "I — had to fight the Martians — but I realized — we're both aliens here. In spite of everything — I felt sorry for them. I myself ... came from space. For all I know ... my world is dying ... like theirs ... it may already be dead. If the Martians hadn't come ... the people of Earth ... might have been running ... from me..." (61). His dying words shame Lois, who vows to make public the sacrifice that Superman made for humanity. The final page of the story shows a grand statue of Superman that reads "Clark Kent (d. 1938) He was born on one world — grew to manhood on another — and saved his adopted planet from the wrath of a third, during the war of the worlds."

In pitting Superman, the good alien/immigrant against the Martians, evil aliens/immigrants, Thomas has retold a classic *Superman* narrative, made popular previously by *Superman II* (1980) and *Superman: The Animated Series* (1996–2000), in which refugees from the destroyed planet Krypton arrive on Earth, as Superman has, only they have the intent to conquer it and remake Earth into a New Krypton, whereas Kal-El merely wants to live as a guest on his adopted home planet. In the first case, the Kryptonian "Phantom Zone criminals," General Zod, Ursa, and Non all use their new powers to try to defeat Superman and seize control of the Earth. In the animated series, Kryptonian super computer Brainiac tries to refashion the Earth itself into a new Krypton. (Kevin Spacey's Luthor attempts a similar metamorphosis of the planet Earth using Kryptonian crystal technology in the 2006 film *Superman Returns*). These stories represent two different models of the immigration experience. Superman represents an immigrant who has chosen the path of enculturation, whereas Brainiac and the Phantom Zone criminals have chosen to remake their new land into a mirror image of their homeland. And yet, as much as Superman tries to fit into American (and Earth) society, he will always be an alien and an outsider, and he (usually) sympathizes

The Phantom Zone criminals begin their bid to take over the Earth in *Superman II* (Warner Bros., 1980). From left to right: Non (Jack O'Halloran), General Zod (Terence Stamp), and Ursa (Sarah Douglas).

with other outsider figures such as himself. Roger Stern's *The Incredible Hulk vs. Superman* (1999) similarly portrays Superman as an alien outsider, and he feels for the persecuted Hulk, even as he feels compelled to defeat Hulk to cut one of the green goliath's angry rampages short.

In evoking audience sympathy for "aliens" and persecuted characters such as the Hulk, these relatively recent Superman comics are acting in the egalitarian tradition of the character forged by his creators Jerry Siegel and Joe Shuster. *Superman* #1 (1939) contains a series of short stories that demonstrate how populist Superman's concerns are, thanks in part to his being a product of two creators from Jewish immigrant families working to earn a living during the Great Depression. Two of the short stories in particular are memorable for Superman's redressing of wrongs in the worlds of industry and college sports.

The first of these stories begins when coal mineworker Stanislaw Kober is trapped in a cave-in. A rescue party of twelve is sent after Kober, but they stumble into a chamber of poison gas and rapidly lose consciousness. Fortunately, Superman arrives in time to rescue Kober and the members of the rescue party, but the injuries Kober sustained in the cave-in have crippled him for life. Superman transforms himself back into Clark and visits Kober in the hospital.

> SUPERMAN: My name is Kent. I represent a powerful newspaper. Tell me: in your opinion, could the mine-tragedy have been averted?
>
> KOBER: Sure! Months ago we know mine is unsafe—but when we tell boss's foremen they say: "No-like job, Stanislaw? Quit!" ... But we no quit—got wife, kids, bills: So back we go to mine ... an maybe to die!

When the mine owner, Thornton Blakely, refuses to arrange a pension for the crippled miner, or to bring the mine up to reasonable safety standards, Superman chooses to intervene. "That night, Superman, clad in a miner's garb, drops out of the skies like some occult, avenging demon, into the barred and closely guarded confines of the Blakely estate." Upon his arrival, Superman discovers that Blakely is throwing a party on his estate to amuse the wealthy and indolent of the city. On a whim, Blakely invites the party-crashing miner, and the assembled guests, to finish out the party in the mine, possibly to demonstrate that the mine is safe after all, as well as to provide cheap thrills for the crowd of *Great Gatsby*–type socialites. Blakely's plan backfires, as the rich party-goers are horrified by the condition of the mine. "Ugh! What a horrid looking place!" a lovely blonde exclaims. "Don't tell me people actually work down here!" a man in a top hat cries. His wife, in turn, says, "George, I—I don't like this filthy mine! We shouldn't have come!"

Taking his chance, Superman deliberately collapses several wooden tunnel supports and causes a cave-in, trapping the wealthy partiers. Panicked, the rich people try to raise the alarm, but it is rusty and in disrepair, so there is no hope of outside rescue. One partygoer nearly strangles Blakely, yelling, "You blasted skinflint! If you'd have had the mine equipped with proper safety precautions, we might have gotten out alive!," but he is pulled away from Blakely. Refraining from using his powers to rescue those he has just trapped, Superman distributes shovels to the rich people, watching as they vainly try to dig themselves free. When little progress is made, death seems certain to come as the air runs out. At the end of his rope, Blakely cries, "Oh, if I only had this all to do over again! I never knew — really knew — what the men down here have to face."

Satisfied that the rich man has reformed, Superman waits until they have blacked out from lack of air and surreptitiously digs a hole to the surface so that, when the dinner party members awake, they would believe that they had been rescued by the miners and not by Superman. In a brief epilogue, Blakely reports to Clark that, "Henceforth, my mine will be the safest in the country, and my workers the best treated. My experience in the mine brought their problems closer to my understanding." Kent replies: "Congratulations on your new policy. May it be a permanent one!" And he thinks to himself, "If it isn't, you can expect another visit from Superman!"

The second story concerns Dale University's football coach who, worried he will lose his job if he loses the next big game against Cordell University, pays gangsters to disable Cordell University's star players. Superman overhears these plans with his super hearing and decides to go undercover as a player on Cordell's team. He changes places with the player he most closely resembles, and during the game not only protects the other players from being attacked, but also easily ensures a Cordell team victory but using his superpowers to outrun and outscore the Dale players. Since the Dale coach is presented in such a starkly evil light, Superman's assistance of the underdog team is not presented as cheating, but as ensuring that the morally righteous team, with the noble coach, wins. While the modern-day version of the Superman character would be too "principled" to cheat, this original conception of the character has no qualms about cheating a cheater if it ensures that the forces of good will win out in the end.

In these two stories, Superman demonstrates a sense of New Deal and Square Deal fairness, if not a socialistic worldview. Also as a champion of oppressed people, he is cut from the same cloth as two archetypal Jewish figures — the prophet Moses and the classic Golem of Hebrew folklore. In fact, of all the parallels drawn between Superman and a figure of Judeo-Christian religious lore, the one between Kal-El and Moses is the most defensible. Consider how Moses' mother placed him in a basket and sent him downriver, giving him up to save him from being slaughtered by Pharaoh along with a host of other Hebrew infants. Moses was found by members of Pharoah's family and raised to adulthood as one of them. Upon reaching adulthood, Moses discovers his kinship with the Jews and discovers his broader destiny — to defend the Jews and liberate them from living in servitude in a foreign land. In the Superman retelling of these events, Moses' mother becomes Jor-El, the slaughter of the innocents becomes the destruction of Krypton, the basket is the Kryptonian rocket, the river is the vastness of space, and Moses' adoptive parents become the Kents. And Pharoah, the bald, tyrannical ruler of Egypt, transforms into Luthor, the bald, tyrannical American robber baron, who would dare to defy a God in order to hold onto the Empire he has built for himself.

In recent years, Jewish Studies scholars have emphasized the idea that superheroes, which were mostly created by Jewish immigrant comic book creators, are based on the a figure from Jewish folklore called the golem. Golems are creatures made of clay that are summoned into life by Hebrew mystics and ordered to protect the Jewish people during times of great strife. They are featured in a variety of Jewish oral and written lore, have been the subject of plays and short works of literature, and inspired the making of the classic German film *Der Golem* (1920).

Several superheroes, some obscure and some famous, are overtly portrayed as golems. For example, the title character of *The Monolith* (2004–2005), a short-lived DC Comics series written by Justin Gray and Jimmy Palmiotti, was a golem who had been animated by Rabbi Rava in the 1930s and was controlled in the present by a recovering drug addict named Alice Cohen. In addition, the Fantastic Four, a team of superheroes with elemental powers created by Jewish comic book legends Stan Lee and Jack Kirby, features a powerful rock-man called the Thing, who looks like a golem, is often called upon to protect the Brooklyn Jewish neighborhood of his youth, Yancy Street, and who finally has his Bar Mitzvah, after years of putting it off, in *The Thing: Idol of Millions* (*The Thing* Vol. 2 #3, 2006).

Characters who have long seemed like golems, but who have never been explicitly identified as such before, have had the title applied to them by comic book writers in recent years. For example, an exclusively female island of Amazons produced its first child when Queen Hippolyta molded a daughter for herself out of clay, and the Greek gods animated the clay, bringing Princess Diana of Themyscira (a.k.a. Wonder Woman) to life in 1941's *Wonder Woman* #1. She was not referred to as a golem at the time. In *Who Is Wonder Woman?* a 2008 graphic novel written by *Sex and the City* script writer Allan Heinberg, Wonder Woman is having an identity crisis in the aftermath of a battle in which she felt compelled to kill Maxwell Lord, a megalomaniacal opponent that she could not negotiate a truce with. At a pivotal moment, she confesses to another of her most implacable foes, Circe, that she wants to be human. "Don't misunderstand me," Wonder Woman says. "I am grateful for the blessings I've been given. But I am not even a real person. I'm a golem. A clay statue brought to life. I have no idea who or what I am. All I know is I'm alone" (114).

As Rabbi Simcha Weinstein explains in *Up, Up, and Oy Vey: How Jewish History, Culture, and Values Shaped the Comic Book Superhero* (2006), even characters who are not made of clay are arguably golems. Weinstein cites a story in which a little Jewish girl identifies the Hulk as a golem (1970's *Incredible Hulk* #134), and an interview with Hulk co-creator Stan Lee, in which Lee observes, "When you think about it, the Incredible Hulk is a Golem." Weinstein also identifies Captain America, the classic enemy of Nazism, as a golem. According to Weinstein, the letter A that Captain America wears upon his forehead evokes not only the A in "America," but the Hebrew symbol "Aleph" that golems also wear upon their heads, and that is the source of a golem's power.

At the time of Captain America's debut appearance in 1940, America was not yet a participant in World War II. According to cultural critic and historian Jason Dittmer, isolationist elements and Hitler sympathizers within the United States meant that Jewish comic book creators Joe Simon and Jack Kirby were taking a risk by creating an American superhero to confront the Nazi menace, thereby endorsing military action against Germany. However, as Dittmer explained, Hitler was a ready-made comic book villain, more realistic and despicable than any comic villain who had come before him. In addition, news of Kristallnacht and the "Final Solution" had reached the members of the predominantly Jewish comic book industry and they found themselves turning against their natural tendency towards pacifism and calling for an immediate American response to the Holocaust. Dittmer supported this claim with an archival quote from Simon, who said, "The United States hadn't yet entered the war when Jack and I created Captain America, so maybe he was our way of lashing out against the Nazi menace" (38–39).

Captain America appeared in print adventures two years after the introduction of Superman, another character created by a Jewish writer, Jerry Siegel, and a Jewish artist, Joe Shuster. He, too, has been interpreted as a golem, for good reason. A February 1940 issue of *Look Magazine*, featured a two-page Superman adventure written and drawn by his creators, Siegel and Shuster, called "What if Superman Ended the War?" The story, which was recently reprinted in *The Greatest Superman Stories Ever Told* (2004) is a simple, evocative wish-fulfillment narrative that suggests that Siegel and Shuster wished that some powerful force would intervene in Europe and stop the advance of both Communism and Fascism, be that force God, the United States, or Superman. In the brief adventure, Superman singlehandedly charges the Siegfried line and dismantles the German position on the Westwall, then rallies the French forces on the Maginot Line, shouting "Come and get 'em!" Once it looks like the French have things well in hand, Superman races off to Hitler's hideout and captures the Fuehrer. "I'd like to land a strictly non–Aryan punch on your jaw," Superman declares as he grabs Hitler about the neck and lifts him into the air. "But there's no time for that! You're coming with me while we visit a certain pal of yours." Superman then places Hitler under his arm like a sack of potatoes and flies to Moscow, where he apprehends Josef Stalin. He then flies the two men to Geneva, Switzerland, and brings them before the League of Nations. "Gentlemen, I've brought before you the two power-mad scoundrels responsible for Europe's present ills. What is your judgment?" A white-haired judge replies, "Adolf Hitler and Josef Stalin — we pronounce you guilty of modern history's greatest crime — unprovoked aggression against defenseless countries."

As the story illustrates, Superman could have easily ended the war single-handedly. A nearly instantaneous Allied victory would have been even simpler in the expanded "DC Universe" of the fictional Earth-2, in which Batman, Superman, Wonder Woman, Green Lantern, the Flash, and the expanded superhero team All-Star Squadron (formed by order of President Franklin Delano Roosevelt, who was also president on Earth-2) could have worked together to destroy the Axis forces in a heartbeat. Feeling compelled to explain why the superheroes did not take it upon themselves to defeat Hitler, either on Earth-2 or in our own reality, a variety of comic book writers have written stories suggesting that Hitler had used magic to protect himself, and his armies, from direct superhero interference. According to DC Universe folklore, originally established in February 1977's *Weird War Tales* #50, Hitler had somehow acquired the Spear of Destiny — the spear of Longinus, which had pierced Christ's heart during the crucifixion — and found a way to warp its magical powers, and naturally benign powers, to serve his evil ends. The indestructible spear, charged with magical energy because it had been bathed in Christ's blood, gave Hitler the power to brainwash any superheroes that invaded Axis territory, transforming them into Nazis and making them subservient to his will. Once the superheroes of the DC universe realized that Hitler could conceivably turn them against the Allies and use them to conquer the world, the superheroes collectively agreed to sit out the war overseas, focusing instead on rooting out Axis spies on the American mainland.

(This narrative of the Third Reich's employment of divine relics as weapons of mass destruction stands in sharp contrast to the way George Lucas and Steven Spielberg depict such projects in the Indiana Jones films. In *Raiders of the Lost Ark* (1981), the Nazis attempt to use the Ark of the Covenant to secure an Axis victory, but the wrath of the Hebrew God smites them for their hubris. In *Indiana Jones and the Last Crusade* (1989), all those who seek the Holy Grail for their own personal gain are destroyed by their greed and selfishness.)

In a departure from the *Weird War Tales* treatment of World War II, 1998's *Superman* #80–82 featured a dream-like tale in which the contemporary Superman finds himself living the life of the Earth-2 Superman, only this time he is granted the opportunity to participate more directly in actions against the Nazis than he was able to in the "Spear of Destiny" depiction of World War II in the DC Universe. The story begins with a Fascist rally hosted on American soil by a blond-haired-and-blue-eyed Hollywood actor (who is modeled on suspected Nazi sympathizer Errol Flynn). When he is almost killed in a freak accident by a giant decorative swastika, Superman intervenes and saves the actor's life. Thanking Superman, the actor tries to enlist Superman to the Nazi cause on the spot, claiming that Superman is the true Aryan "Superman" and a natural born Nazi. Superman vehemently refuses the attempt to co-opt him as a symbol for Nazism, telling the assembled American Fascists, "Listen up folks. Call me what you want, but I will never be a champion of Nazism! I will not be anyone's symbol of hate, racial prejudice and genocide! I am an American like all true Americans; I must strive to be a champion of tolerance and diversity ... justice and kindness!" In subsequent issues, Superman travels to Poland in the guise of his reporter persona, Clark Kent, to determine the nature of the Nazi occupation. Staying undercover, and refusing to use his superpowers even when the Nazis arrest him, Kent finds himself ordered (alongside two young boys named Moishe and Baruch) to bury Jews in mass graves. Afterwards, Superman learns that Lois has been captured and is being transported to Treblinka by cattle car. Shedding his Clark Kent disguise, Superman rescues Lois and the Jews from being transported to the infamous concentration camp. Finally, Superman joins real-life Jewish resistance fighter Mordecai Anielewicz in the Warsaw Ghetto uprising.

The three-part story, written and drawn by Jon Bogdanove, was met with a degree of criticism for omitting the word "Jew" and for showing the fictional Superman rescuing historical Jews from the real-life horrors of the Holocaust. Rabbi Weinstein, however, seemed approving of the story in his treatment of it in *Up, Up, and Oy Vey*, enjoying the tribute to Superman's strongly Jewish origins in time for the character's sixtieth anniversary, and approving of the tribute to Anielewicz and the treatment of the evils of Nazism (30–32).

Between 1941 and 1943, the Superman cartoons of Max and Dave Fleischer were seen on movie screens across America and helped make the character a household name. These cartoons were among the first to feature "super" villains for Superman to confront, including a mad scientist who orders an army of robots to steal precious jewels and a Tyrannosaurus Rex that awakens from hibernation after the iceberg encasing its flesh is accidentally thawed. Unlike the comic books, they showed Superman on the World War II battlefield, fighting alongside American soldiers against the Japanese. The cartoons were sparse on dialogue and long on action, but they were filled with iconic imagery, including state-of-the-art animation.

As Marek Wasielewski observed in "Industrial Design and the Machine Paradigm in the Fleischer Animated Superman Shorts 1941–1943" (2007), the Fleischer stories present a mechanistic, art deco, future-city Metropolis designed to be an amalgam of architectural concepts found in Fritz Lang's *Metropolis* (1927), the New York World's Fair (1939–1940), the Titan City Project, and a then-contemporary architectural style now known as the

Gernsback Continuum (thanks to William Gibson). The unusual look and feel of the cartoons was beautifully mimicked in Kerry Conran's underappreciated superhero film *Sky Captain and the World of Tomorrow* (2004).

Since many of the villains featured in the Fleischer cartoons were pure fantasy, or enemies of the United States (such as Japanese saboteurs), or were ethnic or racial "others" threatening the status quo, these cartoons were more politically conservative than the comic book adventures of Superman crafted by Siegel and Shuster. In fact, compared to the comic book that had begun seeing print a mere four years earlier, the Fleischer cartoons were arguably reactionary. For example, while few of the villains in the Fleischer cartoons had complex motivations for their crimes, or any motivations at all, the *Electric Earthquake* (1942) adventure, written by Seymour Knietel, featured a Native American who threatened to use an earthquake-generating machine to sink Manhattan Island if it is not returned to his tribe. While this is exactly the kind of underdog, wronged character Superman might well side with in the Siegel and Shuster adventures, in the Fleischer stories the Native American is presented as an irredeemable villain who crosses a line into terrorism when he tries to right a social wrong.

In addition to not always being as sensitive towards racial issues as he could, Superman has a spotty record in his treatment of women, despite (or because of) the fact that his main love interest is a pioneering feminist reporter with kinship to Margaret Fuller and Edith Kinney Gaylord. The Fleischer cartoons are notable in representing a Lois that seems inspired by Rosalind Russell's tough female reporter Hildy Johnson from *His Girl Friday* (1940). The formula for most of the Fleischer adventures involved Lois (voiced by Joan Alexander) hoping to beat her fellow reporter Clark Kent (Bud Collyer) out of a scoop, her rushing to follow a lead without him, and then her proving her mettle as a reporter by uncovering a secret criminal plot against the United States. She would soon find herself captured however, and her screams for help would alert Superman, who would then show up, rescue her, and punch the villains out. The epilogue usually involved Lois meeting Clark back at the offices of their newspaper, with Lois gloating that she got the scoop and Clark didn't, and Clark maintaining his cover as Superman by saying something disparaging about the superhero, or doubting Lois' interpretation of events.

According to Wasielewski, the Lois in these cartoons seems tough at first, aggressively flying a plane on her own despite Clark's fears that she is going on an assignment that is too dangerous for a woman. She also brazenly fires a machine gun at a group of train robbers, but her efforts inspire them to shoot back and hit the train's control panel, so her ineffectual attempts to stop the robbery merely send the train hurtling out of control. Luckily, Superman arrives to save the day from both the robbers and Lois' incompetence. Wasielewski writes, "the Fleischer Superman was depicted as an alien, defined by masculine and technological perfection originating from a futuristic, corporate, and industrially designed Utopia. Lane, in the Fleischer shorts, on the other hand, represents the anti-technological nature. Lane is the feminine gremlin tampering with the mechanics of a streamlined plane. The design of the biplane she flies in the first episode is already hopelessly out of date" (12).

Considering she is one of the most famous characters in the history of comic books, Lois has a great number of detractors in both the fan community and the realm of critics and scholars.[8] Bradford W. Wright, author of *Comic Book Nation: The Transformation of Youth Culture in America* (2001), is one of several critics who views Lois negatively:

> Although arguably a protofeminist character of sorts, Superman's romantic interest, Lois Lane, had few admirable qualities from a contemporary male perspective. While physically

> attractive and spunky, she put her career ahead of romance with the kind but boring Clark Kent and pined after Superman, whom she could never possess. Superman, on the other hand, was too strong and self-assured to succumb to the allure of a beautiful woman. Invariably, Lois's chief function was to be captured and await rescue by her hero [9].

Other complaints commonly leveled against Lois are that she is "bitchy," snidely needles Clark by calling him "Smallville," and shallowly prefers the muscle-bound Superman to the sensitive Clark. There are several possible rebuttals for these accusations. Firstly, if one looks at Lois as she was originally conceived—the only female reporter at the *Daily Planet*, and the star reporter at that—then she has clawed her way to the top of her field, presumably against the unified opposition of a sexist male establishment, and proven her worth by being a tenacious investigative journalist capable of breaking stories of corporate and government corruption most other reporters are too timid or ineffective to take on. A heroine who could have been created by Stieg Larsson, she had to have been tough and unwomanly to get to where she is in the first place. Secondly, Perry humiliates Lois by hiring Clark to join her on the newspaper's prime news beat. Kent is an inexperienced journalist, mild-mannered, and a new arrival to Metropolis from rural Kansas with no understanding of the city or what it takes to survive in an urban environment. While Perry seems to want to portray Clark as a partner, what he has done is maneuver a male newcomer into a competitive position, suggesting that he is preparing to fire Lois and is in the process of grooming her replacement. Under these circumstances, Lois' hostility to Clark is understandable; it is a hostility many of us would feel ourselves in her position. Indeed, in the Kirk Alyn serial, Clark uses his powers as Superman to follow Lois to a story she has already done all the research on; he relies on his super-hearing to get the breaking story she has been striving to get for months, and he uses his super-speed to get back to *The Daily Planet* before her and scoop her out of her own story. This is exactly the kind of unfair play that Superman usually condemns football coaches and mine owners for employing, yet he uses it himself against Lois.

Examining the Lois debate from another vantage point, it can be argued that the two are, in many ways, partners despite themselves. Lois is Superman's infallible compass, only she unerringly points at evil instead of north. Lois unearths evil conspiracies, invariably stumbles upon Luthor's secret hideout, and summons Superman to discover the villain that she has unmasked without assistance from anyone else. In this borderline psychoanalytic construction, Lois and Superman are two halves of the same single superhero character, with Lois acting as the brain and Superman the brawn.

A publicity still of Margot Kidder as Lois Lane from *Superman: The Movie* (Warner Bros., 1978).

There are also those who tease Lois for being fooled by Superman's feeble disguise: When he wears glasses and parts his hair on the side, he is Clark Kent, when he does not wear glasses, and has a spit curl over his forehead, he is Superman. And yet, those who make such jokes forget that Lois has repeatedly figured out the truth about Superman. By the end of the first *Superman* film, mere weeks after first meeting Clark, Lois (Margot Kidder) has almost put it together. By the middle of *Superman II* (1980), she has the mystery solved. In one of the best scenes in the history of superhero stories, Lois says to Clark, "I gotta admit, you know your disguise is nearly perfect. You had me fooled and I am nobody's fool, believe me." He protests that she has an overactive imagination and she cuts him off. "Listen, I'm so sure that you're Superman that I'm willing to bet my life on it." And, with a shout of "Bye, bye baby!" she leaps into a raging river. Clark cleverly manages to rescue her without turning into Superman, but feels guilty enough about continually lying to her that he tells her almost immediately afterward that she had figured out the truth after all. Scenes such as this, as well as Lois' tearful confession of love to the dying Superman in *Superman IV: The Quest for Peace* (1987) and her own brutal death scene in the first *Superman* movie make Margot Kidder's performance as Lois the definitive portrayal of the character on film. (Like most segments in superhero stories involving the revelation of a secret identity and a major character's death, these scenes were almost immediately "invalidated" or "removed from continuity" by *deus ex machina* plot devices, invariably involving time-travel and/or convenient amnesia. Nevertheless, these scenes with Kidder—like the "invalidated" scenes in Spider-Man comics when Aunt May tells Peter Parker she knows his secret—remain some of the best moments in superhero history, whether or not their consequences were "permanent.")

Unfortunately, Kidder's Lois has more than her share of detractors. One of the main reasons is that her Lois, like the comic book Lois, insults the sensibilities of the nerdy comics fan by turning her nose up at the romantic advances of the nerdy Clark. Still, one must remember that Lois is responding in disgust to an insincere persona that Kal-El of Krypton has devised to keep his true identity as Superman a secret. Yes, when Clark is in the privacy of his family home in Smallville, with only his adoptive parents and his confidant Lana in sight, he can be the "real" Clark—the alien boy raised to adulthood by the kindly Methodist Kents. The "Clark Kent" who lives in Metropolis, however, is a buffoon, and—as Jules Feiffer and Quentin Tarantino have argued—is Superman's satirical take on the cowardice, vulnerability, and weakness of the average American male (see Feiffer 347–349 and *Kill Bill Part 2*). So why would Lois fall for a caricature of a weakling?

However, the anti–Lois faction has at least one strong argument to support their claim that she should love Clark more. When Superman loses his powers in *Superman II*, and seems to become, in actual fact, the absurd weakling he had been pretending to be all along, that alteration is too much for Lois to process, and she looks upon him with crushing disappointment. It is a moment many can relate to, especially those who have looked upon their parents or lovers with pained eyes the first time they can plainly see the flaws in a once seemingly flawless façade. (The 2006 Superman-themed film *Hollywoodland* is entirely concerned with that moment of disappointment, and the difference between our heroic image of our parents, and of Superman, and the harsh reality we face when we realize that our parents are mere human beings, and Superman is merely a depressed, typecast actor named George Reeves.) The lack of charity Lois shows a humbled Clark in *Superman II* is, for many viewers, an unforgivable moment of weakness. That reaction from fans is understandable, but so is Lois' disappointment that a man who could one push a planet out of orbit with his finger now has trouble beating a hick in a fistfight in a 24-hour diner. It is also important to note that, once Clark decides to become Superman again, Lois knows she has lost him forever to his career as Superman, and the Kidder Lois tragically spends the rest of her life single, unable to move on from her love for Superman.

The Lois in the comic book is not always as complex, funny, or charismatic as Kidder's—or as well written—but she is often easy to empathize with in her own way. In Scott McCloud's "Balance of Power" (1998), the female supervillain Livewire strikes back at the American patriarchy by taking over the mass media and refusing to broadcast images of men over televisions. As she planned, the moment television stations realize that they need to show only women on television screens to stay on the air, women who were kept in subordinate positions to men in the television industry—underpaid actresses, "sidekick" anchorwomen, and female politicians—are suddenly given a dominant, unprecedented voice in the mass media. When Superman acts to stop Livewire, he is doing so to protect the male status quo. Lois accepts, on some level, that Superman is stopping an act of terrorism, but even she, famous as she is in her own right in a man's world, is sympathetic to Livewire.

LIVEWIRE: It seems to me our little community—the world community—has been dominated by men just a little too long.

LOIS: So, what else is new?

LIVEWIRE: What's new is I've decided to do something about it. You see, I think men and women should have equal time. As in, they had the last few thousand years; we should have the next [102–103].

Superman confronts Livewire and fights her for control of the airwaves, but seems to be holding back, as if he doesn't really want to defeat her. Then Luthor arrives and shoots Livewire, nearly killing her. He tells Superman that his intervention was "a present from the old boy's network." Superman is enraged, and chases Luthor away from the barely breathing Livewire. Meanwhile, Angela Chen, a television reporter who had finally been allowed to cover crime and politics instead of gossip and fashion, has the microphone taken away from her, and a male reporter covers the aftermath of the story without any further assistance from Chen.

Different Superman sagas project starkly conflicting futures for Lois and Superman. *Whatever Happened to the Man of Tomorrow* (1986), written by Alan Moore and drawn by longtime Superman artist Curt Swan, gives the whole series a happy ending, revealing that Superman ultimately retires, lives out a happily married life with Lois, and the two have a super-powered baby. A far less cheerful turn of events unfolds in *Superman Returns* (2006). In that film, audiences discover that Lois (Kate Bosworth) has given birth to Superman's child, but has chosen to marry Perry's nephew Richard (James Marsden) and raise the baby without Superman's help. Several Elseworlds comics posit that Lois is eventually murdered by a supervillain, or is killed when her half–Kryptonian unborn child delivers a superpowered kick to her womb. Some Elseworlds suggest, as both *Hancock* (2008) and *Superman II* (1980) do, that Superman cannot even have sex with a human woman, for fear that his ejaculating sperm would perforate a woman like bullets. In several of these Elseworlds, Superman marries Wonder Woman because she is the only woman on earth who is physically strong enough to survive sex with Superman and bear his child. In official, post–*Crisis* DC continuity, however, writers Geoff Johns and Richard Donner have established that Superman and Lois *can* have sex, but that their incompatible DNA means that they can never have children. The couple's infertility is one of the reasons why, in *Last Son* (2008), Superman and Lois decide to adopt the son of Ursa and General Zod, and rename him Christopher Kent after the boy flees from his abusive parents.

Longtime Superman fans who dislike Lois have often tended to wish that Superman had settled down with Lana, his childhood sweetheart. Lana has appeared in *The Adventures of Superboy*, played by Stacy Haiduk; in *Superman III*, played by Annette O'Toole, and in *Smallville*, played by Kristin Kreuk. She is most often portrayed as a sweet, redheaded girl from a small town who wants to join Clark in the big city, but is scared to leave Smallville behind. She is also in love with Clark, but never made peace with his identity as Superman. Her preference for the nerdy Clark over the hunky Superman makes her a favorite of nerdy comics fans, and the fact that she is "the one that got away" and suffers from pangs of loss since the marriage of Clark and Lois makes her a sympathetic and relatable character. Her vulnerability is another source of her appeal. However, the counterargument can be made that Lana, as a stereotypical girl next door, is somewhat dull next to the more complex and provocative Lois.

The final major female character in the Superman universe also has two "L"s in her name: Linda Lee. Linda Lee, of course, is better known as Supergirl.

Supergirl, like other female counterparts of male heroes — including Spider-Woman, She-Hulk, and Batwoman — is often disparaged for being unoriginal and a bit cheesy. Interestingly, all the above-mentioned women wear costumes that are similar, to varying degrees, to those of their male counterparts, and they have derivative names, but they are quite innovative in all other respects. For example, as an impressionable adolescent Spider-Woman was recruited by the terrorist organization Hydra and brainwashed into hating America — until Nick Fury turned her against her masters. (That doesn't sound much like Spider-Man.) She-Hulk is an intelligent, good-humored criminal defense lawyer with the Hulk's green skin and super strength. (She isn't much like Hulk.) Batwoman Kate Kane is a wealthy Jewish lesbian who was expelled from a military academy for becoming romantically involved with a female student. (She isn't much like Batman.) Later, during the storyline *52*, she drew upon her military training to become Batwoman to replace Batman during a year when he went mysteriously inactive. Supergirl is equally unusual when compared to Superman.

Supergirl has traditionally been more of a fantasy genre character than Superman, who occupies a science fiction world. Created by Otto Binder, Superman's cousin, Kara Zor-El, was introduced into the comic book world during one of its most whimsical, trippy periods, in *Action Comics* #252 (1959). She was an instant sensation as a guest star in *Superman*, but has had difficulty flying solo in her own monthly comic books. Her name and origin story have often been tweaked over the years — sometimes her name has changed and she even had Heavenly, angelic origins instead of a Kryptonian background in a series written by Peter David — but she always wears the Superman "S" logo on her chest and consistently brings a sense of ebullience to a sometimes po-faced DC Universe.

Consequently, the 1984 film *Supergirl*, written by the *Dark Crystal* (1982) screenwriter David Odell, emphasizes the magical and fairy tale qualities of the character. The story begins in a magical floating city, Argo, which detached from Krypton before it was destroyed and has been traveling slowly through space during the period that Superman was coming of age on Earth. At the start of the film, Superman's naïve cousin Kara performs the classic role of the fairy tale heroine by being the initiator of the conflict. She accidentally loses the magical, crystalline power source of Argo City, the Omegahedron, when it is sucked out into space and sent hurtling to Earth. Eager to atone for what she has done, Kara chases after it, hoping that recovering it will save her people. Not knowing exactly where it landed, and unaccustomed to the culture of 20th century earth, Kara adopts the identity of Linda Lee and enrolls in Midvale School, using it as a base of operations from which she can search for the Omegahedron. What Kara doesn't know is that the crystal has been found by a witch,

Selena (Faye Dunaway), who first uses the device to cast simple love spells and then employs it to conquer the town of Midvale and build a fortress home for herself on a nearby mountaintop. But, in order to hold on to her newfound power, Selena has to find a way to defeat a mysterious blonde woman, dressed like Superman, who wants her Omegahedron back.

The film was panned upon its initial release and was a financial failure, but it has two ardent supporters in longtime fans Christopher and Sean Stefanic, who lobbied for years to see an extended cut of the film released on DVD instead of the incomprehensible, heavily edited theatrical version that most people saw in 1984. They are particular fans of the moody, restored segment in which Kara is exiled to the Phantom Zone, and to the "new" character development scenes in which Kara discovers that she has the ability to fly on Earth, and is awestruck by her own newfound abilities. Chris said that he looks up to Kara as a heroine because she is more vulnerable than Reeve's Superman, and has to overcome the difficulties of arriving alone, on earth, as an adult—the ultimate fish-out-of-water. And yet, Chris argues, she proves herself to be a stronger character than Superman by coming back from total defeat—exile in the Phantom Zone—and emerging victorious. Sean hopes that comic readers will give the original film another look, and if a new *Supergirl* film is made, the character will continue to be pure of heart and the film uplifting. "We don't need more films reflecting the sick sadness of society and politics. Leave that for another film." Instead of being as tonally bleak as *The Dark Knight*, he argues, a new *Supergirl* film should be "a real adventure about courage, strength, and intelligence."

Unfortunately for Supergirl, the failure of her theatrical film had disastrous, and long-reaching consequences for her and the rest of the Superman comic book universe. And things would not be the same for years to come.

A World Without Superman

As much as many critics, fans, and scholars find Superman to be a passé, if not highly problematic figure, there is an extent to which a world without Superman scarcely bears contemplating.

Cynical on the surface but idealistic underneath, *Superman* fan Mark Millar has stared the evils of modern society directly in the face and painted an accurate picture of what a world without Superman—and without a new generation of heroes in the mold of King, Gandhi, and John Lennon—looks like. It is our world. *Wanted* (2003–2004) takes place in a reality in which all of the supervillains of the world teamed up at once, handily defeating the minority of superheroes that stood in their way. The villains stripped the defeated heroes of their powers, and

Lex Luthor (Kevin Spacey) examines the dagger-like piece of Kryptonite he will use to stab Superman to death in *Superman Returns* (Warner Bros., 2006).

hypnotized the world into thinking that real superheroes were fictional characters, and that historical events were merely movies, comics, and TV series episodes. Thanks to this mass hypnosis, Superman — who was actually crippled in his final battle with Luthor — is led to believe he is the actor Christopher Reeve, and falsely thinks that he had received his life-changing injuries in a horse-riding accident. The former Wonder Woman has a drinking problem and thinks she is the actress Lynda Carter, who merely played Wonder Woman on television. And Batman and Robin think themselves to be Adam West and Burt Ward. The supervillains all find this hilarious, although the Joker decides, for old times' sake, to murder a powerless and ignorant Adam West and Burt Ward. Before they die, West and Ward scream in protest that it was all just a TV show. "No. No, it wasn't," the Joker insists, and puts them to death.

Aside from being a bizarre in-joke in questionable taste, and the fantasy of a comic book fan who grew up thinking that there was no distinction between these actors and the characters they played, *Wanted* works astonishingly well as a commentary on a real world in which, as Leonard Cohen observed in 1988, *Everybody Knows* that "the good guys" never win.

Superman has certainly never gone away. His old adventures are all available on video, he remains a figure on pajamas and underwear for little children, new Superman tales are released in comic book stores every Wednesday, and he has starred in a new television series every few years, sometimes twice at once, for the past several decades. And yet, he appears to remain unpopular, unsung, and a shadow of his former self. Why?

The Superman comic books produced during the 1980s and 1990s were a stripped-down version of the pre–*Crisis on Infinite Earths* Superman stories, free of Superboy, Supergirl, the Fortress of Solitude, and Superman's dog Krypto. They represented an attempt to place Superman in the same kind of naturalistic world he inhabited in the Reeve films, but what worked brilliantly on screen was incredibly dull in the comic books. Lex Luthor had once been a tragic villain and a brilliant scientist, very much like the characters of Doctor Doom and Doctor Octopus that he inspired. In this new continuity, Luthor was a Donald Trump or a Gordon Gekko robber baron, which brought an incisive, anti–Reaganomics criticism into the comics, but oddly diminished Luthor's grandiosity. (While some fans detested Gene Hackman's comic portrayal of Luthor in the Superman films, it is far and away superior to the bland, corporate Luthor of the post–*Crisis* universe, who only achieved true gravitas when he conned the American people into electing him President of the United States and he became a commentary on Nixon, Reagan, and George W. Bush in stories by Loeb and Joe Kelly.)

In *The Myth of Superman* (1972), Umberto Eco warned that Superman stories can never be effectively grounded in a realistic human history, or timelines, as it would strip Superman of his mythic status, humanizing him and causing his readers to contemplate his inevitable demise. Eco also warned against any Superman story that makes an irreversible status change to Superman's life — such as one in which he marries Lois — because giving him an extended, event-filled past beyond the story of his formative years, and marrying him, compounds the problem of humanizing Superman and pointing to his mortality. The post–*Crisis* Superman has a complex continuity underscored by years of "Triangle numbers" that sort his adventures rigorously. He has also married Lois, an act that humanized him to the degree that there now seems little difference between him and Spider-Man, the Marvel Comics character who was designed to be an accessible, satirical Superman.

It is also significant that the post–*Crisis* Superman is something of a bore. He has lost all of the edge that was imbued in the character by his creators, and was stripped of Reeve's liberal sensibilities by John Byrne, who viewed Superman as a "card-carrying Republican." Frank Miller lampooned Byrne's bland and domesticated Superman as a stooge of Reagan in his futuristic Batman story *The Dark Knight Returns* (1986). The story is remarkably like *Watchmen,* which was published around the same time, in that it takes place in a world in which superheroes cannot operate on their own, but must work directly for the White House, or not at all. Superman has capitulated to the demands of the American government, and Reagan orders him to spearhead the American invasion of Corto Maltese, a Cuba-like fictional island nation occupied by Soviet forces. For his part, an aging Batman refuses to take orders from Reagan, and comes out of retirement to tame a Gotham City that has degenerated into anarchy since Reagan had forced him into retirement. (Significantly, the conflict between Superman and Batman on this issue will later be reflected in the conflict between Iron Man and Captain America in Marvel's 2006–2007 *Civil War* storyline, with Iron Man taking Superman's position and Captain America taking Batman's.)

Reagan orders Superman to stop Batman from defying his authority, but Batman is prepared for Superman's intervention. Armed with Kryptonite, Batman beats Superman to a bloody pulp, proclaiming that, "it is way past time [Clark] learned what it means to be a man." While Miller's story asks readers to accept that Batman is working *against* Reagan and Superman *for* Reagan, most readers reject this idea on a fundamental level and read the scene as being an illustration of how handily badass Republicans like Batman (and Reagan) can defeat wimpy Democrats like Superman (or Jimmy Carter). In effect, the scene plays like an allegorical representation of Reagan's landslide 1980 electoral victory against Carter. Certainly, both contests are widely regarded as a trouncing of epic proportions. Unfortunately for Superman, *The Dark Knight Returns* is one of the most famous Superman stories of the past twenty-five years — one in which Superman is a foolish reactionary who is bested by the more macho Batman. No wonder his status amongst comic fans plummeted after *Crisis on Infinite Earths.*

Indeed, as dull as the 1980s and 1990s comic book Superman is in his own book, when he is a guest star in another character's book, serving as the main character's foil, or when he is part of the Justice League ensemble cast, he is still more dull and establishment. In the *Justice League* cartoon (2001–2006), Superman is little more than a dumb muscle man who takes laser beam hits for his teammates while they strategize and win the day. In a variety of Wonder Woman stories, he preaches paternalistically to Wonder Woman, and comes off remarkably sexist. Indeed, in the Christopher Priest story *The 18th Letter* (2000), Superman learns that the despotic leader of a Third World Nation has promised to end his campaign of ethnic cleansing against his own people if Wonder Woman will agree to spend the night with him. Superman is appalled by this indecent proposal, not just because he is worried that other criminals will try to blackmail Wonder Woman in the same way, but because he can't imagine anyone having sex with Wonder Woman but himself— even though he is already married to Lois. In this Wonder Woman story, as in *Spirit of Truth* and *New Frontier*, Superman seems naïve, moralistic, and self-centered.

What is interesting about Superman's portrayal as paternalistic blowhard is that other "macho" counter-culture figures, especially those from the 1960s such as Captain Kirk and James Bond, also did not fare well in the 1990s. The aged Captain Kirk was equally despised by liberal *Star Trek* fans, who saw Kirk as warlike and sexist next to the neutered, pacifist Jean-Luc Picard, and by conservatives, who were tired of Kirk making speeches about the beauty of world peace and socialism in stories like "Day of the Dove" and "The Undiscovered

Country," and who could not forgive him for growing old and fat. So Kirk was unceremoniously killed off in the appalling *Star Trek: Generations* (1994). As disliked by liberals as Kirk, James Bond fared little better in the 1990s. For example, Pierce Brosnan's debut as James Bond, *GoldenEye* (1995), counterintuitively declared the character obsolete — a sexist, mysognist dinosaur ... a relic of the Cold War. This seemed, at the time, to be an odd way for the filmmakers to assert the character's continuing relevance.

Some of this anti-womanizer rhetoric gained traction during the Bill Clinton Administration, in which a pro-feminist, pro-choice president had the unusual distinction of being one of the most famously horny men on the planet. In 2001, Brian Michael Bendis wrote a *Powers* storyline in which the public discovers that Olympia — a superhero drawn to resemble both Bill Clinton and Superman — has had sex with virtually all of the women he has saved from muggers, car accidents, and natural disasters. During one such encounter, Olympia has a heart attack and dies in the midst of casual sex with a virtual stranger. Like other storylines in *Powers*, the superhero is viewed through the lens of modern American celebrity and tabloid culture, and reminds readers that, if they existed in the real world, superheroes would have groupies (like those described in Pamela Des Barres' book *I'm with the Band*), superheroes would not be moral paragons, and the members of the Justice League would hate each other as much as the band members in the Sex Pistols and the Clash hate one another. The story is also indicative of the level of respect the American people had for liberal champions Bill Clinton and Superman in 2001.

In 1997, the James Bond spoof, *Austin Powers: International Man of Mystery* also commented on the fall from grace of womanizing '60s icons James T. Kirk and James Bond (and womanizing 1990s liberal Bill Clinton) through the character of Austin Danger Powers, an amalgam of Bond, John Steed, and Jon Pertwee's Doctor from *Doctor Who*. The story, written by and starring Mike Meyers, was about the conflict between the philosophies of the heroic Austin Powers (Meyers) and the evil Dr. Evil (Meyers). Austin, champion of free love, drugs, rock n' roll, and the hippie ethic, was a hero of the 1960s, while his arch nemesis, Dr. Evil, represented corporate greed, militarism, and the right-wing agenda that the counter culture movement despised. Both of them are put into cryogenic sleep in the 1960s and awaken in the archconservative 1990s, where Dr. Evil is regarded as heroic by the American people, and placed in command of Starbucks, Enron, and a slew of multinational corporations. For his part, Austin Powers has a harder time adjusting to the "mojo-killing" present, where Austin is sneered at by Puritanical feminist Miss Kensington for being an affront to women everywhere. (When the film was released in 1997, many viewers had little difficulty imagining Bill Clinton attempting to seduce Miss Kensington as Austin Powers did, by asking playfully: "Shall we shag now or shall we shag later?") By the end of the film, Austin Powers understands why his mode of liberalism is out of fashion, but he insists that his heart was in the right place in the chaotic 1960s. Consider the climactic conversation between Austin Powers and Dr. Evil:

> DR. EVIL: We're not so different you and I. However isn't it ironic that the very things that you stand for ... free love, swinging, parties are all now in the '90's considered to be ... evil?
>
> AUSTIN: No man, what we swingers were rebelling against is uptight squares like you, whose bag was money and world domination. We were innocent, man! If we'd known the consequences of our sexual liberation we would have done things differently, but the spirit would have remained the same. It's freedom baby, yeah.
>
> DR. EVIL: Face it. Freedom failed.

AUSTIN: No man. Freedom didn't fail. Right now we've got freedom and responsibility. It's a very groovy time.

DR. EVIL: There's nothing more pathetic than an aging hipster.

Maybe. On the other hand, one might argue that it is too bad there aren't more aging hipsters roaming America in modern times promoting both freedom and responsibility.

Like James Bond, Captain Kirk, and Superman, the classic DC characters did not fare well during the 1990s. Beginning with the deaths of Supergirl and the quaint, straight-laced Flash Barry Allen in *Crisis on Infinite Earths*, DC continued its campaign of purging its roster of heroes, leaving all of the grimmest, darkest characters untouched and maiming and killing all the fun characters. Over the course of the next ten years, Batman comics in particular got progressively darker. The Joker beat Robin to death with a crowbar (1989's *A Death in the Family*), raped and crippled Batgirl (*The Killing Joke*, 1988), and broke up the blossoming romance and crime-fighting partnership between Batman and Catwoman by hypnotizing Selina Kyle and turning her evil, thereby making Bruce Wayne a celibate, humorless loner for the next several decades (see Mike W. Barr's *Detective Comics* #569–570, 1986).

Meanwhile, DC editors and storytellers stripped Aquaman of his extended family and his trusty Seahorse steed and gave Wonder Woman the power of flight in order to remove her much derided Invisible Jet from continuity. Green Lantern Hal Jordan, who had begun his career in 1959 as a suave, reckless Paul Newman–type hero, had aged into a depressed, graying veteran in the 1980s before unexpectedly (and absurdly) transforming into the insane Fascist Parallax (1994). And the success of the dark Tim Burton *Batman* films caused a fan backlash against the 1960s *Batman* series, and encouraged film studios to cease making child-friendly superhero movies such as *Flash Gordon* (1980) and *The Rocketeer* (1991), which underperformed at the box office anyway.

By 1992, all of the bestselling comic book characters on the market were variants of the Punisher—mentally deranged murderers who killed their enemies without remorse. These characters included Wolverine, Lobo, Deadpool, Cable, Venom, and the newly minted Image Comics anti-hero Spawn. Faced with a comic-reading public that found Superman, Wonder Woman, and even Batman to be too kindly and antiquated in their morality, DC writers removed Clark Kent, Diana Prince, and Bruce Wayne from their positions of prominence and replaced all three with Punisher-inspired variants. When the supervillain Doomsday beat Superman to death in *The Death of Superman* (1992), an evil, Cyborg Superman with the human face of Christopher Reeve torn partly away to reveal the battle-damaged Terminator-style skeleton underneath appeared to replace Kal-El. Cyborg symbolically enacted the replacement of the Reeve heroic ideal with the Arnold Schwarzenegger ideal, making him extremely popular. In 1994, the Amazons stripped Diana Prince of her Wonder Woman title and named the more militant Amazon, Artemis of Bana-Mighdall, her replacement. In 1993, the supervillain Bane (who looks like the Mexican Luchador enmascarado Santo) broke Batman's back over his knee and took control of Gotham City. Batman's protégée Jean-Paul Valley, an assassin-in-training of the Order of St. Dumas, takes over the role of Batman and wipes the floor with Bane, proving conclusively to most comics readers that the world would be a better place if all superheroes, including Batman, Wonder Woman, and Superman, were like the Punisher after all. After spending a year or so as supporting characters in their own comics, Bruce Wayne, Clark Kent, and Diana Prince reclaimed their positions of prominence. Bruce Wayne regained the ability to walk through magical means, Clark Kent returned from the grave, and Diana became Wonder Woman again after Artemis was killed in battle.

Distressed by the state of their childhood heroes in the 1990s — especially Superman, Green Lantern, Aquaman, and other DC characters — Alex Ross and Mark Waid crafted the fully painted miniseries *Kingdom Come* (1996) as a means of resurrecting them from pseudo-death — or cryogenic sleep. The "Elseworlds" story was set in an alternative future in which an aged Superman, Batman, and Wonder Woman come out of retirement to take the world back from the new generation of superheroes, all of whom are super-powered versions of the Punisher led by the insane Magog. The irony is that Superman, still bitter and confused that the Joker had murdered Lois — and that Magog had been the one to finally kill the Joker — has returned a meaner, bitter version of his older self; Wonder Woman had become more militant than even Artemis, and billionaire Bruce Wayne has seemingly allied himself with Luthor. So, while the story ostensibly represented a return to simpler times and more noble depictions of heroism, what it really did was portray the members of the Justice League as even more morally flawed than the Watchmen.

However, Ross's beautifully painted art in this project — and on a series of follow-up works, such as *Superman: Peace on Earth* (1999), *Shazam: Power of Hope* (2000), *Wonder Woman: Spirit of Truth* (2001), and *(Absolute) Justice* (2009) — reminded comics readers how rich and beautiful the DC Universe was before it was ravaged by *Crisis on Infinite Earths* and its follow-ups. Ross even made Aquaman's giant Seahorse, Wonder Woman's Invisible Jet and the adorable Captain Marvel family seem hip and relevant to the 21st century — no mean feat indeed. These projects, and the nostalgic elements of the concurrent *Justice League* cartoon (2001–2006), inspired the DC executives, and writers such as Waid, Johns, and Loeb to gradually reverse the effects of the *Crisis on Infinite Earths* and restore to life Hal Jordan, Barry Allen, and Kara Zor-El —*and even turn Barbara Gordon back into Batgirl*— in stories such as *Green Lantern: Rebirth* (2005), *Final Crisis* (2008), and *Flashpoint* (2011).

And yet, while Superman comics continued to be published during the 1990s, and he appeared in several television shows since the release of the final Reeve film in 1987, there was still a feeling that Superman had been absent from the public eye, largely because Batman and Spider-Man had headlined feature film franchises for years while Superman appeared to be enjoying his retirement from the silver screen. Americans may also have felt that Superman had abandoned them, on some level, because he was clearly not around to prevent the September 11 attacks in the real world. Hence, the aptness of the seemingly counterintuitive title of the Bryan Singer film *Superman Returns* (2006). As the film explains, Superman was indeed absent from Earth for an extended period following the events depicted in *Superman II* (1980). He left Earth looking for more Kryptonian survivors after experiencing disappointment that the first refugees he has met since his arrival on Earth were the evil General Zod, Ursa, and Non. Discouraged to find Krypton a dead planet with no survivors, he returned to Earth. The round trip takes Superman away from Earth for a total of five years. Upon his return, Superman discovers that America has become a much darker place under the rule of George W. Bush, and he is no longer wanted. Even Lois, who has given birth to the child they conceived in *Superman II*, has forsaken him, and won a Pulitzer Prize for her editorial "Why the World Doesn't Need Superman."

SUPERMAN: I read the article, Lois.

LOIS: Yeah, so did a lot of people. Tomorrow night, they're giving me the Pulitzer...

SUPERMAN: Why did you write it?

LOIS: How could you leave us like that? I moved on. So did the rest of us. That's why I wrote it. The world doesn't need a savior. And neither do I.

When they meet a second time, Superman takes Lois on another flight, in memory of the first flight they took in *Superman* (1978). Still holding Lois, he stops in mid air, as high in the sky as possible without leaving the Earth's atmosphere.

> SUPERMAN: Listen; what do you hear?
>
> LOIS: Nothing.
>
> SUPERMAN: I hear everything. You wrote that the world doesn't need a savior, but every day I hear people crying for one.

But the film, sad as it is in tone, does not provide a model for a savior. Its Superman, like the chastened and defeated Superman of *Kingdom Come,* is a shadow of his former self. As much as it tries to be a direct sequel to the Reeve films, all audience members could think of was how much better Reeve was than Brandon Routh as Superman, and how superior Kidder was to Kate Bosworth as Lois. Even if more accomplished actors had been cast in the lead roles—say Mark Wahlberg and Robin Tunney—there would have been no guarantee that a Superman film with such a bleak tone would inspire anyone. In the end, it simply didn't feel as if Superman had really returned after all. The other problem, of course, was that Bush was still president when *Superman Returns* was released, and there is a sense in which Superman can only truly return when the Democrats return to the White House and let the spirit of Superman back into the American psyche. Like Captain America, the Marvel Comics equivalent of Superman, Kal-El can only inspire half-hearted patriotism in an age of militarism and unrestrained corporate excess. This is why Superman died in 1992, during the end of twelve years of Republican rule, and was resurrected in a story that was published after Bill Clinton's inauguration. Similarly, Captain America was killed off at the end of the Marvel *Civil War,* during the final years of the Bush presidency, and was resurrected after Obama's inauguration. The deaths of Superman and Captain America were meant to comment upon the limits placed

A scene from *Superman: Secret Origin* #3 (DC Comics, 2009), that recreates the first encounter between a bashful Superman and a terrified and shocked Lois Lane, who has just been rescued from falling to her death. Written by Geoff Johns and drawn by Gary Frank.

upon individual freedoms under the three Republican Administrations in the name of national security and the free market, and their resurrections symbolized a return to sanity in American politics. It is also unsurprising that, during the Reagan years, Superman acted as a replacement American president in *Superman IV*, and that Captain America was featured as an alternative president to Reagan in Mike W. Barr's "What if Captain America Had Been Elected President?" (1981).

Interestingly, at the same time the film *Superman Returns* was released, the comic books had finally begun to rediscover how to tell proper Superman stories. So, while Superman failed to return effectively to the big screen, he did indeed, seem to be back on the printed page as he was meant to be. The Man of Tomorrow was rejuvenated in two of the best Superman storylines in decades. Instead of being ashamed of Superman's colorful, pre–*Crisis* universe, Grant Morrison — and his equally imaginative artist-collaborator, Frank Quitely — reveled in it. Morrison's "non-canonical" *All-Star Superman* (2005–2008) series is a vibrant, imaginative, and psychedelic read, replete with stories in which Lois and Jimmy improbably gain superpowers, Luthor is once again an over-the-top mad scientist, the Bizarro world is fantastic fun, and Superman meets future versions of himself in gloriously convoluted time-travel narratives. It is comic book gold.

Slightly more sober, but within continuity, Johns was more adept at distilling the essence of the Reeve Superman into the comic books with the help of Superman film director Richard Donner in the contemporary-set *Last Son* (2008), which introduced General Zod, Ursa, and Non into the comic book world. Johns also retold Superman's origin in a way that perfectly blended the well-known origin narratives from the first Reeve film, the TV series *Smallville*, the *Superboy and the Legion of the Superheroes* comics, and the smallest dash of Steve Ditko's *The Amazing Spider-Man* to make a compelling, refreshing read out of seemingly over-familiar material. With *Secret Origin* (2009–2010) Johns distilled a single narrative from multiple, irreconcilable *Superman* biographies, in a far more successful manner than his predecessors, Byrne and Waid. The comic is also deeply affecting because artist Gary Frank draws Superman to look remarkably like Christopher Reeve.

After all, Christopher Reeve *is* Superman.

SIX

The Special Relationship: Britain and America in James Bond, Doctor Who *and* Hellblazer

About Superman and Batman: the former is how America views itself, the latter, darker character is how the rest of the world views America.—Michael Caine[1]

Discussion Question ... In *Star Wars: Episode II*, Chancellor Palpatine convinces the Galactic Senate to grant him emergency powers in order to squelch the Separatist movement's droid army, led by Count Dooku. But Palpatine ultimately abuses his authority, disbanding the Republic and appointing himself the lone ruler of a new Galactic Empire. Could it happen here?—Jon Stewart[2]

You know, the very powerful and the very stupid have one thing in common. They don't alter their views to fit the facts. They alter the facts to fit their views. Which can be uncomfortable if you happen to be one of the facts that needs altering.—The Doctor[3]

The Three Plagues of Britain: Thatcherism, Reaganism, and Murdochism

Americans who are accustomed to thinking of themselves as the "good guys" might be surprised to see how they are represented in superhero adventures and science fiction allegories from overseas, in which they are frequently portrayed as villainous, not just by filmmakers from sometimes rival nations, but by writers and artists from America's staunchest allies.

Most Americans do not know that the invincible dragon Gojira (a.k.a. Godzilla) is Japan's representation of the merciless, unstoppable military might of the United States. In *Gojira* (1954), the 167-foot monster rains radioactive flame breath down upon Tokyo, laying waste to the city in an allegorical recreation of President Truman's atomic bombing of Hiroshima and Nagasaki. While many *Gojira* sequels were children's movies featuring amusing wrestling matches between dinosaurs, some retained the somber tone and political commentary of the original Ishiro-Honda film. For example, *Godzilla versus Hedorah* (1971) criticized U.S. and Japanese industries for polluting the oceans, while *Godzilla versus King Ghidora* (1991) subtly condemned Americans for growing racist and xenophobic following the purchase of Rockefeller Center by a Japanese firm.

Dubbed "the most anti–American movie ever made," *Mr. Freedom* (1968) was a diatribe against American imperialism, consumerism, and national stupidity made in France with a mostly European cast by expatriate American fashion photographer William Klein. Mr. Freedom — a racist, moronic superhero dressed in a red-white-and-blue football uniform — goes to Paris to defeat Communist agents and win back the support of the French people, who have turned on America over Vietnam and shown a distressing tendency to embrace socialism. Mr. Freedom's corporate supervisor, Dr. Freedom (Donald Pleasence), warns him that the French may be beyond help, since they "are fifty million mixed-up, sniveling cry-babies who haven't stood on their two feet since Napoleon.... We've had to carry them through two world wars already, and we're damn well gonna have to carry them through the next."

Knowing the odds are stacked against him, Mr. Freedom dons a friendly white cowboy uniform, makes contact with French anti-communist supporters, and rallies them with a series of satirical speeches that tout freedom and democracy. (Chillingly, these "joke" speeches sound remarkably like several seriously intended speeches that President George W. Bush made decades later in defense of the war on terror.) Contrary to the lip service Mr. Freedom pays to democracy, his real objective is to conquer France and force American consumer products upon the French people. When they refuse to submit to his demands, Mr. Freedom bombs most of the country into oblivion and accidentally destroys himself with one of his own weapons.

Mr. Freedom continues to offend conservative American viewers, but liberal film enthusiasts often find themselves enraptured by the similarities between Bush and Mr. Freedom.[4] As IMDB.com reviewer Matthew Janovic observed:

> What's really boring is how whenever someone has the "temerity" to criticize American foreign policy, they're somehow being "pedantic" and "preachy," while the excesses of our corporate owned media get a free pass. It's a hollow argument whose lies are showing, and we've got a lot of criticism coming-our-way these days, even from our "allies" in the EU. We've earned it.[5]

Of course, America's staunchest ally in the EU is Great Britain, and the British people have come to question the virtue of that special relationship in recent years. Although America began its life as a country by fighting two wars against Britain, an alliance between the two world powers gradually developed, and was cemented when America joined Britain's side in World War II, thereby saving its mother country from defeat at the hands of the Nazi menace. In 1946, Winston Churchill had described the bond of friendship and shared cultural heritage between Britain and the United States as a "special relationship" that should never be broken, especially in a nuclear age in which such an alliance could ensure international stability. Although various British and American political administrations since World War II have had their share of conflicts, and presidents and prime ministers (such as Democratic President Bill Clinton and Tory Prime Minister John Major) have personally disliked one another, the alliance has stayed essentially firm. British and American administrations have tended to interact best whenever the president and the prime minister are from the same ideological stock: the two staunchly anti–Soviet, champions of the free market, Reagan and Thatcher, were close friends, as were the left-leaning centrists "New Labour" Tony Blair and "New Democrat" Bill Clinton.

Blair and Clinton's partnership produced notable international achievements, including the signing of the landmark peace agreement in Ireland and the successful conducting of the Kosovo War, but things changed with the election of President Bush and the 9/11 attacks. Blair threw his wholehearted support behind America, in sympathy for the suffering caused by the attacks, and committed British forces to the war in Afghanistan. These decisions were, by and large, not very controversial. However, it was Blair's decision to support Bush's push for an invasion of Iraq on the basis of dubious evidence linking Iraqi President Saddam Hussein to al-Qaeda and 9/11 that gradually turned the British people against Blair and the United States. A 2006 *Cracker* episode effectively dramatizes this growing anti–American sentiment. In the story, written by Jimmy McGovern, a British serial killer murders several expatriate Americans to punish them for voting Bush into office. And this is only one example of such a story.

Comic books by British writers (*John Constantine: Hellblazer*), British spy novels (*The Ghost* and *Devil May Care*), and prominent British television series (*Doctor Who*) released during the Bush-Blair years all paint a decidedly negative portrait of Americans. These popular culture artifacts collectively suggest that England is beset by three plagues: the extreme conservatism of the American government, the omnipresent threat represented by domestic conservatives, and the far-reaching influence of monopolistic, multinational corporations. The arch villains who have become the personification of these plagues, and their deadly effects, are former American President Ronald Reagan, British Prime Minister Margaret Thatcher, and mass media mogul Rupert Murdoch—as well as any and all of their heir apparents, including George W. Bush, Tony Blair, and James Murdoch.

To British writers such as Alan Moore (*Watchmen*) and Russell T. Davies (*Doctor Who*), Reagan and Thatcher, as charming as they may be on camera, represent a conspiracy of self-serving Anglo-American corporate and military interests that will cause any havoc and crush any opposition in their quest to obtain a wider profit margin for their stockholders. While talking extensively of freedom, fiscal responsibility, and the virtues of low taxes and limited government, these figures cut funds to social programs, crush labor unions, stymie environmental protection measures, undermine world peace initiatives, and forestall efforts to mitigate global hunger and poverty. They are, to *Hellblazer* writers such as Jamie Delano and Garth Ennis, smiling demons tempting the British and American people on a path to economic, social, and military hell. And Bush and Blair are no better, writers Davies and Warren Ellis have argued.

Consider how British superspy James Bond's opinions of the United States have altered over the years. He was never enamored of Americans, but his opinion has grown far worse since the Bush Administration.[6] In *Live and Let Die* (1954), Bond urbanely describes Manhattan as "the fattest atomic-bomb target on the whole face of the world," and in "For Your Eyes Only" (1960), he reveals that it is easy for him to pose as American, even though he can't imitate the accent, because Americans don't really speak at length, but grunt a lot and confine themselves with saying "Hi!" "Guess so," "That so?" and "Sure" (68).

In the original Ian Fleming novels, written between 1953 and 1964, Bond was an expression of Fleming's disappointment that the American Empire was eclipsing the British Empire. Bond was Fleming's wish-fulfillment means of demonstrating that Britain could still rule the world, even if only by proxy, since Americans didn't really understand the Empire they had inherited from their parent country, and needed advice on how to run it. Consequently, Bond, British secret agent, would invariably fly to the rescue of C.I.A. agent Felix Leiter, an agreeably unintelligent Texan who liked Bond too much to resent the man for always showing him up.[7] Consider how Felix was too inept a gambler to defeat the terrorist LeChiffre in a card game of astounding political import, so he funded Bond, the better player, to ensure that "good" would triumph (*Casino Royale*). Felix was also too stupid to realize that Bond needed rescuing from Goldfinger's private residence, so Bond had to secure his own release by seducing villainess Pussy Galore (the film *Goldfinger*). Most astoundingly, in a segment in the novel *Live and Let Die* that inspired the movie *Licence to Kill*, Felix was incautious enough to be captured by a henchman of SMERSH agent Mr. Big, and lost an arm and a leg to Big's pet shark. Fortunately, Bond was available to avenge Felix by feeding Big and his guilty henchman to a shark and a barracuda. As unintelligent and incompetent as Felix was, he was still one of the "good guys," and America was a country of well-intentioned ignoramuses in Fleming's books.[8]

But that is no longer the case. In both Bond adventures released in 2008, the film *Quantum of Solace* and the Sebastian Faulks novel *Devil May Care*, Bond finds himself pitted against evil American spies. Taking place the year it was released, the film concerns a conspiracy between high-ranking British and American government officials and the super-secret terrorist organization Quantum to steal Bolivia's water supply. As historian Juan R. I. Cole observes, director Marc Forster presents filmgoers "with a new phenomenon in the James Bond films, a Bond at odds with the United States, who risks his career to save Evo Morales's leftist regime in Bolivia from being overthrown by a General Medrano, who is helped by the CIA and a private mercenary organization called Quantum. In short, this Bond is more Michael Moore than Roger Moore" and is more in the spirit of Graham Greene than Ian Fleming.[9] Set in the 1960s immediately after the final Fleming novel, *Devil May Care* involves a wealthy drug trafficker named Gorner who plots to ignite a war between England and the Soviet Union by framing the UK for terrorist attacks on Soviet territories that he himself orchestrated. His efforts are aided by amoral C.I.A. agent J.D. Silver, who wants to see England destroyed by the Soviet Union because the British have voiced opposition to the Vietnam War. In this novel, as in *Quantum of Solace*, Felix Leiter uncovers the fact that his allies in the C.I.A. are conspiring to commit acts that he finds morally repugnant, and he works with Bond against his colleagues in a surreptitious effort to reform the C.I.A. from within. But Americans are not the only subjects of satire in *Devil May Care*. The book also contains a segment in which Gorner ruminates about how he has also considered destroying England by taking over its major journalism outlets, in Rupert Murdoch fashion:

> Suppose I had bought the most distinguished paper of your Establishment hypocrites, *The Times*. Then I could have put it in the hands of some malleable editor who shared my hatred of Britain and attacked the country from its own mouthpiece. I could have bought television channels, other papers ... I could have piped in pornography and propaganda through every inlet until.... But, no, Bond, it would have taken too long [180].

Casino Royale **(Columbia Pictures, 2006) depicts international politics as an elaborate game of poker, in which the stakes are world domination. Sitting at the 12:00 position is Felix Leiter (Jeffrey Wright), incompetent American CIA Agent. At 2:00 is James Bond (Daniel Craig, with hands clasped), British Secret Agent, and at 10:00 is LeChiffre (Mads Mikkelsen), evil terrorist financier.**

This dialogue is a clear swipe at Murdoch, owner of, among other things, *The New York Post, The Sun, Star Magazine, 20th Century–Fox, Fox News, The Wall Street Journal, Harper-Collins, IGN Entertainment*, and *MySpace*. Critics have characterized his mass media outlets as being beholden to his worldview alone, and have collectively saturated the American and British public with right-wing propaganda, lurid advertising, ubiquitous (nearly) naked women, simplistic language and ideas, and intolerance for progressive thinking. Gorner's dialogue comments upon Murdoch's destructive influence on British culture, but it is not the first time Murdoch served as inspiration for a Bond villain. In the Pierce Brosnan Bond film *Tomorrow Never Dies* (1997) actor Jonathan Pryce played the evil Elliot Carver, a media mogul demagogue who was clearly intended to spoof Murdoch. In 2010, characters that were clearly inspired by Rupert and James Murdoch also appeared as villains in the Christopher Nolan film *Inception* and the *Doctor Who* episode *A Christmas Carol* by Steven Moffat. In *Inception*, Cillian Murphy played James Murdoch's double, Robert Fischer—a man on the verge of inheriting a vast empire from his dying father, Maurice Fischer (Pete Postlethwaite as an ersatz Rupert Murdoch). Cobb, the film's wily superhero protagonist (played by Leonardo DiCaprio), is charged with the task of subtly brainwashing Robert into breaking up his father's monopoly in the interest of making a more free and just marketplace. Cobb hopes to prove to Robert that breaking up the empire is also in his own interest so that he can finally "be his own man." At the end of the film, it is not clear if Cobb has succeeded in pricking Robert's conscience or not.

Almost the exact same narrative and political subtext is at work in the *Doctor Who* adventure made the same year. In *A Christmas Carol*, James Murdoch is represented as an Ebenezer Scrooge–like character called Kazran Sardick (Michael Gambon). Acting in the same superhero role as Cobb, the Doctor seeks to convince Kazran to relinquish his total dominion of the "sky" over the planet in order to literally save lives and give greater freedom to the people of his world. (The literal "sky" in the episode is a jokey reference to Murdoch's British Sky Broadcasting Group.) Unlike *Inception*, the *Doctor Who* episode makes it clear that the Doctor succeeds in his goal—Kazran effectively dismantles the empire he inherited from his father, Elliot (also Gambon), and becomes his own man.

On the surface, one would expect British popular culture to be of little interest to American audiences who do not regularly watch PBS or listen to NPR, but there have been interesting cultural moments when obscure British entertainers have exploded onto the American mainstream, or taken over an American niche market completely.[10] For example, the British Invasion of the rock 'n' roll era brought the Beatles, the Rolling Stones, and more than a dozen other memorable British acts to American shores between 1964 and 1966, fundamentally changing the American popular music industry for years to come. A second British invasion occurred during the late 1980s, when British writer Alan Moore and British artists Brian Bolland and Dave Gibbons produced the enormously successful DC comic books *Swamp Thing* (1984–1987), *Watchmen* (1986–1987), and *Batman: The Killing Joke* (1988). The success of these stories opened the floodgates to a wave of British writers to write and draw "American" comic books.

Far from condescending to their audiences or assuming a child reader, Alan Moore's stories were mature, deconstructionist narratives that explored the limits of the superhero worldview and provided incisive criticism of the 1980s political landscape. *Watchmen* argued that Ronald Reagan was functionally the same president as Richard Nixon, only more photogenic, and was every day bringing the U.S. closer and closer to nuclear war with Russia thanks to his reckless, belligerent anti–Communist policies. Moore's *V for Vendetta* (1982–

1989) was a diatribe against 1980s British culture that pondered the merits of anarchism and pitted a modern-day Guy Fawkes figure against the appalling leadership of the Tories, symbolically represented by the futuristic, fascistic "Norsefire" party. Both Moore stories were brilliant and effective political commentaries, which explains why they were both adapted into films during the Bush Administration — *V for Vendetta* (featuring Stephen Fry) was released in 2006, and *Watchmen* began production the same year and was released in 2009. Both stories were handily refitted to skewer Bush and Blair as the right wing, 21st century equivalents of Reagan and Thatcher.

Following Moore's success, several other notable British writers and artists were recruited by DC, including Neil Gaiman, Grant Morrison, and many others who had worked on *Judge Dredd* and the *Doctor Who* spinoff comic books. Like Moore, these writers were mostly left-wing, edgy, and unafraid to write comic books for intelligent adults, resulting in stories that were replete with violence, nudity, cursing, and angry, leftist political commentary. To discourage children from buying these comic books, and to provide a forum for their new, avant-garde talent, DC created the Vertigo publishing imprint. One of the greatest, most political comic books to spearhead the Vertigo imprint was *John Constantine: Hellblazer.*

Created by Moore and artists Steve Bissette and John Totleben as a supporting character in *Swamp Thing*, Constantine was a working class magician drawn to look like Sting and function as the polar opposite character to Marvel's Doctor Strange. Whereas Dr. Strange was an aristocratic figure informed by Steve Ditko's Objectivist politics, Constantine was a drunken, foul-mouthed populist with angry socialist views and union sympathies. He was the perfect mouthpiece for the disenfranchised members of the Labour Party who looked on in horror during the 1980s at what Thatcher was doing to England. Therefore, it was no surprise that he won his own spinoff comic book, *John Constantine: Hellblazer*, and saw his adventures written by an array of furious British writers.[11]

Overall, the *Hellblazer* comic book's Gothic overtones and nightmarish imagery serve as a commentary on the urban and rural decay England suffered thanks to Thatcher's social and economic policies. Upper-class British aristocrats, businessmen, politicians, and military leaders were presented as being attractive and well-dressed ... on the surface. But Constantine would cleverly scratch their respectable veneers, and reveal the bloated, pimpled, pus-filled demons hidden underneath, covered in diarrhea and the blood of dead babies. In contrast, the foul-mouthed, penniless, drunken cab drivers and prostitutes that Constantine befriended were invariably presented as beautiful on the inside, and more worthy of love and respect than any solicitor, clergyman, or prime minister. But these people were all damned, like Constantine himself, through no fault of their own, save failing to prevent the right wing from rising to power in the 1980s. While Constantine's wanderings tend to take him across the decrepit British landscape, which is nowhere near as beautiful as it is in Jane Austen inspired films, his travels sometimes take him to the unholy landscape of America, as in Garth Ennis' *Damnation's Flame*, and several graphic novels by American writer Brian Azzarello. All in all, according to *Hellblazer*, Dante's Inferno would not be found in the afterlife, but in our time, in our home country, in our neighborhoods, thanks entirely to Reaganism and Thatcherism.

In Jamie Delano's "Going for It" (1987), a *Hellblazer* adventures set on the eve of the 1987 general election, Constantine pits himself against Yuppie demons plotting to gentrify a working-class neighborhood. The demons capture Constantine, hang him upside-down from their living room ceiling and force him to watch the depressing returns. Appropriately enough, when a seemingly upside-down Margaret Thatcher addresses the nation, it is as if the world has turned upside down as well, and all that she says has an inverted, secret meaning.

THATCHER: I intend to win this election and go on and on. My government will provide the freedom for private enterprise to flourish — to create wealth, so that we can afford to care for the sick and disadvantaged.

CONSTANTINE: [thinking] Jesus, damned to the "help yourself society"—where the strong help themselves to whatever they want and the weak are left to help themselves....

THATCHER: With our guidance, Britain will be great again, a nation of growth and opportunity — a symbol of strength.

CONSTANTINE: Isn't she marvelous? [94].

Constantine escapes the demons, and barely manages to avoid being literally dragged to Hell. However, when Thatcher wins a third term in office with a landslide conservative majority in government, Constantine thinks that there is, after all, "More than one road to hell" (98).

Given the overwhelmingly negative portrayal of Thatcher in these comic books, readers might well be surprised that she was successfully elected to three terms as prime minister. On some level, her stated mission to "destroy socialism" must have appealed to some voters, and certainly many British were proud to have finally elected their first female prime minister. However, her success in politics has long been a source of contention for feminist historians, who believe that her election was by no means a victory for feminists.[12] As Amsterdam based political bloggers Martin Wisse and "Palau" have aptly observed, Thatcher was technically not a feminist:

> Thatcher merely profited from feminism and its accomplishments, without which she would not have been able to enter politics in the first place, let alone become prime minister. In her long political career she did nothing to advance feminism; in fact did more to harm it through her anti-working class, anti-welfare state politics. Yes, she was the first women to become p.m. and hence could be seen as an example to others, but feminism is more than just breaking the glass ceiling. If your politics are reactionary you don't get to be called a feminist just because you were lucky enough to be successful.[13]

Iconic British musicians Roger Waters and Elvis Costello both despised Thatcher for her economic policies and instigation of the Falklands War. In "The Post War Dream," a song included on Pink Floyd's 1983 album *The Final Cut,* "Maggie" is asked "What have we done to England?"[14] The titular dream was that World War II would be the final war the British people would ever have to endure, and Thatcher had ended that dream. According to Waters, "The Final Cut was about how, with the introduction of the Welfare State, we felt we were moving forward into something resembling a liberal country where we would all look after one another ... but I'd seen all that chiseled away, and I'd seen a return to an almost Dickensian society under Margaret Thatcher" (Blake 294–295).

Elvis Costello portrayed Thatcher as a madam who had made England the "whore of the world" in "Tramp the Dirt Down," a song on his 1989 album *Spike.* He cast her as the personification of greed, and railed against the folly of disenfranchised British voters who failed to vote on Election Day because they believed that one British P.M. was just as good or bad as another. The title of the song indicated Costello's hope to outlive Thatcher so that, one day, he could stand upon her "grave and tramp the dirt down."[15] BBC interviewer Tracey Macleod observed in a 1989 interview with Costello that the lyrics were uncharacteristically violent for him, and that the song was, paradoxically, sad and melodious. Costello agreed, noting that he wrote the lyrics in a rage and then composed the music to it in sadness over the fate of his country. He also acknowledged how ugly and violent the central image of the song was:

> I think everybody's capable of the most monstrous violence. [Thatcher] seems like a perfectly reasonable person ... in some manifestation. She certainly looks fairly benign. She's a middle-aged woman with hair like candy floss but she does some of the most monstrous things and shows not just two faces, but shows any face that suits her at the time and then tells you that it's a completely honest way to be.[16]

Thatcher's economic legacy is felt with keen bitterness in Northern England and Wales, where she is blamed for the collapse of the coal industry and the downfall of the British labor unions. She effectively outmaneuvered the National Union of Mineworkers (NUM) during their yearlong strike (March 12, 1984 to March 3, 1985), allowing her to proceed with her plan to close 20 mines and gradually privatize the industry. The devastating effects of this clash were dramatized in two British films, *Brassed Off!* (1996) and *Billy Elliot* (2000).

In addition to skewering Thatcher, the *Hellblazer* comics have condemned the British Royal Family, the American military, and the conservative sympathies of New Labour politicians. In a story by Garth Ennis, Constantine discovers a plot orchestrated by conservative members of the Hellfire Club who hope to restore an absolute monarchy to Britain.[17] The head of the conspiracy, Marston, hopes to "man up" Prince Charles by infusing him with the demonic spirit of Jack the Ripper:

> MARSTON: I wanted a king who would have the iron will to rule absolutely.... There would be no parliament. No opposition.... No liberals. No thinkers. No immigrants. There would simply be the rulers and the ruled ... and we could do anything.
>
> CONSTANTINE: You're talking about putting the thing that used to be Jack the Ripper in charge of us? The bastard eats people, you headcase!
>
> MARSTON: Ah, but Constantine ... what has our Royal Family ever done except feed off the blood of the people? [*Bloodlines* 205–206].

In Grant Morrison's "How I Learned to Love the Bomb" (1990), Constantine visits a town torn apart by the news that an American missile base located nearby on the moors was going to be expanded, thereby providing a spike in local employment.[18] An activist informs Constantine that the Campaign for Nuclear Disarmament (CND) membership is enraged by the expansion. He replies, "I don't blame them. This country is turning into an aircraft carrier for the bloody Yanks" (43). In Jamie Delano's "Pandemonium" (2010), members of the C.I.A. and MI-5 coerce Constantine into aiding the war effort in Iraq by interrogating a detainee who is possessed by a djinn. At the end of the tale, Constantine unleashes the djinn upon his captors and leaves them to their fate, satisfied that he has, on some level, avenged the people of the Middle East for the suffering they endured at the hands of British and American imperialists.

When Blair became prime minister in 1997, ending 18 years of Tory rule, the British people were ecstatic, expecting sweeping changes in national policy. And, for some time, Blair's popularity soared, as he established a minimum wage, signed the Freedom of Information Act, and eulogized Princess Diana as the "people's princess" after she was killed in a car crash in Paris on August 31, 1997. However, by 1999, some traditional Labour Party supporters found themselves disappointed that the center-left politician wasn't a little more liberal.

A wounded John Constantine travels though a section of hell that looks like the United States, where he encounters the ghosts of Native Americans slaughtered during the "Westward Expansion." From "Damnation's Flame" (DC Comics, 1994) written by Garth Ennis and illustrated by Steve Dillon.

This history of Blair's first five years in office has been dramatized in a trilogy of films written by Peter Morgan that star Michael Sheen as Blair. *The Deal* (2003) chronicles how Blair became prime minister by seizing control of the Labour Party from the brilliant but unelectable Gordon Brown in the run-up to the 1997 general election. *The Queen* (2006) shows the newly elected Blair striving to shelter Queen Elizabeth II from widespread public outrage over her perceived refusal to share in the nation's grief over the unexpected death of Princess Diana. *The Special Relationship* (2010) chronicles the friendship between Blair and Clinton, and their interactions concerning Ireland, Kosovo, and the Monica Lewinsky affair. A common theme of all of these films, two of which were released during Blair's time in office, is that Blair is a complicated figure, with a dark, secret side that his Cheshire Cat grin often hides. Labour Party characters repeatedly accuse him of being a stealth Tory, someone who is too in love with religion, the free market, military might, and the Royal Family to ever properly represent the beliefs of his far more liberal constituency. Comic writer Warren Ellis had John Constantine express similar opinions on the matter.

In Ellis's *Hellblazer* story "Haunted," Constantine tours a London that remains plagued by poverty and a sizable gap between the wealthy and the poor. In many ways, on the streets, it was as if little had changed from Thatcher's time. When Constantine goes to a corner deli to buy cigarettes, he gruffly tells the proprietor, Sanjay, that he can keep his National Lottery tickets, and that Blair's New Labour has let the country down on a number of levels, not the least of which is failing to abolish the National Lottery. After all, the lottery amounts to a tax on gullible working-class dreamers and merely adds to their financial burden.

Sanjay asks him, "Didn't you vote for 'em, John? Thought you were a Labour man from way back."

John replies, "This ain't Labour how I bleedin' remember it, Sanjay. More like bleedin' Thatcher how I remember it" (16).

The left wing of the party was disappointed in his economic policies, which included instituting higher tuition fees for universities, but was also worried about his doctrine of humanitarian interventionism, and his relationship to Clinton and Bush. Blair's relationship to the United States Executive Branch had had a promising beginning in the friendship he had forged with President Bill Clinton. Together, the two men successfully helped broker the 1998 Good Friday Agreement in Ireland, brought the genocidal reign of Slobodan

Milošević to an end, and came closer than anyone had in years to developing a peace accord between the Israelis and Palestinians. All of this was done according to their belief in the doctrine of humanitarian interventionism, which involved the use of American and British led forces to intervene within other nations' borders to end genocidal campaigns, civil wars, or other humanitarian crises. Thanks to their perceived successes, the British and American press was largely supportive of the Clinton-Blair efforts in Serbia, Ireland, and Israel, even if Clinton was savaged on a daily basis over domestic scandals and his attempts to push forward a liberal agenda.[19]

However, several notable voices were raised in opposition to the doctrine of humanitarian interventionism. America's ally, Israel, was uncomfortable with it, as was Nelson Mandela. Noam Chomsky observed in *Hegemony or Survival: America's Quest for Global Dominance* (2003) that America and Britain only support humanitarian intervention in other nations when they are the ones doing the intervening, and their governments have a history of objecting when other nations make similarly, supposedly altruistic, interventions.[20] When the doctrine became intertwined with the justifications offered for the Iraq War, its credibility was further undermined.

The debate over humanitarian intervention in Iraq surfaced in a 2006 *Justice League* story by Gail Simone called "The Hypothetical Woman." The United Nations Security Council asks the Justice League to depose a military dictator from his position as head of a South American nation. General Tuzik has committed acts of genocide, is developing weapons of mass destruction by manufacturing superheroes, and is standing in the way of the rightful ruler of the nation assuming power. Nevertheless, when the League deposes him, some of their most ardent supporters worldwide begin to fear that superheroes have become too involved in international affairs, and are on the verge of becoming global dictators themselves. Despite Tuzik's evil, the public fear of the league is presented as understandable, even in a scenario far less morally ambiguous than Operation Iraqi Freedom.

Mark Waid's *Authoritative Action* (2004) saw the Fantastic Four conquer the Eastern European nation of Latveria for similar reasons, only they acted in defiance of U.N. wishes, and were themselves deposed by U.N. military forces (see Chapter Seven).

Peter David's "War and Pieces" (*The Incredible Hulk* # 390–392, 1991–1992) concerns the Hulk's unilateral decision to invade the Middle Eastern nation of Trans-Sabal and overthrow the American supported dictator, Farnoq Dahn. The Hulk's goal is to end the sexual enslavement of Trans-Sabal's women and Dahn's acts of genocide. He recruits his young, somewhat naïve friend Rick Jones to help him, and unintentionally allows Rick to witness firsthand the atrocities Dahn commits daily.

The American government sent the superhero Havok to stop the Hulk's one-man military campaign. Havok hates Dahn as much as Hulk does, but he opposes Hulk's attempt to orchestrate regime change:

> HAVOK: So what's next for you, then? Take out every leader on earth who doesn't measure up to your definition of morality? And where do you stop? Until you're running things? ... By what right do you decide who's in charge and who's not? By force? The guy doing the most good is the guy with the biggest gun?
>
> HULK: You make it sound like its wrong to do something about evil. Isn't it more wrong to do nothing?
>
> HAVOK: I don't know. But I do know this: I can't start setting myself up as a one-man judge of international affairs. Overthrowing governments, Hulk ... its not right. Look into your heart. You *know* it isn't.[21]

At the end of the story, a distraught Rick Jones assassinates Dahn when he realizes the Hulk is on the verge of backing down. Only then, when Hulk sees how he is responsible for staining his formerly innocent best friend's hands with blood, does he question his own self-righteous motivations for invading Trans-Sabal.

The Hulk story suggests that, once one goes down a militarist path, even with the best of intentions, it is only a matter of time before motivations are corrupted, military scenarios grow out of control, and the would-be liberators find themselves becoming the very evil force they had initially set out to fight. That, arguably, is what happened to Blair when he supported Bush's decision to invade Iraq in a pre-emptive war designed to prevent Hussein from one day masterminding a nuclear attack on the United States.

Before she assumed the role of Secretary of State, Condoleezza Rice was a national security advisor to President Bush. She outlined the administration's rationale for preemptive war with Iraq during a lecture she gave at the Manhattan Institute on Oct 1, 2002:

> We will break up terror networks, hold to account nations that harbor terrorists, and confront aggressive tyrants holding or seeking nuclear, chemical, and biological weapons that might be passed to terrorist allies. These are different faces of the same evil. Terrorists need a place to plot, train, and organize. Tyrants allied with terrorists can greatly extend the reach of their deadly mischief. Terrorists allied with tyrants can acquire technology allowing them to murder on an ever more massive scale. Each threat magnifies the danger of the other. And the only path to safety is to confront both terrorists and tyrants.
>
> For these reasons, President Bush is committed to confronting the Iraqi regime, which has defied the just demands of the world for over a decade. We are on notice. The danger from Saddam Hussein's arsenal is far clearer than anything we could have foreseen prior to September 11th. And history will judge harshly any leader or nation that saw this dark cloud and sat by in complacency or indecision [Rice 54].

Certainly, other European nations, especially Germany and France, were strong opponents of the war, and accused the United States of doctoring the evidence it presented that Hussein had weapons of mass destruction, was ready to use them, and provide them to his alleged allies in al-Qaeda. It has since been confirmed that some of the key evidence provided by the Bush Administration was extracted under torture from one terrorist suspect, who may have been telling his tormentors what they wanted to hear to get the torture to stop (see Chapter Seven). Questionable evidence notwithstanding, other critics of the war asserted at the time that, even if Hussein posed a grave threat to American national security, preemptive war was not the appropriate response. As Arthur Schlesinger, Jr., argued, preemptive warfare was an insane idea rightly repudiated during the Cuban Missile Crisis by Bobby Kennedy.[22]

Meanwhile, in response to French and German opposition to the war, Rupert Murdoch's lurid American tabloid, *The New York Post,* ran photos of the German and French Ambassadors to the U.N. with weasel heads photoshopped onto their bodies on February 14, 2003, with the headline U.N. MEETS: WEASELS TO HEAR NEW EVIDENCE. Other conservative commentators, like the highly biased Post journalists, said that one nation of ex–Nazis and another nation of "cheese-eating surrender monkeys" should have little of interest to say to the United States and Great Britain.

While *The New York Post* was strongly pro-war during this period, many newspapers seemed to be neutral or incurious concerning Bush's motivations for pushing the Iraq invasion, and the French and German objections to war. As Lisa Finnegan contends in *No Questions Asked: News Coverage Since 9/11,* "In the midst of the chaotic 9/11 hijackings and in the years that followed the first major foreign terrorist attack on U.S. soil, members of the press forgot that their role is to observe what happens, to ask difficult questions, and to report what they see and hear. Instead, journalists minimized alternative viewpoints, amplified the administration's perspective, and presented half-truths that misled the American public" (xvii). Quoting scholar John Pilger to drive her final point home, Finnegan argues that true journalism is the first casualty of war. It is killed and replaced by a perverted form of censored journalism that acts as "a weapon of war" with a power that "could mean the difference between life and death for people in faraway countries such as Iraq" (155).

What were Bush's true motivations in instigating the war? Liberal conspiracy theorists have posited the notion that the war was a classic "wag the dog" tactic designed to give Bush another decisive military victory. With two successful military campaigns under his belt, the argument goes, Bush would handily win re-election, despite the fact that the 2000 presidential election that placed him in the White House was widely disputed and many Americans had initially not considered him a legitimately elected president.

The concept behind the term "Wag the Dog" comes from a 1997 Barry Levinson movie based on Larry Beinhart's novel *American Hero*. The satirical novel posited that President George H. W. Bush initiated the first Iraq War, Desert Storm, as a ploy to ensure his own re-election, when such a conflict was quite clearly unnecessary. The film *Wag the Dog* features a fictional president, and a dramatically staged war with Albania, but the concept is the same in essence. The term "Wag the Dog" was popularized in the summer of 1998 by conservatives in Washington and the media who were skeptical of President Clinton's claims that Osama bin Laden and al-Qaeda represented a legitimate threat to the United States. They argued then that Clinton was merely inventing a menace to distract the public from the Monica Lewinsky scandal, but many of these same critics hoped the public would forget their dreadful mistake following the 9/11 attacks, which clearly demonstrated that Clinton was correct, and not "Wagging the Dog."[23]

Unconcerned about being proven similarly wrong, liberal critics of the Bush-Blair Iraq War suggested that it was a crass, "Wag the Dog" attempt to cement the political power of neo-conservatives in Washington, D.C. Two notable science fiction political allegories that advance this thesis are *Star Wars: Episode III—Revenge of the Sith* (2005), which casts Darth Vader and Supreme Chancellor Palpatine as Bush and Vice President Dick Cheney, and *Justice League: Starcrossed* (2004), which shows how the aptly named Hawk people seize control of Earth by duping the Justice League into mobilizing for a bogus alien invasion.

British Labour Member of Parliament Michael Meacher advanced a somewhat different conspiracy theory in "This War on Terrorism Is Bogus: The 9/11 Attacks Gave the U.S. an Ideal Pretext to Use Force to Secure Its Global Domination" (2003). He argued that the seeds of the Iraq invasion were planted in 2000, well in advance of 9/11, when future high-ranking Bush Administration officials and the neoconservative think-tank Project for the New American Century (PNAC) drafted the imperialist document "Rebuilding America's Defenses" (40). The document is one of several key pieces of evidence that prove, Meacher contends, that America, not Hussein, was the real aggressor in the Iraq conflict. All other stated motivations for the Iraq invasion, including plans to bring democracy to the Middle East and prevent the spread of weapons of mass destruction, amounted to a political smokescreen. He writes:

> The overriding motivation for this political smokescreen is that the U.S. and U.K. are beginning to run out of secure hydrocarbon energy supplies. By 2010 the Muslim world will control as much as 60% of the world's oil production and, even more importantly, 95% of

> remaining global oil export capacity. As demand is increasing, so supply is decreasing, continually since the 1960s...
>
> ... the "global war on terrorism" has the hallmarks of a political myth propagated to pave the way for a wholly different agenda—the U.S. goal of world hegemony, built around securing by force command over the oil supplies needed to drive the whole project [44–45].

Certainly this is the view of the Iraq war that the James Cameron science fiction epic *Avatar* (2009) promulgates. That film allegorically retells the Iraq war as a conflict between Earth colonial troops of the 22nd century and the native Na'vi tribes of the green planet Pandora. The marines have been ordered to use "shock and awe" tactics to crush Na'vi resistance and plunder Pandora's natural resources to shore up corporate profits and dwindling energy supplies back on Earth. One marine, Jake Sully, defects to the Na'vi side when he has a crisis of conscience, taking several other humans with him.

According to Cameron, the film is meant to open American eyes about the effects of the Iraq War:

> We went down a path that cost several hundreds of thousands of Iraqi lives. I don't think the American people even know why it was done....
>
> We know what it feels like to launch the missiles. We don't know what it feels like for them to land on our home soil, not in America. I think there's a moral responsibility to understand that.[24]

Reginald Hudlin's superhero graphic novel *Who Is the Black Panther?* (2005) is crafted to make much the same political point. That story has U.S. Secretary of State Condoleezza Rice order an American invasion of Wakanda, a wealthy African nation rich in the natural resource vibranium, which can be used by the military to produce weapons of mass destruction and artificially generate superpowered soldiers. Wakanda was a U.S. ally, and its leader, Black Panther, a member of the Avengers and friend to both Captain America and Iron Man, so the attack was clearly unprovoked, self-serving, and evil.

Stories such as these, which dismiss the Iraq War cover story of a tie between Hussein and al-Qaeda, beg the question, why would Blair support the Iraq War if it is merely a means for Americans to secure oil resources and solidify their global power base? Is it because he wanted to play James Bond to Bush's Felix Leiter, ruling the world by proxy through a less intelligent President of the United States? Is it because he and Bush, both religious men, had more in common ideologically than anyone would have ever suspected, and were both, indeed, of like minds on the war on terror? Is it because he feared a rift with the world's only superpower, and ignoring Winston Churchill's exhortation to never betray Britain's "special relationship" to the United States?

Thriller writer Robert Harris wrote *The Ghost* (2007) shortly after Tony Blair resigned as prime minister in 2007 and handed the reigns of power over to fellow New Labour founder Gordon Brown. The novel concerns Adam Lang, a disgraced former British Prime Minister who committed war crimes and human rights violations by engaging in a global war on terrorism alongside the unnamed President of the United States. The story depicts Lang as smart, but not very deep, and largely beholden to the advice of his wife, Ruth. His goal, throughout the book, is to avoid being brought to trial at the Hague, and to rehabilitate his tainted international image by hiring an expert ghost writer to craft a sympathetic "autobiography" for him. At the climax of the novel, the ghost writer discovers that Ruth had secretly been recruited by the C.I.A. years before to manipulate her husband into perpetually doing the bidding of the United States throughout his entire political career.

Since Adam Lang is a thinly veiled commentary on Tony Blair, and Ruth bears much in common with Blair's real-life wife, Cherie, Blair supporters have publicly wondered if Cherie might one day sue Harris for defamation of character. After all, as realistic as much of the book is, it is absurdly unlikely that Cherie is more of an American spy and a master manipulator than she is wife to Tony. Harris collaborated with director Roman Polanski to adapt the book into film, and it was released under the title *The Ghost Writer* in 2010 with Pierce Brosnan playing Adam and Olivia Williams as Ruth.

Harris, a real-life former friend and supporter of Tony Blair, broke with Blair over the Iraq war. He has hedged a little in interviews, but explains that the Langs are intended to be fictional characters who behave far more badly than the Blairs ever would. However, he half expected the book's publication to be halted, or to be sued for libel by the Blairs over its contents. But if Harris doesn't really believe that "C.I.A Agent" Cherie Blair was behind securing her husband's support for Bush, then what motivated the prime minister?

In an interview with NPR, Harris explained:

> I don't think a lot of world leaders these days are very well read. I don't think Mr. Blair knew very much about the Middle East. I think he assumed that invading Iraq would be a walkover or at least that the Americans would sort it all out, and its that kind of isolation and shallowness that's bred by the modern media age where we seem to have lost depth in our politicians....
>
> In a curious way, Tony Blair ... made Bush's case [for war] almost better than Bush made it and adopted a sort of subservient role to the President of the United States, which I don't think was in the interests of my country or yours either particularly...
>
> [Like Harris' fictional Prime Minister Adam Lang, Blair is] rather a noble man, a tragic figure, not vicious, not mean, not a liar, either. I think it's important to remember about Tony Blair — I don't think that he ever consciously lied. I think he believed the case, or at least, like a good lawyer, convinced himself.[25]

Hugh Laurie (left) and Stephen Fry (right) have affectionately satirized Americans for being opinionated, conservative, and abrasive in TV shows such as *A Bit of Fry and Laurie*, *House M.D.*, *Stephen Fry in America*, and *Jeeves and Wooster* Season Three (1992), from which this photograph is taken. In *Jeeves and Wooster*, a dim-witted rich British man (Laurie) is taught the facts of life by his supernaturally brilliant butler, Jeeves (Fry).

Blair has stated, time and again since leaving office, that he regretted none of his policy decisions, either concerning his handling of British homeland security or the Iraq War, or the war crimes he has been accused of committing in conducting the war on terror alongside Bush. He has also maintained that Bush never pressured him to participate in the war on terror, and that he was an enthusiastic participant. However, there are those who, despite his claims to the contrary, believe he was coerced into supporting the war, as Colin Powell was.

For example, Blair also appears as a character in *W.* (2008), Oliver Stone's biographical film portrait of George W. Bush, in which Blair (Ioan Gruffudd) is shown to be pushed into supporting Operation Iraqi Freedom by a jovial, subtly menacing Bush.

Richard Curtis' film *Love Actually* (2003) included a similar scene, in which a fictional American President modeled after both Bush and Clinton (Billy Bob Thornton) menaced a British Prime Minister who was a clear stand-in for Tony Blair (Hugh Grant). After the two men find themselves competing for the attentions of the same mistress, the Prime Minister finally asserts his manhood and shifts British government policy away from an American-approved-only direction. His sudden development of a spine wins him the affection of the girl, and the eternal gratitude of the British people. Many American viewers of the film complained of its anti–American subtext on Internet Movie Database discussion boards, but a patient British film viewer explained that Richard Curtis has been skewering conservative British politicians for years, so it was only a matter of time before he lampooned American ones. Consequently, the film was anti–right-wing, not anti–American.

Similarly, long-running British science fiction series *Doctor Who* has also consistently skewered both British and American militarism and conservatism. Angry references to the Falklands war, the Thatcher legacy, and Tony Blair's support of the Iraq invasion abound in the series. For example, "The Happiness Patrol" (1988) concerned a futuristic British society in which a sexy, all-female death squad wanders the streets executing anyone who seems publicly unhappy. The squad acts on the orders of the female leader of the society, Helen A, who has been often interpreted as a Thatcher parody. Blair in particular is a target of derision. In "Aliens of London," alien gangsters called the Slitheen surprisingly, and unceremoniously, murder him. He is also featured as — allegorically — the villain of the three-part storyline "The Sound of Drums" (2007), in which the Doctor's archenemy, the Master, becomes Prime Minister of England. The Moriarty-like Time Lord was first introduced as a suave, goatee-sporting Latin gentleman in a 1971 adventure by Robert Holmes, but his contemporary counterpart, played by John Simm, looked — and even smiled — like the young, charismatic Blair. While the Master was not supposed to *be* Blair, his destructive reign as Prime Minister "Harold Saxon" was intended to make viewers wonder if an alien villain had, indeed, taken over their country in the real world.

However, the Master is allowed one "heroic" moment in his Prime Minister Harold Saxon persona. At a decisive point, when American President Arthur Coleman Winters appears to be making a play for world domination, Saxon declares, "I'm taking control, Uncle Sam! Starting with you!" And then he orders his alien minions to vaporize Winters. The scene when Winters is murdered before the eyes of the world represented a form of burning in effigy of another American president with a prominent "W" in his name. It also served as a wish-fulfillment fantasy for a British public disgusted with Tony Blair for being too deferential to American interests and angry that he did not stand up to the Americans as the Master did.

War and Political Allegory in Five Decades of *Doctor Who*

For the uninitiated, *Doctor Who* is a British television series listed in Guinness World Records as both the longest-running and "most successful" science fiction series of all time.

It ran from 1963 to 1989 and was revived in a sequel series in 2005. The series is about a time-traveling alien with thirteen lives called "The Doctor"—a bohemian, anti-imperialist figure who fights Nazis, demons, zombies, and killer robots, usually accompanied by female human traveling companions to whom he acts as a friend and mentor. The show has had more than thirty seasons' worth of episodes since its premiere in the 1960s, and eleven actors have starred as the Doctor. The fondest remembered of the original Doctors, Tom Baker, played the character as a brilliant Harpo Marx figure who wore an incredibly long, multicolored scarf to stress the character's humor, otherworldliness, and staunch individualism. Christopher Eccleston sported a crew-cut and a black leather jacket, and played the Doctor as if he were, essentially, John Constantine as an alien in the first season of Russell T. Davies' 2005 revival. Other actors, such as Jon Pertwee, projected a serious, Sherlock Holmes–style air, while wearing Edwardian, Victorian or other dated-and-recognizably British heritage clothes. However, as traditional as the Doctor's clothing often is, there is usually something "off" about it to stress his individuality, such as the tenth Doctor's insistence on wearing a shirt-and-tie, a pinstriped suit, and ... red sneakers? In a similar symbolic and counterintuitive outfit alteration, the only actor to play the Doctor in an American made-for-television film, Paul McGann, dressed like Wild Bill Hickok but very deliberately did not wear a gun.[26]

Illustrator Kevin Bolk's caricatures of four actors who have played "the Doctor" in *Doctor Who*. Back to front: William Hartnell, Jon Pertwee, Christopher Eccleston, and Matt Smith (courtesy Kevin Bolk, www.kevinbolk.com).

The series has been successful enough to produce spin-offs in other media, including full-cast audio plays from a company called Big Finish and comic books published by IDW and Panini presses. In addition, there is some striking cross-pollination between the TV show and the comic book world. Fondly remembered *Doctor Who* comic book adventures have been written by Grant Morrison (*We3*) and drawn by Dave Gibbons (*Watchmen*), *Doctor Who* TV series writer Paul Cornell and director Joe Ahearne have written issues of Marvel's *Fantastic Four* comic book, and renowned comic writer and novelist Neil Gaiman (*Coraline*, *Stardust*) wrote an episode of *Doctor Who* for the revival series' sixth season in 2011.

According to Tom Baker, the actor who became a household name in England playing the Doctor between 1974 and 1981, "the series has survived a string of leading actors supposedly playing the same role" because the Doctor's character stays basically the same with only cosmetic changes. "The Doctor is a moral being—you know exactly what he's going to do and why. ... [He] is a heroic stereotype who conforms to the patterns of behavior you expect him to conform to."[27]

As Baker explained, the greatest challenges associated with playing the role were keeping it fresh, and living as scandal-free a life as possible. "I had ... to carry the concept of this semi-perfect man into my own life, so that if there were children around I wouldn't be seen by them as a disappointment. As in the show, I didn't smoke, drink or swear—I was literally on my best behaviour, which was very, very exhausting at times but rewarding as well.... My friends used to think it was unnecessary, but then they didn't have my sense of responsibility to the image of the show—I know that sounds very pompous but it was something I thought very consciously and carefully about."[28]

As John Tulloch and Manuel Alvarado argue in *Doctor Who: The Unfolding Text*, the show's mostly male production team, male star, melodramatic conventions, and Western-Christian-centric worldview often make it establishment in tone, although they point out that some liberal and anarchic creative influences from script writers, producers, and performers have sometimes pushed the show dramatically into the realm of the subversive and the left-wing (8). Indeed, the show was offensive enough to right-wing tastes that it was the target of semi-regular criticism from Mary Whitehouse's National Viewers' and Listeners' Association (now known as Mediawatch-uk), a conservative and religious pressure group in Great Britain that monitors the mass media for "offensive content" and lodges protests against programs that contain too much sex, violence, profanity, and blasphemy (Tulloch and Alvarado 3).

While many of the show's episodes seem purely apolitical, or escapist and unrelated to any obvious political message, others were clearly direct commentaries on real world events.[29] For example, the 1972 serial "Curse of Peladon," featuring Jon Pertwee as the Doctor, was about the planet Peladon, a feudal, superstitious society whose politically progressive leader was weighing whether or not he should join the secularist, collectivist Galactic Federation. His high priest objected that Peladon's sovereignty and culture would vanish the moment it made the alliance, but the king believed it would be best for his planet's economy and social evolution. The story was clearly a commentary on moderate Conservative Prime Minister Edward Heath's (1970–1974) intention to join the European Economic Community, despite objections from both the political right and left. Two years later, Brian Hayles, writer of the first Peladon story, penned a sequel, "Monster of Peladon." This adventure chronicled the fall of Edward Heath's government, which failed to bring rapid closure to a miner's strike that brought coal production to a standstill for a month. In that story, the miners of Peladon refused to use advanced mining machinery supplied by the Galactic Federation because they feared it meant job loss, and that it would anger the God of Peladon, Aggedor, who hated science. (When Thatcher crushed another miners' strike years later, it was seen, in part, as retaliation for Heath's humiliation, as well as a do-or-die moment for her administration.)

While the tone and the politics of the franchise may shift from the left to the right, the tradition of liberal political allegory in *Doctor Who* dates as far back as the original series' first script editor, David Whitaker (1963–1964). Whitaker, working with groundbreaking female producer (and series co-creator) Verity Lambert, strove to make the series an educational adventure show with more enlightened political sentiments than the conservative Flash Gordon adventures it sometimes imitated. When Whitaker wrote his own

Doctor Who adventures, he portrayed war as a form of madness; and the Muslim characters he created for the time-travel adventure "The Crusade" (1965) were arguably as likeable as his Christian characters, if not more so. The serial suggests that there are no winners in war, only survivors and good men on both sides caught up in an evil conflict.[30] That is why the story has no apparent ending: the Doctor and his companions can do little more than flee the battlefield with their lives and accomplish nothing substantial. As Paul Cornell, Martin Day, and Keith Topping observed in *The Discontinuity Guide: The Unofficial Doctor Who Companion,* "The Crusade" is "[a]n ambitious project (some of the script is in iambic pentameter) which ... manages to avoid racism, presenting Arabic culture with integrity."

As a script editor, Whitaker would sometimes moderate the more conservative political sentiments expressed by other scriptwriters; and the result was a more nuanced, complex script, instead of a watered-down one. In fact, by incorporating his own views into the serial "The Daleks" (1963–1964), he helped script a morally ambiguous classic that remains a favorite episode to this day. An early draft of Terry Nation's script for "The Daleks" introduced the title characters as obviously allegorized Nazis obsessed with racial purity and dedicated to a policy of genocide. The Daleks were pitted against the Thals, misguided pacifists modeled on those battle-weary veterans of the First World War who advocated a policy of appeasement of Hitler in an effort to prevent another devastating global conflict. The Doctor's challenge was to enlist the Thals in his quest to attack the Daleks and prevent the mass slaughter of the Thals, who mistakenly believe that they can negotiate with the fanatical Daleks.

Since the screenplay was clearly anti-pacifist, Whitaker moderated it in two key ways: (1) he emphasized the horror of combat and the heavy death-toll caused by war, and (2) he cast into question the Doctor's motivations in inciting the conflict, suggesting that the Doctor's true reason for encouraging the Thals to attack the Daleks was not because they needed to defend themselves, but because he wanted to secure fuel for his time machine — fuel that was stored in the heart of the Dalek city. The Doctor's companion, Ian, is the most eloquent in his defiance of the Doctor's selfish plan, standing firm in his "No-blood-for-oil" policy. Ian only relents in his opposition when he is convinced that the Daleks are too dangerous to ignore because they plan to detonate a weapon of mass destruction that will wipe out all non–Dalek life on the planet.

The next notable left-wing writer of *Doctor Who* serials crafted several adventures in the 1970s for Jon Pertwee's depiction of The Doctor. Scriptwriter Malcolm Hulke, an atheist and a one-time member of the British Communist Party, wrote several episodes that boasted multi-layered characterization portraying aliens who were sometimes friendly and always complex figures. Even if Hulke's aliens proved hostile to humans, they had a graspable motivation and were not purely evil. For example, in 1970, Hulke created the Silurians, a race of intelligent reptiles who ruled the earth in the time before humanity evolved. They went into hibernation during the prehistoric era and awoke to find humans the dominant species. Their distress at their displacement encouraged the more militant Silurians to advocate a war to overthrow or annihilate humanity, while moderate Silurians favored negotiation with humans and peaceful coexistence ("Doctor Who and the Silurians"). Some American viewers might find themselves drawing a parallel between the Silurians and displaced Native Americans planning to retake the land stolen from them by the European settlers, but Hulke crafted the Siluarians in a way that they might just as easily represent any displaced people, be they Palestinians, Jews, or other victims of conquest, colonialism, natural disaster, or Diaspora.

While most classic *Doctor Who* villains look like monsters, Hulke's villains were more often all-too-human figures, especially in the episodes "Invasion of the Dinosaurs," "The Sea Devils," and "Doctor Who and the Silurians." They are often high-ranking members of the military who would prematurely kill friendly aliens out of a desire to protect Britain from foreign threats when negotiation should have been used instead. Hulke casts his military villains as well-intentioned and ultimately wrong, but not evil. The perfect example of this kind of villain is the often-heroic Brigadier Alistair Gordon Lethbridge-Stewart, who buried alive an entire colony of Silurians, some of whom were good, when he feared they would unleash a disease that would wipe out all of humanity. While the threat the Silurians represented was legitimate, the Doctor, on the other hand, was horrified that a fear of the *potential* use of a weapon of mass destruction would inspire a usually good man, his friend Alistair, to commit an act of genocide. The episode is politically balanced enough that it would allow a more conservative viewer to favor the Brigadier's position over the Doctor's, but Hulke clearly wants viewers to side with the Doctor.

Another writer who tended towards political allegory was Robert Holmes, a military veteran who served in Burma during World War II and also had a background as a police officer and as a journalist before breaking into television writing. Holmes' genre of choice was gothic horror, and his stories tended to be far more conservative than either Whitaker's or Hulke's. For example, "The Talons of Weng-Chiang" (1977) and "Pyramids of Mars" (1975) have been criticized for trotting out the old-school gothic villains of Chinese opium dealers and Egyptian religious fanatics, even as they are often praised for being among the best-written episodes of the series, and those villains are often cited as being excellent, charismatic adversaries for the Doctor.[31] Also, Holmes' version of the Doctor has no problem killing villains at the end of a given storyline—sometimes quite brutally, as in the adventures "The Ribos Operation" (1978) and "The Two Doctors" (1985) in which the Doctor blows up one irredeemable enemy with a grenade and uses cyanide to poison another.

However, Holmes did create feminist companions Elizabeth Shaw (Caroline John), a Cambridge University physicist, and Sarah Jane Smith (Elizabeth Sladen), an investigative journalist in the mold of Lois Lane who graduated to stardom in her own spinoff series *The Sarah Jane Adventures* in 2007. Holmes also wrote excellent adventures featuring Leela (Louise Jameson), a strong-willed, savage warrior dressed in leather skins and armed with a dagger and poison blowgun. Sexier and deadlier than even legendary television "super-heroine" Emma Peel, Leela never showed fear or screamed, had keen intuitive powers, and won most of her battles without the Doctor's aid. Still, there was a power imbalance in their relationship, as the Doctor played Henry Higgins to Leela's Eliza Doolittle as he strove to civilize her. There were also hints that Leela was attracted to the Doctor, and he did not reciprocate those feelings. Extraordinarily popular with the British viewership, the Leela character had her detractors. Mary Whitehouse's National Viewers' and Listeners' Association found her too sexy and too violent, objecting in particular to a scene in which she murdered a villainous Rutan and shouted, "Enjoy your death, as I enjoyed killing you!" Even Tom Baker had reservations, revealing in an interview, "I find it very disconcerting acting alongside near naked people."[32]

Holmes' *Doctor Who* scripts cannot easily be pigeonholed as purely left-wing or right-wing. His political satire "The Sunmakers" (1977), often classified as a rant against the tax-happy Labour government of the 1970s, has dialogue and plot developments evoking Karl Marx, and a populist, anti-corporate message that might well make Michael Moore proud. Indeed, Jeremy Bentham, cultural critic and author of *Doctor Who: The Early Years*, observed that the serial "was heavily laced with left wing propaganda" (Tulloch and Alvarado 149).

"The Two Doctors" has a conservative political message opposing the foolishness of the First World giving technology to violent Third World cultures that aren't ready for it, while simultaneously mocking Europe and America for jealously guarding their power against developing nations. The episode also boasts of being one of the most violent in the history of the series, while concurrently promoting vegetarianism. It is an odd mix of conservative and liberal sentiments that makes confusing and entertaining food for thought. Indeed, some viewers might wonder if Holmes himself had a consistent political worldview, or if he was working out his own mixed feelings about international politics and imperialism as he wrote his scripts.

In perhaps his greatest episode, "The Caves of Androzani" (1984), Holmes allegorically posits the possibility that greedy Western corporate moguls are responsible for much of the violence in the Middle East. It is they who wish to keep the conflict brewing because the longer it goes on, the longer the price of the oil they market can remain high and the more guns they can surreptitiously sell to their supposed terrorist enemies through gun-running middle-men.[33]

From Left: The savage Leela (Louise Jameson), the Doctor (Tom Baker), and their trusty robot dog K-9 in a publicity still from *Doctor Who: The Sunmakers* (BBC, 1977), a Marxist fable in which the Doctor instigates a worker-rebellion against an evil corporate oligarchy.

It is in the tradition of "The Caves of Androzani," long considered one of the best-ever episodes of *Doctor Who*, that Russell T. Davies wrote his episodes of the series. The man who helped bring *Doctor Who* back to British television in 2005 after a 16-year hiatus, Davies has great respect for the writers of the original series, and attributes the franchise's longevity to the brilliance of its writers, especially Holmes. "Take 'The Talons of Weng-Chiang,' for example," Davies explained in a 2007 *Telegraph* interview. "Watch episode one. It's the best dialogue ever written. It's up there with Dennis Potter.... When the history of television drama comes to be written, Robert Holmes won't be remembered at all because he only wrote genre stuff. And that, I reckon, is a real tragedy" (qtd. in Johnson).

As a political satirist, Davies' targets of derision are similar to those of Whitaker, Hulke, and

Holmes, but he also imitates other left-leaning *Doctor Who* writers, such as Robert Sloman and Barry Letts, who advocated Buddhism, vegetarianism, and sustainability while condemning corporate pollution of the environment in "The Green Death" (1973). Overall, Davies skewers a media intent on fostering a hawkish, commercialized culture of ignorance and regularly attacks former American President George W. Bush and former British Prime Minister Tony Blair for their imperialist policies.[34] In a column he wrote for *The Guardian* on June 13, 2005, Davies himself said that he enjoyed helming the revival of *Doctor Who* primarily because he was able to resurrect science fiction characters and concepts he loved as a child for the benefit of old fans and to have the opportunity to create a new generation of fans. However, he stops just short of asserting that his second greatest joy in writing *Doctor Who* is the opportunity to recast real-world political figures as monstrous and grotesque villains.[1] As he explains, "[A]s a writer, I have had a ball. This programme gave me the chance to swing from New Labour to Dalek armies, taking in plastic surgery, Fox News, religious fanatics and farting obesity along the way" ("Alien Resurrection").

Earlier in Davies' career, between 1988 and 1992, he produced the television show *Why Don't You?* which, almost counterintuitively, exhorted children to stop watching television and do something constructive with their time. The minor hypocrisy of the message—"Thanks for watching my television show, now stop watching television"—has followed Davies into his career on *Doctor Who.* In the first episode of the new series, "Rose," the Doctor (Christopher Eccleston) criticizes his new teenage companion, Rose Tyler (Billie Piper), for being a typical human, content to "eat chips, go to bed and watch telly, while all the time underneath you there's a war going on." When the Doctor finds her, Rose is a directionless, working class department store clerk living with her widowed mother in a council housing complex in London. However, after the Doctor teases her with the possibilities of a life traveling in the TARDIS, she stops watching "the idiot's lantern" and joins the Doctor's mission to fight evil throughout time and space.

Unfortunately, the Doctor's second companion, Adam (Bruno Langley), acts as a negative example and a condemnation of those who can't stop immersing themselves in television, the internet, iPods, and other non-stop broadcasters of what the Doctor calls "useless information." During his very first adventure into the future with the Doctor ("The Long Game") Adam gets a cybernetic implant enabling him to soak up limitless amounts of information. He absorbs the information, but he does not understand it, gaining a mountain of facts but no wisdom; nor does he have any ethical sense, wanting the information only to make money. And yet, the joke is on Adam because all of the information he downloaded into his brain was controlled, censored, and rewritten by the Jagrafess, a loathsome alien being clearly intended to represent mass media mogul Rupert Murdoch. Thus, all Adam succeeds in doing is becoming a spy and a stooge for the Jagrafess.

The political satire here is amongst Davies' most successful from a dramatic perspective, and his most accurate from a sociological one. Davies is not alone in his concerns that Fox News distorts the truth and is, functionally, the Republican Party's (un)official television station, as documentaries such as *Outfoxed: Rupert Murdoch's War on Journalism* (2004) and satirical books by Jon Stewart, Stephen Colbert, and Al Franken have brought such concerns to the attention of the American public. Davies' satirical attack on contemporary journalists is not only accurate but also a breath of fresh air and a call to greater public awareness of how much of the news is not just biased but practically fiction. But Davies' satiric treatment of contemporary social ills does not stop with news venues, as he tackles topics such as commercialism, global warming, and the pharmaceuticals industry in other episodes.

One of the Doctor's most despicable opponents in the revival series is the Lady Cassandra, a Texas widow who has had so much plastic surgery that she is as thin as a trampoline. As part of an elaborate stock market scam intended to raise money for her next wave of plastic surgeries, Cassandra murders a living tree (one of the last descendants of the Amazon rain forest) and plots to murder other aliens whom she sees as not "human" enough. The episode ("The End of the World"), takes place on the day the Earth dies, but the characters are so engrossed in fighting for their own survival and in listening to Britney Spears music that they neither prevent the destruction of the earth nor watch as it burns. Here again, the criticism is that humans in general, and Americans in particular, are more interested in investing in the trappings of a consumer culture — pop music, plastic surgery, fast food — than they are in preventing global warming and other ecological disasters from destroying the Earth.

After the Lady Cassandra's appearance on the series, another ruthless American capitalist emerges: Utah multi-billionaire Henry van Statten, who presumably owns the Internet, Area 51, and the cure for the common cold — which he has prevented from being released to the general public because it is more profitable to sell a million palliatives instead of one single cure. Clearly, here is another rich American who places profits above the value of human life. He also cares little for his personal army of soldiers, who lay down their lives in an attempt to secure him a profitable artifact, the last living Dalek in the universe (Shearman).

Davies' writing was at its most outrageous in a two-part adventure, "Aliens of London" and "World War Three" (2005).[35] In this storyline, capitalist aliens, the Slitheen, infiltrate the British government, taking possession of the heads of state and the military. In their new positions of respectability, they fake a global emergency and con the public into believing that a race of alien pigs is about to destroy the planet. The alien pigs don't exist, but the Slitheen give their argument credibility by crashing a spaceship into Big Ben. Once the world is whipped into a panic by the sight of Big Ben in flames, the Slitheen work to start a world war that will destroy human civilization but also allow them to make a tidy profit from the spaceship fuel resources that will be left behind when the smoke clears.

If one were to imagine that the American government was the one infiltrated by the Slitheen, that the World Trade Center was destroyed by a plane instead of Big Ben by a spaceship, and crude oil was the Slitheen's goal instead of spaceship fuel, then the episode would play as an allegorized dramatization of the 9/11 conspiracy theory presented by Thierry Meyssan in the book *L'Effroyable Imposture* (*The Appalling Deception*); in which Meyssan claimed that Bush himself staged 9/11 to start an unnecessary series of wars in the Middle East over oil (qtd. in Hagen). Meyssan's book, which was a bestseller in France, was criticized by *Skeptic* columnist L. Kirk Hagen for not being "even marginally plausible" in its theories, and for its misguided attempt to exonerate al-Qaeda for the crime. After all, as Hagen states in a 2002 book review, a left-wing critic like Meyssan should not be expressing solidarity with al-Qaeda, a group that is "about as far-removed from leftist values as anyone can get. They are anti-democratic, anti-secular, unabashedly homophobic, and they openly endorse one of the cruelest forms of gender apartheid in the world" (38). Since Meyssan's book angered Americans and certain conservative British nationals, it is hardly surprising that the *Doctor Who* episodes that seem to be inspired by it were targets of equal ire. "Aliens of London" and "World War III" were lambasted on the internet by bloggers such as Christianus (the pen-name of an anonymous Essex-based art history Ph.D. student) who observed in a post dated June 26, 2005:

> Throughout the two episodes, the aliens are shown as war-crazy, greedy, unscrupulous, fat politicians, laughing as Armageddon approaches. Of course, the fact the loathsome capitalist aliens have replaced, what we might assume to be, a more dignified host of British politicians, is a rather crude comment on the American influence on British foreign policy. Watching and listening to the constant parade of unsubtle political innuendo, we know precisely what we are meant to think of these green abominations: That they are like neo-conservatives and capitalists of the real world, right?
>
> ...
>
> Crass leftist bias is typical of journalists of the mainstream media. It has been so for decades, and it seems that it is something we must try to tolerate. Nevertheless, should we also have to accept that even innocuous entertainment programs like *Doctor Who* are being transformed into platforms for leftist agendas? It would be sad.

As a counter-argument to these kinds of criticisms, the writers of *Doctor Who: The Completely Unofficial Encyclopedia*, Chris Howarth and Steve Lyons, crafted this sarcastic encyclopedia entry:

> **Anti-Americanism:** Charge laid against the new series on the US Sci-Fi Channel's message boards—based, as far as we can tell, solely on the fact that, er, Henry Van Statten was American and he wasn't very nice. Yeah, and decades of British villains in Hollywood films count for nothing, we suppose [12].

All in all, Davies' scripts are not truly anti–American, but offer reasonable criticism of American public policy. The only times the show, under his direction, appears to drift a little too closely to anti–American sentiment occur whenever the Daleks are symbolically linked with the Americans, such as in the episodes "Dalek," "Bad Wolf," and "The Parting of the Ways." The Dalek episodes of the new series take place in New York and Utah, and one of the adventures featured Americans who were recruited to become a new generation of Daleks. These new Daleks also exhibit a religious reverence for their leader, the Emperor Dalek, and are portrayed as zealots, a flaw often attributed to certain religious fundamentalist citizens of the United States with a penchant for revering President Bush as a messianic figure. The suggestion that the Americans are the new Daleks is, in the world of *Doctor Who*, an implicit suggestion that the Americans are the new Nazis, bent on global domination and religious purity.

However, the seemingly mathematical formula of Davies' first season—Nazis = Daleks = Americans—breaks down somewhat in the third season storyline "Daleks in Manhattan" (2007), in which a utopian, multiracial community of disenfranchised Americans living in Central Park represents a cell of "good Americans" (read: Americans opposed to imperialism and sociopath capitalists) and is contrasted to the Daleks, who are the "ugly Americans." Following the broadcast of this episode, written by series script editor Helen Raynor, liberal American fans found it easier to watch the series knowing that the existence of Americans opposed to the Bush doctrine was being acknowledged and saluted.

It is also important to note that Davies created the character Captain Jack Harkness to be a heroic American figure. Indeed, as a regular on the show, Jack consistently threatens to rehabilitate the portrayal of Americans on *Doctor Who*. However, since Harkness seems to be primarily a satirical character, spoofing Tom Cruise's tabloid persona and Harrison Ford's 80s film personalities Indiana Jones and Han Solo, he often fails to register as a believable character, despite his funny one-liners and actor John Barrowman's natural charisma in the part. In "The Empty Child" and "The Doctor Dances" (written by Stephen Moffat), Harkness is introduced as a pseudo-villainous figure since, like Henry van Statten, his greedy pursuit of a valuable alien artifact almost destroys the world. While Capt. Jack dies heroically fighting the Daleks and is later resurrected so that he can star in his own *Doctor Who* spin-off series, *Torchwood*, Harkness is an amazingly ancillary figure in *Doctor Who*, interesting only in the fact that he is a daringly bisexual character. The Doctor himself often seems unsure what to make of Harkness but has recently accepted him as a friend.[36]

When Davies left as series producer in 2010, he was succeeded by Stephen Moffat, the writer of some of the best episodes in the series' history—including "The Girl in the Fireplace," "Blink," and "Silence in the Library." Moffat's episodes have featured fascinating time-travel paradoxes, star-crossed lovers, and truly horrific villains that include stone angel statues that come to life, clockwork men, and airborne piranha that lurk in the shadows. In an interesting moment of pan–Atlantic symmetry, as Davies passed the baton of creative control of *Doctor Who* to Moffat, Bush passed the baton of the American presidency to Obama.[37]

In stark contrast to President Bush, who shared personality traits with the Emperor Dalek, some fans and reporters have noticed that Obama is uncannily like both the Doctor *and* Mr. Spock from the *Star Trek* franchise. As the argument goes, both Obama and the Doctor are articulate, self-aware intellectuals, of mixed racial descent (the Doctor's mother was British and his father Gallifreyan, and Obama comes from both a Kenyan and an American heritage).[38] Reporters have also suggested that Obama and the Doctor both believe in science, negotiation, and peaceful, imaginative solutions to problems. They are both citizens of the universe, not of one insular, prejudiced society. Spock shares these traits, as well, and detractors who wish to see Obama demonstrate more emotion, especially during times of national crisis, have called him President Spock in a disparaging manner.

Arguably, if Obama had a British accent, and wore slightly more outlandish clothing, he might have made a good Doctor. At least, that is what some fans and reporters contend. Consequently, after tenth Doctor David Tennant announced he was leaving the show with Davies, and it would soon be time for the Doctor to regenerate into an eleventh incarnation, the British press speculated that Obama's election would inspire the casting of the first black actor to play the part. That was not to come to pass.

When white, 26-year-old unknown Matt Smith landed the role, cultural commentator Matthew Sweet was disappointed "that the Obama effect hasn't reached Gallifrey yet" and that the "idea of a black or woman Doctor is something we only seem to enjoy as a tease" for a gossipy press, but not something to be realized on screen (qtd. in Davies and Smith). In response, executive producer Piers Wenger stated that he and Moffat, "[auditioned] a dozen or so people, some of them black. There was never any resistance to the idea of a black Doctor and it would have got us all sorts of headlines and brownie points, but we set out to cast the best actor for the role irrespective of ethnicity or age, and that was Matt" (qtd. in Singh).

Ironically, while Smith's Doctor looked younger than any previous Doctor's regenerated body, he was technically playing the Doctor at his oldest, at well over 953. Still, he acted young and inexperienced, recklessly diving into scenarios he was unprepared to face, bluffing his way to success by trading off his intergalactic popularity and intimidating his enemies with stories of his previous remarkable achievements. He also exhibited an odd inability to communicate with everyday people, constantly talking over their heads at length, using technical words and occasional catch phrases, almost as if he were thinking aloud to himself and uninterested if he were understood.

For his part, Moffat was less concerned with American politics during his first season as producer than he was British. Even as American society struggled mightily to drag itself politically to the left — despite the best efforts of Fox News pundits, Tea Party activists, and filibustering Republican Senators to stymie the Obama agenda — Great Britain was beginning to move more to the right. The British people, weary of Labour Party leadership after thirteen years of Prime Ministers Blair and Gordon Brown, seemed finally ready to return the Tories to power during the 2010 General Election. There was some hope in moderate circles that the third party candidate, Nick Clegg of the Liberal Democrats, might gain enough votes to become Prime Minister, and serve as a genuine alternative to both the Tories and the Labour Party. However, Moffat feared that the election would result in conservative David Cameron taking residence in 10 Downing Street. In an interview, Moffat predicted a nightmare scenario in which a victorious Cameron would slash the BBC operating budget and functionally hand control of the British mass media over to Rupert Murdoch and his son James. The budget cuts would turn the BBC from a "brilliant organisation to shit.... Are we really going to put James Murdoch in place of [the BBC]? Can you imagine how shit it would be? Never mind the fine and glorious things that the BBC does. Stuff would be shit. Let's not have really good restaurants, let's have Kentucky Fried Chicken."

In the months running up to the general election, Moffat found *Doctor Who* suddenly under greater scrutiny, as his vision of the show garnered loud criticism from conservative watchdog group Mediawatch-uk because new companion Amy Pond wore short skirts and was portrayed as sexually aggressive. Unlike Lucy Westenra, the female character in Bram Stoker's *Dracula* whose soul was damned for loving more than one suitor at a time, Amy Pond is a woman in love with both the Doctor and her husband, and neither the Doctor nor Moffat morally condemn her for those feelings. In "Flesh and Stone" (2010), Amy is nearly killed, and she is so delighted to be alive when the Doctor saves her from death that she begins ripping his clothes off and demanding sex then and there. The shy Doctor fights her off and runs away. The scene divided viewers evenly between those who wondered what was wrong with the Doctor and those who wondered why such a seduction scene would be featured on a show marketed to children. For her part, Karen Gillan, the actress who plays Amy, was offended that viewers were offended by the sight of her legs — and by Amy's willingness to try to seduce the Doctor and not wait around for him to make the first move.

In *Doctor Who: Victory of the Daleks* (2010), the Doctor helps Winston Churchill escape from an unholy alliance with the Daleks during the darkest days of World War II. From the left: a "good" Dalek, cyborg scientist Bracewell (Bill Paterson), Churchill (Ian McNeice), the Doctor (Matt Smith), and Amy Pond (Karen Gillan).

"Short skirts show that Amy is confident and comfortable about her look. You have to have confidence to wear something like that," she said, noting that, in real life, many young women wear even sexier outfits unabashedly in public.

Executive Producer Piers Wenger said that Moffat always intended for Amy Pond to be "feisty and outspoken and a bit of a number. Amy is probably the wildest companion that the Doctor has travelled with, but she isn't promiscuous. She is really a two-man woman and that will become clear over the course of the episodes. Sci-fi has a long and happy history of sexy female characters and long may that continue."

Interestingly, viewers who seemed unoffended by the wildest stories Davies wrote appeared ready to be offended by scenes in Moffat's series that were arguably not as daring. The recent spike in thin-skinned viewers is yet another sign of Britain's growing conservatism. Delivering BAFTA's annual TV lecture on June 15, 2010, British comedian and intellectual Stephen Fry argued that quality television in England has become a thing of the past, largely because television writers are afraid of offending conservatives, and of failing to promote intelligent content to a public interested only in escapist programming. As an example, Fry mocked the record numbers of angry British television viewers who called the BBC to complain about an edgy prank call comedy sketch by Russell Brand and Jonathan Ross (in an incident known as "Sachsgate"), saying that "People who have nothing better to do than phone a television station at night are, by definition, desperately in need of help."[39]

According to Fry, quality television "requires a confident producer class, and that calls for people of real creative talent, intelligence, courage, resource and imagination, for my fear is that almost everyone I have encountered in production in the making of programmes is afraid. They have much to be afraid of, and much to cage, confine, cripple and constrain them. Fear is everywhere in the television business in this country. When you are afraid, it is a great deal easier to say no than to say yes."[40]

One of the sources of the fear was the possibility of a return to a Tory government. After all, as Fry observed, Thatcher had spent years attacking the BBC in retaliation for its left-wing programming:

> Liberalism, permissive media encroachments on decency, disrespectful satire, outright socialistic dramas and documentaries were all cited as proof of the BBC's undemocratic doctrinaire partiality. The trick was conceived in which the BBC could be blamed for being at one and the same time old-fashioned, stuck in the mud, reactionary, elitist, hidebound, de haut en bas, patriarchal, top/down, patronising and simultaneously left-wing, trendy, bien pensant and unpatriotic, because radical now meant right-wing. Modern and progressive meant consumer-led and market-oriented. The ... Thatchers of this world were not about to allow intellectuals, artists, liberals and Oxbridge nomenclatura of decadent self-appointed cultural apparatchiks to decide what was good for the public. The nanny state was bad enough in their eyes but the schoolmaster state, the don state was even worse.[41]

For Fry, the end result of this assault on intellectual television in general and the BBC in particular is that all television programming is marketed at children, even shows that are supposedly for adults are simple-minded melodramas where the heroes and villains are clearly delineated, the resolutions are contrived, and no thinking is required of the audience. Interestingly, Fry maintained, as much as the British tend to think of Americans as "vulgar" and "stupid," many of America's recent television programs (presumably shows like *The Wire*) show "maturity" and surprise the audience.[42] Fry singled out *Doctor Who* as an excellent series that is clearly intended for children, yet it is what adults watch instead of more intellectually challenging fare.[43]

In typical tabloid journalism fashion, newspapers the following day disregarded the substance of Fry's lecture and merely publicized the fact that Fry had "attacked" *Doctor Who*. The irony of all this is that Fry, who once was commissioned to write a script for the series, was essentially making the same political point that Moffat was—the quality of British mass media is crumbling, the quality of national discourse on political issues has been "dumbed down," and the BBC is under renewed threat from a regenerated Thatcherism, championed by the Murdoch clan and David Cameron.

As a last-ditch effort to convince the British public to vote Labour in the 2010 General Election, despite a general disappointment with the legacies of Blair and Brown, Moffat wrote the *Doctor Who* episode "The Beast Below." In it, the Doctor describes Election Day as an exercise in mass amnesia in which voters collectively choose to forget what conservatives have done time and again in the past to make society virtually unlivable. This amnesia allows voters to, inexplicably, cast their vote for the Tories once again. The episode uses symbolism and direct address to the viewer to simultaneously plea for greater support for animal rights and environmental causes as well as sympathy for the working classes. Moffat's message in "The Beast Below" is clear: vote Cameron in, get Thatcher 2.0.

And that's exactly what the British people did. The elections saw votes divided between the three parties, Tory, Labour, and Liberal Democrat, resulting in a hung parliament. Gordon Brown resigned as Prime Minister and the Tories formed a center-right coalition government with the Liberal Democrats. On July 19, 2010, the newly minted Tory Prime Minister David Cameron unveiled his "Big Society" plan to privatize public services and use volunteers to run post offices, libraries, and public transportation. In response, volunteer groups and the Labour Party have questioned where the money would come from the fund these initiatives. For their part, union leaders wondered whether unpaid volunteers would provide quality public service, or even enough of a work force to keep programs running.

"Make no mistake, this plan is all about saving money," Dave Prentis, general secretary of Unison, said. "The government is simply washing its hands of providing decent public services and using volunteers as a cut-price alternative."[44]

Supporters of Cameron's plan claimed that it was an excellent way of controlling public spending. Naturally, other ways of controlling public spending would include cutting funds to the BBC news office, letting the Murdochs run the media, and making sure that British people who dine out don't have to eat at posh restaurants, but can save money by enjoying fine dining at Kentucky Fried Chicken.

No doubt, Moffat was not pleased by the results of the election, and fears that it will result in the BBC's budget being slashed to such a degree that it will no longer be possible for it to produce expensive shows such as *Doctor Who*. However, the series is, at the moment, still alive. And, as the Moffat-Smith era continues to unfold, it will undoubtedly be unique in many respects but recognizably part of the same, nearly fifty-year narrative that is *Doctor Who*. In that manner, the Moffat-Smith era will be like all the others that have come before, whether they were shaped by a David Whitaker, a Robert Holmes, a Malcolm Hulke, or a Russell T. Davies. The series will blend action, humor, and mystery, entertain and instruct children with the moral example of the Doctor, and encourage adults to continue voting for the Labour candidates on Election Day, even if Tony Blair and Gordon Brown both left something to be desired.

SEVEN

Tortured Consciences: Jack Bauer, the Invisible Woman, and George W. Bush's America

I have killed two people since midnight. I haven't slept in over 24 hours. So maybe you should be a little more afraid of me than you are now.—Jack Bauer[1]

Doesn't it bother you? All the worlds and innocent people you've helped destroy?—The Invisible Woman[2]

I'm the commander—see, I don't need to explain.... That's the interesting thing about being the president. Maybe somebody needs to explain to me why they say something, but I don't feel like I owe anybody an explanation.—George W. Bush[3]

Jack Bauer and Donald Rumsfeld's Torture Memo

U.S. Secretary of Defense Donald Rumsfeld authorized eighteen interrogation techniques that were regarded as torture by international law when he signed his name to "the Rumsfeld Memo" on December 2, 2002. In defiance of both the Geneva Convention and the Torture Convention, these "techniques" were soon employed in Abu Ghraib, Afghanistan, Guantanamo, and the extraordinary rendition program sites overseas. In *Torture Team: Rumsfeld's Memo and the Betrayal of American Values* (2008), Philippe Sands documented how these torture techniques were initiated by Rumsfeld, President Bush, and Vice President Dick Cheney, in tandem with high-ranking White House lawyers. Among the torture methods approved were waterboarding (simulated drowning), exposure to extremes of temperature, and the use of the implied threat of the torture and imminent execution of the detainee and members of the detainee's family.

As alarming as the United States' decision to officially legalize and expand the use of torture was, perhaps the most bizarre and grotesque element of the torture initiative was the role that a fictional character played in the proceedings. Jack Bauer, the preternaturally effective Counter Terrorism Unit agent from Fox TV's series *24*, was the inspiration for a number of the torture techniques named in the memo. Furthermore, his actions were sometimes cited in lieu of legal precedent when White House advocates strove to justify the effectiveness of torture as a means of extracting information.

During the course of eight seasons of *24,* Jack Bauer has prevented the nuclear destruction of Los Angeles, halted the release of the deadly Cordilla virus, and stalled a neo-conservative conspiracy to push the U.S. into a war with a country under false pretences. Bauer achieved all these ends using a series of highly questionable tactics, including occasionally torturing and killing civilians and suspects who were later proven to be innocent.[4]

While Bauer may be a fictional character, his actions on television had surprising consequences in the real world. According to Sands, Diane Beaver, a lawyer for the Army's Judge Advocate General Corps, hosted a conference on interrogation techniques and national security to mark the one-year anniversary of the September 11, 2001 attacks.[5] The list of recommended techniques that were finally included in the legal memo Beaver drafted for use at Guantanamo Bay have since come under harsh international criticism for being, effectively, torture, and a direct violation of the principles of the Geneva Convention. Some of the interrogation techniques listed in Beaver's memo were employed by Jack Bauer.[6]

> Bauer had many friends at Guantanamo Bay. Beaver said, "he gave people lots of ideas." ... The first episode [of *24* season two] opened with a scene of a man being tortured, apparently with chemicals. The information he divulged—that a nuclear device was to be exploded in Los Angeles within the next twenty-four hours—was the basis for the series. The message was clear: torture works.... "We saw it on cable," Beaver explained. "People had already seen the first series. It was hugely popular." She believes the scene contributed to an environment in which those at Guantanamo were encouraged to see themselves as being at the frontline—and to go further than they otherwise might. Nowadays she can't watch *24* any more [62].

Journalist and novelist Robert Harris called Sands' exposé "shocking," and observed that "the parallel with Nazi Germany's descent into immorality is impossible to escape."[7]

The cast of Season Eight of *24*, standing patriotically before the United Nations Building. From left to right: the Counter-Terrorism Unit operatives Arlo Glass (John Boyd), Dana Walsh (Katee Sackhoff), Brian Hastings (Mykelti Williamson), Chloe O'Brian (Mary Lynn Rajskub), and Cole Ortiz (Freddie Prinze, Jr.), as well as FBI Agent Renee Walker (Annie Wersching), Jack Bauer (Kiefer Sutherland), Kamistan President Omar Hassan (Anil Kapoor), U.S. President Allison Taylor (Cherry Jones), and presidential aide Rob Weiss (Chris Diamantopoulos).

After all, it was the mistreatment of prisoners of war by German and Japanese forces during the Second World War that inspired the adoption of the Geneva Convention in 1949.[8]

Making matters still worse, as executive director of Amnesty International USA William Schultz observed, "Citizens around the world suffer the consequences when the U.S. defaults on its responsibility to promote human rights.... The actions of the U.S. government provide a de facto green light for other nations to ignore fundamental human rights standards."[9]

One of the most persistent critics of the Bush torture policy was Arizona Senator and U.S. Presidential candidate John McCain. During the Vietnam War, McCain was captured and tortured by the North Vietnamese, who used some of the same "interrogation techniques" currently employed by the CIA, including sleep deprivation and the forcing of "stress positions." A Republican, McCain further solidified his reputation as a maverick by defying his own party on this issue, consistently speaking out against the CIA's use of these techniques, as well as the employment of waterboarding. He also revealed that he and other POWs would routinely lie to their Vietnamese torturers, telling them what they wanted to hear rather than the truth.[10] By and large, despite McCain's best efforts to discourage the use of torture by the Bush administration, the violations of human rights continued. While the CIA has stated that it has discontinued the use of waterboarding, several Democrats who have been briefed by the CIA have condemned the organization for continuing to use immoral and illegal methods of interrogation.[11]

However, both the Bush White House and Jack Bauer have an unwavering defender in Supreme Court Justice Antonin Scalia, a personal friend of Cheney's who considers liberals who oppose torture under extreme circumstances smug, unrealistic ideologues. In 2007, during a law conference hosted in Ottawa, a Canadian judge expressed relief that not all international security agencies "subscribe to the mantra 'What would Jack Bauer do?'" This comment offended Scalia, who replied, "Jack Bauer saved Los Angeles.... He saved hundreds of thousands of lives.... Are you going to convict Jack Bauer? Say that criminal law is against him? 'You have the right to a jury trial?' Is any jury going to convict Jack Bauer? I don't think so."[12]

Polls conducted by Fox News in 2008 and by Gallup in 2009 have suggested that the American people are evenly split in their opinion of the Bush White House's use of torture. The split falls largely along party lines, with the majority of Republicans favoring the use of torture and supporting the Bush White House, with the majority of Democrats opposing torture. Independents are split between them, but leaning towards favoring the use of torture in extreme circumstances. However, Gallup polls have indicated that these same independents favor a probe of the Bush administration's use of torture to make sure that it was justified and justly implemented.[13]

The Parents Television Council, a watchdog group, revealed that representations of torture on television rose dramatically in the wake of 9/11, from 102 scenes of torture depicted between 1996 and 2001, to the 624 scenes shown between 2002 and 2005. One of the essential differences between the two periods was that, before 9/11, Nazis and drug dealers were the ones doing the torturing while, after 9/11, it was most likely the hero of the program. While Jack Bauer's name became inextricably linked to torture, and his series, *24*, featured 67 scenes of torture its first five seasons on the air, heroes of the past would never torture their enemies.[14]

"It's unthinkable that Capt. Kirk would torture someone," said David Danzig, director of Human Rights First's "Prime Time Torture Project." He explained that his organization is "not opposed to having torture on television, but 98 percent of the time when it is shown, it's 'Bing, bang, boom,' and it works.... Frankly, it's unrealistic and it's kind of boring."[15]

As Danzig attests, aside from the moral issues involved in torture, frequent reports have emerged from within the F.B.I. and C.I.A. that have revealed that torture is an ineffective means of protecting national security. In 2008, a seasoned counterterrorist agent at the F.B.I. revealed to journalist David Rose that information extracted via torture has provided false leads that have wasted time and eroded company morale:

> At least 30 percent of the F.B.I.'s time, maybe 50 percent, in counterterrorism has been spent chasing leads that were bullshit. There are "lead squads" in every office trying to filter them. But that's ineffective, because there's always that "What if?" syndrome. I remember a claim that there was a plot to poison candy bought in bulk from Costco. You follow it because someone wants to cover himself. It has a chilling effect. You get burned out, you get jaded. And you think, "Why am I chasing all this stuff that isn't true?" That leads to a greater problem—that you'll miss the one that is true. The job is 24-7 anyway. It's not like a bank job. But torture has made it harder.[16]

Other national security sources interviewed by Rose contested that they were forced to employ torture techniques they did not believe in, morally, did not believe yielded genuine results, and which they had no training to administer. The consequence is that many agents who performed interrogation techniques that clearly violated international torture law fear that they will face prison terms thanks to an Obama-administration-led torture probe, while the high-ranking Bush administration officials that compelled them to carry out torture, including the president and vice president, will never go to trial.[17]

Finally, and most damningly, another of Rose's sources believed that the Bush administration used torture as a means of getting key prisoners, particularly Guantanamo Bay detainee Abu Zubaydah, to offer up bogus information that would justify an unjustifiable U.S.–led invasion of Iraq. "It seems to me they were using torture to achieve a political objective," the source said.[18] The information extracted from Abu Zubaydah was central to the Bush Administration's case for war with Iraq, and its validity has been repeatedly and convincingly challenged.[19] Furthermore, stories have surfaced that the administration applied constant, mounting pressure to interrogators to "find" evidence linking Iraq and al-Qaeda.[20]

As *Harper's Magazine* journalist Scott Horton wrote on March 29, 2009, "President Bush's torture techniques provided our terrorist adversaries with their most compelling recruitment theme ever. Thousands were mustered to their side as a result. Four thousand Americans died in Iraq as a consequence, and thousands of other Americans suffered severe injuries from IEDs [Improvised Explosive Devices, or roadside bombs] and other attacks. And the balance? Did America secure any meaningful, actionable intelligence through the use of torture?" Despite Cheney's unsubstantiated claims to the contrary, Bush's FBI director, Robert Mueller, has revealed that the answer to that question is *no*.[21]

Alfred W. McCoy, Professor of History at the University of Wisconsin–Madison, observed in *A Question of Torture* (2006):

> As a people, Americans are now faced with a choice that will influence the character of their nation and its standing in the world. They can honor their commitments under law and treaty to ban torture unconditionally. Or, they can agree with the Bush administration's decision to make torture a permanent weapon in America's arsenal. If they adopt this latter policy, they should be mindful of a sober assessment by former White House adviser Arthur Schlesinger, Jr.: "No position taken has done more damage to the American reputation in the world—ever."
>
> As a powerfully symbolic state practice synonymous with brutal autocrats, torture—even of the few, even of just one—raises profound moral issues about the quality of America's jus-

> tice, the character of its civilization, and the legitimacy of its global leadership. "Cruelty disfigures our national character," warned Alberto Mora, the U.S. Navy's general counsel who fought to stop the Pentagon's psychological torture at Guantanamo. "Where cruelty exists, law does not" [225].

The questions raised by torture in the name of national security are not new. For years, fictional heroes have asked themselves whether extreme measures are justified in extreme cases. And, as Scalia and Beaver have demonstrated, how fictional heroes grapple with these dilemmas is significant, because fictional heroes have the potential to influence decisions made by real people in the real world.

In 2004, the heroes of the DC Universe — who had long been presented as moral paradigms — showed that they were not above using ruthless tactics when they believed that the lives of their friends and family were at stake. In Brad Meltzer's *Identity Crisis* (2004), supervillain Dr. Light discovers the secret identity of Elongated Man and rapes his wife, Sue Dibny. When Light brags that he will reveal their identities to others if sent to prison, the members of the Justice League (including Atom, Flash, Hawkman, Green Arrow, Green Lantern, and Black Canary) pressure the sorceress Zatanna into erasing Light's memory and, functionally, lobotomizing him. Batman discovers the conspiracy and is enraged by how supposed superheroes treat their prisoners. When it becomes clear that he will take action against them, the Justice League members compel Zatanna to erase Batman's memory as well. While the spell was not supposed to have an effect on his character, merely his memory, it is this moment that signaled the change in Batman's personality from kindly Caped Crusader to the Dark Knight.

In Brad Meltzer's *Identity Crisis* (2004), the sorceress Zatanna (above) magically lobotomizes the rapist Dr. Light. When Batman attempts to intervene, Zatanna casts a spell to erase his memory of the incident. This story is indicative of the ruthless actions DC Universe heroes resorted to in comic books published during the Bush administration. Illustration by Dave Hoover (courtesy Dave Hoover).

When the secret gets out that this subset of Justice League members has consistently conspired to erase the memories of villains who discover secret identities, the members of the supervillain community band together as one massive army and attack the League in retaliation for the inhumane treatment of their fellow supervillains. The tone of the story is dark and morally ambiguous. The narrative suggests that the actions of the League members were necessary given how dangerous supervillains are to the families of superheroes, but that they had to pay a high emotional price of guilt. On the other hand, the story seems to indicate that their actions were fundamentally inexcusable, and caused them to turn on their own, punishing the innocent Batman merely because he couldn't condone their methods.

Other hero narratives over the years have raised the question of whether a hero can or cannot adhere to a strict moral code while fighting adversaries who have no qualms about raping, torturing, and killing their opponents. During the climax of Ian Fleming's *Casino Royale* (1953), a Communist agent named LeChiffre attempts to extort money from his British counterpart, James Bond, by lashing Bond's groin with hemp. When Bond refuses to disclose the location of the cache, LeChiffre threatens castration. Only the timely intervention of a third party spares Bond, and he is taken to the hospital for treatment of his savagely wounded testicles. For days, Bond fears permanent impotence, but eventually heals enough to make love to fellow spy Vesper Lynde.

While Bond is convalescing, he expresses doubts about his newly minted career in espionage to René Mathis, a member of the French secret service. Bond explains that he earned his status as a Double O agent by killing villainous agents. And yet, the term "villain" is problematic, because everyone can be a villain from a certain point of view. After all, from a Communist perspective, isn't he the enemy agent and LeChiffre the hero agent? What really sets them apart?

"Of course," Bond says, "patriotism comes along and makes it seem fairly all right, but this country-right-or-wrong business is getting a little out-of-date. Today we are fighting Communism. Okay. If I'd been alive fifty years ago, the brand of Conservatism we have today would have been damn near called Communism and we should have been told to go and fight that. History is moving pretty quickly these days and the heroes and villains keep changing parts" (159–160).

Mathis teases Bond, asking if LeChiffre had actually whipped Bond's brains and not his testicles. Bond chooses a different track, arguing that one thing the British could learn from LeChiffre was how not to behave.

> "LeChiffre was serving a wonderful purpose, a really vital purpose, perhaps the best and highest purpose of all. By his evil existence, which foolishly I have helped to destroy, he was creating a norm of badness by which, and by which alone, an opposite norm of goodness can exist. We were privileged, in our short knowledge of him, to see and estimate his wickedness and we emerge from our acquaintance better and more virtuous men."
>
> "Bravo," said Mathis. "I'm proud of you. You ought to be tortured every day" [162].

Many of Bond's doubts about his career vanish after he discovers that the Communist spy organization SMERSH is responsible for Vesper's death. He rededicates himself to his career as a spy and vows to avenge himself upon SMERSH by hunting down as many of their agents as he can. The motivation is personal, having nothing to do with whether Russia is an enemy of the United Kingdom or an ally during a given political moment. Indeed, as Bond predicts, during the course of his career, the Communists do change from his adversaries to his unlikely allies. In the film series inspired by the Fleming novels, Bond's mission brief changes from hunting SMERSH agents to destroying the members of the rogue terrorist organization SPECTRE who threaten the fragile détente between Russia and China and the U.S. and Great Britain.[22]

While Bond regrets some of his conversation with Mathis in the aftermath of Vesper's death, what he does not regret is his desire to be morally superior to his opponents. However ruthless Bond can be in the service of queen and country, the implication of this exchange is that, as a British gentleman, Bond would not resort to the same brutal interrogation tactics that LeChiffre employed. Yes, the Bond of the Fleming novels would kill brutally on many occasions—impaling SPECTRE stormtroopers with ski poles, sinking enemy ships with limpet mines, and feeding SMERSH agents to sharks—but he would draw the line at torture, since torture is beneath him, and something that villains do.

A different interpretation of Bond for a different era, *Quantum of Solace* (2008) shows

Bond (Daniel Craig) and his MI6 supervisor M (Judi Dench) more than willing to torture Mr. White (Jesper Christensen), a high-ranking officer of "Quantum" for information about the mysterious terrorist organization. Since Mr. White is one of the people responsible for Vesper's death, Bond has no qualms about White's torture "not being cricket," and M warns White, "The longer it takes [for you to talk], the more painful we'll make it."

Another example of a ruthless screen hero is the fictionalized depiction of real-life law enforcement officer Elliot Ness (Kevin Costner) in *The Untouchables* (1987). In the film, Ness swore to do "anything and everything in my power" to bring mob boss Al Capone to justice using "all legal powers at my disposal." However, like Fleming's Bond, Ness initially felt it was as important to remain pure of heart as it was to combat the moral corruption that Capone represented. Ness' mentor Malone (Sean Connery), a veteran police officer with a lifetime of knowledge of the seamier side of life in Chicago, both envied and disdained Ness' idealism. According to Malone, the only way to win a street fight is to keep escalating the violence until you beat your opponent by becoming more ruthless and deadly than he.[23] Ness initially resists the notion that he must become evil in order to succeed at fighting evil, but his war against the Chicago underworld gradually corrupts him. In one key segment he watches, approving, as Malone torments a gangster into testifying against Capone. The scene is played largely for laughs and elicits audience approval for Malone's extreme methods.

By the end of the film, Ness has gotten civilians killed in the crossfire of gun battles, murdered a prisoner, and blackmailed a judge in order to ensure Capone's conviction for tax evasion. Ness' final statement on his own descent into moral corruption is, "I have foresworn myself. I have broken every law I have sworn to uphold, I have become what I beheld and I am content that I have done right!"[24] It is a speech that has been given new life and meaning during the war on terror, and has been quoted repeatedly by conservative bloggers to justify torture, extreme rendition, and the detention without trial of enemy combatants in the war on terror.

Quantum of Solace and *The Untouchables* are both violent films, but their depictions of torture and murder are almost quaint when compared to the visceral, relentless depictions of torture featured in the disturbing horror subgenre of "torture porn" that rose to popularity during the first decade of the 21st century. The inspiration for the genre may be Japanese director Takashi Miike's *Audition* (1999), in which a seemingly demure woman avenges herself upon her insincere lover by torturing him with dozens of needles and sawing off his left foot.[25] American director and Miike enthusiast Eli Roth strove to recreate *Audition*'s emotional impact in his own films, *Cabin Fever* (2002), *Hostel* (2005), and *Hostel: Part II* (2007), knowing full well that his target audience of contemporary teenagers "want to see people getting' fucked up — bad" (Sharrett 36).

There are several possible reasons why 21st century teenagers have an enthusiasm for observing torture. One may be that, since the Reagan era, horror films lost their subversive content and became intense roller-coaster rides and endurance tests for their audiences (Sharrett 33). As each new horror film has more gore, more suspense, and more killings than the one before, horror fans could brag to one another about surviving the experience of watching the film.

Another reason may be that teenagers who have lost their fears of traditional, supernatural monsters, have retained their fear of serial killers, maniacs, and Jack Bauer. While many Americans tacitly approve of the Bush torture program, and root for Jack Bauer while watching *24*, they secretly fear falling into the hands of an expert torturer like Bauer, whether a horror movie riff on Bauer is an all–American Homeland Security agent who has targeted them by mistake, or an enemy agent who is avenging himself upon all Americans for the crimes of the U.S. government.

While several of these torture films take place on American soil, some exploit American fears of foreign locales. Such films often involve American students studying abroad who are captured and tortured while visiting a Third World beach resort community that exists uncomfortably near extremely poor communities, or a formerly friendly European nation, such as France or Italy, that Bush has effectively turned against America. The films in this vein—*Turistas* (2006) being a prime example—are "inspired"/"justified" by real-life accounts of raped and murdered study-abroad students. The tourist cautionary tale film may also involve plotlines in which the fish-out-of-water teens contract a deadly disease far worse than Montezuma's Revenge (2008's *The Ruins*) or are sold into prostitution by Arabs and Eastern Europeans with machine guns (2008's *Taken*).[26]

Perhaps most troubling of all is the idea that the scenes of torture featured in "torture porn" films enrapture some audience members, who believe that pain is redemptive and makes one appreciate life. These beliefs may be rooted in a form of Christianity that promotes the idea that, to be truly holy, one must suffer as Christ did, and contemplate his wounds through prayer and repeated viewings of *The Passion of the Christ* (2004). Scenes of torture may also have appeal for a generation of teenagers that has embraced "cutting" and deliberate self-harm as a form of self-expression, therapy, and rebellion against a repressive home life and broader social environment.

Other viewers might enjoy watching scenes of torture for the same reason they enjoy vigilante films, to watch evil characters get their comeuppance in new and inventive ways. Hence the appeal of *Hard Candy* (2005), in which a vengeful Lolita figure tortures and threatens with castration a character who may or may not be a pedophile and a murderer. But the most popular films in this vein are those in the ubiquitous *Saw* franchise, which began in 2004. The hero/villain of the series is Jigsaw (Tobin Bell), a character who resents the amoral, manic-depressive vapidity of the average American and intends to teach them to value being alive in the greatest country in the world by torturing them. A more deadly variation of the Riddler from the *Batman* comic books, Jigsaw sets elaborate deathtraps for his prey, which can be escaped only if the victim shows a redeeming trait or a desire to reform. For example, following the advice of Matthew 18:9 ("And if your eye causes you to sin, gouge it out and throw it away. It is better for you to enter life with one eye than to have two eyes and be thrown into the fire of hell") Jigsaw seems to be doing God's work when he compels a voyeur to destroy his own eyeballs in order to survive a deathtrap.

As film critic Christopher Sharrett observed in "The Problem of *Saw*: 'Torture Porn' and the Conservatism of Contemporary Horror Films."

> The notion of teaching the good old-fashioned values through torture and murder might tend to make one read the *Saw* films as a parody of the Bush years, were there any real signs of intelligence on display, including a touch of humor given a manifestly ridiculous character and situation. But the filmmakers are far too smitten by the idea that Jigsaw might "have something" to his morality... [33].
>
> Although Jigsaw's project seems to be one of "reformism," his course is one of obliteration, including self-annihilation. The impulse toward destruction and suicide has been basic to the conservative vision of America since its inception, preferring conflagration to rational social change [35].

When female victims of Jigsaw and other Grand Inquisitors are eventually "reformed" several of them become torturers themselves, sometimes turning on their former tutors and torturing the torturers; it is unclear if such a transformation is meant to be applauded as a moment of feminist empowerment, or greeted with despair as another reactionary Inquisitor has been refined in the fires of pain. Female torture victims, to a somewhat greater degree than male victims, also raise the question of the sadomasochism of torture porn films. The distinctions between rape, sadomasochism, and prostitution are often either blurred or eliminated in hardcore pornography.[27] Torture porn films, with their simulated torture and rape scenes, are also troubling, not because the sex and torture might be real, but because they encourage some viewers to fantasize about committing rape and others to fantasize about being raped.

Rape fantasies and sadomasochism also often employ deeply troubling imagery from the African slave trade and the Holocaust, with the sexually dominant partner assuming the role of slave trader or leather-clad S.S. Commandant, while the sexually passive partner accepts punishment as if imprisoned in a concentration camp, slave ship, or plantation. Films that have recreated "Nazi sex" relationships have been critical of them (1974's *The Night Porter*) or are examples of extreme exploitation employed as entertainment (1974's *Ilsa: She Wolf of the S.S.*), but they are always disturbing, and the question of authorial intent is a vexed one. Certainly jokes about sadomasochism and Nazi-rape-sex remain a strong social taboo. For example, the Nazi villain of Mark Millar's *Wanted* (2003–2004) makes a statement that is burned forever in the memory of many of those who read the graphic novel: "You [call me a] Fascist like its some kind of insult, but people *love* Fascists, man. You ever meet a woman who fantasized about being tied up and raped by a liberal?"

The America portrayed in Millar's *Wanted* is a fallen world in which there are no heroes, only a corporate oligarchy comprised of supervillains that runs the country. In this America, middle-class Americans are wage slaves on antidepressants with no hope of achieving happiness or fulfillment in life, and the working classes are mindless slaves who exist to be exploited, raped, and killed. While some critics have accused Millar of showing a perverted streak in his representation of an "alternate reality" United States, the implication of the story is that it is representing America *as it truly is*— a Fascist state in which the only erotic relations are S&M relations, and the only chance one has of becoming wealthy and powerful is to sell one's soul and join a paternalistic organization such as the U.S. Chamber of Commerce. The satire is savage, but flies over the heads of most people who read the comic book.[28]

While many readers felt that Millar was out of line with his story, he is not alone in worrying over the dark, Gothic state of fin de siècle and early 21st century American society. As Mark Edmundson observed in *Nightmare on Main Street: Angels, Sadomasochism, and the Culture of the Gothic* (1997), Americans have become more and more cynical since the 1960s, embracing a purely gothic worldview in which hope, virtue, and love are nonexistent, society is in a state of perpetual decay, empathy is for fools, and all that matters is power and self-defense.

According to Edmundson, the great American tradition of Transcendentalism has often risen to challenge the more Gothic elements of American culture. Iconic Transcendentalists such as Ralph Waldo Emerson, Henry David Thoreau, and Walt Whitman famously called for an embracing of hope, the advancement of social reforms, the education of the mind, and the nourishment of the soul. Sadly, writing in the mid–1990s, Edmundson believed that there was little evidence of Transcendentalist feeling in Clinton-era America. He asks, "What happens if the culture of Gothic goes uncontested? What if its influence grows, it becomes sharper, more subtle, more pervasive, and what if nothing comes along to counter the Gothic drive?" (125).

The answer Edmundson provides to his own questions certainly describes the America portrayed in *Wanted* and arguably describes what America was like under the leadership of George W. Bush:

> A culture approaching pure S&M Gothic would be one where human relations, especially erotic relations, would always be defined as power relations. Equality in love, as well as in politics and social life generally, would no longer be a tenable ideal. It would be impossible in such a culture to conceive of any relation, with husband, with child, with neighbor, or with friend, except in terms of domination and submission; in an S&M culture, love (if one could still use that word) would always be love of power [131].

Edmundson's S&M Gothic America is one in which there is no hope of redemption or regeneration through Transcendentalism. But were there any Transcendentalists—in reality or in fiction—during the Bush years to offer an alternative worldview to the S&M Gothic? To oppose the fear-mongering, militarism, and anti-intellectual fanaticism of Team Bush? To promote hope, peace, empathy, and freedom? Who, when faced with the same dilemmas confronted by Donald Rumsfeld and Jack Bauer, would choose a radically different path each and every time?

Democratic-Farmer-Labor Party Senator Paul Wellstone was one of the few elected officials who consistently defied Bush's most militarist and inhumane policies, but he was killed in a plane crash on October 25, 2002, leaving the campaign against the invasion of Iraq without a strong champion in the Senate. Liberal activist and gonzo journalist Hunter S. Thompson committed suicide shortly after Bush was elected to a second term in the White House because, as Thompson explained, living through President Nixon and Vietnam once was bad enough, having to do it all over again with Bush and Iraq was just too much to bear. Friends and family members wished he had forestalled his suicide, and criticized Bush in print with the same vigor and passion that he had lambasted Nixon and lionized George McGovern, but he just didn't have it in him anymore.[29] Other notable critics of the Iraq invasion and the Bush torture policy included retired newsman Walter Cronkite, documentary filmmakers Alex Gibney and Eugene Jarecki, cultural critics Howard Zinn and Barbara Ehrenreich, and Hollywood activists such as Susan Sarandon, George Clooney, Maggie Gyllenhaal, Alec Baldwin, and Sean Penn. These voices were passionate, but not widely heeded, and were roundly condemned by conservative commentators, including the screenwriters of the surprisingly reactionary superhero satire *Team America: World Police* (2004), who suggested that the whiny Alec Baldwin was a bigger threat to American national security than Kim Jong-il and al-Qaeda.

While several individual superhero stories were strongly critical of the Bush administration, very few American superheroes *consistently* stood firm against the excesses of the Bush administration, passionately opposing torture, the Iraq invasion, the Patriot Act, and even Bush's disastrous environmental policy. But one superhero in particular bravely confronted these issues head on, despite opposition from the President of the United States, the majority of the American people, and even her own husband, Reed.

That superhero was Susan Storm Richards, the Fantastic Four's Invisible Woman.

The Invisible Woman: Cold Warrior Turned 21st Century Conscientious Objector

In the film *Fantastic Four: Rise of the Silver Surfer* (2007), a mysterious, shimmering alien soars across the globe, spreading environmental chaos by freezing oceans, draining the Thames, and creating seemingly bottomless pits in international locales. After the Fantastic Four helps capture the "Silver Surfer," the scientist team leader, Reed Richards (Ioan

Gruffudd) asks to question the being, but the U.S. military head of operations, General Hager (Andre Braugher), instead wants a Jack Bauer–type master interrogator to conduct the "interview." The film presents this interrogator, Mr. Sherman, as a cardboard villain totally lacking in Bauer's charisma, conflicted emotions, or burning self-righteousness. Confronting the restrained Silver Surfer with an enormous syringe, Mr. Sherman offers an oily smile: "There are certain things I'm not permitted to do because they're considered human rights violations. Fortunately, you're not human." Like Bush, Rumsfeld, and Cheney, Sherman is adept at defeating the spirit of the law with the letter of the law.

Unexpectedly prisoners themselves, the Four stew in a cell of their own. Reed is angry primarily because he has been cheated of being the first human to directly address a sentient alien being. Johnny Storm (Chris Evans), the team's young hothead, is largely indifferent to what is going on and is more concerned with flirting with a sexy woman in uniform. Ben Grimm (Michael Chiklis), the Four's Golem-like muscle, feels that the Surfer probably deserves to be imprisoned and tortured because he has already done incalculable damage to the Earth's environment and would commit further acts of aggression if freed.

Only Susan Storm (Jessica Alba), Johnny's older sister and Reed's fiancée, expresses horror at the thought of the Surfer being tortured. As she sees it, torture is not the way to treat a visitor from the stars, or any sentient being for that matter. Nor, she thinks, is it likely to garner real answers from the prisoner, especially if the torture is administered before a genuine overture of friendship is made. Also, the Surfer has shown some sign of compassion, as he rescued Sue from being killed by military "friendly fire" shortly before he was captured. In Sue's mind, that gesture of good will demands returning.

Activating her invisibility powers, Sue sneaks past the guards posted at the Four's cell, and at the Surfer's, and finds the Surfer alone, recovering from his encounter with Mr. Sherman. The Surfer senses her presence and is not alarmed. Sue introduces herself to the Surfer and offers to help him if he tells her why he is attacking the planet. He tells her that his master, the planet-eater Galactus, is coming to destroy the Earth, and he is merely a powerless emissary. The Surfer reveals that he serves Galactus reluctantly; some time ago he had convinced Galactus to spare his own world, Zenn-la, and his true love, Shalla-Bal, provided that he help Galactus find other worlds to devour. The Surfer tells Sue that he had protected her before, and is speaking with her now, because she reminds him of Shalla-Bal.

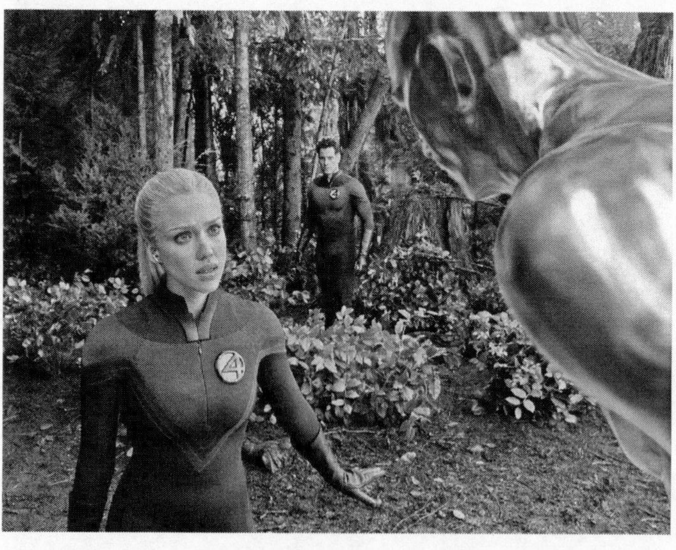

In *The Fantastic Four: Rise of the Silver Surfer* (20th Century–Fox, 2007), the Invisible Woman (Jessica Alba, left) asks the Silver Surfer (Doug Jones, right) why he is attacking the Earth as Mr. Fantastic (Ioan Gruffudd) looks on.

In a reversal of *24*, compassionate treatment of a prisoner, rather than torture, is the only thing that garners the interrogator key information on the eve of the apocalypse. The scene is arguably as contrived as any in *24*, especially because of the enormous coincidence of Sue's resemblance to Shalla-Bal. However, the film acts as a much needed corrective to the far-too-influential *24*.

After this exchange, Sue convinces the rest of the Four to take the drastic step of freeing the Silver Surfer, partly to rescue him from further torture, partly as a gambit to secure his help against Galactus. When she continues to be kind to him, and nearly dies saving his life from perennial Four villain Dr. Doom, the Surfer responds in kind by renouncing his allegiance to Galactus and defecting to the side of Earth. During the climax of the film, the Surfer confronts the planet-eater alone. There is a spectacular cosmic battle that appears to result in the mutual destruction of the Surfer and Galactus, and the Earth is saved.

The film is an adaptation of two landmark stories in the 1960s *Fantastic Four* comic books by Stan Lee and Jack Kirby (featured in numbers 48–50 and 57–60).[30] By that point, the comic book had been in print for several years, and Lee was interested in raising the threat level of the Four's opponents as much as he could to keep readers engrossed. After a moment of inspiration, he sent visual storyteller Kirby a "'plot' which consisted of nothing more or less than for words: 'Have them fight God.'"[31] Rather than have the Four *literally* fight God, Kirby created Galactus, an impersonal destroyer of worlds motivated by hunger and a survival instinct. In contrast, the God in the Torah is a personal God, who converses with his peoples, acts directly in history, and destroys cities and peoples who displease Him. Galactus' actions seem inspired by those of the Hebrew God who destroyed Sodom and Gomorrah with fire and brimstone, flooded the world of Noah, killed the first-born children of Egypt, and smote the builders of the Tower of Babel. While His personality is nothing like Galactus', there is a subtext to most Galactus tales that suggests the planet-eater is acting, consciously or not, as an agent of divine retribution against a humanity that has grown corrupt.

Christian readings of the Sodom and Gomorrah narrative notwithstanding, the dominant Hebraic interpretation holds that the inhabitants of those cities were guilty of unrestrained greed, hostility to strangers, lack of compassion for the poor and homeless, and a propensity for violence and bloodshed. In *Genesis*, God had heard reports of these evildoings but assured Abraham that He would spare Sodom if He could find but ten righteous people living in it. When God's angelic emissaries went to Sodom, they found that the kindly Lot and his family were protective of strangers, and good hosts, but they were alone in practicing proper hospitality etiquette. Consequently, God destroyed Sodom and Gomorrah and spared Lot and his children. In the *Fantastic Four: Rise of the Silver Surfer*, the Silver Surfer plays the role that the angelic emissaries play in the Bible, only he finds Four righteous people left on Earth who, thanks to Sue, show him the proper hospitality etiquette and protect him from harm. This angel demands that his God not destroy the Earth and his efforts on behalf of the human race spare the planet. The moral of the film, therefore, is that Americans in the real world need to end their support for U.S. torture policy and extreme rendition or risk suffering divinely inspired retribution for being as ruthless, greedy, and bloodthirsty as the people of Sodom.[32]

It is noteworthy, however, that Reed is initially slow to object to the Surfer's treatment, showing tacit support of the Bush torture program, while Sue is the one who takes the lead and frees the alien. This is consistent with the way Reed was portrayed between 2000 and 2008. Throughout the eight years President George W. Bush was in office, Reed Richards, leader of the Fantastic Four, took the president's side on virtually every policy decision, and his wife took the opposite. Sometimes Sue's opposition was slight and sometimes Reed's support was enthusiastic, and vice versa. Most dramatically, in *Fantastic Four: Authoritative Action* (2005), Reed orders the Four to conquer the Eastern European nation of Latveria to bring democracy to Dr. Doom's people and confiscate his weapons of mass destruction. These actions symbolically show Reed to be in sympathy with the Bush Administration's publicly stated motivations of the Iraq invasion, and act as an allegorical restaging of Operation Iraqi Freedom in the Marvel Universe.[33] Reed's family members and teammates are initially supportive of the invasion, but soon realize that he has become as much of a despot as Doom ever was. This time, the Thing is the first to rebel against Reed, and Sue reluctantly follows his lead. Finally, in *Fantastic Four: Civil War* (2007), Reed is a firm believer in the Patriot Act, and the Marvel Universe counterpart to the law, the Superhero Registration Act, while Sue actively participates in a violent superhero uprising against the Bush Administration, in staunch opposition to those very laws, inspiring Johnny and the Thing to take her part against Reed's. All of these stories deserve closer attention, but they can only be fully understood when considered in the broader context of the *Fantastic Four* saga.

To some extent, the modern, liberal interpretation of Sue is a notable departure from the character's roots as a devoted Kennedy era anti–Communist. Indeed, in general, the recent film adaptations and comic books take notable liberties with the comic book's roots. They depict the *Fantastic Four* as 21st century cosmonauts and genetic researchers who were accidentally transformed into superheroes while doing research on a space station orbiting the earth. The origin of the Four featured in their 1961 debut comic book was notably different in its Cold War historical and political context, and cast the Four as pioneers of a fledgling, dangerously experimental space program.

On May 25, 1961, President John F. Kennedy declared before the United States Congress, "I believe that this nation should commit itself to achieving the goal, before this decade is out, of landing a man on the Moon and returning him safely to the Earth."[34] In the newly created fictional world of Marvel Universe, Dr. Reed Richards responded to Kennedy's call to action in November of that year by planning a hastily prepared trip to the stars in a space shuttle of his design. Soviet astronaut Yuri Gagarin had become the first human in space mere months before, and Reed was determined to exceed Gagarin's accomplishments by breaking free from Earth's orbit and reaching the stars.

Reed's pilot, Ben Grimm, was worried that the space race was causing them to act hastily and recklessly, and that Reed had neglected to install proper shielding to protect the crew from cosmic rays. Feeling Ben was being overcautious, Reed was determined to commandeer his own vessel that night without wasting time waiting for bureaucratic clearance. Reed's girlfriend, Sue, goads Ben into participating: "Ben, we've *got* to take that chance ... unless we want the Commies to beat us to it. I — I never thought that *you* would be a coward." His manhood questioned by a woman he was secretly attracted to, Ben agreed to join Reed, Sue, and her brother, Johnny, as the makeshift crew of America's first mission to the stars. The flight was a success, but the ship was, indeed, vulnerable to cosmic rays, which penetrated the hull and instantly began mutating the crew.

"Ben was right!" Reed realized too late. "We should have waited ... should have gotten heavier shielding!"

They lost control of the shuttle and crash landed in a forest back on Earth. Relieved beyond belief that they had survived the crash, the four soon discover that the cosmic rays had bestowed near magical powers upon them. Incredibly, the powers matched their personalities. The sometimes shy and subservient Sue developed the power to turn invisible, and called herself The Invisible Girl. Her brother, Johnny, was a teenage "hot shot," transformed into the Human Torch, a man who could burn as hot as a supernova without so much as singeing the hair on his body. Reed Richards, the scientist with the ever-expanding intellect, could stretch and bend his body to an incredible degree. Tragically, Ben Grimm was severely disfigured by the transformation that granted him incredible strength and near-invulnerability. He became the Thing, a man with a body of living, moveable rock. The Four instantly grasp that it is their responsibility to use their powers to defend America from Communism, and the Earth from alien menaces, and publicly take up residence in Manhattan's Baxter Building as the Fantastic Four.

Furious with Reed and Sue for pressuring him into participating into the flight that mutated him so tragically, Ben Grimm reluctantly joined the fledgling group so that Reed could work night and day to find a means of reversing his mutation. Gradually, as it became clearer that Reed would never find a cure, Ben came to accept his grotesque new body as a bizarre gift that granted him the opportunity to explore the universe and fight evil alongside the Four. As a superhero, the Thing could lead a wondrous life that would never have been open to Ben Grimm, working-class "mook" from Brooklyn. Furthermore, he found acceptance, and a family, as a member of the Four that he has been denied elsewhere, as well as a "Beauty and the Beast" style love with a blind sculptor, Alicia Masters. On some level, the Thing feared losing all of this should he ever be permanently cured. Consequently, he is a tragic figure, but not as tragic as the Incredible Hulk, the character whose creation was inspired by the Thing's runaway popularity with early Marvel readership. (The Thing has frequently fought the Hulk, but the two are kindred spirits and have even embarked on a Douglas Adams–style outer space "road trip" in Jim Starlin's hilarious buddy story "The Big Change.")

During the fifty-year history of the comic book, Reed, the patriarch of the Fantastic Four, has been portrayed as a cold, capable Mr. Spock figure, a wimpy nerd with a useless superpower, and as a grizzled adventurer. Artist Alex Ross has painted Reed to look like "The Professor" from *Gilligan's Island*, while the handsome, graying George Clooney has often been touted as the ideal actor to play the character in a film. However he has been portrayed since, Lee and Kirby created Reed to be both a manly adventurer and an intellectual—a blending of Allan Quatermain and Victor Frankenstein. Limited neither to the active nor the contemplative life, Reed is a bold explorer who leads the Four into outer space, the past and future, and other-dimensional realms such as the Negative Zone. He also regularly secludes himself in his lab to develop new medicines, technologies, and scientific proofs. Spending time with his wife and children takes third place for Reed, but he makes time for that as well, if not as much as Sue would like.

Of the Four, Sue's younger brother was the only one to embrace his powers immediately, loving his newfound ability to fly and set objects aflame. A fun-loving, girl-chasing car enthusiast, the earliest depictions of Johnny were reminiscent of a young Steve McQueen or Bobby Darin. Chris Evans brilliantly portrayed the character as an extreme sportsman and savvy merchandiser whose only ambition in life is to be famous for being famous (Sue laments in Mark Millar's "World's Greatest" that "My brother is Paris Hilton"). While Johnny is often portrayed as perennially immature, writer and artist John Byrne did much to transform the brash teen into a seasoned, responsible man. In Byrne's "Hero" (1985), Johnny almost gives up being the Human Torch when he finds out that his biggest fan, a little boy named Tommy Hanson, has set himself on fire with rocket fuel in imitation of his hero. When the boy dies, Johnny dedicates his future actions as a member of the Four to Tommy, and decides to act more maturely and soberly from then on.[35]

For her part, "Invisible" Sue is the glue that holds the family together — the maternal figure who makes sure that the Thing and Human Torch don't destroy the entire city in one of their recurring "play" fights, that Reed occasionally eats, and that her children, Franklin and Valeria, are not forgotten in the chaos of their daily lives.

According to cultural historian Robert Genter, Lee "tapped into popular discourse about the nuclear family" with their portrayal of the Four as a symbolic family. In the 1960s, the nuclear family was seen as providing hope, happiness, and shelter in an unstable world rocked by wars, economic uncertainty, and cultural instability. The pro-family movement had conservative motivations in promoting "everything from rising consumption levels to traditional gender roles to Cold War foreign policy" (957). The Lee-Kirby comics involved the Four constantly making contact with friendly alien beings and protecting Earth from invading menaces. While Reed and Ben had war records — during World War II, Reed fought behind enemy lines as an underground member of the O.S.S. and Ben Grimm was a "marine fighter ace over Guadalcanal and Okinawa" — their expeditionary group was a domesticated vanguard, more a perfectly imperfect "average American family" than a commando unit. Consequently, the Lee-Kirby Four was "a morality tale about the power of the nuclear family to defeat intruders" (Genter 959).

The Four's greatest and most implacable foe has always been Doctor Doom, an Eastern European despot who rules the feudal nation of Latveria. Dressed in a grey suit of armor, an expressionless iron mask, and a dark green cloak, Doom resides in a Romanian-style Castle equipped with futuristic technology that includes robot guards, ray guns, and a working time machine. The operatic and humorless archvillain is a bizarre amalgam of several Gothic archetypes: disfigured recluse, mad scientist, gypsy magic user, and brooding aristocrat. This odd assemblage of personality traits should not work, and yet Doctor Doom is widely recognized as the greatest comic book villain of all time. Indeed, along with Toshiro Mifune's iconic screen "samurai," Doom was *the* central inspiration for George Lucas' Darth Vader, arguably the greatest movie villain of all time.

One of the reasons Doom is such an effective antagonist is that he has occasionally triumphed. In Jim Shooter's *Secret Wars,* he successfully stole the powers of the God-like Beyonder (1984–1985). In David Micheline's *Emperor Doom* (1987), he hypnotized the entire world into obeying his every whim, and then grew bored with world domination, ultimately surrendering control of his own accord. Most significantly, in Roger Stern's *Doctor Strange and Doctor Doom: Triumph and Torment* (1989), Doom succeeds in his life-long quest to rescue his mother's damned soul from hell. As previous storylines revealed, Doom first began his study of the black arts, and his descent into evil, when he witnessed his mother dragged to hell by demons when he was a child. Tragically, at the end of *Triumph and Torment,* as his mother's soul rises to heaven, she observes Doom and tells him, tearfully, that she is horrified by what he has become — he has damned himself to save her.

Having succeeded in his schemes to save his mother and conquer the world, Doom's remaining motivation is his obsessive desire to prove himself smarter than Reed Richards and destroy the Fantastic Four. Doom has always blamed Reed, his old college rival, for the accident that left him hideously disfigured. The lab explosion was caused by Doom's first failed attempt to blend science and magic to create a gateway to Hell and rescue his mother. It was a gambit that Reed warned would never work because Doom's mathematical equations were off; the fact that Reed was right about the shoddy mathematics added fuel to Doom's rage rather than abate it.

For all of his attacks on the Richards family, Doom has never been able to defeat them when they have stood united against him. He has only ever come close to crushing their spirit by employing psychological warfare, blithely asking the Thing why Reed hasn't bothered to cure him yet or expressing sympathy to the others that Reed loves playing in his lab more than he loves his family. In Chris Claremont's *The Fantastic Four versus the X-Men* (1987), Doom planted a forged "Journal of Reed Richards" where Sue could find it. The journal contained the manifestly false revelation that Reed knew the cosmic rays would mutate the family, but took them on the voyage to deliberately turn them into superheroes. Sue and the others briefly believed that the forged journal was genuine, and it caused one of the greatest rifts in the family's history.[36]

In the 1980s, writer-artist John Byrne made Sue Storm Richards a central character in the *Fantastic Four* comic books. Here she bravely confronts the evil Doctor Doom in a story featured in *The Trial of Galactus* (Marvel Comics, 1990).

Aside from the preternatural threat to the family represented by Doom, the Four have seen their secure home life threatened by more mundane forces in recent years. For example, the frequency of supervillain attacks on their home in the Baxter Building have caused them to be evicted, and the Department of Social Services has also tried to take Sue's children away on the grounds of reckless endangerment and parental neglect. However, it is the allegorical clash between the ultimate evil represented by Doom and the ultimate good represented by the Four that made for some of the most dramatic superhero comic books ever published. In fact, the Lee and Kirby stories that comprised the first several years of the comic book are widely considered the pinnacle of achievement in the genre, making the *Fantastic Four* "The World's Greatest Comic Magazine."

For novelist Jonathan Lethem, the first 102 *Fantastic Four* issues were the result of a unique collaboration between Lee, "a coddled fifties striver" and "wannabe beatnik," and Kirby, a child of the Depression and a frontline combatant in World War II. These two very different men collaborated to produce art in an unlikely, John Lennon–Paul McCartney style partnership that set the same high benchmark in comics that the Beatles set in music.

> Lee and Kirby were full collaborators who, like Lennon and McCartney, really were more than the sum of their parts, and who derived their greatness from the push and pull of incompatible visions. Kirby always wanted to drag the Fantastic Four into the Negative Zone—deeper into psychedelic science fiction and existential alienation—while Lee, in his scripting, resolutely pulled them back into the morass of human lives, hormonal alienation, teenage dating problems and pregnancy and unfulfilled longings to be human and normal and loved and not to have the Baxter Building repossessed by the City of New York. Kirby threw at the Four an endless series of ponderous fallen gods or whole tribes and races of aliens and antiheroes with problems no mortal could credibly contemplate: Galactus and the Silver Surfer, the Inhumans, Doom, etc. Lee made certain the Four were always answerable to the female priorities of Sue Storm, the Invisible Girl, Reed Richard's wife and famously "the

weakest member of the Fantastic Four." She wanted a home for their boy Franklin, she wanted Reed to stay out of the Negative Zone, and she was willing to quit the Four and quit the marriage to stand up for what she believed [11–12].

Lethem observed that few comic fans he knew growing up in the 1960s and 1970s had sexual fantasies about the maternal Sue Richards the way they did about Valkyrie and other female superheroes, but there was something indispensable about Sue. Since the first decade of *Fantastic Four* stories were widely recognized by fans as the greatest superhero comic books of all time, and Sue was the audience identification character in a grand space opera, that made "one single character, our squeaky little Sue, the most important superhero in the Silver Age of Comics" (22).

Sue Storm, the Invisible Girl, began as the kindest member of the Four with the least impressive powers.[37] Judged purely on the basis of their combat skills, Sue, like several Marvel comic heroines, was useless in the extreme. During the early days of her career, Sue was only good at turning invisible to sneak past guards, acting as a spy or thief, or mounting prison breaks. In a fight, there was little she could do, other than sneak up to a foe and hit him over the head with a vase.[38] Apparently, a number of readers wrote complaint letters to the editors of the *Fantastic Four* during the first year of publication, expressing the wish that Sue be written out of the comic book. Addressing these complaints, Lee and Kirby produced a fourth-wall breaking segment in which Sue showed herself to be heartbroken over these letters and Reed and Ben come gallantly to her defense by pinpointing specific instances in which Sue was "useful" in a combat situation.[39] What Reed and Ben (and Lee) fail to mention in Sue's defense is the important point that, for some readers, female superheroes with "unimpressive" powers were approachable and engaging precisely *because* they were sensitive, imaginative, negotiators offering an alternative worldview and personality type to the Alpha male superheroes who headlined the superteam comics they were featured in.[40] Thankfully, as comic book stories have become more psychologically complex, and have played up interpersonal relations and political strife over the kind of extended combat sequences that used to characterize Marvel Comics in particular, female characters with more "subtle" abilities have had expanded roles.[41]

Nevertheless, it is important to note that Sue is a far more formidable physical combatant now than she was in the 60s. Following her marriage to Reed, and the birth of Franklin, Sue's superpowers began to mature. In addition to turning invisible, Sue could manipulate invisible "forcefields" in a Green Lantern–like manner that enabled her to create from thin air invisible projectiles, cages, bomb shelters, slides, elevators, oxygen tanks, and deadly air bubbles within the bodies of her opponents. In one fell swoop, these new abilities upgraded Sue from "the weakest member of the Fantastic Four" to the strongest. Along with her new powers, Sue changed her name from the Invisible Girl to the Invisible Woman, reflecting her newfound empowerment and maturity. (Jessica Alba played a younger, Invisible *Girl* Sue Storm in two theatrical films, while demonstrating many of the Invisible *Woman*'s more evolved powers. In the Pixar animated movie *The Incredibles*, Holly Hunter voiced ElastiGirl, a wonderful, if highly derivative, character who looks and behaves much like the married Sue Richards, while exhibiting *Reed* Richard's superpowers. Meanwhile, ElastiGirl's daughter Violet has Sue's powers.)

In the world of comics, Sue Storm Richards is also rare in that she is a female superhero who can adequately control her amazing powers. Unfortunately, in another sign of the sexism inherent in comic books, many heroines who were gifted with awe-inspiring abilities — ranging from the Scarlet Witch's world-shaping spells to Jean Grey's world-destroying telekinesis to Vixen's ability to channel the physical traits of any animal—would often find themselves unable to control those abilities, or possessed by the potency of their raw power and driven insane. Supremely powerful, the modern-day Sue can perform nearly any feat her ethical code will permit her to. She is an amalgam of sitcom "wife" (i.e., June Cleaver, Samantha Stephens, and Debra Barone) and James Cameron action heroine (Ellen Ripley and Sarah Connor), and is one of the most nuanced and realistic female characters in comic books.

All told, the 21st century comic book version of the Fantastic Four is hip and modern, blending psychedelic science fiction concepts with savage political satire, but it is also very much in the spirit of the early Lee-Kirby adventures, and the characters are recognizably the same ones Marvel fans have known and loved for years. Lethem was correct that it is the odd juxtaposition of the epic and the domestic that is the core of what makes the *Fantastic Four* great; it is, indeed, the clash of Reed's and Sue's values that generates the drama.[42]

While the Reed and Sue of today are generally portrayed as happily married characters, they have had some dramatic falling outs in recent years. In the past, their arguments were artificially created for dramatic purposes, as when the shape-shifting villain the Brute posed as Reed, or when Sue was demonically possessed. However, recent clashes between the two come from legitimate personality and political differences, and are not explained away by "possession."[43] After suffering a miscarriage, Sue secretly turned to religion for comfort, but never disclosed her newfound piety, or the exact nature of her religious beliefs, to her staunch atheist husband (Starlin *Infinity Crusade* 1993). For her part, as much as Sue is willing to explore space and time with Reed, she has no interest in working with him in the lab, which leaves her vulnerable to romantic competition from Alyssa Moy, Reed's old college girlfriend. Essentially Reed in female form, Moy likes nothing better than to spend days on end secluded in the lab, just as he does. As a rival for Reed's affections, Alyssa is Sue's worst nightmare, but Reed has reassured her that Alyssa is not a threat to their relationship.[44] For her part, Sue is occasionally tempted to have an adulterous affair with the hunky Namor, Prince of Atlantis, who boasts a Byronic demeanor and six-pack abs, but those flirtations never go far.

Politics, however, is a very real threat to their marriage.

In *Authoritative Action* (written by Mark Waid and illustrated by Mike Wieringo) Reed decides to lead the Four into Latveria to fill the power vacuum left by Doom when his living body was consigned to Hell at the end of their last, most brutal conflict. Reed argues that the swift, unilateral move—done without the blessing of either the U.N. or the U.S. government—was necessary because the armies of bordering nations Hungary, Serbia, and Symkaria are poised to invade and confiscate Doom's time-travel technology. Reed is also certain that the indomitable Doom would, against all odds, find a way to escape Hell and reclaim his throne. Should Doom achieve such a miracle, Reed would want him to return to a Latveria where the people were free and all of his weapons of mass destruction have been removed. Since Sue, Ben, and Johnny know—as do all regular readers of the comic book—that Doom's return to power is a mathematical certainty, Reed's logic seems unassailable.[45]

The Four effectively keep all the invading armies at bay, and attempt to bring democracy to the people of Latveria. Reed reveals, and destroys, the secret guillotine and crematorium Doom used to kill political dissidents, allows the people to ransack Doom's castle, and promises to disband Doom's oppressive robot police force. However, the Four do not speak

Latverian, and they are better at destroying Doom's artifacts than building a new nation. Before long, a suicide bomber tries to kill Reed and his family, shouting, "Free Latveria! This is our country and we will reclaim it!"[46]

He is subdued with ease, but his show of passion shakes Ben. He tells Reed, "It's astoundin'. That fella was willin' to give his life ta say somethin'. His *life*. If you ain't proved him wrong yet, whose fault is that?"[47]

Sue, who initially maintained that the Latverians were free under their rule and just didn't know it yet, begins to agree with Ben. "Put yourself in their place. Yes, Doom ruled without mercy, but zero percent unemployment and universal healthcare buy a lot of devotion. They want to believe life is good. It is easier to live in ignorance than in constant fear."[48]

But Reed, whose face was recently scarred in his final battle with Doom, has begun to look and act like his archenemy. Contrary to his initial promise, he keeps Doom's robot army functional and uses it to uproot insurgents. He also shows no compassion, eagerly seeing to it that the portrait of Doom's mother in the throne room is destroyed because it is the cruelest thing he can do to Doom. As Reed grows ever more militant, Sue and Johnny join the Thing in opposing his tactics.[49]

"These people aren't a social experiment and Latveria isn't your laboratory!" Sue declares.[50]

However, Reed takes positive steps towards genuinely liberating Latveria. He diverts funds once intended for Doom's personal coffers into a national trust for export revenue, and for "training and selecting locals capable of internal leadership." He does not believe the country is ready for immediate democratic elections, however, arguing that, while West Germany and Japan swiftly installed successful democratic regimes after World War II, "Vladimir Putin was elected but rules Russia like an autocrat."[51]

Michael Chiklis plays Ben Grimm, the Jewish "mook" from Brooklyn who is transformed by cosmic rays into the super-powered Golem known as the Thing, in two *Fantastic Four* films.

In the end, Reed is not allowed to make the final call as to when or how elections are to occur. Ultimately, a U.N. Peacekeeping force led by Nick Fury of S.H.I.E.L.D. removes Reed from power, and replaces him with a provisional U.N. government. The tragic tone of the story suggests that, while Reed's intentions were good, he was ultimately corrupted by his own imperial agenda. However, an unexpected epilogue muddies the waters of the message considerably, demonstrating that Reed may not have been as unpopular as Sue, Ben, and Johnny thought. As Fury walks through the main street of Latveria's capital shortly after deposing Reed, a young Latverian woman accosts him, demanding that Reed be restored to power. Fury protests that Reed violated international law.[52]

"Stinking hypocrite!" the Latverian woman yells. "For how many years did Doom commit worse crimes every day? Yet you granted him diplomatic immunity even as he brutalized us — ruled us through fear and cruelty! Now we at last have a sovereign who wishes to give us a voice in our own government — and *him* you cart away? Who are you to proclaim what is best for us?"[53]

The scene symbolically acknowledges that there are some outsiders genuinely trying to improve the quality of life for the people of U.S.-occupied countries — outsiders whose efforts are appreciated and saluted by the local communities. Is Reed one such outsider? Maybe. Is Greg Mortenson? Maybe not. However, *Authoritative Action* as a whole also demonstrates how easy it is for a liberating army to gradually morph into an occupying, conquering army. Consider also how difficult a time Reed has maintaining order and winning over the hearts and minds of the Latverians in a situation that is far more ideal and far less morally ambiguous than the Iraq invasion. As Reed indicated, unlike Iraq, Latveria is self-sufficient, has "no racial issues, and a stable economy." Also, Reed invaded the country after its despotic leader vanished and no one was left in charge as a successor. He also intended to protect it from imminent invasion and *knew for a fact* that Doom had weapons of mass destruction. Nor was Reed at all interested in acquiring for himself access to any oil that might or might not be under the Latverian soil.[54]

This well-written, timely story provided much for readers to think about, and was far from the usual escapist *Fantastic Four* space adventure. It signaled a change in the direction of the comic book that meant the Four would now be dealing far more heavily with political issues, and the Bush administration, than it had the actions of any previous American administration.

The next story that questioned and criticized the Bush administration followed not long afterwards. During the Marvel Universe *Civil War* storyline, Reed signs on with Tony Stark, and the Bush Administration, in a campaign to arrest and detain any superhero who refuses to reveal his secret identity and act as an official member of S.H.I.E.L.D., the Initiative, or the office of Homeland Security. Far more than a sideline supporter of Stark's faction, Reed is a central figure in the crackdown. He helps build and organize a prison in the Negative Zone in which superheroes who refuse to register their powers and secret identities with the U.S. government are detained without trial as enemy combatants. He also designs weapons for Tony Stark to use as a means of rounding up rogue superheroes for questioning and imprisonment.

Reed has several reasons for supporting Superhero Registration. The first is that he genuinely believes that a world in which superpowered beings run rampant without any form of government regulation overseeing their actions would inevitably descend into chaos and nuclear destruction. The second is that, as a respected war veteran, prominent member of several think tanks, and a rich, respected scientist with the grant money and facilities he needs to conduct research in peace, the last thing Reed wants to do is risk everything he has built for himself and his family by challenging the system. After all, he has seen his defiant artist uncle tell the House Un-American Activities Committee (HUAC) "to go to hell" when they demanded to know if he or anyone he knew was a member of the Communist Party. His uncle's artistic career ended on the spot, and Reed's father refused to ever speak with the "traitorous" uncle again. The last thing Reed wants is to suffer the same fate.[55]

As soon as Sue learns of her husband's prominent role as active Tony Stark supporter in the Civil War, she voices strong moral opposition to his actions:

SUE: [This] law is wrong.

REED: Fine. Then change it. But until you can do that, you have to obey it. That's what we do, remember?

SUE: ... Isn't that what they said when the Nazis took whole sections of the population they didn't like, Jews and gypsies and troublemakers, and herded them into cattle cars for train rides to places like Auschwitz and Treblinka?[56]

When Sue realizes that she has failed to shame him into turning against Stark, she decides that he isn't the man she married. That man feared nothing, least of all losing his wealth and reputation. She leaves her husband and children that night to join the resistance movement led by Captain America. Her brother Johnny joins her shortly thereafter. The Thing, unwilling to choose between Reed and Sue, but also unwilling to remain in America under a government he finds morally reprehensible, moves to France. "Corny as it is," the Thing tells Reed before he leaves, "I'm a patriot. I won't fight my own government. Thing is, if I stay here, if I stay silent, it is as good as saying that I condone what they're doing. I hafta make some kind of statement. So I'm goin'."[57]

After sitting out most of the war, the Thing ultimately decides that he can't remain neutral forever and returns to the United States, joining Sue and Johnny on Captain America's side in time for the final battle of the Civil War. In the midst of the pitched battle, Reed Richards realizes that one of his comrades-in-arms is about to shoot Sue, so he jumps in the way to take the bullet. Sue drags her husband to safety, as the battle rages on. At a key moment, Captain America realizes that his side was on the verge of winning the military battle, but losing the political war, as the fight decimates private property and terrifies the civilians around them. He decides to surrender then and there, ending the war and ensuring victory for Iron Man's side. Captain America is assassinated shortly thereafter.

When a general amnesty is declared, Sue, Johnny, and Ben are pardoned and decide to try to patch the family back together. Meanwhile, Spider-Man and other radical superheroes go underground to continue the war beyond the armistice as a resistance movement Sue no longer has the heart to participate in. Ironically, in the aftermath of the *Civil War*, a miraculously resurrected (but still deposed) Dr. Doom publicly condemns Reed for having "built and maintained secret prisons, contributed to the dissolution of your country's habeas corpus" and participated in imperial endeavors that have "destabilized the political balance of the entire world."[58] Interesting that, in this case, Dr. Doom is more of a voice of moral authority than Reed Richards.

Even though Sue failed in her rebellion against the Bush Administration in this particular instance, she enjoyed greater success in exposing the secret of his nonexistent environmental policy. While scientists, environmentalists, and social activists were flabbergasted by the Bush Administration's denial of climate change, insistence on loosening environmental protection regulations, and allowing oil drilling on formerly protected lands, none of them could know what the fictional George W. Bush was planning in "The Death of the Invisible Woman," written by Mark Millar and illustrated by Bryan Hitch.[59]

In the comic book, Bush was one of four hundred members of a secret organization of super rich businessmen, politicians, and scientists, called the Earth-Trust. Using the massive finances at their command, the Earth-Trust commissioned the building of Nu-World, a duplicate Earth intended to replace our native planet when it suffers total environmental collapse within the decade. Alyssa Moy, now married to Earth-Trust member Ted Castle, attempts to recruit Reed to the Nu-World construction project, but he refuses, preferring to work to save the real Earth from catastrophe instead of giving up on it.[60]

After Reed leaves, Alyssa is shocked to discover that Nu-World is only intended to act as an Ark, or planet-sized lifeboat, for a half-million politicians and super rich global elite hand-picked by the four hundred Earth-Trust board members. The remaining 6.8 billion people would be condemned to stay behind, metaphorically going down with the ship like the steerage passengers on the *Titanic*. Not feeling that she can tell her secret to Reed, Alyssa confides in Sue, expressing hopelessness that she has no means of going public with her knowledge, since all governments, news organizations, and businesses are operated by board members.[61]

Incredibly, an elderly, time-traveling Sue Richards from 2509 arrives at this critical moment in human history to reveal to the Four what will happen to the earth, and those left behind by the Earth-Trust, in the future:

> The good news is that the earth didn't die in the early part of the twenty-first century. It actually survived another five hundred years, thanks to the efforts of Doctor Reed Richards. But when the end times came, it was worse than we imagined. Twelve billion people starved to death. Half the world's cities drowned in the seas and cancer and disease affected almost every living creature. The rich and powerful disappeared overnight, leaving behind a lawless mess that the world's remaining superheroes bound together to protect. But it was hopeless and we knew it. Hence the reason I built the big machine.[62]

The elderly Sue constructs an enormous time machine on present-day Earth, powered by the Human Torch and a kidnapped Galactus and Dr. Doom. She conspires with her younger self and Alyssa to transport through time all eight billion surviving refugees from 2509 to the Nu-World of the present day. Hence, the planetary lifeboat intended to serve only the few super-rich becomes a shelter for the masses well before the Earth-Trust members have the opportunity to occupy it.[63]

Alyssa tells her shocked husband that it is payback, "Eight billion asylum seekers running away from the world you left them to die in."

Ted screams at her, "What have you done, you stupid witch? Have you any idea what the board is going to say about this?"

"What are they going to do, Ted? *Evict* them?"[64]

The massive time machine drained enough power from Galactus to kill him, but left the Human Torch and Dr. Doom merely shaken. The elderly Sue frees both and approaches Dr. Doom to offer her apology for kidnapping him.

> SUE: You know it was nothing personal, Victor. I only did what I had to do.
>
> DOOM: Likewise.

Then Doom vaporizes the elderly Sue Richards, declaring that his honor has been restored with the death of the Invisible Woman. This turn of events leaves the Sue of the present day in the grotesque position of having to deliver a eulogy for her future self at a funeral held in the present day, attended by both residents of 21st century Manhattan and refugees from 2509. Younger Sue now knows exactly how she is going to die, but she is comforted with the knowledge that she will have a long life and die saving the people of the world from the secret plans of Ted Castle and George W. Bush.[65]

The ending of "The Death of the Invisible Woman" is bittersweet because of the murder of the elderly Sue. Nevertheless, there is also something wonderfully subversive and exultant about the end of the tale, especially following on the heels of *Authoritative Action* and *Civil War*. Of course, it would have always been a foregone conclusion that the *Civil War* and *Authoritative Action* stories would have tragic endings, for the Iraq War rages on, Guantanamo Bay remains open, and the destructive environmental policies of the Bush Administration remain largely unaltered. In fact, the writers of Marvel comics showed great wisdom in never having Bush "brought to justice" in their own fictional world, since he was never impeached and never resigned from office. In contrast, DC comics made an enormous dramatic miscalculation when President Lex Luthor went conveniently mad and was removed from office in Jeph Loeb's *Superman/Batman: Public Enemies*. The happy ending did not ring true since Luthor was clearly intended to be a Bush stand-in, and Bush was so obviously still in power in the real world. Consequently, that story lacked artistic integrity.

Since the plot of "The Death of the Invisible Woman" placed President Bush in a fictional scenario, it was now suddenly possible for Mark Millar to write a story in which Sue is *at long last triumphant* against the man who had corrupted her husband and plagued her family, and America, for eight years. (And the Transcendentalists finally get to win a major skirmish against the collective forces of S&M Gothic America.)

Indeed, as a *Fantastic Four* story, and as a wish-fulfillment narrative celebrating the final days of Bush in the White House, there could be nothing more dramatically satisfying than reading "The Death of the Invisible Woman"—a story in which Sue, after suffering years of defeat after defeat at the hands of American neo-conservatives, finally has her chance to stick it to the Man.

EIGHT

Gay Rights, Civil Rights, and Nazism in the X-Men Universe

Morality is simply the attitude we adopt towards people we personally dislike.— Mrs. Cheveley, from Oscar Wilde's *An Ideal Husband*[1]

The [Marx] Brothers are egalitarian. In *Monkey Business*, Harpo kisses a line of people at the boat's railing. These include several women and a man; however, after kissing the man, there is no double-take, no grimace. It's not a joke based on homophobia; there's an inclusiveness to Harpo's inappropriate behavior. He invades the personal space of everyone.— Joseph Mills, *A Century of the Marx Brothers* (2007)[2]

The X-Men, Gay Rights, and Reader Identification

Marvel comic books have long invited direct reader identification with Marvel heroes, who are designed to be as flawed and "human" as the reader. Consider the shallow and vainglorious Human Torch, the angry antihero known as the Incredible Hulk, and the recovering alcoholic Iron Man. All of these characters have a vulnerability that the more aristocratic paragons of virtue at DC Comics sometime seem to lack. However, as much as readers have enjoyed relating to characters such as Iron Man, the Hulk, and the Human Torch, they have, in recent decades, expressed a highly personal love for the enormous cast of "mutant" characters that comprises the universe of the X-Men.

Like other superheroes, mutants don't exist in the real world, and yet the *X-Men* comic books and films that feature mutant characters are surprisingly popular across a broad demographic of readers. Presumably, the super-powered mutants allegorically represent real-world people; otherwise, they would not have resonance in a world in which superpowers don't exist. The allegory is clearly there, but what makes it so compelling is that it is a flexible allegory. The story of the X-Men is the story of the oppressed and the disenfranchised striking back against their oppressors, so any reader who feels oppressed may relate to the X-Men, regardless of the nature of the oppression, or its level of severity. Another reason that the allegory is so flexible is the vast, multicultural cast of characters who comprise the mutant community enables readers of different ethnic and racial backgrounds, sexual orientations, genders, and religious beliefs to see themselves in the *X-Men* narratives and to see the X-Men "story" as being primarily about "their" particular life conflict.

Consider Tabitha Smith, the runaway "white trash" punk rocker called Boom Boom because she has the power to mentally create energy grenades. She fled from home when her father began beating her and has, effectively, been homeless ever since. Because she has such an explosive personality she often does not stay long with one group of friends before moving on to another one (see *Secret Wars II* and *X-Men: Inferno*). In contrast, Sean Cassidy is a wealthy, middle-aged Irishman whose wife Maeve was killed in an IRA bombing. In his superhero life, he is known as Banshee thanks to his formidable sonic scream, but he vacillates between acting as an older mentor to the youthful X-Men and as a man who prefers a civilian life to a heroic one. Piotr Rasputin (Colossus) is a Détente-era Russian atheist with the physique of a professional wrestler, the metal skin of an android, and the soul of an artist. John and James Proudstar are brothers and Native American X-Men who are superhumanly strong, fast, and resistant to injury, and who are called by the somewhat politically incorrect names Thunderbird and Warpath. Each of these characters has the potential to speak to real-life readers who can relate to them due to their age, gender, culture, or personal story (see *Marvel Masterworks: Uncanny X-Men* Vol. 1–3).

German Americans and religious Roman Catholics weary of seeing their respective groups portrayed poorly in popular culture can take comfort in Nightcrawler. A furry blue demon-man with a forked tail and yellow eyes, Nightcrawler (a.k.a. Kurt Wagner) is a religious Roman Catholic German who was raised by gypsies and performed in the Munich Circus before joining the X-Men. Despite looking like a demon, Nightcrawler is amazingly well-adjusted, funny, and seems to spend much of his time acting like a brash, Errol-Flynn style swashbuckler and ladies' man (see *Excalibur Classics* Vol. 1–5 and *Excalibur Visionaries: Alan Davis* Vol. 1 and 2). In contrast, the X-Men universe has not been particularly kind to Italians. Writer Scott Lobdell created Omerta (whose given name was Paul Provenzano) to be a homophobic U.S. army veteran who is recruited by the X-Men as a reserve member before he has completed his bid to take over the Brooklyn Mafia. He shows his true colors by tormenting gay X-Man Northstar, but it isn't long before Omerta learns his lesson — Northstar soon saves his life. Fortunately, the television show *Heroes*, which is inspired in large part by the *X-Men* comic books, created famous, interesting, and three-dimensional Italian American superheroes, the brothers Peter and Nathan Petrelli, to make up somewhat for Omerta.

As these more obscure X-Men characters demonstrate, there are, indeed, enough mutants in *X-Men* for virtually every conceivable reader to relate to. On the other hand, most of these secondary mutant characters, such as Boom Boom and Omerta, are unimportant in the grand scheme of the *X-Men*. Hence their absence from the films, and the frequency with which they, and characters like them, are written out of the comic book, killed, or suddenly (and often inexplicably) turned into villains. Indeed, given the personal backgrounds of the men who have written *X-Men*, and the subtexts of *X-Men*'s most famous adventures, it is fair to say that the fans who read *X-Men* as being primarily about the fight for gay rights, the oppression of Jews, the black power movement, and the feminist movement are those who have the most textual evidence to support their claims.

Despite the varied cultural background of the supporting character mutants, the principal characters form a fairly select group representing very specific peoples. Two of the most important characters in the narrative are Jewish (Magneto and Shadowcat), both the time-traveling Bishop and the X-Men team leader Storm are African American, and the vast majority of famous X-Men are women (Storm, Rogue, Shadowcat, Mystique, Jean Grey, Jubilee, Psylocke, Emma Frost, and Dazzler). Northstar is gay in the comic book and the *X-Men* films suggest symbolically that Angel and Magneto are gay. In addition, the film *X2: X-Men United* features a centerpiece scene in which heterosexual character Bobby Drake has to "come out" to his parents as a mutant and his mother asks him if he can "just ... *stop* being a mutant?"

The basic *X-Men* narrative is deceptively simple, and somewhat similar to the narrative of the Harry Potter adventures. Teenage humans who suddenly demonstrate a seemingly magical ability at the onset of puberty frighten their families with their newfound powers. They are summoned to a special school by a friendly headmaster who seeks to teach them how to control—and to love—their unique gifts. However, an evil magician who hates humans for being prejudiced against his kind hopes to wipe them out and establish wizard kind as the dominant life form on Earth. The wise-but-imperfect headmaster agrees that humans are prejudiced, but stands against the evil wizard's plan for genocide. As powerful as the headmaster is, he sends his young students to fight the evil wizard in his stead while he watches from the sidelines. The headmaster, then, as much shelters his students from the dangerous world as turns them into a paramilitary unit, whether it is called Dumbledore's Army or, in the case of the Marvel universe, the X-Men (and their various subordinate groups).

This barebones plot summary describes both *Harry Potter* and *X-Men* equally well. The Harry Potter saga has been interpreted by critics and fans as, alternatively, an allegory about World War II, the British class system, absent fathers, and what it is like to come-of-age in the British public school system. Regardless of what themes individual *X-Men* storytellers develop in the adventures they craft, critics and fans of the films, cartoons, and comics have their own reasons for embracing the X-universe. Some fans see the *X-Men* story as being generically and universally about the emotional scars of puberty, while others are more interested in what *X-Men* says about immigration, terrorism, gay rights, and race relations.

Many of the writers and artists most associated with crafting the comic books have been Jewish—Stan Lee, Jack Kirby, Chris Claremont, Brian Michael Bendis, Peter David, Jeph Loeb, Adam Kubert, and Andy Kubert—so the comic book understandably often focuses on issues of anti–Semitism and frequently includes flashbacks to the Holocaust. Horrific, recurring conflicts include a series of pogroms and ethnic cleansing campaigns against mutants in the modern day, often led by white supremacists and Christian fanatics.

Aside from Magneto, the most significant Jewish character in the comic book is Kitty Pryde, a teen from suburban Illinois introduced in *Uncanny X-Men* #129 (1980) by John Byrne. She has a mutant power known as "phasing," which allows her to turn intangible and walk through solid objects like a ghost, and has been known by the superhero names Sprite, Ariel, and Shadowcat. Drawn to resemble a young Sigourney Weaver, Kitty has served as an accessible, audience viewpoint character in the mold of Robin, only she soon became more popular than the Boy Wonder ever was.

In the comic book world, the sensitive mutant artist Colossus was Kitty's first love. In the real world, many comic book readers found themselves developing their first crushes on the fictional Kitty. In fact, in the more than thirty years since Kitty's creation, *X-Men* fans have written a steady stream of letters to the editor proclaiming their love for Shadowcat, wishing ardently that she were a real person. The nerdy girl next door, Kitty is a pretty-but-decidedly-normal-looking girl who wears reading glasses, is a computer geek, and enjoys making nerdy jokes about *Star Trek*. Gifted, funny, and neurotic about her physical appearance, Kitty prefigures the personality traits that would later find themselves in heroines such as Hermione Grainger, Buffy Summers, and Juno MacGuff. The source of her appeal is obvious.

Notably, *Wizard Magazine* named her the greatest female comic book character of all time—handily beating Wonder Woman and Buffy the Vampire Slayer—and the 13th greatest comic book character of all time. She is also a personal favorite of writers Joss Whedon and Chris Claremont, who consistently use her as a central character when they write *X-Men*. Her popularity has remain fixed, despite (or because of) the fact that she has adopted a purple dragon, Lockheed, as a pet, served with Captain Britain as defender of England and the Multiverse in the fantasy comic book *Excalibur*, and gotten a little sexier and more aggressive as she has grown older — to the point of even having a torrid affair with John Constantine (a.k.a. Pete Wisdom). The character had cameo appearances in the first two *X-Men* films and was a major supporting character in the third, *X-Men: The Last Stand* (2006) when she was played by Ellen Page. In 2005, writer Brian Michael Bendis introduced Kitty as a love interest for Peter Parker in *Ultimate Spider-Man* Annual #1 (2005), and the two have an on-again, off-again romance.

Kitty Pryde's lack of centrality to the *X-Men* films is one of the factors that underscores the shift between the Jewish-centric focus of the comic books and the gay-theme focus of the films. The *X-Men* film franchise certainly includes Jewish themes, but is arguably more concerned with dramatizing the struggle for GLBTQ acceptance in America. At least two of the major creative figures behind the *X-Men* films are gay actor Ian McKellen and gay director Bryan Singer, who is also Jewish, which accounts for the films' interest in gay rights.

In *X-Men*, a percentage of the human population unexpectedly begins developing superhuman powers at the onset of puberty. The powers range from the modest (the ability to leap far) to the extreme (the power to destroy an entire planet with but a mere thought). An almost preternaturally beautiful physique or a horrifyingly disfigured appearance sometimes accompanies these abilities. The causes of the sudden onset of these powers have changed over time. In the original 1960s era comic books, *X-Men* co-creators Stan Lee and Jack Kirby posited that the powers were a result of the mutation of children born in the nuclear age. These beings were called, respectively, "mutants," "children of the atom," and "x-men" because of the radioactive source of the powers, and because they have "eXtra power" than the average person. During the 1990s, the comic books began discussing the mysterious, recessive "mutant x gene," which somehow coded the powers of the gods into the DNA of select offspring, which are proudly called *homo superior* by mutants rights activists. The initial trilogy of films based on the comic books (helmed by directors Bryan Singer and Brett Ratner, and written by Singer, Tom DeSanto, David Hayter, Simon Kinberg and Michael Dougherty, Dan Harris, and Zak Penn) suggest that the mutants are the next step in human evolution, and the rest of the human race, so-called "normal" *homo sapiens*, need to do real catching up.

Kitty Pryde, a Jewish teenager, has the mutant power to turn intangible and walk through walls. Sometimes known as Ariel or Sprite, Kitty wore this costume and adopted the codename Shadowcat when she joined the British superhero team Excalibur (1988–1998). Illustration by Dave Hoover (courtesy Dave Hoover).

In both the films and the comic books, "normal" people (the "Muggles" of Harry Potter's universe) are afraid of the mutants, partly because the mutants are different, but also because the mutants are powerful and the "normal"s fear their own subjugation and eventual extinction. Consequently, normal *homo sapiens* are perpetually trying to solve the "mutant problem," either by trying to mandate by law a mutant census called the Mutant Registration Act (an initiative spearheaded by Senator Robert Kelly, a Republican from Kansas), building giant robots called Sentinels to use as weapons against mutants, or developing a drug that will "cure" mutants of their powers and restore them to "normal" (in a storyline introduced by writer Joss Whedon). In response to these hostile moves on the part of humanity, two mutant leaders have emerged, the radical terrorist and mutants' rights activist Erik Lehnsherr, and the more moderate, philosophical teacher Charles Xavier.

Erik Lehnsherr, also known as Magneto, has responded violently to the prejudice of humans. A member of the World War II generation and a Jew, Magneto survived the Holocaust because he developed the power to control metal, which enabled him to escape from a Nazi concentration camp. Fearing that a new Holocaust is coming, perpetrated by *homo sapiens* against *homo superior*, Magneto wishes to strike first. He begins his war on humanity with a tactical strike against a U.S. army base, and soon starts actively recruiting embittered mutants into his Brotherhood of Mutants. In the first *X-Men* film (2000), Magneto posits that all prejudice will end if all of humanity finally evolves into mutantkind, and there is no longer a division between mutant and non-mutant. He believes that, inevitably, everyone on earth will become a mutant, but that something has gone wrong and the evolutionary process is going in fits and starts, and not everyone is evolving, neatly, at the same time. As Magneto puts it, "God works too slowly." He attempts to force the evolution of humanity, starting with the leaders of the world, who will become much more pro-mutant in their governmental policies once they themselves experience a mutation and understand how the other half lives. However, Magneto's machine does not work—it kills instead of mutates. Learning that the machine is deadly, Xavier sends his X-Men to destroy the machine and arrest Magneto.

A powerful mutant telepath the same age as Magneto, Xavier founded his School for Gifted Youngsters in Westchester, New York, specifically to teach frightened teenage mutants how to accept, adapt to, and use their newfound powers. He tracks down newborn mutants with a computer called Cerebro, and sees to the training of the most powerful (and most emotionally disturbed) mutants himself. The older students, who have already become experts at controlling their powers and who are, essentially, happy to be mutants, mentor the younger students. In addition to their roles as mentors, the older students comprise a military strike force called the X-Men. These X-Men confront and capture rogue mutants who endanger human/mutant relations through acts of selfish criminality or acts of terrorism against humans. In doing so, they protect *homosapien* lives from *homosuperior* aggression, and create a more stable political environment from which Xavier can negotiate for mutant rights and improve the general public's perception of mutants. An adherent of Ghandi's philosophy of passive resistance, Xavier hopes that humans will respond to mutants with less fear and more acceptance when they see how nice and reasonable most law-abiding mutants are.

For his part, Magneto believes that Xavier is living in a fantasy world, and that "Professor X" and his X-Men are a group of misguided, "Uncle Tom" figures. "A Tale of Two Mutants," a 1999 story by Alan Davis and Joe Kelly featured in *X-Men* #85, features two parallel stories that illustrate well the difference between the two men, their philosophies, and their expectations. In the first narrative, Xavier sends the X-Men to rescue patients trapped in a burning hospital, especially the babies in the maternity ward. They succeed in containing the fire and rescuing the children, but the police who arrive fear that the mutants caused the fire in the first place and are holding the children hostage. The X-Men leader, a black female mutant named Storm, steps forward, holding two swaddled infants and says to the police, "Officers, we are the X-Men and we are here to save your children. Please lower your weapons." The officer in charge, a human who also happens to be a black woman, confronts Storm. After a tense moment, the officer orders her men to stand down and allow the X-Men to continue their rescue and clean-up efforts. When all is done, the officer says to Storm, "X-Men, huh? Never been this close to a real mutant before." Storm replies, "Get closer, officer. We do not bite." Observing this moment from afar, Xavier thinks to himself, "The greatest part of being a teacher is learning from one's students. The dream is alive. Thank you, my X-Men."

Magneto's counter-narrative is far different in tone and climax. Dressing in a fine white suit, he disguises himself as the board member of a corporation and approaches the foreman of a construction site — a likeable man named Bill Jones who Magneto describes as being of "average" intelligence, from an "average" family, living an "average" life who Magneto admits he might even like personally, if Magneto didn't feel "instinctual loathing of his kind." Magneto's goal is to determine the extent to which the foreman is mutant phobic. The stakes of the test are high, as Magneto thinks, "Today Bill Jones determines whether humanity lives or dies." Magneto tests Bill by suggesting there is concern among board members that one of the construction workers is a mutant. Bill seems to pass the test, appearing uncomfortable with the anti-mutant slurs Magneto slips into his speech and objecting to the idea of starting a mutant witch-hunt on his construction site. As Magneto continues to ask Bill blunt, probing questions to uncover Bill's true political views, Bill balks and says, "If you want to figure somebody out with the question game you have to be more subtle ... like ... if you could go back in time and kill Hitler as a baby, would you do it? See? Not so easy when the answer's not black-and-white."

But Bill has made a mistake evoking Hitler as a good example of a hypothetical evil, as Magneto himself lived through the tyrant's reign. At that moment, he unmasks himself as Magneto, levitates himself above Bill's head, and shouts, "You're *wrong*, Mister Jones. It's not a difficult question *at all*. The answer is yes. To save millions of lives I would track the child down at his home and smother him where he lay. Then I would destroy his family, his family's family, *I would raze an entire city from the ground and scatter his ashes from the earth!*" Now revealed as a powerful, furious mutant, Magneto asks Bill, "Face your fear, my friend. Face the truth. [Mutants] were meant to rule. Tell me, Bill, do you still want to share coffee and a dirty joke?" Crying, Bill yells back, "No! I want you dead! Dead!"

Magneto looks down upon Bill silently for a long moment. Then he says, quietly, "Thank you, Bill. Your honesty is appreciated. I have my answers. Even an everyman with a kind heart becomes a rabid beast at the sight of that which he does not understand. It's simply human nature."

Recovering a little, and absorbing the ramifications of what he himself has said, and of Magneto's condemnation, Bill replies, "No.... It doesn't have to be like this ... you could have ... if you had just said something instead of— I'm just a man! What choice did I have after what you did? I was scared! Not because you were a mutant — but because you're a monster! A sick and twisted monster!"

Magneto leaves abruptly without replying, and returns to his secret base of operations, convinced of his own fundamental correctness. "Given the chance, they'd see our kind swept from the earth," he says to himself. "I ... do not want to do this ... but they've forced my hand. There can never be peace."

The story builds upon concepts introduced by Stan Lee and Jack Kirby, but molded and developed by Chris Claremont and John Byrne during a fruitful period of collaboration on the comic book *Uncanny X-Men* in the early 1980s. Their work, more than Lee's and Kirby's, has influenced the shape of the *X-Men* films and cartoons, and the writers who have followed their examples in the ensuing decades. A Jewish writer, Claremont was the person who revealed Magneto's Jewish background, as well as his tortured childhood as a victim of Nazi brutality, and he has consistently imbued Magneto with a tragic, often sympathetic quality. His stories with Magneto sometimes suggest that mutants are right to fear humans, especially since some time-traveling mutants have discovered possible futures in which there are, indeed, Holocausts for mutants (see the classic *Days of Future Past* storyline and its many sequels). Other stories are more critical of Magneto, citing him for hypocrisy and condemning him for becoming a mirror image of Adolf Hitler, a madman bent on genocide in the name of preventing genocide.

Directly tackling the contentious portrayal of Magneto as a vengeful Jew, Ami Eden observed in a 2003 article for *Forward: The Jewish Daily* that the conflict between Xavier and Magneto in the *X-Men* films paralleled the "post–Holocaust theological divide" between Rabbi Irving "Yitz" Greenberg and Rabbi Meir Kahane. Greenberg advocated a secularist, globalist, and pacifistic future for the Jewish people, while Kahane argued that Jews should defy persecution — especially Islamic antagonism — by becoming devout, militarist, and isolationist. Eden argues that, in a post–9/11 world, Kahane's worldview is particularly seductive, but that Greenberg's approach is the only sane one, and the only one that will lead to a stable world.

In "Israel Invades Gaza," liberal Jewish playwright, actor, and cultural critic Wallace Shawn (*My Dinner With Andre*) argues much the same thing, explaining that the emotional scars of World War II have made some Jewish militarists incapable of recognizing that the Palestinian people are not blindly anti–Semitic as Hitler was, but have a legitimate grievance against Israel and the United States. After all, Shawn argues, the Western powers that assuaged their guilt over the Holocaust by granting the Jews a homeland in an area that was already occupied was not, in the end, an act of kindness. He adds that the creation of Israel was clearly motivated, in part, by the West's desire to place a friendly regime in an oil-rich region of the world (*Essays* 93–96).

Sentiments such as these are deeply controversial, and have been hotly contested by other thinkers, such as Alan Dershowitz, who believes that such views are sympathetic to terrorists and undermine the sovereignty and legitimacy of Israel as a nation. Notably, Jews who are politically in sympathy with Dershowitz might have a very different reading of the *X-Men* saga as a commentary on Jewish life. For example, a Jewish reader might interpret the mutant-killing Sentinels as symbolically representative of Muslim fundamentalist terrorists, or interpret the total annihilation of Genosha, the mutant homeland, as a possible apocalyptic future for Israel, and as a warning against taking a complacent view of anti–Israel sentiments in the Middle East. Interestingly, in the comic book, Magneto spends little or no time discussing the Israeli-Palestinian conflict, and confines himself with fighting Republican Senators, grassroots bigot organizations, and evil Christian televangelists. This is perhaps because the Israeli-Palestinian conflict is so fundamentally controversial that Marvel doesn't want to go near it.

As valid, intriguing, and politically explosive as these divergent interpretations of the *X-Men* saga as Jewish narrative are, they are merely two examples of the many intelligent, deeply personal interpretations of a source material that is as malleable as it is politically provocative. Indeed, while Eden has a liberal reading of the *X-Men*, some *X-Men* fans, Jewish and non–Jewish alike, are politically conservative. Generally speaking, conservative *X-Men* fans tend to relate most strongly to a violent Canadian X-Man who "is the best there is at what he does, but what he does best isn't very nice."

Wolverine, the final major character in the *X-Men* saga, has sided with Xavier but has Magneto's bitter, vengeful personality. He is also the most reluctant to discuss, at length, "the mutant cause," and sometimes seems detached from the X-Men's mission. Indeed, Wolverine sometimes boasts of his lack of devotion to the X-Men, but he is the one most likely to mentor its youngest, most vulnerable member (in the comic books, Shadowcat and Jubilee, in the movies, Rogue), and he seems to be in more *X-Men* adventures than any other mutant. He also has reasons to be militant, as the government has exploited him because of his mutant abilities. He has been experimented on by the Canadian military and greeted with fear by the general public, yet he has a reluctance to declare his allegiance to the X-Men similar to the reluctance Han Solo showed in joining the rebellion in *Star Wars*. His insistence that he is not a victim when he obviously is, his undisclosed past, and his too-cool-for-school attitude sometimes do more to limit him as a character, and distance him from the reader, than make him compelling.

Although he calls himself Logan, Wolverine is not sure what his real name is and most often goes by his apt code-name, which he shares with a small-but-tenacious-wild-animal. Wolverine is easy to wound, but his ability to heal almost instantly from multiple gunshot wounds makes him seem, at times, even more invincible than Superman on the battlefield. He has the gruff personality and tough-love values of Clint Eastwood's "Man with No Name" character, Freddy Krueger's knife hands growing out of his metal skeleton, and he consistently demonstrates a near–Punisher-level willingness to kill his enemies.

Wolverine is, in some ways, amazingly ancillary to the core plot — the conflict between Charles Xavier and Magneto — but he is also the mutant who is most beloved by the general *X-Men* readership. He is popular, perhaps, because he is in the mold of a Clint Eastwood or Charles Bronson action hero, so he appeals to conservative, macho readers who might not find the comic books' otherwise liberal sensibilities palatable if he were not a cast member. Thematically, Wolverine is there to reassure the heterosexual male readership of their primacy — by being relentlessly "cool," abrasive, and in lust with Jean Grey — even as the majority of the characters in the comic book are strong-willed women and gay rights activists. Dramatically, Wolverine proves his usefulness, and protects his centrality in the narrative, by often being the one to win victory for the X-Men on the battlefield, even though one might assume that Storm the weather witch, or Jean Grey the telepath, should be able to bring about a more conclusive victory more rapidly than a scrappy guy dressed in yellow with perpetual five-o'clock-shadow and knives for hands. However, as appealing as Wolverine can be (especially when he is portrayed on film by actor Hugh Jackman) and as much as he likes to try to steal the spotlight from the other mutants, whose stories are more complex, emotional, and thematically relevant, he cannot overshadow the power of the central story, which celebrates the rights of the individual, and the beautiful diversity of humanity in the face of prejudice, oppression, and the horrors of genocide, both within the American borders and abroad.

When writer and director Bryan Singer assumed the responsibility for adapting the *X-Men* comic books into a film franchise, he emphasized the political elements of the comic books and minimized their more outlandish science fiction elements (surgically removing the cheesy robots and aliens) to help foreground the themes of tolerance versus prejudice, terrorism versus passive resistance, and the perpetration and prevention of genocide. Since Bryan Singer is both Jewish and gay, he had a vested interest in making the movies as serious and dramatically effective as possible, despite the first film's low budget and the public's lack of knowledge of the *X-Men* comic books, which were famous only in comic book fan circles and to viewers of Saturday morning cartoons.

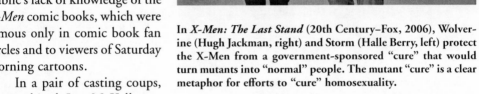

In *X-Men: The Last Stand* (20th Century–Fox, 2006), Wolverine (Hugh Jackman, right) and Storm (Halle Berry, left) protect the X-Men from a government-sponsored "cure" that would turn mutants into "normal" people. The mutant "cure" is a clear metaphor for efforts to "cure" homosexuality.

In a pair of casting coups, Singer hired Ian McKellen—Best Actor Oscar nominee for playing legendary *Bride of Frankenstein* director and gay film icon James Whale in *Gods and Monsters* (1998)—as Magneto and Patrick Stewart—another Shakespearean actor who starred in *I, Claudius* and became famous in America playing Captain Jean-Luc Picard in *Star Trek: The Next Generation*—as Xavier. The then-unknown Hugh Jackman was perfectly cast as Wolverine, and two Oscar-winning actresses, Anna Paquin and Halle Berry, brought the characters of Rogue and Storm to life. The high quality of the writing, acting, and directing, coupled with the personal stake the actor's felt in the political sensibilities of the film, conspired to make the first *X-Men* movie one of the best and most serious superhero movies. The 2000 film, and the two sequels that followed, took on prejudice of all kinds, but—thanks to the specific concerns of Bryan Singer and Ian McKellen—was particularly strong in its condemnation of anti–Semitism and homophobia.

In October of 2003, in a BBC interview with Stephen Applebaum, Bryan Singer revealed that he relates strongly to the X-Men as outsider figures because he is not only Jewish (like Shadowcat) and gay (like Northstar), but adopted; with little knowledge of his personal history (like Wolverine), he grew up feeling alienated at school because he was a poor student. Singer grew up with a dread of intolerance that caused him to become deeply obsessed with the Holocaust. This fascination and horror at man's inhumanity to man inspired him to direct the *X-Men* films, as well as World War II–themed films *Apt Pupil* (1998) and *Valkyrie* (2008).[3]

Singer was particularly intent on exploring gay themes in the *X-Men* films because he saw homosexuals as the ultimate outsiders. According to Singer, a Jewish or African American child can still grow up within the comfort zone of a Jewish or African American family or community, whereas gay youths often lack that safe haven, discovering their sexual orientations as adolescents and finding themselves with the challenge of having to live amongst straight parents and classmates, sometimes never figuring out how to live their lives. In the interview, Singer laughingly admitted that he was using the *X-Men* films as a vehicle to explore his own personal situation. "I could think of no better place to spill out one's own personal problems and foist them onto the world" he said "than in a giant, action, summer event movie!"

Certainly, the seriousness of the political commentary in the film, and the earnest performances by a cast with an excellent acting pedigree, elevates the material. The films can be uneven at points, causing film critic Roger Ebert to observe that he preferred the dramatic and political segments to the action segments. He also raised the possibility that superhero narratives were not sophisticated enough to tackle serious issues such as genocide, and that attempting to comment on real-life atrocities in a glorified action story is arguably in bad taste. As he wrote, in his 2001 review of *X-Men*:

> *X-Men* is at least not a manic editing frenzy for atrophied attention spans. It's restrained and introspective for a superhero epic, and fans of the comic books may like that. Graphic novels (as they sometimes deserve to be called) take themselves as seriously as the ones without pictures, and you can tell that here when the opening scene shows Jews being forced into death camps in Poland in 1944. One could argue that the Holocaust is not appropriate subject matter for an action movie based on a comic book, but having talked to some *X-Men* fans I believe that in their minds the medium is as deep and portentous as, say, *Sophie's Choice.*

By the time *X-Men 3: The Last Stand* is released in 2006, Ebert is more accustomed to *X-Men*'s seemingly incongruous pairing of superhero battle scenes with political commentary, and has grown more thoughtful about the issue. He has made note of the same provocative themes that the notion of "curing" mutants raises, but believes that the film is only partial successful at treating these issues thoughtfully and honestly:

> There are so many parallels here with current political and social issues that to list them is to define the next presidential campaign. Just writing the previous paragraph, I thought of abortion, gun control, stem cell research, the "gay gene" and the Minutemen. "Curing" mutants is obviously a form of genetic engineering and stirs thoughts of "cures" for many other conditions humans are born with, which could be loosely defined as anything that prevents you from being just like George or Georgette Clooney. The fact is, most people grow accustomed to the hands they've been dealt and rather resent the opportunity to become "normal." (Normal in this context is whatever makes you more like them and less like yourself.)
>
> *X-Men: The Last Stand* raises all of these questions in embryonic form, but doesn't engage them in much detail, because it is often distracted by the need to be an action movie.

Although the incongruous mix of action and politics might not appeal to a sophisticated filmgoer like Ebert, who has seen far more art and independent films than the average multiplex attendee, it is arguably the perfect mix of action and activism to win over a mainstream audience and awaken an interest in politics in an adolescent viewer. While there are some viewers who are not attuned enough to social issues to even catch some of the political references, and others who choose to ignore the liberal propaganda and focus on how cool it is when Wolverine disembowels someone, there are other viewers who are drawn to *X-Men* precisely because it is sensitive to issues of prejudice and challenges racism, xenophobia, and homophobia.

The *X-Men* films are remarkable in that they are far more overtly pro-gay than most superhero stories, which market themselves to a straight audience. This is surprising because Frederic Wertham condemned comic books for their gay themes, and fans have often speculated that certain heroes are secretly gay, such as Batman, Wonder Woman, and the Doctor, but those speculations usually happen outside of the comic books themselves. Certainly, there have been jokes along these lines. When Dr. Strange was reunited with "the girl next door," Amanda Payne, the two were instantly attracted to one another, but Payne worried that "y'know, with those clothes and that beard ... living in Greenwich Village and all—are you gay?" When asked this, Dr. Strange laughed heartily.[4] In *Mark of Zorro* (1940), Don Diego Vega (Tyrone Power) poses as gay to convince the evil overlords of Southern California that he couldn't possibly be the people's hero Zorro that has been bedeviling them. The sensitive Bruce Banner of the Hulk has been often regarded as gay, and the Hulk the manifestation of the anger that General "Thunderbolt" Ross' homophobia created (or, alternatively, rage at Ross' anti–Semitic reaction to a "nice Jewish boy" courting his daughter Betty, and not a Protestant, John Wayne–type like himself). Tony Stark (Iron Man) has also been read as gay. When a war wound forced Tony to live out his life with artificial body parts imbedded in his chest and around his heart, his former womanizing days came to an end. He then spent years playing the part of the playboy, but not acting on it, nursing a secret shame—and an inability to consummate sexual love with a woman—that made him seem like one of Rock Hudson's closeted lotharios.

In J. Michael Straczynski's "Interlude," Aunt May discovers that her nephew, Peter, is Spider-Man. She is angry with him for hiding his secret identity from her for years, but admits that she knew he was keeping some kind of secret from her. "On top of that, you were quiet and sensitive, you didn't like sports, you were awkward around girls, and ... to tell you the truth, Peter, for a while I thought maybe you were gay, which I was prepared to accept either way, because you were still you. I mean, I knew something was in the closet. Could've been chiffon. Who knew it was a costume?"[5] While this kind of humor might not appeal to everyone, Aunt May is a model of tolerance and acceptance that is truly moving.

Peter Parker did spend twenty years (our time, not his) married to Mary Jane Watson in the comic books, but he also spent ten years (our time) living a celibate life after the death of Gwen Stacy, vowing never to endanger another woman again by being involved with her. *Slate* commentator Chris Suellentrop described Spider-Man's celibacy as a "superhero calling" and "a voluntary priesthood" that comments symbolically on celibacy in the Catholic Church, and speaks directly to its pedophilia scandals. According to Suellentrop, the message of Spider-Man's celibacy is: "Only superheroes are fit for lives of celibacy, and as we've learned, not all priests are superheroes."[6]

Playwright Rona Munro wrote the final episode of the original *Doctor Who* series, "Survival" (1989), which explored a lesbian relationship between the Doctor's traveling companion, Ace, and the warrior Karra of the Cheetah People. The story also condemned the human tendency to give into animal instincts and "fight or flight" responses instead of negotiating disputes like properly evolved beings and resolving problems peacefully. Indeed, one of the villains of the tale is a bully of a self-defense instructor who teaches troubled teens that social Darwinism is the law of the land and only the strong triumph. In "Survival"'s climactic moment, the Doctor engages in a fight to the death with his archenemy, the Master. When the Doctor gets the upper hand, and has the opportunity to bash the Master's skull in with a rock, he feels himself literally devolving into a wild animal. He drops the rock, offering the Master a truce, and proclaims, "If we fight like animals, we die like animals!" The lesbian love depicted between Ace and Karra is another possible redemptive force in the story, offering a loving existence as an alternative to a kill-or-be-killed one.

Since major franchises such as *Star Trek* are also not known for consistently advocating gay causes or featuring gay and lesbian characters, it leaves gays in the position of having to rewrite the established narrative—either in their imaginations or through slash fiction—to imagine Kirk and Spock, for example, in a gay relationship. The television series *Xena:*

Warrior Princess (1995–2001) played with the relationship between Xena and Gabrielle for years, tantalizing lesbian viewers until the characters were finally outed in the series finale. Other oft-appropriated characters include Samwise and Frodo from the *Lord of the Rings* and Sherlock Holmes and Doctor John Watson. Some historians have challenged queer readings of these British classics, on the basis that Americans don't understand British friendships, or the World War I concept of the "batman," which is clearly the position of fiercely loyal servitude that Samwise occupied in relation to Frodo.

The Holmes and Watson relationship has been particularly controversial, and has inspired a number of memorable — and completely irreconcilable — "readings." This is possibly partly due to the fact that Watson reveals little about his wives or his married life, which muddies the narrative waters enough that many scholars and fans are confused as to how many times Watson was married, and to whom. They all agree, however, he was married once to Mary Morstan, the heroine of *The Sign of Four* (1890). June Thompson maintains that Holmes and Watson were merely wonderful friends, and that was the nature of their relationship:

> It was not, I believe, homosexual, although some evidence in the canon might suggest, upon first reading, a homoerotic relationship, such as the fact that Holmes and Watson share a double bed during the Man With the Twisted Lip inquiry or that Holmes bundles Watson out of sight in the Dying Detective Case with the words, "Quick, man, if you love me!" Although on occasions he might have been naïf, Watson possessed a great deal of common sense and, knowing, as he must have done, the penalties of social ostracism should sexual deviation be suspected, or imprisonment should he be found engaging in homosexual activities, he would hardly have risked arousing suspicion by publishing these admissions unless he knew his own and Holmes' sexual behavior was beyond reproach.
>
> Watson, one of whom's most endearing qualities was an inability to lie convincingly, was incapable of carrying out such a sustained deception on his readers [10–11].

Thomson theorized that Watson was happily married twice — to Mary Morstan and Grace Dunbar.[7] William S. Baring-Gould posited that Holmes and Irene Adler had a son together, Nero Wolfe, and that Watson was thrice married and thrice widowed (to Constance Adams, an American, then Mary Morstan, and then Lady Francis Carfax).[8] Other authors (including Rex Stout and Marilyn MacGregor) have suggested that Holmes and Watson were lovers, but that either Holmes or Watson was secretly a woman.[9]

Laurie R. King has written a series of novels in which a 59-year-old Sherlock Holmes marries a *very* young, Jewish, cross-dressing Oxford University theology student, Mary Russell, and the two solve cases together with the occasional help of "Uncle John" Watson and "Brother-in-law" Mycroft. Like Baring-Gould, King's books also reveal that Holmes and Adler had a child, only in King's version that child is the surrealist painter, and possible criminal, Damien Adler.[10] When Holmes and Russell share their first, passionate kiss in *A Monstrous Regiment of Women* (1995), the two characters are presented as being in complete ecstasy — but they still manage to tease one another in between kisses:

> "By God," he murmured throatily in my hair. "I've wanted to do that since the moment I laid eyes upon you." ...
>
> "Holmes," I objected when I could draw breath, "when you first saw me, you thought I was a boy." ...
>
> "And don't think that didn't cause me some minutes of deep consternation," he said [273].

That bit of dialogue is odd — a mixture of phobic and funny that makes it unclear where King's version of Holmes falls on the Kinsey scale. He certainly likes girls, but how much he likes boys is not revealed. In her fiction there is an extent to which King is striving to dramatize a classic female sex fantasy—in which a strong, alluring young woman melts the heart of a male-chauvinist, Henry Higgins–style lover (see Haskell)—without completely spoiling interpretations of Holmes as being bisexual or gay.

While these are the straight depictions of Holmes, there are several notable gay ones. Billy Wilder's *Private Life of Sherlock Holmes* (1970) and the BBC series *Sherlock* (which is, interestingly, set in modern day) both play with the possibility that Holmes is gay. More daring, Rohase Piercy's novel, *My Dearest Holmes* (2007), suggests that Watson married Mary Morstan to fool the homophobic British public about the mutual love he and Holmes shared. Bisexual actor Jeremy Brett played homes as bisexual in the Granada *Sherlock Holmes* series (1984–1994) and in love with Watson, Adler, and Enrico Firmani. Rupert Everett played Holmes as in love with Watson and jealous of Watson's American bride in *Sherlock Holmes and the Case of the Silk Stocking* (2005). Robert Downey, Jr., joked in interviews that his Holmes and Jude Law's Watson were a couple, and that Morstan was Watson's "beard" in *Sherlock Holmes* (2009), but nothing overt was depicted on screen.

Like the divergent readings of the *X-Men* comic books, these different versions of Holmes, presented by critics, pastiche writers, and film and television adaptations, show how rich a character Holmes is and how invested certain people are in his sexual orientation. Many of these portrayals work on their own terms, but the least convincing portrayals of Holmes are the ones when he is the most romantic heterosexually, as in the silent film *Sherlock Holmes* (1922), where John Barrymore plays the detective as a virtual Romeo. The Mary Russell novels are good enough that they work despite the occasional nagging feeling that something isn't right about the romance.

Indeed, it is difficult to come up with a "reading" of Holmes' sexuality that seems to accurately take into account his asexual, emotional scientist inclinations, his unclear feelings for Irene Adler, his deep friendship with Watson, and his flirtation with Charles Augustus Milverton's maid, among other things. Arguably, Jeremy Brett's bisexual portrayal of Holmes solves all of these problems, even making all of the above narratives fit together to a degree. Brett's bisexual Holmes has a kinship with his Victorian contemporary, Oscar Wide, whom Holmes expressed sympathy for (in the 1976 Nicholas Meyer pastiche *The West End Horror*) after Wilde's life was ruined by the public revelation of his affair with Lord Alfred Douglas. Unlike the sanitized, dull, heroic ideal version of Holmes portrayed by Basil Rathbone in the World War II era Hollywood films, Brett's Holmes was a very real, very exciting variant of the character. As Steven Doyle and David A. Crowder wrote in 2010:

> Brett's performance came like a thunderclap to viewers used to the traditional interpretation of Holmes. Whereas previous Sherlocks tended to fix on individual characteristics of Holmes's complex personality, Brett presented the full character, warts and all. Not only did Brett's performance finally replace Rathbone's as Sherlock Holmes in the public mind, but it also changed the public's understanding of Holmes. No longer was Sherlock a stuffy old-fashioned straight arrow, saying, "Elementary, my dear Watson," while being followed around by a doddering old duffer. No, Brett's Holmes was mesmerizing, brilliant, moody, drug-abusing, and, to be honest, a bit scary [279].

Indeed, Brett is so superb as Holmes that he is not only the best screen Holmes of all time, but arguably the most compelling, charismatic bisexual character in the history of popular culture. As much of a mess as Holmes' life is, he is arguably not a great role model for young gays or bisexuals per se, but he is sympathetic, and that goes a long way.

According to Phil Jiminez, a writer and artist who is also gay, there is a lot at stake when it comes to the sexuality of characters such as Holmes:

> I think it matters very much; some disagree with me, but I think the way we self identify absolutely affects the way we receive and process fiction. When we learn characters are more or less like us in very personal, and some times socio-political ways, it affects our affection for them. I always think the sexuality of characters should be an organic, natural outgrowth of the character and not foisted upon them; however, if it hasn't been established one way or the other and it makes sense, I think it's always fair game to tweak a character's back story for such a reveal.
>
> I do think it's worth noting that I'm one of those people that parses language — male, female, masculine, feminine, gay, queer, etc. I think a character can have a gay sensibility but still be "straight," sexually; I think a character can be totally straight in their social sensibilities but be physically attracted to someone of the same gender.

Jiminez doesn't name Spider-Man here, but that is a very valid reading of Peter Parker — a straight man with a classically female personality. This would also explain why his personality translates so well to the personalities of female superheroes who act a lot like him: Buffy Summers and Kitty Pryde.

Jiminez's goal is to create more GLBTQI characters for comic books than there are currently, but he admits that there are many challenges to writing gay characters in a way that will appeal to a broad range of readers:

> most minority characters of any kind get stuck with representing whole swaths of people..., there are as many different kinds of gay people as there are people on the planet, from all walks of social, racial, and economic life. I don't think any character should be saddled with representing the entire gay population; I also think it's absolutely impossible, and usually dooms a character to oblivion. Same with minority characters, same with female characters.
>
> [t]he only gay character I've ever written extensively — Kevin Zapada in "Otherworld" — was based on a couple of gay friends of mine (and me, when I was younger). The intent ... was to explore the rejection many gay people feel from religious or spiritual institutions and their embrace instead of secular, commercial ones.... Ultimately, none of it feeds our spiritual selves. It's stuff we vigorously invest in and defend, but what does it do for us, really, except carve out an acceptable niche?
>
> In "Otherworld," Kevin ends up so enraptured by the secular, technological-driven world to which he and his friends are taken, which doesn't judge him for his sexuality or his ethnic background, and actually celebrates him or it — and rejects his allies and misguidedly sides with the main villain to defend this Land, free of the intolerance and harsh religious dogma he's known his whole life. I'd consider that flawed; However, most gay journalists who interviewed me ... wanted to know if the character was going to get

In the television series *The Adventures of Sherlock Holmes* (1984), Jeremy Brett played Sherlock Holmes (left) as a bisexual in love with both Dr. John Watson (David Burke, right) and Irene Adler (Gayle Hunnicutt, not pictured).

> a boyfriend and kick ass. ... I realized that for many gay readers, all they wanted to see was a gay character in romantic situations who could do some damage to villains.... I realized that I'd leapt right over some basics — the simple desire to see a "normal" out, gay super-hero that could maybe end up on the Justice League one day.

Jiminez does cite Hulking and Wikkan of the *Young Avengers* as two of the best mainstream gay characters in comic books, and worth greater exposure to the general public.

Similarly, while they are imperfect in many ways, the literally gay and symbolically gay characters in the *X-Men* films tell GLBTQI members of the audience that they are not alone. It is a rare message indeed, even in an era following Ellen DeGeneres' coming out and the inclusion of gay characters in supporting roles in a variety of sitcoms, reality TV shows, and dramas.[11] McKellen's complex performance as Magneto with a threefold grudge against mainstream American culture as a persecuted gay man, a Jew, and a mutant, casts him at times as a villain, at times as a revolutionary, and sometimes even as a hero. Again, while he may not necessarily make a wonderful role model for a given viewer — irrespective of sexual orientation, he is clearly in the upper-echelon of excellent gay or bisexual characters in mainstream American popular culture.

In fact, while most comic book fans do not share the opinion, the *X-Men* films are distinguished by being superior to their source material. They benefit from excellent writing and acting, and boast representations of Wolverine, Xavier, Magneto, Rogue, Ice Man, Jean Grey, and the Beast that are infinitely superior to their comic book incarnations. Shadowcat and Cyclops (James Marsden) are very good in the films as well, but they have comparatively little screen time, making their biggest fans less likely to embrace the films. The only real disappointment is Storm, who should have been played by Angela Bassett, and who should have exuded more strength and maturity. Still, there are only so many X-Men the films can portray at once, and the central characters are pitch-perfect.

Magneto in particular is a screen triumph. The Magneto of the printed page, like too many comic book characters, is a steroid-enhanced, over-the-top supervillain dressed in red spandex and a silly red helmet. In deference to the comics, McKellen is briefly saddled with this helmet in a handful of scenes in each film, and that is unfortunate. Otherwise, he is a far better physical fit for what the character Magneto would be like in real life — a frail, older man who survived the Holocaust and is, paradoxically, infinitely powerful thanks to his control of all of the magnetic forces around the globe. Like Yoda, McKellen's Magneto is far stronger than he looks, and that makes for superb dramatic effect.

McKellen is also adept at playing Magneto because Magneto is designed to be a sympathetic antagonist in the mold of Shakespeare's charismatic villains, and McKellen is the Shakespearean actor Harold Bloom praised for giving the best ever stage performance of Richard III. Traditionally, Shakespeare's villains Edmund, the bastard son of the Earl of Gloucester, and Shylock, the Jewish moneylender from *The Merchant of Venice*, have been played as demonically evil or comic, but many actors have found in Shakespeare's original prose evidence that these figures have reason to be angry, and can justify their violent actions as retaliation for past wrongs. Edmund's speech proclaiming that he, a child conceived in passion, should be Gloucester's true legal heir, while his "legitimate" brother Edgar, who was the issue of a marriage of convenience, is the true abomination, is excellent drama. Similarly, several of Shylock's speeches about the abuses he suffered from Italian anti–Semitism are deeply affecting, and his speech "If you prick us do we not bleed?" has been viewed as an unlikely inspiration for Martin Luther King, Jr.'s, "I Have a Dream" speech. One should not overstate the sympathetic aspects of Shylock who, like Marlowe's *Jew of Malta*, is tainted by anti–Semitism, but Shylock remains an excellent character nonetheless, unlike Dickens' Fagin from *Oliver Twist*, who is simply too loathsome to stomach. One of the things that helps distinguish Magneto from Shylock and Fagin is that he is consistently written by Jews who understand his anger and empathize with him. Also unlike Shylock, Magneto has been portrayed as a hero on several occasions — including during the first half of *X2: X-Men United* (2003) — and even led the X-Men at one point during a period after he and Xavier's teams had been at each other's throats for years.

As anyone who has visited discussion boards and chat rooms on the World Wide Web knows, there are a host of unintelligent, snarky, sexist, and racist comments made by anonymous posters online every day. The internet is both blessed and cursed by the fact that it is a realm in which the id may be unchained, and individuals hiding behind the safety of assumed names and avatars can use their newfound freedom to express themselves for good or ill. Fortunately, Ian McKellen's personal web site is one of the few places where one can find intelligent comments from comic book fans on the political content of comic books and on the ethical code and morality that comic books promote. Part of the reason for this is that the abhorrent feedback is screened out, but that doesn't mean that all of the messages published on the page are universally positive.

Many of the posters are sympathetic to McKellen's efforts to promote gay rights and frame their remarks thoughtfully and sensitively. The most interesting comments posit different ways in which viewers interpret what "mutants" mean to them in a real-world context; many posters comment on similarities between Magneto and real life activists, whether they be Malcolm X or British gay rights activist Peter Tatchell, while others wonder to what extent McKellen is comfortable with the representation of Magneto as a villainous Jewish figure, or villainous gay man. As correspondent James Veldon argued, "I don't think Magneto, Toad etc give young gay people, black people, Jews, the disabled, non-nationals or non–Christians positive role models (a topic you discuss in relation to this movie) and neither do the inoffensive, closeted, self-loathing good guys. If you accept this reading, even as a possibility, then was your experience as a gay man used to perpetrate straight propaganda?"

In the first *X-Men* film trilogy, gay actor Ian McKellen played Erik Lehnsherr (Magneto) as a man who has suffered a lifetime of racist persecution because he is Jewish, gay, and a mutant. Seeking to destroy those who have wronged him and his people, Magneto leads a leftist terrorist campaign against the governments of the world in the hopes on installing a new, mutant world order and make "normals" into the powerless minority. From *X-Men: The Last Stand* (20th Century–Fox, 2006).

McKellen replied:

> I am certain that the story devised by Bryan Singer and Tom De Santo was not intended to demonise Jews, gays et al. Rather they might simply be illustrating that institutionalised ill-treatment of innocents can breed violence a generation later. Magneto's conscious response to Auschwitz (where significantly he discovers his mutancy), is to be

> alert to other legalised discrimination. His decision to match mutant-bashers with military force is explained but not lauded in the movie...
>
> Some might be persuaded by Magneto's violent politicking as, without his intervention, the wicked senator's prejudice could have prevailed. Others may be troubled about the film's representation of minorities. I'm heartened by mailers who say they use *X-Men* in the classroom to debate the issues it raises.

He further summed up his feelings on the role of the Magneto character in reply to a separate Veldon letter:

> The central disagreement between Magneto and Professor Xavier can be related to the divide evident in all human rights struggles between those who are prepared to use violence and those who are not. Beyond that, I wouldn't look to the film or the original comics' storylines to illuminate the particular problems of gay activism. As for my own sympathies, they lie with the Professor's concern to give mutants pride in their abilities.

Veldon and McKellen both have equally understandable and compelling reactions to the *X-Men* films as gay narratives. There is an extent to which the films are very effective at promoting tolerance for gays, especially the third installment, *X-Men: The Last Stand*, in which the discovery of a drug that "cures" mutants and makes them human enrages the X-Men as much as it angers Magneto. There is an extent to which the humans are granted understandable motivations for wanting to create the drug—it can be used to power-down mutants who have God-like, uncontrollable powers, such as the Dark Phoenix (see also *The Dark Phoenix Saga*), and it can liberate mutants from a mutant ability that is more of a curse than a blessing, as in the case of Rogue, whose vampire-like powers make it impossible for her to touch another human being without sucking their life away.[12]

In fact, Rogue herself wants to take the drug because she sees her mutanthood not as a badge of honor but as a form of leprosy. To the extent that she does not define herself by her mutant power, she does not work well as an allegorically gay character, unless viewers were prone (like Storm) to see her as a gay person who was ashamed of her own homosexuality. It is very difficult to view Rogue in this fashion precisely because the extreme nature of her powers should predetermine her feelings about them. In addition, I have long been uncomfortable with efforts to use vampire-like characters as stand-ins for gays because of how murderous and destructive vampires are often portrayed as being, even in gay vampire stories such as *Interview with the Vampire*. Like Dark Phoenix, the very extreme nature of Rogue's powers reminds us that gays in the real world, whatever *True Blood* suggests, are neither vampires nor God-like beings capable of vaporizing cities at will. The only way that Rogue might work as a pseudo-gay character is to see her vampire-state as representing her as a gay character with AIDS who can only be cured of AIDS if she was also cured of being gay. The ideal solution for Rogue, of course, would be if her mutant powers' negative side effects could be controlled or eliminated, and their positive side—her ability to read other people's minds and mimic their powers—could be retained. The fact that Rogue is also presented as heterosexual attracted to Wolverine and involved in a love triangle with Iceman and Shadowcat further invalidates this reading.

However, the problematic instances of Rogue and Dark Phoenix notwithstanding, the humans' efforts to "cure" mutants are fundamentally offensive and Nazi-like. Viewers recall similar, real-world efforts to "cure" homosexuality, such as Christian camps that brainwash homosexuals into embracing a heterosexual lifestyle, and they shudder. "Why would anyone in their right mind want to 'cure' a gay person?" the film asks. It celebrates the beauty of the mutant, Angel, a handsome man with a divine pair of angel wings growing from his back that give him the gift of flight. His father invented the cure for mutantcy specifically because the wings offended him and because he couldn't see the beauty, and the glory, of the gift of flight his son had been given. In choosing Angel as its prime example of a beautiful "gay" mutant, *X-Men 3* also condemns religious fundamentalists who deny that gays are close to God and divine creations in their own right.

While McKellen is interested in the *X-Men* as an allegory for gay rights, he respects posters on his web site who suggest alternative readers, even the comparably apolitical interpretation of "mutants" as awkward teenagers going through puberty and feeling alienated from their parents, peers, and society. In a July 7, 2004 post, McKellen offers comfort to an intellectual high school student who feels out of step with youths his age, reassuring the boy that things change in college, when people are freer to chose their own friends and become more comfortable with themselves, as he did. Fan posts, such as those by the high school student, and McKellen's thoughtful and compassionate replies, indicate that there are several individuals who have clearly invested a lot of thought and emotion into a comic book universe that, from afar, might seem trivial at first glance.

After all, to many of the uninitiated, *X-Men* comic books and movie posters seem like lurid ads for a lowbrow form of entertainment akin to professional wrestling. However, these commentators, such as the 16-year-old teen quoted above, take great comfort from the *X-Men*, see themselves in the characters, and consider themselves the real-world equivalent of X-Men. If such readers of *X-Men* comics, and viewers of the films, have few friends in the real world, they can at least find friendship and support by imagining themselves as fellow students of Xavier's School for Gifted Youngsters, and that is no small comfort.

On the other hand, many commentators, such as James Veldon, find the political content of the *X-Men* films highly dubious and question their effectiveness as the bearers of a socially progressive message. Veldon objected specifically to the characterization of gay mutants in the first *X-Men* film. Other concerned posters objected to the portrayal of Magneto as a Holocaust-survivor turned would-be mass murderer. However, McKellen objected to posters who characterized Magneto as being, essentially, the same as Hitler. "Hitler's power used constitutional power to oppress minorities," McKellen explained. "Magneto is a political subversive fighting for freedom. The rhetoric might be similar but their beliefs are not."

McKellen wrote on his web site that, while he knows the comic books explicitly identify Magneto as Jewish, the script for the first *X-Men* film does not, so he assumed Magneto could also be either a gypsy or gay or a member of any other group targeted by Hitler. While he is more in sympathy with Xavier's pacifist approach to activism than Magneto's more militant one, there is an interesting real-life parallel between McKellen and Magneto. The first *X-Men* film sees Magneto launch a campaign to prevent the passage of the Mutant Registration Act, a deeply racist law proposed by a conservative Senator Robert Kelly (read: Joseph McCarthy). In real life, McKellen came out to the British public in 1988 on a BBC Radio 3 program to protest the homophobic and reactionary British law "Section 28," which banned the "promotion" of homosexuality and the teaching of schoolchildren that homosexuality is acceptable "as a pretended family relationship."

In an interview, McKellen revealed that his own participation in the anti–Section 28 campaign was "a focus for people [to] take comfort that if Ian McKellen was on board for this, perhaps it would be all right for other people to be as well, gay and straight."[13] Unfortunately, the reactionary initiative of Margaret Thatcher's Tory-led government was enacted on May 24, 1988, causing a large number of gay and lesbian support groups in schools and colleges to close, and fueling homophobia and AIDS paranoia in England for many years.

McKellen co-founded Stonewall, a gay and lesbian rights advocacy group, to fight the legislation, and Tatchell founded OutRage! Meanwhile, comic book writers and artists Alan Moore, Frank Miller, Robert Crumb, and Neil Gaiman raised $17,000 through AARGH (Artists Against Rampant Government Homophobia) to fund anti–Section 28 activists.[14] Even after the Tories left power in 1997, Labour Party Prime Minister Tony Blair seemed slow to repeal Section 28, and McKellen was a vocal and persistent critic of Blair's on this point. The law was finally repealed on June 21, 2000 in Scotland, and on November 18, 2003 throughout Great Britain.

Even after this victory, McKellen has continued to campaign for gay rights internationally, donated funds to gay charities, and participated in gay pride events. Certainly, there is plenty of homophobia left in the world to combat, as the 2008 passage of Proposition 8 in California — which provided that "only marriage between a man and a woman is valid or recognized in California" — has clearly illustrated. Since the pro–Proposition 8 movement has been largely funded by religious groups, especially Mormons and fundamentalist Christians, McKellen has consistently dared to challenge Christianity's validity and condemn the religions for homophobia. This opposition to conservative Christianity was, in part, the reason he took the role of the villain in *The DaVinci Code* (2006), a film that condemned Christianity for its long history of male chauvinism and advocated a historical reassessment of the centrality of women to the founding of Christianity. McKellen has also made a point of tearing out all of the anti-gay passages in the Bible whenever he finds one in the drawer of a hotel room he is staying in, because it is, he says, dangerous leaving pornography like that lying around to corrupt innocent people.

Also significant is the fact that, in the late 1990s, McKellen campaigned to get a statue of Oscar Wilde built in England because, at the time, there were no statues honoring the bisexual playwright, novelist, and poet. It was an important, symbolic means of getting the British people to apologize to Wilde for imprisoning him for two years for being homosexual (and arguably killing him indirectly with the hard labor that destroyed his health), and to, at long last, recognize Wilde as a national hero.[15]

A campaign such as that is worthy of any gay man, and any member of the X-Men.

Where Are All the Black Superheroes?

Laudable as the first three *X-Men* films were as political statements condemning discrimination on the basis of religion and sexual orientation, there was an extent to which issues of racial discrimination were sidelined. Indeed, while Storm (Halle Berry) has more screen time than team leader Cyclops, she was highly peripheral to the plot, and the screenwriters clearly had little idea of what to do with her. Nor were other black members of the X-Men, including Bishop, Gateway, Cloak, and Shard, anywhere to be seen. On the one hand, this is not surprising, as the black characters named above are rarely featured prominently in the comics, and Storm's role has diminished in the X-Men universe since the 1980s, when she was both team leader and mentor to Shadowcat in *Uncanny X-Men*. However, this lack of centrally important black characters in the *X-Men* franchise is odd, especially given the oft-drawn parallel between Xavier and Martin Luther King and Magneto and Malcolm X. If that parallel is supposed to be strong, then where are the black X-Men?

Aaron McGruder explored this theme with angry gusto in his *Boondocks* comic strips, in which he voiced criticisms of the absence of black X-Men, as well as Storm's straight white hair and general irrelevance. In *Fresh For '01 ... You Suckas: A Boondocks Collection* (2001) McGruder depicted several exchanges between his young *Boondocks* protagonists Huey and Riley Freeman in which they wondered aloud if white comics fans would like it if they had to read about characters named "White This" and "White That" and were drawn with "nappy hair." Riley Freeman admits that Lee and Kirby probably did not create the original X-Men to be commentaries on the civil rights movement, nor did Len Wein's "new X-Men" of 1973 seem to have such a commentary embedded, but he did have Riley Freeman maintain that "it's well known that around the 80s the comic book began to increasingly draw upon the civil rights and Black Power movements for inspiration — the pivotal moment of change being *God Loves, Man Kills,* published in 1982" (90).

Aside from the Martin Luther King and Malcolm X parallels, there is another link between the world of the Marvel mutants and the real-life world of blacks that lived under Jim Crow. Prominent African American writer and intellectual W.E.B. Du Bois argued in "Does the Negro need Separate Schools?" (1935) that blacks who attend predominantly white schools are subject to such racism that it undermines their ability to learn, achieve recognition, and develop a healthy self-image. Consequently, he argued against the ideal of integration that would later be the cornerstone of the Brown vs. Board of Education Supreme Court Case, and advocated that blacks should attend schools of their own, which could be just as good as traditionally white schools, or better, and would be free of prejudice. Du Bois agreed that integration was preferable, but would only be possible when racism in America had abated. In recent years, similar arguments have been made about the necessity of founding separate high schools for gay students to give them a safe haven from persecution.

Clearly, Charles Xavier was thinking along these same lines when he founded Xavier's School for Gifted Youngsters. Only by segregating mutants out of mainstream American society and giving them a safe haven to develop their powers, intellects, and worldviews as free of oppression as possible could they hope to lead fulfilling lives as adults. While these students learned, Xavier would work on improving the image of mutants in the non-mutant community, in the hopes of creating a better world outside the walls of the school so that, some day, his school would no longer be necessary. It was a dream Xavier had spent all of his life achieving, and many *X-Men* fans have wondered what kind of life Xavier led before the events of *X-Men* #1 (1963). In 2011, the film *X-Men: First Class* finally revealed Xavier's hidden past.

When he conceived the story for *X-Men* trilogy prequel *X-Men: First Class* (2011), Bryan Singer set the film in the 1960s, during the height of the civil rights era, and chose to feature Malcolm X, Martin Luther King, Jr., and John F. Kennedy in the narrative.[16] Filmed in England, the United States, and Russia, the *First Class* is designed to have a 60s aesthetic inspired by the Sean Connery James Bond films and Silver Age Marvel Comics. James McAvoy and Michael Fassbender play the younger versions of the characters created on film by Patrick Stewart and Ian McKellen, and Matthew Vaughn (*Kick-Ass*) inherited the director seat from Singer.[17] "Before Charles Xavier and Erik Lehnsherr took the names Professor X and Magneto, they were two young men discovering their powers for the first time. Before they were archenemies, they were closest of friends, working together, with other Mutants (some familiar, some new), to stop the greatest threat the world has ever known. In the process, a rift between them opened, which began the eternal war between Magneto's Brotherhood and Professor X's X-Men."[18]

Charles Xavier makes an impassioned plea on behalf of mutant rights to a hostile audience in Central Park. Moments later, he is shot and almost assassinated. From "X-Cutioner's Song Part 1" in *Uncanny X-Men* #294 (Marvel Comics, 1992). Written by Scott Lobdell and illustrated by Brandon Peterson.

Singer and his fellow screenwriters incorporated into the *X-Men: First Class* team Caucasian X-Men Havok and Banshee, as well as a crimson-skinned character, Azazal, and the blue-skinned returning characters Beast and Mystique. Unfortunately, despite the claims of pre-production publicity, the theatrical cut of the film featured neither Malcolm X nor Martin Luther King. Another failure of *First Class* is that the much-hyped bi-racial mutant Darwin (Kenyan-born Edi Gathegi) had a minimal part and was, essentially, cannon fodder for the villains.[19] In the end, an *X-Men* movie that was expected to explore African American issues in greater depth skirted them yet again to privilege Singer's laudable-but-now-familiar gay allegory.

Elwood Watson, professor of History and African American Studies at East Tennessee State University and author of *Outsiders Within: Black Women in the Legal Academy After Brown v. Board* and co-editor of *The Oprah Phenomenon* (both 2009), has written extensively about the portrayal of African Americans in popular culture.[20] According to Watson, while representations of black men and women have improved somewhat over the years, "there are still too many instances where Black men are represented as sambos, buffoons, pimps, thugs, immature, oversexed men, etc. You can see this on the nightly news. Interestingly, if you look at more recent commercials, it seems that the Black guy is always the smartest guy in the room. He knows where to get matches, how to fix a tire, how to get the best hotel room rates, how to solve mathematical equations, and it is often his White buddy who is the lame one. There have been a number of positive representations such as Sidney Poitier (for the most part), Denzel Washington, Blair Underwood, Colin Powell and our current Commander-in-Chief, Barack Obama.

"Black women have been seen as sassy, oversexed, often obese, those who are physically attractive are usually saddled with so many emotional issues—paranoid, temperamental, always angry, in some cases, confused—that they are unable to have a healthy, functional relationship with anyone (think Tara in *True Blood*, Thelma on *Good Times*, Omarosa on *The Apprentice*). Every now and then we get a character like Dominique Devereux on the 1980s hit nighttime soap opera, *Dynasty*, who was played by the incomparable Diahann Carroll, Claire Huxtable on *The Cosby Show*, which was also an 80s/early 90s show. This show was also a pleasant departure from the traditional image of Black families as being either poor, on welfare, dysfunctional, always up against it."

Regarding superheroes, Watson sees little change. He said he never recalled seeing black superheroes on television when he was growing up, and there seem to be very few black superheroes that have penetrated the mainstream media from the comic book world. "I always looked at my parents, relatives and my older siblings as my Black superheroes," he said. "I do not mean to be flippant, but I did."[21]

Even in comic books, black superheroes are rare figures. They often operate as "sidekick" supporting characters to other heroes — usually white, male heroes like Tony Stark — or as background members of team books who are sometimes interesting in their own right and sometimes "token black guys." Black characters that star in their own books, as Black Panther does in a comic that has been written by Reginald Hudlin and Christopher Priest, are rare. Spawn is another rare exception that headlines his own comic book. However, he is a disfigured, demonic African American who wears a mask that he rarely seems to take off, so his value as a black role model is questionable. There is also the odd phenomenon of the African American cyborg, seen in Marvel's *Deathlock* comics and DC's *Teen Titans* hero, Victor Stone (a.k.a. Cyborg).

The black Iron Man, James Rhodes, and the black Green Lantern, John Stewart, were both briefly the main characters of their own books, deputized during periods when their white bosses, Tony Stark and Hal Jordan, were incapacitated by alcoholism and self-doubt. (Please note: This John Stewart is not to be confused with *Daily Show* host Jon Stewart, who is not currently a Green Lantern. However, his persistence in standing up to Fox News shows that he has strong willpower and the ability to overcome great fear, so perhaps the Oans should consider recruiting him.) Several other attempts have been made to replace traditionally white male superheroes with men of color, or with women, but they have tended not to remain in the role for long, usually only until the characters they have replaced are resurrected from the dead or emerge from retirement. In one case the Atom (Asian Ryan Choi) first replaced — and then was replaced by — white man Ray Palmer. In another case, the black, pinch-hitter Firestorm (Jason Rusch) didn't sell many comic books, so the original, white Firestorm (Ronnie Raymond) returned from the grave to take over. In the 1970s, Gloria Steinem campaigned for the creation of a black Amazon in the *Wonder Woman* comics, but *The Crisis on Infinite Earths* wiped the character of Nubia from continuity in the 1980s. She was reintroduced briefly in 1999 as Nu'Bia, but remains a minor, minor character.

One of the few successful transformations of a traditional white character into a black one was the refitting of white, cigar-chomping, eye-patch-wearing World War II veteran Nick Fury into the bald, black, eye-patch-wearing Samuel L. Jackson, founder of the 21st century incarnation of the Avengers and director of S.H.I.E.L.D. This radical alteration succeeded because the new Nick Fury was part of the justification for the creating of a parallel Marvel Universe called the Ultimate Universe, and he was featured as a supporting player in two enormously popular comic books, *The Ultimates* by Mark Millar and Bryan Hitch and *Ultimate Spider-Man* by Brian Michael Bendis and Mark Bagley. The fact that Samuel L. Jackson consented to play the character that was now drawn to look *exactly like him* in the *Iron Man* and *Avengers* films helped the change stick. If Jackson had been less popular with comic book readers, or the black Nick Fury had not been drawn to look like an already famous black man, the alteration might not have been as successful.

(Interestingly, while the black Nick Fury has dealings with the X-Men in the Ultimate

Universe, it is the white Nick Fury who is a member of the X-Men, and a friend of Xavier's, in Chris Claremont's monthly comic *X-Men Forever*.)

In contrast to Samuel L. Jackson's success remaking Nick Fury, black actresses who have played Catwoman have not inspired comic book artists to draw the character as black, and the majority of Batman fans seem to prefer Michelle Pfeiffer and Julie Newmar to Eartha Kitt and Halle Berry in the role. On a related note, in early 2011, Christopher Nolan assembled a cast for his third Batman film, *The Dark Knight Rises*, which included Caucasian actress Anne Hathaway as Catwoman and English actor Tom Hardy as the Hispanic villain Bane. Nolan was also rumored to be considering French actress Marion Cotillard for the role of a major Arab character, Talia al Ghul.

Blade, an African American vampire hunter who was himself part vampire and the child of a prostitute, is an anti-hero figure who was popular as a supporting character in Marvel's 1970s era *Tomb of Dracula* comic book, but has never generated enough money for the company to maintain his own monthly title. He achieved mainstream fame in the 1990s by appearing in a series of violent, modestly budgeted *Blade* horror films starring Wesley Snipes, but the superhero's film success did not translate to success on the small screen (a spinoff television series was short lived) or the comic book world (he still does not have a monthly title). However, to give the character a home, Marvel made him a member of the X-Men in 2010.

The Falcon, Luke Cage, Vixen, Black Lightning, and (the appallingly dull character) Triathlon have helped bring some racial diversity to the traditionally all Aryan teams the Avengers and the Justice League—as have blue-skinned, red-skinned, and green-skinned characters, such as the Beast, Vision, She-Hulk, and Martian Manhunter, all of whom represent a free-floating "otherness" that could stand-in for any "minority" or "disenfranchised" American figure. Blue and green characters can sometimes reach black audience members (as Dave Chappelle said about the Hulk: "He's green. I'm black. It's close enough."), but it isn't the same as seeing a bona fide black character on the screen to relate to.

Despite her silly name, Bruce Banner's cousin She-Hulk is a superb character who can be seen as "pseudo-black," in part because she is occasionally drawn to resemble a green Angela Bassett. Created by Stan Lee and John Buscema, the character was introduced as Jennifer Susan Walters, the shy daughter of a Los Angeles Sherriff, who was shot and nearly killed by a vengeful crime lord. Fortunately, her cousin Bruce was in town to save her life with a blood transfusion. He passed his "Hulk condition" on to Jennifer, but she has had far more success controlling the powers than he. Indeed, she has spent years as She-Hulk, preferring being tall, strong, and beautiful, to being small and plain as a regular "human." She even remains in her She-Hulk form when working in the courtroom as a criminal defense lawyer. She-Hulk has appeared in several of her own monthly comic books, all of which had brief tenures before being cancelled, but she has had the advantage of appearing in an excellent string of *Fantastic Four* comics by John Byrne and in several *She-Hulk* graphic novels by Dan Slott that were legitimately among the best comic books produced in the first decade of the 2000s.

The television series *Doctor Who* has not, traditionally, cast many actors of color, and the few appearances black actors made in the series have often been embarrassing, forgettable, or racially problematic at best. However, the Doctor has had three black traveling companions throughout the franchise's history—Sharon Davies, Mickey Smith, and Martha Jones—with Mickey being the most memorable of the three, and the most embraced by fans, thanks largely to Noel Clarke's nuanced acting and charismatic screen presence. Martha Jones, a wealthy black doctor who heroically saves the world from the Master, was a little too defined by her unrequited love for the Doctor, and actress Freema Agyeman's performance was sometimes uneven.[22] But

Mickey and Martha are both sidekicks, and the black character's lot in superhero stories is to be the oft-sidelined sidekick or ensemble cast member.

Truly, black characters are often sidelined, and of little interest to readers of ensemble superhero narratives. Still, it is refreshing to note that, thanks in large part to African American writer Dwayne MacDuffie, John Stewart was essentially the most important member of the *Justice League* in the 2000s animated series, and has been regarded by a generation of fans as the one, true Green Lantern as a result. Created by Dennis O'Neil and Neal Adams, Stewart was an out-of-work architect invited to join the Green Lantern Corps to provide backup for a burnt out Hal Jordan in his first appearance in *Green Lantern* vol. 2 #87 (1971). Jordan was uneasy about Stewart's ghetto background and leftist political views. He also felt that Stewart had a chip on his shoulder, and reveled too much in one small part of the Green Lantern Corps oath that Stewart seemed to verbally italicize as he uttered it, "In brightest day, in blackest night, no evil shall escape my sight. For those who worship evil's might, *beware my power*, Green Lantern's light."

Stewart's first assignment as Green Lantern was, provocatively, to prevent the assassination of a racist presidential candidate, Senator Jeremiah Clutcher (who seemed to be a transparent commentary on George Wallace). Despite a reluctant Jordan second-guessing his every move, Stewart first prevents a black assassin from shooting Clutcher, then reveals to the public the truth about the "assassination attempt"—Clutcher himself had staged it to turn the American people against the black power movement and get himself elected president. After this turn of events, Jordan reassesses Stewart and apologizes for being so skeptical. The two Green Lanterns become friends (see O'Neil, "Beware My Power").

While Hal Jordan was written out of the Green Lantern comics for years, giving Stewart and Metrosexual Green Lantern Kyle Rayner the spotlight, Jordan's return to prominence as the central Green Lantern in the DC universe in 2004 took much of the attention away from Stewart. Indeed, while Stewart was going to be the Green Lantern featured in a mooted *Justice League* film project, and played by rapper Common, that project was scuttled and replaced by a *Green Lantern* feature film in which Caucasian actor Ryan Reynolds played Hal Jordan. At this point, Stewart seems to be a pinch-hitter at best as Green Lantern in the DC Universe.

Outside of the comic book world, the greatest wellspring of African American superheroes was the Blacksploitation film genre of the 1970s, which produced female vigilantes Coffy and Foxy Brown as well as larger-than-life male figures Shaft, Superfly, Dolemite, the Mack, Watermelon Man, and Petey Wheatstraw: The Devil's Son-in-Law. Pam Grier found stardom as the title character in *Coffy* (1973), a tough nurse who initiates a war on drugs, and the pseudo-sequel, *Foxy Brown* (1974) in which Grier infiltrates a sex-slave ring to save black women from a life of drug addiction and prostitution. (Coffy was remade with an all-white cast in 1981 as *Lovely But Deadly*.)

Melvin Van Peebles' *Watermelon Man* (1970) is a supernatural Blacksploitation film in which a racist white insurance salesman named Jeff Gerber finds himself mysteriously transformed into a black man. His neighbors effectively drive him out of the upscale suburban community in which he lives because they fear his presence will drive property values down, and his supposedly liberal wife leaves him and takes their children with her because she can't handle the public scrutiny that comes with an interracial marriage. Ironically, by the end of the film, the once racist Jeff radicalizes and joins the Black Panthers, seemingly ready to rebel against an oppressive white regime.

Perhaps the most famous male Blacksploitation hero was Shaft, due in no small part to Richard Roundtree's charismatic performance, and the funky main theme provided by Isaac Hayes. *Shaft* (1971) and *Shaft's Big Score* (1972) introduce John Shaft, a ladies' man detective who pits himself against an Italian Mafia bent on seizing violent control of Harlem. These films were followed up by *Shaft in Africa* (1973) and a CBS television series (1973–1974). In 2000, John Singleton directed *Shaft*, a continuation of the Shaft saga starring the original Shaft's nephew, also named John Shaft (Samuel L. Jackson), and including a cameo by Roundtree's Shaft. The story involves a rich, racist young murderer, Walter Wade, Jr. (Christian Bale), who escapes from justice because his father is wealthy and the murder victim was black. An idealistic police officer, Shaft vows to bring Wade to justice to prove that the system works, but the more stymied he is in his efforts, the more disillusioned he becomes.

Years after the heyday of Blacksploitation films came to a close, Quentin Tarantino embedded elements of the genre in *Pulp Fiction* (1994) and *Jackie Brown* (1997), bringing Jackson mainstream superstardom and offering Pam Grier one of her greatest film roles in decades. Elwood Watson finds black exploitation films, new and old, fascinating—especially *Superfly*, the definitive film in the genre, as well as *Uptown Saturday Night*, and *Bucktown*—but sees the depiction of blacks in these films as highly problematic. "The perception of Blacks as violent, immature and less disciplined than Whites seems to emerge in many of these movies. *Watermelon Man* was rife with racism. *Jackie Brown* was not as blatant in its stereotypes as some of the other movies, but they must use the N-word at least 30 times in the movie. I loved Samuel Jackson in the movie. He is probably my favorite actor."[23]

Oddly, despite the success of these neo-blacksploitation films, Hollywood seemed reluctant to offer Grier or Jackson a starring role as a traditional, Marvel or DC style superhero, even though there were characters they could have easily played. Jackson voiced Frozone, a character inspired by the Caucasian *X-Men* member Iceman, in the *Incredibles*, and later starred as Nick Fury in a supporting role in *The Avengers* and *Iron Man* films, but has yet to headline a film as a traditional superhero. An oft-mooted Luke Cage film has had similar difficulty getting made, and the plug was pulled on a *Justice League* film starring John Stewart. Notably, *Hancock*, a film ultimately starring Will Smith, languished in development hell for years before executives finally took a chance with it.

Race issues are sublimated in *Hancock* (2008), but they are there to see if viewers look for them. Modeled on Marvel's Spider-Man and DC Comics' Hawkman, John Hancock is an incompetent, publicly vilified superhero with the powers of flight, superhuman strength, and near invincibility. He dresses in stereotypical urban ghetto clothes, drinks while he flies, curses in front of children, frequently makes homophobic remarks, and destroys billions of dollars in property in his efforts to protect public safety.

For the first half of the film, Hancock is depicted as deserving public scorn because he is incompetent, misanthropic, and scornful of authority figures. When he saves public relations expert Ray Embrey (Jason Bateman) from being struck by a train, Embrey chooses to show his gratitude to Hancock by making it his mission to change the anti-hero's public image. He gives Hancock a 21st-century-style superhero costume—skin-tight, monochromatic, and sporting a subtle hawk logo—and demands that Hancock take responsibility for his actions by serving a prison term for the crimes he has committed while, paradoxically, fighting crime. When Hancock demonstrates his humility by accepting punishment at a penal institution he could escape from at any time, public opinion turns in his favor and he is soon pardoned and deputized by the District Attorney's office into stopping a deadly bank heist in progress.

If the film ended there, it would arguably lay the blame for Hancock's alienation from society on Hancock himself. The first half of the film suggests that, if only Hancock had dressed better, stayed off the drink, and not been such an "ornery nigger," then he would have never run afoul of the law. The second half of the film presents the alternative view that Hancock did not choose to separate himself from society, but that he was forced to live, segregated from the world, by racist Americans. At the film's midpoint, the audience learns that Hancock suffers from amnesia and does not know who he is or how old he is. He knows only that he does not age, and that his earliest memory was waking up in a hospital in 1931 after being nearly beaten to death by white supremacists outside of a movie theater showing James Whale's *Frankenstein*.

What Hancock does not know, or remember, is that Embrey's wife Mary (Charlize Theron) is really a closeted superhero, Superwoman, who used to be married to Hancock. This revelation is unexpected, and completely alters Mary's motivations as a character, but it sets up a dramatic love-triangle storyline and brings the racial subtext of the film closer to the surface. Like Hancock, Superwoman is thousands of years old, only she remembers their many lifetimes worth of married life together. As she ultimately reveals to Hancock, the fact that he is black and she is white has caused generations of racists to ambush them when they are at their weakest—when they are together and in love. Time and again, lifetime after lifetime, racial purists were offended by their love and repeatedly tried to murder them for their forbidden, interracial marriage. When KKK sympathizers attacked them both in 1931, and nearly killed Hancock, Superwoman decided it was time they lived apart, so she left him at the hospital to wake up alone, an amnesiac, with no sense that anyone in the world loved him. And that was the beginning of his alienation from society.

From *Hancock* (Sony Pictures, 2008): "Black Superman" John Hancock (Will Smith) rescues civilian Ray Embrey (Jason Bateman) from being struck by a train. This moment is reminiscent of the cover of the first *Superman* comic book, *Action Comics* #1 (1938), in which Superman lifts a car. Throughout the film, Hancock is criticized for being incompetent and overly aggressive, but he is bitter and alone because murderous racists broke up his interracial romance with Superwoman (Charlize Theron).

Consequently, the message of the second half of the film repudiates the message of the first half of the film, underscoring the feeling that many viewers had that the film turns on a dime tonally and thematically at midpoint. In the second half of the film, it is not Hancock in particular, or black men in general, who emerge as the reason for racial strife in America, but intolerant white Americans. Gone from the second half of the film is all neo-conservative suggestion that militant black men are "reverse racists." When Hancock and Superwoman are together in a hospital at the end of the film, and are once again beset by working-class white criminals, the suggestion is that, no matter how savvy Hancock is at public relations, no matter how well he dresses or speaks, no matter how polite and well-spoken he is, racists will continue to hate him merely because he is black.

The following year saw the release of a retro-style spoof of Blaxploitation films set in the 1970s, co-written by and starring former *Spawn* star Michael Jai White. The title character of *Black Dynamite* (2009) is a former CIA agent who transforms urban ghettos into suburban utopias by single-handedly cutting off the drug trade at its source—the Nixon White House. Black Dynamite defeats Nixon is a kung fu fight in the Oval Office and accuses "Tricky Dick" of working to destroy the black community simply because he is jealous of the prodigious sizes of black men's dicks. The scene is hilarious and outrageous, but is based on a genuine hostility between Nixon and the black community chronicled in Rick Perlstein's history *Nixonland: The Rise of a President and the Fracturing of America* (2008). First Lady Pat Nixon is wowed by Black Dynamite's manhood, and falls at his feet as the hero strikes a heroic pose in the Oval Office. The moment is symbolically appropriate for a film released the year that the mantle of the Presidency of the United States was assumed by an African American male.

Some cultural critics and historians have speculated that Barack Obama's path to the White House was paved by positive popular culture representations of black men, especially depictions of black male presidents from 1998's *Deep Impact* (Morgan Freeman's President Beck) and the series *24,* which featured two black presidents (Dennis Haysbert's President David Palmer and D. B. Woodside's President Wayne Palmer) at the urging of its politically left-leaning star Kiefer Sutherland. The breakaway popularity of movie stars Will Smith and Samuel L. Jackson, the mainstreaming of rap music, and other signs of the growing acceptance and "coolness" of African Americans and what is perceived to be black American culture may also have contributed to his success.

However, as surprised as many members of the African American community were that an inexperienced black man succeeded in becoming the president of a country they perceived to be inherently racist, there were signs that Obama's presidency will never be viewed as legitimate by a large percentage of Americans who cling to racist ideologies of the past. To that extent, the message of the film *Hancock* seems apt. No matter how smart, well-dressed, and even-tempered a black man is, he cannot earn the respect or affection of a fundamentally racist white American.

Xavier's Dream Fulfilled: A Mutant in the White House

In the first *X-Men* film, Magneto argued that life for mutants in America would change substantively if the President of the United States, and all the leaders of the world, were suddenly transformed into mutants. After all, Christianity had been a persecuted, underground cult in Ancient Rome until the Emperor Constantine converted to Christianity and established it the official religion of the Roman Empire. What the mutants needed, Magneto felt, was an Emperor Constantine. But he was trying to artificially transform all of the world leaders through an aggressive act of terrorism, and Xavier and his X-Men argued that no act of terrorism would ever lead to an oppressed group finding true acceptance. Indeed, Xavier rightly feels that all terrorism ever achieves is bolstering the power and popularity of the very same oppressive, conservative regimes that terrorism is trying to unseat.

However, Magneto is not patient enough to wait for American public opinion to change, and racism to abate to the point that a mutant is actually elected President of the United States. The idea is preposterous, anyway. So Magneto continues a career of making terrorist attack after terrorist attack against humanity. During one such campaign, when he aggressively sinks a Soviet submarine, killing everyone on board, the X-Men redouble their efforts to end his destructive campaign. In the heat of combat, Magneto strikes out wildly and accidentally wounds Kitty Pryde (see *Uncanny X-Men* #150). Believing he has killed an innocent teenage girl who is, like him, both Jewish and a mutant, Magneto wonders if he has finally gone too far and become exactly like the insane Nazis he has always hated. At this moment, he has an epiphany and announces his reform.

From the moment she was introduced in 1980, Kitty clearly represented the symbolic hope of a better future. Unlike Magneto and Xavier, Kitty did not live through World War II or the turbulent 1960s. She did not have their emotional scars and could look at the world with fresh eyes and begin contemplating how to remake it. A member of Generation X, literally and figuratively, Kitty embraced the X-Men's mission while still making time to live a normal life, go to college, date, and even spend time exploring the multiverse with *Excalibur* and giving the mutants rights cause a rest. As much as Kitty had to be bitter about — and she had a lot because most of her friends and family members have been killed in anti-mutant hate crime attacks — she somehow manages to maintain her good humor, sense of justice, and kind heart.

When long-time *X-Men* writer Chris Claremont was commissioned to write a story set in the near future that would bring the *X-Men* saga to a close, he found an incredibly fitting climax. In *X-Men: The End* (2004–2006), a thirtysomething Kitty Pryde is running against racial purity advocate Alice Tremaine for the position of mayor of Chicago. Though African American, Tremaine is a violent racist and her entire election campaign is based on demonizing Kitty. During a live, televised debate, Tremaine asks the voters of Chicago if they want "the next mayor of this great city to be a human being, or a monster?" A brief look of cold fury passes over Kitty's face and then vanishes. She then beams, theatrically placing a hand upon her breast, and says, "Well, I'm a monster? What I am, ladies and gentlemen, by accident of birth, is a mutant. In my case, I can walk through walls." And she demonstrates the power by passing right through her podium, startling everyone watching. By not hiding her true nature, and by showing a sense of humor in the face of Tremaine's hateful attacks, Kitty gradually starts to turn the tide of the election in her favor during the course of

A grown-up Katherine Pryde is the liberal candidate in the Chicago mayoral election. Her opponent, Alice Tremaine, is a racist politician who calls Katherine "a monster" because she is a mutant. Notably, Katherine's head is bandaged during this live, television debate because one of Tremaine's supporters hit her with a rock during one of her rallies. From *X-Men: The End* (Marvel Comics, 2004–2006), written by Chris Claremont and illustrated by Sean Chen.

one debate. Each time Tremaine tries to make the election about Kitty's mutant background, Kitty turns the public's attention to the fact that Tremaine has spent no time outlining her positions on "the real concerns of real people," such as taxes, education, transportation, health care, housing, and jobs. Ignoring Tremaine's ad hominem attacks, Kitty lays out a series of practical plans for dealing with each of these issues that assures the voting public that she has a well-thought-out agenda. When Tremaine suggests that, as mayor, Kitty would only represent the interests of mutant over humans, Kitty proclaims that idea nonsense.

"I'm a Jew. Does that mean I favor my faith over all the others?" she asks. "Do I favor women over men? White over non-white? Geeks over jocks? A community is people working together for the common good. We don't achieve that by casting some out."

The unlikely outcome of the election is that Kitty Pryde becomes the first mutant mayor of Chicago.

But the story does not end there.

An epilogue that takes place 20 years later, finds Katherine Pryde, the former X-Men neophyte Shadowcat, serving her first term as President of the United States. In the time that has passed since the Chicago mayoral election, she has won Alice Tremaine's respect. However, Speaker of the House Tremaine is still a member of the opposing political party, so they will remain political adversaries even if they have made peace personally. The epilogue does not establish if she is the first female president, or the first Jewish president, but she is certainly the first mutant president. Readers are also introduced to her children, but no husband is referenced or seen.

In the final segment of the story, President Shadowcat, the pride of the X-Men, make a speech on the White House lawn in honor of how far the cause of mutant's rights has come since the passing of Magneto and Xavier — both of whom would have voted for her had they lived to do so. Since America had shown itself to be capable of electing a liberal Jewish woman mutant President of the United States, it had clearly demonstrate its capacity for growth and tolerance. With her election, the age of the X-Men was over, and the need for segregated institutions of learning like Xavier's School for Gifted Youngsters had passed. The age of mutant segregation, both enforced and voluntary, was at an end. The era of integration, inter-species tolerance, and intermarriage had begun.

Magneto had believed that the only way to change the United States, make it a genuinely free country, and purge it of the legacy of racism, was to take the White House by force. Kitty Pryde, using Charles Xavier's methods, won over the hearts and minds of the American people, and was democratically elected president. The Oval Office was given to her by a nation of mutants and non-mutants alike.

And the dreams of both Charles Xavier and Erik Lehnsherr were finally realized in President Kitty Pryde.

As were the dreams of Martin Luther King and Malcolm X with the election of President Barack Obama...

NINE

In Brightest Day, in Darkest Knight: President Obama vs. the Zombie Apocalypse

When there's no more room in hell, the dead will walk the earth.— George A. Romero, *Dawn of the Dead* (1978)

All this talk of the end of the world isn't appealing is it? Doesn't it seem childish and irreligious?— G.K. Chesterton

The Coming Zombie Apocalypse

President Obama stands in the midst of Arlington National Cemetery, surrounding by a horde of flesh-eating zombies bent on tearing him apart. Realizing that his wonderful powers of persuasion cannot work on the mindless, Obama activates his "self-defense suit" with a touch of his American-flag lapel pin; a Green Lantern–like energy glow cloaks him in an invulnerable field and he is fueled with superpowers to beat the zombies into submission. In that moment, Obama is instantly transformed from politician and world leader to comic book superhero. The comic book, written and drawn by David Hutchinson, is called *President Evil* after the *Resident Evil* zombie video game and film franchise. The story is intended to be satirical, but the main characters are all recognizably the presidential and vice presidential candidates of America's 2008 election, with their names misspelled or turned into puns. Issue #1 (released July 2009) begins shortly after President Obama's inauguration, when an outbreak of the swine flu virus mutates and reanimates the corpses of the dead. Air Force One crash-lands in Washington, D.C., and Obama emerges from the wreckage, eager to find his wife and children, whom he has been separated from. Characters clearly intended to be Sarah Palin and John McCain arrive to help Obama. Palin is an insane survivalist armed with an array of weapons, and John McCain's elderly form is augmented with an eight-hundred-million dollar battle suit, which Palin cites as a bargain price. They are better than Obama at dispatching zombies, as is Hillary Clinton, who transforms into a powerful, incredible Hulk figure whenever she thinks of her husband's infidelities. As "Hillary Hulk," she does some serious damage to the zombie hordes. However, Obama ultimately saves the day by summoning his secret weapon, the seemingly harmless Stephen Colbert, who destroys all of Obama's enemies effortlessly.

In issue #3 (November 2009), the press alternates between fawning over Obama's heroism during the zombie uprising and blaming him for causing the infestation. Obama reminds the reporters that he did not cause the zombie plague; he inherited it from George W. Bush.

President Obama faces off against zombies in Arlington National Cemetery in *President Evil* #1 (Antarctic Press, 2009), written and illustrated by David Hutchison.

However, the president maintains that most zombies are not evil flesh-eaters, but actually law-abiding citizens who can almost all become productive members of society if granted citizenship, respect, and access to social programs. In response, conservative forces led by Rush Limbaugh, Bill O'Reilly, and Glenn Beck convince the American people that Obama is to blame for the zombie invasion and stage a coup d'état.[1] Limbaugh is named the new president and O'Reilly vice president. Working in collusion with zombie Ronald Reagan, Limbaugh orders the globe to be purified by fire to cleanse it of zombies. All of the world's nuclear weapons are launched and the planet is bathed in radiation. After the nuclear blasts subside, Obama, Palin, and McCain are left standing before the ruins of the Statue of Liberty, half buried in sand *Planet of the Apes*–style, aware they are now living in a post-apocalyptic world.

President Evil depicts Barack Obama as a superhero figure who is the only man standing between the American people and Armageddon. It also depicts as evil-to-the-core the leadership of the Republican Party, and its corporate sponsors, which will do everything in its power, legal and illegal, to humiliate Obama, reclaim the government, and destroy democracy. Simultaneously funny and depressing, this *President Evil* storyline gains frisson from its real-life parallels. These parallels are the core concern of this chapter, which will begin by exploring the apocalyptic threats facing the nation in the 21st century, continue with an exploration of the notion of Obama as a superhero, and end with an analysis of the increasingly abhorrent and frightening tactics employed by the radical right wing to prevent Obama's social reforms from seeing the light of day.

Representations of the zombie apocalypse in popular culture have been pervasive in recent years, bringing to mind that it is the horror genre's closest analogue to the science fiction genre's traditional insistence on dystopian, apocalyptic, and post-apocalyptic narratives. As Ursula K. Le Guin explained in the introduction to her book *The Left Hand of Darkness* (1969):

> Science fiction is often described, and even defined, as extrapolative. The science fiction writer is supposed to take a trend, or phenomenon of the here-and-now, purify and intensify it for dramatic effect, and extend it into the future. "If this goes on, this is what will happen." A prediction is made ... [that generally arrives] somewhere between the gradual extinction of human liberty and the total extinction of terrestrial life.
>
> This may explain why many people who do not read science fiction describe it as

> "escapist," but when questioned further, admit they don't read it because "it's so depressing."[2]

So, for example, the film *Soylent Green* (1973) takes several worrying trends of the Cold War era — the rise of fast food, the overcrowding of cities, the growing gulf between rich and poor, and the ever-expanding suburban sprawl replacing America's invaluable farmland — and posits a future in which the American food industry mass produces Soylent Green rations made from the recycled remains of dead humans. These rations are fed to a ravenous, undernourished, shambling mass of people, who do not know that they might be eating their own relatives and, consequently, have symbolically become flesh-eating zombies. Given the contemporary parallels, an absurdist science fiction concept suddenly seems quite plausible.

Soylent Green is a science fiction pseudo-zombie story. The horror genre, in contrast, employs actual zombies to make much the same kind of social and political commentary that *Soylent Green* does about social degeneration. In many ways, it was no wonder that popular culture was replete with apocalyptic imagery during the first decade of the new millennium, as the civilized world did, indeed, seem to be besieged on every level, and on the verge of total collapse. The zombie apocalypse that George Romero had envisioned as a result of racism, class warfare, and American imperial policies in his *Night of the Living Dead* (1968–present) series of films had gradually come to symbolize an apocalypse initiated by any number of causes, from germ warfare to foreign invasion. Liberal zombie movie fans tend to gravitate to films that depict the zombie apocalypse as being caused by evil multinational corporations (*Resident Evil*), the military industrial complex (as in proto-zombie-apocalypse narrative *Day of the Triffids*), or a rebirth of the Nazi movement (*Shock Waves*). Conservatives see the zombie invasion as a natural consequence of runaway immigration (*Zombi 2*, *Doctor Who: The Unquiet Dead*) or an uprising of the urban poor, especially the homeless and black populations (*C.H.U.D.*, *Land of the Dead*). The male chauvinist *Evil Dead* trilogy (1981–1992) symbolically pins the coming end of days on feminism. Each film in the series conspires to put women back in their pre-feminist place by casting all the female characters as rape victims, withered witches, walking bodies without heads, or aggressive, giggling zombies bent on devouring the affable funnyman who once loved them, Ash (Bruce Campbell).

Since the 1996 release of the video game *House of the Dead*, zombies have become more of a mainstream fixture of American popular culture than they had been in previous generations, when they were relegated to unrated cult films shown in grindhouse theaters and on Heavy Metal band T-shirts. Throughout the Bush Administration, zombie movies and video games grew ever more popular and mainstreamed, and bookstores sold many a copy of Max Brooks' zombie opuses, *The Zombie Survival Guide* (2003) and *World War Z: An Oral History of the Zombie War* (2006). The zombie film that most directly commented upon the Bush Administration and its policies was *Land of the Dead* (2005). The George A. Romero film took place in and around Fiddler's Green luxury high rise, a small, elite community of the super rich that lives cordoned off from the rest of an impoverished, zombie-infested America. Fiddler's Green chief, Mr. Kaufman (a George Bush–like Dennis Hopper) believes that, as long as his constituents are healthy, wealthy, happy, and safe, it is unimportant if the rest of the world falls into poverty, illness, despair, and chaos. But the rest of the world wants what the people of Fiddler's Green have, and they are desperate to be invited to the party.

Significantly, despite President Obama's oft-repeated message of the importance of embracing hope, even in these terror-filled times, the existential dread embodied by zombie narratives remain popular, and their ubiquitous presence shows little sign of vanishing. Indeed, Obama's first two years as president saw the release of Seth Grahame-Smith's *Pride and Prejudice and Zombies* (2009), a rewrite of Jane Austen's classic novel "improved" with the insertion of zombies into the narrative, and Alan Goldsher's *Paul Is Undead: The British Zombie Invasion* (2010), a book in which Yoko Ono and Mick Jagger team up to save America from the zombie Beatles. A promotional video for the fake movie *Jim Henson's Resident Evil 5* has made a circuit of the internet, showing Muppets shooting the heads off shambling zombies, and Cookie Monster dying horribly at the hands of the undead. In a similar vein, a "Disney Zombies" fashion show was a centerpiece of the Midlands MCM Expo 2010, and included a Zombie Tinkerbell and Zombie Captain Jack Sparrow. And, in October 2010, a television series based upon the zombie apocalypse comic book *The Walking Dead* premiered on AMC.

President Obama's supporters saw him as a nearly Messianic figure during his campaign and first year in office. He represented the dawn of a new age of progressivism that would empower the average American, reform Wall Street, curb environmental abuses, revitalize the economy, and fix a broken health care system. In contrast, archconservatives celebrated the election of the United States' first African American president by disingenuously blaming him, and him alone, for a series of economic, military, social, and environmental crises that were caused by his predecessor's government and its corporate masters. In his first two years in office, Obama was faced with the challenge of ending two wars, combating global warming, curbing illegal immigration, finding alternative fuel resources, and dealing with both the devastating repercussions of the Deepwater Horizon oil spill and the worst economic crisis since the Great Depression.

On the one hand, proponents of reform had much to celebrate in the steps Obama took to improve the image of the United States abroad. They could also cheer the historic legislation he passed reforming health care (The Patient Protection and Affordable Care Act of 2010), and reigning in the abuses of an out-of-control corporate America (The Dodd-Frank Wall Street Reform and Consumer Protection Act of 2010). However, fears that the United States, if not the world, was on the verge of total financial, environmental, social, and technological collapse have pervaded the mass media and popular culture. As Al Gore continually strove to convince supremely skeptical Americans that the scientific establishment was correct in its consensus that climate change was a genuine threat, James Howard Kunstler warned that the world's oil resources are being depleted at a rate that will soon make industrialization a thing of the past. Former CNN cultural commentator Lou Dobbs has consistently warned of the "war on the middle class" waged by the forces of globalism, job outsourcing, and rampant illegal immigration, while other reporters have represented China as a game-changing threat to the American way of life thanks to its poisoned food exports and expertise at cyber warfare. Recently failed terrorist plots related to an international Delta Airline flight and a Times Square car bomb have kept alive fears of a repeat of the 9/11 terrorist attacks, and persistent fears of a future nuclear war with Korea, Iran, or Pakistan have made many Americans fearful of an irradiated Armageddon. Swine flu and West Nile outbreaks have joined the AIDS virus as national health safety risks, and the widely televised devastation caused by 2005's Hurricane Katrina, the 2010 Haiti earthquake, and the volcanic eruptions of Eyjafjallajökull in Iceland have renewed fears of natural disasters of varying scope and nature. The 2010 Deepwater Horizon oil spill that occurred during an offshore drilling exercise in the Gulf of Mexico has caused even non-environmentalists to worry that the worst environmental disasters to come will be caused by humans, not God or Mother Nature.

For many liberal commentators, Obama is doing the best job he can, and has achieved more in less than two years than Bill Clinton achieved in two terms in the face of similarly implacable right-wing opposition. However, many fear that Republicans will stymie his efforts enough to make him seem weak and ineffective to the general public, and allow another destructive Republican administration, as bad as or worse than George W. Bush's, to seize control of the government and further exacerbate the environmental and economic forces that threaten to end peace and prosperity in America and abroad for the foreseeable future. This coming apocalypse — that many liberals fear will be brought about by Republican demagoguery — has often been symbolically represented by a zombie horde shambling across the ruins of a decimated Manhattan cityscape.

One of the appeals of the zombie figure as the physical manifestation of cultural anxieties about a number of abstract issues — ranging from fears of death to economic hardships created by difficult-to-identify culprits — is that they give angry Americans something to shoot at. Killing zombies in video games and watching zombies killed in movies may not solve America's social, political, and economic woes, but it makes people in the audience feel a little better watching zombies get shot in the head or chopped up by helicopter blades.

As zombie novelist Brooks observed:

> You can't shoot the financial meltdown in the head — you can do that with a zombie. [...] All the other problems are too big. As much as Al Gore tries, you can't picture global warming. You can't picture the meltdown of our financial institutions. But you can picture a slouching zombie coming down the street [qtd in Gross par. 4–5].

Since the pleasure provided by killing a zombie is escapist and regressive, it offers little hope of any real solution to such abstract problems. However, zombie stories can sometimes offer theories as to why Americans are so angry and depressed, and why they feel like the world will, or already has, succumbed to a zombie invasion.

One of the humorous conceits of the movie *Zombieland* (2009) is that the zombie apocalypse has already happened and many of us haven't noticed it. This is underlined by one of the film's establishing scenes, which shows a desolate looking Texas town comprising an empty main street and a dilapidated gas station. As this shot is held, the urbane narrator remarks that the zombies did not do this to his hometown in Texas; the town already looked like this *before* they arrived. (Hint, hint.) The same joke informs *Shaun of the Dead* (2004), a film written by Simon Pegg and Edgar Wright, which offers no explanation as to how the zombie apocalypse occurred, but suggests that economic Thatcherism is to blame. In a world where unions no longer exist, upward social mobility has been halted, and the British people see no meaning in their lives, all that remains for the average Brit, including heroes Shaun and Ed, is a choice between toiling mindlessly at a minimum-wage job in a grocery or electronics store, sitting dully on the couch playing video games, or sitting sullenly at the bar sipping ale and eating chips. When zombies begin showing up in the alley outside the pub, or shambling along suburban streets, Shaun completely fails to notice the flesh-eating undead because they look exactly like regular people — unthinking, tired, and directionless.

Just as zombies are sometimes hard to distinguish from people, they are also often hard to distinguish from vampires. The line between zombies and vampires has blurred in recent years, as it was in Richard Matheson's 1954 novel *I Am Legend*, one of Romero's central inspirations for *Night of the Living Dead.* While Stephenie Meyer's *Twilight* series has returned to prominence the conception of the vampire as Romantic hero — an idea popularized before by *Dark Shadows* (1966–1971), *Horror of Dracula* (1958), and John Badham's *Dracula* (1979) — the depiction of the vampire as plague carrier from F.W. Murnau's *Nosferatu* (1922) is alive and well, and central to *The Strain* (2009), a pandemic-themed vampire novel by Guillermo del Toro and Chuck Hogan. As a disfigured, slow-moving plague carrier leading an army of rats into an urban population, the vampire can be remarkably similar to the zombie and recent vampire films have been replete with apocalyptic imagery.

For example, an arguably recent addition to the vampire genre is the vampire "war film," which has the urgency and brutality of war movies, and often involves a small town, or fortified building, that is besieged by an enemy force of far superior strength and numbers. In films such as these, the defenders are either massacred, in an outcome akin to the battle of the Alamo, or, incredibly, prevail, as in the Battle of Rorke's Drift in the Anglo-Zulu War. In such films, the human defenders are clearly the "heroes" and the attacking vampire army the "villains," so vampire "war movies" are rarely as morally ambiguous as the circumstances behind the real-life battles that inspired them. Nevertheless, the depiction of mass killings and burning of homes evokes real-life war crimes, genocides, and wars of attrition in an often serious and sobering manner. This scenario is more common to zombie films, westerns, and science fiction blockbusters inspired by *Aliens* (1986), but it is featured in notable vampire films *From Dusk Till Dawn* (1996), *30 Days of Night* (2007), and *I Am Legend* (2007). The most recent additions to this genre are, unsurprisingly, replete with 9/11 and war on terror imagery.

Previous adaptations of *I Am Legend,* including *The Last Man on Earth* and *The Omega Man*, starred Caucasian actors Vincent Price and Charlton Heston in the role of protagonist Robert Neville. Will Smith's muscular military man iteration of the character was charismatic and appealing to mass audiences, making his adaptation the most financially successful of the three. Images of Smith walking with his pet dog across an abandoned Times Square, littered with burnt and battered cars, reminded the world that Americans, and New Yorkers, remain afraid that civilization as they know it can end at any time.

In 2009, the vampire film *Daybreakers,* written and directed by Michael Spierig and Peter Spierig, was even more explicitly about the end of the American Empire. The film took place in 2019 in a world where virtually everyone on earth has been transformed into a vampire, and a vampire corporation that provides blood to the masses keeps the few surviving humans in food pens. Unfortunately, the corporation is rapidly running out of blood as the few remaining humans on earth die in captivity, and the whole vampire population of earth is becoming malnourished and withering into a primal, death-like state as the food is rationed. Faced with rampant rioting and total social collapse, vampire scientist Edward Dalton (Ethan Hawke) seeks a cure for vampirism to end the need for blood while the corporate head Charles Bromley (Sam Neill) schemes to find new supplies of blood, no matter the cost in human suffering. When Dalton finds a cure for vampirism, Bromley suppresses it, because he knows that a cure would liberate the world from its dependence upon his corporation for sustenance and severely cut into his profits.

The vampires in the film are symbolic representations of modern-day Americans and Europeans, whose prosperity and social stability is entirely dependent upon dwindling oil resources dominated by Middle Eastern regimes and dwindling water supplies that have been quietly bought up and siphoned off by massive corporations such as the Coca Cola Company. The film raises questions about this situation that it cannot completely answer, but it is a warning to viewers to encourage the development of alternative fuels and to embrace the environmental legislation that will protect the world's endangered natural resources and share them equitably worldwide. Like *Avatar* (2009), which also concerns a resource-starved Earth of the future, *Daybreakers* makes it apparent that the wars in the Middle East are, indeed, far more about securing oil than they are about establishing democracies or preventing future nuclear attacks on American soil.

Like the vampire film *Daybreakers*, recent zombie films also succeed in bringing the wars in Iraq and Afghanistan unerringly back to the American home front. In Robert Rodriguez's *Grindhouse* feature *Planet Terror* (2007), Bruce Willis plays Lt. Muldoon, an American soldier whose unit successfully assassinated Osama bin Laden in Afghanistan only to be accidentally exposed to a deadly biochemical agent that transformed him and his men into zombies. Written off by the Bush Administration and their accomplishments left largely unknown by the American public, Muldoon's unit unleashes the same chemical agent on a small Texas town. The zombie army created by the gas attacks the town, tearing off the limbs of local residents, and the shapely leg of go-go dancer "Cherry Darling" (Rose McGowan), making everyday Americans experience the same crippling, mutilating injuries that unsung American soldiers suffered in the war on terror.

In *Masters of Horror: Homecoming* (2005), the "unidentified" President of the United States (a.k.a. George W. Bush) is seeking re-election while waging an unpopular war overseas. The leader of the anti-war movement, Janet Hofstader (Beverly Breuer), is the mother of one of the slain soldiers and a character obviously inspired by real-life anti-war activist Cindy Sheehan. The president seeks to discredit Hofstader, so he sends two of his best political consultants to face off against her on a news commentary program: David Murch (Jon Tenney) and Jane Cleaver (Thea Gill), a conservative female pundit modeled on Anne Coulter. Murch uses feigned emotion and verbal sophistry to humiliate Hofstader on national television, and declares that anti-war activists are disgracing the memories of the soldiers who died overseas to protect our freedoms. Indeed, Murch argues, if such soldiers could somehow come back to life to vote in the upcoming election, they would vote for the man who sent them to their deaths because they have all carried their enduring belief in the justness of the war into the afterlife with them. The President overhears this effective argument and, taking his cue from Murch, begins using it in his speeches. This crass campaign strategy enrages the spirits of the dead soldiers, who were shipped home to America secretly, at night, so that no news cameras could film their arrival. Their bodies return to life and the zombies peacefully proceed to vote against the president on Election Day, and for the candidate who promises to end the war overseas. The president's opponent wins the election by a landslide, but the president's well-placed supporters rig the results, and invalidate the zombie vote. Enraged that their votes no longer count, the once peaceful zombies radicalize and proceed to walk across the country, devouring every supporter of the president they can find, taking special pleasure in killing Murch and his Anne Coulter–like friend.

Zombies had been a fixture of comic books in the 1950s, especially the E.C. Comics horror periodicals *Tales from the Crypt* and *Vault of Horror*, but they were driven out of the medium by the creation of the Comics Code Authority in the wake of the Frederic Wertham hearings. The weakening of the power of the Comics Code in recent decades and the mainstreaming of comics for adults in the 1980s meant that it was only a matter of time before the undead walked the pages of comic books once again. The popular *Marvel Zombies* line of comic books features undead incarnations of all of the company's most famous heroes, and includes a revolting segment in which a zombie Spider-Man kills and eats Mary Jane.

There are also a line of collector's statues and action figures being sold to tie in with the comic book, depicting zombie Hulk, zombie Captain America, and so on. Other comic book forays into zombie lore are more appealing, however.

Watch out! The zombie wants to eat your flesh! A scene from *The Walking Dead* (2010), an AMC television series developed by Frank Darabont from the comic book by Robert Kirkman.

Eric Powell's *The Goon* is a horror-comedy about two invincible mob extortionists who protect a small town from being overrun by an encroaching, ever-expanding zombie horde. Powell's retro artistic style, gleeful enthusiasm for violence, and strain of anti-intellectualism earmark the comic book as conservative and nostalgic, but its anarchic, almost Marx Brothers style humor makes it a favorite of many liberal comics readers. The same can be said of *Hellboy*, a comic book about a loveable red demon who fights traditional monsters such as Nazis, vampires, and zombies, but specializes in protecting our reality from invading, other-dimensional, H.P. Lovecraft–style tentacle monsters. Like *The Goon*, *Hellboy* is a celebration of old-world, blue-collar machismo, a Jack Kirby–style breed of manhood that has arguably vanished since the dwindling of the World War II Generation and the fall of organized labor.

Indeed, Hellboy creator Mike Mignola has said that the inspiration for his character was his cabinet-maker father, who was injured daily on the job and merely shrugged off his array of wounds to press on and get the job done.[3] Guillermo del Toro, who directed two *Hellboy* films and produced two *Hellboy* animated movies, called Mignola a "genius" and praised the comic creator for celebrating a working-class male character.[4] Del Toro has himself made Lovecraft inspired films such as *Chronos* (1993) and *Pan's Labyrinth* (2006), both of which were violent political allegories that condemned corporate greed and imperialism while sensitively portraying children and social outcasts as victims of Fascistic regimes. In del Toro's *Hellboy II: The Golden Army* (2008), the American public discovers Hellboy's existence and is, as a whole, terrified of his crimson skin, massive stone hand, and sawed-off demon's horns. Unimpressed that Hellboy, and Hellboy alone, has stood between Earth and the apocalypse on a multitude of occasions, the American people are too prejudiced against demons to accept that notion that one could possibly be redeemable and "one of the good guys." Therefore, they shun Hellboy, making him doubt whether he was right to choose to live his life serving a populace that hates and fears him. While possibly unintentional, there are parallels with President Obama, who does not possess Hellboy's blue-collar charm, but has been similarly demonized by a significant minority of Americans despite his efforts to stave off the fall of the American empire.

Berni Wrightson's *Captain Sternn: Running Out of Time* (1993) takes place on a future earth in which everyone who dies comes back to life as a zombie. The world has become so overpopulated that a massive space catapult has been built to launch the legions of the living dead into the sun. Amoral intergalactic con man Lincoln Sternn discovers that the cause of the zombie plague is the soda pop Cosmic Coola, the only beverage available to humanity. Cosmic Coola Company CEO Fillmore Coffers has laced his product with a highly addictive plant extract that ensures his company's continued monopoly on drink, but has the unfortunate side affect of reanimating the dead. When Coffers realizes he has caused this problem, he does not stop adding the plant; instead, he silences Sternn and his friends by exiling them in the far-flung past of the Jurassic era where they can do him and his company no harm. However, Coffers' problems begin to spiral out of control when Sternn finds a way to return to the present, as do a series of man-eating dinosaurs who, once they consume enough Cosmic-Coola–drinking humans, become zombie dinosaurs after they are shot by the earth military. The over-the-top comic storyline is Wrightson's satire of the rise of the Coca-Cola Company, which initially introduced its soda products to the world with cocaine and caffeine as its two central ingredients (the cocaine was reportedly removed in 1903).[5]

Another futuristic satire of the sugary-drinks-industry is the zombie-free *Idiocracy* (2006) by *King of the Hill* creator Mike Judge. The story charts the sharp decline in intelligence of the average American thanks to plummeting reading scores, cuts to education funding, sinister corporate manipulation, the abominable stupidity of modern-day movies and television shows, and the refusal of intelligent, professional Americans to breed as many children as "hicks" breed. The result is a world of moronic compulsive shoppers with the inability to think in anything but three-word-slogans supplied by the corporate advertisements plastered all around their world, including "Money is good" and "Plants need electrolytes."

As health awareness blogger Mike Adams has written:

> What's so great about *Idiocracy* is not merely how funny it is, but rather how accurate it is at constructing a future society extrapolated from the real trends of modern-day America. Today, for example, corporations have taken over control of the Food and Drug Administration. In *Idiocracy*, a sports drink company simply buys the FDA and replaces the entire Food Guide Pyramid with sports drink ads.
>
> Water is no longer consumed at all in the *Idiocracy* world — consumers have been taught that water is only for toilets — and sports drink liquid is used to water the crops (which are mysteriously dying). This is much like modern medicine today, where doctors, sunscreen manufacturers and even the American Cancer Society insists that sunlight is bad for your health, and that what you really need are expensive prescription medications to solve your health problems.

When moderately intelligent everyman Joe Bauers (Luke Wilson) is discovered to be the smartest man on the planet, he is named the new U.S. Secretary of the Interior, despite the fact that everyone he meets thinks he is pompous and "faggy" because he is capable of speaking in complete sentences. He demands that American crops be irrigated with water instead of a Gatorade-like sports drink, and suggests that people should consider drinking water again, too. This attack on the sports drink industry causes the stock market to go into free fall, and the country turns on Bauers, demanding his blood. He is only saved at the last moment when plants begin growing again, demonstrating that water is, indeed, healthy after all.

While the film was released before Obama was elected president, Bauers' dilemma is much like Obama's. As hard as it was for Bauers to convince Americans that water is better for them than sports drinks, it is still harder for Obama to convince the American people that seeking alternative fuel sources, protecting the environment, and eating right is more important than continuing to funnel billions of dollars into oil companies, the dietary supplements industry, McDonald's, and the businesses associated with the U.S. Chamber of Commerce. However, against all odds, Bauers does indeed succeed in helping the idiocracy take the first few baby steps towards restoring health, intelligence, and a decent quality of life to America. Obama represents a similar hope for the world of the present. To that extent, these zombie apocalypse narratives may not signal the inevitable end of civilization as we know it, but may be a sign that the dawn of a new age is approaching.

In *The Dark Knight*, heroic politician Harvey Dent proclaims to his constituents, "The night is darkest just before the dawn. And I promise you, the dawn is coming." The line of dialogue transforms the film's title into a pun, signifying both Batman's feudal moniker as well as the idea that the Joker's reign of terror causes Batman's "dark night of the soul"—and Gotham City's as well. But Dent suggests that night's end is coming, and the mutual pain experienced by Batman and the city he protects will subside and be replaced by hope and fulfillment.

There is, though, little hope to be found in *The Dark Knight*. The film takes place over an indeterminate period, but suggests that the Joker is at large long enough to plan a series of crimes against the city, including the assassination of a mayor, the bombing of a hospital, and the burning of the Mafia's secret stockpiles of money. As in the classic Alan Moore and Brian Bolland saga *The Killing Joke*, the Joker's overarching plan throughout is to prove that, deep down, people are only as "good" and "decent" as circumstances allow them to be, and if they had had his childhood, they would be just as horrific a figure as he is. His main target in the film is the idealized public figure Harvey Dent, who is too noble and handsome for the Joker to stomach, and who the Joker mistakenly believes to be Batman. Consequently, the Joker launches a campaign to destroy, discredit, and drive Harvey Dent insane, and his tactics make Glenn Beck's and Rush Limbaugh's respective public crusades against Barack Obama seem tame in comparison. Significant, also, is the Joker's white face, seemingly bloody mouth, and shambling gait, which gives him an even more zombie-like appearance than he has in the comics. Consequently, in *The Dark Knight*, a single, malevolent figure of chaos and destruction represents the same apocalyptic-level threat posed by an entire horde of flesh-eating zombies in other, similarly apocalyptic films.

In a subplot apparently inspired by the comic book *Dark Detective* (2005), Batman has to protect Harvey Dent from the Joker and the Mafia even as he is tempted to have an affair with Dent's fiancée, Rachel. When the Joker ultimately murders Rachel and mutilates Harvey's once-handsome face, he destroys Harvey's sanity. Since the inspiring, idealistic Dent bore a striking resemblance to Barack Obama, some critics feared that the film suggested that Obama would crack under the relentless pressure placed upon him by his enemies, and unexpectedly reveal a weaker, darker side.

In "Art of Darkness," a *New York Times* editorial published on September 20, 2008, shortly before the presidential election, Jonathan Lethem wondered if the runaway success of *The Dark Knight*, and the parallels between Batman and the Bush Administration pointed out by certain critics, indicated an inevitable McCain-Palin victory. Ultimately Lethem argued that—whether or not Batman was supposed to "symbolize" Bush—the film's incoherent plot and depressing tone indicated little more than that the Joker was an excellent representation of the American people. Like us, the Joker is angry, confused, bitter, and completely against seeing a fundamentally broken society *actually mended*. Like us, the Joker wants to destroy any would-be hero who actually tries to change things for the better. So anyone who tries to offer Harvey Dent–style "hope" for a new dawn better watch out for the American people — all Jokers and zombies to a man. As Alfred Pennyworth tells Bruce Wayne in *The Dark Knight*, "Some men just want to watch the world burn."

And yet, despite Lethem's fears, Obama won the election, suggesting the possibility that Harvey Dent might not, in the real world, lose his mind or be killed after all. Perhaps the dawn truly is coming, as Dent predicted.

Like the fallen, Gothic world portrayed in *The Dark Knight*, the DC and Marvel Universes have been a grim and violent place to visit for more than twenty years. The popularity of anti-hero characters such as the Punisher and Lobo, the deconstructionist view of heroism represented by *Watchmen*, and the fury liberal writers have consistently felt living under decades of conservative governance conspired to strip all of the joy, innocence, and imagination from superhero comics, and ensure they are not safe places for many children or optimists to visit. However, shortly after Obama's election victory, both Marvel and DC announced major editorial changes in their comic book lines, highlighting hope over fear and heroism over anti-heroism. Finally, a transcendentalist sensibility was making a return to comic books through Marvel's "Heroic Age" and DC's *Brightest Day*.

Since transcendentalism is only credible if it directly confronts Gothic sensibilities and proves the stronger in a straight contest, the story that directly preceded DC's *Brightest Day* was the superhero vs. zombie war comic book *Blackest Night*. In Geoff Johns' *Blackest Night*, Green Lantern Hal Jordan rallies the heroes of the DC Universe against the flesh-eating, reanimated corpses of their former opponents and comrades-in-arms. Zombie Aquaman, Zombie Hawkman, Zombie Maxwell Lord, and Zombie Dr. Light were a few of the legions of the deceased Black Lantern Corps members waging war against creation. Hal Jordan decides to rally not only the entire Green Lantern Corps — which has a membership dedicated to preserving the will to act decisively in the face of overwhelming fear — but the members of other "Color Spectrum" Corps as well. Representing an "emotional spectrum" based on the colors of the visible spectrum are the Blue Lanterns, who channel hope; the Indigo Lanterns, who embrace compassion; and the Violet Lanterns, who spread love throughout the cosmos. These "positive emotions" joined forced with the more traditionally "negative" emotions — rage (the Red Lantern Corps), avarice (The Orange Lanterns), and fear (the Yellow Lanterns led by classic Green Lantern villain Sinestro) to take on the Black Lanterns, the physical embodiment of death.

These united Corps members, fighting alongside Superman, Wonder Woman, and all the DC heroes, beat back the zombie menace. While they were at it, they completed Geoff Johns' multi-year project to resurrect from the dead (not as zombies but as "real" people) many of the kind, whimsical superheroes who had been written out of continuity for decades because they were too "cute" or idealistic to be an integral part of the post–*Watchmen* DC Universe. Thanks to Johns, DC Vice President Dan DiDio, Grant Morrison, and several others, many nostalgic faces have returned in the DC Universe roll call of heroes. Back again is the sweet, seahorse-riding Aquaman, as well as the whitebread Flash Barry Allen, and the mythic fantasy characters Hawkman and Hawkgirl. The moment in *Blackest Night* when many heroes return to life is triumphant, and occurs in tandem with the unveiling of the White Lantern, the wellspring of the Entity, the embodiment of all life in the cosmos. The light radiated by the White Lantern is the central image of 2010's *Brightest Day* storyline, and heralds a new dawn of hope for the DC universe as the zombie apocalypse has been finally, conclusively, averted by the power of positive emotion.

In Brightest Day: A Heroic Age of New Transcendentalism

In fearful day,
In raging night,
With strong hearts full,
Our Souls Ignite.
When All Seems Lost
In the War of Light,
Look to the Stars,
For hope burns bright!
—The Blue Lantern Oath[6]

In 2009, independent comics publisher DDP released a "sword and sorcery" genre comic book starring a muscle-bound Barack Obama as title character *Barack the Barbarian*. The comic, written by Larry Hama and illustrated by Christopher Schons, was an in-joke reference to the fact that Obama grew up enthusiastically reading Marvel's *Conan the Barbarian* and relating to the hero. The story takes place in a future America, caught in the grip of an Ice Age caused by climate change. One of the old, wise men of a surviving Arctic tribe regales his people's children with stories of the world before the great freeze. Commenting on the stunning brutality of Washington politics, the old wise men tells stories of the 2008 presidential election and the 2009 healthcare debate as if they are literally sword-fight battles to the death, and relates them as if they were Conan-style adventure stories.

The wise man's story begins when Barack of Shikhago, "dark-skinned ... glib of tongue ... with unflappable coolness and ironic sensibility," comes to the feudal town of Warshington to liberate it from the rule of the Despot Boosh (George Bush) and his evil vizier Harry Burden (Dick Cheney). Boosh and Burden rule Warshington from atop the Tower of the Elephant, where they are guarding the mysterious "Treasure of the Stimuli." Barack decides to raid the tower, depose Boosh, and liberate the secret treasure, but he faces competition from Red Sarah, a sexy red headed warrior woman dressed only in glasses and a chain mail armor bikini, and her supposed employer, whom she constantly defies, known as "The old soldier." Red Sarah is a character based on both the *Conan* character Red Sonja and Sarah Palin, while the Old Soldier, who lost much respect by teaming up with Red Sarah, is clearly a commentary on John McCain.

Barack teams with the Valkyrie Hilaria (Hilary Clinton) and the two try to beat Red Sarah and the Old Soldier to the top of the tower. They meet nearly life-ending challenges in the Labyrinth of Pundits, where Barack slices the tongue off the screeching enchantress Choler (Anne Coulter), and has to face the bloated demon AIGh (the corporation AIG), and the rampaging Elephant God. When faced with the Elephant God, Hilaria asks what it is and how they can defeat it. Barack replies that it is "A conflation of failed policies, delusional political theory, and wretched excess." Barack notes that the monster is "just bellowing in inchoate rage ... flailing aimlessly with no positive strategy." He concludes, that the monster "will defeat itself. All we have to do is stay out of its way." However, the Cult of the Elephant successfully disguises itself by trading its elephant heads for giant tea bag emblems, and wins over a legion of new supporters by "rallying the geriatric, the uninformed, and the easily swayed" (see issue #3).

At the end of the story, Barack and Hilaria defeat Boosh and his Vizier and liberate the treasure—the chained, haggard, and beaten Statue of Liberty, whose torch has gone out. Barack manages to reignite the torch, a symbol of freedom and enlightenment, by returning balance to the magical Scales of Justice he found hidden in a pile of rubbish in Bush's secret lair (issue #4).

In the sequel story, *Barack the Barbarian: The Fall of Red Sarah* (2009), Barack comes upon a city riddled with plague and disease in which the inhabitants hope to find medical treatment but lack the money needed to pay the doctors and the insurance companies for health care. Barack tries to help the people find affordable medicine, but they are afraid of him since they had heard prophecies of a roving "Death Panel" that would come to their city and commit murder while posing as physicians. Barack laughs off the wild accusation and tries to help. Meanwhile, Red Sarah, humiliated by the defeat she and the Old Soldier suffered in the campaign to take the Tower of the Elephant, accepts a massive treasure chest of money as a bribe to help the evil wizard HMO and his greedy corporate backers (symbolically portrayed by a giant Spider God and a loathsomely fat demon) dispose of Barack.

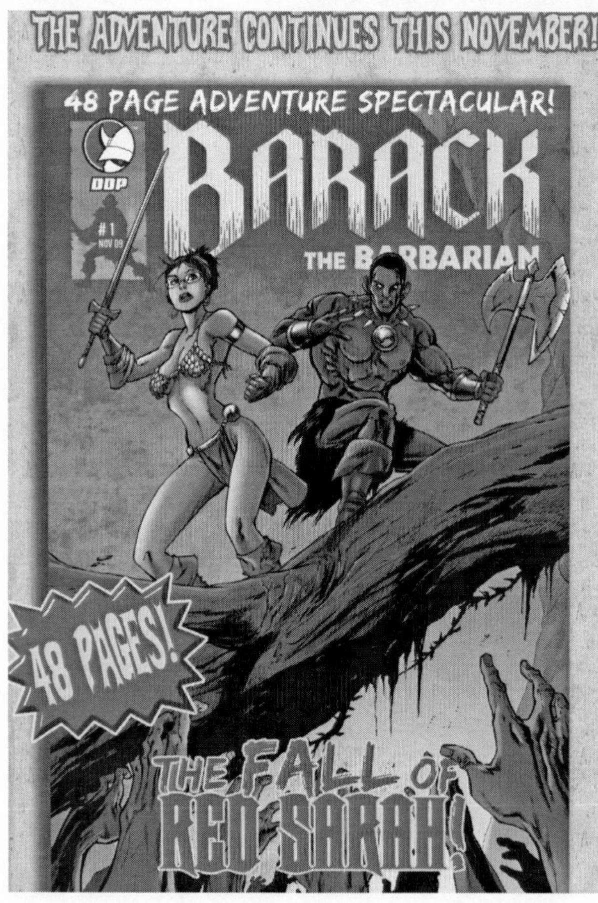

Advertisement for *Barack the Barbarian: The Fall of Red Sarah* (Devil's Due Publishing, 2009). The comic, written by Larry Hama and illustrated by John Christmas, dramatizes President Obama's successful passage of health care reform despite overwhelming opposition led by his election-year opponent, Sarah Palin. Obama is dressed to resemble Conan the Barbarian and Palin is depicted in the chain-mail bikini normally worn by the Robert E. Howard character Red Sonja.

Barack is soon captured and chained up. He confronts his enemies, howling with indignation: "You've enriched yourselves by seeing to it that only the wealthy can afford health care! Have you no conscience?"

The wizard HMO kicks Barack in the face, shouting, "Conscience! Don't you believe in free enterprise and allowing the market to regulate itself? What are you, a socialist!"

Barack eventually escapes and tries to rally the oppressed masses against the demons. "Okay, I'll lead you. But who here is willing to put their lives on the line for real change? Who will follow me on an assault on the citadel of the triumvirate?"

Four citizens raise their hands to volunteer and the rest skulk away in embarrassed terror.

"So be it," Barack says. "If this is what we have to work with, this is what we have to work with."

Ultimately, Barack defeats HMO and the two demons, and provides affordable health care access to the people. Unfortunately, Red Sarah escapes with vast supplies of money, living to fight Barack another day.

Obviously, this allegorical history of Obama's battle to pass 2010's Patient Protection and Affordable Care Act despite Republican filibusters and relentlessly negative press from Fox News and conservative radio outlets represents a positive view of health care reform. It lampoons Palin's real-life insistence that the Act would fund euthanasia and abortion panels and transform America into a Communist country, while supporting the views of health care reform represented by Nicholas D. Kristoff, Paul Krugman, Jon Stewart, and Michael Moore.

One of the things that is interesting about the Barack the Barbarian series is that its depiction of Obama as a muscle-bound warrior stands in stark contrast with the slim, civilized figure President Obama cuts in real life. While it is amusing to think of Obama reading *Conan* comics as a child, that background information is not sufficient to explain the dramatic power of seeing Obama portrayed as a literal warrior. Why does the image of "Conan Obama" simultaneously make sense and not make any sense at all?

The answer lies in our culture's complete inability to recognize heroism in its modern form. Americans have no tradition of respecting intelligence, or of applauding the reforming of outdated legislation, or of appreciating the moral courage and fortitude it takes to stand in opposition to corporate moguls and members of the military industrial complex. Americans, by and large, simply don't understand that kind of heroism, so they don't know how to identify it, how to celebrate it, or how to represent it dramatically. They do, however, understand sports metaphors and war metaphors, so they can grasp bravery as a man suiting up to do battle, whether in strapping on a football uniform, a battleaxe, or a rifle. And that is where the image of Barack as Conan comes in.

As Leo Braudy explains in *From Chivalry to Terrorism: War and the Changing Nature of Masculinity* (2003):

> ... we now seem to be living in a debased if modern chivalric world, still fascinated by the solitary knight sallying forth to cure the evils of the world. Something of the medieval obsession with the knight in armor returned especially in the 1980s and 1990s with the simultaneous minting of two popular images: the buffed and muscular human body as a rugged container from within which to meet the challenges of life; and, in science fiction and action films, the image of the armor-plated cyborg or robotic hero, like Ripley in *Aliens*, climbing inside a full-body prosthesis to combat the monster. Superman is no longer a being of special powers from another planet; with the right technology, he can be created right here on earth. The films of Arnold Schwarzenegger, Sylvester Stallone, and Jean-Claude Van Damme, for example, combine the two images: the omnicompetent body complete with the paraphernalia of advanced technical weaponry. In part, such characters harken back to a more personal style of medieval warfare in the face of the dehumanization of modern war. Perhaps in an unknowing tribute to Joan of Arc, this neomedieval body is not always masculine—as Ripley and other heroines like her indicate—nor must it always be in armor to be armored in effect. Yet it remains almost the sole way of demonstrating heroism, for men and women alike [114].

To add to Braudy's examples, some of the most famous moments in recent film memory include heroes arming themselves for battle in Quentin Tarantino films, especially when Bruce Willis carefully selects the most deadly weapon available from a variety of alternatives in *Pulp Fiction*, and when the Bride ritualistically claims possession of a perfectly crafted, Hattori Hanzō Samurai Katana sword in *Kill Bill*.

Like many liberals, feminist film critic Molly Haskell expresses impatience with the American inability to see heroism in progressive politics, passive resistance, or the bravery it takes to assume a peaceful, multicultural attitude in an embattled, pluralistic world. As she observes in *From Reverence to Rape: The Treatment of Women in the Movies* (1973), popular culture is replete with heroic narratives that celebrate Batman and Robin style friendships in which two "good old boys" fight evil together and go on daring adventures. But she sees these adventures as a form of cultural regression, and evidence of the contemporary man's unwillingness to face up to his responsibilities to society (and to women) in the real world of today:

> The irony is that the greatest risks are not in riding the rapids or bearhunting or bullfighting, where the fight is clean and the results can be tabulated. For better or for worse, these belonged to an earlier, simpler world, and to reenact them now in the name of virility is to seek security and peace of mind by obsolete definitions. Men have been deprived of the physical grounds for the testing of their virility and those magical mirrors women hold up to their egos. It is, still, a painful transition period. And they haven't yet adjusted to a new definition of masculinity, one that would include courage and bravery in personal relationships, endurance of a [Howard Hawks "cowboy"-style] professionalism transferred to other areas, courage to speak when one would be safer silent, to question the scruples of one's superiors (a quality that Watergate showed to be in short supply), guts, even, to admit weakness. By underrating these virtues, we fail, also, to see heroism when it appears. It is all around us, but in different guises. And so the real risks (and thus, the test of "masculinity" is the same as the test of "femininity"—it is the test of character) lie in the rising to meet other challenges, the challenge of another human being, of someone different but equal, in a love that relishes separateness, grows stronger with resistance, acknowledges its own mortality [24–25].

Indeed, today's most iconic superhero stories involve teenagers who escape the hell of high school into a fantasy world of combat and heroism (*Harry Potter, Buffy the Vampire Slayer, Spider-Man, Kick-Ass*) or who leave their middle-management, cubicle job behind to become a hero (*Wanted, The Matrix, The Incredibles*). All of these stories represent fantasy escapes from reality, but offer no real guideposts to how to live in the real world. One of the few superhero stories that encourages people to try to find new kinds of heroism, and embrace new forms of bravery fit for the modern world, is the Japanese manga and anime series *Salaryman Kintaro* by Hiroshi Motomiya.

Blending two popular Japanese genres — the "salaryman" office-set drama (akin to *The Office*) and the Yakuza film —*Salaryman Kintaro* is about a motorcycle gang leader who assumes a white collar job in an office after his lover dies and leaves him to raise their child alone. The newly "responsible" Kintarō Yajima is appalled by office culture — the passive-aggressive relationships, the gossip, the lying, and the rampant corporate corruption. In contrast, his "criminal" Bōsōzoku bikers all lived by a firm ethical code that put the amoral office environment to shame. Kintaro soon proceeds to imbue his office environment with the Bōsōzoku ethic. He publicly shames people who lie, tirelessly exposes corporate corruption, refuses to take bribes, and calls people out into the street for a fist-fight when they engage in gossip and passive-aggressive shenanigans. While probably still too macho for Haskell, this story, nevertheless, goes a long way towards meeting her demands for a new form of heroism. Consequently, in many ways, *Salaryman Kintaro* is a far better depiction of the heroic ideal that Barack Obama represents than *Barack the Barbarian*.

As Haskell feared, many people do not recognize modern heroism when they see it. In Obama's case, his ability to sneak progressive legislation past Republican filibustering is perceived as evil and unscrupulous, his decision to end Operation Iraqi Freedom is seen as a sign of his treasonous sympathy for Muslims, and his oratory skills are perceived as womanish and fueled by teleprompters and professorial speechwriters.

On the other hand, a great many progressives do recognize Obama's form of heroism, and see him as the liberal movement's greatest hope since the assassinations of John F.

Kennedy, Bobby Kennedy, Malcolm X, Martin Luther King, and John Lennon; hence the jubilation upon Obama's election, and the widespread portrayal of him as a form of superhero in the comics industry. For many liberals, the fact that he would be America's first African American president was merely icing on the cake. As *DMZ* creator Brian Wood argued, after eight years of Bush's transparently unconstitutional agenda, it was an enormous relief to see a professorial liberal in the White House instead of a corrupt conservative (Hudson).

The day after Obama's victory, Laura Hudson of MTV News reported the general euphoria among comic book writers and artists. Comic creators Fred Van Lente (*Marvel Zombies*), Alex Ross (*Kingdom Come*), Mike Mignola (*Hellboy*), Eric Powell (*The Goon*), Jaime Hernandez (*Love and Rockets*), Jimmy Palmiotti (*The Punisher*), and Amanda Conner (*Vampirella*) had raised $5,000 for the Democrat's campaign via The Comics Industry for Obama by auctioning off their comics work. Hernandez was distressed at the passing of Proposition 8, but was otherwise "a giddy schoolboy" over the results. Keith Knight (*K Chronicles*), who famously condemned racist tactics used by the right against Obama in his comic strip, was also delighted, but admitted that "many cartoonists will miss Bush and Cheney, because they made our job so easy." According to Hudson, even libertarian Peter Bagge (*Hate*) said he believed the symbolic importance of a non-white male being elected president "can't be underestimated, especially regarding how we're perceived in the rest of the world," and noted that "the Republican Party has so thoroughly disgraced itself that they needed to be sent to exile."

In celebration of Obama's victory, *Kingdom Come* and *Justice* artist Alex Ross painted portraits of Obama tearing open his shirt to reveal an "O" logo on a superhero outfit underneath, Superman-style, and rendered portraits of the first family for the cover of industry magazine *Wizard*.

While *Saturday Night Live*, and many Obama opponents, had consistently failed to find an apt, amusing way to lampoon the new president, the "fake newspaper" *The Onion* came up with the brilliant idea of poking fun at him for being a comic book geek. In "Obama Disappointed Cabinet Failed to Understand His Reference to 'Savage Sword of Conan' #24" (Issue 45–05, January 27, 2009), *The Onion* "reported" that Obama

> is expected to meet with Secretary of Defense Robert Gates on Friday to discuss Afghanistan. A holdover from the Bush administration, Gates told reporters he may have gotten off on the wrong foot with the new president, citing an occasion when Obama asked him what he knew about 1984's *Secret Wars*, a 12-issue limited Marvel release. Gates then handed a visibly confused Obama 1,400 classified pages on covert CIA operations in El Salvador.

Since many Obama-supporting writers and artists worked for Marvel and DC, they had not been able to endorse him overtly in their comic stories, but independent comic book creators were not so hamstrung. In August 2008, the cover of *Savage Dragon* #137 featured the reptilian superhero's official endorsement of Barack Obama. As Erik Larsen, *Savage Dragon* creator, explained, "This was unheard of. It was not something comic book characters typically did. Generally ... folks in editorial were hesitant to have [superheroes] take a stand on much of anything for fear of alienating readers. But it was ... an important election ... [and] made good storytelling sense to do it.... As you might expect, I'm pleased as punch to see that Obama made it to the White House. With any luck and a little cooperation I hope he can help get us out of the downward spiral we seem to be caught in. We should all wish him well in his endeavors. Liberal or conservative, we all benefit from a strong economy and a strong country."[7]

Interestingly, at the same time the *Savage Dragon* comic debuted, Scottish comic book writer Mark Millar's satirical election-year comic book *War Heroes* posited a science fiction future in which John McCain emerged victorious in the contest. However, if the writer had had the right to vote in American elections, he revealed in a pre-election interview that he would not be casting his vote for the McCain-Palin ticket:

> I quite like McCain, but he's the shiny berry on a plant that's going to poison you. He's dangerous because he's the acceptable face of something just completely unacceptable to almost everyone now, but is likable enough to possibly pull this off. I'd obviously vote for Obama, just as I'd have picked Kerry, Gore, Clinton, Dukakis, Mondale, or Carter over any of their Republican opponents. But I worry about the messianic hope America has invested in [Obama]. He's a good orator and I agree with him on most things, but he's still just a guy from Chicago. Let's not go overboard....
>
> [As for Palin, she's] terrifying. America has a habit of selecting the candidate we Europeans most likely balk at. So I can't even laugh. She represents that side of your country we can't even begin to understand.[8]

Many Obama supporters knew, on some level, that Millar was correct to assert that Obama was human, and not a superhero after all. However, knowing this and feeling this were two different things. Professional artist Paul Richmond explained that he grew up watching reruns of the Adam West *Batman* series, and the series protagonists represented a set of ideals to him as a child that he has since attempted to seek out in the more complicated world he inhabits as an adult. When, at long last, Obama, someone who represented the kind of heroism Richmond had always hoped to see operating in the real world, appeared on the scene, it was only natural that Richmond would pay tribute to Obama by painting him as Batman and his vice-presidential running mate, Joe Biden, as Robin in "BatmObama and RoBiden." Richmond included their election-year opponents in the painting as well, depicting John McCain as the Penguin and Sarah Palin as Catwoman.

In 2008, Erik Larsen received extensive press attention for being the first comic book writer-artist to have a superhero from a major publisher, Image Comics, endorse a real-life political candidate on the cover of *Savage Dragon* #137 (courtesy Erik Larsen).

> While this painting certainly represents my support of the Democratic ticket and my hope

> for victory over the "bad guys," I also wanted to capture the campiness and spectacle of the political process as a whole.
>
> Batman seemed like an ideal match for the heroic status that Obama's achieved, and when Biden joined on as his running mate, the "Dynamic Duo" parallel was complete. I felt that McCain and Palin were also well cast as Penguin and Catwoman not only because of their uncanny physical resemblance to the characters, but also [because of] their roles in the campaign.
>
> I have great hopes and expectations for our heroes, Obama and Biden. As for the "villains," they make great caricatures but frightening prospective leaders.[9]

Amusingly, around the same time that Richmond was depicting Obama as a black Batman, comedians on the Comedy Central series *The Daily Show* were hard at work spoofing the recurring media question, "Is America ready for a black president?" by asking a series of African American cultural critics, "Is America ready for a black Batman?" Meanwhile, in England, the British tabloid press speculated (in all seriousness) that David Tennant's replacement on the series *Doctor Who* might be the first black British actor to play the Doctor, effectively asking, "Is the United Kingdom ready for a black Doctor?"

In 2008, artist Paul Richmond depicted Barack Obama as Batman, and Joe Biden as Robin in "Batmobama and Robiden." Their election-year opponents John McCain and Sarah Palin are pictured as Penguin and Catwoman (courtesy Paul Richmond).

Like DC Comics, which seemed ready to produce more optimistic comics following the election through its *Brightest Day* story arc, Marvel Comics Group also celebrated the election of President Obama with a series of humorous, triumphant, and hopeful stories. The first of these was a meeting between Spider-Man and Obama (featured in *Amazing Spider-Man* #583) that took place during Obama's inauguration on Tuesday, January 20, 2009. The story, written by Zeb Wells and drawn by Todd Nauck, involved an attempt by the Chameleon, a shape-shifting Spider-Man villain, to impersonate Obama and get himself sworn in as the 44th president instead. Spider-Man recognizes one of his oldest foes handiwork and unmasks the imposter just in time. Still a wanted man thanks to the events of the Marvel *Civil War*,

Spider-Man expects to be apprehended by the Secret Service instead of thanked for his intervention. He moves to flee the scene, but Obama stops him. The president elect says, "I've been a big fan of yours for a long time and, before you go I just want to say thanks ... partner." And the two men fist bump in solidarity and mutual respect.

This bestselling, oft-reprinted issue was a one-off event designed by Marvel Comic's Editor in Chief Joe Quesada to publicly thank Obama for declaring in interviews his love of Spider-Man and Conan the Barbarian, two classic Marvel properties. While subsequent Marvel stories featuring a fictionalized Obama were sometimes less widely publicized, many of them were far less silly in tone and far more dramatically significant.

For example, the resurrection of Steve Rogers, the original Captain America, took place in *Captain America Reborn* (2009–2010), a story written by Ed Brubaker and drawn by Bryan Hitch. As the living embodiment of faith in the American Dream, Captain America's resurrection was symbolically facilitated by Obama's election, which liberal comic writers viewed as a referendum on the Bush presidency. In Brubaker's *Two Americas* (2010), a story that deeply offended the political pundits at Fox News, the resurrected Captain America prevents a homegrown terrorist organization with ties to the Tea Party from blowing up the Hoover Dam in protest against Obama's socialist policies. Captain America also commanded all of the Marvel superheroes, registered and unregistered alike, in a campaign against Norman Osborne, preventing him from starting a destructive, unnecessary war between America and the Gods of Asgard in Brian Michael Bendis' *Siege* (2010).

In gratitude for Captain America's service, the fictional Obama featured in the Marvel Universe appointed the Captain head of American national security. Captain America asked several favors of Obama before he accepted the post. He asked that the Superhero Registration Act that ignited the superhero Civil War be repealed, that all of the superpowered beings held without trial in the Negative Zone be released, and that pardons be granted all superheroes wanted for treason (including Spider-Man, Dr. Strange, Wolverine, Falcon, and Luke Cage) because they acted in defiance of the SRA. Obama granted all of these

In *The Amazing Spider-Man* #583 (Marvel Comics, 2009), Spider-Man prevents the shape-shifting villain Chameleon from replacing President-Elect Obama moments before the inauguration. Afterwards, Obama — a lifelong Spider-Man fan — thanks his rescuer. Written by Zeb Wells and illustrated by Todd Nauck.

requests, at long last bringing to a happy ending the years of suffering caused by Tony Stark and the fictional President Bush of the Marvel Universe. This act made Obama a pivotal character in the Marvel Universe. This pardoning also paved the way for Spider-Man to join Jonathan Hickman's revamped Fantastic Four (*FF*) and helped give Peter Parker the boost he needed to, at long last, find career success as a scientist at a think tank in Dan Slott's *Big Time*.

It is interesting to consider the legal ramifications of the use of real-life political figures, ranging from Obama to Palin to unelected media pundits such as Limbaugh and O'Reilly. In *Barack the Barbarian* and *President Evil*, the names of characters are changed, the tone of the comics are satirical, and the drawings of the individuals are exaggerated, suggesting that the publications are commentaries on public figures and protected by the First Amendment. The comically beleaguered Barack Obama stand-in who appears as a lead character in *Godzilla: Kingdom of Monsters* is represented sympathetically, but placed in an unbelievable science fiction reality context. Still, it arguably acts as a commentary on what his leadership represents in the real world. However, according to Jeff Trexler, Wilson Professor of Social Entrepreneurship at Pace University, companies that have seemed to make money licensing the image of a real person without commenting upon them have run into some difficulties.

"The appearance of Obama in *Licensable Bear* was arguably a paradigmatic protected comment, using Obama to satirize the commoditization of public life," said Trexler. "Obama's appearance in *Spider-Man* was arguably little more than a commercial appropriation of Obama's likeness and thus, it could be argued, less protected."[10]

Of all of the commentaries on Obama provided by the comics industry, perhaps the most seriously intended is Mark Powers' *Drafted: One Hundred Days* (2009). Like *President Evil* and *Barack the Barbarian*, it takes place in a post-apocalyptic world, but it is a story told in a far more somber style. The world has been devastated by a serious of earthquakes, has suffered the most bitter winter in a century, and civilization has fallen. Aliens have drafted the surviving humans into an army in a war against a second alien race. When the enemy aliens are repelled from an attempted takeover of Earth, the human's mysterious alien masters disappear as well, leaving a group of humans with virtually no food or supplies in the snow-covered ruins of Chicago. The leader of the small band of humans is former Senator Barack Obama. He had been running for president when human civilization, as it was known, came to an end so, clearly, the fault for the calamity was not his. His intelligence, integrity, and reassuring smile made him a natural leader, and he kept the humans' spirits up, even as their food depleted and the bitter winter made them exhausted and ill. One woman, a nurse, remembers that Bill O'Reilly once characterized Obama as a dangerous Muslim, and she asks him about this. Obama smiles at her, and she realizes that she has said something deeply foolish and apologizes. The two become fast friends.

A conflict emerges when Obama urges the humans to try to rebuild the ruined Chicago. A splinter group of humans breaks off, declaring it foolhardy to waste time and resources trying to rebuild a fallen civilization. Instead, the leader of the second faction argues, it is wiser to become a roving band of scavengers and pirates, and try to live off what is left of the natural food and resources in the area. Obama fears that the splinter group will raid the resources his faction needs to rebuild the city, but he tries to ignore the other group and focus on the task at hand.

Weeks go by, food supplies dry up, and those who stayed with Obama begin to wonder if they should have joined the other faction. Gradually, all Obama's supporters defect, including his closest personal aid, and Obama is left alone. Suddenly feeling enormous guilt, but realizing that the mistake he has just made cannot be undone, Obama's former aide is horrified when he takes another, closer look at the leaders of both factions, Obama and the pirate leader. He thinks:

> All this time I've been asking myself what separates leaders from followers. Is it charisma? Pragmatism? A willingness to act when others don't? No. The ones who make the biggest mark come in two forms: those who demand your best, and those who indulge your worst...
>
> We need to believe in something — a person, the future, a vision of perfection. And the darker the times, the more fervent that need is. I invested all my faith in Obama — and when he couldn't make things the way I wanted them to be, I felt betrayed...
>
> The dynamic between a group and its chosen leader is complex — equal parts emotion and practicality. Go too far in either direction and disaster follows. But if you can keep the balance long enough, with the right give and take, sometimes, it is enough to get through the worst of times.

While exiled from all human contact, Obama climbs the highest snowdrift he can and risks dying of exposure to contact their alien commanding officers for new food and supplies. He nearly freezes to death when the aliens arrive with eleventh hour assistance. Obama is able to return to the human base and reassure them that help has arrived. The pirate captain tries to assassinate him, but Obama's old right-hand-man leaps forward and stops the pirate. The two old friends reconcile.

By setting all of the cataclysmic events of *Drafted* before Obama became president, and setting the story in an alternate reality where he is a mere former Senator, Powers suggests that all of the major crises Obama faced his first years in office were caused before he arrived on the scene. In a sense, the Apocalypse happened, and Obama has arrived too late to stop it. All he can do is damage control on a decimated economy and two impossible-to-win wars. Under these circumstances, it does, indeed, seem like too much pressure to put on a man (who is human after all) to act as a Messiah for all of human civilization. In a way, the story's two climaxes represent two possible futures for Obama as Powers seems to see them: Obama sent into exile by a broken-spirited public that chooses to throw their lot back in with the Republicans instead of the Democrats, and Obama miraculously victorious against all odds. In a way, those two melodramatic moments are not as important as the thoughts expressed by the traitorous aid. That inner monologue, coupled with the traitor's realization that Obama is a human being after all, and not a God, makes *Drafted: One Hundred Days,* a thoughtful and sensitive read.

On Persian Flaws and Outfoxing the Republican Noise Machine

As Mark Powers observed in *Drafted,* Obama faced a series of seemingly insoluble problems the moment he was sworn into office, and the majority of the plans he presented to the legislative branch designed to address these plans were opposed by the Republican Party — whose membership consistently voted unanimously against Obama's proposals, no matter their relative merit. Conversely, the left wing of the Democratic Party viewed Obama as too cautious, too conservative, and too conciliatory towards the Republicans. They condemned him for retaining several of George W. Bush's military and economic advisors in the name of bi-partisanship and continuity in a time of military and economic upheaval, especially Bush's Chairman of the United States Federal Reserve Ben Bernanke and Defense Secretary Robert Gates. (In fact, Brian Michael Bendis seems to be criticizing Obama for appointing conservatives to his administration when he depicts the unnamed black President of the United States unknowingly appointing the Green Goblin the head of U.S. National Security in 2008's *Secret Invasion.*)

Obama famously stated, "I am not an ideologue"—a fact that right wing ideologues find hilarious and hypocritical—but Obama's continual opposition from both the left wing of his party and the entire Republican Party validates the view that he is a centrist besieged by attacks from both the left and right wings. Some of Obama's critics have genuine reservations about his policies, and cannot make the ideological leap needed to approve of policies that he presents as "pragmatic" and "necessary." However, former President Jimmy Carter has stated that he believes most of the opposition against Obama is motivated by white racism against blacks. Media coverage of overtly racist Tea Party protester signs and the upswing in enrollment in militia and white supremacist groups since Obama's elections seem to bear Carter's view out, but Obama has consistently refused to credit the claim.

During Obama's presidential campaign, some voters became concerned about the then–Senator's close personal connection to the Rev. Jeremiah Wright, Jr., pastor of the church Obama attended for years, Trinity United Church of Christ, in Chicago. Wright, who officiated at Obama's wedding, controversially condemned American racism and imperialism, and suggested that the 9/11 attacks were a deserved retaliation against American imperial policies in the Middle East.

Responding to the controversy, Obama made the speech "A More Perfect Union" on March 18, 2008, at the National Constitution Center in Philadelphia. In the speech, he talked broadly about the history of racial tension in America, from the time of the Founding Fathers up through the Civil War, the civil rights movement, and the present. He characterized American Democracy as a work in progress in which American society continually struggles to evolve and improve in an effort to live up to its ideals of equal rights under the law—whether it is in the ending of the legacy of slavery and Jim Crow, the granting of women's rights, or the closing of the yawning economic gap between the rich and the poor. He cited Wright's views as inflammatory and an overly negative characterization of American history and society that he did not share. Obama also noted that those views were new and shocking to many white Americans because they are largely unfamiliar with the understandable resentments that African Americans have about the enduring racial inequalities in America. Those resentments, he argued, should not be dismissed as purely black racism against whites. However, Obama noted that African Americans also have to heed the legitimate grievances white Americans have about society, and criticisms they have of the African American community, and not dismiss those as racist either. As Obama observed:

> Most working- and middle-class white Americans don't feel that they have been particularly privileged by their race. Their experience is the immigrant experience—as far as they're concerned, no one handed them anything. They built it from scratch. They've worked hard all their lives, many times only to see their jobs shipped overseas or their pensions dumped after a lifetime of labor. They are anxious about their futures, and they feel their dreams slipping away. And in an era of stagnant wages and global competition, opportunity comes to be seen as a zero sum game, in which your dreams come at my expense. So when they are told to bus their children to a school across town; when they hear an African-American is getting an advantage in landing a good job or a spot in a good college because of an injustice that they themselves never committed; when they're told that their fears about crime in urban neighborhoods are somehow prejudiced, resentment builds over time.
>
> Like the anger within the black community, these resentments aren't always expressed in polite company. But they have helped shape the political landscape for at least a generation. Anger over welfare and affirmative action helped forge the Reagan Coalition. Politicians rou-

> tinely exploited fears of crime for their own electoral ends. Talk show hosts and conservative commentators built entire careers unmasking bogus claims of racism while dismissing legitimate discussions of racial injustice and inequality as mere political correctness or reverse racism.
>
> Just as black anger often proved counterproductive, so have these white resentments distracted attention from the real culprits of the middle class squeeze — a corporate culture rife with inside dealing, questionable accounting practices and short-term greed; a Washington dominated by lobbyists and special interests; economic policies that favor the few over the many. And yet, to wish away the resentments of white Americans, to label them as misguided or even racist, without recognizing they are grounded in legitimate concerns — this too widens the racial divide and blocks the path to understanding.

This speech, given before Obama was elected president, accurately predicted two of the greatest challenges he would face as president — the average middle class swing-voter's mounting anger over the Great Recession and the jobless economic recovery that followed, and the constant interference by a corporate oligarchy in Obama's attempts to make America an even more democratic and egalitarian country. While the steps he took in getting an Economic Stimulus Bill passed, unemployment benefits extended, and abusive credit card company practices tamed may have collectively helped prevent the country from falling into another Great Depression, these initiatives did not do enough to generate long-term, well-paying jobs for many Americans suffering from years of unemployment. The jobless recovery, then, eroded public support for his presidency, especially in light of the costly Bush-initiated wars in Iraq and Afghanistan that he seemed insistent on continuing to fight, and the role he played in bailing out failing Wall Street businesses.

The outrage over the Enron scandals was largely overshadowed by other Bush-era controversies until the Great Recession (a.k.a. the financial crisis of 2007–2010), which reawakened populist anger at corporate excess. While many have argued that the corporate bailouts presided over by the Bush and Obama administrations were a necessary evil, others were angered that companies that were "too big to fail" had endangered the entire economy through reckless investments and the insatiable pursuit of profit at the expense of the nation as a whole. Indeed, many have argued that if a company is "too big to fail," it shouldn't exist in the first place and should be broken up into smaller units.

Writing on the eve of the Obama Administration bailouts, economist Paul Krugman felt that the bailouts represented "a classic exercise in 'lemon socialism': taxpayers bear the cost if things go wrong, but stockholders and executives get the benefits if things go right." Krugman's main disappointment was that President Obama was giving corporate America the same royal treatment as his Republican predecessor, only throwing a few more harsh words in for good measure. "When I read recent remarks on financial policy by top Obama administration officials, I feel as if I've entered a time warp — as if it's still 2005, Alan Greenspan is still the Maestro, and bankers are still heroes of capitalism."[11]

In March 2009, further populist anger was stoked when it was publicized that the American International Group (AIG), a beneficiary of $170 billion in taxpayer bailout money, paid out $218 million in salary bonuses to executives during the same year the company lost $61.7 billion.[12]

Obama's 2009 decision to escalate the war in Afghanistan further eroded his support in the Democratic Party's base. This unpopular decision was made still more problematic when he was awarded the Nobel Peace Prize the same year. There was a graspable logic to the Nobel Committee's granting him the award, but the timing was dreadful. The Nobel Committee was recognizing Obama's efforts to reduce the number of American troops in

Iraq, close the Guantanamo Bay internment camp, and replace the G8 international forum with the more inclusive G20, as well as to thank him from the tonal shift his administration represented in the wake of George W. Bush's. Liberal commentators such as Rachel Maddow applauded this thinking. In contrast, liberal bloggers felt that the honor was prematurely granted to a world leader who, ironically, would decide to escalate the war in Afghanistan one week before accepting his prize. Consequently, as Paul Craig Roberts argued, a warmonger had won the Nobel Peace Prize in an Orwellian nightmare come true:

> The Nobel Committee has awarded the 2009 Peace Prize to President Obama, the person who started a new war in Pakistan, upped the war in Afghanistan, and continues to threaten Iran with attack unless Iran does what the US government demands and relinquishes its rights as a signatory to the non-proliferation treaty....
>
> No Bush policy has changed. Iraq is still occupied. The Guantanamo torture prison is still functioning. Rendition and assassinations are still occurring. Spying on Americans without warrants is still the order of the day. Civil liberties are continuing to be violated in the name of Oceania's "war on terror."
>
> Apparently, the Nobel committee is suffering from the delusion that, being a minority, Obama is going to put a stop to Western hegemony over darker-skinned peoples.[13]

In "A Just and Lasting Peace," the Nobel Prize acceptance speech he delivered on December 10, 2009, Obama tried to reconcile his ideals, which embraced the peaceful teachings of Gandhi and Martin Luther King, with the decision he made to escalate the war in Afghanistan in response to the reality of the violent and imperfect world Americans live in. For some, his speech was eloquent, passionate, and honest, as well as deeply moral. For others, the hypocrisy evident in his not refusing the honor, and in the sophistry of his speech, was unforgivable. In either case, the moral ambiguity evident in his speech, and in the Nobel controversy he was embroiled in, was confusing and offensive to many.

For many Americans, Obama's bailout of Wall Street and escalation of the Afghanistan War constitute legitimate reasons to disapprove of his performance as president that have nothing whatsoever to do with his race. Liberal Americans also criticized Obama for attempting to build a bi-partisan coalition with Republicans on healthcare, when the Republican record on bipartisanship is abysmal, giving conservatives the time they needed to scuttle the "public option" part of the health care plan and turn the public at large against health care reform so that the signing of the Health Care Act into law became as much of a public relations defeat for Democrats as it was a legislative and civil rights victory. Other critics of Obama felt he should have done more to ensure that the special election held to replace the deceased Senator Edward Kennedy would result in a Democratic victory. Since Republican Scott Philip Brown won the election, it gave the Republican Party the key vote it needed in the Senate to filibuster a notable percentage of Obama's domestic agenda, threatening to turn him into an ineffective, lame-duck president a mere one year into his presidency. It is, perhaps, no surprise that, following Brown's election, immigration reform, environmental legislation, and the movement to construct an American high-speed rail system all stalled, and health care reform was only signed into law when Obama used arcane procedural laws to circumvent a Republican filibuster.

The danger here is that Obama's presidency will wind up resembling Clinton's. Thanks to the Newt Gingrich–led Republican Revolution, the Democrats lost control of the Legislative Branch two years into Clinton's presidency, ensuring his ineffectiveness as a domestic social reformer for the next six years. Indeed, all the major legislation he signed into law following the Republican Revolution was either part of Gingrich's Contract with America or had a conservative seal of approval, making Howard Zinn declare Clinton's presidency a waste of potential and Michael Moore declare Clinton "The greatest Republican President in American history."

And yet, despite all this, Michael Moore urged Obama supporters not to give up too soon on their president, or fold too quickly, even when Obama makes an obvious mistake, or capitulates too much to conservative interests. Moore wrote in 2009:

> All I ask of those who voted for Obama is to not pile on him too quickly. Yes, make your voice heard (his phone number is 202-456-1414). But don't abandon the best hope we've had in our lifetime for change. And for God's sake, don't head to bummerville if he says or does something we don't like. Do you ever see Republicans behave that way? I mean, the Right had 20 years of Republican presidents and they still couldn't get prayer in the public schools, or outlaw abortion, or initiate a flat tax or put our Social Security into the stock market. They did a lot of damage, no doubt about that, but on the key issues that the Christian Right fought for, they came up nearly empty handed. No wonder they've been driven crazy lately. They'll never have it as good again as they've had it since Reagan took office.
>
> But — do you ever see them looking all gloomy and defeated? No! They keep on fighting! Every day. Our side? At the first sign of wavering, we just pack up our toys and go home.[14]

And yet, for Obama's supporters, the honeymoon following the inauguration was short-lived. There was much to be depressed about. Mere months into Obama's first year, it was already apparent that the conservative media was determined to break the public's faith in Obama and erode his presidency with slander and gossip. The hopes Obama entertained that the Republican Party had mellowed since the Clinton Administration were false hopes indeed.

Throughout the Clinton Administration, the conservative American press savaged President Clinton on a nearly daily basis, offering extensive, relentless coverage of scandal after scandal, some of which were more worthy of news coverage than others. These scandals included accusations that Clinton had Vince Foster murdered, that he accepted campaign donations from China during the 1996 election, and that he shut down LAX airport for hours so he could have his hair cut on the runway. Other Clinton-era scandals included Nannygate, Paula Jones' sexual harassment lawsuit, the Monica Lewinsky affair, and the Whitewater controversy. During an interview with Matt Lauer on *The Today Show* on January 27, 1998, First Lady Hilary Clinton declared that the press and the Republican Party formed part of "a vast right wing conspiracy that has been conspiring against my husband since the day he announced [he was running] for president." Some critics accused her of paranoia and hypersensitivity. Others declared that the Clintons were a pair of blue-collar career criminals who had conned their way into the White House — thanks in large part to the third-party presidential candidacy of Ross Perot — and were guilty of all of the infractions the press had nailed them to the wall for committing. In contrast, Clinton supporters argued that most of the scandals were based on false or misleading evidence and that the Clintons couldn't truly be called paranoid if everyone, indeed, was out to get them.

In *The Republican Noise Machine: Right-Wing Media and How It Corrupts Democracy* (2005), David Brock explained that, contrary to popular belief, the mass media is not liberal, but fueled by conservative interests that began a campaign to systematically seize control of the media during the Nixon Administration. Once a former member of the "vast right-wing conspiracy" that besieged the Clintons himself, Brock had a change of heart. He wrote the book to expose to the public an attack machine comprised of radio shows, think tanks, web pages, publishing companies, and cable news channels such as Fox. Brock linked the funding of these organizations to a handful of multibillionaire bankrollers, and cited Grover Norquist as the mastermind behind the "the noise machine." According to Brock, traditional journalists have become too frightened (or are too poorly funded) to take on this well-organized, well-funded, and unified opposition, so they merely repeat the rumors, smears, and highly questionable studies and statistics that are passed on to them by the "noise machine," helping to ensure as many Republican victories as possible in every election cycle.

The corporate and religious-right opposition to Obama has been implacable. The Republican noise machine's anti–Clinton campaign involved establishing him as being, simultaneously, a bumbling hick and elitist intellectual while painting him as a womanizing draft dodger and self-centered glory hound. Obama, in contrast, has been criticized for being an emotionless "President Spock," and conservatives have attempted to alienate the American people from him by crafting tabloid stories that suggest he was not born in the United States and is secretly Muslim and homosexual.

The Muslim rumors, which began shortly after Obama announced his candidacy in 2007, and were immediately debunked, have, nevertheless, haunted Obama for years. As Bill Tancer established in *Click: What Millions of People Are Doing Online and Why It Matters* (2008), statistical evidence suggests that Americans do not vote for their governmental leaders on the basis of platform, but most Internet-enabled voters care only about physical appearance and religious affiliation. In 2007, a Fox News report falsely accused Obama of attending an Islamic madrass with ties to the Taliban in his early childhood, from 1967 to 1971, Tancer revealed. While that report was debunked four days later, the consequences of it have endured, Tancer said, demonstrating clearly the astonishingly devastating effect of one single false news report.[15]

In 2007, a puppet-animated adaptation of *Dante's Inferno* was directed and co-written by Sean Meredith. Set in modern-day America, the film searched for contemporary analogues of many of the sinners and monsters found in Dante Alighieri's original, written in feudal Italy in the early 1300s. George Sanders, Dick Cheney, and Strom Thurmond (the man who led a one-man, non-stop, 24-hour filibuster against the Civil Rights Act of 1957) were featured prominently in the movie as souls damned for suicide, war profiteering, and racism. In the original epic poem, Dante depicted the personification of Rumor as a demon with a multitude of eyes, ears, and tongues that was hellbent on destroying individual reputations and undermining society. In the 2007 adaptation, Meredith aptly depicted the Rumor demon of today as a Fox News helicopter. The 2007 Fox News–inspired rumor that Obama was Muslim is merely one example of why this satire seems spot on.

The "Obama is Muslim" rumor resurfaced anew, and with a vengeance, in 2010, when Fox News led a campaign against the construction of an Islamic cultural center in Manhattan several blocks away from Ground Zero, near a strip club and an out-of-business Burlington Coat Factory. Several widows of the victims of the 9/11 attacks opposed the construction of the center, and Fox News sought to condemn President Obama for not taking a stand against the center. Fox news commentators criticized Obama for citing the First Amendment as a reason to stay out of the debate, and insinuated that his refusal to condemn the cultural center—which it described as a "9/11 mosque"—was further evidence of his Islamic sympathies and secret Muslim faith.

In *The Daily Show*'s coverage of the controversy, Jon Stewart made the startling revelation that Fox News' attempts to not-so-subtly imply that mosque builder Imam Rauf is funded by terrorists are complete sophistry because Rauf's principal backer is Saudi prince

Al-Waleed bin Talal, a business partner of Rupert Murdoch and shareholder in Fox News itself. "That's right, the guy they're painting as a sinister money force OWNS Fox News," Stewart exclaimed. He later added, "If we want to cut off funding to the terror mosque, we must, together as a nation, stop watching Fox."[16]

Using the mosque controversy and the 2010 election year as a springboard to begin the race for the 2012 presidential election, the Republican Party faithful seemed eager to see Sarah Palin, Newt Gingrich, Glenn Beck, or Mike Huckabee in the White House. Gingrich had the advantage of years of political experience to promote, Palin could promote herself as a Margaret Thatcher–style conservative feminist who would be America's first female president, Glenn Beck had ardent supporters in his niche viewership, and Mike Huckabee had the ability to make people forget how far-right his political platform was because he was the most likeable and charismatic candidate of the group.

Feminist blogger Holly Ord has been angered by Republican claims that Palin is a feminist role model because Ord sees those claims as deliberately designed to mislead American women:

> Not only is Sarah Palin not a feminist, she is as anti-woman as Bush and McCain combined. That is the reason why McCain picked her; not because she is a woman and he wanted to be underhanded (which he totally did,) but because she's a Republican, conservative man who just happens to be in a woman's body.
>
> Feminism means to stand up for human rights; it means to stand up for equality and the freedoms and liberties of people and Sarah Palin is disgustingly right wing, anti-choice and has no record of representing women's interests; though her record in general is quite minuscule.[17]

Making similar complaints about the charismatic Huckabee, *Democratic Underground.com* blogger Nicole Belle wrote in 2008: "While I was watching and transcribing Mike Huckabee's appearance on *SNL* this weekend, I kept thinking he is so good at being likeable that if you don't have a clear sense of what he really stands for, it would be easy to be swayed by Huckabee. But then a story like this [in which Huckabee endorses a constitutional amendment that defines a person as a human being from the moment life begins at conception] comes down the wires and you realize that it is really, really important to know *exactly* what candidates do stand for."

Certainly, the more time the electorate spends wondering whether or not Obama is a Muslim, the less time they spend looking carefully at the pedigree of those running against him and his fellow Democrats across the country. So, the "9/11 Mosque" controversy has all the earmarks of an election year ploy that has served to exacerbate tensions between Christians and Muslims in America and abroad.

Frank Rich noted in an August 21, 2010, *New York Times* column that the neoconservatives who deliberately stirred up anger over the mosque are the few remaining supporters of the war in Afghanistan, and they harmed their own cause overseas by demonizing Islam as a religion and further turning the Afghan people against Gen. David Petraeus. Rich also cited Palin's hypocritical concern over New York City's wounded psyche when she has consistently demonstrated little interest in, or affinity with, the people of New York before.[18]

Alarmed by a *Newsweek* poll that stated one-third of the American people believe Obama sympathizes with Muslim radicals who want to convert the world to Islam, and 24 percent believe that Obama is a Muslim, film critic Roger Ebert wrote an open letter to John McCain and George W. Bush calling upon them to publicly declare, as they have done before, that they know Obama to be a Christian. Ebert also called upon Sarah Palin, Rush

Limbaugh, and Glenn Beck to produce conclusive evidence that Obama is Muslim, or "shut up." Ebert also observed that America should be a country of religious freedom, protected by the First Amendment, and that it shouldn't even matter to Americans if Obama is Muslim. But it does, and it frightens many of them. As Ebert wrote on September 1, 2010:

> These figures sadden me with the depth of thoughtlessness and credulity they imply. A democracy depends on an informed electorate to survive. An alarming number of Americans and a majority of Republicans are misinformed. The man who was swept into office by a decisive majority is now considered by many citizens to be the enemy. Some fundamentalists believe he is the Antichrist named by Jesus in the Bible....
>
> This many Americans did not arrive at such conclusions on their own. They were persuaded by a relentless process of insinuation, strategic silence and cynical misinformation...
>
> These opinions have an agenda. They seek to demonize the Obama Presidency and mainstream liberal politics in general. The conservatism they prefer is not the traditional conservatism of such figures as Taft, Nixon, Reagan, Buckley or Goldwater. It is a frightening new radical fringe movement, financed by such as the newly notorious billionaire Koch brothers, whose hatred of government extends even to opposition to tax funding for public schools.[19]

Shortly after Ebert published his letter, the Koch brothers to whom he referred were the subject of an August 20, 2010, *New Yorker* exposé by Jane Mayer, "Covert Operations: The Billionaire Brothers Who Are Waging a War Against Obama."

According to Mayer, Charles and David Koch, owners of Koch Industries, have donated more than $100 million to archconservative causes, and are major funders of the Tea Party movement. Koch Industries was named one of the top ten air polluters in the United States and have been the leading voices in climate science denial. Between 2005 and 2008, the Koch brothers also outspent ExxonMobil in

> giving money to organizations fighting legislation related to climate change, underwriting a huge network of foundations, think tanks, and political front groups. Indeed, the brothers have funded opposition campaigns against so many Obama Administration policies—from health-care reform to the economic-stimulus program—that, in political circles, their ideological network is known as the Kochtopus.
>
> ... Charles Lewis, the founder of the Center for Public Integrity, a nonpartisan watchdog group, said, "The Kochs are on a whole different level. There's no one else who has spent this much money. The sheer dimension of it is what sets them apart. They have a pattern of lawbreaking, political manipulation, and obfuscation. I've been in Washington since Watergate, and I've never seen anything like it. They are the Standard Oil of our times."

One of the Obama Administration's frustrations is that many of the events funded by the Koch brothers, including Tea Party leadership training rallies, do not name the Kochs as their underwriters. So, while the Tea Party is ostensibly a populist movement, Obama officials believe that nothing could be further from the truth. "David Axelrod, Obama's senior adviser, said, 'What they don't say is that, in part, this is a grassroots citizens' movement brought to you by a bunch of oil billionaires'" (Mayer).

Meanwhile, the Supreme Court's Citizens United ruling in 2010 now allows corporations the right to spend any amount of money they wish on election campaigns, and that opened the floodgate on corporate donations in the 2010 election. Rupert Murdoch's News Corporation, the owners of *Fox News*, *The New York Post*, and *The Wall Street Journal*, donated one million dollars to the Republican Governors Association in August 2010, garnering accusations from liberal group Media Matters for America that the News Corporation is functionally "an appendage of the Republican Party."[20] The department store Target's parent company donated $150,000 to a group actively campaigning for Tom Emmer, a Republican conservative gubernatorial candidate in Minnesota, inspiring a grassroots boycott of Target led via Facebook. Democratic efforts to pass the DISCLOSE Act, which would make public the sources and recipients of large corporate donations, were blocked by Senate Republicans on July 27, 2010.[21]

George Bernard Shaw, the Pulitzer Prize–winning and Oscar-winning Irish playwright, famously derided the United States for never living up to its potential as a true democracy. Instead, he believed, the country was ruled by a wealthy elite that buys every election, rigs the courts, and writes the laws, all the while convincing a gullible electorate that they are the ones running the country.[22]

Certainly, during the summer of 2010, many American liberals were firmly convinced that they were witnessing the plots of *Mr. Smith Goes to Washington* (1939) and *A Very British Coup* (1982) playing out in real life in contemporary America. In *Mr. Smith*, media mogul and political powerbroker Jim Taylor realizes that he cannot buy the loyalty of Jefferson Smith, the callow-but-principled junior Senator from his home state, as he did the senior Senator, Joseph Paine. In retaliation, Taylor and Paine join forces to discredit Smith by accusing him of sponsoring a public works project, ostensibly for children, that Smith himself would profit from. Smith believes that he will be able to prove his innocence by laying his case out to the public, but his earnest, honest, and eloquent speeches are filtered to the electorate through newspapers and radio stations owned by Taylor, who distort Smith's words and cleverly insinuate his guilt. Only when Paine has an eleventh hour change of heart is Smith exonerated, but Taylor's hold over the mass media, and the democracy, remains strong despite this minor defeat.

A Very British Coup, a 1982 novel by future Tony Blair cabinet minister Chris Mullin, was also adapted into a 1988 Channel Four miniseries with Ray McAnally. "In the novel, Harry Perkins, a socialist, is elected Prime Minister of the United Kingdom in 1989 and tries to effect genuinely socialistic policies, but is brought down by a conspiracy involving the media, business interests, and a hostile American administration. The fact that Mullin's publishers brought out a new edition of the book in 2001 is suggestive of its contemporary resonance" (Peatling 1078).

Against opposition such as this in the real world, from men named Koch and Norquist and Murdoch, if not Taylor, it is no surprise that Obama's message has often not gotten through to the American people, and that much of his legislation has been stalled by Republican filibusters and relentless bad press. And yet, two years into Obama's presidency, Paul Richmond, the artist who painted "Batmobama and Robiden," revealed that he stood by his portrayal of Obama as a superhero, and believed there was still reason to hope. "I continue to be an ardent Obama supporter," Richmond said. "He certainly has his critics, but I think it's important to factor in the countless jokers who have climbed out of the woodwork to thwart his plans too. Who could have predicted the wacky tea parties and diabolical schemes of the right-wing archenemies? But I believe Batmobama will triumph in the end."[23]

Literary and cultural critic S.T. Joshi agrees that, however Obama's presidency plays out in the end, the tide of history is against the ardent conservatism represented by the right wing that still vainly hopes to see unrestrained capitalism rule the day, women return to the kitchens, gays go back into the closet, and black people stay safely on the margins of society. As he argued in *The Angry Right* (2006):

> Americans, even if to a lesser extent than Europeans, are willing to encompass restrictions of freedom in the economic sphere — another core value of liberalism — because these seeming

> restrictions actually enhance the freedom of the individual: with immense corporations already wielding disproportionate power and influence, Americans are becoming aware that the deck is stacked against them and that government is the only power strong enough to restrain big business.... [I]t is only this restrain of free market capitalism that has allowed the middle class in America to gain what prosperity it has. That prosperity is now threatened by a conservatism that, even more crassly than in the past, has sided with the superrich as the guardians of American capitalism seeking to stave off the dreaded bugaboo of socialism, but it is evident that the generality of Americans are losing patience with this new Gilded Age and beginning to wonder why they are not sharing in the immense profits that are lining the pockets of corporate executives.
>
> One suspects, indeed, that the tide is turning against conservatism in general—thanks in no small part to the reactionary, corrupt, deceitful, and incompetent administration of George W. Bush. His regime has laid bare the manifold inadequacies of the conservative agenda: tax breaks for the rich that have not produced general prosperity; aggressive militarism that has backfired upon itself; the idea of "small government" leading to blundering inability to deal with natural disasters and other matters that are manifestly the responsibility of the federal government; degradation of the environment in the interest of monetary profit for the few and well-placed [294–295].

During his "A More Perfect Union Speech," Obama revealed that he was not naïve enough to believe that all of the problems of race in America could be solved "in a single election cycle, or with a single candidacy—particularly a candidacy as imperfect as my own." The same thing could be said of any number of issues. Whether Obama ultimately succeeds or fails in passing key legislation, or making the world a more peaceful and egalitarian place to live, the rest of us are not absolved from our responsibility of doing our part as well.

What he also seems to be saying is, while progressives might feel discouraged by an election year defeat for Obama, it isn't the end of the world. Nor is it the end of the fight.

When we look to real world heroes to solve our problems for us the way that superheroes solve problems for Americans in comic books, in a Messianic fashion, then we allow ourselves to avoid taking action ourselves or proving that we stand by our convictions. Then, when our real world heroes fail to deliver on our overinflated expectations, we find ourselves tearing down the idols we once worshipped—often unjustly and viciously, like real-world J. Jonah Jamesons. It is a vicious cycle and one we tend to get caught up in with almost all of our real-life heroes who, frustratingly, tend to be far less perfect than Superman.

A far better thing to do than continue this cycle of cheering and heckling from the sidelines is to contribute our own special gifts and abilities to make the world a better place to live. Then we would use our heroes as an inspiration to act ourselves—while being fully aware of their limitations, as well as of our own. Instead of continuing to sit in front of a glowing computer or television screen, hoping against hope that a series of self-aggrandizing talking heads will think, act, and solve all of our problems for us, we should pull ourselves away from the hypnotic and all-consuming influences of the internet, the television, and the shopping mall and rediscover how to empathize with others, how to think for ourselves, and how to act for ourselves. Then, we can begin to work together to build a better future for ourselves, for America, and for the world.

That is what heroes, real and fictional, can—and should—inspire us to do.

Chapter Notes

Introduction

1. See Harris, "The Ghost of Tony Blair" on *NPR Morning Edition*, October 31, 2007.

2. See Dave Chappelle on *Dr. Katz, Professional Therapist*, episode 35, Electric Bike, Comedy Central, June 29, 1997.

3. The Incredible Hulk #390–392, reprinted in "The Incredible Hulk: War and Pieces." *X-Factor Visionaries* Vol. 2.

4. For the moment, they are posted at <http://www.bravenewwave.com/2008/11/27/sickly-superheroes/>

5. See Vanetta Rogers, "FATHOM Helps Clean Up the Gulf ... For Real." *Newsarama.com*. August 4, 2010. September 4, 2010.<http://www.newsarama.com/comics/fathom-gulf-spill-issue-100804.html>

6. See <http://www.batmanforpresident.com/2008/01/25/b4p-08-you-cant-stop-the-signal/>

7. See *Deviantart.com* at <http://browse.deviantart.com/?qh=§ion=&global=1&q=obama>

8. See Edward Douglas, "Andrew Garfield's First Words on Spider-Man."

9. See J. Michael Straczynski, "The Amazing Spider-Man #36." Illus. John Romita, Jr. *The Amazing Spider-Man: Ultimate Collection 1.* New York: Marvel Comics, 2009.

10. Historian Leo Braudy has a slightly different take on the creation of the Golden Age of Superheroes. As he explains:

> There were many Messianic figures whose myths drew fans and followers during and after World War I—d'Annunzio, T.E. Lawrence, Charles Lindberg, Mussolini, Hitler, Roosevelt, Churchill, Stalin—along with such fictional creations as the detective, the benevolent alien Superman, and Batman, the socially conscious and defanged version of Dracula. But, although there were fascist movements in countries like France and England, often with leaders who aspired to quasi-divine status, the more characteristic democratic response to post-war disillusionment was skepticism about national calls to action. The national rituals of masculinity characteristic of totalitarian regimes contrast intriguingly with more individualist fantasy figures like the detective and the cowboy. They also correspond to two visions of chivalry; the solitary champions Gawain and Don Quixote, knights-errants sallying forth to correct the world, and the Crusaders or the samurai obeying an overriding authority.
>
> We may reasonably prefer the lone avengers to the murderous dictators, but all—whether fictional characters or real people with programs and policies—were fantasy figures whose presence salved the sense of individual failure and inadequacy. Essential to both was the idea of a code based in some way upon the soldier's experience in war: for the totalitarians, a code modeled on the frontline camaraderie that excluded anyone who had not taken part; for the democrats, an internalized code of individual morality [437].

11. See *Stan Lee, Origins of Marvel Comics*; Jim Arehart and the Wizard Staff, "The Secret History of Marvel Comics;" and Kevin Smith, *Stan Lee's Mutants, Monsters, and Marvels*.

12. See Martin Anderson, "The Den Of Geek interview: Mark Millar." Den of Geek! Jul 20, 2008. September 4, 2010. <http://www.denofgeek.com/comics/88459/the_den_of_geek_interview_mark_millar.html>

13. See Nisha Gopalan. "Mark Millar on Sarah Palin: 'Terrifying.'" io9.com. September 23, 2008. September 4, 2010. <http://io9.com/5053777/mark-millar-on-sarah-palin-terrifying>

14. See Sylvester Stallone, "Sly bleeds some more answers in anticipation of RAMBO—Day 2." AintItCoolNews.com. January 15, 2008. September 4, 2010. <http://www.aintitcool.com/node/35284?q=node/35286>

15. From an interview with the author conducted over e-mail on January 11, 2009.

16. *Ibid.*

17. See Mark Kirby, "Megan Fox Was a Teenage Lesbian! Plus Other Confessions from the Lips of Hollywood's New Favorite Temptress." *GQ*. September 2008. September 6, 2010. <http://www.gq.com/women/photos/200809/actress-model-transformers-sexiest-woman-in-the-world>

18. "Famke Janssen Biography Page." *Internet Movie Database*. 1990–2010. August 12, 2010. <http://www.imdb.com/name/nm0000463/bio>

19. See Dave Chappelle on *Dr. Katz—Professional Therapist*, "Episode 35: Electric Bike." Broadcast June 29, 1997 on *Comedy Central*.

Chapter One

1. See Chuck Dixon, "The Beginning of Tomorrow!" Illus. Graham Nolan. *Detective Comics: Featuring Batman*, #0. New York, DC Comics: Oct. 1994.

2. Page 255.

3. See also Paul Starobin's "The Angry American," in *The Atlantic*, January/February 2004 and James Heskett's "Will the Societal Effects of Enron Exceed Those of September 11?" in *Harvard Business School's Working Knowledge for Business Leaders*, February 2, 2002. <http://hbswk.hbs.edu/cgi-bin/print>

4. Finnegan page 33.

5. "Falwell apologizes to gays, feminists, lesbians." CNN.com. September 14, 2001. June 28, 2010. <http://archives.cnn.com/2001/US/09/14/Falwell.apology/>

6. *Ibid.*

7. Dialogue from *Batman Begins* spoken by Christian Bale and Liam Neeson.

8. Despite my the joy at seeing Batman as a member of the Justice League along with Aquaman and Wonder Woman, I essentially agree with Denny O'Neil, longtime writer and editor of the *Batman* comics, that Batman works best when he is the only "superhero" in his universe. O'Neil liked to present Batman as if he existed in a world apart from the other DC Comics heroes as often as he could, although corporate marketing and "cross-over" stories sometimes stymied his efforts. As O'Neil said, "I'm a realist. Batman should not exist in the same world as Superman and Green Lantern. You've got Superman, who can juggle planets and Batman who is ... quite strong!" (Interview with critic Will Brooker from *Batman Unmasked*, 277).

9. Interestingly, Batman's surname, Wayne, is Scottish, and a common Scottish word for child is "wean." Wean means the "wee one" and is pronounced "Wayne."

10. Dialogue spoken by Moran Freeman, playing the role of Batman's weapons designer, Lucious Fox, in *Batman Begins.*

11. *Iron Man* Vol. 3 number 74, January 2004.

12. Personal interview, Monday, March 26, 2006.

13. *Batman Begins* also made the formerly ancillary comic-book character of Lucius Fox, an African American executive who runs Wayne Enterprises, an important member of Batman's inner circle of allies. The character's first appearance was in Batman #307 (1979), and Len Wein and John Calnan created him. Although Fox's new centrality to the Batman saga is a significant step in making the Batman universe less uniformly "white," Gotham remains significantly less multiracial than Spiderman's New York. As Dave Chappelle joked, "...you'd never see Batman in a housing project wasting his time." (*Dr. Katz — Professional Therapist Episode 35: Electric Bike.* Broadcast June 29, 1997 on Comedy Central).

14. Since Batman's worldview is Medievalist, is it unsurprising that one of his most famous devotees is a literary character obsessed with the Middle Ages. In John Kennedy Toole's *A Confederacy of Dunces*, the protagonist, Ignatius J. Reilly, a contemporary Don Quixote who loves Medieval philosophy, feels one way to "understand the crises of our age" is to read *Batman* comics.

15. The classic version of the Two-Face character is simpler and less interesting. He was traditionally portrayed as a mere thief who enjoys committing crimes around the number two (ie: stealing a statue of Janus, the two-faced Roman God, or lifting the first editions of both Ralph Ellison's *Invisible Man* and H. G. Wells' *The Invisible Man* — two different books with the same title. Clever, but not deep stuff.

16. *Batman* (1989), directed by Tim Burton.

17. Pesca, Mike. "When 'I Hate Mondays' Means Murder." January 29, 2009. www.NPR.org

18. Tucker, Reed. "Holy Liplock! Slash Fiction Puts Pop Icons in Steamy Settings." New York Post. August 20, 2006. See also: "Gallery Told to Drop Gay Batman." BBC News Online. August 19, 2005. <http://news.bbc.co.uk/2/hi/entertainment/4167032.stm>

19. New York State Coalition Against Sexual Assault. "Penal Codes: A Summary of New York State Penal Code 130. Sex Offenses as of 2008." New York. 2007. June 11, 2010. <http://nyscasa.org/understanding/penalcodes.>

20. Roger Ebert made a similar observation in his review of the film.

21. See Dixon, Chris. "The California Recall: Voters Recall Just Who Started This Thing, If You Will." *The New York Times*, October 8, 2003 and John M. Broder, "Davis Seeks a Debate; Schwarzenegger Camp Says No." *The New York Times*. September 27, 2003. See also the documentary film *Enron: The Smartest Guys in the Room* (2005).

22. Holleran, Scott. "Wing Kid: An Interview with Christopher Nolan." *Box Office Mojo*. October 20, 2005

Chapter Two

1. *Wonder Woman*, Vol. 3, number 25 (2008). "A Star in the Heavens Scene 2: Personal Effects." Written by Gail Simone and illustrated by Bernard Chang.

2. Thomas, Matt. "Comic Con Q&A with Wonder Woman, Gail Simone." *The Torontoist*. March 29, 2010. Viewed online at http://torontoist.com/2010/03/comic_con_qa_with_wonder_woman_gail_simone.php on June 15, 2010.

3. Quoted in Trina Robbins' *The Great Women Superheroes*, page 7.

4. According to historian Sue Blundell, author of *Women in Ancient Greece* (1999), the mythical Amazons referenced by Homer shunned marriage and family while embracing traditionally masculine pursuits such as hunting and warfare. As Blundell argues, ancient Athenian women could have interpreted the legend of the Amazons as containing "heartwarming messages about the empowerment of women," but, more likely, "the majority of women subscribed to the prevailing view" that the Amazons were barbaric figures and "rejected the warrior woman's example" (61–62).

5. Well, maybe not the only offspring. Some stories — in comics and in the 1970s television series — have featured Donna Troy, who is sometimes presented as Diana's sister ... but not always. The explanation for Donna's presence has changed repeatedly and is, frankly, confusing beyond belief. In any event, the character more often appears outside of *Wonder Woman* comic books (as a major figure in the pages of *The Teen Titans*, for example) than she does in the *Wonder Woman* title proper, so I like to disregard her presence when I can.

6. This comic book was reprinted in *DC Archive Editions: Wonder Woman Archives* Vol. 1. New York: DC Comics. 1998.

7. As historian Jill Stephenson wrote in "The Wary Response of Women," "[i]t is generally safe to say that in the Nazi view, women were to be 'wives, mothers, and homemakers'; they were to play no part in public life, in the legislature, the executive, the judiciary, or the armed forces. Hitler himself frequently expressed opposition to women's participation in politics, claiming that it sullied and demeaned the female nature, as he saw it. It was partly Hitler's personal attachment to the image of women as 'mothers of the nation' which delayed and then vitiated the introduction of labor conscription for women during the Second World War, although in his Gotterdammerung mentality early in 1945 he was prepared to see women enlisted as soldiers and sent to the front" (168–169).

8. That having been said, as a possible consequence of the comic never going out of print (and of her story cycle constantly being "rebooted," retelling her adventures from the beginning), Wonder Woman has not, to my knowledge, ever really had to face the consequence of giv-

ing up her immortality. To this day, she remains eternally young. Even in stories set in the future, such as the non-canonical miniseries *Kingdom Come*, she still appears to be in her prime. Menopause never seems to be an issue for her either, as she gives birth to Superman's child after they are married in the novel version of the story.

9. While American culture was hardly free of sexism, it was, in contrast with Nazi Germany, a much more feminist-friendly culture during the World War II era, lending credence to Marston's thesis that a feminist's natural allegiance would be to the Allied Forces and not the Axis. As Susan M. Hartmann, author of *American Women in the 1940s: The Home Front and Beyond*, explained, "The [wartime] need for female labor lent a new legitimacy to the women worker.... While the women who replaced men in aircraft factories, ordinance plants and shipyards were most numerous and visible, the labor shortage also opened doors for women musicians, airplane pilots, scientists, athletes, and college professors." And, for the first time, discussions of pay equity were taken seriously (20–23).

10. Marston's suggestion that the Nazi thirst for warfare was fueled by sexual repression carries some weight when one considers biographical evidence which points to Hitler's own bloodlust being fueled by his sexual inadequacies. Historians such as Ken Anderson, in his 1995 essay "Hitler and Occult Sex," have argued that Hitler's horror of Jews, and thirst for conquest, were outgrowths of his own sexual repression, and fear of women (159–160). Also, the connection between Hitler and Ares evokes Hitler's real-world fascination with the Occult and paganism, and the fact that, between 1940 and 1945 paganism was "publicly commended by the Nazis and publicly practiced. Nazi-sponsored pagan 'cults' revived the pre-Christian shrine to Wotan [German God of War] at the Heiliger Berg near Heidelberg.... The old stone gods of the Germanic race had been taken out of storage, dusted down and revitalized" (Prittie 74).

11. This story is featured in the reprint hardcover called *DC Archive Editions: Wonder Woman Archives* Vol. 2. New York: DC Comics. 2000.

12. *Ibid.*

13. The content of Marston's early *Wonder Woman* adventures, as drawn by Harry (H.G.) Peter, has given many commentators pause, largely because of the bondage imagery that can be seen throughout, which has sometimes been viewed as an indication of Marston's sexual kinkiness, while other times explained as a convention of the superhero narrative, since villains almost always tie up the heroes they capture. See Smith, Robbins, and Steinem. Also, during the 1990s, "bad girl" comics such as Brian Pulido's *Lady Death* took their lead from the tradition of bondage imagery Marston set the precedent for, producing kinky representations of tied-up women that few feminists would take kindly to.

14. Reprinted in *DC Archive Editions: Wonder Woman Archives* Vol. 1. New York: DC Comics. 1998.

15. *Ibid.*

16. See *DC Archive Editions: Wonder Woman Archives* Vol. 1. New York: DC Comics. 1998.

17. *Ibid.*, 42.

18. That having been said, there is something very romantic, and very comical, about two sexist, sexually repressed warriors doing an awkward mating dance. Although they traditionally operate in different comic book universes, and have been kept separate for decades, recent years have seen Batman and Wonder Woman together and acting like a dysfunctional couple in the *Justice League* and *Justice League Unlimited* cartoons, as well as in issues of the *JLA* comic book by Joe Kelly. Wonder Woman and Batman have also been adversaries in physical conflicts with an erotic undercurrent, as in the graphic novels *Trinity, Wonder Woman: The Hiketeia*, and *JLA: A League of One*.

19. See rumor postings on *The Comic Bloc Forums*, especially on http://www.comicbloc.com/forums/archive/index.php/t-11159.html

20. See Wikipedia entry on Rama (comics) at http://en.wikipedia.org/wiki/Rama_(comics). The Rama romance was central to comic books scripted by the underrated Eric Luke.

21. The Cathy Lee Crosby *Wonder Woman* television movie, which preceded the production of the more faithful, Lynda Carter television series, is not widely regarded as a "legitimate" *Wonder Woman* film by fans of the character. The controversial I Ching stories that inspired the Crosby film were reprinted in Volumes One through Four of *Diana Prince: Wonder Woman* by DC Comics in 2008.

22. "The New Original Wonder Woman." *Wonder Woman: The Complete First Season. Prod.* Douglas S. Cramer. Develop. Stanley Ralph Ross. Perf. Lynda Carter and Lyle Waggoner. 1975–1977. DVD. WarnerHome Video, 2004.

23. See "Beauty, Brawn, and Bulletproof Bracelets: A Wonder Woman Retrospective."

24. "Fausta: The Nazi Wonder Woman." *Wonder Woman: The Complete First Season*. Prod. Douglas S. Cramer. Develop. Stanley Ralph Ross. Perf. Lynda Carter and Lyle Waggoner. 1975–1977. DVD. Warner Home Video, 2004.

25. To that extent, this version of the character is more her own woman than the comic book heroine seen since the series, who not only has to answer to female gods, but feels great reservation whenever she is asked to pay homage to the male chauvinist and tyrannical likes of Zeus in comic book stories written by Eric Luke, George Perez, John Byrne, and Greg Rucka.

26. "Wonder Woman: The Ultimate Feminist Icon." DVD Special Feature. *Wonder Woman: The Complete Third Season*. Warner Home Video, 2005.

27. "The Feminum Mystique: Part 1" and "The Feminum Mystique: Part 2." *Wonder Woman: The Complete First Season*. Prod. Douglas S. Cramer. Develop. Stanley Ralph Ross. Perf. Lynda Carter and Lyle Waggoner. 1975–1977. DVD. Warner Home Video, 2004.

28. "The Last of the Two-Dollar Bills." *Wonder Woman: The Complete First Season*. Prod. Douglas S. Cramer. Develop. Stanley Ralph Ross. Perf. Lynda Carter and Lyle Waggoner. 1975–1977. DVD. Warner Home Video, 2004.

29. "The Return of Wonder Woman." *Wonder Woman: The Complete Second Season*. Perf. Lynda Carter and Lyle Waggoner. 1977–1978. DVD. Warner Home Video, 2005.

30. See the DVD special feature "Revolutionizing a Classic: From Comic Book to Television — the Evolution of Wonder Woman from Page to Screen."

31. *Ibid.*

32. Gail Simone and Aaron Lopresti. "Rise of the Olympian." *Wonder Woman* (vol. 3) #33. New York: DC Comics. 2009.

33. See Gail Simone and Ed Benes' *Birds of Prey: Sensei & Student*.

34. Simone, Gail and Aaron Lopresti. "Birds of Paradise." *Wonder Woman* (vol. 3) #34. New York: DC Comics. 2009.

35. Simone, Gail and Aaron Lopresti. "Warkiller." *Wonder Woman* (vol. 3) #36. New York: DC Comics.

2009.

36. Simone, Gail and Bernard Chang. "A Star in the Heavens." *Wonder Woman* (vol. 3) #24–25. New York: DC Comics. 2008.

37. Simone, Gail and Aaron Lopresti. "A Murder of Crows." *Wonder Woman* (vol. 3) #40–41. New York: DC Comics. 2010.

38. Rogers, Vaneta. "JMS Talks WONDER WOMAN's New Look and New Direction." *Newsarama*. June 29 2010. June 30, 2010. <http://www.newsarama.com/comics/jms-talks-wonder-woman-100629.html>

39. *Ibid.*

40. *Ibid.*

41. The hope is that this shakeup in the *Wonder Woman* status quo will rescue the book's sales figures — which are plummeting as of the time of writing. The reboot is also intended to make the character more palatable to studio executives, who have thus far refused to risk making a *Wonder Woman* movie because they are uncertain a character dressed like her would be taken seriously on screen, and because they are concerned by the box office failures of female-centric superhero movies such as *Catwoman* (2004), *Elektra* (2005), and *Aeon Flux* (2005). Indecision about whether the tone should be dark or campy, and whether the film should be set in World War II or the present, has further complicated production plans. Previous attempts to make new *Wonder Woman* movies and telefilms based on scripts by Joss Whedon, Laeta Kalogridis, and David E. Kelley were scuttled by executives with no faith in the projects. Actresses bandied about by fans as ideal casting choices for Wonder Woman — including Monica Bellucci, Angelina Jolie, Jennifer Connelly, Rachel Weisz, Adrianne Palicki, Jessica Biel, Selma Hayek, and Megan Fox — have either grown too old to play the part or fallen out of favor with the public.

42. "Wonder Woman: The Ultimate Feminist Icon." DVD Special Feature. *Wonder Woman: The Complete Third Season*. Warner Home Video, 2005.

43. In her article "Superwomen? The Bad-Ass Babes of Sin City — Or Are They?" Dana Leventhal criticizes the portrayal of women in the film adaptation of Frank Miller's *Sin City*. As she observes, "On the one hand, the women can be seen as warrior-goddesses, magnificent and luminous; on the other, they are morally dubious prostitutes and strippers, victims and servants of debased male gratification.... In the end, the women are simultaneously exalted and loathed as the objects of male fantasy."

Chapter Three

1. From *Batman & Spider-Man: New Age Dawning* by J.M. DeMatteis, Graham Nolan, and Karl Kesel.

2. See "Barack Obama: My Pop Culture Favorites," *Entertainment Weekly*.

3. At the end of the classic novel *The Great Gatsby*, the narrator, Nick Carroway, decides that his dream to become a wealthy playboy is an empty one and returns to his humble western roots. Unlike Nick Carroway, Peter Parker has never managed to leave his dream of fame and fortune completely behind, and his residual ambition surfaces just frequently enough to get him into regular trouble.

4. See Ken Tucker, "Book Review: *The Megalomaniacal Spider-Man*."

5. See the documentary *Enron: The Smartest Guys in the Room*, Tom Fowler's "Judge vacates Ken Lay's Enron conviction," and Mark Sherman, "High court hears ex–Enron CEO Skilling's appeal."

6. See, Barbara Ehrenreich, "The Enron Tea Party."

7. *Ibid.*

8. See Tom Fowler's "Judge vacates Ken Lay's Enron conviction," and Mark Sherman, "High court hears ex–Enron CEO Skilling's appeal."

9. In the *Spider-Man* movies directed by Sam Raimi, Spider-Man's webbing is not a chemical compound fired from a "webshooter," but is an organic goo that sprays from a fleshy aperture in his wrists, since the genetically engineered spider granted him the power to spin organic webbing from within. Also, in the first *Spider-Man* film, the spider that bit Peter was not accidentally bathed in radiation, but was a genetically engineered "super-spider" with mysterious physical properties.

10. To continue the *Great Expectations* analogy, Pip is at his most unlikable when he is too embarrassed by his guardian, the blacksmith Joe Gargery, to welcome Joe properly into his posh London lifestyle after he comes into money. In a similar fashion, any scene of Spider-Man belittling, or "forgetting," Uncle Ben is equally unpleasant, as in the aforementioned scene from the *Spider-Man* film and the agonizingly depressing alternate reality story "Jumping the Tracks" (a 2006 adventure written by Peter David and reprinted in *Friendly Neighborhood Spider-Man Vol. 1: Derailed*), which posits that, had Uncle Ben not died, Peter would have become a rich entertainer in his Spider-Man persona and used Uncle Ben as a doormat throughout his entire career.

11. Class issues permeate the film, but the theme of class is second to the film's concern with vengeance and how it darkens the soul. When Peter exposes Brock's fraud, thereby ruining his career in journalism, Brock swears vengeance, but he has no real justifiable reason to hate Peter, since he did, indeed, commit fraud. Harry Osborne is obsessed with avenging his father's death and killing Peter, but his anger isn't justified because his father was evil and had accidentally killed himself with a fatal trap that he had laid for Peter. For his part, Peter becomes obsessed with the idea of killing Flint Marko when he learns that Flint was the one who really shot Uncle Ben. However, Flint had unintentionally killed Ben when his handgun went off by accident, so even though he was technically guilty of killing Ben, he was not necessarily morally responsible. All of these characters are consumed with grief and rage, and are looking to kill. They are beyond reason, and are too furious to realize that they have, by and large, all chosen the wrong targets for their anger. Still, by the end of the film, most of the characters realize their mistakes, and that their quest for vengeance is eating away at their souls, and most of the principal players forgive one another. Only Eddie Brock (who becomes the supervillain Venom towards the end of the film) is wedded to his plan for revenge, and he ultimately destroys himself in the process. Unpopular as the film was with its target audience, the message of the importance of admitting one's own fallibility and forgiving the trespassers of others was a surprising and poignant one for a summer blockbuster marketed to males with adolescent sensibilities.

12. In contrast, the irredeemable Eddie Brock (who becomes the supervillain Venom) destroys himself thanks to his own hunger for power, and inability to accept that he is, in the final analysis, mediocre. Many critics believe that the film is mediocre as well. The final installment of the trilogy is dramatically uneven, leaves Sandman's storyline unresolved, and has two unforgivable plot loopholes involving a meteor and a butler, but it is the very bravery

it demonstrates in concluding an action movie with a moment of reconciliation that makes the film unusual and intriguing. To that extent, at least, the film is under-appreciated, especially when compared to legitimately awful superhero films such as *X-Men Origins: Wolverine, The Spirit, Elektra*, and *Catwoman*, that have nothing whatsoever to offer.

13. Although, given the rent in New York City, this is not surprising, as his rent circa 2004 is likely upwards of $1,300 for a loft in a poorly maintained neighborhood.

14. Although the supernatural has not traditionally played much of a role in Spider-Man, Ditko did develop a friendship between Spider-Man and the sorcerer Doctor Strange that Straczynski has returned to. Straczynski has also introduced a more mystical, more horrific backstory to Spider-Man's origin which has resulted in a lot of Ditko-like gothic imagery being returned to the comic, including giant talking spiders and Escher-like landscapes. The new origin story maintains that Parker was chosen by mystical forces beyond the realm of his understanding to be Spider-Man because he was worthy of the honor. He was not, then, an incompetent and a fool granted powers by a quirk of fate. He is also one of many great Spider-Man chosen throughout history, and is part of a heritage that recalls Buffy Summers and her place in the Slayer lineage.

15. This "New Avengers" is not to be confused with the British superhero team the New Avengers, featuring John Steed, Mike Gambit, and Purdy.

16. See "Skin Deep: Part 1." *The Amazing Spider-Man* 515, February 2005.

17. As Stephen Grey wrote in *Ghost Plane: The True Story of the CIA Torture Program*, "America's programs of extraordinary renditions and harsh treatments of prisoners have not, when considered strategically, been weapons against terrorism. Every time a new repressive measure is approved by Congress or the president, Osama bin Laden must cheer. Ultimately, those are tactics which must encourage terrorism and help lose the war. Ignoring human rights helps recruit terrorists, justifies terrorism, and defeats the best thing we have going for us — the fact that we stand for something better: for freedom, tolerance, and laws that protect all" (268).

18. See *The Amazing Spider-Man: Civil War*.

19. Driving him to make a deal with Mephisto to save her life, and causing his entire life to change in *One More Day*. But that is a bit much to go into right here.... For more, see J. Michael Straczynski's "One More Day" (Illus. and Co-writ. Joe Quesada) and Joe Quesada's "One Moment in Time."

20. See Stan Lee and Steve Ditko, *Marvel Masterworks Amazing Spider-Man* Vol. 1.

21. See "Glenn Beck: Obama Is a Racist." The Associated Press.

22. Consider how Parker's characterization has varied over the years, from writer to writer, medium to medium, since his creation in 1962. Is he a high school kid with an egg-shaped head and glasses that can't get a date with prom queen Liz Allen? Or is he a handsome, James Dean type married to the supermodel-turned-B-movie-actress Mary Jane Watson? Is he the veteran fighter who has defeated demigod-like opponents Firelord and the Juggernaut, or is he the weakling who can't even defeat the feeble Stilt Man? And, most importantly, is he a hero who saves children from fires and stops runaway trains, or is he a reckless adventurer who tends to get the people he loves most killed, including his Uncle Ben, and his first love, Gwen Stacy?

Could the discrepancies in the character be boiled down to bad writing or inconsistent characterization? Possibly, one could make such a claim, if one has a mind to be uncharitable. However, it would be more accurate to observe that these inconsistencies in Parker's behavior and personality speak to his realism, and roundness as a character.

23. The academic essay collection *Superheroes and Philosophy* (2005) contains several essays that praise Spider-Man for his morality and heroism, essentially because of his flaws and inner turmoil, not in spite of them. In "Comics and the Ring of Gyges," Jeff Brenzel discusses two classic narratives in which an unremarkable person accidentally discovers a magic ring that makes him all-powerful. In one, Plato's *Republic*, Gyges is a shepherd from Lydia (modern-day Turkey) who finds a magic ring in a cave following an earthquake and uses it to seduce Lydia's queen, kill the king, and seize control of the country. In *The Lord of the Rings*, the simple hobbits that find themselves in possession of the One Ring of Sauron realize that it has the power to absolutely corrupt anyone who comes into contact with it, no matter how innocent and kindhearted, and opt to destroy it at the advice of their wizard friend Gandalf. According to Brenzel, the Spider-Man and Superman stories offer an alternate take on this myth, in which a person entrusted with great power is tempted to evil, but ultimately chooses to do good. As Brenzel argues, their decision to be good and powerful, however, does not come without cost, or much soul-searching on their parts, making their stories eminently moral and thought-provoking, instead of simple-minded or merely escapist.

In "Spider-Man, the X-Men, and Kierkegaard's Double Danger," Stephen C. Evans, argues that Superman and Spider-Man are true Christians who genuinely love their neighbors and, as Kierkegaard explains, surrender "self-loving desires and cravings" and surrender "self-seeking plans and purposes" so that they "work unselfishly for the good — and then, for that very reason, put up with being abominated almost as a criminal, insulted and ridiculed" (Kierkegaard qtd. in Evans 164). Evans' connection between Superman, Spider-Man and Kierkegaard's theory works well, except that Superman's love for humanity is purer than Spider-Man's, and he is spared the hatred of the press and the public (with Lex Luthor being the lone exception), while Spider-Man's intellectual snobbery and anger issues makes him reluctantly help his fellow New Yorkers and — thanks to a public turned against him by J. Jonah Jameson — he is repaid with scorn for his efforts at assisting them.

24. See p. 20.

25. From cinema.com's article "Spider-Man: Interview with Tobey Maguire."

26. Now, there is some controversy over how large a role Lee's artistic collaborators on that first issue played in creating Spider-Man. For example, it isn't clear whether or not interior artist Ditko or cover artist Jack Kirby designed the classic Spider-Man costume, but Lee has said that he thinks the designs were Ditko's. For his part, Ditko claims that Kirby's initial story draft was vastly different from Ditko's, as it featured a boy who finds a magic ring that gives him spider powers, and Kirby's designs for Spider-Man's costume were radically different than the design Ditko ultimately produced. "The Spider-Man pages Stan showed [that were drawn by Kirby] me were nothing like the published character," Ditko said in 2002 (Theakston 13).

In describing the thought process that led to the creation of the Spider-Man that we know today, Ditko revealed that the decision to give Spider-Man a full-face mask was his, as were other key design elements. "One of the first things I did was to work up a costume. A vital, visual part of the character. I had to know how he looked ... before I did any breakdowns. For example: A clinging power so he wouldn't have hard shoes or boots, a hidden wrist-shooter versus a web gun and holster, etc. ... I wasn't sure Stan would like the idea of covering the character's face but I did it because it hid an obviously boyish face. It would also add mystery to the character...." See Steve Ditko, "'Jack Kirby's Spider-Man.' Robin Snyder's *History of Comics* #5 (May 1990)." Alter Ego: The Comic Book Artist Collection. Ed: Roy Thomas. TwoMorrows Publishing, 2001.

27. These included the Lizard, Sandman, Doctor Octopus, the Green Goblin, Kraven the Hunter, Mysterio, Electro, the Vulture, the Scorpion, Betty Brandt, Harry Osborne, Gwen Stacy, Flash Thompson, Liz Allen, J. Jonah Jameson, Aunt May, and Uncle Ben.

28. *Amazing Spider-Man* #38, reprinted in *Marvel Masterworks: The Amazing Spider-Man Vol. 4.*

29. *Ibid.*

30. *Ibid.*

31. As Evanier argues on Steve Ditko.com: "[Ditko] was unhappy because he believed Marvel's then-owner was reneging on certain promises about sharing in the revenues of the characters Ditko co-created, Spider-Man and Dr. Strange. He was upset with the way his comics were then produced, feeling that he was doing most of the writing work on the comics he did with Stan Lee, but that Lee — as dialogue writer — was getting too much of the credit and money.... In any case, at the time Ditko left Marvel, he was well aware that his co-creation had been sold for a TV show and that there would likely be a flood of Spider-Man toys and merchandise, and that he wouldn't be sharing in that windfall.... So is it really that huge a mystery as to why Steve Ditko quit Spider-Man?"

32. Certainly, royalties were an issue for Kirby. Despite the questions concerning his role in the development of Spider-Man, it is widely accepted that he designed the title characters and supporting casts of The Incredible Hulk, The Fantastic Four, The X-Men, and Thor, justifying his feelings of propriety over the characters, and his anger that his "work for hire" position at Marvel did not entitle him to a dime of the fortune in merchandising royalties that Marvel Comics Group has made in the decades since. Obituaries published in *The New York Post* and *The Daily News* in 1994 revealed that Kirby refused to walk into stores such as Toys 'R Us because it was too painful for him to see his characters' action figures on display, knowing that he was not profiting from the sales of those figures.

In March 2010, Kirby's children sued Marvel to terminate its current control of the rights to the characters and their profits. The lawsuit acknowledged that many of the key characters at the center of the lawsuit were created collaboratively, so it appealed that, in future, the Kirby estate share the rights to Jack Kirby–co-created characters with Marvel. Marvel Comics Group, backed by its owners, the Walt Disney Co., leveled its own lawsuit against the family, arguing that the company had exclusive rights to the characters thanks to Kirby's "work-made-for-hire" contract and the dictates of the 1909 Copyright Act (See Gardner. "It's on! Kirby Estate Sues Marvel; Copyrights to Iron Man, Spider-Man at Stake." The Hollywood Reporter, Esq. March 15, 2010. July 11, 2010.) According to Eriq Gardner, "The suit, filed in U.S. District Court in Los Angeles, follows the September move by the estate to send out 45 notices of termination to Marvel and owner the Walt Disney Co., as well as Sony, Universal, Fox and others, hoping to recapture control of much of Kirby's work.... The complaint seeks declaratory relief, including copyright termination and profits."

According to *Hollywood Reporter Esq.* reporter Eriq Gardner, the complaint "describes the backstory of Kirby's creative period, particularly from 1958 to 1963, when Marvel existed in a tiny office with few employees and relied upon 'freelancers to which they had little or no obligation.' Kirby disputes Marvel's work-for-hire theory." The Kirby lawsuit follows on the heels of the Siegel family's astonishingly successful legal bid to reclaim the rights to Superman's origin story in August of 2009, and Stan Lee's 2002 lawsuit against Marvel, which sought ten percent of the profits "from any film and television production using his characters and that Marvel has already received 'enormous windfalls' from X-Men and Spider-Man films and related merchandise." See Marc Graser's "Superman co-creator's family given rights: Siegels now control character's Krypton origins." (Variety. August 13, 2009.) and Kit Bowem's "Stan Lee Sues Marvel." (Hollywood.com. November 13, 2002).

33. See Kevin Smith, *Stan Lee's Mutants, Monsters, and Marvels* (DVD).

34. The question of buttons comes up again during the "Cult of Love" storyline, when a member of a religious cult tries handing Spider-Man a lapel pin advertising the organization, and Spider-Man demurs, saying, "I try not to wear anything that makes me stand out in a crowd" (see Peter David, "Cult of Love").

35. From *Batman & Spider-Man: New Age Dawning* by J.M. DeMatteis, Graham Nolan, and Karl Kesel. New York: DC Comics, 1997.

36. See Jim Shooter, "Superman and Spider-Man." Illus. John Buscema. *The Marvel/DC Collection — Crossover Classics, Vol. 1.*

37. The storyline is one of the darkest to have emerged at the time and one that Conway himself sees as laying the groundwork for the darker and grittier stories that would appear in the following decades, including *Watchmen* and *Daredevil: Born Again*. As Gerry Conway has explained in the book *Comic Creators on Spider-Man* (2004), the bitter tragedy of the storyline is that, while Uncle Ben died because Peter had refused to use his great power to fight crime, Gwen Stacy died because Peter had refused to back down against a master criminal. The two deaths of people Peter held most dear leave him stuck in a logical and emotional trap (47). No longer truly enjoying being Spider-Man, Peter nevertheless cannot give it up, and the fundamental contradiction leaves him a bitter and neurotic mess for much of the rest of Conway's run.

38. See *The Spectacular Spider-Man* #s 137–142, 149–153, 155–157, 161, 163, 165, and 166.

39. See Brian Michael Bendis' *House of M* graphic novel for a fuller exploration of this concept.

Chapter Four

1. Dialogue spoken by the title character, played by Thomas Jane, in *The Punisher* (2004).

2. See Orwell, "Politics and the English Language."

3. See Daniel King, "Chasing Zodiac," *San Francisco Chronicle*. October 5, 2005.

4. *Roman Polanski: Wanted and Desired.* Director: Marina Zenovich. THINKfilm. 2008.

5. Mark Hamilton Lytle. *America's Uncivil Wars: The Sixties Era from Elvis to the Fall of Richard Nixon* (New York: Oxford University Press, 2006) 336.

6. Pauline Kael. "Dirty Harry." *5001 Nights at the Movies*. New York: Henry Holt and Company, 1991. 191.

7. As David Chase's landmark HBO television series *The Sopranos* came to an end, select television critics proclaimed it "the greatest TV show of all time," columnist Peggy Noonan called it "a masterpiece," and — despite some dissatisfaction with the open-ended finale — there was great public mourning over the passing of the gritty crime soap opera. However, a solid contingent of Italian Americans were just as glad to see yet another mass-media portrayal of their people as degenerate Mafia killers fade into memory. Traditionally, American movies and television shows featuring those of Italian descent in "non–Mafia" roles are few and far between. The restaurant owners of *Big Night* and *For Roseanna*, the various fake Italians played by Chico Marx, and the military men in *Crimson Tide, Band of Brothers,* and *From Here to Eternity* are the exceptions that prove the rule. Fortunately, while Sylvester Stallone's character Rocky Balboa spent a brief stint as hired muscle for Italian loan sharks, he was too nice to break legs to collect on loans and quit the Mafia early in the first *Rocky* movie to become a professional boxer. In addition, a small-but-notable subset of Italian American characters on film and television fight crime rather than commit crimes. Though not Italian American himself, actor Peter Falk played the brilliantly intuitive homicide investigator Lt. Columbo in the 1968 telefilm *Prescription Murder*. He continued to play the character for decades afterward in a series of *Columbo* television movies, continuing to outsmart rich, establishment villains who underestimate his intelligence because his slovenly appearance tricks them into thinking that he is a poor, unintelligent, immigrant cop. Film and television followed up with further examples of noble Italian American police officers, including Al Giardello, Yaphet Kotto's half-Italian American, half-African American protagonist from *Homicide: Life on the Streets* (1993–1999), space station security chief Michael Garibaldi in the science fiction series *Babylon 5* (1993–1998), and portrayals of real-life Italian crime fighters in the movies *Serpico* (1973), *The Untouchables* (1987), *Rudy: The Rudy Giuliani Story* (2003), and *Donnie Brasco* (1997).

8. According to Barry Harvey, a twenty-four year veteran of the Pennsylvania State Police's Organized Crime Division, it is difficult to ascertain how many (and what percentage) of Italian Americans were a part of the mafia throughout its history, from the Prohibition era to the present. "As the mafia is a 'secret' organization it usually is very difficult to determine accurate numbers. There are members and then there are associates. Most figures are merely estimates by law enforcement agencies or writers who specialize in organized crime.... [However, t]here is no doubt that the percentage of Italian-Americans belonging (actually 'made members') to the mafia is very small." As Harvey observes, "The original mafia came about as a pseudo government when there was none in Sicily. The local don was the most respected man in the village and functioned as a government would. The mafia, or men of respect, formed around this don to perform services for the community. It was a tradition and part of the heritage. When groups of Sicilians and Italians immigrated to the United States they found themselves living in overcrowded cities where once again the real government ignored them so the men of respect once again became very powerful in the little Italys, etc. They viewed themselves as honorable men bringing with them a tradition, rules, and a structure. For the most part these men were looked up to in the neighborhoods.... They would not exist if they were not supported by the public through the use of their "services" and through the support and respect of the Italian/Sicilian people who live in the neighborhoods. So on the one hand they do not like the depiction of all Italians as mafia but on the other hand the mafia is supported and held up as something special in the neighborhoods where they thrive."

9. In the Punisher universe, there's no such thing as "Untouchables," or noble Italians. Still, one of the first notable real-life Italian crime fighters is Frank Basile, a man who understood underworld culture and joined Eliot Ness' squad of Untouchables during the Prohibition era to help bring down the empire Al Capone built on illegal alcohol trafficking. While Ness and Oscar Fraley do not do much to develop Basile's character in their book-length account of the mob war, they express admiration for Basile and terrible anger at Capone for ordering Basile's murder. Presumably, Capone targeted Basile for assassination because he was angry that Basile worked against his own people. Capone may have also felt it would be easier to get away with killing a mere Italian than a member of the U.S. Treasury Department (although he would later try to kill Ness as well). Basile is not widely remembered by the American public, and is hardly a household name, but he was the inspiration for Andy Garcia's character in Brian De Palma's *The Untouchables* (1987). In the film, Garcia is a dedicated member of the team who had attempted to distance himself from Italian criminals, and from his Italian heritage, by changing his name from Giuseppe Petri to George Stone. Sean Connery's character, Irish cop Jim Malone, admits to having some prejudices against Italians, and calls Capone's men Dagos and WOPs, but admonishes Stone for changing his name, and insists on affectionately calling him Giuseppe. Stone, thankfully, is more fortunate than the real-life inspiration for his character and survives to see Capone jailed for tax evasion. The film presents Stone as being a more righteous Italian American than Capone mainly because Capone is a cruel, murderous, unelected "head" of Chicago, and Stone is bravely defiant of Capone's unjust rule. Consequently, the film virtually sidesteps a very natural audience caveat that few Americans feel that Prohibition was a just or enforceable law, and that Capone was merely providing the public "what they wanted."

10. While the police are often ineffective at collaring rich and powerful criminals, there is one wish-fulfillment, folk hero character who is particularly effective at arresting seemingly untouchable opponents — Lt. Columbo. Unlike Pistone, the fictional television detective Lt. Columbo only infrequently found himself investigating Italian criminals. An evil vineyard owner and wine connoisseur played by Donald Pleasance in the episode "Any Old Port in a Storm" (1973) springs to mind as a rare Italian adversary. However, Columbo's Italian heritage was mentioned repeatedly during the course of the series, and was often the subject of light-hearted humor. One of the most memorable conversations in the history of the show takes place between Columbo and his Italian American dentist, Dr. Perenchino, in the story "Candidate for Crime" (1973). As Perechino examines Columbo's wisdom teeth and listens to opera playing on the radio, he launches into a monologue about anti–Italian prejudice in America "when people talk about Italians, do they think cops, dentists, tenors? The Pope, not even? The Pope is Italian, ain't he? They think ... they think Mafiosa, Mafiosa, Mafiosa."

At the time the episode was broadcast, the Pope was Italian: Pope Paul VI. The script involved a Senatorial hopeful (Jackie Cooper) killing his controlling campaign manager and blaming the death on members of the underworld whom he has sworn to bring down. Amusingly, when Dr. Perenchino hears on the radio that the famous public figure was killed, he predicts that the real killer will likely be a rich white guy who tries to pin it on the Mafia. As Columbo leaves the dentist's office to begin his investigation, Perenchino says, "You are an Italian cop. No matter who you catch for this murder, they're still gonna say it's the Mafia and that you're covering for them.... Take my advice, lieutenant, change your name!"

Columbo has no comment. Nor does he change his name. He merely proceeds to prove that the senator was the killer and makes a successful arrest at the end of the episode. Interestingly enough, Perenchino is convinced that, as an Italian American on the police force, Columbo is in constant danger of becoming a victim of his own ethnicity, but the series never presents Columbo's status on the force, or his reputation, as being threatened by his class or culture. In fact, Columbo's entire modus operandi works because he follows Sun Tzu's dictum, "Appear strong when you are weak and weak when you are strong." He appears weak, but his position in the fabric of the criminal justice system, and in American society, is secure. He is able to fool his criminal adversaries into underestimating him by pretending to be on the margins of society when, in actuality, he commands the respect of his superiors and the power to jail white collar criminals who, in the real world, oftentimes would be beyond the reach of a mere working-class homicide investigator. In fact, Columbo is unassailable, even when wealthy murderers, like the psychiatrist played by Gene Barry in "Prescription Murder," are friends with the district attorney, or use bribes or threats to shake Columbo off their trail. Columbo is never taken off the case, and never faces an opponent too rich or politically powerful to buy his way to freedom. Indeed, this almost counterintuitive consistency of outcome makes some viewers wonder if Columbo is secretly wealthy himself, has some kind of politically invincible ally, or if his whole persona as a frumpy, poor cop is a put-on and he only pretends to drive a broken-down car and wear a hand-me-down raincoat when he's off-duty.

11. In recent years, the growth of the discipline of Italian American studies in academia has inspired the writing of several excellent books about the Italian American experience by members of the "baby-boom" generation. These works, which include Robert Viscusi's *Buried Casears* (2006) and Alfred Lubrano's *Limbo* (2004), have used autobiographical anecdotes, historical research, and sociological data to chronicle the journey of enculturation that many Italian American families made over a period of several generations. Such works invariably begin with a discussion of the arrival of the main wave of immigrants at Ellis Island and follow the displaced Italians to urban centers such as Rochester or Brooklyn, where they survived in an alien land by clustering together in "Little Italy" neighborhoods and toiling in jobs involving hard physical labor and unjustly low pay. From such humble beginnings, these working-class Italians saved enough to send their children to college, or to enable their progeny to begin their own small businesses. Within the span of two or three generations, many Italian Americans felt that they had finally achieved the much-vaunted American Dream when the descendents of immigrants began trading in their one-bedroom city apartments for (semi-attached) homes in the suburbs of places like New Jersey and Staten Island.

Both Viscusi and Lubrano speak of the present-day Italian American as a middle-class figure, often a college professor in the humanities, or an executive with one home in Park Avenue and another in Tuscany, who is weary of the immigrant stereotype of the Mafia don that haunts the Italian American public image and who has a love-hate relationship with films like *The Godfather*. For these authors, the greatest problem facing their contemporaries are identity issues tied up with the fact that, as financially and socially successful as Italian Americans are, they do not feel "at home" anywhere. For Lubrano, the feeling of "Limbo" is one of class. Italians who were the first members of their family to graduate college never felt at home in the Protestant, middle-class communities they moved into (or the "WASPy" occupations they entered), nor could they ever feel at home again in the working-class communities they left behind. According to Viscusi, national identity remains the most contested problem as Italian Americans are still not truly accepted either by the Italy they left behind or the America they came to. As he writes:

> ... consider the difficulties immigrant Italians needed to face in developing a discourse of their own entitlement in the millennial European project called America [after the Italian explorer Amerigo Vespucci]. These new arrivals in no way could identify themselves directly with the ruling peoples. The Anglo-Americans had resisted the entry of the Irish Catholics. But now these groups began to cooperate in the definitive marginalizing of the Italians, who found themselves forming, and still do, a part of the vivid and highly decorated frame of American society, along with the blacks, the Latinos, and the Eastern European Jews. Naturally, a society as mobile as that of the United States always has room to absorb some members of these border peoples into the operating centers, but much larger proportions remain, as before, to a greater or lesser degree visibly tattooed with their tribal or racial otherness. For Italians this exclusion has been less rigid than for blacks or Latinos, but more rigid than for Jews and Irish Catholics. In short, to the regional and class divisions of Italy has been added in the United States the machinery of ethnic boundary markers. The borders are such that Italians who cross them must do so at the risk of losing their own possibilities of historical self-awareness.
>
> ... Not surprisingly, many Italians have refused to pay this price [146–147].

Despite the obvious anxiety in evidence here, the general narrative arc presented by both books suggests that, despite the presence of many obstacles — such as anti-Catholic bigotry, first-generation immigrant poverty — the Italians have succeeded in improving their lot in America with each successive generation.

As Viscusi observes,

> Italians now come to New York, not to organize garbage trucks and cocaine dealers, but to represent major manufacturers, traders, and banks. They have offices along Park Avenue. They win lucrative contracts to build bridges and pipelines all over the world.... From Greenwich, Connecticut, to Palo Alto, California, Italian American professionals have the financial and educational capital to appreciate the finer — that is, the more socially dominant — meanings of the word Italian.... These graduates of Stanford and Harvard do not resemble the candy store bookies and Brooklyn torpedoes who populate American Mafia films. As Italian Americans move toward the notion

that Italian means something central and authoritative, their impatience with the immigrant stigma grows. Some spend huge amounts of money protesting the Mafia mythology. Others simply buy themselves villas in Tuscany [31].

However, despite the fact that previous generations of Italian Americans have seen their quality of life improve, and have seen the creation of a class of Italian Americans who can afford to buy a house in Tuscany, this is the first generation in which Italians appear to be losing ground in their quests to finally achieve, and retain, their status as full-fledged Americans while holding on to their Italian heritage. Lubrano and Viscusi both effectively end their discussion with the "baby-boom" generation, and do not consider how members of Generation X, or the Millennial Generation, have fared in the face of additional problems such as the dissolution of the American family, the political polarization of the Culture Wars and the War on Terror, and the slowdown of the American economy. Naturally, all of these issues plague the baby boomers as well, but they are having a particularly disastrous effect on young Americans in general, who have not yet made their careers or begun their families.

Even as Rudolph Giuliani failed his 2008 bid to become the first Italian (and the second Roman Catholic) U.S. president, middle-class suburban Italian families seem to be fighting to keep up with their mortgages, health care and utility bills, and debt from college loans and credit cards used to help keep the family up with inflation. The financial strain has caused many Italian Americans in their twenties and thirties to wonder why they bothered going to college when all that is open to them is a middle management job that involves sitting in a cubicle in an understaffed office entering data into a computer for more than forty hours a week with no health benefits and no chance of promotion. Truly, they are members of the *Generation Debt* described by Anya Kamenetz in her 2006 book of that title. As such, many Italian Americans wonder whether they will ever earn enough money so they can marry, buy a house of their own, or have children, and some males lament the possibility of ever meeting a woman who has not been so scarred by her parents' divorce that she is even willing to consider marriage. Also, while Italians have traditionally not been big drinkers, reserving their alcohol intake for a glass or two of wine at dinner, the younger generations of Italian Americans have taken, in recent years, to succumbing to the youth party culture and, on Staten Island, are now part of a demographic of "Northeast ... white, middle-class, teenage" Catholics who are "one of the highest demographics of underage drinkers" who "drink, and drink savagely" (Zailckas xv).

It is also interesting to try to trace the migratory patterns of Italian Americans, many of whom cannot afford to be homeowners, but do not feel at home returning to the apartment buildings their families owned in the past, since new ethnic groups have moved in and the neighborhoods are less "Italian," or, in the case of Greenwich Village, far too expensive for most. However, the richer Italians are part of an intriguing white-flight pattern. Some have moved off of Staten Island over the years, searching for greener pastures in New Jersey, joining other former Brooklyn residents who bypassed New York's least famous borough. Other Italians moved to Florida, but later grew tired of Florida and decided to take a home in North Carolina. (Local lingo dubs these North Carolina transplants from Florida "half-backs" because they moved half-way back to Brooklyn.) Despite these maneuvers, there is a general sense among Staten Islanders that there's no place to move to. Partly due to economic factors, partly due to a lack of imagination or a general sense of fear, they feel fundamentally trapped on Staten Island, as if it were some kind of black hole. They are not very interested in Italy, or most of the rest of the country, or even Manhattan, which is expensive and a pain to commute to given the lack of subway access, affordable parking, and the erratic bus schedule. If they do move, they want it to be to another "Little Italy," for fear that, should they try moving to a town without a sizable Italian populace, they will be greeted with disdain by the non–Italian neighbors. In addition, as Italians disperse across America, it becomes harder to maintain their traditional culture in any meaningful way.

12. Joseph D. Pistone, an American of Sicilian extraction and another real-life crime fighter, helped bring down New York's Bonanno crime family by operating undercover as one of their number for six years during the 1970s. Pistone's book *Donnie Brasco*, named after the alias he assumed while working undercover, inspired the Johnny Depp vehicle *Donnie Brasco* (1997), the independent film *10th & Wolf* (2006), several fiction novels featuring the further adventures of Donnie Brasco, and the short-lived television series *Falcone*. Consequently, Pistone has become as much of a folk hero in the annals of crime drama as he is a real person, prompting *New York Post* entertainment critic Linda Stasi to complain of his ubiquitous presence during the turn of the century. In the film *Donnie Brasco,* Depp plays Pistone as a figure who spies upon his fellow Italians with great reluctance. He relates strongly to mob culture and is in danger of embracing the gangster personality. He feels like a Judas figure when he betrays his mobster friend "Lefty" Ruggiero. He also butts heads with his "WASP," establishment superiors in the FBI.

However, the Joe Pistone in the book *Donnie Brasco* is vastly different from the one in the film. Pistone's own written account of his feelings — both at the time he was undercover and since — seems far less conflicted. In fact, Pistone appears almost detached in his attitude towards the two hundred criminals that were indicted for crimes based on evidence that he gathered. Aside from voicing disapproval of their lifestyle, their corrupting influence, and their lack of intelligence, Pistone claims to have felt neither malice nor great sympathy for those he spied on. Their Italian-American heritage was irrelevant, he wrote.

Pistone has not voiced objections to Depp's portrayal of him as more conflicted than he seems in the book. It is possible that both portrayals of Pistone are, to an extent, true, representing two very different reactions for someone in Pistone's position. The Pistone in the film sees what he is doing as a crime against his own people and feels guilty for it, while the Pistone of the book sees the case in terms of law-breakers versus law abiders and feels no such conflict. Both reactions are fascinating.

Barry Harvey, a former undercover agent and a twenty-four-year veteran of the Pennsylvania State Police's Organized Crime Division in Philadelphia, noticed the discrepancy between the book and the film and believes that the truth is somewhere in between. He suspects that Pistone feels the most guilt over the fact that the several of the individuals who brought him into the inner circle of the mob — not knowing that he was an undercover agent — were later killed by other gangsters as punishment for the mistake. As Harvey explained in an October 8, 2008 e-mail "I have personally used individuals such as Lefty who I certainly did not care for but still had some reservations about using them and what would happen to them.... [W]orking undercover requires lies and deceit. You must 'like' someone no matter if you do or not if that person is useful. Relationships are formed, and just because someone is a criminal does not necessarily mean they are not likeable. I will never forget a long-term undercover assignment I had in which I became friendly with a group of people and one in particular. At the end of the investigation when this one person was arrested, he cried and told me 'I thought we were friends.' ... [So] even if Pistone did not like Lefty he knew that he, Pistone, would be directly responsible for Lefty's death. Maybe that is where the 'guilt' comes from [more than from being Italian like Lefty]."

13. Barry Harvey e-mail interview on March 25, 2008.

14. See Req Seeton and Dayna Van Buskirk. "Screenwriting Punishment with Michael France." *UGO Screenwriter's Voice.* April 06, 2004. June 25, 2010. <http://screenwriting.ugo.com/interviews/michaelfrance_interview.php>

15. *Ibid.*

16. *Ibid.*

17. "Boondock Saints" entry in Wikipedia.org, obtained on June 22, 2010. (http://en.wikipedia.org/wiki/The_Boondock_Saints).

18. This perspective is a contentious one, especially since the many Italian Americans who are not prone to racist feelings do not deserve to be painted with the same broad brush as those who do. Arguably, there is an inconsistency in any article that disavows one stereotype (the mafia stigma) while reinforcing another (the racist Italian American). While there are statistically few Italian Americans in the mafia, the question of Italian American racism is raised consistently and convincingly enough in the media, and in sociological works, and is harder to refute. Recent articles published online at the Italian American Digital Project (www.i-italy.org) have taken a strong stand against Italian and Italian American racism, and cover topics ranging from the election of Barack Obama to the extent to which the media coverage of the 1989 murder of African American teenager Yusef Hawkins in Bensonhurst justifiably painted the Brooklyn Italian American community as essentially racist.

Martin Scorsese and Robert DeNiro have both directed films that were based on true stories in which an Italian American male faces his own prejudice, and the prejudice of his peers when he contemplates dating a black woman —*Mean Streets* (1973) and *A Bronx Tale* (1993). These films hint that anti-black sentiments are common in Italian American communities. In addition, Spike Lee has nailed Italian Americans to the wall for being anti-black, and has been strident enough, and persistent enough in his criticism that he has been accused of being himself racist anti–Italian and painting them in too broad, and negative a brush. (For example, Lee's attempt to cast an Italian American cop as moderately likeable despite being racist in the 2006 film *Inside Man* is still a bitter pill for many Italian American viewers to swallow, as the police officer, once again, is a racist Italian American.)

Films like those in the *Rocky* franchise portray the good and the bad about Italian American and African American relations. Eddie Murphy has a famous comedy routine where he makes fun of Italian Americans for investing too much in the myth of Rocky Balboa, and accuses the film series of race-baiting and escalating tensions between blacks and Italians because three of Rocky's main opponents are formidable African Americans whom audience members are invited to root against. While I see where he is coming from, the friendship that Rocky eventually cultivates with Apollo Creed in *Rocky III* and *IV*, the training he does under Tony Burton, the affection he gives to Little Marie's son Steps, and the respect he ultimately gives the Mason "the Line" Dixon, who defeats Rocky at the end of *Rocky Balboa*, is an infinitely preferable model of black/Italian relationships than those seen just about anywhere else in the popular media.

And, coming at it from another angle, unlike most Italian American characters in film, Rocky has the advantage of being a really nice guy.

19. See Nancy Mills' article, "'Punisher' Star Says Frank Castle is No Superhero." *The Reading Eagle.* December 5, 2008. June 25, 2010. <http://readingeagle.com/article.aspx?id=116368>

Chapter Five

1. See John Arcudi's *JLA: Superpower.* 1999.

2. See Martin Anderson, "The Den Of Geek interview: Mark Millar." *Den of Geek!* Jul 20, 2008. September 4, 2010. <http://www.denofgeek.com/comics/88459/the_den_of_geek_interview_mark_millar.html>

3. See Mark Juddery "5 Comic Superheroes Who Made a Real-World Difference," Steven D. Levitt and Stephen J. Dubner's *Freakonomics*, and Stetson Kennedy's "StetsonKennedy.com."

4. *Ibid.*

5. *Ibid.*

6. While some readers might question the necessity of an in-depth discussion of a superhero that has, functionally, fallen from grace, in many ways it isn't possible to write a book about superheroes without discussing Superman. This is true for a number of reasons. First of all, he is an American institution and deserves serious treatment. Secondly, he was not always as bland a figure as he has been in recent years, and there are many legitimately good Superman stories out there. Thirdly, some of the first, and greatest academic essays written about superheroes focus on Superman, ranging from Umberto Eco's "The Myth of Superman," to essays by Marshall McLuhan and Jules Feiffer. Academics remain fascinated by Superman to this day, even if he appears passé to the general public. Finally, and most importantly, Superman was the first superhero as we understand the term, and all others that were created afterwards either built upon concepts first introduced in the Superman mythology, or reacted against them. In a very real way, when one discusses superheroes as a broad concept, one necessarily discusses Superman as an individual superhero at the same time. The reverse is also true.

7. Despite the exemplary role he played in the Stetson Kennedy vs. KKK affair, Superman's record on racial issues has not always been this exemplary. *Daily Planet* reporter Ron Troupe is an intellectual black man, social activist, and adversary of conservative Planet Sports Editor Steve Lombard. Introduced in *Adventures of Superman* #480 (1991) by Jerry Ordway and Tom Grummett, Troupe was involved in a prominent storyline in which he got Lois Lane's sister Lucy pregnant and later married her.

A toned-down and painfully unfunny Richard Pryor played a gifted computer hacker who has to choose between being Superman's friend and adversary in *Superman III* (it was an odd role that appeared to be designed originally for Ned Beatty's Otis character).

A mysterious government agent in a stereotypically fat "mammy" body, Amanda Waller is sometimes a boring stuffed shirt but she is often an intriguing figure — sometimes a villain, sometimes establishment anti-hero—who has had dealings with Superman in the comics and *Justice League* cartoon.

John Henry Irons, a.k.a. Steel, is a man in a metal Superman suit that began his career as an heir to the Superman legacy when he thought Superman was dead and buried in the *World Without a Superman* storyline (see 1993's *Adventures of Superman* #500). A black Superman created by Louise Simonson, Steel is also inspired by one of America's very first superheroes, the brawny black railroad spike driver John Henry. The *Superman* saga is the natural outgrowth of this folk tale, in which humans prove their superiority to machines after all by being "faster than a speeding bullet, more powerful than a locomotive, and able to leap tall buildings in a single bound" without dying of a heart attack from the effort.

While John Henry may have been one of the folklore inspirations for Superman, it is notable that there have been very few black Supermen in comic history. *The Final Crisis* (2008) storyline masterminded by Grant Morrison includes a segment set in an alternate reality in which a black Superman is President of the United States. In Jeph Loeb's "What Can One Icon Do?" (2002), Superman encounters Muhammed X, the black superhero protector of Harlem, who tells Superman he is not welcome in their neighborhood because he has not done anything of note to help black people. Superman feels guilty, and quizzes children, both black and white, about whom they look up to; the white children look up to him and the black children respect black superheroes. The racial divide disturbs Superman, who can find no better solution to the problem than to be color-blind himself in the hope of creating a color-blind society in the future (*Superman* #179).

Movies that explore the theme of an African American Superman include *Black Supaman* (2007), *Abar, the First Black Superman* (1977), and *Meteor Man* (1993), the last of which represented the fulfillment of Robert Townsend's wish to play a black Superman, expressed in *Hollywood Shuffle* (1987). There were also rumors that Denzel Washington might play Clark Kent and Beyoncé Knowles would be Lois Lane in a *Superman* film mooted before the release of *Superman Returns* (2006), but that project never materialized.

Historically, there have not been many black Kryptonians in the comic books. However, 2009's *New Krypton* storyline depicted a multiracial cast of 100,000 Kyrptonian refugees coming to Earth years after Superman's arrival as an infant, including "Asian" and "African" Kryptonians (see Brady "Supermen of Color").

This storyline represents the most diverse portrait of Krypton yet, trumping 1971's introduction of a non-white Kryptonian in *Superman* #234 and the unveiling of a segregated society of black Kryptonians—called "Vathlo Island, Home of a Highly Advanced Black Race"—in issue #239. Expressing embarrassment at these first awkward steps towards racial diversity, Superman writer and historian Mark Waid noted that he felt it would be too harsh to call earlier *Superman* writers racist. "A lack of ethnicity was an error of omission, and I'm not sure given the time that it's fair to call that 'racist,'" he said (see Brady "Supermen of Color").

Supporting Waid's point, reporter Matt Brady wrote that the science fiction of the 1930s did tend to cast alien races as having one, monolithic culture, unless the storyline concerned some form of alien civil war. Therefore, Jerry Siegel and Joe Schuster were arguably following others' leads in their crafting of Kryptonian culture. Brady also cited the Civil Rights Act of 1964 as the initiating incident that made pop culture as a whole finally decide to begin recognizing all races and ethnicities, and diversifying the people portrayed in films, comics, television, and advertising (see Brady "Supermen of Color").

8. One of the reasons it is difficult to find a literary or cultural critic who would act as an apologist for Lois Lane, as I do, is that many of them approach the subject matter of women in popular culture with a knowledge of both art and literature that "the average American" in the mass media age does not have. I agree that, next to Angela Carter's *The Bloody Chamber*, the novels of Margaret Atwood, the short stories of Jane Smiley, the films of Gillian Armstrong, and the wonderfully intellectual women one encounters while listening to NPR, the many iterations of Lois Lane seen over the years, generally speaking, do not seem anywhere near feminist enough. However, even critics who approach the material from this vantage point have granted that Lois can be an appealing character at times, with a noticeable feminist streak at her core. And, if one begins with, as a point of comparison, how women are portrayed in popular culture instead of with how women are portrayed in literature or by academics, then Lois Lane quickly emerges as a breath of fresh air. Compare the Lois Lane portrayed by Margot Kidder in the Superman films to the Lolitas featured in the average MTV-music-video-harem; the moronic and neurotic women of *Friends* and most soap operas; the marriage-obsessed daddy's girls of reality television and films such as *27 Dresses* and *Bride Wars*, and the leather-clad killer prostitutes of *Sin City*. If Lois comes up short of a more ideal feminist character (such as the heroine of *My Brilliant Career*), she still stands head and shoulders above the nightmarish role models available for young women today. As rock singer Pink laments in her song "Stupid Girls," girls who, in former generations, dreamed of one day becoming president, are now content with performing an erotic dance in a rapper's music video.

Chapter Six

1. See Jemma McFatBack, "BATMAN BEGINS rated R Gary Oldman spills interesting beans...." *AintIt CoolNews.com*. May 28, 2004. September 8, 2010. <http://www.aintitcool.com/display.cgi?id=17668>

2. See Jon Stewart and the Writers of *The Daily Show*. *The Daily Show with Jon Stewart Presents America (The Book) Teacher's Edition: A Citizen's Guide to Democracy Inaction* page 79.

3. *Doctor Who: The Face of Evil* (1977).

4. At the time of the film's release, everyone was offended by it, including the French, so it languished in obscurity until The Criterion Collection chose to release it in 2008 as part of *The Delirious Fictions of William Klein* DVD set. Criterion has also released and championed other prescient and newly relevant films, such as *The Lost Honor of Katarina Blum* and *The Battle of Algiers*.

5. See Matthew Janovic. "Mr. Freedom." Internet Movie Database. September 1, 2008. August 12, 2010. <http://italy.imdb.com/title/tt0064674/usercomments>

6. In *Live and Let Die* (1954), Bond describes the retirement communities and trailer parks that dot the Florida landscape as ghastly. In "007 in New York" (1964), Bond teases Americans for being germ phobic, lacking taste in cuisine, and building womb-like cars that insulate the driver from the experience of driving.

7. The Felix character is a fixture in the vast majority

of Bond movies, but he is not as memorable as Miss Moneypenny (Lois Maxwell/Samantha Bond) or Boothroyd of "Q" Branch (Desmond Llewelyn) because the same actor has so infrequently played him. Hawaii Five-O star Jack Lord originated the role in *Dr. No* (1962), David Hedison played Felix in *Live and Let Die* (1973) and *License to Kill* (1989), and Jeffrey Wright made the role his own in *Casino Royale* (2006) and *Quantum of Solace* (2008). Otherwise, Felix has been played only once by a variety of other actors.

8. Americans who chafe at this description of how the British portrayed Felix might take into consideration that the very first filmed dramatization of a Bond novel was a 1954 episode of the American series "Climax!" It adapted the novel *Casino Royale*, recasting superspy "Jimmy Bond" as an American and portrayed Bond's ineffective overseas partner "Clarence Leiter" as British.

9. Cole, Juan R. I. "A Quantum of Anti-Imperialism." Informed Consent. Nov. 16, 2008. July 8, 2010. <http://www.juancole.com/2008/11/quantum-of-anti-imperialism.html>

10. While comparatively few Americans watch or listen to BBC news, unless they listen to NPR or watch the cable network BBC America, they have had access to British news and entertainment for years. Certainly, PBS has syndicated BBC BritComs such as *Black Adder*, *Fawlty Towers*, *The Office*, and *Are You Being Served?* for decades, while the (occasionally renamed) *Masterpiece Theater* and *Mystery!* have long provided a home for a variety of BBC and ITV British novel adaptations (*Poldark*, *Jeeves and Wooster*), short series (*State of Play*, *Reckless*), and crime dramas (*Prime Suspect*, *Inspector Morse*).

11. Unfortunately, the comic book is so fundamentally British in its class-consciousness that it took years for it to be made into a film. When it was, American Keanu Reeves played the title character in *Constantine* (2005), a film that offered an in-depth exploration of the Roman Catholic laity's anxiety concerning the seemingly unjust doctrine of the damnation of suicides. The film had little to say about politics, economics, or any other non-theological issues.

12. The very same arguments heard about Thatcher began anew when American presidential hopeful Sarah Palin dubbed herself a feminist and promised that, should she become the first woman president of the United States, it would be a symbolic victory for all women. Traditional feminists were largely unconvinced by these claims, for the same reasons Wisse and Palau deny Thatcher's status as a feminist.

13. See Martin Wisse and "Palau." "No, Thatcher was not a feminist."

14. Pink Floyd. "the post war dream." the final cut. CD. Capitol, 2004.

15. Costello, Elvis. "Everything You Wanted To Know About Spike." BBC2 Late Show. Perf. Tracey Macleod. BBC 2. February 20, 1989.

16. *Ibid.*

17. Garth Ennis is most famous for his work on the comic book series *Preacher*, which shares many themes and artistic sensibilities with *Hellblazer*, only it is a series set in the United States. Ennis also wrote *The Punisher: Born*, which is covered in Chapter Four.

18. Anti-nuke, anti-imperialist protesters arrived from London to protest the expansion, but several locals objected to the political interference, calling the activists "middle class yuppie bastards" who are sticking their noses into things that aren't their business (40).

19. Throughout the Clinton Administration, the conservative American press savaged President Clinton on a nearly daily basis, offering extensive, relentless coverage of scandal after scandal, some of which were more worthy of news coverage than others. These scandals included accusations that Clinton had Vince Foster murdered, that he accepted campaign donations from China during the 1996 election, and that he shut down LAX airport for hours so he could have his hair cut on the runway. Other Clinton-era scandals included Nannygate, Paula Jones' sexual harassment lawsuit, the Monica Lewinsky affair, and the Whitewater controversy. During an interview with Matt Lauer on *The Today Show* on January 27, 1998, First Lady Hilary Clinton declared that the press and the Republican Party formed part of "a vast right wing conspiracy that has been conspiring against my husband since the day he announced [he was running] for president." Some critics accused her of paranoia and hypersensitivity. Others declared that the Clintons were a pair of blue-collar career criminals who had conned their way into the White House — thanks in large part to the third-party presidential candidacy of Ross Perot — and were guilty of all of the infractions the press had nailed them to the wall for committing. In contrast, Clinton supporters argued that most of the scandals were based on false or misleading evidence and that the Clintons couldn't truly be called paranoid if everyone, indeed, was out to get them.

20. He added:

> While Western powers and intellectuals were admiring themselves for having established the new norm of humanitarian intervention in the late 1990s, the rest of the world also had some thoughts on the matter. It is illuminating to see how they reacted, say, to Tony Blair's repetition of the official reasons for the bombing of Serbia in 1999: failure to bomb "would have dealt a devastating blow to the credibility of NATO" and "the world would have been less safe as a result of this." The objects of NATO's solicitude did not seem overly impressed by the need to safeguard the credibility of those who had been crushing them for centuries. Nelson Mandela, for example, condemned Blair for "encouraging international chaos, together with America, by ignoring other nations and playing 'policemen of the world'" in their attacks on Iraq in 1998 and Serbia the next year. In the world's largest democracy — which, after independence, began to recover from the grim effects of centuries of British rule — the Clinton-Blair efforts to shore up NATO's credibility and make the world safe were also not appreciated, but official and press condemnations in India remained unheard. Even in Israel, the client state par excellence, the pretensions of the Clinton-Blair and a host of domestic admirers were ridiculed by leading military and political analysis as a return to old-fashioned "gunboat diplomacy" under the familiar "cloak of moralistic righteousness," and as a "danger to the world" [23–24].

21. See Peter David, *The Incredible Hulk* #392, page 14. Reprinted in "The Incredible Hulk: War and Pieces," *X-Factor Visionaries* Vol. 2.

22. In "The Immorality of Preemptive War," a 2002 article for the *New Perspective Quarterly*, Schlesinger wrote:

> During the Cold War, advocates of preventive war were dismissed as a bunch of loonies. When Robert Kennedy called the notion of a preventive attack on the Cuban missile sites "Pearl Harbor is reverse," and added "For 175 years we have not been that kind of country," he swung the ExCon — President Kennedy's special group of advisors — from an airstrike to a blockade.

> The policy of containment plus deterrence won the Cold War. After the collapse of the Soviet Union, everyone thanked heaven that the preventive-war loonies had never got into power in any major country.
> Today, alas, they appear to be in power in the U.S. [77].

23. Clinton had ordered the bombing of an al-Qaeda training camp in Afghanistan on August 20, 1998, mere days after issuing a public apology to the American people over the Monica Lewinsky affair, on August 17. His critics thought this military strike was a transparent attempt to get Lewinsky off the front page of newspapers and make himself look good as a defender of homeland security in a transparent, "wag the dog" public relations maneuver. These same conservative critics remained unconvinced that al-Qaeda was a credible threat to the United States, even after bin Ladin's promise to attack the American mainland, made in the aftermath of the USS *Cole* bombing in Yemen on October 12, 2000.

24. See Nile Gardiner. "Is Avatar an attack on the Iraq War?" *Telegraph*. December 12, 2009. August 15, 2010. <http://blogs.telegraph.co.uk/news/nilegardiner/100019656/is-avatar-an-attack-on-the-iraq-war/>

25. See Robert Harris, "The 'Ghost' of Tony Blair."

26. The "off"ness of the Doctor's clothing not only contributes to the "alien"ness of the character but makes a determination about the Doctor's economic class and sexual orientation difficult to pin down. For example, the Doctor has been presented as, paradoxically, heterosexual, homosexual, bisexual, and asexual during the course of the series in a manner that is sometimes overt and sometimes pure subtext. It is also left deliberately unclear whether he is a thief, con artist, and gadabout who left his home world out of boredom with its stagnant society of "door mice" (see "The War Games") or an aristocrat and co-developer of time travel technology who was exiled from his home planet for political reasons (see "An Unearthly Child" and "Remembrance of the Daleks").

To further muddy matters, throughout the series the Doctor's accent shifts by class and region, while remaining forever British, suggesting that he is, simultaneously, one-hundred-percent British as well as a "pure"-blooded Time Lord from the planet Gallifrey. In a sense, the Doctor's fictional origins are a muddle and a mess more than they are a mystery, a natural consequence of decades of script writers who defied one another's vision of the series and sometimes neglected to read one another's work.

Eric Saward, Marc Platt, Kim Newman, and an array of fan fiction writers have crafted several possible "origin" stories set before the start of the series. Naturally, these origins are all irreconcilable, but the best of them include Newman's book *Time and Relative* (2002), which focuses on the Doctor's granddaughter, Susan, and the audio play "Auld Mortality" (2003), which is a far more comprehensive origin. However, one scholar, Jon Preddle, has come closer than anyone else to providing a comprehensive biography of the Doctor, and history of the Doctor Who universe, by writing *Timelink*, a book that resolves all narrative inconsistencies in the series, but is successful largely because it rejects clues to the Doctor's past provided by the American Doctor Who made-for-TV-movie starring Paul McGann. One might well argue that the series' narrative inconsistencies — though accidental — are oddly appropriate for a protagonist who resists revealing too much about himself to even his closest friends, who travels under an alias, and who defies authority at every turn, refusing to be controlled, psychoanalyzed, or domesticated by anyone.

Like the Doctor's wardrobe and persona, *Doctor Who*'s aesthetic "feel" has changed radically over the years, partly due to the changing times but primarily because of the radically different creative sensibilities of its regularly changing roster of producers, stars, and scriptwriters. Some episodes, such as "The Web of Fear," have sensibilities similar to those of *The Twilight Zone*, while others, like "The Aztecs," seem more like a lost episode of *Masterpiece Theatre*. Other creative influences include steampunk, the fantasy films of Jim Henson, the comedy of *Monty Python* and Douglas Adams, the science fiction of Ursula K. Le Guin, and the post-modern cynicism and hip sensibilities of *Buffy the Vampire Slayer*. Because the series was on the air for so many decades, there are those who love different eras of the show. Oftentimes viewers will like the Doctor they grew up with best. Some will choose their favorite episodes based on whether their tone is more Gothic horror or campy farce. Others choose their favorite Doctor based on whether he is a belligerent killer of aliens or a pacifistic, multicultural figure.

27. See "Tom Baker Interview." *Doctor Who Magazine* #92. 1984. TomBaker.com. August 12, 2010. <http://www.tom-baker.co.uk/pages/content/index.asp?PageID=185>

28. *Ibid.*

29. For other scholar's views on *Doctor Who*, consult *The Greatest Show in the Galaxy: The Discerning Fan's Guide to Doctor Who* by Marc Schuster and Tom Powers.

30. In 1968's "Enemy of the World," Whitaker portrays the Doctor as one who will use violence only as a last resort. When a group of rebels tries to recruit the Doctor in their terrorist campaign against the Fascist ruler Salamander, the Doctor needs proof positive that Salamander is evil before he will consider joining their cause. This characterization of the Doctor stands in stark contrast with the Doctor of the Big Finish audio play "Project: Twilight" (first released on compact disc in 2001), who rushes into a conflict only to find out after-the-fact that he's joined the wrong side and is working for vampires.

31. For more information on Robert Holmes, see the special features included with the DVD *Doctor Who: The Two Doctors*.

32. The Leela character was married off to a kindly Captain of the Chancellory Guards on the Doctor's home planet of Gallifrey. Leela departed the series far from domesticated, with her warrior's spirit intact. Indeed, she is far more likely to change Gallifrey, and her husband, than Gallifrey and her husband is likely to change her.

33. It is an idea ahead of its time, predicting the controversial thesis of George Clooney's *Syriana* (2005), which, upon its release, was roundly condemned by Republican critics as being anti-American. But "Caves of Androzani" was more subtle than *Syriana*. Rather than state this highly charged theory overtly, Holmes sets "Caves" on Androzani Major, an alien planet which represents the rich West, and Androzani Minor, a pseudo-Middle Eastern wasteland. In the adventure, the Doctor finds himself trapped on Androzani Minor, caught in the middle of a guerilla war between an army of robots led by fanatic and duped colonial marines who don't know they're fighting for rich traitors back home instead of for the high ideals they thought they were upholding. Furthermore, in "Caves of Androzani," the symbolic stand-in for oil is Spectrox, a gooey substance that is poisonous in its natural state but an elixir of youth when refined. It is referred to as "the most valuable substance in the universe" and, like the spice in Frank Herbert's *Dune*, is an

obvious allegorizing of the central importance of oil in our own reality.

34. Of course, Davies has always mixed entertainment with activism, most notably in his miniseries *The Second Coming* (2003), a political fantasy in which he posited what would happen if a new Messiah would be born into modern-day England. By the end of the story, the Messiah's girlfriend convinces him that God, and all organized religion, holds humanity back by fostering a global culture of ignorance and violence. In response, the savior obliges her, and humanity, by killing himself. Davies is also famous for writing the series *Bob and Rose*, about a gay man who falls in love with a woman. In the series, the couple encounters prejudice from members of both the gay and the straight communities. As Davies explained in a 2001 article he wrote for *The Observer*, he intended to surround Bob and Rose with an array of "cardboard" villains but fleshed out the characterizations of their enemies by revealing that everyone has something to hide, and everyone has some "coming out" to do ("A Rose by any other name").

35. Even though Davies specializes in over-the-top, snarky political commentary in his stories, some of his best work on the series is subtler and more somber in tone. Indeed, Davies' crowning artistic achievement on the series may well be "Midnight," an episode which condemns racism, stupidity, and paranoia more effectively than any other Davies episode because the allegory is smarter, the plot tighter, and the writing less self-conscious. When a tourist shuttle falls under attack by an invisible alien menace, a group of otherwise "normal" and "everyday" civilians experiences a fit of paranoia and are almost driven to murdering the innocent Doctor because he is "different."

36. Indeed, on the whole, *Doctor Who* has never had many interesting American characters. Morton Dill, the silly cowboy from "The Chase," is an appalling minor player who is one of the few "Americans" in the series; but it can at least boast 1980s–era Peri Brown, a popular traveling companion of the Doctor — sweet, smart, and strikingly gorgeous in the great episodes "Caves of Androzani" and "The Two Doctors." Nicola Bryant, the British actress playing Peri, occasionally pronounces a key word here and there the British way and once deviated from a Midwestern American accent to a Brooklyn accent, but she is, overall, a solid, charismatic actress creating an American character to be proud of. Other nice Americans appeared in the *Doctor Who* episodes "The Claws of Axos" and the made-for-television movie starring Paul McGann. In a sense, *Doctor Who* portrays dangerously amoral American cowboys as negatively as American science fiction show *Battlestar Galactica* portrays dangerously amoral British intellectuals. Gaius Baltar is a poorly realized character because the American script writers caricature British figures in much the same way that Davies' team of writers caricatures Americans, making turnabout fair play. Baltar also demonstrates why *Doctor Who* has never achieved mainstream popularity in the United States: Americans traditionally tend to think of smart people as evil and have often been reluctant to watch a series with an intellectual protagonist, *House M.D.* being one exception.

37. Obama did appear in Davies' final episode, "The End of Time" (2009), which was broadcast as Moffat was filming the first season of Smith episodes. In Davies' swan song, the Master hijacks an internationally broadcast television transmission through which President Obama was slated to announce the end of the global recession. The Master uses the broadcast to possess the entire population of the world, and remake the global populace in his image. The story was odd, and certainly a jab at Obama's global popularity, but it seemed also to be Davies once again criticizing how much time everyone on Earth spends sitting in front of the television.

38. I would be remiss if I did not note that this fact, established in the American *Doctor Who* television film, has been widely disputed by fans, and undermined by televised adventures written by Davies. The idea that the Doctor might well be part human is born from his tendency to dress in distinctly British clothing, his boyhood love of trains ("Black Orchid"), and the provocative fact that the Doctor teleports himself to Earth when he wishes himself "home" in "Survival" (this last event was explored more fully in an earlier draft of "Survival"'s script, but the key dialogue was struck when the producer's realized "Survival" might well be the final episode). In the Paul McGann film, the Doctor describes himself as "half human, on my mother's side," and is revealed to have human eyeballs. In the adventure, the Doctor visits an Earth research center with a name that is an anagram of TARDIS, and reveals that his TARDIS is designed to respond to human commands. These clues suggest that the Doctor's Gallifreyan father and human mother (presumably an employee of that laboratory) co-created time travel technology. The clues, left unexplained, seem gratuitous, but were inserted because producer Philip Segal hoped that the one-off film would lead into a series that would see the Doctor on a quest through space and time to find his long lost parents. Some published reports indicate that the series would have revealed that the Doctor's father was Homer's Odysseus, and that Odysseus was a Time Lord. This storyline could have been excellent, or awfully cheesy, but it would have likely eliminated all mystery from the Doctor's past. It also remains a lost chapter in *Doctor Who* history, since the McGann series never became a reality.

All this aside, the Big Finish audios, IDW comic books, *Doctor Who* magazine comic strips, and BBC novels featuring the Paul McGann Doctor have collectively repudiated the idea that the Doctor's mother was human, and suggested that the Doctor had used a device called a Chameleon Arch to trick the Master into thinking he was half-human as a bizarre (and, frankly, completely ineffective) ploy to gain time to recover from a regeneration. Episodes of the revival series have also suggested that Gallifreyans are unable to mate with any other species, which is why the Doctor never tries to father a child with his human companions, even when he finds himself the "Last of the Time Lords" and rapidly running out of regenerations. Also, the Doctor's mother (Claire Bloom) makes an appearance as a disgraced Gallifreyan in "The End of Time." Since she is living on Gallifrey and is allowed to vote on important issues, the implication is that she is a pure-blooded Gallifreyan. After all, the xenophobic society has a rule against humans (or aliens of any kind) residing on Gallifrey. However, the Doctor repealed that law when he was Lord President of Gallifrey, so it is still possible that his mother is a human who has been granted honorary Time Lord status. But, given the reputation of the McGann film in fan circles, that theory is not likely to find many adherents, since it is designed only to reconcile it with the series continuity established later by Davies.

Some of the resistance to the idea that the Doctor is half-human is also based on the idea that it is too American and too "Star Treky." Dual heritage is a dreadfully overused (and often dramatically irrelevant) character-development concept meant to imply divided cultural loyalties (and personalities) in various Star Trek storylines: Spock is half-human and half–Vulcan, Deanna Troi is half-human and half–Betazoid, B'Elanna Torres is half-human and half–Klingon, and Saavik is half–Vulcan and half–Romulan. After all this, a half-human Doctor seems like something of a joke.

However, I am not annoyed by the "revelation" at all, and do not disregard it, despite the fact that it came somewhat out of left field. The paltry evidence provided concerning the Doctor's past elsewhere, and the lost potential of a possibly intriguing McGann storyline, makes me less inclined to disregard a vexing piece of the puzzle, and more eager to make it fit with the little that is known of the hero's biography. In a similar fashion, I disregard any attempt to suggest that Susan is not the Doctor's granddaughter, especially since Verity Lambert and others clearly intended her to be just that.

39. See Anita Singh, "Television is only made for children, moans Stephen Fry."

40. See Stephen Fry. "Stephen Fry's Bafta speech."

41. *Ibid.*

42. See Anita Singh, "Television is only made for children, moans Stephen Fry."

43. *Ibid.*

44. See "David Cameron launches Tories' 'big society' plan."

Chapter Seven

1. "24: 8:00 A.M.–9:00 A.M." *24*. Season One, Episode 9. 2002.

2. See *The Fantastic Four: Rise of the Silver Surfer*.

3. Bob Woodward, *Bush at War*, New York: Simon and Shuster, 2002, p. 145–146.

4. In one dramatic moment, Jack threatens to murder an innocent woman, Jane Saunders, by exposing her to the deadly Cordilla virus, gambling that the threat would compel her terrorist father, Stephen Saunders, into helping CTU officers halt the spread of the virus. The gambit pays off, but there are other occasions when Jack feels compelled to follow through with his threats when his bluff is called.

As blogger John Kubicek has observed, "There's nothing Jack wouldn't do to defend the homeland. He'd torture a terrorist. He'd torture an innocent bystander. He'd torture a member of his own family. If there's a rule, Jack would break it. Here's a short list of just how far outside the Geneva Convention he's willing to stray.... Kidnapping the President [of the United States], hacksawing the head off a witness, torturing Paul Raines [a suspected terrorist who was proven innocent], torturing someone as a private citizen, threatening a Dept of Justice attorney."

5. Beaver invited representatives of the Defense Intelligence Agency, Central Intelligence Agency, and members of the military with training in SERE (Survival, Evasion, Resistance and Escape) to offer ideas for harsher interrogation techniques that technically did not constitute torture by the standards of international law.

6. See Sands 61–62.

7. From a review of Sands book published on its back cover and on its Amazon.com sales page.

8. The document demanded that prisoners be spared torture, physical punishment, and humiliation, and dictated the provision of food, shelter, and medicine. Harris' disgust that the U.S. has striven to undermine a document that was drawn up to protect POWs from the kinds of treatment they received at the hands of the Nazis is representative of international and domestic opposition to America's torture policy. See also Sands and McCoy.

9. See "Detainees' Rights." *Facts on File: Issues & Controversies*.

10. See Michael Scherer. "Has McCain Flip-Flopped on Torture?"

According to Scherer, McCain has advocated that the American military and security forces adhere to interrogation guidelines laid out in the Army Field Manual, a document whose guidelines do not contravene the Geneva Convention. He also opposed attempts by torture advocates to suggest that harsh methods of interrogation that were employed for brief moments might be acceptable.

11. *Ibid.* Scherer's article has also revealed that, after several of his initiatives to outlaw waterboarding and other extreme interrogation techniques were defeated and circumvented by the Bush White House, McCain showed some signs of fatigue in his anti-torture crusade. Furthermore, as it became clearer that he would win the Republican Party nomination for the 2008 Presidential Election, he further softened his opposition to torture, and even opposed some initiatives by the Democrats to outright ban the CIA's use of torture. Some speculated that this was a play to garner votes rather than a reflection of his true convictions.

12. See Peter Lattman "Justice Scalia Hearts Jack Bauer." *Wall Street Journal Law Blog*.

A year later, Scalia elaborated further on his position during a BBC interview: "Seems to me you have to say, as unlikely as that is, it would be absurd to say that you can't stick something under the fingernails, smack them in the face. It would be absurd to say that you couldn't do that. And once you acknowledge that, we're into a different game.... How close does the threat have to be, and how severe can an infliction of pain be?" (See Jan Crawford Greenburg, "Does Terror Trump Torture?")

13. See Jeffrey Jones. "Slim Majority Wants Bush-Era Interrogations Investigated."

14. Martin Miller, "24 and Lost get symposium on torture."

15. *Ibid.*

16. See David Rose. "Tortured Reasoning."

17. *Ibid.*

18. *Ibid.*

19. See Andrew Sullivan, "One tortured lie" and Scott Horton. "Information Secured Through Torture Proved Unreliable, CIA Concluded."

20. See Frank Rich. "The Banality of Bush White House Evil."

21. Scott Horton. "Information Secured Through Torture Proved Unreliable, CIA Concluded."

22. See John Storey.

23. Malone's famous speech from *The Untouchables* (1987) is as follows:

> If you open the can on these worms you must be prepared to go all the way because they're not gonna give up the fight until one of you is dead.... You wanna know how you do it? Here's how, they pull a knife, you pull a gun. He sends one of yours to the hospital, you send one of his to the morgue. That's the Chicago way, and that's how you get Capone! Now do you want to do that? Are you ready to do that?

24. *Ibid.*

25. It is also possible that Quentin Tarantino's films paved the way for the cult success of torture porn, as his *Reservoir Dogs* (1992) famously included a scene in which

villainous Vic Vega (Michael Madsen) sliced the ear off of a police officer while dancing to the Stealers Wheel song "Stuck in the Middle." His subsequent films all showcase torture scenes of varying degrees of intensity, with some of the most excruciating examples being featured in the *Kill Bill* films.

26. See Susan Donaldson James. "In College Study Abroad the Risk Increases the Reward."

27. This is true especially when one considers that porn star Jenna Jameson was gang raped as a teenager, Linda Lovelace was reportedly coerced into filming *Deep Throat*, and the women who film live sex for the Bang Bus appear horrified and confused when the sex act turns violent and abusive.

28. Sadly, the film adaptation featuring Angelina Jolie and Morgan Freeman retains no trace of the angry satire or ironic humor and plays like a recruitment video for Eric Harris' and Dylan Klebold's Trenchcoat Mafia.

29. See *Gonzo: The Life and Work of Dr. Hunter S. Thompson* (2008).

30. With Sue playing a role that the blind sculptor Alicia Masters had played in the original tale. For affordable, recent reprints, see Stan Lee and Jack Kirby, "The Fantastic Four Nos. 41–50 & Annual No. 3" *Marvel Masterworks: The Fantastic Four* Vol. 5, and "The Fantastic Four Nos. 51–60 & Annual No. 4" *Marvel Masterworks: The Fantastic Four* Vol. 6.

31. From John Byrne's introduction to *Fantastic Four: The Trial of Galactus.*

32. While some might argue that these themes are too buried in subtext to be the true way of interpreting the film, Stan Lee makes these very same issues central to "World's End: The Last Fantastic Four Story" (2007), in which the Four convince a cosmic tribunal to spare the Earth by demonstrating limitless compassion, even to their deadliest enemies.

33. See Condoleezza Rice, "A Balance of Power That Favors Freedom."

34. See Richard Stenger. "Man on the moon: Kennedy speech ignited the dream

35. See John Byrne, "Hero."

The inescapable problem is that a mature Johnny Storm would no longer have any need to live with his older sister's family but can go off on his own. Consequently, there have been several stories in which he appears to find maturity (such as "Hero"), and true love (as with Chrystal of the Inhumans), only to find himself left alone and humiliated when his lover leaves him or turns out to be an alien Skrull in disguise. In Joe Ahearne's "A Little Stranger" (2010), the womanizing Johnny seriously considers becoming a responsible husband and father after he impregnates a woman he meets at a bar. Worried that the child will not have a normal life as a superpowered baby, the woman employs the Four's time travel technology as a means of going back in time to prevent the baby's conception, though it is unclear if she ultimately goes through with the "retroactive abortion."

36. See Grant Morrison's "1234" *Marvel Knights: Fantastic Four* (2001–2002). This scene is the basis for a similar segment in the 2005 *Fantastic Four* film. In "1234," Doom briefly convinces Ben to turn on Reed with an eloquent speech in which he argues that Reed has made monsters of both of them:

> Like Prospero, [Reed] finds true beauty only in his own rigorous attempts to comprehend and master the universe. With John Storm as his impetuous and fiery Ariel. And you his monstrous Caliban....
>
> My people love me. I love and protect them in return, as legitimate head of a sovereign European state. And yet he has made an international devil of me.

Like most lies told by devils, there is an element of truth in what Doom says about Reed, especially in the way in which the self-styled Mr. Fantastic often neglects his family duties in favor of his scientific research.

37. The personalities of superheroes often dovetail with their powers. Kindly superheroes tend to have defensive powers and cruel superheroes boast offensive powers. For example, Spider-Man and Wonder Woman have defensive powers, dodging and deflecting their opponent's attacks while using harmless snares to tie up their opponents. The aggressive Wolverine, in contrast, carves up his enemies with his indestructible claws and does not bother dodging attacks because his "healing factor" makes him invulnerable to weaponry, as well as most recognizable human emotions.

38. Other heroines created by Stan Lee and Jack Kirby in the 1960s were similarly unimpressive on the battlefield. The "winsome" Wasp's sting was, more often than not, totally ineffective against opponents such as Ultron, Kang, and the Grim Reaper. (However, in Mark Millar's *The Ultimates*, she did shrink small enough to fly into the inner ear of the rampaging Hulk, sting him, and force him to transform back into Bruce Banner. She used a similar technique to some effect against Godzilla in *Godzilla: King of the Monsters* #23, 1979, during the brief period Marvel Comics Group had the license to publish comic books featuring the radioactive dinosaur.)

Created by John Byrne and Chris Claremont in 1980, nearly two decades after Sue and the Wasp, the teenage member of the X-Men, Kitty Pryde, was another gentle soul with equally passive powers. Her ability to walk through walls made her, like Sue, a spy and a jailbreaker first and foremost. While comic book fans warmed to Kitty right away, and developed significant crushes on her, many young male comic book readers were impatient with characters such as Sue and the Wasp because they were not more formidable on the battlefield. Indeed, most gamers familiar with the HeroClix Superhero Miniatures war game know that it is not often good strategy to choose Wasp, the Invisible Woman, or Kitty Pryde for a team since they are likely to be slaughtered by the soldiers on the opposing team, especially if they have more formidable abilities. But there is more to a superhero, and a superpower, than its application in a combat scenario.

39. The scene is a bit quaint, but fascinating reading for anyone interested in representations of gender.

40. The Wasp, for all of her heiress affectations, could be highly intuitive and empathic. For example, in *Secret Wars*, she found a wounded supervillain, the Lizard, nursed him back to health, and befriended him, showing that his human side, Dr. Connors, was still buried within.

41. For classic examples of combat-centric storylines, Jim Shooter's *Secret Wars*, John Byrne's *Fantastic Four: The Trial of Galactus* and the Jeff Youngquist edited anthology *Wizard Masterpiece Edition Spider-Man: The Ten Greatest Spider-Man Stories Ever.*

42. This is why it is no surprise that any team of writers and artists that grants too much primacy to either Reed's worldview or Sue's throws both the family and narrative dynamic out of balance. Any Fantastic Four in which Reed is merely a wimpy nerd or a "space cadet" does not ring true, and any iteration of the Fantastic Four in which Sue is merely a whiner, harpy, or happy homemaker falls apart completely. And that has been the case with the title for fourteen years — either one or the other

character has been dreadfully cartooned or mischaracterized, to the detriment of the whole series.

After Lee and Kirby left the comic book, their successors were reasonably accomplished at characterizing the leads, if showing less innovation in storylines and villains, and the comic book remained an excellent read under John Byrne, Roy Thomas, Steve Englehart, and Marv Wolfman. However, the comic book took a turn for the worse after *Fantastic Four* #296 (Nov. 1986) and was essentially unreadable for the next fourteen years, which is why, as an act of desperation to boost sales, the original Fantastic Four was briefly replaced by Spider-Man, Wolverine, Ghost Rider, and the Hulk in Walter Simonson's tongue-in-cheek "New Fantastic Four" story (*Fantastic Four* #347–349, 1990–1991). Except for three issues by Scott Lobdell and Alan Davis, the comic book remained largely awful until Carlos Pacheco took over as storyteller in 2000 (See *Fantastic Four* vol. 3 #35–41, 44, 47–49). His arrival signaled a new golden age for the comic book, and the writers who have followed, Mark Waid, Mark Millar, Jonathan Hickman, J. Michael Straczynski, Grant Morrison, and Roberto Aguirre-Sacasa, have once again allowed the monthly title to earn its former boastful marketing tagline "the world's greatest comic magazine!"

43. Also, while Reed has no interest in fiction whatsoever, Sue is an ardent devotee of British literature, particularly the works of Jane Austen. Since she herself has been torn romantically between Namor, the perfectly sculpted, Byronic ruler of Atlantis, and the cerebral moralist Reed, she can relate to any Austen heroine who is compelled to choose "between dashing, moody villains and rather uptight heroes who have trouble talking about their feelings" (see Paul Cornell's "True Story" 2009). In Roberto Aguirre-Sacasa's series *Marvel Knights 4*, Sue took on a job as an English teacher at the Pembrooke Academy in New York's West Side when the family fell upon hard economic times.

44. See Mark Millar's "World's Greatest."

45. See Mark Waid, "Authoritative Action." This book has no page numbers, so all future references cannot be to specific pages, but to the story, generally.

46. *Ibid.*

47. *Ibid.*

48. *Ibid.*

49. *Ibid.*

50. *Ibid.*

51. *Ibid.*

52. *Ibid.*

53. *Ibid.*

54. *Ibid.*

55. See J. Michael Straczynski's "Civil War: Fantastic Four."

56. *Ibid.*

57. *Ibid.*

58. See Dwayne McDuffie's "Civil War."

59. Reprinted in Mark Millar's "World's Greatest." The book has no page numbers, so all future references to events in this story, and quoted dialogue, are from this source.

60. *Ibid.*

61. *Ibid.*

62. *Ibid.*

63. *Ibid.*

64. *Ibid.*

65. *Ibid.*

Chapter Eight

1. Page 67.

2. See page 4.

3. Applebaum, Stephen. "X-Men 2 Interview: Bryan Singer." *BBC.* October 2003. September 10, 2010. <http://www.bbc.co.uk/films/2003/04/25/bryan_singer_x_men_2_interview.shtml>

4. See J.M. DeMatteis. "Walking Into Yesterday." Illus. Mark Buckingham. *Doctor Strange: Sorcerer Supreme* Vol. 1, No. 86. New York: Marvel Comics, 1996.

5. See J. Michael Straczynski, "The Amazing Spider-Man." Illus. John Romita, Jr. *The Amazing Spider-Man: Ultimate Collection 2.* New York: Marvel Comics, 2009.

6. See Chris Suellentrop, "Sex and the Single Superhero." *Slate.* June 4, 2002. September 8, 2010. <http://www.slate.com/id/2066513/

7. See June Thomson, *Holmes and Watson.* New York: Carroll & Graf Publishers, 1995.

8. See William S. Baring-Gould. *Sherlock Holmes of Baker Street: A Life of The World's First Consulting Detective.* New York: Bramhall House, 1962.

9. See Rex Stout. "Watson Was a Woman." *The Saturday Review of Literature,* Vol. 23 No. 19, March, 1941. See also Marilyn MacGregor. "Dr. Watson's Mistress: A Story for Which the World is Not Yet Prepared." *Ladies, Ladies: The Women in the Life of Sherlock Holmes.* Ed: Patricia Guy and Katherine Karlson. Aventine Press, 2007. 96–100.

10. See Laurie R. King, *The Beekeeper's Apprentice* (1994), *A Monstrous Regiment of Women* (1995), *The Language of Bees* (2009), and *The God of the Hive* (2010).

11. Notable works of scholarship that explore the representations of gay, lesbian, bisexual, transgender, queer, and intersex persons in the mass media include Vito Russo's *The Celluloid Closet: Homosexuality in the Movies* (1987, revised ed.), Harry M. Benshoff's *Queer Images: A History of Gay and Lesbian Film in America* (2005), and the edited anthologies *A Queer Romance: Lesbians, Gay Men and Popular Culture* (Ed: Paul Burston and Colin Richardson, 1995), *New Queer Cinema: A Critical Reader* (Ed: Michele Aaron, 2004), *Queer Popular Culture: Literature, Media, Film, and Television* (Ed: Thomas Peele, 2007), and *Oscar Wilde and Modern Culture: The Making of a Legend* (Ed: Joseph Bristow, 2009). There have also been a number of excellent documentaries produced recently that broadly comment upon the GLBTQI experience, as well as their portrayal in the media, but two of the most innovative and iconoclastic are *The Films of Su Friedrich: Vol. 4—Hide and Seek* (2007) and *Rock Hudson's Home Movies* (2003), directed by Mark Rappaport.

12. Vampires frequently hope for redemption, or a cure for their condition, but are rarely granted any form of peace beyond being decapitated or pierced through the heart by a wooden stake. Barnabas Collins, the reluctant vampire of television's *Dark Shadows* (ABC, 1966–1971), was granted several "remissions" from his curse, but he had better luck than *Dracula's Daughter* (1936) Countess Zeleska, who begged God, psychiatry, and science for redemption but ended up being killed with a bow and arrow. The possibility of a vampire redeeming himself through prayer is raised in *Kiss of the Vampire,* but it is not depicted. Vampires in more recent films are often not evil and in need of redemption, but are members of a misunderstood, persecuted minority.

13. See Bruce C. Steele. "The Knight's Crusade." *The Advocate.* December 11, 2001. pp. 36–38, 40–45

14. See Barry Kavanagh, "The Alan Moore Interview: Brought to Light—deep politics/AARGH." *Blather.net.*

October 17, 2000. September 10, 2010. <http://www.blather.net/articles/amoore/brought-to-light2.html>

15. As Wilde himself demonstrated time and again in his plays, moralists and overly earnest society figures often find humor difficult to fathom, view it as a sign of moral bankruptcy, or condemn it as a lack of sympathy with the sufferings of the world. Many social and aesthetic critics of the Victorian and Edwardian eras demonstrated an inability to recognize the moral and progressive in the work of Wilde and his fellow "decadents," both before and after Wilde was brought to trial and sentenced to two years in prison for "gross indecency" in 1895. As early Wilde critic Holbrook Jackson observed in his literary and cultural history The Eighteen Nineties (1914), Wilde's "intellectual playfulness destroyed popular faith in his sincerity, and the British people have still to learn that one can be as serious in one's play with ideas as in one's play with a football" (77).

A critic closer to our own age, Ruth Robbins, has interpreted Wilde's writing as still more subversive and revolutionary. In 2003's *Pater to Forster*, Ruth Robbins discussed the notion of Wilde as a figure of "double vision," who tended to choose "both/and" when faced with an "either/or" decision in his career, was at heart a bisexual man, and was — as a writer of the fin de siècle — one who kept one eye on the ebbing Victorian value system and another on the emerging modernist aesthetic. As she explains, "Wilde stands neatly as a transitional figure precisely because he also looked backwards towards the conventions of the past, which he had internalized to an amazing degree, and forwards, away from them; because he had internalized them he could see their limitations" (126). For Robbins, conservative Victorians did not regard Wilde's duality as a sign of wisdom or complexity, but as a sign of mental illness, sexual deviance, and a character divided against itself akin to the protagonist in Robert Louis Stevenson's then-contemporary story of Dr. Jekyll and Mr. Hyde. "It is a grim irony that a playwright who tried to make a virtue out of having it both ways has also come to stand for continuing double visions. Double vision can be subversive, playful, a game: it can also represent two-faced hypocrisy. I think we know which Wilde 'intended': but his message was not always received" (127).

16. See Harry Knowles. "So Bryan Singer just called regarding Matthew Vaughn's X-MEN: FIRST CLASS.... I'm quite excited now." AintItCool.news. August 20, 2010. September 10, 2010. <http://www.aintitcool.com/node/46217>

17. *Ibid.*

18. "Plot Details Revealed for X Men First Class." The Film Stage. June 21, 2010. September 10, 2010. <http://thefilmstage.com/>

19. See Mike Fleming, "'X-Men: First Class' Drafts Twilight Vampire Edi Gathegi To Play Biracial Mutant Darwin." Deadline New York. July 27, 2010. September 10, 2010. <http://www.deadline.com/2010/07/x-men-first-class-drafts-twilight-vampire-edi-gathegi-to-play-biracial-mutant-darwin/?utm_source=twitterfeed&utm_medium=twitter>

20. Other scholars and works that chronicle the history of African Americans in popular culture include *From Sambo to Superspade: The Black Experience in Motion Pictures* (1976, 2nd ed.) by Daniel J. Leab, *Blacks and White TV* (1992, 2nd ed.) by J. Fred Mac Donald, *Say it Loud!: African American Audiences, Media and Identity* (2002) edited by Robin Means Coleman, and *Brown Sugar: Over 100 Years of America's Black Female Superstars* (2007, 2nd edition) and *Toms, Coons, Mulattoes, Mammies, and Bucks: An Interpretive History of Blacks in American Films* (2001, 4th ed.), by Donald Bogle.

21. From an interview conducted over e-mail on September 10, 2010.

22. One indicator of the political sensibilities of a production team on *Doctor Who* is the way it portrays "aliens." Barry Letts, who served as series producer for Jon Pertwee's Doctor (1970–1974) and as scriptwriter Robert Sloman's uncredited collaborator on four serials, was a Buddhist who often ensured that alien characters were presented sympathetically. These characters included the Tharils, Draconians, Mutts, Ambassadors, Bellal, Alpha Centauri, and the reformed villains the Ice Warriors. Patrick Troughton's Doctor (1966–1969), under producers Innes Lloyd and Peter Bryant, was much more likely to encounter hideous, monstrously evil aliens, earmarking his era as more conservative in sensibility than Letts'. Generally speaking, the series usually addressed issues of race and multiculturalism through the introduction of green aliens, who symbolically represented any number of racially "othered" peoples.

23. From an interview conducted over e-mail on September 10, 2010.

Chapter Nine

1. These characters are called Crush Limbo, Bill O'Smiley, and Glen Speck to underline the point that this is just a satire, and that the real men who inspired these satirical figures might not actually do something like this in our world.

2. See Ursula K. Le Guin, "Introduction." The Left Hand of Darkness. New York: Ace Books, 2003.

3. See interviews included as special features on the DVD *Hellboy: Sword of Storms.*

4. *Ibid.*

5. See Liebowitz.

6. See Geoff Johns, "Blackest Night 0–8." Illus. Ivan Reiss. *Blackest Night.* New York: DC Comics, 2010.

7. See Erik Larsen, "Force of One." *Savage Dragon* #145. Berkeley: Image Comics, 2009.

8. See Nisha Gopalan. "Mark Millar on Sarah Palin: 'Terrifying.'" io9.com. September 23, 2008. September 4, 2010. <http://io9.com/5053777/mark-millar-on-sarah-palin-terrifying>

9. From an interview conducted via e-mail on 12/31/2008

10. Brady, Matt. "How is Obama Appearing in Comic Books?" *Newsarama.com.* January 28, 2009. September 1, 2010. <http://www.newsarama.com/comics/010928-Obama-Comics.html>

11. See Paul Krugman, "Bailouts for Bunglers."

12. See Brady Dennis and David Cho. "Rage at AIG Swells As Bonuses Go Out."

13. See Paul Craig Roberts. "Warmonger Wins Peace Prize." *CounterPunch.* October 9–11, 2009. June 20, 2010. <http://www.counterpunch.org/roberts10092009.html>

14. See Michael Moore. "Get Off Obama's Back ... second thoughts from Michael Moore." MichaelMoore.com. October 10th, 2009. July 12, 2010. <http://www.michaelmoore.com/words/mikes-letter/get-obamas-back-second-thoughts-michael-moore>

15. Tancer writes:

> On January 27, 2007, less than a month before his announcement to run for president, a news report appeared on Fox News saying that Barack Obama had attended an Islamic madrass in his early childhood,

from 1967 to 1971. The Fox New story was discredited in a CNN segment that aired four days later, on January 23. The CNN reporter visiting the Basuki School, which Barack had attended in Indonesia, found no evidence that the school was teaching radical Islamic principles. Basuki was a public school that did not focus on religion....

One of the most remarkable aspects of the Barack Obama madrass misinformation incident is the half-life of associations created by a story that had only four days before it was discounted. If we look at search behavior one year later, three of the top ten search terms that contain "Barack Obama" reference his religion or the Muslim religion, and if we look at the searches that contain "Muslim," six of the top ten terms contain a mention of Barack Obama [34–36].

16. See Katla McGlynn,. "Stewart: FOX Failed to Mention Co-Owner Is One They Accuse of 'Terror Funding.'" Huffington Post. August 24, 2010. September 6, 2010. <http://www.huffingtonpost.com/2010/08/23/stewart-fox-prince-alwaleed_n_692234.html>

17. Holly Ord, "Sarah Palin is not a feminist." *Menstrual Poetry.com.* August 30, 2008. September 7, 2010. <http://menstrualpoetry.com/sarah-palin-feminist>

18. See Frank Rich, "How Fox Betrayed Petraeus." *The New York Times*. August 21, 2010. September 6, 2010. <http://www.nytimes.com/2010/08/22/opinion/22rich.html>

19. See Roger Ebert, "Put Up Or Shut Up." *Roger Ebert's Journal.* September 1, 2010. September 6, 2010. <http://blogs.suntimes.com/ebert/2010/09/put_up_or_shut_up.html>

20. See Eric Lichtblau and Brian Stelter. *The New York Times*. "News Corp. Gives Republicans $1 Million." August 17, 2010. September 6, 2010. <http://www.nytimes.com/2010/08/18/us/politics/18donate.html>

21. See Brian Montopoli. "Target Boycott Movement Grows Following Donation to Support 'Antigay' Candidate." CBSNews.com. July 28, 2010. September 6, 2010. <http://www.cbsnews.com/8301-503544_162-20011983-503544.html>

22. As Shaw scholar Dan H. Laurence observed in "'That Awful Country': Shaw in America:"

> The United States was, to Shaw the socialist, a great experiment gone wrong, a golden opportunity squandered. "America broke loose from us at the end of the eighteenth century," he remarked in 1910; "[e]ver since that it has been proving its utter unfitness to govern itself." America, he charged, had never been successful in politics: "It was made independent largely in spite of its own teeth by a declaration if sentiments which it did not share and principals which it barely grasped the narrow end of. Even today," he said in 1907, "neither its ordinary security nor its liberty is up to the monarchical standard of central Europe." Americans had long deluded themselves into believing that it was the people who governed. But how, Shaw inquired, can you call a thing a government "which every railway king or mammoth pigsticker can buy or bully and every lynching mob defy?" "You haven't realized yet," he told the Americans, "that it's your money kings that rule. You think it's a government of the people, by the people, and for the people. That's how you get your mob passion when anyone attacks the government. It's reflected in the courtroom and on the bench, as well as in the street" [280].

23. From an e-mail interview conducted on 8/10/10.

Bibliography

Aaron, Michele, editor. *New Queer Cinema: A Critical Reader.* New Jersey: Rutgers University Press, 2004.

Abnett, Dan and Andy Lanning. "The Punisher: Year One." Illus. Dale Eaglesham. *The Punisher.* New York: Marvel Comics, 1994.

Adams, Mike. "Movie Review: *Idiocracy* starring Luke Wilson, directed by Mike Judge. February 05, 2007. August 27, 2010. <http://www.naturalnews.com/021558_Idiocracy_Hollywood.html>

The Adventures of Sherlock Holmes. Dir. Alan Grint *et al.* Writ. John Hawkesworth, Jeremy Paul, et al. Perf. Jeremy Brett, David Burke, and Edward Hardwick. 1984–1994. *Jeremy Brett as Sherlock Holmes: The Complete Granada Television Series.* DVD. MPI Home Entertainment, 2007.

The Adventures of Superboy. Dir. David Nutter. Writ. Migdia Chinea-Varela, Fred Freiberger, et al. Perf. Gerard Christopher, Stacy Haiduk, and Sherman Howard. Warner Bros. 1988–1992.

The Adventures of Superman. Dir. Thomas Carr et al. Writ. David T. Chantler, Jackson Gillis, et al. Perf. George Reeves, Jack Larson, Noel Neill, and Phyllis Coates. 1952–1958. DVD. *The Adventures of Superman* (Six Complete Season Volumes). Warner Home Video, 2006.

Aguirre-Sasca, Roberto. "Wolf at the Door." Illus: Steve McNiven. *Marvel Knights 4.* New York: Marvel Comics, 2004.

Ahearne, Joe. "A Little Stranger." Illus. Bryan Hitch. *Fantastic Four Annual No. 32.* New York: Marvel Comics, 2010.

_____. *Ultraviolet.* Perf. Jack Davenport, Susanna Harker, Idris Elba, and Philip Quast. 1998. DVD. Palm Pictures/Umvd, 2001.

All-New Super Friends Hour. Dir. Charles A. Nichols. Writ. Orville H. Hampton, Elana Lesser, et al. Perf. Danny Dark, Shannon Farnon, Casey Kasem. 1977–1978. DVD. Warner Home Video, 2008.

'Allo 'Allo! The Complete Collection. Writ. Jeremy Lloyd and David Croft. Perf. Gorden Kaye and Vicki Michelle. DVD. BBC Home Video, 2008.

American Psycho. Dir. Mary Harron. Writ. Mary Harron and Guinevere Turner. Perf. Christian Bale, Willem Dafoe, and Reese Witherspoon. DVD. Lions Gate, 2000.

Anderson, Ken. "Hitler and Occult Sex." *Hitler and the Occult.* New York: Prometheus Books, 1995. 159–166.

Anderson, Martin. "The Den Of Geek interview: Mark Millar." *Den of Geek!* Jul 20, 2008. September 4, 2010. <http://www.denofgeek.com/comics/88459/the_den_of_geek_interview_mark_millar.html>

Applebaum, Stephen. "X-Men 2 Interview: Bryan Singer." *BBC.* October 2003. September 10, 2010. <http://www.bbc.co.uk/films/2003/04/25/bryan_singer_x_men_2_interview.shtml>

Arcudi, John. "Superpower." Illus. Scot Eaton. *JLA.* New York: DC Comics, 1999.

Arehart, Jim and the Wizard Staff. "The Secret History of Marvel Comics." *Wizard: The Comics Magazine.* Number 162. April 2005. New York: Wizard Entertainment, 2005.

"Army of One: Punisher Origins." *The Punisher.* DVD special feature. Lions Gate, 2004.

Ashcroft, John. "USA Patriot Act 'Honors' Liberty and Freedom." *Peace, War, and Terrorism.* Ed: Dennis Okerstrom. New York: Pearson, 2006. 96–103.

The Avengers. Dir. Roy Ward Baker et al. Writ. Brian Clemens, Philip Levene, Dennis Spooner, et al. Perf. Patrick Macnee, and Diana Rigg. 1961–1969. DVD. *The Avengers—The Complete Emma Peel Megaset.* A&E Home Video, 2008.

AVP: Alien vs. Predator. Writ.-Dir. Paul W.S. Anderson. Perf. Sanaa Lathan, Raoul Bova, and Lance Henriksen. 2004. DVD. 20th Century–Fox, 2005.

"The Aztecs." *Doctor Who.* Dir. John Crockett. Writ. John Lucarotti. Perf. William Hartnell, Jacqueline Hill, William Russell. 1964. DVD. BBC Video, 2003.

"Balance of Terror." *Star Trek.* Dir. Vincent McEveety. Writ. Paul Schneider. Perf. William Shatner, Leonard Nimoy, and DeForest Kelly. 1966. DVD. *Star Trek: The Original Series—Season One.* Paramount, 2007.

"Barack Obama: My Pop Culture Favorites." *Entertainment Weekly.* August 6, 2008. July 8, 2010. <http://www.ew.com/ew/article/0,,20217406_2,00.html>

Bardsley, Alison. "Batman/Election Returns." *Bad Subjects* no. 3. Nov. 1992.

Baron, Mike. "Intruder." *The Punisher.* Illus. Bill Reinhold. New York: Marvel Comics, 1989.

_____. "The Iris Green Saga." Illus. Erik Larsen. *The Punisher* Vol. II #s 21–25. New York: Marvel Comics, 1989.

Baring-Gould, William S. *Sherlock Holmes of Baker Street: A Life of The World's First Consulting Detective.* New York: Bramhall House, 1962.

Barnes, Brooks and Michael Cieply. "A Custody Battle, Supersized. An Artist's Heirs Vs. Marvel." *The New York Times.* Business 2 and 8. March 21, 2010.

Barr, Mike W. "Batman: Son of the Demon." Illus. Jerry Bingham. *Batman.* New York: DC Comics, 1987.

_____. "Batman: Year Two." Illus. Alan Davis and Todd McFarlane. *Batman.* New York: DC Comics, 1990.

_____. "Catch as Catscan." Illus. Alan Davis. *Detective Comics* #569–570. New York: DC Comics, 1986.

_____. "What if Captain America Had Been Elected President?" Illus. Herb Trimpe. *What if—?* #26. New York: Marvel Comics, 1981.

Barry, Dave. *Dave Barry's Complete Guide to Guys*. New York: Random House, 1996.

Batman. Writ. Victor McLeod, Leslie Swabacker, and Harry Fraser. Dir. Lambert Hillyer. Perf. Lewis Wilson, Douglas Croft, J. Carrol Naish.1943. DVD. Columbia Pictures, 2005.

Batman. TV series. Dir. Robert Butler, et al., Unavailable on DVD. 1966–1968.

Batman. Dir. Tim Burton. Writ. Sam Hamm. Perf. Jack Nicholson and Michael Keaton. DVD. Warner Home Video, 1989.

Batman Begins. Writ.-Dir. Christopher Nolan. Perf. Christian Bale and Liam Neeson. DVD. Warner Home Video, 2005.

Batman Beyond. Prod: Alan Burnett, et al. Television Series. Warner Bros, 1999–2001.

Batman for President. Web master: BT Domenech. January 25, 2008. August 29, 2010. <http://www.batmanforpresident.com/2008/01/25/b4p-08-you-cant-stop-the-signal/>

Batman Returns. Dir. Tim Burton. Writ. Daniel Waters. Perf. Michael Keaton and Michelle Pfeiffer. DVD. Warner Bros., 1992.

Batman: Mystery of the Batwoman. Dir. Curt Geda and Tim Maltby. Writ. Michael Reaves. Perf. Kevin Conroy and Kyra Sedgwick. DVD. Warner Home Video, 2003.

Batman: The Complete Animated Series. Dir. Kevin Altieri *et al.* Writ. Paul Dini, et al. Perf. Kevin Conroy. 1992–1999. DVD. Warner Home Video, 2008.

Batman: The Laughing Fish. (See entries for *Batman: The Animated Series* and Steve Engleheart's *Batman: Strange Apparitions*.)

Batman: The Movie. Dir. Leslie H. Martinson. Writ. Lorenzo Semple, Jr. Perf. Adam West, Burt Ward, Lee Meriwether. DVD. Warner Home Video, 1966.

Batman versus Dracula. Dir. Michael Goguen. Writ. Duane Capizzi. Perf. Rino Romano and Peter Stormare. DVD. Warner Home Video, 2005.

Batman XXX: A Porn Parody. Dir. Axel Braun. Perf. Dale DaBone, James Deen, and Tori Black. DVD. Vivid Video, 2010.

Battlestar Galactica. Dir. Michael Rymer, *et al.* Writ. David Eick, Ronald D. Moore, *et al.* Perf. Edward James Olmos, Mary McDonnell. Television series. The Sci-Fi Channel, 2004–2009.

"Beauty, Brawn, and Bulletproof Bracelets: A Wonder Woman Retrospective." *Wonder Woman: The Complete First Season*. DVD special feature. Warner Home Video, 2004.

Beck, Bernard. "The Myth That Would Not Die: *The Sopranos*, Mafia Movies, and Italians in America." *Discovering Popular Culture*. Ed: Anna Tomasino. New York: Pearson, 2007. 122–130.

Beerbohm, Max. "A Defence of Cosmetics." *The Yellow Book: An Illustrated Quarterly*. Volume I. London: Elkin Mathews & John Lane. April 1894. 65–82.

_____. "A Letter to the Editor." *The Yellow Book: An Illustrated Quarterly*. Volume II. London: Elkin Mathews & John Lane. July 1894. 281–284.

Belle, Nicole. "Huckabee Endorses 'Egg As Person' Concept." *Democratic Underground.com*. February 26, 2008. September 7, 2010. <http://www.democraticunderground.com/discuss/duboard.php?az=view_all&address=389x2925150>

Bendis, Brian Michael. "House of M." Illus. Oliver Copiel. *House of M*. New York: Marvel Comics, 2008.

_____. "Learning Curve." Illus. Mark Bagley. *Ultimate Spider-Man,* Vol. 2. New York: Marvel Comics, 2001.

_____. "Secret Invasion." Illus. Leinil Francis Yu. *Secret Invasion*. New York: Marvel Comics, 2009.

_____. "Siege." Illus. Olivier Coipel. *Siege*. New York: Marvel Comics, 2010.

_____. "Ultimate Spider-Man and His Amazing Friends." Illus. Stuart Immonen. *Ultimate Spider-Man,* Vol. 20. New York: Marvel Comics, 2008.

_____. "Olympia." Illus. Michael Avon Oeming. *Powers: Little Deaths*. Reprinted from *Powers* #12–14. Orange, CA: Image Comics, 2001 and 2003.

Benshoff, Harry M. *Queer Images: A History of Gay and Lesbian Film in America*. Rowman & Littlefield Publishers. New York: 2005.

Bigger, Stronger, Faster. Documentary. Writ.-Dir. Christopher Bell. DVD. Magnolia Home Entertainment, 2008.

Billy Elliot. Dir. Stephen Daldry and Tom Sheerin. Writ. Lee Hall and Daniel Dowdall. Perf. Jamie Bell, Gary Lewis, and Julie Walters. BBC Films. 2000. DVD. Universal, 2001.

The Bionic Woman. Dir. Alan J. Levi, Alan Crosland, Jr., et al. Writ. Martin Caidin, Kenneth Johnson, et al. Perf. Lindsay Wagner and Richard Anderson. Television series. ABC and NBC, 1976–1978.

Birds of Prey. Dir. Chris Long et al. Writ. Laeta Kalogridis, Melissa Rosenberg, Nora Kay Foster, et al. Perf. Ashley Scott, Dina Meyer, and Rachel Skarsten. 2002. DVD. *Birds of Prey—The Complete Series*. Warner Home Video, 2008.

Black Dynamite. Dir. Scott Sanders. Writ. Michael Jai White, Byron Minns, and Scott Sanders. Perf. Michael Jai White and James McManus. 2009. DVD. Sony, 2010.

Blake, Mark. *Comfortably Numb—The Inside Story of Pink Floyd*. Pennsylvania: Da Capo Press, 2008. 294–295.

Blundell, Sue. "Women in Myth: Amazons." *Women in Ancient Greece*. Cambridge, MA: Harvard University Press, 1995. 58–62.

Bogle, Donald. *Brown Sugar: Over 100 Years of America's Black Female Superstars*. New York: Continuum, 2007.

_____. *Toms, Coons, Mulattoes, Mammies, and Bucks: An Interpretive History of Blacks in American Films*. New York: Continuum, 2001.

The Boondock Saints. Writ.-Dir. Troy Duffy. Perf. Sean Patrick Flanery, Norman Reedus, Billy Connolly. DVD. 20th Century–Fox Home Video, 2008.

"The Boondock Saints." *Wikipedia*. June 22, 2010. <http://en.wikipedia.org/wiki/The_Boondock_Saints>

Bowem Kit. "Stan Lee Sues Marvel." *Hollywood.com*. November 13, 2002. July 11, 2010. <http://www.hollywood.com/news/Stan_Lee_Sues_Marvel_/1696116>

Bowen, Mark. *Censoring Science: Dr. James Hansen and the Truth of Global Warming*. New York: Plume, 2008.

Brassed Off! Writ.-Dir. Mark Herman. Perf. Pete Postlethwaite, Tara Fitzgerald, Ewan McGregor. 1996. DVD. Miramax, 1999.

Brady, Matt. "How Is Obama Appearing in Comic Books?" *Newsarama.com*. January 28, 2009. September 1, 2010. <http://www.newsarama.com/comics/010928-Obama-Comics.html>

_____. "Supermen of Color: The Non-White Kryptonians." *Newsarama.com*. January 6, 2009. September 3, 2010. <http://www.newsarama.com/comics/010906-Supermen-Color.html>

Braudy, Leo. *From Chivalry to Terrorism: War and the Changing Nature of Masculinity.* New York: Alfred A. Knopf, 2003.

The Brave One. Dir. Neil Jordan. Writ. Roderick Taylor, Bruce A. Taylor, and Cynthia Mort. Perf. Jodi Foster and Terrence Howard. 2007. DVD. Warner Home Video, 2008.

Brenzel, Jeff. "Why Are Superheroes Good? Comics and the Ring of Gyges." *Superheroes and Philosophy: Truth, Justice, and the Socratic Way.* Ed: Tom Morris and Matt Morris. Chicago: Open Court, 2005. 147–160.

Bristow, Joseph, editor. *Oscar Wilde and Modern Culture: The Making of a Legend.* Ohio: Ohio University Press, 2009.

Brock, David. *The Republican Noise Machine: Right-Wing Media and How It Corrupts Democracy.* New York: Three Rivers Press, 2005.

Broder, John M. "Davis Seeks a Debate; Schwarzenegger Camp Says No." *The New York Times.* September 27, 2003. June 22, 2010. <http://www.nytimes.com/2003/09/27/us/davis-seeks-a-debate-schwarzenegger-camp-says-no.html>

Brooker, Will. "Batman: One Life, Many Faces." *Adaptations: From Text to Screen, Screen to Text.* Ed: Deborah Cartmell and Imelda Whelehan. London and New York: Routledge, 1999. 185–198.

_____. *Batman Unmasked.* New York/London: The Continuum Publishing Group, 2000.

Buffy the Vampire Slayer—Collector's Set. Writ. Joss Whedon, *et al.* Perf. Sarah Michelle Gellar, Anthony Stewart Head. DVD. 20th Century–Fox Home Video, 2006.

Burston, Paul, and Colin Richardson, editors. *A Queer Romance: Lesbians, Gay Men and Popular Culture.* New York: Routledge, 1995.

Busiek, Kurt. "A Journey Into Mystery." Illus. George Perez. *JLA/Avengers* (1 of 4). New York: Marvel Comics, September 2003.

_____. "So Smart in Their Fine Uniforms." Illus. Carlos Pacheco. *Arrowsmith,* Book 1. New York: Wildstorm, 2004.

Byrne, Ciar. "Russell T Davies: The saviour of Saturday night drama." *Independent,* 10 April 2006. June 22, 2010. <http://www.independent.co.uk/news/media/>

Byrne, John. "Hero." *The Fantastic Four* #285. New York: Marvel Comics, 1985.

_____. *Fantastic Four: The Trial of Galactus.* New York: Marvel Comics, 1989.

"Candidate for Crime." *Columbo: The Complete Third Season.* Dir. Boris Sagal. Writ. Irving Pearlberg, Alvin R. Friedman, Roland Kibbee, Dean Hargrove, and Larry Cohen. Perf. Peter Falk and Jackie Cooper. DVD. California: Universal Studios Home Entertainment, 2005.

"Casino Royale." *Climax!* Dir. William H. Brown, Jr. Writ. Charles Bennett and Anthony Ellis. Perf. Barry Nelson and Peter Lorre. 1954. DVD. *Casino Royale* (1967). MGM, 2002.

Chapelle, Dave, writer. "Episode 35: Electric Bike." *Dr. Katz, Professional Therapist.* June 29, 1997. *Dr. Katz, Professional Therapist: The Complete Series.* DVD. Comedy Central, 2007.

Charlie's Angels. Dir. Dennis Donnelly, Allen Baron, et al. Writ. Ivan Goff, Ben Roberts, et al. Perf. Jaclyn Smith, David Doyle, John Forsythe, Cheryl Ladd, Kate Jackson, and Farrah Fawcett. Television series. ABC. 1976–1981.

Chatman, Seymour. *Story and Discourse: Narrative Structure in Fiction and Film.* Ithaca: Cornell University Press, 1978.

Chomsky, Noam. *Hegemony or Survival? America's Quest for Global Dominance (The American Empire Project).* New York: Metropolitan Books, 2003. 22–24.

Christianus. "WMD and Doctor Who?" *Christianus.* June 26, 2005. August 19, 2009. <http://christianus.blogspot.com>

Claremont, Chris. "The End." Illus. Sean Chen. *X-Men.* New York: Marvel, 2009.

_____. "X-Men vs. Fantastic Four." (a.k.a. *Fantastic Four vs. X-Men.*) Illus. Jon Bogdanove. *Fantastic Four vs. X-Men.* New York: Marvel Comics, 2010.

"The Claws of Axos." *Doctor Who.* Dir. Michael Ferguson. Writ. Bob Baker and Dave Martin. Perf. Jon Pertwee, Katy Manning. 1971. DVD. BBC Video, 2005.

A Clockwork Orange. Writ-Dir. Stanley Kubrick. Perf. Malcolm McDowell. 1971. DVD. Warner Bros Home Video, 2007.

Cole, Juan R. I. "A Quantum of Anti-Imperialism." Informed Consent. Nov. 16, 2008. July 8, 2010. <http://www.juancole.com/2008/11/quantum-of-anti-imperialism.html>

Collins, Judy. "Foreward." *DC Archive Editions: Wonder Woman Archives* Vol. 1. New York: DC Comics, 1998.

Coleman, Robin R. Means, editor. *Say It Loud!: African American Audiences, Media and Identity.* New York: Routledge, 2002.

Comic Bloc Forums. Copyright (c)2000–2010, Jelsoft Enterprises Ltd. June 28, 2010. <http://www.comicbloc.com/forums/archive/index.php/t-11159.html>

Conan the Barbarian. Writ.-Dir. John Milius. Perf. Arnold Schwarzenegger, James Earl Jones, and Max von Sydow. 1982. "Collector's Edition" DVD. Universal, 2000.

Constantine. Dir. Francis Lawrence. Writ. Frank A. Cappello and Kevin Brodbin. Perf. Keanu Reeves, Rachel Weisz, Djimon Hounsou, and Shia LaBeouf. 2005. DVD. Warner Home Video, 2005.

Conway, Gerry. "Death of Gwen Stacy." Illus. Gil Kane and John Romita. *Spider-Man.* New York: Marvel Comics, 2002.

_____. "Death Sentence." Illus. Tony Dezuniga. *Classic Punisher.* New York: Marvel Comics, 1989.

_____. "Gerry Conway." *Comic Creators on Spider-Man.* Ed: Tom DeFalco. Cornwall: Titan Books, 2004.

_____. "The Punisher Strikes Twice." Illus. Ross Andru and John Romita, Sr. *Amazing Spider-Man* #129. New York: Marvel Comics, 1974.

_____. "Superman Vs. Wonder Woman: An Untold Epic of World War II." Illus. Jose Luis Garcia-Lopez. *All New Collector's Edition Volume 7, No. C-54.* New York: DC Comics, 1978.

Cook, David. *A History of Narrative Film.* New York: W. W. Norton & Company. 1996. 705.

Cooke, Darwyn and Dave Stewart. *DC: The New Frontier—Volume One.* New York: DC Comics, 2004.

_____. *DC: The New Frontier—Volume Two.* New York: DC Comics, 2005.

Cornell, Paul (with Martin Day and Keith Topping). *The Discontinuity Guide: The Unofficial Doctor Who Companion.* Texas: MonkeyBrain Books, 2004. August 19, 2009. <http://www.bbc.co.uk/doctorwho/classic/episodeguide/crusade/detail.shtml>

_____. "True Story." Illus. Horatio Domingues. *Fantastic Four.* New York: Marvel Comics, 2009.

Costello, Elvis. "Everything You Wanted To Know About *Spike.*" *BBC2 Late Show.* Perf. Tracey Macleod. BBC 2. February 20, 1989.

_____. "Tramp the Dirt Down." *Spike.* CD. Rhino Records, 2009.

Costello, Matthew J. *Secret Identity Crisis: Comic Books & the Unmasking of Cold War America.* New York: Continuum International, 2009.

Curtis, Richard. "Vincent and the Doctor." *Doctor Who.* Perf. Matt Smith, Karen Gillian. 2010. DVD. *Doctor Who: The Complete Fifth Series.* BBC, 2010.

Daniels, Les. *Wonder Woman: The Complete History.* San Francisco: Chronicle Books, 2000.

"David Cameron launches Tories' 'big society' plan." *BBC.com.* July 19, 2010. August 12, 2010. <http://www.bbc.co.uk/news/uk-10680062>

David, Peter. "Cult of Love" Illus. Alex Saviuk. *Web of Spider-Man* #40–43. New York: Marvel Comics: 1988.

_____. "The Incredible Hulk: War and Pieces." Illus. Dale Keown. *X-Factor Visionaries* Vol. 2. New York: Marvel Comics, 2007.

_____. "Jumping the Tracks." Illus. Roger Cruz and Mike Wieringo. *Friendly Neighborhood Spider-Man, Vol. 1: Derailed.* New York: Marvel Comics, 2006.

_____. "Point of View." Illus. Mike Harris. *Web of Spider-Man* #13. New York: Marvel Comics, 1986.

Davies, Caroline and David Smith. "Dr Who? Big names lose out to Matt Smith." *Guardian,* 3 January 2009. August 19, 2009. <http://www.guardian.co.uk/>

Davies, Russell T, writer. "Alien Resurrection." MediaGuardian, p. 8. *Guardian.* 13 June 2005, p. 8. August 19, 2009. <http://www.guardian.co.uk/media/2005/jun/13/mondaymediasection7>

_____. "Aliens of London." *Doctor Who.* Perf. Christopher Eccleston, Billie Piper. 2005. *Doctor Who: The Complete First Series.* DVD. BBC Video, 2005.

_____. "A Rose by any other name." *The Observer,* 2 September 2001. August 20, 2009. <http://www.guardian.co.uk/theobserver/2001/sep/02/features.review67>

_____. "Bad Wolf." *Doctor Who.* Perf. Christopher Eccleston, Billie Piper. 2005. *Doctor Who: The Complete First Series.* DVD. BBC Video, 2005.

_____. *Bob and Rose.* Perf. Lesley Sharp, Alan Davies, Jessica Stevenson. Television series. ITV, 2001.

_____. "The End of the World." *Doctor Who.* Perf. Christopher Eccleston, Billie Piper. 2005. *Doctor Who: The Complete First Series.* DVD. BBC Video, 2005.

_____. "The Long Game." *Doctor Who.* Perf. Christopher Eccleston, Billie Piper. 2005. *Doctor Who: The Complete First Series.* DVD. BBC Video, 2005.

_____. "Midnight." *Doctor Who.* Perf. David Tennant, Catherine Tate. 2008. *Doctor Who: The Complete Fourth Series.* DVD. BBC, 2008.

_____. "The Parting of the Ways." *Doctor Who.* Perf. Christopher Eccleston, Billie Piper. 2005. *Doctor Who: The Complete First Series.* DVD. BBC Video, 2005.

_____. "Rose." *Doctor Who.* Perf. Christopher Eccleston, Billie Piper. 2005. *Doctor Who: The Complete First Series.* DVD. BBC Video, 2005.

_____. *The Second Coming.* Perf. Christopher Eccleston, Lesley Sharp. DVD. ITV, 2003.

_____. "The Sound of Drums." *Doctor Who.* Perf. David Tennant, Freeman Agyeman. 2007. *Doctor Who: The Complete Third Series.* DVD. BBC, 2007.

_____. "World War Three." *Doctor Who.* Perf. Christopher Eccleston, Billie Piper. 2005. *Doctor Who: The Complete First Series.* DVD. BBC Video, 2005.

_____. *Why Don't You?* Television series. BBC, 1988–1992.

Davis, Alan. *Excalibur Visionaries: Alan Davis 1.* New York: Marvel Comics, 2009.

Daybreakers. Writ.-Dir. Michael Spierig and Peter Spierig. Perf. Ethan Hawke, Sam Neill, and Willem Dafoe. 2009. DVD. Lionsgate, 2010.

Death Wish. Dir. Michael Winner. Writ. Wendell Mayes. Perf. Charles Bronson, Hope Lange, and Vincent Gardenia. 1974. DVD. Paramount, 2006.

DeFalco, Tom. *Spider-Man: The Ultimate Guide.* New York: Dorling Kindersley, 2001. 84–85.

Delano, Jamie. "Going for It." Illus. John Ridgway and Alfredo Alcala. *John Constantine: Hellblazer — Original Sins.* 1987. New York: DC Comics, 1992.

_____. "Pandemonium." Illus. Jock. *John Constantine: Hellblazer.* New York: DC Comics, 2010.

DeMatteis, J.M. "New Age Dawning." Illus. Graham Nolan and Karl Kesel. *Batman and Spider-Man.* New York: DC Comics, 1997.

_____. "Walking Into Yesterday." Illus. Mark Buckingham. *Doctor Strange: Sorcerer Supreme* Vol. 1, No. 86. New York: Marvel Comics, 1996.

Dennis, Brady and David Cho. "Rage at AIG Swells as Bonuses Go Out." *The Washington Post.* March 17, 2009. July 24, 2010. <http://www.washingtonpost.com/wp-dyn/content/article/2009/03/16/AR2009031602961.html>

"Detainees' Rights." *Facts on File: Issues & Controversies.* April 15, 2004. July 17, 2010. <http://www.2facts.com/icof_story.aspx?PIN=i0701760&term=detainees'+rights>

DeviantArt.com. "Obama." August 2000. September 4, 2010. <http://browse.deviantart.com/?qh=§ion=&global=1&q=obama>

De Villiers, Marq. *The End: Natural Disasters, Manmade Catastrophes, and the Future of Human Survival.* New York: Saint Martin's Press, 2008.

Diana Prince: Wonder Woman. Volume One. Writ. Mike Sekowsky. Illus. Dick Giordano. New York: DC Comics, 2008.

Diana Prince: Wonder Woman. Volume Two. Writ. Mike Sekowsky. Illus. Dick Giordano. New York: DC Comics, 2008.

Diana Prince: Wonder Woman. Volume Three. Writ. Mike Sekowsky. Illus. Dick Giordano. New York: DC Comics, 2008.

Diana Prince: Wonder Woman. Volume Four. Writ. Dennis O'Neil et al. Illus. Dick Giordano. New York: DC Comics, 2008.

Dini, Paul and Alex Ross. *Wonder Woman: Spirit of Truth.* New York: DC Comics, 2001.

Dirty Harry. Dir. Don Siegel. Writ. Harry Julian Fink, Rita M. Fink, and Dean Riesner. Perf. Clint Eastwood. 1971. DVD. Warner Home Video, 2008.

Ditko, Steve. "The Amazing Spider-Man." Co-Illus. Jack Kirby. Co-Writ. Stan Lee. *Marvel Masterworks: The Amazing Spider-Man* Vol. 1. New York: Marvel Comics, 2003.

_____. "The Amazing Spider-Man." Co-Writ. Stan Lee. *Marvel Masterworks: The Amazing Spider-Man* Vol. 2. New York: Marvel Comics, 2003.

_____. "The Amazing Spider-Man." Co-Writ. Stan Lee. *Marvel Masterworks: The Amazing Spider-Man* Vol. 3. New York: Marvel Comics, 2003.

_____. "The Amazing Spider-Man." Co-Writ. Stan Lee. *Marvel Masterworks: The Amazing Spider-Man* Vol. 4. New York: Marvel Comics, 2003.

_____."'Jack Kirby's Spider-Man.' Robin Snyder's *History of Comics* #5 (May 1990)." *Alter Ego: The Comic Book Artist Collection.* Ed: Roy Thomas. TwoMorrows Publishing, 2001.

Dittmer, Jason. "Retconning America: Captain America in the Wake of World War II and the McCarthy Hearings." *The Amazing Transforming Superhero!* North Carolina: McFarland, 2007.

Dixon, Chris. "The California Recall: Voters Recall Just Who Started This Thing, If You Will." *The New York Times*. October 8, 2003. June 22, 2010. <http://www.nytimes.com/2003/10/08/us/the-california-recall-voters-recall-just-who-started-this-thing-if-you-will.html>

Dixon, Chuck. "The Beginning of Tomorrow!" Illus. Graham Nolan. *Detective Comics: Featuring Batman*. #0. New York, DC Comics: Oct. 1994.

_____. "Joker's Last Laugh." Illus. Scott Beatty. *Batman: Joker's Last Laugh*. New York: DC Comics, 2008.

Doughty. Robbie. "Letter to the Editor." *The Amazing Spider-Man* #579. New York: Marvel Comics, 2009.

Douglas, Edward. "Andrew Garfield's First Words on Spider-Man." *SuperheroHype.com*. September 6, 2010. September 6, 2010. <http://www.superherohype.com/news/articles/106701-andrew-garfields-first-words-on-spider-man>

Doyle, Steven and David A. Crowder. *Sherlock Holmes For Dummies*. New York: Pearson, 2010.

Dr. Mabuse: The Gambler. Dir. Fritz Lang. Writ. Fritz Lang, Norbert Jacques, and Thea von Harbou. Perf. Rudolf Klein-Rogge. Germany. 1922. DVD. Kino Video, 2000.

Du Bois, W. E. Burghardt. "Does the Negro need Separate Schools?" *The Journal of Negro Education*, Vol. 4, No. 3, The Courts and the Negro Separate School. July 1935. 328–335.

Ebert, Roger. "Batman Begins." *Chicago Sun-Times*. June 13, 2005. June 25, 2010. <http://rogerebert.suntimes.com/>

_____. "Batman Returns." *Chicago Sun-Times*. June 19, 1992. June 25, 2010. <http://rogerebert.suntimes.com/>

_____. "Kick-Ass." *Chicago Sun-Times*. April 14, 2010. June 25, 2010. <http://rogerebert.suntimes.com/>

_____. "Put Up Or Shut Up." *Roger Ebert's Journal*. September 1, 2010. September 6, 2010. <http://blogs.suntimes.com/ebert/2010/09/put_up_or_shut_up.html>

_____. "Wanted." *Chicago Sun-Times*. June 26, 2008. July 11, 2010. <http://rogerebert.suntimes.com/apps/pbcs.dll/article?AID=/20080626/REVIEWS/294566124>

_____. "Watchmen." *Chicago Sun-Times*. March 4, 2009. June 25, 2010. <http://rogerebert.suntimes.com/>

_____. "X-Men." *Chicago Sun-Times*. July 14, 2000. June 25, 2010. <http://rogerebert.suntimes.com/>

_____. "X-Men: The Last Stand." *Chicago Sun-Times*. May 26, 2006. June 25, 2010. <http://rogerebert.suntimes.com/>

Eco, Umberto. "The Myth of Superman." *The Role of the Reader: Explorations in the Semiotics of Texts*. Bloomington: Indiana University Press, 1979. 107–125.

Eden, Ami. "(Orthodo)X-Men: Marvel's Mutant Split Parallels the Post-Holocaust Theological Divide Between Kahane and Greenberg." *Forward: The Jewish Daily*. May 23, 2003. July 12, 2010. <http://www.forward.com/articles/8878/>

Edmundson, Mark. *Nightmare on Main Street: Angels, Sadomasochism, and the Culture of the Gothic*. Massachusetts: Harvard University Press, 1997.

Ehrenreich, Barbara. "The Enron Tea Party." *Barbara's Blog*. May 26, 2006. July 24, 2010. <http://ehrenreich.blogs.com/barbaras_blog/2006/05/the_enron_tea_p.html>

Ellis, Warren. "Haunted." Illus. John Higgins. *John Constantine: Hellblazer*. New York: Vertigo/DC Comics, 2003.

Engleheart, Steve. "Dark Detective." *Batman: Dark Detective*. New York: DC Comics, 2005.

_____. "*Detective Comics* #467–479. 1977–1978." Illus. Marshall Rogers. *Batman: Strange Apparitions*. New York: DC Comics, 1999.

Ennis, Garth. "Bloodlines." Illus. Steve Dillon, Mike Hoffman, and Will Simpson. *John Constantine: Hellblazer*. New York, DC Comics, 2007.

_____. "Born." Illus. Darick Robertson. *The Punisher: Born*. New York: Marvel Comics, 2004.

_____. "Damnation's Flame." Illus. Steve Dillon and Mike Hoffman. *John Constantine: Hellblazer*. New York, DC Comics, 1999.

_____. "Punisher: The Tyger." Illus. John Severin. *Punisher: The Tyger*. New York: Marvel Comics, 2006.

Enron: The Smartest Guys in the Room. Dir. Alex Gibney. Writ. Peter Elkind, Alex Gibney, and Bethany McLean. Narrator. Peter Coyote. 2005. DVD. Magnolia, 2006.

Evans, C. Stephen. "Why Should Superheroes Be Good? Spider-Man, the X-Men, and Kierkegaard's Double Danger." *Superheroes and Philosophy: Truth, Justice, and the Socratic Way*. Ed: Tom Morris and Matt Morris. Chicago: Open Court, 2005. 161–177.

Evil Dead. Writ.-Dir. Sam Raimi. Perf. Bruce Campbell and Ellen Sandweiss. 1981. DVD. Anchor Bay, 2002.

"Falwell apologizes to gays, feminists, lesbians." *CNN.com*. September 14, 2001. June 28, 2010. <http://archives.cnn.com/2001/US/09/14/Falwell.apology/>

"Famke Janssen Biography Page." *Internet Movie Database*. 1990–2010. August 12, 2010. <http://www.imdb.com/name/nm0000463/bio>

Faulks, Sebastian. *Devil May Care*. USA: Vintage, 2009. 180.

"Fausta: The Nazi Wonder Woman." *Wonder Woman: The Complete First Season*. Prod. Douglas S. Cramer. Develop. Stanley Ralph Ross. Perf. Lynda Carter and Lyle Waggoner. 1975–1977. DVD. Warner Home Video, 2004.

Feiffer, Jules. "'Introduction' from *The Great Comic Book Heroes*." *The Conscious Reader*, 1st edition. Ed: Caroline Shrodes, Harry Finestone, and Michael Shugrue. New York: Macmillan, 1974. 347–349.

"The Feminum Mystique: Part 1" and "The Feminum Mystique: Part 2." *Wonder Woman: The Complete First Season*. Prod. Douglas S. Cramer. Develop. Stanley Ralph Ross. Perf. Lynda Carter and Lyle Waggoner. 1975–1977. DVD. Warner Home Video, 2004.

Fingeroth, Danny. *Superman on the Couch: What Superheroes Really Tell Us About Ourselves and Our Society*. New York/London: Continuum, 2004.

Finnegan, Lisa. *No Questions Asked: News Coverage Since 9/11*. London: Praeger Publishers, 2007.

First Blood. Dir. Ted Kotcheff. Writ. Michael Kozoll, William Sackheim, and Sylvester Stallone. Perf. Sylvester Stallone. 1982. DVD. Artisan, 2002.

Fleming, Ian. *Casino Royale*. London: Penguin Books, 2002.

_____. *For Your Eyes Only*. London: Penguin Books, 2002.

_____. *Live and Let Die*. London: Penguin Books, 2002.

_____. *Octopussy & The Living Daylights*. London: Penguin Books, 2002.

_____. *Diamonds are Forever*. London: Penguin Books, 2002. 23, 231

Fleming, Mike. "'X-Men: First Class' Drafts Twilight Vampire Edi Gathegi to Play Biracial Mutant Darwin." *Deadline New York*. July 27, 2010. September 10, 2010. <http://www.deadline.com/2010/07/x-men-first-class-drafts-twilight-vampire-edi-gathegi-to-play-biracial-mutant-darwin/?utm_source=twitterfeed&utm_medium=twitter>

Forbidden Planet. Dir. Fred M. Wilcox. Writ. Cyril Hume. Perf. Leslie Nielsen and Anne Francis. 1956. DVD. Warner Home Video, 2006.

Forman, Lillian. *Stem Cell Research.* Minnesota: ABDO Publishing Company, 2008.

Fowler, Tom. "Judge vacates Ken Lay's Enron conviction." *Houston Chronicle.* Oct. 17, 2006. July 24, 2010. <http://www.chron.com/disp/story.mpl/special/enron/4265806.html>

Fraction, Matt. "Civil War." Illus. Ariel Olivetti. *The Punisher War Journal.* New York: Marvel Comics, 2007.

Freddy vs. Jason. Dir. Ronny Yu. Writ. Damian Shannon and Mark Swift. Perf. Robert Englund and Monica Keena. 2003. DVD. New Line Home Video, 2004.

Freiman, Barry. "Superman IV: The Quest for Peace." *The '80s Movie Rewind.* 2003. July 8, 2010. <http://www.fast-rewind.com/supermaniv.htm>

The French Connection. Dir. William Friedkin. Writ. Ernest Tidyman. Perf. Gene Hackman and Roy Scheider. 1971. DVD. 20th Century–Fox Home Video, 2005.

Friday the 13th. Dir. Sean S. Cunningham. Writ. Victor Miller. Perf. Betsy Palmer, Adrienne King, and Kevin Bacon. 1980. DVD. Paramount, 2009.

Frus, Phyllis and Christy Williams. "Introduction." *Beyond Adaptation.* North Carolina: McFarland, 2010.

Fry, Stephen. "Stephen Fry's Bafta speech." *Guardian.co.uk.* June 16, 2010. July 8, 2010. <http://www.guardian.co.uk/media/2010/jun/16/stephen-fry-bafta-lecture>

Furcht, Leo. *The Stem Cell Dilemma: Beacons of Hope or Harbingers of Doom?* New York: Arcade Publishing, 2008.

Fussman, Cal. "What I've Learned: Christopher Reeve." *Esquire.* December 31, 2003. July 12, 2010. <http://www.esquire.com/features/what-ive-learned/ESQ0104-JAN_SUPERHEROES_1>

Gaiman, Neil. "Whatever Happened to the Caped Crusader?" Illus. Andy Kubert. *Batman: Whatever Happened to the Caped Crusader?* New York: DC Comics, 2009.

"Gallery Told to Drop Gay Batman." *BBC News Online.* August 19, 2005. June 22, 2010. <http://news.bbc.co.uk/2/hi/entertainment/4167032.stm>

Gandhi, Mohandas K. "My Faith in Nonviolence." *The Conscious Reader, 12th edition.* Ed: Caroline Shrodes, Marc DiPaolo, et al. New York: Pearson, 2010.

Gardiner, Nile. "Is Avatar an Attack on the Iraq War?" *Telegraph.* December 12, 2009. August 15, 2010. <http://blogs.telegraph.co.uk/news/nilegardiner/100019656/is-avatar-an-attack-on-the-iraq-war/>

Gardner, Eriq. "It's On! Kirby Estate Sues Marvel; Copyrights to Iron Man, Spider-Man at Stake." *The Hollywood Reporter, Esq.* March 15, 2010. July 11, 2010. <http://thresq.hollywoodreporter.com/2010/03/kirby-marvel-lawsuit.html>

Genter, Robert. "'With Great Power Comes Great Responsibility': Cold War Culture and the Birth of Marvel Comics." *The Journal of Popular Culture.* Vol. 40, Issue 6. Massachussetts: Blackwell Publishing, 2007. 953–978.

Gerbner, George. "Reclaiming Our Own Cultural Mythology; Television's Global Marketing Strategy Creates a Damaging and Alienate Window on the World." *In Context, A Quarterly of Humane, Sustainable Culture, Ecology of Justice,* no. 38 (Spring 1994): 40.

Ghost Rider. Writ.-Dir. Mark Steven Johnson. Perf. Nicholas Cage and Eva Mendes. DVD. Sony Pictures Entertainment, 2007.

The Ghost Writer. Dir. Roman Polanski. Writ. Robert Harris and Roman Polanski. Perf. Ewan McGregor, Olivia Williams, and Pierce Brosnan. 2010. DVD. Summit Entertainment, 2010.

"Glenn Beck: Obama Is a Racist." *The Associated Press.* New York: CBS News.com. July 29, 2009. July 8, 2010. <http://www.cbsnews.com/stories/2009/07/29/politics/main5195604.shtml>

The Godfather. Dir. Frances Ford Coppola. Writ. Mario Puzo, Francis Ford Coppola and Robert Towne. Perf. Marlon Brando, Al Pacino, James Caan, and Diane Keaton. 1972. DVD. Paramount, 2004.

Godzilla: King of the Monsters. Dir. Terry O. Morse. Writ. Al C. Ward. Perf. Raymond Burr and Takashi Shimura. 1956. DVD. *Gojira/Godzilla Deluxe Collector's Edition.* Sony, 2006.

Godzilla: King of the Monsters #23. Writ. Doug Moench. Illus. Herb Trimpe. New York: Marvel Comics, 1979.

Godzilla versus King Ghidora. Writ.-Dir. Kazuki Omori. Perf. Kosuke Toyohara, Anna Nakagawa, Megumi Odaka. 1991. DVD. Sony, 1998.

Godzilla versus Hedorah. Dir. Yoshimitsu Banno. Writ. Yoshimitsu Banno and Takeshi Kimura. Perf. Akira Yamauchi and Toshie Kimura. 1971. DVD. Sony, 2004.

Gojira. Dir. Ishiro Honda. Writ. Shigeru Kayama, Ishiro Honda, and Takeo Murata. Perf. Takashi Shimura. 1954. DVD. *Gojira/Godzilla Deluxe Collector's Edition.* Sony, 2006.

Gonzo: The Life and Work of Dr. Hunter S. Thompson. Writ.-Dir. Alex Gibney. Perf. Hunter S. Thompson, Johnny Depp, Pat Buchanan. DVD. Magnolia Home Entertainment, 2008.

Goossen, Rachel Waltner. *Women Against the Good War: Conscientious Objection and Gender on the American Home Front 1941–1947.* Chapel Hill and London: The University of North Carolina Press, 1997.

Gopalan, Nisha. "Mark Millar on Sarah Palin: 'Terrifying.'" *io9.com.* September 23, 2008. September 4, 2010. <http://io9.com/5053777/mark-millar-on-sarah-palin-terrifying>

Gordon, Margaret T. and Stephanie Riger. *The Female Fear: The Social Cost of Rape.* Chicago: University of Illinois Press, 1991.

Gould, Stephen Jay. "A Biological Homage to Mickey Mouse." *The Panda's Thumb: More Reflections in Natural History.* New York: W. W. Norton, 1992. 95–107.

Grand Theft Auto. New York/London: Rockstar Games, 1997.

Grant, Alan. *The Batman Judge Dredd Files.* Co-writer. John Wagner. New York: DC Comics, 2004.

_____. "Engram." Illus. David Roach. *Psi-Judge Anderson: Engrams* #1 and 2. London: Fleetway, 1992.

_____. "The Possessed." Illus. Brett Ewins. Judge Anderson: Death's Dark Dimension. London: Titan Books/2000 AD, 2002.

Grant, Steven. "Circle of Blood." Illus. Mike Zeck. *The Punisher* Vol. I #1–5. Marvel Comics, New York: 1986.

Graser, Marc. "Superman co-creator's family given rights: Siegels now control character's Krypton origins." *Variety.* August 13, 2009. July 11, 2010. <http://www.variety.com/article/VR1118007269.html?categoryid=13&cs=1>

Greenburg, Jan Crawford. "Does Terror Trump Torture?" *ABC News.com.* February 12, 2008. July 17, 2010. <http://blogs.abcnews.com/legalities/2008/02/does-terror-tru.html>

Grey, Stephen. *Ghost Plane: The True Story of the CIA Torture Program.* New York: St. Martin's Press, 2006.

Gross, Doug. "Why We Love Those Rotting, Hungry, Putrid Zombies." *CNN*. Turner Broadcasting System. Oct 2, 2009. August 27, 2010. <http://www.cnn.com/2009/SHOWBIZ/10/02/zombie.love/index.html>.

Guggenheim, Marc. "Flashbacks." Illus. Barry Kitson. *The Amazing Spider-Man* #574. New York: Marvel Comics, 2008.

Guglielmo, Jennifer. "White Lies, Dark Truths." *Are Italians White? How Race is Made in America*. Ed: Jennifer Guglielmo and Salvatore Salerno. New York: Routledge, 2003.

Gustines, George Gene. "Out of the Closet and Up, Up and Away." *New York Times*. April 16, 2010. September 8, 2010. <http://www.nytimes.com/2010/04/18/fashion/18comics.html>

Hagen, L. Kirk. "French Follies: A 9/11 Conspiracy Theory Turns Out to Be an Appalling Deception." *Legends, Lore, and Lies: A Skeptic's Stance (A Longman Topics Reader)*. Ed: Joseph Calabrese. New York: Pearson/Longman, 2007. 32–39.

Haimson, Leonie, Michael Oppenheimer, and David Wilcove. "The Way Things Really Are: Debunking Rush Limbaugh on the Environment." *The Environmental Defense Fund*. Reprinted from *Our Environment Online*. 2005. September 18, 2010. <http://www.bestofmaui.com/rush.html>

Hama, Larry. "The Fall of Red Sarah." Illus. John Christmas. *Barack the Barbarian*. Chicago: Devil's Due Publishing, 2009.

_____. "Quest for the Treasure of Stimuli." Illus. Christopher Schons. *Barack the Barbarian* #1–4. Chicago: Devil's Due Publishing, 2009.

Hamilton, Clive. *Requiem for a Species: Why We Resist the Truth About Climate Change*. London: Earthscan Publications, 2010.

Hancock. Dir. Peter Berg. Writ. Vince Gilligan and Vincent Ngo. Perf. Will Smith and Charlize Theron. 2008. DVD. Columbia, 2008.

Happy Feet. Writ.-Dir. George Miller, Warren Coleman, and Judy Morris.Perf. Elijah Wood, Nicole Kidman, Hugh Jackman. Warner Bros. Pictures, 2006.

Harris, Robert. *The Ghost (Writer)*. New York: Pocket, 2010.

_____. "The 'Ghost' of Tony Blair." *NPR Morning Edition*. October 31, 2007. June 25, 2010. <http://www.npr.org/templates/story/story.php?storyId=15776253>

Hartmann, Susan M. *American Women in the 1940s: The Home Front and Beyond*. Boston: Twayne Publishers/G.K. Hall & Co, 1982.

Harvey, Barry. E-mail interview. March 25, 2008.

Haskell, Molly. *From Reverence to Rape: The Treatment of Women in the Movies*. 2nd edition. Chicago: The University of Chicago Press, 1987.

Hayles, Brian. "Curse of Peladon." *Doctor Who*. Dir. Lennie Mayne. Perf. Jon Pertwee and Katy Manning. 1972. DVD. 2 Entertain, 2010.

_____. "Monster of Peladon." *Doctor Who*. Dir. Lennie Mayne. Perf. Jon Pertwee and Elizabeth Sladen. 1974. DVD. 2 Entertain, 2010.

Hedges, Chris. *American Fascists: The Christian Right and the War on America*. New York: Free Press, 2006.

Heinberg, Allan. "Who Is Wonder Woman?" Illus. Terry Dodson. *Wonder Woman*. New York: DC Comics. 2008.

Heller, Anne C. *Ayn Rand and the World She Made*. New York: Doubleday, 2009.

Herbert, Frank. *Dune*. New York: ACE, 1990.

Herman, Susan. "The U.S.A. Patriot Act and the Department of Justice: Losing Our Balances?" *Peace, War, and Terrorism*. Ed: Dennis Okerstrom. New York: Pearson, 2006. 103–110.

Heroes. Dir. Greg Beeman et al. Writ. Tim Kring, Nora Kay Foster et al. Perf. Sendhil Ramamurthy, Masi Oka, Hayden Panettiere. 2006–2010. DVD. *Heroes—Season One*. Universal, 2007.

Heskett, James. "Will the Societal Effects of Enron Exceed Those of September 11?" Harvard Business School Weekly. Working Knowledge for Business Leaders. February 2, 2002. June 25, 2010. <http://hbswk.hbs.edu/cgi-bin/print>

His Girl Friday. Dir. Howard Hawks. Writ. Charles Lederer, Ben Hecht, and Charles MacArthur. Perf. Cary Grant, Rosalind Russell, Ralph Bellamy. 1940. DVD. Sony Pictures, 2000.

Hogan's Heroes: The Komplete Series, Kommandant's Kollection. Dir. Gene Reynolds *et. al*. Writ. Bernard Fein, Albert S. Ruddy et al. Perf. Bob Crane. 1965–1971. DVD. Paramount Home Video, 2009.

Hoggan, James and Richard Littlemore. *Climate Cover-Up: The Crusade to Deny Global Warming*. Canada: D&M Publishers, 2009.

Holleran, Scott. "Wing Kid." *Box Office Mojo*. Oct. 20, 2005. June 25, 2010. <http://boxofficemojo.com/features/?id=1921&p=.htm>

Hollywoodland. Dir. Allen Coulter. Writ. Paul Bernbaum. Perf. Adrien Brody, Diane Lane, Ben Affleck, and Robin Tunney. 2006. DVD. Universal, 2007.

Holmes, Robert, writer. "The Caves of Androzani." *Doctor Who*. Perf. Peter Davison, Nicola Bryant, 1984. DVD. BBC Video, 2002.

_____. "Pyramids of Mars." *Doctor Who*. Perf. Tom Baker, Elizabeth Sladen. 1975. DVD. BBC Video, 2004.

_____. "The Ribos Operation." *Doctor Who*. Perf. Tom Baker, Mary Tamm. 1978. DVD. BBC Video, 2002.

_____. "The Sunmakers" (1977), *Doctor Who*. Perf. Tom Baker, Louise Jameson. 1977. VHS. BBC Video, 2002.

_____. "The Talons of Weng-Chiang." *Doctor Who*. Perf. Tom Baker, Louise Jameson. 1977. DVD. BBC Video, 2003.

_____. "The Trial of a Time Lord." *Doctor Who*. Perf. Colin Baker, Nicola Bryant. 1986. DVD. BBC Video, 2008.

_____. "The Two Doctors." *Doctor Who*. Perf. Colin Baker, Patrick Troughton, Nicola Bryant. 1985. DVD. BBC Video, 2004.

Horton, Scott. "Information Secured Through Torture Proved Unreliable, CIA Concluded." *Harper's Magazine*. March 29, 2009. July 17, 2010. <http://harpers.org/archive/2009/03/hbc-90004644>

Housel, Rebecca. "Myth, Morality, and the Women of the X-Men." *Superheroes and Philosophy: Truth, Justice, and the Socratic Way*. Ed: Tom and Matt Morris. Chicago and LaSalle Illinois: Open Court Publishing Co, 2005. 75–88.

House of the Dead. Video Game. Ota: Sega, 1996

House M.D. Dir. Deran Sarafian, et al. Writ. David Shore, Russel Friend and Garrett Lerner, et al. Perf. Hugh Laurie. Television series. Fox, 2004–present.

Howarth, Chris and Steve Lyons. *Doctor Who: The Completely Unofficial Encyclopedia*. Des Moines, IA: Mad Norwegian Press, 2006.

Howe, David J. and Steven James Walker. *The Television Companion: The Unofficial and Unauthorized Guide to Doctor Who*. Surrey: Telos Publishing, 2003.

Hudlin, Reginald. "Who Is the Black Panther?" Illus. John Romita, Jr., Black Panther. New York: Marvel Comics, 2005.

Hudson, Laura. "Comic Book Industry Celebrates Barack Obama's Historic Presidential Win." *MTV News.* November 5, 2008. September 1, 2010. <http://splash page.mtv.com/2008/11/05/comic-book-industry-cele brates-barack-obamas-historic-presidential-win/>

Hutchison, David. *President Evil* #1–3. Texas: Antarctic Press, 2009.Huver, Scott. "Jon Favreau on the Iron Man Franchise!" ComingSoon.Net. September 12, 2008. July 12, 2010. <http://www.comingsoon.net/news/movienews.php?id=48774>

Hulke, Malcolm. "Doctor Who and the Silurians." *Doctor Who.* Perf. Jon Pertwee, Nicholas Courtney. 1970. DVD. *Doctor Who — Beneath The Surface (Doctor Who And The Silurians/The Sea Devils/Warriors Of The Deep).* BBC Video, 2008.

_____. "Invasion of the Dinosaurs." *Doctor Who.* Perf. Jon Pertwee, Elizabeth Sladen. 1974. VHS. BBC Video, 2003.

_____. "The Sea Devils." *Doctor Who.* Perf. Jon Pertwee, Katy Manning. 1972. DVD. *Doctor Who — Beneath the Surface (Doctor Who and the Silurians/The Sea Devils/Warriors of the Deep).* BBC Video, 2008.

Hultkrans, Andrew. "Steve Ditko's Hands." *Give Our Regards to the Atomsmashers.* Ed: Sean Howe. New York: Pantheon Books, 2004.

The Incredibles. Writ.-Dir. Brad Bird. Perf. Craig T. Nelson, Holly Hunter, Samuel L. Jackson, and Brad Bird. 2004. DVD. Walt Disney Home Entertainment, 2005.

Iron Man. Dir. Jon Favreau. Writ. Mark Fergus, Hawk Ostby, Art Marcum, Matt Holloway, and John August. Perf. Robert Downey, Jr., Gwyneth Paltrow, Jeff Bridges. Paramount, 2008.

I Spit on Your Grave. Writ.-Dir. Meir Zarchi. Perf. Camille Keaton. 1978. DVD. Elite Entertainment, 2004.

Isaacson, Walter. *Benjamin Franklin: An American Life.* New York: Simon & Schuster, 2004.

Jaffe, Nina. *Wonder Woman: The Journey Begins.* New York: HarperFestival, 2004.

James, Susan Donaldson. "In College Study Abroad the Risk Increases the Reward." *ABC News.com.* Nov. 8, 2007. July 17, 2010. <http://abcnews.go.com/US/story?id=3835147&page=1>

Janovic, Matthew. "Mr. Freedom." *Internet Movie Database.* September 1, 2008. August 12, 2010. <http://italy.imdb.com/title/tt0064674/usercomments>

Jiminez, Phil. "Amazons Attack!" *Wonder Woman Vol. 2 #173.* New York: DC Comics, 2001.

Jiminez, Phil and Joe Kelly. "She's a Wonder." *Wonder Woman Vol. 2 #170.* New York: DC Comics, 2001.

Johnson, Richard. "Master of the universe." *Telegraph.* March 11, 2007. Aug. 20, 2009. <http://www.telegraph.co.uk/culture/3663738/Master-of-the-universe.html>

Johns, Geoff. "Blackest Night 0–8." Illus. Ivan Reiss. *Blackest Night.* New York: DC Comics, 2010.

_____. (with Peter Tomasi). *Brightest Day.* Illus. Ivan Reis et al. New York: DC Comics, 2010–2011.

_____. (with Richard Donner). "Last Son." Illus. Adam Kubert. *Superman.* New York: DC Comics, 2008.

Jones, Gerard. *Killing Monsters: Why Children Need Fantasy, Super Heroes, and Make-Believe Violence.* New York: Basic Books, 2002.

Jones, Jeffrey M. "Slim Majority Wants Bush-Era Interrogations Investigated." *Gallup.* April 27, 2009. July 17, 2010. <http://www.gallup.com/poll/118006/Slim-Majority-Wants-Bush-Era-Interrogations-Investigat ed.aspx>

Joshi, S.T. *The Angry Right: Why Conservatives Keep Getting It Wrong.* New York: Prometheus Books, 2006.

Juddery, Mark. "5 Comic Superheroes Who Made a Real-World Difference." *Mental Floss.* November/December 2008. 32–35.

Judge Anderson: Death's Dark Dimension (2000 AD Presents). Writ. Alan Grant and John Wagner. Illus. Brett Ewins, Cliff Robinson, and Brian Bolland. UK: Titan Books, 2003.

Judge Dredd. Dir. Danny Cannon. Writ. Michael De Luca, Steven E. de Souza, and William Wisher, Jr. Perf. Sylvester Stallone and Diane Lane. DVD. Walt Disney Video, 1998.

Judge Dredd: Featuring Judge Death. Writ. Alan Grant. Illus. Brian Bolland. UK: Titan Books, 2004.

Jurgens, Dan, Jerry Ordway, Louise Simonson, Roger Stern, et al. *The Death of Superman.* New York: DC Comics, 1993.

Justice League (a.k.a. *Justice League Unlimited*). Producers: Bruce W. Timm, Rich Fogel, Dwayne McDuffie, *et al.* Directors: Dan Riba, Butch Lukic, et al. Cartoon Network, 2001–2006.

Justice League: Starcrossed. Dir. Butch Lukic and Dan Riba. Writ. Rich Fogel and Dwayne McDuffie. Perf. Phil LaMarr, Kevin Conroy, Maria Canals-Barrera. Warner Bros., 2004.

Kael, Pauline. "Dirty Harry." *5001 Nights at the Movies.* New York: Henry Holt and Company, 1991. 191.

Kamenetz, Anya. *Generation Debt: Why Now Is a Terrible Time to Be Young.* Riverhead Books. New York: 2006.

Kavanagh, Barry. "The Alan Moore Interview: Brought to Light — deep politics/AARGH." *Blather.net.* October 17, 2000. September 10, 2010. <http://www.blather.net/articles/amoore/brought-to-light2.html>

Kelly, Joe. "Golden Perfect." Illus. Doug Mahnke. *JLA.* New York: DC Comics. 2003.

Kennedy, Stetson. "StetsonKennedy.com." *Stetson Kennedy.* 1998–2010. September 18, 2010. <http://www.stetson kennedy.com/>

King, Daniel. "Chasing Zodiac." *San Francisco Chronicle.* October 5, 2005. July 8, 2010. <http://www.sfgate.com/cgibin/article.cgi?f=/c/a/2005/10/05/DDG7OF1T 4R71.DTL&type=movies>

King, Laurie R. *The Beekeeper's Apprentice.* New York: Picador, 1994.

_____. *The God of the Hive.* New York: Bantam Books, 2010.

_____. *The Language of Bees.* New York: Bantam Books, 2009.

_____. *A Monstrous Regiment of Women.* New York: Picador, 1995.

King, Stephen. *The Mist (Previously Published as a Novella in "Skeleton Crew").* New York: Signet, 2007.

Kirby, Jack. "The Fantastic Four Nos. 1–10." Co-writer. Stan Lee. *Marvel Masterworks: The Fantastic Four* Vol. 1. New York: Marvel Comics, 2003.

_____. "The Fantastic Four Nos. 11–20 and Annual No. 1." Co-writer. Stan Lee. *Marvel Masterworks: The Fantastic Four* Vol. 1. New York: Marvel Comics, 2003.

_____. "*The Fantastic Four* Nos. 41–50 & Annual No. 3." Illus. Jack Kirby. *Marvel Masterworks: The Fantastic Four* Vol. 5. New York: Marvel Comics, 2004.

_____. "*The Fantastic Four* Nos. 51–60 & Annual No. 4." Illus. Jack Kirby. *Marvel Masterworks: The Fantastic Four* Vol. 6. New York: Marvel Comics, 2004.

Kirby, Mark. "Megan Fox Was a Teenage Lesbian! Plus other confessions from the lips of Hollywood's new favorite temptress." *GQ.* September 2008. September 6, 2010. <http://www.gq.com/women/photos/200809/

actress-model-transformers-sexiest-woman-in-the-world>

Klock, Geoff. "The Bat and the Watchmen: Introducing the Revisionary Superhero Narrative." *How to Read Super Hero Comics and Why.* New York/London: Continuum, 2002. 25–77.

Knowles, Harry. "So Bryan Singer just called regarding Matthew Vaughn's X-MEN: FIRST CLASS.... I'm quite excited now." *Aint It Cool News.* August 20, 2010. September 10, 2010. <http://www.aintitcool.com/node/46217>

_____. "Why my friend, Roger Ebert is dead wrong about KICK ASS." *Ain't It Cool News.* April 15, 2010. June 25, 2010. <http://secure.aintitcool.com/node/44670>

Krugman, Paul. "Bailouts for Bunglers." *The New York Times.* February 1, 2009. July 24, 2010. <http://www.nytimes.com/2009/02/02/opinion/02krugman.html>

Kubicek, John. "Jack Bauer's Top 5 Human Rights Violations." *BuddyTV.* March 29, 2010. July 17, 2010. <http://www.buddytv.com/articles/24/jack-bauers-top-5-human-rights-35581.aspx>

Larson, Erik. "Force of One." *Savage Dragon* #145. Berkeley: Image Comics, 2009.

Larsson. Stieg. *The Girl with the Dragon Tattoo.* Trans. Reg Keeland. Massachusetts: Vintage, 2009.

The Last House on the Left. Writ.-Dir. Wes Craven. Perf. Sandra Cassel and Marc Sheffler. 1972. DVD. MGM, 2002.

"The Last of the Two-Dollar Bills." *Wonder Woman: The Complete First Season.* Prod. Douglas S. Cramer. Develop. Stanley Ralph Ross. Perf. Lynda Carter and Lyle Waggoner. 1975–1977. DVD. Warner Home Video, 2004.

Lattman, Peter. "Justice Scalia Hearts Jack Bauer." *Wall Street Journal Law Blog.* June 20, 2007. July 17, 2010. <http://blogs.wsj.com/law/2007/06/20/justice-scalia-hearts-jack-bauer/>

Laurence, Dan H. "'That Awful Country': Shaw in America." *Shaw: The Annual of Bernard Shaw Studies Vol. 5: Shaw Abroad.* Eds: Stanley Weintraub and Rodelle Weintraub. University Park: Pennsylvania State University Press, 1985.

Leab, Daniel J. *From Sambo to Superspade: The Black Experience in Motion Pictures.* New York: Houghton Mifflin Co, 1976.

Lee, Stan. *Origins of Marvel Comics.* New York: Simon and Schuster/Fireside Books, 1974.

_____. "*The Amazing Spider-Man* Nos. 1–10 and *Amazing Fantasy* No. 15." Illus. Steve Ditko and Jack Kirby. *Marvel Masterworks: The Amazing Spider-Man* Vol. 1. New York: Marvel Comics, 2003.

_____. "*The Amazing Spider-Man* Nos. 11–20 and Annual No. 2." Illus. Steve Ditko. *Marvel Masterworks: The Amazing Spider-Man* Vol. 2. New York: Marvel Comics, 2003.

_____. "*The Amazing Spider-Man* Nos. 21–30 and Annual No. 3." Illus. Steve Ditko. *Marvel Masterworks: The Amazing Spider-Man* Vol. 3. New York: Marvel Comics, 2003.

_____. "*The Amazing Spider-Man* Nos. 31–40." Illus. Steve Ditko and John Romita, Sr. *Marvel Masterworks: The Amazing Spider-Man* Vol. 4. New York: Marvel Comics, 2003.

_____. "*The Fantastic Four* Nos. 1–10." Illus. Jack Kirby. *Marvel Masterworks: The Fantastic Four* Vol. 1. New York: Marvel Comics, 2003.

_____. "*The Fantastic Four* Nos. 11–20 and Annual No. 1." Illus. Jack Kirby. *Marvel Masterworks: The Fantastic Four* Vol. 1. New York: Marvel Comics, 2003.

_____. "*The Fantastic Four* Nos. 41–50 & Annual No. 3." Illus. Jack Kirby. *Marvel Masterworks: The Fantastic Four* Vol. 5. New York: Marvel Comics, 2004.

_____. "*The Fantastic Four* Nos. 51–60 & Annual No. 4." Illus. Jack Kirby. *Marvel Masterworks: The Fantastic Four* Vol. 6. New York: Marvel Comics, 2004.

_____. "World's End." Illus. John Romita, Jr. *The Last Fantastic Four Story.* New York: Marvel Comics, 2007.

Le Guin, Ursula K. "Introduction." *The Left Hand of Darkness.* New York: Ace Books, 2003.

Lethem, Jonathan. "Art of Darkness." *The New York Times.* September 20, 2008. July 12, 2010. <http://www.nytimes.com/2008/09/21/opinion/21lethem.html>

_____. "The Return of the King, or, Identifying with Your Parents." *Give Our Regards to the Atomsmashers.* Ed: Sean Howe. New York: Pantheon Books, 2004.

"Let That Be Your Last Battlefield." *Star Trek.* Dir. Jud Taylor. Writ. Gene L. Coon and Oliver Crawford. Perf. William Shatner, Leonard Nimoy, and DeForest Kelly. 1969. DVD. *Star Trek: The Original Series—Season Three.* Paramount, 2007.

Leventhal, Dana. "Superwomen? The Bad-Ass Babes of Sin City—Or Are They?" *Bright Lights Film Journal.* Issue 49. August 2005.

Levitt, Steven D. and Stephen J. Dubner. *Freakonomics: A Rogue Economist Explores the Hidden Side of Everything.* New York: William Morrow, 2005. 55–88.

Lieberman, A.J. "The Letter." Illus. Al Barrionuevo. *Batman: Gotham Knights* #72. New York: DC Comics, 2006.

Lichtblau, Eric and Brian Stelter. *The New York Times.* "News Corp. Gives Republicans $1 Million." August 17, 2010. September 6, 2010. <http://www.nytimes.com/2010/08/18/us/politics/18donate.html>

Liebowitz, Michael, R. *The Chemistry of Love.* Boston: Little, Brown, & Co, 1983.

Limbaugh, Rush. *The Way Things Ought to Be.* New York: Pocket Books, 1992.

LoBasso, Randy. "Lehigh Valley Carnival Game Gives You Prizes for Pretending to Murder President Obama." *PhillyNow.* August 5, 2010. September 6, 2010. <http://blogs.philadelphiaweekly.com/phillynow/2010/08/05/lehigh-valley-carnival-game-gives-you-prizes-for-pretending-to-murder-president-obama/>

Loeb, Jeph. "Batman: The Long Halloween." Illus. Tim Sale. *Batman: The Long Halloween* #1–13, New York: DC Comics, 1996–1997.

_____. "Superman for All Seasons." Illus. Tim Sale. *Superman for All Seasons* No. 1–4. New York: DC Comics, 2002.

_____. "What Can One Icon Do?" Illus. Ariel Olivetti. *Superman* #179. New York: DC Comics, 2002.

Love Actually. Writ.-Dir. Richard Curits. Perf. Bill Nighy, Hugh Grant, Emma Thompson, and Laura Linney. Studio Canal/Working Title/DNA Films. 2003.

"Love Actually." *The Internet Movie Database.* August 19 2009. <http://www.imdb.com>

Lubrano, Alfred. *Limbo: Blue-Collar Roots, White-Collar Dreams.* New Jersey: John Wiley and Sons, 2004.

Lytle, Mark Hamilton. *America's Uncivil Wars: The Sixties Era from Elvis to the Fall of Richard Nixon.* New York: Oxford University Press, 2006. 336.

MacDonald, J. Fred. *Blacks and White TV: African Americans in Television Since 1948.* Massachusetts: Wadsworth Publishing, 1992.

MacGregor, Marilyn. "Dr. Watson's Mistress: A Story for Which the World Is Not Yet Prepared." *Ladies, Ladies:*

The Women in the Life of Sherlock Holmes. Ed: Patricia Guy and Katherine Karlson. Aventine Press, 2007. 96–100.

Madigan, Lee and Nancy Gamble. *The Second Rape: Society's Continued Betrayal of the Victim*. New York: Lexington Books, 1989.

Mahedy, William P. *Out of the Night: The Spiritual Journey of Vietnam Vets*. Cleveland, OH: StressPress, 1996. 41, 46–47.

Malcolm X, "A Homemade Education," from *The Autobiography of Malcolm X*. Reprinted in *The Conscious Reader*, 10th edition. Ed: Caroline Shrodes, Marc DiPaolo, etc. New York: Pearson, 2006. 806.

The Man Who Laughs. Dir. Paul Leni. Writ. J. Grubb Alexander and Walter Anthony. Perf. Conrad Veidt. Universal. 1928. DVD. Kino Video. 2003.

The Mark of Zorro. Dir. Rouben Mamoulian. Writ. John Taintor Foote. Perf. Tyrone Power, Basil Rathbone, and Linda Darnell. 20th Century–Fox. 1940. DVD. 20th Century–Fox. 2005.

Marston, William Moulton. "Wonder Woman." Illus. H.G. Peter. *DC Archive Editions: Wonder Woman Archives Vol. 1*. New York: DC Comics, 1998.

_____. "Wonder Woman." Illus. H.G. Peter. *DC Archive Editions: Wonder Woman Archives* Vol. 2. New York: DC Comics, 2000.

_____. "Wonder Woman." Illus. H.G. Peter. *DC Archive Editions: Wonder Woman Archives* Vol. 3. New York: DC Comics, 2002.

Masterpiece Theatre (a.k.a. *Masterpiece*). Television series. WGBH Boston, 1971–present.

The Matrix. Writ.-Dir. Andy Wachowski and Larry Wachowski. Perf. Keanu Reeves, Laurence Fishburne, Carrie-Ann Moss, and Hugo Weaving. 1999. DVD. Warner Home Video, 2007.

The Maxx. Dir. Ilya Skorupsky. Writ. Sam Kieth and Bill Messner-Loebs. Perf. Michael Haley, Glynnis Talken Campbell, and Barry Stigler. 1995. DVD. MTV, 2009.

Mayer, Jane. "Covert Operations: The billionaire brothers who are waging a war against Obama." *The New Yorker*. August 30, 2010. September 6, 2010. <http://www.newyorker.com/reporting/2010/08/30/100830fa_fact_mayer>

McCloud, Scott. "Balance of Power." Illus. Bret Blevins. *Superman: Adventures of the Man of Steel*. New York: DC Comics, 1998.

_____. *Understanding Comics*. New York: Harper Paperbacks, 1994.

McCoy, Alfred W. *A Question of Torture*. New York: Metropolitan Books/Henry Holt, 2006.

McDuffie, Dwayne. "Civil War: Fantastic Four." Illus. Mike McKone. *Fantastic Four*. New York: Marvel Comics, 2007.

McFatBack, Jemma. "BATMAN BEGINS rated R' Gary Oldman spills interesting beans...." *AintItCoolNews.com*. May 28, 2004. September 8, 2010. <http://www.aintitcool.com/display.cgi?id=17668>

McGlynn, Katla. "Stewart: FOX Failed to Mention Co-Owner Is One They Accuse of 'Terror Funding.'" *Huffington Post*. August 24, 2010. September 6, 2010. <http://www.huffingtonpost.com/2010/08/23/stewart-fox-prince-alwaleed_n_692234.html>

McGovern, Jimmy, writer. *Cracker: A New Terror*. Dir. Antonia Bird. Perf. Robbie Coltrane. ITV. 2006. DVD. Acorn Media, 2009.

McGruder, Aaron. *Fresh for '01 ... You Suckas! A "Boondocks" Collection*. Kansas City: Andrews McMeel Publishing, 2001. 90.

McKellen, Ian. "X-Men." *E-Post: Correspondence With Ian McKellen*. November 28, 2000. June 26, 2010. <http://www.mckellen.com/epost/xmen2000.htm>

McLuhan, Marshall. "'Superman' from *The Mechanical Bride*." *The Conscious Reader*, 1st edition. Ed: Caroline Shrodes, Harry Finestone, and Michael Shugrue. New York: Macmillan, 1974. 349–350.

Meacher, Michael. "This War on Terrorism Is Bogus: The 9/11 Attacks Gave the U.S. an Ideal Pretext to Use Force to Secure Its Global Domination." *Peace, War, and Terrorism*. Ed: Dennis Okerstrom. New York: Pearson, 2006. 39–45.

Meltzer, Brad. "*Identity Crisis* 1–7." Illus. Rags Morales. *Identity Crisis*. New York: DC Comics, 2005.

Men Who Stare at Goats. Dir. Grant Heslov. Writ. Peter Straughan. Perf. George Clooney, Ewan McGregor, Kevin Spacey, and Jeff Bridges. 2009. DVD. Anchor Bay, 2010.

Messner-Loebs, William. "Moments." Illus. Mike Deodato, Jr. *Legends of the DC Universe* #4. New York: DC Comics, 1998.

_____. *The Maxx*. Dir. Ilya Skorupsky. Co-Writ. Sam Kieth. Perf. Michael Haley, Glynnis Talken Campbell, and Barry Stigler. 1995. DVD. MTV, 2009.

Meth, Clifford. "Man and Superman: The Christopher Reeve Interview. *Starlog*, February 1987." *Comics Bulletin—The Interviews Archive*. 2004. <http://www.comicsbulletin.com/features/109777928398167.htm>

Meyer, Stephenie. *Twilight*. Massachusetts: Little, Brown, Books, 2008.

Michelinie, David. "Emperor Doom" Illus. Bob Hall. *The Avengers*. New York: Marvel Comics, 1987.

Mignola, Mike. *Hellboy: One for One*. Milwaukee: Dark Horse Comics, 2010.

Millar, Mark. "Civil War." Illus. Steve McNiven. *Civil War*. New York: Marvel Comics, 2008.

_____. "The Master of Doom." Illus. Bryan Hitch. *The Fantastic Four*. New York: Marvel Comics, 2010.

_____. "Red Son." Illus. Dave Johnson. *Superman*. New York: DC Comics, 2009.

_____. "Super Human." Illus. Bryan Hitch. *The Ultimates*. New York: Marvel Comics, 2002.

_____. *Wanted*. Illus. J.G. Jones. California: Image Comics, 2007.

_____. "World's Greatest." Illus. Bryan Hitch. *The Fantastic Four*. New York: Marvel Comics, 2009.

Miller, Frank. *Batman: The Dark Knight Returns*, New York: DC Comics, 1986.

_____. "Batman: Year One." Illus. David Mazzucchelli. *Batman: Year One*. New York: DC Comics, 1987.

Miller, John Jackson. "Iron Man: The Best Defense." Illus. Jorge Lucas. *Iron Man* Vol. 3 #73–78. New York: Marvel Comics, 2004.

Miller, Martin. "*24* and *Lost* get symposium on torture." *Seattle Times*. February 14, 2007. July 17, 2010. <http://seattletimes.nwsource.com/html/television/2003570697_tvtorture14.html>

Milligan, Peter. "The Golem of Gotham." Illus. Jim Aparo. *Detective Comics* #631 and #632. New York: DC Comics, 1991.

Mills, Nancy. "'Punisher' Star Says Frank Castle is No Superhero." *The Reading Eagle*. December 5, 2008. June 25, 2010. <http://readingeagle.com/article.aspx?id=116368>

Milton, John. *Paradise Lost (Norton Critical Editions)*. Ed: Gordon Teskey. New York: W. W. Norton, 2004.

Moeller, Christopher. *JLA: A League of One*. New York: DC Comics, 2000.

Moffat, Steven, writer. "The Beast Below." *Doctor Who*.

Perf. Matt Smith, Karen Gillian. 2010. DVD. *Doctor Who: The Complete Fifth Series.* BBC, 2010.

_____. "The Big Bang." *Doctor Who.* Perf. Matt Smith, Karen Gillian. 2010. DVD. *Doctor Who: The Complete Fifth Series.* BBC, 2010.

_____. "Blink." *Doctor Who.* Perf. David Tennant, Freeman Agyeman. 2007. DVD. *Doctor Who: The Complete Third Series.* BBC, 2007.

_____. "The Doctor Dances." *Doctor Who.* Perf. Christopher Eccleston, Billie Piper. 2005. DVD. *Doctor Who: The Complete First Series.* BBC Video, 2005.

_____. "The Empty Child." *Doctor Who.* Perf. Christopher Eccleston, Billie Piper. 2005. DVD. *Doctor Who: The Complete First Series.* BBC Video, 2005.

_____. "Flesh and Stone." *Doctor Who.* Perf. Matt Smith, Karen Gillian. 2010. DVD. *Doctor Who: The Complete Fifth Series.* BBC, 2010.

_____. "The Girl in the Fireplace." *Doctor Who.* Perf. David Tennant, Billie Piper. 2006. DVD. *Doctor Who: The Complete Second Series.* BBC, 2006.

_____. "New *Doctor Who* boss Stephen [sic] Moffat has said a Tory election victory would spell disaster for the BBC." *Daily Mirror.* March 32, 2010. June 25, 2010. <http://www.mirror.co.uk/news/top-stories/2010/03/23/tories-will-be-disaster-for-beeb-115875-22132113/>

_____. "Silence in the Library." *Doctor Who.* Perf. David Tennant, Catherine Tate. 2008. DVD. *Doctor Who: The Complete Fourth Series.* BBC, 2008.

Montopoli, Brian. "Target Boycott Movement Grows Following Donation to Support 'Antigay' Candidate." *CBSNews.com.* July 28, 2010. September 6, 2010. <http://www.cbsnews.com/8301-503544_162-20011983-503544.html>

Monty Python's Flying Circus. Television series. Dir. Ian MacNaughton. Writ.-Perf. Graham Chapman, John Cleese, Terry Gilliam, Eric Idle, Terry Jones, Michael Palin. BBC. 1969–1974.

Moore, Alan. "Batman: The Killing Joke." Illus. Brian Bolland. *DC Universe: The Stories of Alan Moore.* New York: DC Comics, 2006.

_____. "Superman: For the Man Who Has Everything." Illus. Dave Gibbons. *DC Universe: The Stories of Alan Moore.* New York: DC Comics, 2006.

_____. *Watchmen.* Illus. Dave Gibbons. New York: DC Comics, 2008.

_____. *Whatever Happened to the Man of Tomorrow?* Illus. Curt Swan. *DC Universe: The Stories of Alan Moore.* New York: DC Comics, 2006.

Moore, Michael. "Get Off Obama's Back ... second thoughts from Michael Moore." *MichaelMoore.com.* October 10th, 2009. July 12, 2010. <http://www.michaelmoore.com/words/mikes-letter/get-obamas-back-second-thoughts-michael-moore>

Morgan, David. "Bush: I've Made No Mistakes Since 9/11." *Reuters.* April 14, 2004. July 24, 2010. <http://www.commondreams.org/headlines04/0414-01.htm>

Morgan, Peter, writer. *The Deal.* Dir. Stephen Frears. Perf. Michael Sheen and David Morrissey. 2003. DVD. Miriam Collection, 2008.

_____. *The Queen.* Dir. Stephen Frears. Perf. Michael Sheen and Helen Mirren. 2006. DVD. Miramax, 2007.

_____. *The Special Relationship.* Dir. Richard Loncraine. Perf. Michael Sheen and Dennis Quaid. 2010. DVD. HBO, 2010.

Morning Edition. "Batman Goes After bin Laden." *NPR.* February 16, 2006.

Morris, Matt. "Batman and Friends: Aristotle and the Dark Knight's Inner Circle." *Superheroes and Philosophy: Truth, Justice, and the Socratic Way.* Ed: Tom and Matt Morris. Chicago and LaSalle Illinois: Open Court Publishing Company, 2005. 102–118.

Morrison, Grant. "All-Star Superman." Illus. Frank Quitely. *All-Star Superman 1.* 2007.

_____. "All-Star Superman." Illus. Frank Quitely. *All-Star Superman 2.* 2009.

_____. *Batman: The Return of Bruce Wayne.* Illus. various artists. DC Comics, 2010.

_____. "Early Warning" and "How I Learned to Love the Bomb." Illus. David Lloyd. *John Constantine: Hellblazer—Rare Cuts.* New York: Vertigo/DC Comics, 2005.

_____. "1234." Illus. Jae Lee. *Marvel Knights: Fantastic Four.* New York: Marvel Comics, 2005.

Mr. Freedom. Writ.-Dir. William Klein. Perf. John Abbey, Delphine Seyrig, Donald Pleasance. 1969. DVD. *The Delirious Fictions of William Klien.* Eclipse: Criterion Collection, 2008.

Murder by Decree. Dir. Bob Clark. Writ. John Hopkins. Perf. Christopher Plummer, James Mason, Donald Sutherland, and Genevieve Bujold. 1978. DVD. Anchor Bay Entertainment, 2003.

Nation, Terry, writer. "The Chase." *Doctor Who.* Perf. William Hartnell, Jacqueline Hill, William Russell. 1965. VHS. *Doctor Who: The Daleks Limited Edition Boxed Set—"The Chase" and "Remembrance of the Daleks."* BBC Video, 2001.

_____. "The Daleks." *Doctor Who.* Perf. William Hartnell, Jacqueline Hill, William Russell. 1964. DVD. *Doctor Who: The Beginning Collection.* BBC Video, 2006.

Ness, Eliot Ness and Oscar Fraley. *The Untouchables: The Real Story.* New York: Pocket Books, 1957, 1987.

The New Avengers. Dir. Ray Austin, Sidney Hayers, et al. Writ. Brian Clemens, Dennis Sponer, et al. Perf. Patrick Macnee, Joanna Lumley, and Gareth Hunt. 1976–1977. DVD. *The New Avengers '76* and *The New Avengers '77.* A&E Home Entertainment, 2003 and 2004.

Newman, Kim. *Doctor Who: Time and Relative.* Prestatyn, Denbighshire: Telos Publishing, 2002.

The New Original Wonder Woman. Prod. Douglas S. Cramer. Develop. Stanley Ralph Ross. Perf. Lynda Carter and Lyle Waggoner. 1975. DVD. *Wonder Woman: The Complete First Season.* WarnerHome Video, 2004.

New York: State Coalition Against Sexual Assault. "Penal Codes: A Summary of New York State Penal Code 130. Sex Offenses as of 2008." New York. 2007. June 11, 2010. <http://nyscasa.org/understanding/penalcodes>

Night of the Living Dead. Dir. George A. Romero. Writ. John A. Russo and George A. Romero. Perf. Duane Jones and Judith O'Dea. 1968. DVD. Elite Entertainment, 2002.

Nosferatu, eine Symphonie des Grauens. Dir. F. W. Murnau. Writ. Bram Stoker and Henrik Galeen. Perf. Max Shrek and Greta Schröder. Film Arts Guild, 1922. DVD. Kino Video, 2007.

Novik, Naomi. *In His Majesty's Service: Three Novels of Temeraire.* New York: Del Rey, 2009.

Obama, Barack. "A Just and Lasting Peace." *The Conscious Reader, 12th edition.* Ed: Caroline Shrodes, Marc DiPaolo, et al. New York: Pearson, 2010.

_____. "Transcript: Barack Obama's Speech on Race—A More Perfect Union." NPR. March 18, 2008. September 6, 2010. <http://www.npr.org/templates/story/story.php?storyId=88478467>

"Obama Disappointed Cabinet Failed to Understand His Reference to 'Savage Sword of Conan' #24." *The Onion.* Issue 45-05. Jaunuary 27, 2009. September 12, 2010. <http://www.theonion.com/articles/obama-disappointed-cabinet-failed-to-understand-hi,2648/>

O'Neil, Dennis. *Batman: Tales of the Demon.* Illus. Neal Adams et al. New York: DC Comics, 1991.

_____. "Beware My Power." Illus. Neal Adams. *Green Lantern: The Greatest Stories Ever Told.* Reprinted from *Green Lantern* #87. 1972. New York: DC Comics, 2006.

_____. "Venom." Illus. Trevor Von Eeden. *Batman.* New York: DC Comics, 1991.

Ord, Holly. "Sarah Palin is not a feminist." *Menstrual Poetry.com.* August 30, 2008. September 7, 2010. <http://menstrualpoetry.com/sarah-palin-feminist>

O'Reilly, Bill. *The O'Reilly Factor: The Good, the Bad, and the Completely Ridiculous in American Life.* New York: Broadway Books, 2000.

Oreskes, Naomi and Erik M. Conway. *Merchants of Doubt: How a Handful of Scientists Obscured the Truth on Issues from Tobacco Smoke to Global Warming.* New York: Bloomsbury Press, 2010.

Orwell, George. "Politics and the English Language." *The Conscious Reader, 12th edition.* Ed: Caroline Shrodes, Marc DiPaolo, et al. New York: Pearson, 2010.

Ostrander, John. "The Final Thrust." Illus. Gary Frank. *Bullets and Bracelets.* New York: Marvel Comics, 1996.

Outfoxed: Rupert Murdoch's War on Journalism. Dir. Robert Greenwald. DVD. The Disinformation Company, 2004.

Palmieri, Marco Palmieri. "Best of All." *The Further Adventures of the Joker. Ed: Martin H. Greenberg.* New York/London: Bantam Books, 1990.

Palmiotti, Jimmy and Justin Gray. "Bloody Valentine." Illus. Paul Gulacy. *The Punisher: Very Special Holidays.* New York: Marvel Publishing, Inc, 2006.

_____. "Red X-Mas." Illus. Mark Texeira. *The Punisher: Very Special Holidays.* New York: Marvel Publishing, Inc, 2006.

Paprika. Dir. Satoshi Kon. Writ. Seishi Minakami and Satoshi Kon. Perf. Megumi Hayashibara. 2006. DVD. Sony, 2007.

Peatling, G.K. "Ordinary Relationships: 'Pro-Americans,' 'Anti-Americanism,' and 'Left-Wing Continentalism' in British Cinema and Culture." *The Journal of Popular Culture* Vol. 42, Issue 6. New Jersey: Wiley Periodicals, Inc, 2009. 1073–1092.

Peele, Thomas, editor. *Queer Popular Culture: Literature, Media, Film, and Television.* New York: Palgrave Macmillan, 2007.

Perez, George, writer and illustrator. "Beauty and the Beasts." Co-writ. Len Wein. *Wonder Woman Vol. 3.* New York: DC Comics, 2005.

_____. "Challenge of the Gods." Co-writ. Len Wein. *Wonder Woman Vol. 2.* New York: DC Comics, 2004.

_____. "Destiny Calling." *Wonder Woman Vol. 4.* New York: DC Comics, 2006.

_____. "Gods and Mortals." Co-writ. Len Wein. *Wonder Woman Vol. 1.* New York: DC Comics, 2004.

Pereira, KL. "Female Bonding." *Bitch: Feminist Response to Pop Culture, Issue 33, Fall 2006.* Oakland, CA: B-Word Worldwide, 2006.

Perlstein, Rick. *Nixonland: The Rise of a President and the Fracturing of America.* New York: Scribner, 2008.

Peterson, Scott. "'Smarter' Bombs Still Hit Civilians: In Every War Since Iraq, the U.S. Used More 'Smart' Bombs, So Why Do Civilian Casualty Rates Keep Rising?" Monitor. Oct. 22, 2002. *Peace, War, and Terrorism.* Ed: Dennis Okerstrom. New York: Pearson, 2006. 179–183.

Pfeifer, Will. "Amazons Attack." Illus. Pete Woods. *Wonder Woman: Amazons Attack.* New York: DC Comics, 2009.

Picoult, Jodi. "Love and Murder." Illus. Terry Dodson, Rachel Dodson, and Drew Johnson. *Wonder Woman.* New York: DC Comics, 2009.

Piercy, Rohase. *My Dearest Holmes.* BookSurge Publishing, 2007.

Pink Floyd. "the post war dream." *the final cut.* CD. Capitol, 2004.

Pistone, Joseph D. and Richard Woodley. *Donnie Brasco.* New York: Penguin Books. 1987. 407–408.

Plazza, Jo. "New Wonder Woman Loses Patriotic Costume in Favor of 'Globalized' Duds." *FoxNews.com.* July 01, 2010. July 8, 2010. <http://www.foxnews.com/entertainment/2010/07/01/new-wonder-woman-loses-patriotic-costume/>

"Plot Details Revealed for X Men First Class." *The Film Stage.* June 21, 2010. September 10, 2010. <http://thefilmstage.com/>

Postrel, Virginia. "Superhero Worship." *The Atlantic.* Volume 298. Number 3. October 2006. 140–144.

Powell, Colin. "The Good Soldier." *The Conscious Reader, 12th edition.* Ed: Caroline Shrodes, Marc DiPaolo, et al. New York: Pearson, 2010.

Powell, Eric. "Vol. 1: Nothin' But Misery." *The Goon.* Oregon: Dark Horse, 2003.

Powell, Kerry. *Acting Wilde: Victorian Sexuality, Theatre, and Oscar Wilde.* Cambridge: Cambridge University Press, 2009.

Powers, Mark. "One Hundred Days." Illus. Chris Lie, Junaidi and Faisal *Drafted.* Chicago: Devil's Due Publishing, 2009.

Preddle, Jon. *Timelink: The Unofficial and Unauthorised Guide to the Continuity of Doctor Who.* Prestatyn, Denbighshire: Telos Publishing, 2006.

Priest, Christopher. "The 18th Letter." Illus. Karl Waller. *Legends of the DC Universe* #30–32. New York: DC Comics, 2000.

Prittie, Terrence. *Germans Against Hitler.* Boston/Toronto: Little, Brown, and Company/Atlantic Monthly Press Book, 1964.

"Project Twilight." *Doctor Who.* Dir. Gary Russell. Writ. Cavan Scott and Mark Wright.

Perf. Colin Baker, Maggie Stables. CD. Big Finish Productions, 2001.

Pulido, Brian. *Lady Death: The Reckoning.* Chaos! Comics, 1997.

The Punisher. Dir. Mark Goldblatt. Writ. Boaz Yakin. Perf. Dolph Lundgren, Louis Gossett, Jr., and Jeroen Krabbe. 1989. Live/Artisan DVD: 1999.

The Punisher. Dir. Jonathan Hensleigh. Writ. Jonathan Hensleigh and Michael France.

Perf. Thomas Jane and John Travolta. Lions Gate Films. 2004. *Extended Edition* DVD, Lions Gate, 2006.

The Punisher: War Zone. Dir. Lexi Alexander. Wri. Nick Santora, Art Marcum, and Matt Holloway. Perf. Ray Stevenson, Julie Benz, and Colin Salmon. Lions Gate, 2008.

"The Punisher." Wikipedia entry. June 25, 2010. <http://en.wikipedia.org>

Quayle, Dan. "Restoring Basic Values." *The Conscious Reader, 12th edition.* Ed: Caroline Shrodes, Marc DiPaolo, et al. New York: Pearson, 2010.

Joe Quesada, writ. and illus. "One Moment in Time."

Co-illus. Paolo Rivera and Paul Ryan. Co-writ. Jim Shooter and David Michelinie. *The Amazing Spider-Man.* New York: Marvel Comics, 2010.
Raiders of the Lost Ark. Dir. Steven Spielberg. Writ. Lawrence Kasdan. Perf. Harrison Ford and Karen Allen. 1981. DVD. *Indiana Jones—The Complete Adventure Collection (Raiders of the Lost Ark/Temple of Doom/Last Crusade/Kingdom of the Crystal Skull).* Paramount, 2008.
Rand, Ayn. *The Fountainhead.* New York: Signet, 1952.
Raynor, Helen, writer. "Daleks in Manhattan." *Doctor Who.* Perf. David Tennant, Freeman Agyeman, 2007. DVD. *Doctor Who: The Complete Third Series.* BBC, 2007.
"Religious Affiliation of Comic Book Character Frank Castle, The Punisher." <http://www.adherents.com/lit/comics/Punisher.html>
Resident Evil. Video Game. Osaka: Capcom, 1996.
"The Return of Wonder Woman." *Wonder Woman: The Complete Second Season.* Perf. Lynda Carter and Lyle Waggoner. 1977–1978. DVD. Warner Home Video, 2005.
"Revolutionizing a Classic: From Comic Book to Television — the Evolution of Wonder Woman from Page to Screen." *Wonder Woman: The Complete Second Season.* DVD Special feature. Warner Home Video, 2005.
Ricci, Michael. "Forbidden Gay Frontier: Where Star Trek Hasn't Boldly Gone." *AfterElton.com.* April 20, 2006. September 8, 2010. <http://www.afterelton.com/TV/2006/4/startrek.html>
Rice, Condoleezza. "A Balance of Power That Favors Freedom." *Peace, War, and Terrorism.* Ed: Dennis Okerstrom. New York: Pearson, 2006. 52–59.
Rich, Frank. "The Banality of Bush White House Evil." *The New York Times.* April 25, 2009. July 17, 2010.
_____. "How Fox Betrayed Petraeus." *The New York Times.* August 21, 2010. September 6, 2010. <http://www.nytimes.com/2010/08/22/opinion/22rich.html>
Robbins, Trina. *The Great Women Super Heroes.* Massachusetts: Kitchen Sink Press. 1996.
_____. "The Once and Future Story." Illus. Colleen Doran. *Wonder Woman.* New York: DC Comics, 1998.
Robert Rodriguez, director. *Machete.* Co-Dir. Ethan Maniquis. Writ. Robert Rodriguez. Perf. Danny Trejo, Robert DeNiro, Jessica Alba, and Michelle Rodriguez. 20th Century–Fox. 2010.
_____. *Sin City.* Writ. and Co-Dir. Frank Miller. Perf. Bruce Willis, Jessica Alba, Mickey Rourke, and Clive Owen. Dimension Films, 2005.
Roberts, Paul Craig. "Warmonger Wins Peace Prize." *CounterPunch.* October 9–11, 2009. June 20, 2010. <http://www.counterpunch.org/roberts10092009.html>
Rocky IV. Writ.-Dir. Sylvester Stallone. Perf. Sylvester Stallone, Talia Shire, Dolph Lundgren. 1985. DVD. MGM, 2005.
Rogers, Vaneta, "FATHOM Helps Clean Up the Gulf ... For Real." *Newsarama.com.* August 4, 2010. September 4, 2010.<http://www.newsarama.com/comics/fathom-gulf-spill-issue-100804.html>
_____. "JMS Talks WONDER WOMAN's New Look and New Direction." *Newsarama.* June 29 2010. June 30, 2010. <http://www.newsarama.com/comics/jms-talks-wonder-woman-100629.html>
Roman Polanski: Wanted and Desired. Dir. Marina Zenovich. DVD. THINKfilm, 2008.
Rose, David. "Tortured Reasoning." *Vanity Fair.* December 16, 2008. July 17, 2010. <http://www.vanityfair.com/magazine/2008/12/torture200812>
Rucka, Greg. *Batman: No Man's Land.* New York: Pocket Star, 2001.
_____. "Down to Earth." Illus. Drew Johnson. *Wonder Woman.* New York: DC Comics, 2004.
_____. "The OMAC Project." Illus. Jesus Saiz. *The OMAC Project.* New York: DC Comics, 2005.
_____. "The Hiketeia." Illus. J.G. Jones. *Wonder Woman.* New York: DC Comics, 2002.
Rushdie, Salmon. "'Imagine There's No Heaven': A Letter to the Six Billionth World Citizen." *The Portable Atheist: Essential Reading for the Nonbeliever.* Ed: Christopher Hitchens. Pennsylvania: Da Capo Press, 2007. 380–384.
Russell, Gary, moderator. "The Daleks: DVD audio commentary." Perf. Verity Lambert, Carole Ann Ford, William Russell, etc. *Doctor Who: The Beginning Collection.* BBC Video, 2006.
Russo, Vito. *The Celluloid Closet: Homosexuality in the Movies.* New York: Harper & Row, 1987.
Ryall, Chris and Scott Tipton. The Fantastic Four as a Family: The Strongest Bond of All." *Superheroes and Philosophy: Truth, Justice, and the Socratic Way.* Ed: Tom and Matt Morris. Chicago and LaSalle Illinois: Open Court Publishing Co, 2005. 29–41.
Sachedina, Abdulaziz. "From Defensive to Offensive Warfare: The Use and Abuse of Jihad in the Muslim World." *Religion, Law, and Force.* Transnational Publishers, 2002.
Said, Edward. "Homage to Joe Sacco." Joe Sacco. *Palestine.* Washington: Fantagraphics Books, 2005.
Sands, Philippe. *Torture Team: Rumsfeld's Memo and the Betrayal of American Values.* New York: Palgrave Macmillan, 2008.
Saturday Night Live. Creator: Lorne Michaels. NBC, 1975–present.
Scherer, Michael. "Has McCain Flip-Flopped on Torture?" *Time.* April 10, 2008. July 17, 2010. <http://www.time.com/time/politics/article/0,8599,1729891,00.html>
Schlesinger, Jr., Arthur. "The Immorality of Preemptive War." *Peace, War, and Terrorism.* Ed: Dennis Okerstrom. New York: Pearson, 2006. 76–78.
Schulman, Bruce J. *The Seventies: A Great Shift in American Culture, Society, and Politics.* New York: Free Press, 2001.
Schuster, Marc and Tom Powers. *The Greatest Show in the Galaxy: The Discerning Fan's Guide to* Doctor Who. Jefferson, NC: McFarland, 2007.
Seeton, Req and Dayna Van Buskirk. "Screenwriting Punishment with Michael France." *UGO Screenwriter's Voice.* April 06, 2004. June 25, 2010. <http://screenwriting.ugo.com/interviews/michaelfrance_interview.php>
Shadid, Anthony. "Legacy of the Prophet." Westview Presss, Perseus Books, L.L.C., 2002. *The Conscious Reader* 10th edition. Ed: Caroline Shrodes, Marc DiPaolo, et al. Pearson, 2006.
Shaft. Dir. John Singleton. Writ. Richard Price, John Singleton and Shane Salerno. Perf. Samuel L. Jackson, Christian Bale, Vanessa Williams. DVD. Paramount, 2000.
Shaft. Dir. Gordon Parks. Writ. Ernest Tidyman and John D.F. Black. Perf. Richard Roundtree. MGM, 1971. DVD. Warner Home Video, 2000.
Sharrett, Christopher. "The Problem of Saw: 'Torture Porn' and the Conservatism of Contemporary Horror Films." *Cineaste.* Vol. XXXV, No. 1. New York: *Cineaste* Publishers, 2009. 32–37.
Shawn, Wallace. "Israel Attacks Gaza." *Essays.* Chicago: Haymarket Books, 2009. 93–96.

Shearman, Robert, writer. "Dalek." *Doctor Who*. Perf. Christopher Eccleston, Billie Piper. 2005. DVD. *Doctor Who: The Complete First Series*. BBC Video, 2005.

Sherlock Holmes. Dir. Guy Ritchie. Writ. Lionel Wigram and Michael Robert Johnson. Perf. Robert Downey, Jr., Jude Law, Rachel McAdams. Warner Home Video, 2009.

Sherlock Holmes and the Case of the Silk Stocking. Dir. Simon Cellan Jones. Writ. Allan Cubitt. Perf. Rupert Everett. Warner Home Video, 2005.

Sherman, Mark. "High court hears ex–Enron CEO Skilling's appeal." *Yahoo! Finance*. March 1, 2010. July 24, 2010. <http://finance.yahoo.com/news/High-court-hears-exEnron-CEO-apf-692969977.html?x=0&sec=topStories&pos=5&asset=&ccode=>

Shooter, Jim. "Marvel Superheroes: Secret Wars." Illus. Mike Zeck and Bob Layton. *Secret Wars*. New York: Marvel Comics Group, 1999.

_____. "Superman and Spider-Man." Illus. John Buscema. *The Marvel/DC Collection–Crossover Classics, Vol. 1*. New York: DC Comics and Marvel Comics, 1997.

Siegel, Jerry and Joe Shuster. *DC Archive Editions: Superman Archives* Vol. 1. New York: DC Comics, 2005.

_____. *DC Archive Editions: Superman Action Comics Archives* Vol. 1. New York: DC Comics, 1998.

_____. "What If Superman Ended the War?" *Look Magazine*, Feb. 1940. *Superman: The Greatest Stories Ever Told*. Ed: Anton Kawasaki. New York: DC Comics, 2004.

Simone, Gail. "Birds of Paradise." Illus. Aaron Lopresti. *Wonder Woman* (vol. 3 no. 34). New York: DC Comics, 2009.

_____. "The Hypothetical Woman." Illus. Jose Luis Garcia-Lopez. *Justice League of America*. New York: DC Comics, 2008.

_____. "A Murder of Crows." Illus. Aaron Lopresti. *Wonder Woman* (vol. 3 nos. 40–41). New York: DC Comics, 2010.

_____. "Rise of the Olympian." Illus. Aaron Lopresti. *Wonder Woman* (vol. 3 no. 33). New York: DC Comics, 2009.

_____. "Sensei and Student." Illus. Ed Benes. *Birds of Prey*. New York: DC Comics, 2004.

_____. "A Star in the Heavens." Illus. Bernard Chang. *Wonder Woman* (vol. 3 nos. 24–25). New York: DC Comics, 2008.

_____. "Strange Attractions." Illus. John Byrne. *Superman*. New York: DC Comics, 2006.

_____. "Warkiller." Illus. Aaron Lopresti. *Wonder Woman* (vol. 3 no. 36). New York: DC Comics, 2009.

_____. "Women in Refrigerators." March 1999. June 25, 2010 <http://www.unheardtaunts.com/wir/>

Simonson, Walter. "The New Fantastic Four." Illus. Arthur Adams. *Fantastic Four* #347–349. 1990–1991.

Singh, Anita. "Search for New Doctor Who's Partner Begins." *Daily Telegraph*. Jan. 5, 2009. August 20, 2009. <http://www.telegraph.co.uk/culture/tvandradio/4108697/Search-for-new-Doctor-Whos-partner-begins.html>

_____. "Television Is Only Made for Children, Moans Stephen Fry." June 16, 2010. July 8, 2010. <http://www.telegraph.co.uk/culture/tvandradio/7831560/Television-is-only-made-for-children-moans-Stephen-Fry.html>

Skal, David J. *The Monster Show: A Cultural History of Horror*. New York: Faber and Faber, Inc, 1993.

Skoble, Aeon J. "Superhero Revisionism in *Watchmen* and *The Dark Knight Returns*." *Superheroes and Philosophy: Truth, Justice, and the Socratic Way*. Ed: Tom and Matt Morris. Chicago and LaSalle Illinois: Open Court Publishing Co, 2005. 29–41.

Sloman, Robert, writer. "The Green Death." *Doctor Who*. Perf. Jon Pertwee, Katy Manning. 1973. BBC Video, 2005.

Smiljani, Uros. "Letter to the Editor." *The Amazing Spider-Man* #592. New York: Marvel Comics, 2009.

South, James B. "Barbara Gordon and Moral Perfectionism." *Superheroes and Philosophy: Truth, Justice, and the Socratic Way*. Ed: Tom and Matt Morris. Chicago and LaSalle Illinois: Open Court Publishing Co, 2005. 29–41.

Smallville. Dir. James Marshall, Greg Beeman, et al. Writ. Alfred Gough, Miles Millar, et al. Perf. Tom Welling, Allison Mack, Kristin Kreuk, Michael Rosenbaum, Erica Durance. Television Series. USA: The WB & The CW, 2001–2010.

Smith, Kevin. *Stan Lee's Mutants, Monsters, and Marvels*. DVD. Sony Pictures/Creative Light, 2002.

Smith, Matthew J. "The Tyranny of the Melting Pot Metaphor: Wonder Woman as Americanized Immigrant." *Comics and Ideology. Popular Culture/Everyday Life Series, Vol. 2*. Ed: Matthew P. McAllister, Edward H. Sewell, Jr., and Ian Gordon. New York: Peter Lang, 2001.

Sontag, Susan. "Notes on 'Camp.'" *Against Interpretation and Other Essays*. New York: Picador, 1961,1990.

Spider-Man. Dir. Sam Raimi. Writ. Alvin Sargent and David Koepp. Perf. Tobey Maguire, Kirsten Dunst, James Franco, Willem Dafoe. 2002. DVD. *Spider-Man—The Motion Picture Trilogy*. Sony, 2007.

Spider-Man 2. Dir. Sam Raimi. Writ. Alvin Sargent, Alfred Gough, Miles Millar and Michael Chabon. Perf. Tobey Maguire, Kirsten Dunst, James Franco, Alfred Molina. 2004. DVD. *Spider-Man—The Motion Picture Trilogy*. Sony, 2007.

Spider-Man 3. Dir. Sam Raimi. Writ. Sam Raimi, Ivan Raimi, and Alvin Sargent. Perf. Tobey Maguire, Kirsten Dunst, James Franco, Thomas Hayden Church, Topher Grace. 2007. DVD. *Spider-Man—The Motion Picture Trilogy*. Sony, 2007.

Stallone, Sylvester. "Sly bleeds some more answers in anticipation of RAMBO — Day 2." *AintItCoolNews.com*. January 15, 2008. September 4, 2010. <http://www.aintitcool.com/node/35284?q=node/35286>

Starlin, Jim. "The Cult." Illus. Bernie Wrightson. *Batman*. New York: DC Comics, 1988.

_____. "A Death in the Family." Illus. Jim Aparo. *Batman*. DC Comics, 1989.

_____. "*Infinity Crusade* Vol. 1. Illus. Ron Lim, Tom Raney, Angel Medina, and Tom Grindberg. *Infinity Crusade*. New York: Marvel Comics, 2008.

_____. "The Big Change." Illus. Berni Wrightson. *The Incredible Hulk and the Thing*. New York: Marvel Comics, 1987.

Starobin, Paul. "The Angry American." *The Atlantic*, January/Febuary 2004.

Star Trek. Dir. J.J. Abrams. Writ. Alex Kurtzman and Roberto Orci. Perf. Chris Pine, Zachary Quinto, Karl Urban, and Zoe Saldana. Paramount, 2009.

Star Trek: The Next Generation. Dir. Cliff Bole et al. Writ. Ronald D. Moore, René Echevarria, Michael Piller et al. Perfs. Patrick Stewart, Brent Spiner, and Jonathan Frakes. 1987–1994. DVD. *Star Trek: The Next Generation—Complete Series*. Paramount, 2007.

Star Trek II: The Wrath of Khan. Writ.-Dir. Nicholas Meyer. Co-Writ. Jack B. Sowards. Perf. William Shatner, Leonard Nimoy, Ricardo Montalban, and DeForest Kelly. 1982. DVD. *Star Trek Original Motion Picture Collection*. Paramount, 2009.

Star Trek IV: The Voyage Home. Dir. Leonard Nimoy. Writ. Steve Meerson, Peter Krikes, Harve Bennett, and Nicholas Meyer. Perf. William Shatner, Leonard Nimoy, and DeForest Kelly. 1986. DVD. *Star Trek Original Motion Picture Collection*. Paramount, 2009.

Star Trek VI: The Undiscovered Country. Dir. Nicholas Meyer. Writ. Nicholas Meyer, Denny Martin Flinn, and Leonard Nimoy. Perf. William Shatner, Leonard Nimoy, and DeForest Kelly. 1991. DVD. *Star Trek Original Motion Picture Collection*. Paramount, 2009.

Star Wars Episode II: Attack of the Clones. Dir. George Lucas. Writ. George Lucas and Jonathan Hales. Perf. Ewan McGregor, Natalie Portman, Hayden Christensen, Christopher Lee, and Samuel L. Jackson. 2002. DVD. 20th Century–Fox, 2005.

Steele, Bruce C. "The Knight's Crusade." *The Advocate*. December 11, 2001. pp. 36–38, 40–45.

Steinem, Gloria. "Introduction." *Wonder Woman: Featuring Over Five Decades of Great Covers*. New York: Abbeville Press, 1995. *The Conscious Reader, 12th edition*. Ed: Caroline Shrodes, Marc DiPaolo, et al. New York: Pearson, 2010.

Stephenson, Jill. "The Wary Response of Women." *The Nazi Revolution*. 3rd edition. Ed: Allan Mitchell. USA/ Canada: D.C. Heath and Company, 1990. 167–175.

Stern, Roger. "Double Lives." Illus. Steve Rude. *The Incredible Hulk vs. Superman*. New York: Marvel Comics/ DC Comics, 1999.

_____. *The Death and Life of Superman*. New York: Spectra, 1994.

_____. "Triumph and Torment." Illus. Mike Mignola. *Doctor Strange and Doctor Doom*. New York: Marvel Comics, 1989.

Stewart, Jon and the Writers of *The Daily Show*. *The Daily Show with Jon Stewart Presents America (The Book) Teacher's Edition: A Citizen's Guide to Democracy Inaction*. New York: Grand Central Publishing, 2006. 79.

Stober, Spencer S. and Donna Yarri. *God, Science, and Designer Genes: An Exploration of Emerging Genetic Technologies*. Denver, Santa Barbara, Oxford: Praeger, 2009.

Stoklasa, Mike. "Mr. Plinkett Reviews J.J. Abrams' Star Trek (2009)." *Red Letter Media*. September 1, 2010. September 8, 2010. <http://www.redlettermedia.com/ index.html>

Storey, John. *Cultural Studies and the Study of Popular Culture* (2nd Edition). Athens: The University of Georgia Press, 1996.

Stout, Rex. "Watson Was a Woman." *The Saturday Review of Literature*, Vol. 23 No. 19, March, 1941.

Straczynski, J. Michael. "The Amazing Spider-Man." Illus. John Romita, Jr. *The Amazing Spider-Man: Ultimate Collection 1*. New York: Marvel Comics, 2009.

_____. "The Amazing Spider-Man." Illus. John Romita, Jr. *The Amazing Spider-Man: Ultimate Collection 2*. New York: Marvel Comics, 2009.

_____. *Babylon 5: The Complete Seasons 1–5*. Dir. Richard Compton *et al*. Perf. Bruce Boxleitner, Andreas Katsulas, and Peter Jurasik. DVD. Warner Home Video, 2009.

_____. *The Changeling*. Dir. Clint Eastwood. Perf. Angelina Jolie and John Malkovitch. DVD. Warner Home Video, 2009.

_____. "Civil War: Amazing Spider-Man." Illus. Ron Garney. *Amazing Spider-Man*. New York: Marvel Comics, 2007.

_____. "Civil War: Fantastic Four." Illus. Mike McKone. *Fantastic Four*. New York: Marvel Comics, 2007.

_____. "One More Day." Illus. and Co-writ. Joe Quesada. New York: Marvel Comics, 2008.

_____. "Origin of the Sorceress." *He-Man and the Masters of the Universe*. Season 2, Episode 8. 1985. DVD. *The Best of He-Man and the Masters of the Universe*. Bci/ Eclipse, 2005.

_____. "Sins Past." Illus. Mike Deodato, Jr. *The Amazing Spider-Man* Vol. 8. New York: Marvel Comics, 2005.

_____. "Skin Deep." Illus. Mike Deodato, Jr. *The Amazing Spider-Man* Vol. 9. New York: Marvel Comics, 2005.

Suellentrop, Chris. "How an Obscure Collection of Japanese Action Figures Changed the Way We Play." *Wired*. June 28, 2007. September 6, 2010. <http://www.wired.com/entertainment/hollywood/magazine/15-07/trans_toy>

_____. "Sex and the Single Superhero." *Slate*. June 4, 2002. September 8, 2010. <http://www.slate.com/id/ 2066513/>

Sullivan, Andrew. "One tortured lie: that's all it took for war. Bush needed 'evidence' and used techniques designed to produce lies to get it." The Sunday Times. April 26, 2009. <http://www.timesonline.co.uk/tol/com ment/columnists/andrew_sullivan/article6168270.ece>

Superman. Dir. Dave Fleischer. Writ. Seymour Kneitel and Izzy Sparber. Perf. Bud Collyer and Joan Alexander. 1941. DVD. *Superman Ultimate Collector's Edition*. Warner Home Video, 2006.

Superman. (a.k.a *Superman: The Motion Picture*.) Dir. Richard Donner. Writ. Mario Puzo, David Newman, Leslie Newman, Robert Benton, and Tom Mankiewicz. Perf. Christopher Reeve, Margot Kidder, Gene Hackman, Marlon Brando, and Glenn Ford. 1978. DVD. *Superman Ultimate Collector's Edition*. Warner Home Video, 2006.

Superman II. Dir. Richard Donner and Richard Lester. Writ. Mario Puzo, David Newman, Leslie Newman, Robert Benton, and Tom Mankiewicz. Perf. Christopher Reeve, Margot Kidder, Terrence Stamp, and Gene Hackman. 1980. DVD. *Superman Ultimate Collector's Edition*. Warner Home Video, 2006.

Superman IV: The Quest for Peace. Dir. Sidney J. Furie. Writ. Christopher Reeve, Lawrence Konner, and Mark Rosenthal. Perf. Christopher Reeve, Margot Kidder, and Gene Hackman. 1987. DVD. *Superman Ultimate Collector's Edition*. Warner Home Video, 2006.

Superman: The 1948 & 1950 Theatrical Serials Collection. Dir. Spencer Gordon Bennet and Thomas Carr. Writ. Arthur Hoerl, David Mathews, and George H. Plympton. Perf. Kirk Alyn, Noel Neill, Lyle Talbot, and Tommy Bond. 1948, 1950. DVD. Warner Home Video, 2006.

Superman: Electric Earthquake. Dir. Dave Fleischer. Writ. Seymour Kneitel and Izzy Sparber. Perf. Bud Collyer and Joan Alexander. 1942. DVD. *Superman Ultimate Collector's Edition*. Warner Home Video, 2006.

Superman: The Mechanical Monsters. Dir. Dave Fleischer. Writ. Seymour Kneitel and Izzy Sparber. Perf. Bud Collyer and Joan Alexander. 1941. DVD. *Superman Ultimate Collector's Edition*. Warner Home Video, 2006.

Superman Returns. Dir. Bryan Singer. Writ. Michael Dougherty and Dan Harris. Perf.Brandon Routh, Kate Bosworth, Kevin Spacey, and Parker Posey. 2006. DVD. *Superman Ultimate Collector's Edition*. Warner Home Video, 2006.

Superman: Volcano. Dir. Dave Fleischer. Writ. Bill Turner and Carl Meyer. Perf. Bud Collyer and Joan Alexander.

1942. DVD. *Superman Ultimate Collector's Edition*. Warner Home Video, 2006.

Suspiria. Dir. Dario Argento. Writ. Dario Argento and Daria Nicolodi. Perf. Jessica Harper, Udo Kier, and Joan Bennett. 1977. DVD. Blue Underground, 2007.

Sweeney, David. Personal interview. Monday, March 26, 2006.

Swift, Jonathan. *A Modest Proposal and Other Satirical Works*. Toronto: Dover, 1996.

Syriana. Writ.-Dir. Stephen Gaghan. Perf. George Clooney, Matt Damon. Warner Bros., 2005.

Taken. Dir. Pierre Morel. Writ. Luc Besson and Robert Mark Kamen. Perf. Liam Neeson. 2003. DVD. 20th Century–Fox, 2008.

Tancer, Bill. *Click: What Millions of People Are Doing Online and Why It Matters*. New York: Hyperion, 2008.

Taxi Driver. Dir. Martin Scorsese. Writ. Paul Schrader. Perf. Robert DeNiro, Jodie Foster, Harvey Keitel. Columbia Pictures, 1976.

Theakston, Greg. *The Steve Ditko Reader*. Pure Imagination, Brooklyn, NY, 2002.

Them! Dir. Gordon Douglas. Writ. Ted Sherdeman. Perf. James Whitmore, Edmund Gwenn, Joan Weldon. Warner Bros. 1954. DVD. Warner Home Video, 2002.

30 Days of Night. Dir. David Slade. Writ. Steve Niles, Stuart Beattie, and Brian Nelson. Perf. Josh Hartnett, Melissa George, Danny Huston. 2007. DVD. Sony, 2008.

"This Side of Paradise." Dir. Ralph Senensky. Writ. D.C. Fontana. Perf. William Shatner, Leonard Nimoy, and DeForest Kelly. 1967. DVD. *Star Trek: The Original Series—Season One*. Paramount, 2007.

Thomas, Matt. "Comic Con Q&A with Wonder Woman, Gail Simone." *The Torontoist*. March 29, 2010. June 15, 2010. <http://torontoist.com/2010/03/comic_con_qa_with_wonder_woman_gail_simone.php>

Thomas, Roy. "War of the Worlds." Illus. Michael Lark. *Superman*. New York: DC Comics. 1999.

Thomson, June. *Holmes and Watson*. New York: Carroll & Graf Publishers, 1995.

Thoreau, Henry David. *Civil Disobedience and Other Essays*. New York: Dover Publications, Inc, 1993.

Tolkien, J. R. R. *Lord of the Rings*. Mariner Books, 1999.

Tolstoy, Leo. *What is Art?* New York: Barnes and Noble Books, 2005.

"Tom Baker Interview." *Doctor Who Magazine* #92. 1984. TomBaker.com. August 12, 2010. <http://www.tombaker.co.uk/pages/content/index.asp?PageID=185>

Toole, John Kennedy. *A Confederacy of Dunces*. Grove Press, 1987.

Torchwood. Dir. Euros Lyn et al. Writ. Russel T. Davies et al. Perf. John Barrowman, Eve Myles. Television series. BBC Wales, 2006–present.

"Torture" *Facts on File: Issues & Controversies*. June 27, 2008. July 17, 2010. <http://www.2facts.com/icof_story.aspx?PIN=i0802140&term=torture>

"The Trouble with Tribbles." *Star Trek*. Dir. Joseph Pevney. Writ. David Gerrold. Perf. William Shatner, Leonard Nimoy, and DeForest Kelly. 1967. *Star Trek: The Original Series—Season Two*. Paramount, 2007.

True Blood. Writ.-Dir. Alan Ball et al. Perf. Anna Paquin and Stephen Moyer. HBO, 2008–present.

Tucker, Ken. "Book Review: The Megalomaniacal Spider-Man (2010)." *EW.com*. May 31, 2002. July 25, 2010. <http://www.ew.com/ew/article/0,,249608,00.html>

Tucker, Reed. "Holy Liplock! Slash Fiction Puts Pop Icons in Steamy Settings." *New York Post*. August 20, 2006.

Tulloch, John and Manuel Alvarado. *Doctor Who: The Unfolding Text*. New York: St. Martin's, 1983.

Turtledove, Harry. In the Balance: An Alternate History of the Second World War (*Worldwar*, Vol. 1). New York: *Del Rey, 1994.*

The Twelve Tasks of Asterix. Dir. René Goscinny, Henri Gruel, Albert Uderzo, and Pierre Watrin. Writ. René Goscinny, Albert Uderzo, and Pierre Tchernia. Perf. Roger Carel and Pierre Tornade. France: Dargaud Films, 1976.

25th Hour. Dir. Spike Lee. Writ. David Benioff. Perf. Edward Norton, Philip Seymour Hoffman, and Barry Pepper. DVD. Walt Disney Video, 2003.

The Twilight Zone. Writ. and Perf. Rod Serling. Television series. CBS, 1959–1964.

Ultraviolet. Writ.-Dir. Joe Ahearne. Perf. Jack Davenport, Susanna Harker, Idris Elba, and Philip Quast. 1998. DVD. Palm Pictures/Umvd, 2001.

Underwood, Peter. *Jack the Ripper: One Hundred Years of Mystery*. London: Blandford Press, 1987.

The Untouchables. Dir. Brian DePalma. Writ. David Mamet. Perf. Kevin Costner, Robert DeNiro, and Sean Connery. Paramount Pictures, 1987.

V for Vendetta. Dir. James McTeigue. Writ. "The Wachowski Brothers." Perf. Natalie Portman, Hugo Weaving. Warner Bros. Pictures, 2005.

Vankin, Jonathan and John Whalen. *Based on a True Story (But With More Car Crashes): Fact and Fantasy in 100 Favorite Movies*. Chicago: Chicago Review Press, 2005.

Van Lente, Fred. "The Extremist." Illus. Javier Rodriguez. *Web of Spider-Man* Vol. 2 #8–10. New York: Marvel Comics, 2010.

Vaughan, Brian K. "The Oath." Illus. Marcos Martin. *Doctor Strange: The Oath* #1–5. New York: Marvel Comics, 2006–2007.

"Viewers Think New Doctor Who Is 'Too Sexy.'" *Telegraph*. April 5, 2010. July 8, 2010. <http://www.telegraph.co.uk/culture/tvandradio/doctor-who/7554825/Viewers-think-new-Doctor-Who-is-too-sexy.html>

Viscusi, Robert. *Buried Caesars and Other Secrets of Italian American Writing*. New York: State University of New York: Press, 2006.

Voltaire. *Candide*. Trans. Francois-Marie Arouet. Toronto: Dover Publications, 1991.

W. Writ. Stanley Weiser. Dir. Oliver Stone. Perf. Josh Brolin, Elizabeth Banks, Richard Dreyfuss, James Cromwell, Jeffrey Wright, Toby Jones. 2008. DVD. Lions Gate. 2009.

Waid, Mark. "Authoritative Action." Illus. Mike Wieringo. *Fantastic Four*. New York: Marvel Comics, 2005.

_____. "Kingdom Come." Illus. Alex Ross. *Kingdom Come* nos. 1–4. New York: DC Comics. May–August 1996.

_____. "The Real Truth About Superman: And the Rest of Us, Too." *Superheroes and Philosophy: Truth, Justice, and the Socratic Way*. Ed: Tom and Matt Morris. Chicago and LaSalle Illinois: Open Court Publishing Co, 2005. 3–10.

Wagner, Matt. *Trinity: Superman, Batman, Wonder Woman*. New York: DC Comics, 2004.

Wall, David. "It Is and It Isn't: Stereotypes, Advertising, and Narrative." *The Conscious Reader, 12th edition*. Ed: Caroline Shrodes, Marc DiPaolo, et al. New York: Pearson, 2010.

Walters, Ben. "Why the Obama as Joker Poster Leaves a Bad Taste in the Mouth." *The Guardian*. August 5, 2009. September 12, 2010. <http://www.guardian.co.

uk/film/filmblog/2009/aug/05/obama-as-joker-poster>

Warner, Marina. "Boys Will Be Boys." *Six Myths of Our Time: Little Angels, Little Monsters, Beautiful Beasts, and More.* US/UK: Vintage, 1995.

_____. "Fantasy's Power and Peril." *The New York Times.* Dec. 16, 2001. June 25, 2010. <http://www.nytimes.com/2001/12/16/weekinreview/ideas-trends-fantasy-s-power-and-peril.html>

Wasielewski, Marek. "This Amazing Stranger from the Planet Krypton: Industrial Design and the Machine Paradigm in the Fleischer Animated Superman Shorts 1941–1943." *Film International* issue 26. Volume 5 Number 2. Malmö, Sweden: 2007. 6–14.

Watermelon Man. Dir. Melvin Van Peebles. Writ. Herman Raucher. Perf. Godfrey Cambridge and Estelle Parsons. 1970. DVD. Sony, 2004.

Watson, Polly, ed. *The Villainy of Doctor Doom (From the House of Ideas).* New York: Marvel Comics, 1999.

"The Web of Fear." *Doctor Who.* Writ. Mervyn Haisman and Henry Lincoln. Perf. Patrick Troughton, Frazer Hines, Deborah Watling. 1968. DVD. *Doctor Who—Lost in Time Collection of Rare Episodes—The William Hartnell Years and the Patrick Troughton Years.* BBC Video, 2004.

Weinstein, Simcha. *Up, Up, and Oy Vey: How Jewish History, Culture, and Values Shaped the Comic Book Superhero.* Baltimore: Leviathan Press. 2006.

Whitaker, David, writer. "The Crusade." *Doctor Who.* Perf. William Hartnell, Jacqueline Hill, William Russell. 1965. DVD. *Doctor Who—Lost in Time Collection of Rare Episodes—The William Hartnell Years and the Patrick Troughton Years.* BBC Video, 2004.

_____. "The Enemy of the World." *Doctor Who.* Perf. Patrick Troughton, Frazer Hines, Deborah Watling. 1967–1968. DVD. *Doctor Who—Lost in Time Collection of Rare Episodes—The William Hartnell Years and the Patrick Troughton Years.* BBC Video, 2004.

Who Wants to Kill Jessie? Dir. Václav Vorlícek. Writ. Václav Vorlícek, Milos Macourek. Perf. Dana Medrická, Jirí Sovák, Olga Schoberová. 1966. DVD. Facets, 2006.

Wilde, Oscar. *An Ideal Husband.* South Carolina: BookSurge Classics. 2002.

Wisse, Martin and "Palau." "No, Thatcher was not a feminist." Prog Gold. June 16th, 2010. August 14, 2010. <http://www.cloggie.org/proggold/2010/06/16/no-thatcher-was-not-a-feminist/>

Wolk, Douglas. *Reading Comics: How Graphic Novels Work and What They Mean.* Massachusetts: Da Capo Press, 2007.

Wonder Woman. Dir. Vincent McEveety. Writ. John D.F. Black. Perf. Cathy Lee Crosby and Ricardo Montalban. TV series pilot movie. ABC. 1974.

Wonder Woman. Dir. Lauren Montgomery. Writ. Michael Jelenic. Perf. Keri Russell. Nathan Fillion, Virginia Madsen, Alfred Molina. Cartoon DVD. Warner Home Video, 2009.

Wonder Woman: The Complete First Season. Prod. Douglas S. Cramer. Develop. Stanley Ralph Ross. Perf. Lynda Carter and Lyle Waggoner. 1975–1977. DVD. Warner Home Video, 2004.

Wonder Woman: The Complete Second Season. Perf. Lynda Carter and Lyle Waggoner. 1977–1978. DVD. Warner Home Video, 2005.

Wonder Woman: The Complete Third Season. Perf. Lynda Carter and Lyle Waggoner. 1978–1979. DVD. Warner Home Video, 2005.

"Wonder Woman: The Ultimate Feminist Icon." *Wonder Woman: The Complete Third Season.* DVD Special Feature. Warner Home Video, 2005.

Woodard, Joe. "Pumped, Pierced, Painted, and Pagan." *The Conscious Reader, 12th edition.* Ed: Caroline Shrodes, Marc DiPaolo, et al. New York: Pearson, 2010.

Woodward, Bob. *Bush at War.* New York: Simon and Shuster, 2002. 145–146.

Woolley, Benjamin. "Chapter Six: Cyberspace." *Virtual Worlds: A Journey in Hype and Hyperreality.* Oxford: Blackwell, 1992. *CyberReader.* Ed: Victoria J. Vitanza. New York: Pearson, 2005. 4–16.

Wright, Bardford W. *Comic Book Nation: The Transformation of Youth Culture in America.* Baltimore: Johns Hopkins University Press, 2001.

Wrightson, Berni. *Captain Sternn.* Northhampton, Massachusetts: Kitchen Sink, 1993.

Xena: Warrior Princess. Dir. Rick Jacobson, Mark Beesley, et al. Writ. R.J. Stewart, Steven L. Sears, Nora Kay Foster, et al. Perf. Lucy Lawless, Renée O'Connor, Hudson Leick, and Karl Urban. 1995–2001. DVD. *Xena Warrior Princess—Complete Series (Seasons 1–6).* Anchor Bay Entertainment, 2005.

X-Men. Dir. Bryan Singer. Writ. David Hayter. Perf. Ian McKellen, Hugh Jackman, Patrick Stewart, Anna Paquin, Halle Berry, and Famke Janssen. 2000. DVD. *X-Men Trilogy (X-Men/X2: X-Men United/X-Men—The Last Stand).* 20th Century–Fox, 2006.

"X-Men producer begs DC Comics: Let me do *Wonder Woman.*" SciFiWire. June 25, 2010. June 30, 2010. <http://scifiwire.com/2010/06/x-men-producer-begs-dc-co.php>

X-Men: The Last Stand. Dir. Brett Ratner. Writ. Simon Kinberg and Zak Penn. Perf. Ian McKellen, Hugh Jackman, Patrick Stewart, Anna Paquin, Halle Berry, and Famke Janssen. 2006. DVD. *X-Men Trilogy (X-Men/X2: X-Men United/X-Men—The Last Stand).* 20th Century–Fox, 2006.

X-2: X-Men United. Dir. Bryan Singer. Writ. Michael Dougherty, Dan Harris, and David Hayter. Perf. Ian McKellen, Hugh Jackman, Patrick Stewart, Anna Paquin, Halle Berry, and Famke Janssen. 2003. DVD. *X-Men Trilogy (X-Men/X2: X-Men United/X-Men—The Last Stand).* 20th Century–Fox, 2006.

Youngquist, Jeff, ed. *Wizard Masterpiece Edition: Spider-Man—The 10 Greatest Spider-Man Stories Ever.* New York: Gareb Shamus Enterprises, 2004.

Zailckas, Koren. *Smashed: Story of a Drunken Girlhood.* London: Penguin Books, 2004.

Zodiac. Dir. David Fincher. Writ. James Vanderbilt. Perf. Mark Ruffalo, Jake Gyllenhaal, and Robert Downey, Jr. 2007. DVD. Paramount, 2008.

Index

Page numbers in ***bold italics*** indicate illustrations.